Lake Superior

Lake Huron

Lake Michigan

Lake Ontario

Lake Erie

St. Lawrence R.

(to MASS.)

N.H.

Concord

MASS.

Hudson R.

Albany

Boston

NEW YORK

Hartford

Providence

Newport

New London

Delaware R.

New York

CONN.

R.I.

PENN.

Trenton

Philadelphia

NEW JERSEY

Wilmington

Baltimore

DELAWARE

Ohio R.

MARYLAND

BRITISH
TERRITORY

Potomac R.

VIRGINIA

Williamsburg

Tennessee R.

R.

NORTH
CAROLINA

INDIAN
RESERVE

Wilmington

Mississippi R.

SOUTH
CAROLINA

Charleston

GEORGIA

Savannah

Atlantic
Ocean

WEST
FLORIDA

EAST FLORIDA

Gulf of Mexico

Present-day state borders are shown in gray.

FROM SEA
∽TO∽
SHINING SEA

Books by Robert Leckie

HISTORY

From Sea to Shining Sea: From the War of 1812 to the Mexican War,
the Saga of America's Expansion
George Washington's War: The Saga of the Revolution
None Died in Vain: The Saga of the American Civil War
Delivered from Evil: The Saga of World War II
The Wars of America: Updated and Revised, 1609–1991
American and Catholic: The Catholic Church in the U.S.
Challenge for the Pacific: The Struggle for Guadalcanal
With Fire and Sword (*edited with Quentin Reynolds*)
Strong Men Armed: U.S. Marines Against Japan
Conflict: The History of the Korean War
The March to Glory: 1st Marine Division's Breakout from Chosin

AUTOBIOGRAPHY

Helmet for My Pillow
Lord, What a Family!

BELLES LETTRES

These Are My Heroes: A Study of the Saints
Warfare: A Study of War
A Soldier-Priest Talks to Youth

FICTION

Ordained
Marines!
The Bloodborn
Forged in Blood
Blood of the Seventeen Fires
The General

FOR YOUNGER READERS

The Battle for Iwo Jima
The Story of Football
The Story of World War Two
The Story of World War One
The War in Korea
Great American Battles
The World Turned Upside-Down
1812: The War Nobody Won
The Big Game
Keeper Play
Stormy Voyage

FROM SEA ~TO~ SHINING SEA

*From the War of 1812
to the Mexican War,
the Saga of America's Expansion*

ROBERT LECKIE

HarperCollins*Publishers*

HarperCollins books may be purchased for educational, business, or sales promotional use. For information please write: Special Markets Department, HarperCollins Publishers, Inc., 10 East 53rd Street, New York, NY 10022.

FIRST EDITION

Designed by Jessica Shatan
Maps by Paul Pugliese

Library of Congress Cataloging-in-Publication Data

Leckie, Robert.
    From sea to shining sea: from the War of 1812 to the Mexican War, the saga of America's expansion/Robert Leckie.
        p. cm.
    ISBN 0-06-016802-1
    1. United States—History, Military—To 1900. 2. United States—History, Naval—To 1900. 3. United States—Territorial expansion.
I. Title.
E181.L439 1993
973—dc20   92-56243

93 94 95 96 97 ❖/HC 10 9 8 7 6 5 4 3 2 1

To the Glennons:
The Lovely Marguerite and
Old Reliable Joseph, My Dear Friend
for Sixty-one Years and
Still My Best Man

Contents

Maps

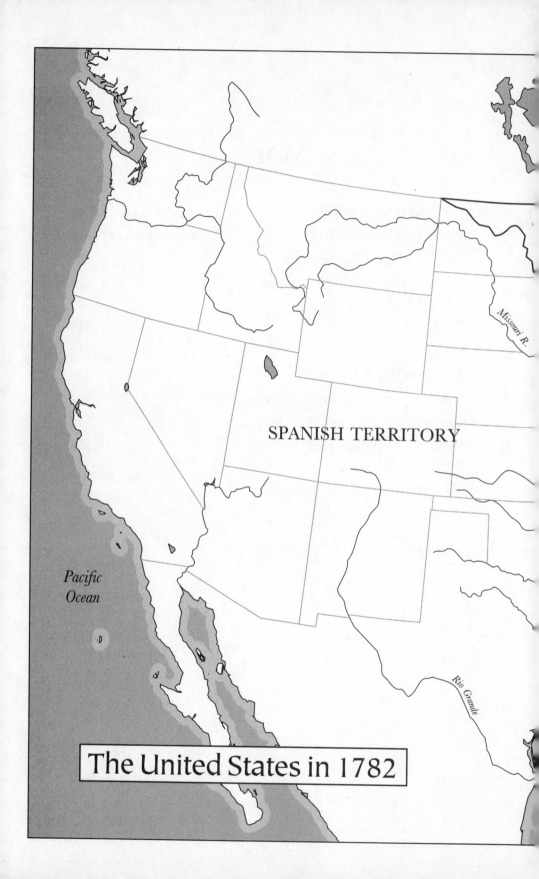

SPANISH TERRITORY

Pacific
Ocean

Missouri R.

Rio Grande

The United States in 1782

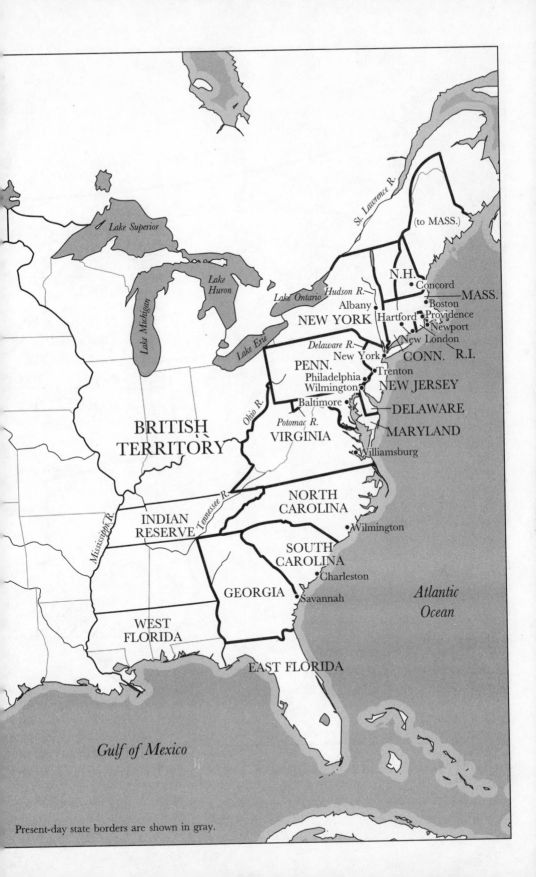

Lake Superior

Lake Huron

Lake Michigan

Lake Ontario

Lake Erie

St. Lawrence R.

(to MASS.)

N.H.
• Concord

Hudson R.
Albany

MASS.
• Boston
Hartford • Providence
• Newport
New London

NEW YORK

Delaware R.
New York

CONN.   R.I.

PENN.
Philadelphia
Wilmington

Trenton

NEW JERSEY

Baltimore

DELAWARE

Ohio R.

Potomac R.
VIRGINIA

MARYLAND

BRITISH
TERRITORY

• Williamsburg

Tennessee R.

NORTH
CAROLINA

INDIAN
RESERVE

• Wilmington

SOUTH
CAROLINA
• Charleston

Mississippi R.

GEORGIA
• Savannah

WEST
FLORIDA

Atlantic
Ocean

EAST FLORIDA

Gulf of Mexico

Present-day state borders are shown in gray.

OREGON
COUNTRY

MINNESOT

Missouri R.

UNORGANIZED
TERRITORY

Arkansas R.

MEXICO

Red R.

Pacific
Ocean

Brazos R.

TEXAS
ANNEXATION

Rio Grande

The United States in 1847

Present-day state borders are shown in gray.

FROM SEA
~TO~
SHINING SEA

∼ I ∼

THE NEW
AMERICAN NATION

If men were angels,
there would be no need of government.

1

From Victory to Anarchy

~ IN THE SPRING OF 1781, GENERAL GEORGE WASHINGTON HEARD alarming reports—later proven to be true—that Charles Gravier, the Comte de Vergennes and King Louis XVI's foreign minister, was planning to end the war with Great Britain by abandoning the American ally and convening a peace conference of European powers friendly to France that would leave the British in possession of land they now occupied—the modern Midwest—thus blocking any westward expansion by the rebellious colonists. French withdrawal from the war would sound the death knell of American independence. Instead of the arrival of a great French fleet as promised, there would come to America only transports to take King Louis's white-coated regulars home. After them King George III's commissioners would probably appear to administer the oath of allegiance to a conquered people, and to take "Mr." Washington along with John Adams, Thomas Jefferson, Benjamin Franklin and other signers of the Declaration of Independence, to London, there to stand trial for treason.

This plan, contained in a secret memorandum to himself drawn up by Vergennes, was never made public at the time, although Vergennes had sounded out the British on the proposal and received enthusiastic support. With Washington, it had the effect of making him yearn more desperately for a single decisive victory that would destroy the

British Crown's will to continue the war. So on May 21 in Wethersfield, Connecticut, he met with General Jean Baptiste Donatien de Vimeur, the Comte de Rochambeau, to plan a summer campaign.

In spite of the Vergennes plan, of which Rochambeau was unaware, the promise of the great French West Indian fleet for use against the British had not been withdrawn. Both Washington and Rochambeau expected it to appear under the Comte Francois Joseph Paul de Grasse, and the American commander wanted desperately to use it in a campaign against New York City held by General Sir Henry Clinton. New York was an obsession with Washington. He had been defeated in and around there three times: on Long Island, in the city itself and at White Plains. Each time, he had saved his army—truly notable feats of generalship, much as successful withdrawals do not excite the public—and would continue to do so throughout five years of defeat and retreat brightened only by such rallies as the brilliant raids on Trenton and Princeton. In May of 1781 it seemed to Washington that his time for vengeance had come, for between them he and the French general commanded 16,600 men: 8,800 Americans and 7,800 French. With de Grasse's powerful fleet this should be enough to overwhelm Clinton.

But then Washington and Rochambeau made an armed reconnaissance of Sir Henry Clinton's New York defenses, finding to their dismay that they were much too strong to be stormed. Their dejection turned to joy, however, when on August 14 they received the electrifying news that de Grasse was enroute to the Chesapeake with twenty-eight big ships and three thousand men!

The Chesapeake! Lord Charles Cornwallis's southern army was there! General Nathanael Greene and the aroused Patriots of the Carolinas had disabused His Lordship of his conviction that he could win the South for King George III. Hastening north to Virginia, with Greene snapping at his heels, he had halted in the little tobacco-trading port of Yorktown, and there taken up a defensive position expecting reinforcements from Clinton in New York and a rescuing British fleet under Sir Samuel Graves.

George Washington now forgot the New York operation and prepared to march south, first notifying the Marquis de Lafayette to keep Cornwallis cornered in Yorktown. Next, efforts were made to convince Clinton that New York was still the Franco-American objective. Staten Island was made to appear the staging area for an assault. Roads toward it were improved. A party of French in nearby Chatham, New Jersey, began making bake ovens as though for a siege. Leaving three thousand men above New York, Washington sent two thousand across the Hudson into New Jersey. The French followed. A leisurely march toward Chatham began. On August 29 the troops were making for Morristown—then New Brunswick—and Clinton still believed them bound for Chatham.

But on the next day the Americans and French began marching briskly south toward Chesapeake Bay and Yorktown.

All the way down to the Head of Elk in Maryland, Washington pondered the question: Where is de Grasse? He had not heard from him since receipt of that letter in mid-August. He had no way of knowing that de Grasse had met and defeated the British rescuing fleet.

Washington still had had no word as his Americans—mostly Continentals with about three thousand militia—reached the Head of Elk and began embarking in boats for Williamsburg on the James. The French followed. As Rochambeau and his elegant aides neared the landing on the Virginia shore they saw a strong, tall figure in blue and buff waving his big hat wildly, and almost capering for joy. Rochambeau stepped ashore and a beaming George Washington rushed up to embrace him. Then French hats went soaring into the air, for Washington had informed them that de Grasse had met the British fleet off the Capes, driving it back to New York, that he now held the Chesapeake, completely cutting off Cornwallis, and had already put ashore three thousand more French regulars under the Marquis Saint-Simon. As one of Washington's generals was to write of Cornwallis: ". . . we have got him handsomely in a pudding bag."

They had indeed. When Cornwallis learned that Admiral Graves had sailed back to New York, he was so distressed that he shortened his front by abandoning a formidable outer work that might have delayed his enemy for at least a week. On September 30 Washington was delighted to find this position empty. Because all these works but the battery were enclosed, they were immediately useful against Yorktown, and the battery was enclosed that night. Meanwhile on the morning of October 1 the French drove in the pickets at the Fusilier's Redoubt near the river.

Five days later work was begun on the first of Washington's parallels about six hundred yards from the lower end of the town. The trench was to run down to the water's edge. Diggers toiled throughout the night, sweating profusely in that moist heat which had already spread sickness through both camps. Heavy guns were dragged into place, and on October 9 a French battery on the left opened up. Then the American battery on the right began blasting, with Washington firing the first shot, and a British frigate on the York was driven to the Gloucester shore.

On the next night two bigger batteries began roaring. The French set another frigate hopelessly afire, and two transports were destroyed. In all, fifty-two guns were battering the town, and Cornwallis wrote ominously to Clinton: "We have lost about seventy of our men and many of our works are considerably damaged: with such works on disadvantageous ground, against so powerful an attack we cannot hope to make a very long resistance. P.S. 5 P.M. Since my letter was written (at 12M.) we have lost thirty men . . . We continue to lose men very fast."

Clinton and the admirals, meanwhile, had only belatedly begun another rescue operation. But the limitations of New York's dockyards made the work of refitting proceed with agonizing slowness. It was hoped to be ready by October 5, then the 8th . . . the 12th . . . But the 12th passed and the fleet still had not sailed. Clinton was beside himself. At last, on October 17, seven thousand troops were embarked and the ships began dropping down Sandy Hook—only to be forced to wait two more days for favorable winds and tides. In the meantime, some sixteen thousand French and Americans drew ever closer to Cornwallis's beleaguered seven thousand, and a second parallel only three hundred yards away from Yorktown was begun by Baron von Steuben and his engineers.

As the trench approached the river edge, its builders were raked by fire from two British redoubts close to the water. Washington decided to storm them. The French took the left in a stirring charge, climbing the parapet with cries of *"Vive le Roi!"* and forcing its garrison of Hessians and British to throw down their arms.

Alexander Hamilton led the Americans against the one on the right. Now grown fond of the bayonet, the Patriots went at it with unloaded muskets, clawing their way through the abatis, crossing the ditch and leaping over the parapets. From all the British lines came a storm of shells and musket balls. Washington, watching the assault, was cautioned by his aide: "Sir, you are too much exposed here. Had you not better step a little back?"

"Colonel Cobb," Washington replied gravely, "if you are afraid, you have liberty to step back."

And so both redoubts were won, the second parallel was extended down to the river and the second nail driven into the British coffin. On the morning of October 16, Cornwallis sent out a force of 350 men to capture and destroy the batteries in the second parallel. In a brave charge, the British succeeded in entering both positions and in spiking some guns, but they were eventually driven back and the guns restored to service.

So desperate now that he was losing his judgment, Cornwallis attempted a wild escape across the river through Gloucester. He expected to burst through the Franco-American force there and proceed to New York by forced marches. That same midnight he began embarking his troops, but a violent storm broke upon him and forced him back into Yorktown.

That was the end.

On the morning of the 17th, two days before Clinton's relief force made the open sea, the allies opened on the town with a dreadful cannonade. One by one the British works collapsed. There was no answering fire, for the British had exhausted their ammunition. Soon a redcoated drummer boy strode onto a parapet and began to beat a parley. He could not be heard in all that thunder, but he was seen. The guns fell silent and a British officer advanced to be blindfolded and led to Washington.

He asked for a twenty-four-hour armistice. Washington granted him two hours. He returned with Cornwallis's surrender terms, including a condition that his army be paroled to Britain. Washington insisted that the enemy surrender as prisoners of war, and Cornwallis submitted.

At noon of October 19, 1781, the gay military music of the French sang out, and for the last time the vivacious white-coated soldiers of France went into line on American soil. Into line opposite them, moving proudly across trampled fields to the Celtic lilt of fifes and drums, went the tall Americans in brown or hunting shirts and here and there in blue and buff. George Washington rode up on a great bay horse and stood at their right. Across from him Rochambeau and Admiral de Barras sat their horses. De Barras was there because Admiral de Grasse was uncomfortable aboard a horse. His deputy was hardly better. As his mount stretched to void itself, he cried: "My God—I'm sinking!" To the right of them Yorktown's main sally port was flung open. Faint on the wind came the mournful beat of drums and the melancholy squeal of fifes. Out rode Brigadier General Charles O'Hara. With stupefyingly bad grace, Cornwallis, pleading illness, had sent a deputy to surrender for him.

Bewildered, O'Hara rode first toward Rochambeau. But the count, by a gracious inclination of the eyes, directed him to Washington. Slightly flustered, O'Hara approached the tall Virginian. Washington indicated General Benjamin Lincoln, after himself the senior American officer present. Deputy must surrender to deputy.

Here was the supreme irony of the war: Benjamin Lincoln, champion of lost battles, a fat and fatuous failure, one of those politicking militia generals that a meddling Congress had promoted over the heads of Greene, Arnold, Knox and John Stark, was to receive the enemy commander's sword symbolic of surrender! But Washington, a stickler for protocol, could do no other. Certainly he would have preferred the gallant and able Nathanael Greene, except that he was too valuable where he was: campaigning in South Carolina with his customary skill. So O'Hara handed Cornwallis's sword to Lincoln, who returned it while calling for the surrender to begin.

Out they came, the scarlet-coated British and their Hessian allies brilliant in blue and green. Out came the German mercenaries, striding briskly, stacking their arms neatly; then the British, moving along slowly, their faces sullen, some of them already weeping. Down went their arms in a disorderly crash. Drummer boys stove in their drums, infantrymen smashed their musket butts and stomped on their cartridge cases. Officers pouting like schoolboys avoided the eyes of their captors.

Above the clatter of grounded arms and the hoarse cursing of broken-hearted soldiers rose the music of the British bands bringing the War of the American Revolution to its effective close with the prophetic notes of "The World Turned Upside Down."

In this last decade of the twentieth century, which has seen the end of the Cold War, the collapse of European and Soviet Communism, and the emergence of the United States as the world's sole superpower, it is difficult indeed to understand the pathetic weakness and petty quarreling that divided the thirteen former colonies which—with the help of France—had just defeated the greatest military power on earth. This new little nation called itself the *United* States of America, but there was no real union anywhere. There was no president and no judiciary except for admiralty courts. The Continental Congress was a rope of sand absolutely unable to exercise those powers of government that the several states with foolish jealousy preserved for themselves. So little was thought of Congress that it was usually described as "a firm league of friendship," and its members regarded it with such contempt that many of them seldom attended meetings.

The states even usurped such national functions as currency, control of interstate commerce and maintenance of armed forces. Since the Americans after their first great victory rushed to disband their armed forces—a policy of beating their swords into drinking goblets, which was to be continued with varying degrees of thoroughness until the onset of the Cold War in 1946—the only military force in those early peacetime years was the various state militia usually called up to protect the frontier against Indian incursions. Because of their bitter experiences with the British military, most Americans regarded a regular, standing army as the enemy of freedom. Having successfully resisted taxes on tea and stamps, they were in no mood to accept national taxation by Congress, even if its members were American. In 1782–83 when Congress asked the states for $10 million, it received less than $1.5 million.

Congress was so universally ignored that some states did not even bother to send their representatives to New York. When John Hancock was elected president of Congress in 1785, he did not bother to attend, an example which led to more empty seats than otherwise. Robert Morris, the superintendent of finance, unable to effect cooperation between the states and Congress, quit in disgust. Washington was so appalled by the universal contempt for authority that he wrote, "No morn ever dawned more favorably than ours did; and no day was ever more clouded than the present. . . . We are fast verging to anarchy."

There was also no real leadership, for the men who were to be known as the Founding Fathers had all returned to private life or were out of the country on diplomatic missions. Washington himself had gone back to Mount Vernon and the planter's life that he loved, Benjamin Franklin preferred his post as president of the Pennsylvania Executive Council and Alexander Hamilton was practicing law in New York City. Thomas Jefferson was in Paris and John Adams in London.

Even if such skillful and experienced hands had been at the helm it is doubtful that they would have captured the loyalty of these stiff-necked sons of freedom—most of them ignorant farmers concerned only with local matters. They called themselves Americans, but still thought of themselves as New Yorkers, Virginians or New Hampshiremen rather than as citizens of the United States. Dispute and division rather than a spirit of unity prevailed among them. Pennsylvania and Virginia came close to armed conflict before they could agree on a boundary. Both New Hampshire and New York claimed present-day Vermont—known first as the "New Hampshire Grants" and then the "Green Mountain Commonwealth"—and Ethan Allen of Green Mountain Boys fame was so incensed by this quarrel that he actually offered the British a treaty making Vermont part of Canada. Threats of secession were common, and it would seem that this divided and unarmed new nation—comprising an area so vast that it was as large as Britain, France, Italy and Spain combined—was ripe for invasion.

Indeed it is surprising that these most covetous of nations—Italy excepted—did not rush to carve out enclaves in this fledgling country so rich in natural resources, in seaports and navigable rivers, populated by an ingenious, enterprising race—but now so weak. Perhaps, as Chancellor Otto von Bismarck of Germany was to remark so sourly, there must indeed be "A special providence for fools, drunks and the United States of America." For all of these predator kingdoms were distracted: Britain was still a government divided between an insane Tory king and those contumacious Whigs and in no way disposed to attempt reconquest over that daunting supply line three thousand miles long; the treasury of the economy-minded King Louis XVI of France was all but empty, and the first faint rumblings of the Revolution that was to cost him his head could be heard in Versailles; and Spain was struggling to hold together what was then the greatest empire since Rome, particularly disturbed by the growing spirit of rebellion in her Latin American colonies. Italy then, of course, was no more than a geographical designation, an area occupied by a congeries of quarreling city-states that would not be united as a kingdom for still another half century.

Nevertheless, the Old World watched with amusement and contempt what appeared to be the dissolution of the American union. None of these nations believed that popular government was possible in an area so vast, with an unruly population growing with such astonishing speed. True, there was the example of the Greek city-states two thousand years earlier—the only precedent—but in these entities both area and population were tiny. Typical of this European attitude was the prediction of Dean Josiah Tucker of Gloucester Cathedral, who wrote: "A disunited people till the end of time, suspicious and distrustful of each other, they will be divided and sub-divided into little commonwealths or principalities, according to natural boundaries."

At first it had been hoped that the Articles of Confederation that had helped the United States wage successful war against Great Britain would save the union. But the Articles could not supply the answer to the problem of how to induce the states to surrender enough sovereignty to form a national government, and they could not be amended except by unanimous consent. In a union already divided by the sectionalism of North versus South and beset by the mutual distrust of large and small states, unanimity was not possible. Congress frightened no one. Driven from Philadelphia in June 1783 by mutineers of the Pennsylvania Line, the capital had wandered like a waif from Princeton to Annapolis to Trenton and finally, in 1785, to New York. Two years later Congress's basic weakness was laid bare by the rising of Massachusetts farmers known as Shays's Rebellion.

A sound money policy supported by heavy taxes had left the Bay State's farmers destitute. Farms and cattle were sold to satisfy court judgments for taxes or debts. The farmers tried to stop the courts from sitting, and they set up committees of correspondence, just as the leaders of the Revolution had acted against Parliament. But now these leaders were conducting the state government and they threatened the farmers with the gallows. The farmers paid no heed. They grew stronger and more aggressive and they called upon Daniel Shays, a distinguished soldier of the Revolution, to lead them. Shays tried to prevent the Supreme Court from sitting at Springfield, and it was here that his attack on both the courthouse and the Confederation arsenal was shattered by artillery fired by loyal state militia. After a few more, lesser defeats, Shays fled to Vermont. Massachusetts wisely treated his followers with clemency, and a newly elected legislature moved to alleviate their hardships.

Nevertheless, Shays's Rebellion alarmed the nation, delighting those Tories who saw in it the first crack in the American facade. Massachusetts had appealed to Congress for help, and Congress had been able to do nothing. Even those Americans who had feared the formation of a strong national government now favored revision of the Articles of Confederation. On May 25, 1787, the Constitutional or Federal Convention was convened in Philadelphia for this "sole and express purpose."

2

United at Last

 THE FOUNDING FATHERS OF THE UNITED STATES (ONLY FOUR OF FIFTY-five Convention delegates were sixty or over) did not so much revise the old Articles as devise an entirely new government as set forth in the Constitution. Congress received taxing and other important powers and was expanded from a single chamber into a House of Representatives elected by the people and a Senate selected by the more conservative state legislatures. A strong executive power vested in a President was also provided, as well as a Supreme Court.

Thus was born the American system of the division of powers—legislative, executive and judicial—acting as checks and balances on one another. In Congress the people, as manifested by the popularly elected House, were balanced against property, as expressed by the Senate. Civilian control of the military was guaranteed by making the president commander-in-chief, and the president in turn was checked by giving the House the power to determine the size of the armed forces. Finally, excesses by either legislative or executive powers could be checked by a Supreme Court empowered to interpret the Constitution.

In four months, then, these political carpenters raised a stout roof over the new nation. They wrote a Constitution that, intended to serve 4 million people and thirteen states for a generation, still guides 253 million Americans and fifty states while remaining, after the tests of nearly two centuries, one of the triumphs of practical politics. Above all, these men were practical. They were not doctrinaires, like the French and Russian revolutionaries who eventually replaced old tyrannies with new ones.

They were experienced in the arts of self-rule. "Experience must be our only guide," farmer John Dickinson told the Convention, "reason may mislead us." Steeped in the political theories of British thinkers, they were eminently practical men and were about to evolve their own concept of viable self-rule, best expressed in the remark of James Madison of Virginia: "If men were angels, there would be no need of government." If there were any single architect of the new government, it would have been Madison, although he could and did rely upon the contributions of such brilliant associates as Thomas Jefferson and George Mason of Virginia, Benjamin Franklin of Pennsylvania and Alexander Hamilton of New York. There was not one of these delegates who did not fear "a man on a horse" such as Oliver Cromwell or Julius Caesar. They also refrained from pretending that their society was not a congeries of conflicting interests: town and country, Northern shippers and Southern planters, seaboard merchants and back-country farmers, creditors and debtors, politicians and people. Rather, they openly strove to reconcile them along the lines proposed by Madison when he said: "All civilized societies are divided into different sects, fashions, and interests, as they happened to consist of rich and poor, debtors and creditors, the landed, the manufacturing, the commercial interests, the inhabitants of this district or that district. . . . The only remedy is to enlarge the sphere, and thereby divide the community into so great a number of interests and parties, that a majority will not be likely to have a common interest separate from that of the whole or of the minority."

Enlarge the sphere and balance the interests, how wise a concept and how different in its result from the contrary concept of the late unlamented experiment of Communism with its narrow and sacrosanct trio of state, party and proletariat. What Madison proposed and what was adopted was nothing less than the first pluralist society. And so these supreme realists proclaimed the rule of law, making no attempt to reconcile such irreconcilables as freedom and authority, populace and property, but rather balancing the one against the other so that neither might gain a clear ascendancy to establish either extreme of anarchy or oligarchy.

More specifically the Convention in shedding the old unicameral legislature of the Continental Congress provided for a two-year term for the House, six for the Senate and four for the presidency, while approving the power of Congress to regulate foreign and interstate commerce, and prohibiting bills of attainder and ex post facto laws. Another achievement was the work of the Congress of the Articles of Confederation known as the Northwest Ordinance, which provided (1) each territory to be governed by a governor, a secretary and three judges appointed by Congress; (2) a bicameral legislature to be established when there were five thousand free adult males in the territory; (3) three to five states to be created eventually with a population of sixty thousand to be achieved before admission to the Union; (4) the new states to be "on an equal footing with the original states in all respects whatsoever"; (5) freedom of worship, right to trial by jury and public support of education; and (6) involuntary servitude (save in punishment for crime) to be prohibited. One unfortunate provision in the new Constitution was that in slave states three-fifths of the bondsmen were to be counted in determining the state's representation in the House. Within half a century this mischievous submission to Southern political power would emerge as one of the root causes of the Civil War.

Nevertheless, the Constitution was adopted, and on September 13, 1788, the Continental Congress passed the resolution ending its own life and putting the new government into operation. The First Congress was chosen, and then the presidential electors who made George Washington their unanimous choice. On April 30, 1789, Washington was inaugurated in New York.

The form of government which, in all its fundamental characteristics still governs the United States of America, had entered history.

The new government began life without money or an administrative system, with no navy or Marine Corps, an army down to 672 officers and men—and with war clouds still hovering over the horizon.

Britain had not withdrawn from her seven northwest posts as she had promised. Rather, after dividing Canada into the provinces of Lower and Upper Canada* (modern Quebec and Ontario), she planted Upper Canada's seat of government at Fort Niagara on the American side of the border. Britain also continued to sell arms to those Indians who were one of the young Republic's chief enemies.

To counteract British influence in the Northwest, the United States proposed to build a fort on the Maumee River in what is now northwest

---

* "Upper" or "Lower" Canada then did not relate to north or south but "up" or "down" the St. Lawrence and the Great Lakes chain. Thus "upper" was actually western and "lower" was eastern.

Ohio. In 1791 about two thousand men—the entire American Army—marched toward the Maumee under General Arthur St. Clair. The Indians, believing the fort aimed at them, prepared an ambush. St. Clair blundered into it and was put to rout with casualties of more than nine hundred men.

Elated, the Indians boasted that they would drive the "long knives" back across the Ohio. Britain encouraged them, for Britain hoped to block American expansion with an Indian buffer state. In the meantime, while the House of Representatives began an investigation that ended in placing the blame for the defeat on no one, the United States began to suffer at sea.

Without a navy to protect them, American merchant ships in the Mediterranean had fallen prey to the pirates of the Barbary Coast, the southern Mediterranean shore extending from Egypt to the Atlantic Ocean and consisting of the Muslim states of Tripoli, Tunis, Algiers and Morocco. Captured American seamen were held for ransom. Until it was paid they languished in prisons or toiled in chains at the oars of Algerian war galleys. Congress, forced to choose between war or tribute, talked belligerently of reviving the navy but actually did nothing. Then it appropriated $54,000 to ransom the sailors at $2,000 a head and appointed John Paul Jones to negotiate a treaty of tribute with the Dey of Algiers. Fortunately for Jones's honor, he died before he could complete his ignominious mission; unfortunately for the seamen, they were to suffer many more years in captivity before the Republic at last faced up to the war-or-tribute decision.

Meanwhile, the first ripples of the tidal wave unleashed by the French Revolution of 1789 were lapping at American shores. American sympathy for their republican brothers in France rose to near-hysterical devotion after the French decreed "a war of all peoples against all kings." That was in 1793, the same year in which Britain and the French Republic went to war. Love for France thereupon became synonymous with hatred for England, especially after British naval vessels began seizing American ships with cargoes bound for France. Britain claimed that any enemy property was a good prize, whether or not it was carried in a neutral ship. The Americans countered with the principle "Free ships make free goods." Actually, the debate was academic; Britain had no intention of allowing America to supply her French enemy, and she had the ships to prevent it.

A war clamor arose in America. Washington, determined to avoid foreign entanglement, sent John Jay to Britain to prevent war, and also to persuade the British to evacuate the Northwest forts. In the meantime, however, Upper Canada had built a new fort on the Maumee.

Indians, grown confident since their defeat of St. Clair, were encouraged to attack American settlements. They did, and Washington called on Anthony Wayne to restrain them.

Wayne spent the winter of 1793–94 at Greenville, Ohio, which he had named for his old friend, Nathanael Greene. In the spring of 1794 he moved out with a force of perhaps 2,500 men, regulars whom he had personally trained, as well as a few hundred mounted Kentucky riflemen. The Indians, between 1,500 and 2,000 from a half-dozen different tribes, retreated back toward the Canadian fort. They turned to fight at Fallen Timbers, a wide swath that a tornado had cut in the woods northwest of present-day Defiance. Hidden among twisted trunks and branches, the Indians were all but invisible. But the Americans in four columns marked by the white, red, yellow or green plumes of their officers' hats were unmistakable targets.

On August 20 the battle began with a charge of American dragoons against the Indian left. White horsehair plumes flying, sabers glittering, the mounted Americans galloped through an intense fire, leaped the timber barricades and fell upon the enemy with flashing steel. On the Indian right, infantry and riflemen fired one volley and charged with the bayonet. It was over in less than an hour. The Indians, as they admitted later, "could not stand up against the sharp ends of the guns."

Thus the critical year of 1794 was crowned with American military success. The prestige of the national government rose higher in 1795 as the Indians ceded the southeastern corner of the Northwest Territory, together with Vincennes, Detroit and the site of Chicago; it soared again in 1796 when the British withdrew from the Northwest forts.

Federalism, however, had reached its high-water mark. The rival theories of Alexander Hamilton and Thomas Jefferson had come out into the open and clashed, and in that collision political parties and the American two-party system were born. Hamilton's Federalists believed in an industrial America run by men of wealth and talent, while Jefferson's Republicans rallied under the standard of agrarianism and democracy. It was rule-by-the-best versus rule-by-the-most. The Federalists, political parents of today's Republicans, were realist and empiricist and they mistrusted the people; the Republicans, from whom the modern Democrats have descended, were idealist and rationalist and they trusted the people too much. Actually, the differences between the parties were never so distinct, shaded as they were by local rivalries and religious, racial and social disparities. But they were crystallized in 1794 when the war between Britain and France found the Federalists opting for Britain's conservative society and the Republicans backing republican France.

That war had repercussions in America, after John Adams became President by a narrow margin and took office in 1797. By then the French Revolution had been drowned in the blood bath of the Reign of Terror and the French Directory had become the arrogant afflictor of the Western world. Its armies, led by that very Napoleon Bonaparte who eventually destroyed the Directory and made France his own, had been victorious everywhere. Of all the Western nations, only Britain, Russia and the United States had not come to terms with France. Cheered on by the Republicans, the French fell upon the American merchant fleet with a ferocity that made previous British spoliations seem comparatively gentle. Distressed, Adams sent a mission to Paris.

It was received coldly. Foreign Minister Talleyrand sent a trio of minor officials (identified only as Messieurs X, Y and Z) to inform the Americans that negotiations would only be opened after a $250,000 bribe had been paid to Talleyrand, and a $10 million loan been granted to France. News of the XYZ Affair enraged America and rocked the Republicans; the rallying cry of "Millions for defense but not one cent for tribute" provided support for President Adams's policy of armed neutrality.

The policy actually was nothing less than declaration of a naval war with France. Congress revived the navy and Marine Corps, expanded the army, and sent such famous ships as the *United States, Constellation* and *Constitution* swaying down the ways. These and other warships were authorized to capture French armed vessels wherever they might be found, and in actual battle they gave far more than they got. Meanwhile, the army prepared to repulse an anticipated French invasion of America. George Washington put on his sword again to command this force of three thousand men, which he found to be a distasteful motley of "the riff-raff of the country and the scape-gallows of the large cities." Fortunately, the British navy bottled up Napoleon in Egypt and there was no French invasion. In 1799 the French government turned conciliatory and the Naval War with France quietly entered history.

The following year the Federalists lost power, never to regain it. Federalist intolerance as exemplified by the Alien and Sedition Acts—attempts to persecute the foreign-born and curb criticism—helped to establish Thomas Jefferson and his Republicans in office.

In Jefferson, the United States got a president eager to save money by reducing the strength of the armed forces; and although Congress authorized the founding of the United States Military Academy during his first term, it was over this pacifist's vigorous opposition. Mr. Jefferson, who also detested the shifting diplomacies of Europe, was to add in 1803 the diplomatic coup of the Louisiana Purchase. Derided as it was at the time, the purchase of the Louisiana Territory for $15 million from Napoleon (who had secretly recovered it from Spain) was a stupendous event that advanced the American frontier to the Rocky Mountains. Out of this huge province came four new states and parts of nine others, and with the Union already expanded to seventeen states through the admission of Vermont, Kentucky, Tennessee and Ohio, the continental expansion of the United States was already in full career not fifteen years after Washington had taken his first oath of office. In 1805 its advance parties penetrated to the Western Ocean, when Captain Meriwether Lewis and Lieutenant William Clark made their overland expedition to and from the Pacific.

So much territory, as loosely defended as it was loosely defined, naturally attracted the attention of adventurers—chief among them former Vice President Aaron Burr. After the Republicans had dropped him in the election of 1804, Burr had entered into a conspiracy with some New England Federalists who hoped to secede from the Union and form a Northern Confederacy. New York State was to be the keystone of this Federalist arch, and Burr tried to capture its governorship. He was defeated, mainly by the efforts of Hamilton. Enraged, Burr seized upon a reported slur on his character made by Hamilton—believed today to have been a charge that Burr was guilty of incest with his daughter Theodosia Burr Alton—and challenged Hamilton to a duel. It was fought in Weehawken, New Jersey, across the Hudson from New York City. Hamilton declined to set the hair trigger of his pistol, suggesting that he did not intend to fire and probably believed that Burr would not either. But Burr took deliberate aim and fired. Hamilton gave a convulsive leap, and as he fell his pistol discharged harmlessly. Thus perished, after thirty hours of intense pain, one of the great men of American history. Even more than Washington, he was the true soldier-statesman, able to write as well as fight, to execute as well as propose.

Indicted for murder, Burr fled into hiding off the Georgia coast. When Congress reconvened in 1804, he calmly resumed his duties as vice president until his term expired in March 1805, after which he went west to organize what seems to have been nothing less than a conspiracy to make himself emperor of Mexico and to set up an independent republic in Louisiana. Yet if plots and conspiracies came naturally to this bold bantam and ruthless charmer, they were also common to the age. Districts run by sturdy and honest men who went "up west" out of disgust with the fumbling Confederation had already flirted with Spain; while the fiercely republican state of Franklin, organized in east Tennessee by Nolichucky Jack Sevier, one of the heroes of the Battle of King's Mountain, often acted as though it had seceded from the Union. Nor were the Creoles of Louisiana happy when the Stars and Stripes were unfurled at New Orleans and the notes of "Yankee Doodle" came squealing into their cultivated ears. Therefore it was not surprising that Burr should win the friendship of such men as Andrew Jackson of Tennessee, that filibusterers should flock to his cause, or that the Catholic bishop of New Orleans should give him his blessing. In such times also it was almost automatic that Burr should find an accomplice in James Wilkinson, then commanding general of the American Army, federal governor of the Louisiana Territory—and Spy No. 13 in the pay of Spain. The conspiracy might very well have succeeded had not Wilkinson—finding even his duplicity unequal to the challenge of remaining a loyal conspirator, citizen and spy at one and the same time—decided to betray Burr.

Thomas Jefferson in his passion to bring about the conviction of his most bitter enemy spared no effort to bring Burr down, even coaching the triple traitor Wilkinson in the testimony he was to give against him. But Chief Justice John Marshall presiding at the trial made certain that the constitutional definition of treason—"levying war against the United States" with proof from "two witnesses to the same overt act"—was strictly observed. From this it followed that the mere gathering of forces without actual assault was not treason, and Burr was acquitted.

Perhaps regretting that he had killed the Federalist Hamilton and not his fellow Republican Jefferson, Burr fled to Europe. Charming as ever, he succeeded in gaining support and money for such wild schemes as the restoration of Canada to France, or to lead American sailors thrown out of work by Jefferson's Embargo Act in a march on Washington and there to set himself up as dictator. Failing in this, but ever resourceful, Burr by some unknown means obtained a passport, returning to New York City where he began practicing law. His final achievement was one not usually associated with a seventy-seven-year-old man: for he married the wealthy and beautiful widow Jumel, whose boast was that she had slept with George Washington *and* Napoleon: after which, having exhausted her fortune, the lady divorced Burr shortly before his death in 1836.

Thus, just as Washington had quietly crushed an incipient plot to set up a military dictatorship, Jefferson in thwarting Burr had effectively destroyed an attempt to organize on American soil a rival government to that of the United States. Ironically, this pacifist president's most popular policy was his decision to fight the pirates of the Barbary Coast of North Africa rather than pay them tribute.

~II~

WAR WITH THE BARBARY PIRATES

*Millions for Defense
but Not One Cent for Tribute!*

3

Thomas Jefferson

~ THOMAS JEFFERSON'S FAMILY WAS ONE OF THE OLDEST IN VIRGINIA, though not socially prominent like the Lees, Carters or Randolphs. His ancestors are believed to have migrated to the Old Dominion from Wales, probably near Snowdon, although the exact date is not known. His father was Peter Jefferson, a surveyor and a man of superb physique and legendary physical strength. He was a magistrate and sheriff of Goochland County, having settled in 1737 on a thousand acres of land among the western fringe of white families on the edge of the wilderness.

Like Abraham Lincoln, Peter Jefferson was a man of little formal education, but possessed of a powerful mind self-instructed through constant reading of the Bible and the plays of Shakespeare, as well as Jonathan Swift and the *Spectator* of Addison and Steele. His influence in the frontier community was great, and when Albemarle County was formed of territory split off from Goochland, he became a magistrate there as well as lieutenant colonel of militia. From 1755 until his death two years later he sat for his county in the House of Burgesses.

A close friend of the Randolphs, Peter Jefferson in 1739 married Jane Randolph, a union that was to mingle the blood of this vigorous, intelligent, gigantic man with that of the aristocratic Randolph clan. Just before his marriage, he bought from Colonel William Randolph, brother of his bride-to-be, a four hundred-acre tract of land in Albemarle County on the frontier of western Virginia. There he built the mansion called Shadwell, to which he eventually brought his nineteen-year-old wife. She gave birth to ten children; the third, called Thomas, was born on April 2, 1743.

Two years later Colonel Randolph died, after naming Peter Jefferson as the guardian for his young son Thomas Mann Randolph, and also as manager of his estate, Tuckahoe, on the James River in tidewater Virginia. Because Tuckahoe was too far away from Shadwell to be properly controlled, Jefferson moved his family to the James, where they lived for seven years. Thus Thomas was nine when he returned to Shadwell, and gazed in delight for the first time on the height called Monticello, or "little mountain," that would be his land of heart's desire. Here he would build his splendid mansion of the same name, but here in 1752 he came only to listen to the evening song of the wood thrushes and try to imitate them on his beloved violin, or else merely gaze in loving awe at the violet mists of dusk descending on the Blue Ridge Mountains. But these moments of reverie were all too infrequent for Thomas: almost immediately upon his return to Shadwell he was sent to board with the Reverend William Douglas to study Latin, Greek and French.

No more than this is known of the young student at this time, but then, five years later, his father died leaving Thomas at fourteen the head of a family now reduced to his widowed mother, one brother and six sisters. He also left him comparatively wealthy, with thirty slaves, 2,750 acres of land and an unknown sum of money that was probably respectable, coming as it did from a leading citizen of sharp business acumen as well as helpful political connections.

Wealthy, well-connected socially and politically, Thomas could look forward to success in any calling that he chose, or to be content with the life of a country gentlemen living off the produce of his estate and amid the quiet republican elegance of which he would become so fond. Moreover, his father had left instructions that he should receive the finest classical education, and to achieve this the youth spent the next two years studying under the Reverend James Maury, whom he later described as "a correct classical scholar."

Thomas was probably unaware that he was growing up on the frontier, the "West" where life was simpler and freer than on the seaboard "East," where blood was bluer and property and privilege the marks of success. He probably did not realize either that the freer but poorer frontiersmen were also willing to risk change—if not actually seek it— for the sake of betterment, while the seignurial families of the Tidewater sought the status quo to protect what they had. Thus there was born in him very early in life a dislike of privilege using authority as a shield and a love of liberty that was the mark of the liberal political thinkers of the day—the great British theorists such as John Locke and Sir Algernon Sidney. This was an unconscious formation of the mind that was also affecting other Blue Ridge boys his age such as Patrick Henry, John Marshall and James Madison. So Thomas, for all his wealth and social connections, probably through no deliberate decision, chose the study of political theory and a political career. In the spring of 1760 he enrolled in the College of William and Mary at Williamsburg, then still the capital of Virginia.

By then Thomas Jefferson had reached physical maturity, having inherited his father's height, though not his physique: he stood six feet two and one-half inches tall, was slender, red-haired, handsome, and extremely poised with a quiet bearing that concealed a voluble conversational gift that burst forth only when he was intellectually aroused. Among his chief characteristics at William and Mary were his ability to converse on almost equal terms with his instructors and his capacity for friendship. His friendship with Lafayette, for instance, endured for half a century; and so did his affection for John Adams and Patrick Henry, though both seemed to be broken either by difference of opinion or political allegiance, yet were both renewed.

After his graduation in 1762 and his decision to study law, Thomas remained abreast of and mostly approved of all those events that were alienating the colonies from the mother country, and he was in the audience at the House of Burgesses on May 29, 1765, when his friend Henry arose to make his famous speech: "Caesar had his Brutus, Charles the First his Cromwell and George the Third"—from somewhere the cry, "Treason!" arose, and Henry continued—"may profit from their example. If *this* be treason, make the most of it."

Although Henry after the war became reactionary and Jefferson remained liberal, he never shed his admiration of his friend's command of language. Of Henry's eloquence, Jefferson wrote: "I never heard anything that deserved to be called by the same name with what flowed from him; and where he got that torrent of language was inconceivable." And yet: "I have frequently shut my eyes while he spoke, and when he was done asked myself what he had said, without being able to recollect a word of it. He was no logician." True, and Thomas Jefferson was no orator, his voice becoming weak and throaty after only a few minutes of public speaking.

It was as a writer and a political theorist that Jefferson made his mark in public life. These skills, together with that genius for friendship and his remarkable political acumen, led him to the Second Continental Congress in Philadelphia—where he wrote the immortal Declaration of Independence, on which his fame has since rested. Because he was a doctrinal pacifist, Jefferson did not take his place on the battlefield along with other Founding Fathers such as Washington, Alexander Hamilton and James Monroe. Rather he was elected first governor of the new Commonwealth of Virginia, where he proved to be a highly unpopular and unsatisfactory executive: the first in a long line of American politicians whose political skills and ambitions outran their administrative ability.

Nevertheless, he did enter public life, being elected to the House of Burgesses and showing in his first session—1769—that he was definitely in favor of that stream of resolutions issuing from Williamsburg to London proclaiming the rights of the colonies as well as their right to unite in pursuit of those rights. Jefferson also made public his lifelong detestation of slavery by introducing a bill granting slave-owners the power to free their bondsmen. It failed to pass, of course, but Jefferson never ceased trying to abolish slavery, although by then he was one of the great slaveholders of Virginia.

Through his marriage on January 1, 1772, to the wealthy widow Martha Skelton, his own holding of thirty slaves and 2,750 acres of land was augmented enormously by her own inheritance of 40,000 acres and 130 slaves, all of which by Virginia law became Jefferson's property.

Jefferson's large slave-labor force is one of the great contradictions of his career. He did indeed detest the pernicious institution of slavery, so far losing his balance on the subject that in his great work—the Declaration of Independence—he unjustly poured vituperation on the head of George III as though that unlovely but much-maligned sovereign were guilty of inventing the dreadful system. Fortunately, this abusive language—which might have issued from a guilty conscience—was deleted. But Jefferson's repeated vows to free his bondsmen—as Washington did quietly, posting the necessary funds to keep them off the public charge as required by Virginia law—never were executed. By then Jefferson had almost completed Monticello, having hurried its construction along after Shadwell burned to the ground in 1770 and he invited his homeless mother and sisters to come live with him in the partially completed mansion. As it says in the Bible, "Where your treasure is, there also is your heart," and it is clear where Jefferson's treasure was when he wrote in grief to a friend: "I calculate the *cost* of the books burned to have been £200 sterling. Would to God it had been the money, *then* had it never cost me a sigh." He did not even liberate his black mistress Sally Hemings, with whom he had become so infatuated after the death of his wife. Probably he may have thought that freeing her alone among all his slaves would set malicious tongues wagging. Some historians and biographers have suggested that by then Thomas Jefferson was so broke he could not have afforded mass manumission, and certainly could not have been able to post the necessary funds required for their welfare. If this is so, then it would seem that Jefferson was not only a poor executive but also could not manage money, not an unusual failing in an intellectual.

Neither was he the original thinker portrayed by his biographers in their desire to crown him prince of the Founding Fathers. This claim is based only on his vast erudition and the Declaration itself, which was actually a rewrite of his friend George Mason's Declaration of Rights written as a preamble to the Virginia constitution. Splendid rewrite though it was, compressing 143 languid words into 73 forming half a dozen ringing and immortal phrases, the ideas were not really Jefferson's or even Mason's but rather those of John Locke. As Jefferson himself freely admitted, Locke's trinity of inalienable rights—"life, liberty and property," the latter changed to "pursuit of happiness" probably for rhythm and felicity, though happiness is not actually a right but a desirable condition—were the "harmonizing sentiments of the day." Thus it is closer to the truth to say that Jefferson was a profound student of political philosophy, but not an original thinker in the way of either Locke or his friend James Madison.

Nor was he "profoundly religious" as James Truslow Adams in his *Living Jefferson* (1936) has maintained, but rather an English deist believing that there might be a Creator God, but that He is unknowable and indifferent to his Creation. Protector of religious freedom he was indeed, for he had the perception to see that religion must be free in every sense of the word: either from the outright hostility of persecution or the corrosive coddling of an established faith.

It is doubtful that any man in American history was more charming or cultivated than Thomas Jefferson, and certainly no man ever rivaled his capacity for "the good life." When he arrived in Paris in 1785 to help John Adams and Benjamin Franklin negotiate treaties between their new country and the European powers, he was pleasantly surprised to learn that his fame had preceded him, and his welcome was almost as affectionate and tumultuous as the reception given Franklin during the Revolutionary War. Here was another rare bird—a sophisticated and cultivated American—to delight the minds of the encyclopedists and the hearts of those same contessas and marchesas who only a few years earlier had gathered each morning around Franklin holding court in bed.

Finally this man of so many contradictions was indeed a pacifist who bitterly opposed the founding of the United States Military Academy at West Point, and also—his horror of war aided and abetted by his passion for saving money—reduced the army to hardly more than a ceremonial battalion while all but scuttling the navy that had done so well in the Naval War with France; yet, for all his pacifist convictions, his red-haired outrage at the torments suffered by his countrymen wasting away in Muslim prisons let his heart get the better of his head and lead him to war with the Barbary pirates.

4

The Barbary Pirates

☙ IF NAUTICAL HISTORY BEGAN ON THE SURFACE OF THE MEDITERRANEAN Sea, as seems likely, then piracy began there also. Homer had Ulysses boast of being "a sacker of cities." Julius Caesar was captured by pirates there, and kept his vow to return and hang them all. Cervantes, the author of the immortal *Don Quixote,* was held captive in Algeria for five years.

Piracy on the Barbary Coast reached its golden age early in the sixteenth century under Khayr ad-Din, the legendary Barbarossa, or Redbeard, who rose to become admiral of the Ottoman Empire. It was he who founded the pirate states of Tunis and Algeria, later joined by Tripoli and Morocco. These four were known as the Barbary Kingdoms after the Greek word *barbarian,* meaning all foreigners who could not speak Greek. They were part of the huge Islamic empire ruled by the sultan in Constantinople, a dominion of subject states so enormous that it threatened to engulf the entire civilized globe; until in 1570 the galleys of Don Juan of Austria defeated those of Sultan Suleyman the Magnificent at Lepanto. Thereafter the Muslim world— never able to construct a system of government other than a simple tyranny, nourished only by loot and hardly capable of building a road—fell into pieces of its own weight.

Four of these pieces formed the Barbary states extending east to west from Egypt to the Atlantic. In the main they were populated by

Arabs and Berbers, a Hamitic people related to Egyptians and southern Europeans and ranging from blue-eyed blondes of the Atlas Mountains to olive-skinned, black-eyed brunets of the seacoasts or black inhabitants of desert oases. Strictly speaking the Barbary pirates were not buccaneers per se. Rather they were citizens or subjects of these four countries at war with other countries. They captured ships as prizes and either enslaved enemy seamen or held them for ransom, just as some but not all of their foes did. They also made rather a good thing of their Muslim faith, prowling the Mediterranean like sea wolves feeding on their Christian enemies. Most of them believed—and the rest pretended to believe—that it was a Muslim's duty to make war on Christians, and any son of Muhammad who fell in a *jihad,* or holy war, against the infidels went straight to a paradise inhabited by obliging and tireless concubines called *houris,* beautiful, perpetual virgins. By the late eighteenth century piracy and its concomitant evil of white slavery had become the major industry of the North African coast.

Each of the seaboard cities held regular auctions in which captive men, women and children were prodded onto the block like so many cattle. The slave market was as crass and calculating as any stock market of today, with pitiless speculators buying in a glutted "down" market and holding their purchases in miserable dungeons until the supply of prisoners slackened and the higher prices of the ensuing "up" market began to appear. If some of those imprisoned died in captivity, the loss was figured into the price of the survivors.

In the beginning the local dey or bashaw confiscated the stronger men as oarsmen on his galleys, but after the shift to sailing ships they were "freed" to become forced laborers on palaces and fortifications. Educated captives were used as clerks. Young and pretty women were sold as concubines and handsome boys peddled to the pederasts so prevalent in the Arab world. Wealthy or titled captives were the outstanding prizes who could bring much more in ransom than on the auction block. The chief beneficiaries of this iniquitous traffic in human flesh were the pirate captains. They became incredibly rich, building palaces rivaling the splendor of those of the Barbary rulers.

These chieftains were nominally the vassals of the sultan in Constantinople, but because of the looseness of the Muslim confederation they were actually absolute and independent despots. They enjoyed unlimited power and ruled by terror, always with a Damoclean sword dangling over their head. To relax their cruel grasp upon their people was to invite some brother or son to rebel and murder them, always by strangulation, because in Islamic law royal blood cannot be spilled.

Punishment was quick and cruel, the mildest being the bastinado, a beating of the bare feet with a stout stick for disrespect or talking back to a palace official. A thief's right hand would be cut off and hung around his neck while he was paraded through the streets riding backward on a donkey with the jeering townspeople pelting him with stones and filth. Among the prisoners caught attempting to escape, the ringleaders were beheaded and their followers given five hundred strokes of the bastinado. If a captive were so audacious and so clever as to seduce a Muslim woman, he was beheaded and the woman taken out to sea where she was tied in a weighted sack and thrown overboard. Blaspheming or disparaging the Koran, the Islamic holy book, was punished by roasting alive, impalement or crucifixion. The crime of treason or of a Christian killing a Muslim brought the most hideous and ingenious penalty: the culprit was hung by his flesh on the huge iron hooks imbedded in the palace wall so that the birds might devour him alive. If, in his writhing, twisting agony, he should free himself, his fall on the jagged rocks below was a blessing delivering him from the flocks of winged harpies following him down. Christians who died were tossed onto the same rocks, their bodies carried out to sea by surging waves. Christians taken prisoner of war were usually led out into view of their comrades and there impaled, sometimes after having been forced to eat their noses and ears.

Obviously such tactics made the people no more loyal to their local ruler than he was to the sultan, and it was only in the narrow confines of the walled seaboard towns that he could enforce his will on his destitute population: so many of them the victims of ubiquitous and numerous Mediterranean diseases, especially the blight of blindness brought on by a combination of burning sun and blowing sand, biting insects and inadequate or nonexistent medical care. Often the pirate towns were in a sense trapped, with a frequently hostile sea to their front and an unfriendly countryside to their rear. So the Barbary rulers came to be dependent for both luxuries and necessities on what they could steal on the sea. Thus, like latter-day Vikings they raided the Christian coasts of the Latin kingdoms on the Mediterranean, foraging as far away as Ireland on the Atlantic or Denmark on the Baltic.

At the outset of their depredations the Barbary pirates were hardly worse than their enemies because there were then no international conventions or treaties prohibiting piracy or covering the treatment of prisoners. When the seafaring states became more civilized and did develop such codes, the various beys or bashaws ruling these kingdoms got around such difficulty by a "declaration of war" against any nation whose ships could be a likely source of loot, and whose citizens could be enslaved or held for ransom. By this transparent legalism their corsairs became privateers, that is, seamen of a warring power licensed to attack enemy shipping, rather than as outlaw pirates. This was a recognized custom of the day, always depending upon a state of war; and to a Barbary ruler no pretext was too flimsy to declare that such a state existed. The most common was that the country chosen for plunder had refused to pay tribute as the price of peace.

Actually these payments were not tribute—a stated sum payed by a vassal state to a superior in acknowledgment of subjugation—but naked extortion extracted under the threat of force. "Tribute" was not only a euphemism used to help the government of the intimidated country save face, but also an expression of the Barbary rulers' unshakable belief that they were the lords of the Mediterranean and any other sea power venturing into their domain was fair game.

The British in 1646 were the first to pay tribute when Parliament sent an emissary to Algiers to ransom hundreds of Britishers enslaved there. This led to a regular system of payments to protect British shipping, and soon other European sea powers adopted the custom. It was cynically believed that these bribes were less costly than going to war with the Barbary powers. In exchange for their forebearance, the pirates developed a system of "passports" issued to the ships and seamen of those countries that had purchased their immunity to attack. Sometimes they were ignored by a rogue Barbary captain seeking to rival his ruler's opulence, but usually they were respected. Sometimes also the greedy Barbary sovereigns would make tribute demands so exorbitant that the European powers would remember their sense of honor and send punitive fleets to the Barbary Coast. Piracy would then subside, until a new European war would erupt and the continent's crowned heads would be too distracted by the sport of kings to endure the higher expense of keeping the nuisance suppressed. So the payments would be renewed, and by the end of the eighteenth century they were regular and unchallenged, not the least because by then the great powers had come to realize that they denied the lucrative trade center of the Mediterranean to lesser rivals who could not afford to pay for their protection.

One of the least of these weaker nations was the fledgling United States of America.

Weak and divided though the United States had been prior to the Constitutional Convention, the merchant marine had not only remained strong but grew stronger. Shipping merchants and shipbuilders ignored the political crisis and resumed the profitable trade that had been halted by the war. Within months after Cornwallis's surrender, the *Empress of China* sailed from New York to Canton, and those sleek, swift American sailing ships that would one day be known as Yankee clippers were soon trading in all the ports of the Old World. There their skippers, shrewd seagoing merchants, peddled American merchandise for a profit, then bought European goods to sell for another profit wherever they could find a market. Typical of these seafaring sharpers was the legendary "Lord" Timothy Dexter of Salem, Massachusetts, who reputedly sold coal to the miners of Newcastle, bed-warming pans in tropical Bermuda and wines in France. In 1783, the year the former British colonies became the United States, a Parliament still so sulky over the Yorktown debacle that it had not yet sent a minister to the new nation, responded to the Yankee competition by an Order in Council prohibiting American trade with British islands in the West Indies.

U.S. shippers countered by scrambling for new markets elsewhere, particularly in the flourishing trade centers of the Mediterranean. Something like a hundred ships employing 1,200 seamen sailed for that inland sea annually, carrying about twenty thousand tons of flour, lumber, sugar and salted fish, while sailing home with cargoes of fruit, olive oil and opium. Protected by no tribute, they inevitably became the prey of Barbary pirates.

In 1784 the Boston brig *Betsey* bound for Tenerife in the Canary Islands was captured by Moroccan corsairs. Fortunately, Emperor Sidi Mahomet of Morocco was an unusually unferocious ruler more interested in trade than piracy and proud of having been one of the first heads of state to recognize the new American nation. So he ordered *Betsey* released with her captain and crew and informed the delighted skipper that he would welcome a U.S. envoy.

Dey Mahomet of Algeria, however, was not so compassionate. Three months later his pirate ships captured the American ships *Maria* and *Dauphin*. A crewman aboard the *Maria* has described the corsairs' tactics. Sailing in a xebec, a small, swift, three-masted shoaling ship favored by Barbary pirates and ideal for boarding, the Algerians came swarming over the gunwales of the defenseless *Maria* to strip its crew and captain of all they possessed down to their underwear. After a prize crew was put aboard *Maria,* the captive Americans were herded aboard the xebec and driven below decks to a dark, verminous hold already overcrowded by thirty-six men and one woman seized in earlier captures. Taken to Algiers, the shivering half-naked prisoners were paraded through winding streets so narrow that they could brush against the snarling, cursing Algerians who welcomed these unclean infidels with the customary foul reception. Flung into prisons, they were auctioned off for the usual purposes while the single woman—being nubile—was shipped off to the sultan's harem in Constantinople as a gift of the dey: the first American to be so favored.

Although enraged by these reports, there was little the inept Continental Congress could do to succor their countrymen, except to bow to the threat of further attacks and negotiate a treaty with Morocco based on small, regular payments of tribute. But with the Dey of Algiers they could do nothing. Despite his contempt for the new American nation he still demanded $3,000 ransom apiece, twice what he asked from any other power. This the penniless Congress simply could not pay, so the helpless Americans—grown in number to 119 by 1793—remained in the clutches of this vile and evil Muslim chief, living a life that can be described as nothing less than a sacrament of hell.

Their story was told by John Foss, a foremast seaman aboard the brig *Polly* captured by Algerian brigands in October of that year. As a foretaste of what to expect in Algiers, the American prisoners were informed by Captain Rais Hudga Mahomet Salamia that they could expect nothing but cruel treatment "for your history and superstition in believing in a man who was crucified by the Jews, and disregarding the true doctrine of God's last and greatest prophet, Mahomet." It was worse ashore where Algerians cursing Jesus and praising Allah—many of them blind and most in rags with their bodies covered by running sores—escorted them to the palace of Ali Hassan, the new Dey of Algeria. He was a light-skinned Turk in his sixties with a flowing beard and a heart full of hate. "Now I have got you, you Christian dogs," he snarled from his throne, "you shall eat stones." Selecting four handsome boys to be palace servants—and probably also love boys—he ordered the rest of the Americans marched into prison.

There they were issued a bundle of clothing that included a prison uniform, hooded jacket, pantaloons and slippers, plus a single blanket for bedding. At 5 P.M. they were fed on a small loaf of sour black bread per man. Breakfast and lunch each day consisted of but a chunk of the same bread which was to be eaten within ten minutes. At 3 A.M. they were awakened, lined up, chained together, and marched off to a mountain. There they were freed from their gang chain but were still confined by a personal chain with a thirty-pound weight at the end. If, during work, a prisoner reached the end of his tether, he had to carry this ball to a new location.

Foss's detail received pickaxes to dig holes in the mountain's rocky base, carrying the debris away in baskets. When the hole was completed, guards filled it with explosive and detonated it, breaking away ten- to twenty-ton chunks that the prisoners rolled down the mountain to waiting sleds. Once a week the captives were fastened to the loaded sleds like oxen and then, driven by goads, made to haul them to the shore, where they were lifted onto barges that carried them out to sea to extend the mole. Other prisoners served as beasts of burden, transporting all portable goods from place to place in the city. More fortunate ones went to work on the docks, cleansing hulls of barnacles and worms, unloading ships or fitting them out.

Whatever the labor, it was unceasing. Overseers of the sled details competed with each other to win the dey's weekly prizes, and so drove their crews unmercifully with whips. One man who had been captured with his seven sons saw one of them fall and be crushed beneath a sled. His pleas for succor were unheeded and the youth died the next day. When a tarantula bit another prisoner so that his head swelled double, he was sent back to work, finally dying in a "hospital" that was actually a charnel house. Two weeks later another man suffered the same horrible end. Undernourished and weakened by unremitting work, the prisoners were prone to every epidemic sweeping the disease-ridden Barbary Coast.

No wonder that these Americans beseeched their countrymen to do something to free them from this living hell. Captain Richard O'Brien of the *Dauphin*, who had become one of the dey's clerks in 1792, wrote a moving plea to the Protestant ministers of New England, New York and Virginia, concluding: "Lift up your voices like a trumpet, cry aloud in the cause of humanity. . . . " Families and friends, politicians and preachers, did rally to the cause of the American hostages. Gradually pressure on Congress to do something became so intense that at the end of 1793 it began to debate the wisdom of building a powerful navy to liberate their countrymen and cleanse the Mediterranean of any necessity to pay tribute. Opinion was evenly and bitterly divided between anti-navy Southern planters and pro-navy Northern shippers, but after four months of argument a compromise was reached providing that a six-ship fleet would be built at a cost of $688,888, but that if an agreement could be negotiated with Ali Hassan, work on the ships would stop. The day President Washington signed the bill was March 27, 1794, now considered the birthday of the U.S. Navy and Marine Corps. The trio of heavier, 44-gun ships were to be named the *United States, Constitution* and *President,* and the lighter 36-gun vessels *Constellation, Chesapeake* and *Congress.* To be sure that all the nautical building skills available on the Atlantic coast would go into their design and construction, and that all regions would profit financially from the work, contracts were given to shipyards from Portsmouth, New Hampshire, to Norfolk, Virginia.

The next step in this momentous program was to find the right architect. Fortunately Secretary of War Henry Knox was the son of a ship captain, and even though he had no naval experience, having been Washington's artillery commander during the Revolution, he knew enough to look for the best and most original shipbuilder and designer he could find.

His choice to supervise construction could not have been happier: Joshua Humphreys, who had built his first ship at twenty-one, and then, at forty-three, was a well-known and highly respected shipbuilder in Philadelphia. Knox also chose his partner, Josiah Fox, a thirty-year-old member of a wealthy British shipbuilding family who was in America to survey its naval-stores supply. Once again Knox made an admirable selection. Humphreys and Fox, though they frequently disagreed, were neither one of them so inflexible that they could see no merit in the other's suggestions. Although Fox had been for smaller ships, he eventually acknowledged the wisdom of building the bigger, speedier vessels envisioned by Humphreys. The result, according to Knox, was to "combine such qualities of strength, durability, swiftness of sailing, and force, as to render them equal if not superior to any frigate belonging to any of the European Powers." Although this combination would be less than ideal for chasing light-draft xebecs in the shallow, shoaly waters of the Barbary coast, Humphreys's long-range view of involvement in the Napoleonic Wars then impending was fortunate foresight. It is not known how the Britisher Fox felt about designing warships that might one day be challenging those of the Royal Navy.

But then in December 1795, with the new ships only half finished, it appeared that an impending peace with Algeria would scuttle the new U.S. Navy before it was even afloat.

Dey Ali Hassan of Algeria was uncomfortably aware of the powerful new fleet a-building in the United States. Although he was considered the strongest of the Barbary pirates, his own flotilla of fewer than a dozen xebecs and four oared-galleys could never hope to meet such formidable vessels in a ship-to-ship, shot-for-shot engagement. His was a hit-and-run navy that would have to scurry for the protection of Algiers Harbor to escape destruction. Even so, an American blockade could starve Algeria to death. Time and distance were Hassan's only weapons: another year or so to complete the half-finished American ships, the vast line of communications between their home ports and his harbor. So he suggested to Captain O'Brien that he convey to the United States government his interests in negotiating a peace at the price of $2.5 million plus two frigates.

This outrageous offer was received by David Humphreys—no relation of Joshua—the U.S. minister to Portugal, who, while intending to discuss no such figure, saw the feeler as the first opportunity to talk of peace. So he sent his assistant Joseph Donaldson to Algiers. Severely stricken by gout, Donaldson arrived in Algiers on crutches and was met by O'Brien and Micaiah Bacri, the dey's money man. Limping painfully to the nearest couch, Donaldson collapsed on it mouthing a string of curses. Bacri was shocked, but O'Brien assured him in lingua franca: "The Ambassador is only saying his prayers, and giving God thanks for his safe arrival." Bacri nodded, murmuring, "His devotion is very fervent."

So were Donaldson's objections to Hassan's absurd demands, so much so that the dey angrily ordered him out of his presence. But O'Brien had briefed the ambassador on the dey's foul temper, and he did not at all depart, but reminded him of that fleet taking shape in America. Eventually, it was agreed that the United States would make a lump-sum payment of $642,000 for the prisoners (of which $240,000 was for Hassan's personal use) and pay annual tribute of only $21,600. On September 5, 1795, the treaty was signed to the roar of a twenty-one-gun salute and the raising of the American flag again in Algiers. At the instance of the dey, Bashaw Yusuf Karamanli of Tripoli signed a similar agreement for an annual payment of naval stores worth $58,000, and Bey Hamouda of Tunis did the same a year later. Yankee skill at bargaining (not to say haggling) had apparently triumphed, much to the angry lashing of the British lion's tail at such a cheap purchase of peace, and to the jubilation of frugal members of Congress anxious to cash what is today called "the peace dividend" resulting from an end to the costly shipbuilding program.

But then President Washington, having been convinced by his former secretary of state, Thomas Jefferson, that force was the only way to end the evil of the Barbary pirates, showed Congress a subtlety not often associated with his august and austere style. Acknowledging that the 1794 bill authorizing the new navy had also stipulated that if peace were to be negotiated, he as chief executive would have to order all work on the six ships stopped, he slyly suggested that before taking such a drastic step he would like to submit the matter to Congress for a decision. In other words if a public howl is raised in the six shipyard states affected by this loss of revenue and employment, blame yourselves, boys—not me. Congress, predictably, decided to continue work on the big frigates, and then, if the president so ordered, on the smaller as well.

Thus, it seemed, war with the Barbary pirates had been avoided, and everyone seemed satisfied—except Thomas Jefferson.

5

Tripoli Declares War

$\sim$ THOMAS JEFFERSON FIRST ENCOUNTERED THE PROBLEM OF THE BAR-bary pirates in 1785 after he arrived in Paris to join Benjamin Franklin and John Adams in negotiating treaties between their new country and the European powers.

Renting a fine mansion on the Champs Elysées, Jefferson indulged his extravagant tastes by filling it with silver, linen, crystal, antiques, paintings and dozens of books he could never have bought in still-unlettered America. He soon set one of the finest tables in Paris, stocking his wine cellar with the great vintages, particularly the wines of the St.-Julien district in Bordeaux, his favorite vineyards. He did not, of course, address himself to such pleasures alone, but went immediately to work with Franklin and Adams, even then struggling with the baffling problem of the Barbary bandits.

Almost at once Jefferson, despite his pacifism, argued for the use of force rather than pay tribute, for he correctly perceived that money would only buy an uneasy peace and lead to higher and higher demands. John Adams disagreed. "We ought not to fight them at all," he told Jefferson, "unless we determine to fight them forever. This thought, I fear, is too rugged for our people to bear."

Jefferson insisted that there were only three options: (1) annual tribute, (2) ransom and (3) force. The first—tribute—the United States could never afford. Britain alone was paying the Dey of Algeria, the most powerful of the Barbary rulers, about a quarter million dollars a year; France about $100,000 annually; and the smaller nations of Denmark, Sweden and Venice roughly $30,000 yearly. Impoverished America could not spare a tenth of that amount. Option two—ransom—was also unthinkable because it would only lead to more and more prisoners and higher demands. Option three—naval force—was the only acceptable answer.

But with what? The United States still had no army or navy and only a little money. Nevertheless throughout the ensuing sixteen years Thomas Jefferson continued to advocate naval force as the solution to the lawless depredations of the Barbary powers; and then, on March 9, 1801, five days after his inauguration as president, he convened his cabinet to discuss just such a policy. Two million dollars in ransom and tribute paid so far to Algiers, Morroco, Tunis and Tripoli had been "money thrown away," he told his secretaries. "There is no end to the demands of these powers, nor any security in their promises." The cabinet became divided, some advocating dispatch of a squadron to the Mediterranean to protect American shipping there, others warning that only Congress—not the executive—could declare war. Four days later Secretary of State Madison received a message from the U.S. consul in Tripoli warning: "The cruisers of this Regency are now fitting out for sea and will sail the beginning of April, probably to capture Americans." This message encouraged the cabinet hawks to argue that Jefferson should openly proclaim that an American squadron would attack any vessel threatening American commerce. Yet, debate on the issue continued for two more months, until on May 15 it was decided to send the squadron. Before then Bashaw Yusuf Karamanli of Tripoli, angered by Jefferson's discontinuance of the tribute, sent his soldiers to the U.S. consulate to cut down its flagpole, the quaint Barbary way of declaring war.

By this decision the bashaw lifted President Jefferson off the horns of a dilemma. A strict constitutionalist, Jefferson was uneasy about sending the squadron to the Mediterranean without a Congressional declaration of war. He did not ask Congress for one because that body was in recess, perhaps providing the president with an opportune moment. Certainly he made no attempt to call a special session, either convinced that most of the members would refuse to come back to Washington, or else because he did not want a public quarrel with Congress so early in his administration. So he let the order stand, and when he learned of Yusuf's flagpole-chopping expedition he may have felt there was now no necessity for America to respond with its own declaration. But he did warn Bashaw Yusuf: "We mean to rest the safety of our commerce on the resources of our own strength and bravery in every sea."

• • •

When Jefferson decided to send the American squadron across the Atlantic to the Mediterranean—the first such expedition in U.S. naval history—it was commonly believed that he would appoint Captain Thomas Truxtun to command it. This was because Truxtun had a great reputation as a valiant fighter who could win battles against superior foes. But Jefferson for some obscure reason did not like him, perhaps because of his deep distrust of violent or angry men. Furthermore, Truxtun, though more intrepid and more famous, was ranked by Captain Richard Dale of Virginia. So Jefferson gave the command to Dale with the rank of commodore.

Dale is something of a sport in American military history, chiefly because he never had a biographer and because during the Revolutionary War he first embraced the Patriot cause, next the British and then finally and forever the Stars and Stripes again. The son of a Virginia shipwright, Dale took to the sea early and when war with Britain erupted he was at nineteen already a chief mate. In 1776 he became a lieutenant on a ship of the little navy of Virginia. Captured by the British, he was thrown into the hold of a foul prison ship where a staunchly Loyalist former schoolmate talked him into switching sides. He joined his friend aboard a British tender and was wounded in the head in a fight with Patriot pilot boats on the lower Rappahannock. Recuperating from his wound, he reflected on his peculiar situation, deciding that if he were to be wounded again or killed, it would best be by his true enemy: the British.

Dale's chance to return to his original allegiance occurred on a voyage to Bermuda when he was captured by "Fighting" Jack Barry, the Irish seaman commanding the sloop of war *Lexington*, who would be known as "the father of the U.S. Navy." Becoming a master's mate under Barry, Dale sailed with him on *Lexington*'s legendary cruise to the West Indies and European waters.

Richard Dale's most glorious moment came in 1779 when he was a lieutenant aboard John Paul Jones's *Bonhomme Richard* during its famous moonlight battle with *Serapis*. With *Richard* foundering, he swung by a rope aboard *Serapis* to lead the boarding party that captured the Britisher. For this valorous deed, Jones gave him the gold-mounted sword he had received from King Louis XVI of France. Throughout the Revolution and the Naval War with France, Dale improved his reputation for valor and nautical skill. In 1794 when George Washington established the rankings for the new navy, Jack Barry was first and Richard Dale fourth.

Some historians have suggested that thereafter the fires of ardor burned lower in Richard Dale's soul. More likely, the hamstringing restrictions placed upon him by Acting Secretary Samuel Smith—probably at the insistence of the pacifist Jefferson and the cautious Madison—severely limited the opportunities for aggressive action. His was to be a "defensive war" based chiefly on blockading the port of Tripoli. If he captured any vessels or seamen of the pirate powers, the ships were to be returned and Dale was to treat his prisoners "with humanity and attention, and land them on some part of the Barbary shore. . . ." If battle could not be avoided, Smith wrote, "we enjoin on you the most rigorous moderation, conformity to right and reason and suppression of all passion. . . ." To cover himself from accusations of "softness," the secretary added that he was to accept no insult or permit no officer of another power to board any of his ships. Nevertheless, the meaning was clear: *wear*—but do not *bare*—the cutlass.

So instructed, Commodore Dale sailed from Hampton Roads on June 2, 1801. His squadron consisted of his flagship, the newly launched *President,* 44 guns; two other frigates: *Philadelphia,* 38; built and equipped by the merchants of that city and commanded by Captain Samuel Barron; and *Essex,* 32, commanded by Captain William Bainbridge. The sloop of war *Enterprise,* 12, was under Lieutenant Andrew Sterrett.

In those days so well-named by C. S. Forester as "The Age of Fighting Sail" the mark of a major sea power was the number of ships-of-the-line-of-battle in its navy. These sea mammoths, famous and formidable, were two hundred feet long carrying three tiers of heavy cannon capable of hurling half a ton of spinning cannon balls or of howling grape and langrage—that is, clusters of small iron balls, or bags containing chain, bolts, shot and nails—in a single devastating "broadside." These capital ships were called ships of the line of battle because of their tactic of sailing in single file in order to concentrate dozens of broadsides upon a single target. Later their name was shortened to *liner* and later still changed to *battleship.* They fired broadsides because all but a few of their guns were mounted on either side of the ship with only a half-dozen or so lighter "bow- and stern-chasers" mounted fore and aft. A liner carried as many as one hundred guns. None of these could be fired from turrets to be swiveled or raised and lowered in either direction as in the new *Dreadnought* class of steam-powered, steel-armored, all-big-gun battleships introduced by Britain in 1906. Instead they were fired straight through fixed gunports that opened along each side of the ship and sighted by the naked eye. Nevertheless, because these great ships fought each other at such close range—usually at "half-pistol shot" or less than fifty yards—they did terrible destruction to each other.

Only the great naval powers could afford such behemoths, certainly not a struggling new nation such as the United States with its fledgling navy. That was why Secretary Knox's selection of Joshua Humphreys to design his ships was such a happy choice. Authorized to build only frigates—fast-sailing ships with a single gun deck—he broke with tradition by giving them two gun decks and more sail. Thus bigger and better armed than European frigates and, with more sail, even faster, they were able to overtake and destroy them, or outrun the ponderous liners.

Dale's flagship *President* was heavily armed with thirty long 24-pounders* on the lower gun deck and twenty long 12-pounders on the upper deck, as well as two long 24-pounders on her forecastle. With the other frigates, she mounted a pair of carronades on bow and stern. These were short, squat guns able to fire a large ball at close range; and because they were so short they could be loaded and fired more rapidly than the long guns. Weighed down by such armament, and with the larger, heavier area of sail, *President* and the other frigates wallowed in heavy seas once they reached the open Atlantic.

About 300 to 350 men—gunner's, carpenter's, surgeon's and boatswain's mates, able and ordinary seamen, midshipmen and Marine marksmen—were crowded cheek-by-jowl into these 175-foot-long warships. Because the Americans had a stormy crossing, most of the men were crammed belowdecks and almost all of them were seasick the first few days.

For *President*, fresh off the ways, it was a maiden voyage and anything that could go wrong did go wrong. Heavily loaded with her guns plus a year's provisions, she lurched headlong into smashing head seas; plunging as though sinking, shuddering as she rose again. Her seams worked open and took on water, and her gunports though closed also leaked. Off-duty men tried to sleep in their hammocks above the guns, but it was not easy in a canvas sling swinging from side to side. Breathing was also difficult in the close air reeking with the stench of bilge and vomit mingling with the sickening odor of excrement and urine issuing from heads seldom cleaned because of the heavy seas. Yet the ordinary duties of officers and crew had to be discharged. At dawn reveille wakened sleeping men, and those slow to tumble from their hammocks were "started" by officers swinging knotted ropes. Hammocks were then folded and stowed in their assigned places along the gunwales, where in battle they would serve as shields against flying steel and wooden splinters every bit as deadly as bolts or bullets. Breakfast consisting of tea and biscuits was first served to the four-to-

* This is not the weight of the gun but of the cannonball it fires.

eight morning watch, and then to their replacements. After breakfast "the smoking-lamp was lit" and men relaxed with their pipes and cigars, or hastened forward to the "head," so called because it was located forward in the bow. A mere grating with seats, it could be a wet and precarious perch in heavy weather, and at all times stinking.

Once fed all hands turned to their specialties: some splicing cable, tarring rigging, making gaskets and mats out of used rope; others pumping the day's accumulation of bilge water into the sea or down on their knees scrubbing decks; the remainder making sails, scraping masts, painting and whitewashing, reeving tackle, or any one of fifty different daily chores necessary aboard a nineteenth-century wooden warship at sea. For every waking moment, it seemed, there was something to do, and there was little time for leisure; except when sailors, obeying the order to be shaved twice weekly, took their turns in the barber's chair. Forward on the starboard gun deck midshipmen were taught arithmetic and navigation in a classroom formed by canvas screens. More often than not the teacher was the chaplain. On the port gun deck aft there was space reserved for off-duty officers to promenade or read. Meals were welcomed as relief from routine.

The main meal was at midday. Officers ate in the wardroom, and the crew on the gun decks in separate messes of eight or ten men each. A common pot and eating utensils were brought from the "caboose," as the galley was then called, by an elected "president" of each mess who would dish out the meal: usually salted meat or fish (soaked the night before), peas or beans, potatoes or turnips, and beer. After dinner the first tot of rum was issued at the grog tub and downed there so that no seaman might hoard his rations and get drunk. Supper came at the four P.M. change of watch, usually consisting of leftovers from dinner with bread, cheese, tea and another tot of grog. Officers dined on finer fare, with wine to wash down their cheese and a sweet for dessert. The mens' only dessert came on Sunday. It was the high spot of the week, known as "duff," made of biscuits, raisins and "slush," the fat scraped from cooking pots. At eight P.M. sailors not on watch took their hammocks down from the rails, slung them from the beams above the guns to fall instantly asleep if the sea were calm, tossing like their ship if it were not, in their ears the steady tramp of the night watch and the Marines patrolling the decks as lookouts.

This was the hard life that an ordinary seaman endured for $9 a month, while the officers—though much more responsible but enduring much less—received much more, ranging up to $75 monthly for the captain. There was also prize money. The worth of any ship and cargo brought into port and adjudged a fair prize was divided among the U.S. government, half; and twenty remaining shares of which three went to the captain (four if he were a commodore); two to the remaining officers; another two for the warrant officers; six for the petty officers and six or seven for the crew.

Short of a storm, gun drill furnished the only excitement. Commodore Dale realized that his squadron faced a type of warfare markedly different from the Revolutionary War tactics of supporting land troops from the sea or escorting the transports from place to place. The Barbary corsairs relied upon ship-for-ship combat, swift and swooping assault, closing with the victim so as to board her with an overwhelming superiority of armed sailors. They had neither the equipment nor the stomach for fleet warfare in which the broadside was king. Such devastating volleys with all guns firing simultaneously could not only keep them terrified and at bay but also sink them before they could turn and flee.

So Dale whenever the seas had become calm would order gunnery practice. Each man in each gun crew had his specific assignment so that by flawless teamwork a simultaneous broadside might be fired from either side of the ship. This meant that of *President*'s forty-four guns there would be eighteen or so on either side that faced the enemy firing at once. The "exercise," as the practice that would perfect this teamwork was called, began with a roll of drums that sent the "powder monkeys"—ship's boys wearing flannel slippers that would not cause a spark—rushing below to the powder magazine and there receiving a black cloth-covered bag of powder to deliver to the chief of his assigned gun.

Next came that worthy's order, "Cast loose your guns," at which the tacklemen moved the lashings holding the gun against the bulwarks, replacing them with breech lashings to contain the gun's massive recoil. "Level your guns" was the order to raise the cannon barrel to fit through the gunport, and upon "Take off your tompions," the stoppers that kept the barrel dry were removed from the muzzle. At "load with cartridge," the bag of powder was pushed down the barrel with a long rammer, after which a wad was shoved behind it to hold it in place. Finally, "Shot your guns" was the command to ram either a cannonball or a bag of langrage in place ahead of the powder and wad. The gun was now ready to fire.

Came the order "Run out your guns!" and all crews bent to the task of shoving the heavy gun forward with its muzzle protruding through the gunport. For this to happen aboard a big ship, a liner, say, with nearly fifty gun muzzles suddenly and simultaneously appearing as though at a genie's command was an unnerving sight indeed. With each gun next secured against recoil by thick ropes, the order,

"Prime!" was issued. At once a bit of powder was sprinkled through the touch hole behind the powder bag in the breech. A gunner would bend over the touch hole blowing on a "slow match," or long, lighted fuse, awaiting the order to fire. This would come with the downward role of the ship in the Anglo-American desire to hole and sink the enemy as opposed to the French tactic of firing on the rise to cripple and capture it by wrecking its rigging and steering gear. When it came—"FIRE!"—the cannoneer touched his match to the hole and with a deafening roar the gun leaped backward while a red-hot cannonball went whirling toward the enemy.

Many such exercises were necessary before both decks of the American frigates were trained to fire in unison, and in the beginning, to conserve ammunition, neither powder nor ball was used, just as in today's Army or Marines a rifleman will spend hours in mock loading and firing of his unloaded weapon—even taking it apart and reassembling it blindfolded—before he makes the exciting march to the rifle range for the real thing. Once the cannons were fired, the next order was, "Sponge your guns," at which a sponge mounted on a long staff was thrust down the barrel to put out any remaining powder or burning cloth so that when a fresh powder bag was thrust into the breech it did not explode prematurely. With the gun re-emplaced and the new powder bag inside, the order "Shot your guns" was repeated and the exercise was begun anew. Eventually the gunners would come to enjoy the pride of teamwork that comes with such practice, developing a camaraderie that would lead them to christen their cannon with such pet names as Hot Stuff, Defiance, Lead Lips or Spitfire.

Meanwhile as the five divisions manning *President*'s guns went through their exercises, the much larger sixth division of sailmakers, carpenters, cooks and surgeon's mates were practicing their own battle speciality. This was to keep the ship responsive to its master's orders and also to prepare for "action" by sprinkling or pretending to sprinkle sawdust on the gun decks to absorb an anticipated wash of slippery blood. Others would simulate carrying "wounded" on stretchers down into the surgery where the surgeon and his mates stood ready with their instruments, bandages, sponges and rum for anesthetic. In combat, bone saws would be heated to reduce the shock of cold steel on warm flesh.

If the ship were holed or her rigging shot away, designated members of the gun crews would leave their posts for damage control, plugging the holes, manning the pumps, clearing the wreckage or fire fighting. Gun crews usually were much larger than needed not only for damage control, but also to replace the dead and wounded or to fire the guns on both sides of the ship should *President* find herself surrounded. If the enemy came close enough to board, all crewmen prepared to repel boarders with pistol and cutlass. After each gun practice the big cannon were stoppered with tompions again and secured to the bulwarks, always a dangerous task for if one of these 7,500-pound monsters were to break free in a heavy sea, careening swiftly about on their little wheels and changing direction like frightened animals, crewmen could be crushed to death or badly maimed.

Marines in "the fighting tops" were always alert to repel boarders with musketry and grenades, and as trained marksmen they would also be expected to take a toll of officers on the enemy quarter deck.* The Leathernecks, as they were called for the leather stocks around their necks, also were expected to be in the forefront of friendly boarding parties. During battle some of them were stationed at the foot of companionways under orders to shoot shirkers trying to flee to safety belowdecks. Although the Marine Corps still claims to have preceded all other services through its recruiting of Leathernecks at Tun Tavern, Philadelphia, in 1775, it also was abolished after the Revolution. It was revived by President John Adams in 1798, and Dale's squadron carried about two-thirds of all Marines recruited since then. Each frigate carried a complement of forty Leathernecks led by a captain and second lieutenant with a couple of sergeants and corporals, and a fifer and drummer to sound or beat the calls.

In 1801 the abrasive friction between seamen and Marines was already in operation: the sailors detesting "the tin soldiers" for their function of policing the ship, the Leathernecks jeering at the sailors as "swab jockeys" good for nothing but menial labor. At sea, of course, the Marine officers were always under the command of the ship's captain, a situation that also was not conducive to cooperation. And Major William Burrows, a stiff-necked Charlestonian and first commandant of the Marine Corps, was forever on guard against insults to his corps by naval officers. If he heard that one of his Marines had been struck by some hectoring naval superior he would immediately write to him ordering him to "call out" his assailant—that is, challenge him to a duel—to "wipe away this insult to the Marine Corps," or face expulsion. Here is a sample of Burrows's style:

> It is my duty to support my officers, and I will do it with my life, but they must deserve it. On board the *Ganges* about 12 months ago Lieutenant Gale was struck by an officer of the navy. The captain took no notice of the business and Gale got no satisfaction on the

---

* The quatrefoil atop a modern Marine officer's hat is a legacy of these days when it identified him to his own sharpshooters.

cruise. The moment he arrived (in port) he called the lieutenant out and shot him. Afterwards, peace was restored.

Thus the Marines, then as now: crusty, cocky and forever seeking "satisfaction." As Commodore Dale entered the Mediterranean, he congratulated himself that if he decided to launch an amphibious operation against Tripoli, he had 120 Marines aboard his frigates.

6

The Funk of Commodore Dale

AT FIRST TRIPOLI WOULD NOT APPEAR TO BE A HARD NUT TO CRACK. Seen from the sea it was a land of enchantment. Under cloudless skies, great hibiscus blossoms flowered red against the gleaming sand of its shoreline. In the afternoon gentle onshore breezes cooled the day's accumulated heat, carrying the sweet scent of jasmine or shaking the white-and-purple blooms of the oleanders, while riffling the variegated blues and greens of the gentle Mediterranean with specks of white. Along the shore also were rows of date palms nodding their star-shaped heads, with here and there among them pomegranates and aloes. Behind these were fields of tobacco, millet and barley with huge watermelons growing among them. These great fruits of Tripoli had been celebrated for centuries, some of them supposedly having weighed one hundred pounds.

For centuries also the rocky reef that formed Tripoli's harbor had protected the city from winter storms, and also hid it from sea rovers roaming the flat African coast. Closer inshore it could be seen that Tripoli was not all that beautiful. The white and buff houses clustering around the great pile of the bashaw's gray fortress castle rising among them were dingy and dirty, and the palace was partly in ruins, although inside it were a series of splendid chambers, arched colonnades and circling courts, brilliant with mosaics. Underneath was a labyrinth of subterranean passages and dungeons where captives were imprisoned, tortured or executed. In those days a wide, circular beach fronted the town, and much of the city was built in a crescent around the tip of the peninsula on which it rested. Around this shore the low mosques could be seen, as well as a disorder of stone buildings that on closer scrutiny turned out to be gun batteries. There were also numerous barracks, suggesting that Bashaw Yusuf fielded a formidable army.

Although the harbor was commodius it was too shallow and too dangerous—at its deepest only about thirty to thirty-six feet—for maneuver by lofty warships such as Dale's big frigates. Offshore shallower waters were filled with shoals and reefs known to the bashaw's seamen but unknown to Dale's.

The name Tripoli was formed by the Greek words *tri* and *polis* meaning three cities, and used by the Romans to designate the province of the three cities: the ancient Oea of the Greeks, Sabratha and Leptis Magna. Only Oea survived, but when it was conquered by the Saracens they mistook Tripoli to be the name of the city, calling it Trablis in their own tongue. Tripoli's population was then an extreme of multitudinous, wretched poor clothed in worn brown homespun and the wealthy few strolling along its narrow, winding streets wearing shawls of the finest texture, or flowing gold-embroidered robes of satin or velvet, or rich furs during winter. Like the forums of ancient Greece, the coffeehouses were their meeting places. Because there were no newspapers, they were the only places to exchange information. Nothing else but coffee was served in them.

Rule of the Turkish sultan ended in Tripoli in 1714 when Hamet Karamanli seized power by surprising and massacring the Turkish garrison there. With this transition the government came under the control of the indigenous Arabs and Berbers. Hamet next raised an army and extended Tripoli's domain across the desert to the borders of Egypt.

Hamet's second son, Mohammed, ascended the throne in 1745 and ruled in relative peace and stability for twenty-one years. Most remarkable of all he did not, in Alexander. Pope's phrase, "Like the Turk, leave no brother near the throne," but actually allowed seven brothers to survive him. But Mohammed's son Ali corrected that enormous oversight by getting rid of six of them for certain and probably the seventh as well. With no other pretenders in sight, Ali sheathed his dagger and ruled with a minimum of the cruelty usually associated with Muslim potentates of the era. He designated his firstborn son, Hassan, as his successor. Hassan quarreled with the second son, Hamet, but instead of menacing each other their eyes should have been on the third son, Yusuf (Joseph). Handsome, ambitious, avaricious and ruthless, Yusuf Karamanli got rid of his older brother Hassan simply by inviting him to their mother's apartment, where he was shot by Yusuf and stabbed about a hundred times by Yusuf's Numidian bodyguards. Brother Hamet was even more easily usurped. Chubby, gentle and gullible, he went into the countryside on some fool's errand trumped up by Yusuf and upon his return found the gates of Tripoli closed against him and his family in Yusuf's power.

That was in November 1796. During the five years intervening between Yusuf's ascension to the throne and his declaration of war against the United States, he consolidated his hold on the country, exiling or executing all the supporters of Hassan and Hamet. He also during this period allowed his fondness for display to run riot.

When receiving the ambassadors or consuls of other powers, or scrutinizing the latest batch of prisoners, Yusuf would be seated majestically on his throne, a beribboned turban upon his head, clothed in a long silk robe embroidered in gold. His ample waist—his corpulence had grown with his opulence—almost covered by a splendid black beard and encircled by a diamond-studded belt into which he had stuffed two gold-mounted pistols, while from it hung a ceremonial saber. His throne was set upon a dais four feet high, inlaid with mosaic and surrounded by a swatch of gold-fringed velvet speckled with jewels.

Yusuf was perhaps even more ostentatious when he made his regular promenades around his regency. Accompanied by a troop of Numidian cavalry and mounted upon a richly caparisoned white horse, he rode at the head of a retinue consisting of smartly striding guards, colorfully clothed ministers, bowing servants and members of his family. All those around him were heavily armed, for Yusuf was haunted by the typical tyrant's paranoid fear of assassination. His personal treasure was almost as dear to him as his life, for two great strong boxes containing all his gold and jewels were protected by a special elite guard. These treasure chests never left his presence, even outside his palace.

Then in his thirties, he was still cruelly handsome in spite of his gluttony and lechery, although his character was an unlovely mixture of rapacious greed, murderous anger, stubborn pride, incredible and uncritical superstition (his chief confidante was an old crone of a sorcerer whose prophecies he swore by), he nevertheless did possess one attractive trait: his love for his children. He coddled and spoiled them outrageously, showering them with gifts and favors, and the apple of his eye was his eldest daughter, who had married the high admiral of his growing fleet, Murad Reis.

• • •

The high admiral of the Tripolitan fleet known as Murad Reis was born Peter Lisle on a Clydebank farm in Scotland. He went to sea at an early age, already physically matured as a powerfully built, blond-haired man with a sandy beard. He is supposed to have seen sea service with the Mameluke rulers of Egypt, where he won a reputation as a skillful and resourceful seaman and an excellent navigator. Later he turned up in Massachusetts, where he became a deck hand on the schooner *Betsey*. In 1796 he sailed out of Boston aboard her bound for the Mediterranean. During this voyage he seems to have suffered some humiliating indignities or injustices—either at the hands of his shipmates or Captain Chapin Sampson—that embittered him forever against Americans. Lisle was aboard *Betsey* when she was captured by Tripolitan pirates. When a peace between Tripoli and the United States was arranged, Captain Sampson and his crew were repatriated, but Tripoli kept *Betsey*, along with Peter Lisle, who refused to return to the land he despised.

Indeed, Lisle "turned Turk," in the derisive phrase for a Christian who becomes a Muslim, taking the name Murad Reis while passing through the elaborate ritual that cleanses an unholy infidel, and then, showing himself such an excellent seaman that Bashaw Yusuf rewarded him with the hand of his daughter and the rank of high admiral. Indeed, Murad Reis was the only seaman in Tripoli who knew how to handle a fleet, and in the Barbary War he would emerge as the chief opponent of the American squadron. But his first encounter with the Yankees was not exactly a harbinger of success.

Although *President* was the fastest of the frigates, the sloop of war *Enterprise* commanded by Lieutenant Sterrett was even faster. With Commodore Dale's permission, Sterrett took *Enterprise* on ahead and entered Gibraltar Harbor alone on June 29, 1801. There to his great delight he sighted the *Betsey*, now coppered and converted to Admiral Murad Reis's 28-gun flagship *Meshouda*. Like all corsair captains, Reis had so lovingly decorated *Meshouda* that she might have been the most colorful ship afloat. Her hull was yellow with a white stripe; her stern was green; painted flowers adorned her stern windows, a woman's head graced its transom and the muzzles of her guns were painted red. She was attended by a 14-gun brig, also decorated but drab by comparison. Because these vessels were in a neutral harbor, Sterrett could not attack them. Neither could Dale when he arrived with the frigates. Instead, he detailed Captain Barron in *Philadelphia* to await Murad Reis outside Gibraltar and "take him when he goes out."

News of Murad Reis's predicament so excited the fiery American Consul William Eaton in Tunis that he immediately dashed off a message to Barron urging him to ignore the niceties of diplomacy and grab Reis and his ships forthwith. He wrote: "This would be an event so fatal to the Bashaw of Tripoli, that it would at once put an end to the war. . . . He can do nothing without the crews of these two corsairs. They are many of them from the first families of Tripoli. Their circumstance, if they fall into our hands, would incite an insurrection in his kingdom and give us the entire command of terms." Eaton was probably right, and the British in Gibraltar might not have protested too vigorously, but Samuel Barron was no fire-eater like the American consul. He was satisfied with bottling up Reis and his two ships. He seemed to believe that because he commanded the harbor mouth, Reis would obligingly sail straight into his arms. Instead, the bashaw's high admiral bribed some local shippers to spirit his 366 officers and men across the Strait to Morocco, whence they marched overland to Tripoli. Then he persuaded—if that is the proper word—British authorities in Gibraltar to allow him to ship out as an ordinary citizen on a British ship bound for Malta. At Malta he paid another captain to take him home.

When Commodore Dale heard this news he was furious, although it must be said that his language though properly salty was not quite as sulfuric as Eaton's.

Dale's next move was to blockade Tripoli Harbor with *President* and *Enterprise*. Although he was unable to keep the shallow-draft feluccas from running along the shoaling coast, he did bottle up the deeper-draft vessels, and this may have been the reason that the Tripolitan pirates were unable to capture a single American ship in 1801. In the meantime, he sent Lieutenant Sterrett in the 12-gun *Enterprise* to Malta to refresh diminishing water supplies. Sterrett had scarcely left Tripoli's coast when his lookouts on August 1, 1801, spotted what appeared to be a Barbary corsair over the horizon. It was the 14-gun *Tripoli* commanded by Admiral Rais Mahomet Rais. Sterrett raised the British ensign and bore down on him. Deceived by Sterrett's ruse, Rais replied to the "Britisher's" hail by explaining that he was cruising for American merchantmen. At once Sterrett lowered the Union Jack and raised the Stars and Stripes, making for *Tripoli* with all guns poking their muzzles through the gunports and beginning to fire.

A three-hour battle began demonstrating the trickery of Tripolitan tactics and the amazing speed and accuracy of American gunnery. Sterrett was a strict disciplinarian who ran a "tight ship," with particular

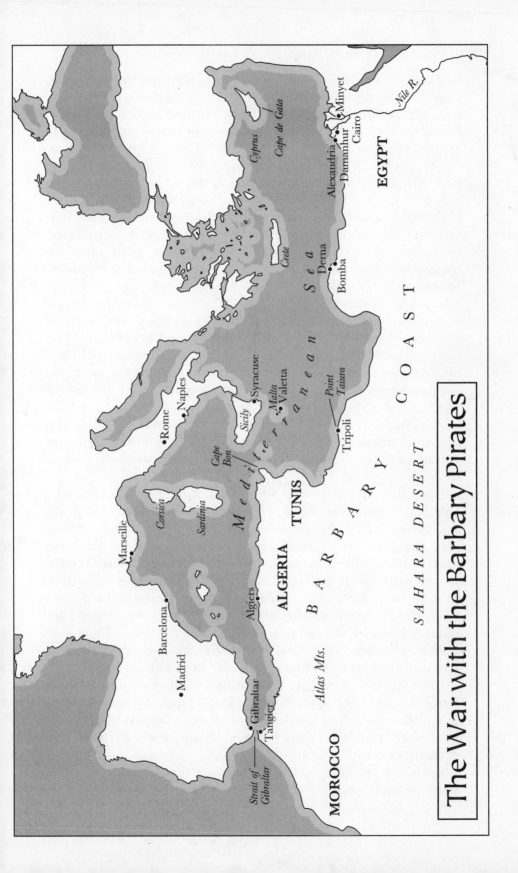

The War with the Barbary Pirates

emphasis on gun drill. As a result, *Enterprise*'s guns were so quickly loaded, fired, cleaned, reloaded and fired again that *Tripoli* soon became a reeling wreck. Unable to match the American onslaught, Rais attempted the customary Tripolitan tactic of coming alongside to grapple and board. But Lieutenant Enoch Lane's Marines were waiting for them. The moment *Tripoli* came within musket range, they swept her gun deck with a fire that rapidly cleared it.

Tripoli now bore away, and Sterrett staggered her with parting broadsides, toppling her masts and holing her above the waterline. Her guns ceased firing and Rais hauled down his flag. With the Americans cheering at the "surrender," Sterrett bore down upon the enemy—and Rais raised his flag again and opened fire. Infuriated, Sterrett shook *Tripoli* with another broadside that sent showers of splinters flying over her decks. Now Rais tried to close and grapple once more, but Lane's Leathernecks were again ready—and Rais bore off, chased by spinning cannonballs. And he tried his surrender ruse again! Sterrett must have chuckled, ordering his grinning crew to bear off. For the third time Rais sought to grapple, and once again Sterrett outmaneuvered him. Like a foolish fisherman believing that a fish will bite four times on the same bait, he actually lowered and raised his flag once more. Sterrett's reply was a thunderous broadside that brought Rais staggering to his shattered rail to hurl his flag into the sea, after which he sank to his knees with arms outstretched in supplication.

Enterprise's guns fell silent while Lieutenant David Porter led a boarding crew aboard *Tripoli*. He found a badly battered ship with thirty of her eighty officers and men killed and thirty more wounded, including Rais and his second-in-command. Because the ship's surgeon had been killed, Sterrett ordered his own surgeon and his mates to tend to the enemy wounded. Aware of Dale's restrictive instructions from Secretary Smith, Sterrett next sent his own sailors aboard *Tripoli* to chop down her remaining masts, give her guns the deep-six, and dump her small arms, cutlasses, pikes, swords, powder, ball and small arms over the side. Then a stubby makeshift mast was raised with a tattered sail attached and Admiral Rais sailed homeward in disgrace.

Upon his arrival in Tripoli, the infuriated Bashaw Yusuf stripped him of his command and sent him riding through a jeering populace mounted backward on a jackass with a sheep's entrails hung around his neck. Just to remind him of his ignominy, he was given five hundred stripes of the bastinado.

Sterrett, meanwhile, continued on to Malta where he took aboard water and sailed back to Tripoli to rejoin Dale. Because *President* was low on provisions, Dale detached his flagship from his fleet to sail to Malta for food. On his return, he halted a Greek ship and took forty-one Tripolitans prisoner. Arriving back off Tripoli he demanded that the bashaw ransom them, evidently willing to play the same dirty game as the pirates. But Yusuf had about as much compassion for his countrymen as he had shown his admiral, telling Dale to keep them until he could swap them for Americans—as soon as he caught a few. Disgusted, Dale sent the Tripolitans ashore and made for Gibraltar, where he learned of Murad Reis's escape. With *President* leaking and still low on provisions and his crew nearing the end of their enlistment, he sent *Philadelphia* to replace him off Tripoli and made for home himself.

After arriving off Norfolk on April 14, 1802, he requested promotion to admiral, a nonexistent rank in the navy of that time, and Congress demurred, whereupon Richard Dale left the sea to become a Philadelphia merchant. Except for Sterrett's single-ship victory, in which he had had no part, Dale had not accomplished much beyond immobilizing a few of the bashaw's ships. He certainly did not frighten Yusuf, who still considered himself to be one of the lords of the Mediterranean and who had lost none of his contempt for Americans.

7

The "Commodoress"
Takes Over

~ PRESIDENT JEFFERSON'S CONTINUING STRUGGLE WITH CONGRESS OVER
the authority to make war was not helped by Commodore Dale's ineffectual Mediterranean cruise, and Jefferson's attempt to make political capital out of *Enterprise*'s bloodless victory over *Tripoli*—though it
provoked a great outburst of patriotic pride among the American public—fell on mostly deaf Congressional ears. Eventually, after much
haggling over the president's request that Congress respond to
Tripoli's declaration of war with one of its own, the legislature on
February 6, 1802, did pass an act authorizing the chief executive to
employ the U.S. Navy to protect American commerce and seamen on
the Atlantic and Mediterranean. Perhaps more important, Jefferson
was to instruct his naval commanders "to subdue, seize and make
prize of all vessels, goods and effects belonging to the Bey of Tripoli or
to his subjects. . . ." This, if not a formal declaration of war, would
serve the same purpose.

Jefferson had already moved to strengthen the U.S. Mediterranean
Squadron. On January 12 Navy Secretary Robert Smith (no relation to
his acting predecessor Samuel Smith) had ordered the frigates *Constellation, Chesapeake, New York, Adams* and *John Adams* to join *Essex* and
Philadelphia still on duty off Tripoli Harbor. *Enterprise,* which had
returned with *President,* was turned around and sent east again with

Sterrett still commanding. The president's next move was to find a replacement for Dale. At first he favored Truxtun, not because he had swallowed his distrust of contentious men, but because he was senior. But Truxtun—predictably—angered Secretary Smith by demanding a captain for his flagship, threatening to resign rather than command both squadron and flagship, as Dale had. To this an immensely relieved Smith replied: "I cannot but consider your notification as absolute." He then thought of Captain Edward Preble, the most revered officer in the U.S. Navy, but Preble was ill. So he chose Captain Richard Valentine Morris.

If the fires of combat had burned low in Commodore Dale, they had never been alight in the heart of the new commodore. He was a pussycat born and a pussycat bred, a sunshine sailor whose rise to captain owed more to his pedigree and political influence than to valor or nautical skill. Most veteran naval officers regarded his selection as a bald bit of presidential prerogative.

Commodore Morris was the son of Lewis Morris, one of the signers of the Declaration of Independence, and the nephew of Gouverneur Morris, a financier of the Revolution and delegate to the Constitutional Convention. Perhaps more persuasive in President Jefferson's mind, his brother was Lewis Robert Morris, a representative from Vermont who, after thirty-six votes in the Congressional stand-off between Burr and Jefferson, had withheld his vote, allowing Vermont to cast the decisive ballot for the man from Monticello. Jefferson could not have made a worse appointment, as Secretary Smith with a sinking heart knew the moment that he opened a letter from the new commodore's wife. She requested permission to sail with her husband, bringing her young son Gerard and his nursemaid along. Smith reluctantly consented, knowing full well that in the navies of the world a woman aboard a warship was regarded as bad luck. Here there would be two women, plus a little boy to trip over. But to refuse, Smith also knew, would be to commit the crime of *lèse-majesté*. So Mrs. Morris and entourage came aboard *Chesapeake*, her husband's flagship; and in no time her influence over her husband had become so apparent to the crewmen in the forecastle that they pinned on her the derisive nickname of "the commodoress."

Upon his arrival in the Mediterranean Commodore Morris showed a brazen indifference to Jefferson's unequivocal orders to blockade Tripoli and thus compel Bashaw Yusuf to return to the negotiating table. But this stick-and-carrot approach inevitably failed because Morris simply refused to be the stick. Instead, he interpreted his orders to mean that he should use his squadron to escort American merchant ships to the various ports on the northern Mediterranean. This, of course, was just what the Commodoress wanted: a pleasant tour of French and Italian harbor cities with prolonged stays ashore to entertain and be entertained. As one naval lieutenant remarked in Washington: "The secretary is much displeased with the conduct of Commodore Morris. His wife it is said *commands* so much as to *lay* five months in port." Whether the lieutenant's choice of verbs was deliberate or not, the fact is that on November 20 *Chesapeake* put into Valletta, Malta, to put the pregnant Commodoress ashore.

President Jefferson was shocked and dismayed by Morris's reports, either casual or complaining, but never indicative of a determination to obey his orders. First Dale had done little, and now Morris had done nothing; if he had not also undone what little Dale had done. Jefferson could remember his days in Paris when Europeans had been impressed by his defiance of the Barbary pirates—and then their smug, smirking supercilious smiles after the new nation paid the tribute after all. Now his failed efforts would be greeted in Europe with the same hilarious contempt. Thus it was a sorrowing Thomas Jefferson who convened his cabinet on May 8, 1803, with the question: "Shall we buy peace with Tripoli?"

The reply was a unanimous vote in the affirmative, and Jefferson notified Consul James Cathcart to try again to reopen negotiations with Yusuf. But the bashaw had nothing but contempt for Cathcart's feelers, telling him to stay away from Tripoli. Jefferson could now do nothing but hope that Morris would obey orders.

In the spring of 1803, Commodore Morris finally decided to sail for the bashaw's stronghold. He sent *Chesapeake* back to the United States for refitting and moved his flag aboard *New York*, and with *John Adams* and *Enterprise* set his course for Tripoli. There were, of course, pleasure calls at Leghorn and then Malta, where he checked on his wife's condition, before he resumed his eastward progress. But then on April 25, a gunner's mate aboard *New York* while stowing signal lanterns in the cockpit storeroom started a small fire that set off an explosion that rocked the flagship, threatening to spread to the nearby powder magazine and thus blow her up. Fire-control parties went into action at once, but the nervous quartermaster who had been ordered to signal FIRE ON BOARD hoisted instead MUTINY ON BOARD, bringing the other ships hastening to *New York*'s rescue with all crews at battle stations. Fortunately lieutenants David Porter and Isaac Chauncey, leading details of fire-fighters wielding wet blankets, buckets of water and axes, were able to put out the fire in an hour and a half and saved the ship. Beyond help were fourteen men, including Morris's secretary, the chief gunner, surgeon's mate and the Marine guarding the magazine—all of whom were killed. Once again, Morris had to return to port.

Thus it was not until May 27—one month short of a year since sailing from Hampton—that the U.S. Mediterranean Squadron hove to off Tripoli, its crewmen rushing to the rails to view the city's beautiful verdant coastline. Morris saw what Dale had seen: feluccas and xebecs slipping along the shoaling shore to elude the blockaders. *Enterprise* now commanded by Lieutenant Isaac Hull went in after one of them, but even his sloop with its shallowest draft drew too much water. Nevertheless, Hull fired a broadside that frightened the felucca's crew into beaching their vessel and fleeing. Hull's request to send ship's boats in after them was rejected by Morris.

At last Morris consented to an amphibious operation against a dozen grain-carrying feluccas that Hull had driven into a shallow bay. On the morning of June 10 nine attack boats shoved off from the frigates. Seven of them carried fifty Marines and the other two were stuffed with flammables to be set afire and driven into the grain boats. Lieutenant Porter was in command, seconded by Lieutenant James Lawrence with Lieutenant Lane leading the Leathernecks. Under a bombardment from the two frigates the boats were rowed ashore.

Awaiting the fifty Marines was an army estimated by Morris at nearly one thousand foot soldiers and cavalry, but this seems high. It would be an obtuse officer indeed who would send an attacking force against a defending enemy twenty times more numerous, especially when the offense usually needs a three to one superiority, and more if the assault comes from the sea. But the American boats came on, the sailor's oars dipping and flashing in the sun-dappled sea, the cannonballs from the bashaw's fortress and beach barricades splashing harmlessly around them. Now the seven attack boats continued straight ahead while the two fireboats veered right to move in among the grain feluccas. Grinding up on the beach with a grating sound, the attackers came to a halt while yelling Marines leaped into the surf brandishing pistols and cutlasses. For a moment the American assault seemed halted by an enemy fire ordered by a dashing officer riding up and down the beach on a black stallion and waving a rifle. A counter volley from the Marines tumbled him from the saddle, and the Americans drove steadily forward to establish a beachhead.

Porter at their head saw that many of the enemy troops were being held back, probably to encircle his men once they had driven too far inland. So he halted them and kept them concentrated, trading gunfire while the sailors in the fireboats set the abandoned feluccas and their cargo ablaze. Then Porter signaled retreat, just as he was wounded in both legs. Crawling into one of the boats he directed a withdrawal until he had lost so much blood that he had to relinquish command to Lawrence. With the oarsmen pulling desperately away, the sea again dimpled by enemy fire, the unscratched boats gradually gained speed and at last reached the safety of the frigates—with the feluccas burning fiercely behind them.

In two hours the Americans had accomplished their mission, although the Tripolitans eventually put out the fires on the feluccas. Because the grain did not burn easily, only half of it had been destroyed. Nevertheless Bashaw Yusuf—who had boasted, "I do not fear war, it is my trade"—was quick to accept Morris's proposal for peace negotiations. But his terms—$200,000 for peace, $20,000 annually to maintain it—so angered Morris that he shouted that the offer was so outrageous, "should the combined world have made it, my nation would have treated it with contempt." Now the bashaw lost his temper, bellowing: "This business is at an end!"

So also ended the career of Captain Richard Valentine Morris, for in mid-September he received a message from Secretary Smith notifying him: "It is the command of the President that you take charge of *Adams*, and that with her you return to the United States."

On his return, Morris faced a board of inquiry convened under Captain Samuel Barron. It found him "censurable for his inactive and dilatory conduct of the squadron under his command," but made no recommendation for punishment. A furious Jefferson considered this but a slap on the wrist, and he angrily revoked Morris's captaincy, while calling upon Secretary Smith to find him a new commodore.

Smith did, choosing the man he had wanted in the first place, for Captain Edward Preble was now fully recovered from his illness and eager to go to sea again.

8

Edward Preble:
A Fighting Commodore

✑ EDWARD PREBLE WAS BORN IN 1761 IN WHAT IS NOW PORTLAND, Maine, the third son by the second marriage of Brigadier General Jedediah Preble (he sired twelve children in all). General Preble had served alongside James Wolfe when that British general fell on the Plains of Abraham and the Union Jack rose above Quebec and thereafter over all of Canada. He also served as a brigadier in the Revolutionary War and is believed to be the first man to have climbed to the peak of Mount Washington. The tradition remains that "Jed Preble went up and washed his hands in the clouds." Tiring of soldiering, Preble retired to a farm and there set his children to work in his potato rows.

As a boy, young Edward was a better athlete than a student, and was known as a superb marksman who once brought down five swallows with five shots. He detested the farm even more than the classroom, so that at the age of sixteen he hurled his hoe to the ground, vowing that he would never again lift that detestable tool. Instead he went down to the docks and shipped aboard a Newburyport privateer then in the harbor. Despite a rough trip across the Atlantic and much seagoing drudgery he loved every minute of it, and his father, despairing of ever luring him back to the farm, wangled him a midshipman's warrant in the Massachusetts State navy in 1779, where he served aboard *Protector*.

Preble's first experience of ship-to-ship fighting was memorable indeed when *Protector* engaged the more powerful British privateer *Admiral Duff.* The two vessels pounded each other for hours, with neither giving way, and when powder became scarce, their crews actually hurled cannonballs against each other by hand. At last the Britisher hauled down her flag, and as Preble prepared to lead a boarding party onto her decks, she exploded and blew herself to bits.

On *Protector's* second voyage Preble was captured and thrown into a hold of the foul and infamous prison ship *Jersey* in New York Harbor. There he sickened with typhoid fever and probably would have died along with hundreds of other Yankees similarly afflicted had not an old friend of his father's interceded with the British authorities, gaining his parole and then his outright release. Preble's next ship was the sloop of war *Winthrop,* on which he served until the peace.

Edward Preble had gone aboard *Protector* a magnificent physical specimen: tall and muscular with piercing blue eyes, a hawkish nose and bulldog jaw. But the ordeal in the prison ship had permanently impaired his health, although it could never suppress his burning spirit of determination. And he still loved the sea, believing that he always felt better with the rolling decks of a ship beneath his feet. So he stayed there, at first as a supercargo in the merchant marine, then a ship captain and finally the owner and master of his own vessel. When the new navy was being organized and its secretary was scouring the seaboard for good officers, one of his first choices was Edward Preble, famous as a fighter, a disciplinarian and a captain who ran a tight ship. In 1798 President Adams made him a first lieutenant. Receiving command of the 14-gun brig *Pickering,* he cruised aboard her under the legendary Fighting Jack Barry on a voyage to the West Indies.

In 1800 Preble was promoted to captain and command of the new 32-gun frigate *Essex.* In January he sailed in *Essex* along with Captain James Sever's 36-gun *Congress* and a large convoy of merchantmen bound for the Cape of Good Hope. They were scarcely on the open Atlantic when a gale dismasted both frigates. Sever ran for the nearest port; Preble re-rigged *Essex* on the run, becoming the first American warship to carry Old Glory around the Cape of Good Hope, and thus enter the Indian and Pacific oceans. In November he returned with eleven of his merchant ships, after passing through more storms and putting down a mutiny. This was impressive enough, but what truly astounded Smith was that Preble had not lost a man to the dreaded malaria of the East Indies. Only ten men were afflicted with the fever, including himself, and he also developed an ulcer.

Actually, Preble became so sick upon his return that when Smith offered him command of *New York*, he declined it and even felt compelled to submit his resignation. Smith wisely refused to accept it, putting him on furlough "until your health should be restored." In May of 1801 he reported that he seemed to be recovered, and Smith promptly replaced Morris with Commodore Edward Preble.

Although President Jefferson had great faith in Preble, many of his advisers were still convinced that peace could only be bought. Just to be prepared for such a disgraceful option, he decided to replace the retired Captain O'Brien with Tobias Lear, who had been Washington's personal secretary and was a man whose diplomatic talents had commanded Jefferson's respect when he was secretary of state. Lear was to accompany Preble to the Mediterranean if it appeared that peace could only be negotiated, i.e., purchased. Lear was not to act on his own but only under Preble's orders, for Jefferson still believed that his valiant new commodore would do all possible to achieve a peace by force.

By the standards of the fledgling United States Navy, Commodore Preble's squadron was huge, consisting of the frigates *Constitution, Philadelphia, John Adams* and *New York*, and the smaller *Nautilus, Vixen, Siren, Argus* and *Enterprise*. All of these ships were rarely if ever brought together, and those he was to lead to the Mediterranean were his own flagship, the 44-gun *Constitution;* the 38-gun *Philadelphia* under Captain William Bainbridge; the 12-gun sloops *Enterprise, Nautilus* and *Vixen;* and the 16-gun brigs *Argus* and *Siren,* both newly built to shallow-draft specifications for the shoaling waters of the Barbary Coast.

It was characteristic of Preble that he received his orders on May 19 and came aboard his flagship at ten the next morning. He immediately called for an inspection, finding *Constitution*'s hull so badly in need of repairs that he ordered them to begin next day. The flagship was careened, that is, laid on its sides while the damaged copper was stripped away, after which the hull was cleansed and recoppered. These and other repairs were completed in the record time of one month, chiefly because Preble, as good at building ships as sailing them, worked his crews mercilessly on a back-breaking day that began at 5:15 A.M. and ended at 7:00 P.M. with time off only for meals or the head or the bo's'n mate's occasional cry, "The smoking lamp is lit." Meanwhile, stores and provisions for the great cruise were packed aboard.

One of Preble's chief difficulties was in signing on American crewmen, so he sent his recruiters into the port cities searching for foreign seamen who might be fearful of impressment by either the British or the French navies and would be eager for the protection of a U.S. Navy ship. One recruiter dispatched to New York City was delighted to find a Royal Navy sloop at anchor in the harbor, signing on eighty men in a single day. By the time *Constitution* was ready to up anchor, Preble could say: "I do not believe that I have twenty native American sailors on board." Finally, on August 14, 1803, the flagship dropped down Boston Harbor and set her course for the Mediterranean. Because Preble's other ships needed fewer repairs, they had sailed earlier. *Constitution* was all alone.

Preble's flagship had hardly reached the open sea before every officer and seaman aboard her realized that the commodore was the master in every sense of the word, for he immediately put her on a war footing, issuing regulations covering every activity and eventuality. Lookouts were posted twenty-four hours daily, and a log was to be cast over the side every two hours to measure the ship's speed.* Any change in wind speed or direction, or the approach of another ship, was to be reported immediately to the commodore. All of *Constitution*'s decks were to be washed down morning and evening. The weather (high) side of the quarterdeck was reserved for the master or the officer of the watch. No one was to be excused for illness without a note from the surgeon. Swearing and "immorality"—sodomy—were forbidden. Muster was to be held every evening and any absent, drunk, dirty or slovenly seamen were to be reported. All hands were to be shaved and changed into clean clothes twice a week, and long hair or unwashed clothing was not to be tolerated. Inspection of the men was to be held daily, with their officers examining every hammock for vermin or kit bag for hoarded rum, and reporting any offenders to Preble, who personally inspected his ship from top deck to hold, bow to fantail, twice a day.

Edward Preble was indeed a martinet as were almost all successful shipmasters of the day. As far as the crew was concerned, the call of the sea was usually not a noble one. Many if not most of these seamen were either recruited by a judge offering a choice between imprisonment or impressment, or else had gone to sea to escape punishment for some crime committed at home. Only the lash could subdue these malingerers and rebels, and Preble ordered it used frequently. But he also treated fairly men who obeyed him. Sundays were days of rest except for necessary duties, the purser was under strict orders to

*This is the origin of the term ship's log.

report any rotten or tainted rations to the commodore and the traditional tot of grog was issued unfailingly at noon and four P.M.

It is not surprising that a man whose body was constantly racked with agony should have an atrocious temper. But Preble's rages were like sea squalls—quick to appear and disappear—and his face, so pinched and peaked with pain, could soften in compassion during his frequent apologies. Preble kept to himself, dining with his officers but once a week, and posted a Marine sentry at his door to admit only senior officers reporting on ship's business. As he took his lonely turns on the quarterdeck no one was allowed to approach him unless summoned or bearing some urgent message such as the approach of a strange ship.

Preble, who was only forty-two himself and would never see forty-seven, was strangely appalled at the youth of so many of his officers, few of whom were yet thirty—an age reached only recently by Captain Bainbridge of *Philadelphia*. The commodore openly complained that he had "nothing but a pack of boys" hung around his neck. What the testy Preble did not realize was that these youngsters for all of his iron discipline actually idolized him and were proud to be known as "Preble's Boys." Isaac Hull and Isaac Chauncey, David Porter and Andrew Sterrett, James Lawrence and William Biddle, Thomas Macdonough and most of all Stephen Decatur, often called "the American Bayard" because of his gallantry and gentle nature, a replica of the great French "Chevalier without fear and without reproach"—these were the men who would study under Preble in his "Nursery of the Navy," and who would distinguish themselves in that larger war less than a decade over the horizon of time.

One reason that Preble's Boys adored their commodore was that they knew he could not be intimidated, as he had shown them the day he arrived in Gibraltar. After darkness fell the shape of a large ship appeared alongside *Constitution*. Preble seized the speaking trumpet and courteously identified himself and his ship, after which he asked the stranger to identify himself. There was no answer. Now Preble's tone turned sharp, and he demanded to know the ship's name and nation and declared he would shoot at it if he received no reply.

Out of the darkness came a British voice snarling: "You fire a shot, and I'll return a broadside."

Infuriated, speaking trumpet in hand, Preble swung himself aloft in the mizzenmast rigging and bellowed: "This is the United States ship *Constitution*, forty-four guns, Commodore Edward Preble. I am about to hail you for the last time. If not answered, I shall fire into you. *What ship is that?"* Lowering his voice, Preble ordered his gunners to blow on their slow matches.

Back came an answer in a more respectful tone: "This is his Britannic Majesty's ship *Donegal,* a razee of sixty guns."

Mollified, but not quite satisfied, Preble replied that he doubted the statement but would lay alongside until daylight, when he would see for himself who his neighbor was. Soon a ship put out from *Donegal* bearing an officer who politely explained that his ship was not actually a razee—a line-of-battle ship with the upper deck removed—but rather a frigate with fewer guns than *Constitution.* Preble's ship had come upon her unawares, he explained, and no reply had been given to gain time to clear her decks for action.

Now Preble was satisfied, both by the explanation and the courtesy of the British officer, and all along the rails of *Constitution* and the other ships of the squadron she had joined, Preble's Boys were also satisfied, for "if he were wrong in his temper, he was right in his heart."

When Preble's squadron entered the Mediterranean it appeared that other Barbary potentates were preparing to join Bashaw Yusuf in declaring war on the United States. Foremost of these was Muley Soliman, the new emperor of Morocco. Outwardly a mild-mannered little man, inwardly a sly deceiver, he had wheedled the *Betsey-Meshouda* away from Commodore Morris on the illogical claim that she had once been his prize. Actually, she belonged to her original Boston owners, but Morris was not the man to challenge the emperor. Captain John Rodgers, who replaced Morris, was. When the cunning Muley Soliman sent the disputed ship to run the Tripoli blockade, Rodgers captured her—and the emperor began rattling his saber.

Enroute to Gibraltar Preble had caught a hint of Morocco's warlike intentions. He had hailed a Moroccan frigate *Maimona,* 30 guns and 150 men. Her captain had said he was on a peaceful voyage from Lisbon to Sallee (now Salé). Preble had not believed him. What was a 30-gun Moroccan frigate doing roaming the Atlantic outside the Strait except to be cruising for American ships? Few if any Yankee vessels were entering the Med in 1803 because of Yusuf's successful defiance of two American commodores. Instead, they were sailing to the Atlantic ports of Portugal and Spain. Because Morocco's chief port of Tangier was on the Atlantic side of the Strait, Muley Soliman could be a greater danger to American shipping than Yusuf. But was the emperor really at war with the United States? The *Maimona*'s captain had said that he was not. Preble had not believed him, but because he had had no proof that a state of war existed, he reluctantly let him go, deciding to clarify the situation by calling on U.S. Consul James Simpson in Tangier.

Putting into the port, Preble had fired a signal gun to summon Simpson, but there was no reply. Through his telescope the commodore could see seven different national flags flying at their consulates but no sight of Old Glory. Mystified, he had continued on to Gibraltar to find *Philadelphia*, which had sailed before *Constitution*, at anchor there. Captain Bainbridge had come aboard the flagship to report to Preble that he had caught a Moroccan warship with a captive American merchantman. Upon his arrival at the Rock he had been informed that Moroccan cruisers were harassing American ships, and had put out to sea again in search of these pirates. Shortly afterward off Spain's Cape de Gata he sighted two vessels. One was the 22-gun Moroccan frigate *Mirboka*, and the other the American brig *Celia* with a Moroccan prize crew on her decks and her Yankee captain and crew imprisoned below. Bainbridge freed *Celia* and took the captive *Mirboka* back to Gibraltar.

Preble had summoned *Mirboka*'s captain, a smooth, ingratiating man named Reis Ibrahim Lubarez who cheerfully handed over his orders to the American commodore. They were from the alcayde (governor or commandant) of Tangier, a man named Hashash, directing Lubarez to take any American ships he sighted. The captain added that the orders had been sealed, only to be opened when at sea; and thus, he did not know whether or not Emperor Muley Soliman had declared war on the United States.

Mystified, and also not a little frustrated at this development at the far western end of the Barbary Coast—that is, his rear—that was distracting him from his objective of Tripoli at the other end, Preble was immensely relieved when ex-Commodore Morris arrived in Gibraltar in *New York* next day. Morris had supplied such other details as the fact that U.S. Consul Simpson had been placed under house arrest by Muley Soliman after he learned that Captain Rodgers had seized *Betsey-Meshouda* trying to run the Tripoli blockade with a cargo of munitions for his friend Yusuf. That explained why Simpson did not respond to Preble's signal gun.

Next day Captain Rodgers himself had arrived in Gibraltar in *John Adams* with *Meshouda* in tow and a complete list of Muley Soliman's gifts to Yusuf. Now Preble was convinced that the Moroccan emperor was either at war with his own country or was on the verge of it. The American commodore knew that Sidi Mahomet, the emperor's father, had in 1786 signed a treaty providing for a small annual tribute be paid to him. Now it appeared that his son had wanted to bluff the United States into upping the ante, so he decided to sail immediately for Tangier with all his squadron and Rodgers's frigate as well.

Captain Rodgers was not enchanted with this new assignment. An aggressive fighter and strict disciplinarian like Preble—which is probably why the two sea dogs were inclined to snarl at each other—he had frigidly informed Preble that he was his senior on the list of captains. To which Preble had replied just as coldly, "Yes, but I am now also a commodore, and these are your orders." With splendid bad grace, Rodgers obeyed, and on the night of September 16—just four days after his arrival at Gibraltar—Preble and his squadron had set sail across the Strait for Tangier, where he requested an audience with the emperor.

Preble might have expected that His Majesty was indisposed—busy with imperial pleasure in the imperial palace, on imperial progress in the countryside, imperial prerogatives—and could not be disturbed. The American commodore had insisted, and Muley Soliman—who had seen the heavily armed frigates *Constitution, John Adams* and *New York* and the sloop *Nautilus* in his harbor, their gunports open and guns run out, their tompions removed—had consented. Preble at once had assembled his officers to warn them that he might be walking into a trap. The ship was to be cleared for action "and if the least injury is offered to my person, immediately attack the batteries, the castle, the city and the troops—regardless of my personal safety." Next he donned his dress uniform with the shining gold epaulets, buckled on his sword, and accompanied by Consul-General Lear, Captain Rodgers and two junior officers, he climbed down the jacob's ladder into a waiting, bobbing long boat and was rowed ashore. There the rooftops were black with townspeople and the narrow streets thronged with them, all awed by the powerful American squadron in the harbor and the sight of this tall, long-striding commodore leading his party to the palace. They had never seen anything like it before.

Joined by U.S. Consul Simpson, just released for the occasion, Preble's party was led by a court attendant into a piazza in which fifty armed guards were stationed. The attendant had placed a cushion at the foot of a flight of stone steps. In a few minutes the door above opened and a little sparrow of a man in a worn woolen cloak had come down to sit on the cushion. "This is the emperor," the attendant had said, and Preble's junior officers had gasped. *This?* This half-pint, this cockleshell of an emperor was challenging *them?* Another attendant had asked Preble to remove his sword, but the commodore politely refused. Through an interpreter the emperor had then greeted Preble and asked him to kneel. Preble refused again, and Muley Soliman had asked:

"Are you not afraid of being arrested?"

"No, sir. If you presume to do that, my squadron in your full view will lay your batteries, your castles and your city in ruins."

The emperor, recalling what he had seen in the harbor, had been quick to assure his visitor that he wanted nothing more in the world than peace with America. With servile charm he reminded Preble that his father had been one of the first heads of state to recognize the new nation. He had blamed his navy's unfortunate depredations against the ships of his valued ally on Governor Hashash, who had unwisely acted on his own, and who, he promised Preble, would be punished "more than to your satisfaction." He also swore that the treaty signed by his father, though intended to last only fifty years, would be observed by him forever. As proof of his eternal friendship, Muley Soliman ordered a celebration in the Americans' honor to be held the moment they had returned to their ships.

When they did, Muley Soliman rode out of his palace on a fine Arabian horse at the head of most of his army, cantering down to the beach. Soldiers lined the shore for nearly three miles. Their officers' mounts pranced in the sand while the Imperial Moroccan Band serenaded the Yankee ships. The emperor sent boats loaded with ten bullocks, twenty sheep, four dozen chickens and ducks and two boatloads of fresh fruit and vegetables out to Preble's squadron. In reply, a twenty-one-gun salute boomed from the American ships.

Convinced at last that his rear was secure, Preble returned to Gibraltar, writing to Secretary of State Madison to inform him that the treaty with Morocco had been re-ratified and that Muley Soliman had promised to treat all American ships as vessels of a favored nation. At Gibraltar the commodore found a message from Secretary Smith ordering him to send *New York* and *John Adams* home for repairs. That left Preble with his own *Constitution* and Bainbridge's *Philadelphia,* together with the smaller craft *Argus, Vixen* and *Nautilus.* But this trio, with their shallow draft, should be most effective against the bashaw's galleys, feluccas and xebecs. So he replied to Smith: "You may rest confidently assured there shall not be an idle vessel in my squadron," predicting that he would win peace with Bashaw Yusuf by the spring of 1804.

So *Constitution* weighed anchor to sail for the port of Tripoli. Enroute on November 4 Preble encountered and hailed the British frigate *Amazon,* which reported the awful news that *Philadelphia* had run aground on a reef and been captured by the Tripolitans with all its officers and crew.

9

Calamity on Kaliusa Reef

 BEFORE COMMODORE PREBLE SAILED TO TANGIER TO SECURE HIS REAR he had ordered Captain William Bainbridge to take his 38-gun frigate *Philadelphia* and the 12-gun sloop *Vixen* to Tripoli and renew the blockade of the port. *Philadelphia*'s great firepower and *Vixen*'s shallow draft and speed should combine to thwart the bashaw's blockade-runners, Preble said, adding that as soon as he settled affairs with Emperor Muley Soliman he would join Bainbridge there.

What Preble probably did not know was that if Bainbridge attempted to sail along Tripoli's shallow and reef-ridden coast, he could not depend on the pilot that had come aboard her a year earlier. That was when Commodore Morris had relieved Commodore Dale, and Dale had remarked: "I recommend that you get a good pilot for the coast of Barbary. Should you meet with *Philadelphia,* you may get a very good one out of her." Presumably Morris did so, for there was no pilot now aboard Bainbridge's frigate. Bainbridge seems to have been relying upon studies of the area made by Lieutenant Porter and an incomplete chart.

Bainbridge arrived off Tripoli on October 7, 1803, cruising on and off the coast in search of enemy ships. Twelve days later he "spoke" an Austrian brig whose captain told him that two Tripolitan warships were roaming the Mediterranean, presumably having sailed before the arrival of Bainbridge's vessels. On October 20 Bainbridge decided to send *Vixen* under Lieutenant John Smith to look for them, ordering Smith to sail west toward Cape Bon, the northern bulge of Tunis that forms a narrow passageway with the island of Sicily. There Smith was to watch for the enemy ships.

Two days later a ferocious gale blew out of the northwest. Heading into it and tacking back and forth, *Philadelphia* fought the storm for nine days, gradually drifting about twenty miles east of her blockade post. At nine in the morning of October 31, a lookout cried, "Sail, ho!" Through his telescope Bainbridge saw a smallish ship sailing west and headed for Tripoli. Concluding that it might be one of those *Vixen* was after, he immediately gave chase.

Although the storm had ended, there were still strong winds blowing and the two ships went skimming over the sea, *Philadelphia* gradually gaining and coming close enough to see that she was indeed a Tripolitan xebec. Within two hours he was close enough to open up with his bow chasers, but the cannonballs fell harmlessly to one side of the enemy. *Philadelphia* had the range, but not the deflection. Now the xebec began running close ashore, and the converging *Philadelphia* swerved with her. She was coming dangerously close to shallow waters, which a good pilot would not have dared to risk—but Bainbridge for some reason believed that he was in safe water. What Bainbridge and Porter did not know was that their chart and Porter's studies did not include Kaliusa Reef: a long, shallow sandbank running parallel to the shore with a channel in its middle. The Kaliusa was well known to local seamen.

So *Philadelphia* went charging along at almost eight knots, her sailors in the forechains still casting their leads and singing out the depths: ten fathoms (sixty feet), eight fathoms, then seven, then back to ten and back to seven again. *Philadelphia* drew eighteen and one-half feet forward and twenty and one-half feet aft, so she was still in safe water. At eleven thirty A.M. with Tripoli's harbor entrance only four miles away, it became obvious to Bainbridge that the xebec was going to get away. So he ordered his bow-chasters to open fire again, but the shots fell harmlessly into the sea once more.

Now there was concern among almost all hands that their ship was in danger. Sailors began exchanging ominous glances and speaking to each other in worried voices. But a Marine private named William Ray heard Porter assure everyone that there "was no danger yet." That seemed to be true, with the soundings holding at a steady forty-eight feet. But that could change quickly. Bainbridge finally ordered the helm up and asked Porter to climb to the mizzentop for a better look at Tripoli as he turned *Philadelphia* away. Porter was halfway up the shrouds when he heard one of the leadsmen call six fathoms, a dramatic drop of twelve feet. This change so alarmed Bainbridge that he promptly ordered his seamen to brace the frigate's yards for tacking away to seaward—and then, with a loud grating noise and a horrible shudder followed by a sudden jolting stop that nearly shook Porter out of the rigging, *Philadelphia* mounted the Kaliusa Reef.

Because Bainbridge depended on his sketchy chart, he had thought he was in safe water—and he was. If he had continued on—thirty-six feet was certainly no difficult depth for a ship drawing only twenty and a half feet aft—he would have passed through the Kaliusa. But upon hearing the leadsman's cry of "six fathoms," a sudden reduction of twelve feet from the previous sounding of eight fathoms, he suddenly veered off to starboard, or north, and climbed the reef. Actually the Kaliusa was not a true reef, that is a huge rock, so that there was no penetration of the frigate's hull. But she was held fast among sand and smaller stones.

Bainbridge's first recourse was to order *Philadelphia*'s yards slanted to the wind, crowding on all sail in that direction in the hope that she would be blown into deep water. But this was exactly the wrong remedy, for the sandbank was too wide, and instead of driving the frigate through it, the wind drove it deeper into the reef and lifted her bow six feet.

Bainbridge then called a council of his officers. It had been noticed that the stern rose and fell with the waves, meaning that it was free, and it was decided to try to have the frigate blown off the reef stern first. All but one anchor was cut free and all guns run abaft to sink the stern deeper in safe water and raise the bow. All sails were then laid back to gain the assistance of the wind, still blowing strongly from the northwest. But the sea was still running strong with heavy waves so that this maneuver only lifted the ship higher on the reef. Now *Philadelphia* listed heavily to port and it became apparent that her guns could not now be aimed or worked properly. Also a small boat put over the side to survey the situation reported that *Philadelphia* was firmly aground in twelve feet of water, six feet less than her draft at the bow, which now was held in a viselike grip of sand and stones. It was then seen that Tripolitan gunboats led by High Admiral Murad Reis were beginning to issue from the harbor mouth, and the horror created by this spectacle may have done much to make Bainbridge commit his third and most dreadful error of all: lighten ship by casting everything portable—cannon, small arms, swords, cutlasses, ammunition, fresh water, all remaining anchors—over the side. Lightened by many tons, Bainbridge ordered the sails trimmed to the wind again—and again *Philadelphia* did not budge.

Now it could be seen that Murad Reis's nine gunboats were making for the mile and a half of open water between *Philadelphia* and the shore. Five more were seen debouching from the harbor.

In desperation Bainbridge ordered the foremast cut down. Axes began to ring and soon the mast came crashing down and over the side in a tangle of sails and rigging, taking the main topgallant mast with it. Once again *Philadelphia* did not budge. Now someone suggested kedging: that is, to carry an anchor forward, drop it and then haul on its chain. But Bainbridge had no boat capable of carrying a heavy anchor, and if he had it would have come under the fire of the enemy gunboats.

So *Philadelphia* was now defenseless, with her remaining guns pointing uselessly skyward. Bainbridge next ordered part of the stern cut away and big guns emplaced there. The first salvo screamed wildly over the heads of the enemy, and because there was no way they could be depressed farther, they also were of no avail. Seeing that *Philadelphia* could not harm them, the Tripolitans opened fire—carefully aiming at the frigate's rigging, for they had no wish to hull such a valuable prize. They sat in their gunboats, bobbing up and down in the swells, patiently waiting, circling their prey like sharks. At four o'clock with the late autumn dusk beginning to descend, Bainbridge called another council of his officers, at which it was decided, in the captain's words: "Upon a deliberate consideration of our situation, it was the unanimous opinion that it was impossible to get the ship off . . . and it was unanimously agreed that the only thing left for us to do was to surrender to the enemy."

This was true, granting the situation then. But that "impossibility" need not have ensued if Captain Bainbridge at the very outset of his predicament had decided to fight his ship. Obviously, it would be folly for the Tripolitans to attempt to sink or burn *Philadelphia*, for then they would lose a ship the like of which no Barbary potentate had ever possessed, together with all those highly ransomable officers and men. If Bainbridge resisted, they would have had to board her to capture her. Before he decided to try to lighten his ship by jettisoning her armament, he should have realized that he had a fighting chance to repel the enemy. If they came too close with their boats, they could be sunk by cannonballs hurled at them by hand—not at all a ridiculous tactic, for this is exactly what Edward Preble and his shipmates aboard the privateer *Protector* had done in their hard-won victory over the

British *Admiral Duff.* Moreover, if they gave battle, time was on their side. It was now twenty-four days since *Philadelphia* and *Vixen* had arrived off Tripoli. Surely Bainbridge had reason to hope that Preble and the rest of his squadron would arrive off the Kaliusa in time to rescue them.

And what was this lame excuse of deciding to surrender "to save the lives of the brave crew." What did the "brave crew" themselves think of that? Judging by their reaction they thought it was unvarnished cowardice. William Ray reported later that many of the seamen argued that there was still time to free the ship. A favorable wind could spring up; the Muslims would not attack at night; in the morning the sails of *Constitution* might be seen over the horizon. What was the all-fired hurry? When a sailor was ordered to haul down *Philadelphia*'s colors, Ray reported, he "positively refused to obey the captain's order," until a midshipman who threatened to run him through "seized the halyards and executed the command (himself) amidst the general murmuring of the crew."

But Bainbridge was determined to execute the decision of his timid council of war. Carpenters were sent below with bits and augurs to drill holes in the frigate's bottom, supposedly to scuttle her—as though Murad Reis once he took possession would not plug them up again. The powder magazine was flooded and shot poured into the pumps so that the ship could not be pumped out; again as though they could not be replaced or cleansed. Bainbridge's code and signal books were brought topside and burned, and then, all the frigate's pistols, muskets and cutlasses that could have been used to defend the ship went over the side, along with the remaining useless big guns—all in view of the silently watching pirates who now would know exactly where to look for them.

According to Ray, many of his shipmates then dashed below to put on all the clothes they could wear—perhaps to have more than a single set to depend on after they went into captivity—emerging on deck looking "like Falstaff." Now the Americans awaited their captors, but they didn't come, even though the sun was about to kiss the fading blue sea. Probably, being pirates, they thought that *Philadelphia*'s flag was hauled down as a trick. Bainbridge had to send a midshipman to announce to them that the ship and 307 Americans were being surrendered.

At dusk the Tripolitans rushed aboard, capering and yelling and brandishing their cutlasses. They stripped their prisoners of their money, watches and clothing, plundering the officers' quarters and Bainbridge's cabin. One swarthy bandit tried to tear a locket containing a miniature of Bainbridge's wife from the captain's neck, but he angrily beat him off. Next Murad Reis came aboard, happy to use his knowledge of English to curse Bainbridge and his officers in their own language. Then the Americans were forced over the side into the waiting boats, which they were compelled to row ashore. Stumbling through the surf, they were led in a torchlit parade through the streets in the customary howling, jeering, spitting reception. About midnight the men were herded into an empty warehouse and Bainbridge and his officers jammed into the consulate quarters vacated by James Cathcart—but not before the captain was relieved of his money, gold watch, sword and epaulets, but not his locket.

Just two days after *Philadelphia*'s surrender, a shrieking November storm sent huge waves sweeping over Kaliusa Reef, enabling the Tripolitans to haul her free—just as the Americans might have done had they fought off their assailants. From a window in the consulate, Bainbridge in consternation saw *Philadelphia* riding at anchor in the inner harbor: refitted and re-armed. Sponge divers had located almost all the jettisoned gear and guns, and they were dredged up. Bashaw Yusuf Karamanli now possessed in his fleet the most formidable warship on the Barbary Coast. Under command of the capable Murad Reis the *Philadelphia*—or whatever she would be renamed—could become the scourge of American shipping in the Mediterranean and beyond. She might even challenge *Constitution*, the only frigate remaining to Commodore Preble.

That terrible-tempered commander flew into a frightful rage when he learned that *Philadelphia* had indeed been captured. "Would to God that officers and crew," he wrote to Secretary Smith, "had one and all determined to prefer death to slavery. It is possible such a determination might (have saved) them from either." Obviously Preble believed that *Philadelphia* had the power to fight off her attackers until a favorable wind helped her off the reef. This seems to be incontrovertibly true. But Preble's bitterness should have been reserved for Bainbridge and his timid officers, not for the frigate's truly "brave crew."

Gradually, as Preble began to receive reports from Bainbridge, his animosity toward the youthful captain began to subside. These dismal documents were eagerly forwarded to the commodore by Bashaw Yusuf, knowing full well that they would be at once dispatched across the Atlantic to Washington where, he confidently believed, their description of the cruel captivity being endured by his American prisoners would so soften President Jefferson's heart that there would be no trouble about ransom, and with it, renewal of the tribute. What the bashaw and his censor did not know—inexplicably so in such cunning, conniving creatures—was that between the lines of his letters, Bainbridge was proposing in invisible ink of lemon juice and water a daring plan to burn *Philadelphia*. When heated, the ink became legible, and Commodore Preble forgot his enmity in his eagerness to conceive a plan to destroy the captured frigate.

10

Decatur Singes
the Bashaw's Beard

~ In December of 1803, three months after Commodore Preble entered the Mediterranean, he arrived off Tripoli in his flagship *Constitution* accompanied by the sloop *Enterprise* under Lieutenant Stephen Decatur to join the American blockaders there. At eight-thirty in the morning of December 23, 1803, Decatur in *Enterprise* sighted another ship east of the port and gave chase, followed by *Constitution*. An hour and a half later Decatur caught up with the stranger, finding her to be the sixty-four-ton ketch *Mastico* flying the Turkish ensign. Her captain insisted that she belonged to the Sublime Porte. But Decatur found her crew, passengers and armament to be a strange mixture indeed for an innocent trading vessel. It consisted of eleven Greek and Turkish sailors, two Tripolitan officers, ten Tripolitan soldiers and forty-two black slaves—men, women, and children—sent as a gift from the bashaw to the sultan. *Mastico* also had two cannon on deck and two more below, as well as a supply of muskets and pistols—not exactly a merchant's stock in trade. When *Constitution* hove to off *Mastico*, Preble ordered her taken as a prize to Syracuse in Sicily, where her Tripolitan origins were confirmed.

Enroute to Sicily, Decatur had become excited when he realized that *Mastico* was a typical Mediterranean ketch—a smallish, low-drafted, lateen-rigged vessel with a large foremast sail and a smaller one aft. Designed for the shallow waters of the Barbary Coast, she could enter Tripoli Harbor unnoticed. At Syracuse Decatur called on Preble to inform him that he thought that they had the perfect vessel to burn *Philadelphia* as she lay at anchor. Now Preble was excited, for this was the same idea that he and Bainbridge had been considering. And Decatur was right. *Mastico,* now renamed *Intrepid,* could be stuffed with flammables and hidden seamen, yet enter the harbor without arousing suspicion. Perhaps just as important, Preble had only recently hired a Sicilian pilot named Salvadore Catalano who spoke not only Arabic but also the *lingua franca* of the Barbary Coast, and was as familiar with those waters as any Tripolitan captain. Thus in *Intrepid* they had the right ship, in Catalano the right "Captain," and in the valiant Decatur the right commander.

Stephen Decatur had been born on January 5, 1779, the son of a prominent and wealthy Philadelphia family. Broad-shouldered, curly-haired, handsome, impeccably polite and charming, at maturity he became a great favorite with the ladies. Yet at nineteen, at the urging of attorneys who had helped to acquit him of a charge of murdering "a woman of doubtful integrity," he went to sea. In those days to begin a nautical career at nineteen was tantamount to a modern man trying to become a professional tennis player at thirty. He was simply too old, and yet, probably through the influence of his father, he was accepted as a midshipman on the frigate *United States.* While briefly ashore he married an heiress who had fallen in love with him before they met, having become infatuated with his portrait. And yet, to paraphrase Lovelace, he seems to have said to her, "I could not love thee, dear, so much / Loved I not Neptune more," whereupon she agreed to allow the U.S. Navy to precede her in his affections. Again, young naval officers in those days were a rare breed indeed, and such an attitude was common.

At twenty-four, as the commander of *Enterprise,* Decatur impressed almost everyone who sailed with or under him. Even William Ray— like most Marine privates a caustic critic of all his superiors, meaning everyone but his fellow rear-rankers—could write of Decatur: "The intrepid Decatur is proverbial among sailors for the good treatment of his men, as he is for his valor. Not a tar whoever sailed with Decatur but would almost sacrifice his life for him." Midshipman Robert Spence, who had sailed with Decatur aboard *United States,* wrote: "I had often pictured to myself the form and look of a hero, such as my favorite Homer delineated; here I saw it embodied."

Decatur also had gained the admiration of the commodore, and it was probably this, as much as his having suggested how to gain access to Tripoli Harbor, that led Preble to give him command of the expedition. This decision disappointed Lieutenant Charles Stewart, commander of the sloop *Siren,* who also volunteered to lead the raid. But Preble placated Stewart by assigning *Siren* to accompany *Intrepid* on her mission.

In tribute to Decatur's reputation among his seamen, when he confronted his crew and asked for volunteers, every man stepped forward. Delighted, Decatur chose sixty-two of the most muscular, who would be best fitted for the hand-to-hand combat he expected with *Philadelphia*'s Tripolitan crew. Eight of these were Marines. Meanwhile, to enhance *Intrepid*'s appearance as an innocent Barbary trader, her guns were taken ashore and her lateen rigging kept in place. Work crews also washed her verminous hold. *Siren* was painted a different color to make it difficult to identify her, her sails rerigged in Turkish style, and her gunports camouflaged.

Preble's plan was simple: *Intrepid* was to be stuffed with combustibles such as boxes of lint, tar, wood shavings and powder. These were to be carried aboard *Philadelphia* and set afire. There would be no attempt to bring the frigate safely out of the harbor. There were also barrels of combustible debris to be set alight if Decatur saw an opportunity to turn *Intrepid* into a fireship and send her in among the other vessels in the harbor. If he did this, he and his men would escape to *Siren* in ship's boats. Lieutenant Stewart was to anchor *Siren* outside the harbor, ready to come to *Intrepid*'s aid if necessary. The attempt would not be made until about ten o'clock at night when there would be the least chance of the enemy recognizing *Intrepid*. Much depended on how well Captain Catalano could deceive *Philadelphia*'s lookouts.

At five P.M. February 3, 1804, *Intrepid* and *Siren* set sail. Midshipman Ralph Izard left a letter behind: "This evening, dear mother, I sail for Tripoli . . . for the purpose of burning the frigate *Philadelphia.* . . . We are certain of success."

Barely out on the Mediterranean Decatur discovered to his dismay that the beef ration was unfit for human consumption. It had been packed in barrels that had contained salt fish and been incompletely cleaned, becoming tainted. The only food left was biscuits and water, but the men were in high spirits—relieved of the boredom of the blockade, delighted to be going on a lark—and did not complain. Perfect weather kept them happy, and both ships made their landfall off Tripoli in four days. On February 7 they separated rather than appear to be sailing together.

Upon the onset of night the wind freshened and soon was blowing a gale with the seas running high. Catalano warned Decatur against trying to negotiate Tripoli Harbor's treacherous entrance, but the dauntless young skipper, impatient at delay, sent the Sicilian pilot and Midshipman Charles Morris ahead to reconnoiter the entrance. Upon their return they reported that high roaring waves were sweeping into the harbor, submerging some reefs and crashing over others. *Intrepid* would be lost in such seas; moreover, it would be impossible to flee the harbor. With reluctance, Decatur headed back to sea to ride out the storm.

Seeing *Intrepid*'s stern lights, Stewart in *Siren* sought to follow—only to have his anchor snagged on rocks. Unable to free it, Stewart ordered the anchor cable cut and it was not until dawn that he was able to seek *Intrepid*. For a solid week the storm pummeled both little ships, driving them eastward into the Gulf of Sidra.

Life aboard the overcrowded *Intrepid* became an ordeal. Both officers and men prayed for survival, the *Philadelphia* mission forgotten. Decatur and four other officers were crammed into a tiny cabin. Catalano and six midshipmen stowed on a makeshift platform above the water casks were so cramped they could not sit up. The eight Marines on a similar perch on the other side of the ship were similar sardines, and seamen jammed into a small hold were pummeled by rolling provision crates and barrels. Worse, the hold had not been thoroughly fumigated and was still inhabited by rats and other vermin. All hands, meanwhile, trembled to hear the mountainous seas thundering against the ship's hull. Bobbing like a cockleshell on the roaring, boiling water, the ketch shipped aboard tons of green seawater, so that the pumps had to be worked continually to keep *Intrepid* afloat. At last, on February 15, the shrieking wind began to slacken and fall silent. Soon it subsided and Decatur called for more sail and set a westward course for Tripoli Harbor. Before dark that night both ships had reached Point Taiura, just east of the harbor mouth. Rather than be detected, Decatur decided to sail farther seaward. At 9:30 P.M. both ships turned and headed harborward once more, but could not find the entrance in the dark.

At 11 A.M. the next day—the sixteenth—Decatur set sail for the harbor again, this time towing a drag of wood to slow his progress. Well behind him purposely lagging was *Siren,* and soon she was out of sight. The British ensign was fluttering from *Intrepid*'s mast as she approached the outer harbor, her sails flapping lazily to give the impression of a trading vessel. At dusk Decatur slipped into the entrance, his eye fastened on the setting sun, trying to calculate exactly how much light would remain when he reached *Philadelphia*. His ketch was moving too fast, he thought, and would reach the frigate too soon. Rendezvous with the *Siren*'s boat had been set for 10 P.M., and Decatur needed to wait to be sure *Siren* was on station, for he might need her should his mission require a rescue.

Accordingly, he called for more drags. Large buckets fastened to the rails went over the side and *Intrepid* slowed. Fortunately, for they were approaching the narrow, twisting entrance to the inner harbor. In the growing darkness, Catalano lying forward on the boom anxiously studied every reef. Though the wind had fallen, white water still frothed over them. At eight o'clock Decatur ordered the drags brought aboard, his wary eyes making out the silhouette of approaching boats. They were from *Siren,* and Decatur let out his breath. The boatmen were eager to join the raid, the Decatur let thirty of them come aboard and instructed the others to remain on station with their boats.

Decatur next ordered all hands to their assigned hideouts, commanding strict silence. At his signal, all were to rise up and rush aboard *Philadelphia*. Only cold steel—swords, cutlasses and daggers— would be used, although a few reliable Marines carried firearms for an emergency. Decatur, two other officers and fourteen men were to seize the frigate's spar deck, while other detachments captured the berth deck, forward and after storerooms and the cockpit. As soon as the ship's crew was subdued, the men remaining aboard *Intrepid* to repel a possible counterattack would begin handing up the combustibles to be placed throughout the *Philadelphia*. When they were in position, Decatur would give the command and all would be lighted at once, after which everyone would rush back to *Intrepid*. Again and again, Stephen Decatur had rehearsed his officers and crew in these maneuvers, and now he was confident that they would succeed.

At nine o'clock *Intrepid* was moving slowly in a near calm, seeming to slide over the glassy surface of the harbor. Decatur, in Arabic robes like all the other officers and men erect on deck, could see the winking lights of the city. Then, silhouetted against them, seeming to rise from the water like a great sea monster, there loomed the hull of *Philadelphia*. No other ship in the harbor was so big. Silently, the helmsman guided the ketch toward the frigate. Now lights could be seen aboard her. They shone through open gunports, showing the cannon with tompions removed. Decatur thought in momentary dread: *They're loaded!* Had the bashaw been warned? One salvo from *Philadelphia* would blow *Intrepid* and everything and everyone aboard her into bits. But Decatur could see no crouching gunners blowing on their slow matches. Only an occasional turbaned head passing the open ports. Otherwise, there was no sign of anyone on her high, darkened deck.

At nine-thirty the ketch was under nearly two hundred guns—thirty-eight aboard *Philadelphia,* forty in the bashaw's fortress castle and another hundred in the Tripoli shore batteries. The harbor was still, except for the sound of wavelets lapping against the wooden sides of anchored ships, the creak of blocks and the louder groan of the ketch's long lateen boom and the croak of tackles. A moon had risen and the surface of the harbor glinted as though it were an obsidian sea.

At ten an Arabic voice full of suspicion came down from the frigate. Catalano whispered to Decatur that it was a lookout ordering *Intrepid* to bear off. Decatur nodded silently, and Catalano called back with the prearranged explanation that he was a trader from Malta who had lost his anchor in the storm. He requested permission to tie up alongside *Philadelphia* for the night. Still suspicious, the lookout asked what Catalano's cargo was. The Sicilian's reply is unknown, but it apparently satisfied the sentry. His next question concerned another ship outside the harbor.

It was, of course, *Siren,* but Decatur had prepared Catalano for this query. He knew that the Tripolitans had purchased the brig *Transfer* in Malta and were awaiting its arrival. So Catalano replied that it was *Transfer,* and that satisfied the lookout. Slowly, *Intrepid* drifted closer. . . . She was now but twenty yards from the side of looming *Philadelphia.* . . . Then the breeze died, and the ketch went dead in the water.

Decatur could see turbaned men climbing down into one of *Philadelphia's* boats. They rowed around to the bow, seized a line, and turned toward *Intrepid.* Decatur stiffened. He didn't want these men to get too close. They might give an alarm and *Intrepid* would be blown to smithereens. He called softly for one of the ketch's boats to take a line toward the frigate. When the two boats met, the men spliced the ropes. Decatur now whispered to his robed Americans to haul on the line, bringing *Intrepid* slowly under the frigate's stern, when a line was thrown aboard and made fast. But then the lookout saw the anchor that the "Maltese" boat supposedly had lost, and raised the cry: "*Americani!*"

Catalano panicked, and shouted: "Board, Captain, board!" But Decatur quieted him, waiting for *Intrepid* to be pulled still closer and calling to his men: "No order to be obeyed but from the commanding officer!" Slowly . . . with agonizing slowness . . . the remaining few feet of water between the two vessels shrank. . . . There was a bump and a sharp crack as the two hulls met, and Stephen Decatur roared:

"BOARD!"

Instantly, *Intrepid*'s deck was filled with racing shadows leaping for hand-holds on the chain plates on the side of the frigate's hull. Decatur was at their head, stumbling as he too lunged for a hand-hold. He nearly fell. Beside him Midshipman Alexander Laws, grabbing a gunport lid, got his sword tangled in his clothing—and it was Midshipman Morris who was first aboard. Decatur was now also safely on the frigate's deck, lifting his cutlass to slash at Morris, whom he mistakenly took for a Mussulman. Only Morris's quick gasp of the password—"*Philadelphia*"—saved him. Now *Intrepid*'s men were pouring aboard the frigate, yelling and slashing with their cutlasses, thrusting with swords, stabbing with daggers, forcing the ship's defenders back, back, and ever backward, until at last most of them dove overboard in fright, unused scimitars flying from their hands.

Now there ensued between Decatur and Catalano a conversation that, had it ended differently, almost certainly would have changed the course of the War with the Barbary Pirates. A beaming Catalano told Decatur that they had an excellent opportunity to take the frigate they had just recaptured out of the harbor. The situation was perfect, Catalano said: the ship had been cleared of Tripolitans, there was a fair and favorable breeze, a moonlit night, double-shotted guns, no opposition likely from the bashaw's gunboats along the shore, and in Catalano himself they had a pilot who knew the harbor. True, the enemy had more guns, but few as powerful as *Philadelphia*'s, and by the time they realized that the frigate was running for it, she would be beyond their range. Also because *Intrepid* and the *Siren*'s boats would be accompanying their flight, if something unforeseen did appear to doom the attempt, *Philadelphia* could still be set on fire. Even as Catalano spoke, the combustibles were already being handed up from *Intrepid* to the details trained to set them afire. But Decatur could not bring himself to disobey Preble's unequivocal orders to burn the frigate. Twenty-one years later, long after Decatur had been killed in a duel with James Barron, Catalano made an affidavit stating that he believed that Decatur was strongly tempted to seize this golden moment. But he did not, and turned to supervising the distribution of the flammables.

Each man carried a small sperm-oil candle, and each squad-leader had a lantern slung over his shoulder. When Decatur gave the command to set *Philadelphia* ablaze, each man lighted his candle from the lantern and hurled it into his carefully secured charge. As many as a half-dozen fires were thus lighted simultaneously.

Philadelphia was tinder dry, and her open ports and hatches provided a strong updraft. She seemed to explode in flame as though lighted by giant matches. Midshipman Morris and his men, down deepest in the cockpit, were almost trapped by the flames as they rushed up the companionway. As they emerged on deck, dozens of men were swinging over *Philadelphia*'s side to land in safety aboard *Intrepid,* leaving behind twenty Tripolitan bodies to be cremated in what would soon be a roaring inferno. Now Decatur made his escape, having made certain that all hands had safely fled the ship. Once again he stumbled, nearly falling overboard. But he managed to grab the ketch's rigging, sliding down it onto her deck just as she swung away from the fiery frigate.

It had taken but twenty-five minutes to set *Philadelphia* ablaze, but now the bashaw's batteries were opening up: not at *Philadelphia,* of course, which they still thought of saving, but at *Intrepid.* Although the shocked enemy gunners were firing wildly, one ball tore through the ketch's topsail. Now the Americans were desperately trying to free their ship from flaming *Philadelphia.* Then as the fire burned through the bowline holding the two vessels together, someone remembered that the stern line had not been cut. Even as seamen rushed to cut it, sizzling tar poured down into *Intrepid,* and tongues of flame shot through *Philadelphia*'s gunports, threatening to ignite the barrels of combustibles to be used if *Intrepid* were turned into a fireship.

At last the stern line was cut, and Decatur called for the sweeps. But then *Intrepid*'s long boom caught on the frigate's stern. Heat was browning the ketch's sails which might burst into flames at any moment. Roaring like huge, live devouring dragons from Hades, the fires coalesced into a single towering torch that lighted the entire harbor. Flames ran up masts and sails like fiery snakes, and burning brands and cotton fell hissing into the water. The frigate was now a firestorm whirling and crackling with such intensity that it threatened to suck *Intrepid* into its center. At last the boom was freed, and with the help of seamen pulling so desperately at their oars that perspiration gleaming in the firelight streamed like water from their overheated bodies, the ketch moved slowly away to safety.

Now the menace came from the bashaw's batteries, for *Intrepid* was perfectly silhouetted in the frigate's flames, and the gunners redoubled their fire. Then, to the amazement of the Americans and the consternation of the Tripolitans, *Philadelphia*'s double-shotted guns were touched off by the heat. Roaring one after another as though in a martial fugue, they sent their cannonballs spinning into the bashaw's castle fortress, silencing its guns and so confusing the gunners that it might have seemed to them that Allah had joined the enemy. Now *Intrepid* began to gain speed, impelled by a providential breeze that assisted the men at the sweeps, and the ketch raced out of range.

At that moment the flames reached *Philadelphia*'s powder magazine. With a deafening roar the frigate seemed to rise from the water by its own power, before it disintegrated into thousands of brilliant sparks and flaming debris forming a cascading, descending fire fountain that at last vanished in the glistening surface of the sea. Out at the harbor mouth, *Intrepid*'s men gaped in awe at this splendid spectacle. They watched in silence as the flames still flickered astern. Then *Siren* joined *Intrepid* and the two American vessels set sail for Syracuse. As dawn of February 17 began to glow pinkish to starboard, they could still see a flame-colored sky astern.

Philadelphia was no more, at a cost to Decatur's force of exactly one man slightly injured.

11

Preble Shivers
the Bashaw's Timbers

◠ IF THERE IS ANY NOBLE EMOTION THAT CAN BE DISARMING AND MIS-
chievous it is gratitude, and even the flinty, hard-headed Edward Preble had no defense against this deceptive feeling when, upon receiving Stephen Decatur's report of the successful burning of *Philadelphia,*
he wrote to Secretary Smith a separate account of the exploit praising
the youthful officer beyond belief. "The important service he has rendered," he wrote, "would in any navy in Europe insure him the instan-
taneous promotion to the rank of port captain."

Smith accepted this recommendation and Jefferson, also carried
away, approved it—both unmindful of the discontent such an unheard-
of elevation would cause among the seven lieutenants senior to
Decatur. Preble, the Instigator, now became Preble the Stubborn,
ignoring the wise advice of his old friend Charles Goldsborough, chief
clerk of the Navy Department, who suggested that Decatur decline the
promotion rather than provoke resentment among his seniors. It is
almost certain that the gracious officer whom all hands called the
American Bayard would have done so, but Preble never mentioned the
proposal to him, and so a delighted Stephen Decatur, veteran of only
six years service, became at twenty-five the youngest captain ever. As
Goldsborough had feared, indignation was rife among the young captain's former seniors; and Lieutenant Andrew Sterrett, victor of the
only ship-to-ship battle of the war, angrily handed in his resignation.

• • •

Upon his return to Syracuse Stephen Decatur confirmed Captain Bainbridge's earlier report from prison that the bashaw's shore guns were "in bad order, and they are very bad gunners." Bainbridge had also written in his invisible ink that Preble could "destroy the place" if he could put three or four thousand troops ashore to march on the capital. But he didn't say where they might be had, and Preble knew that the United States could never mount an amphibious operation of that size. He was also aware that Tripoli's best defense was its gunboats, squat, shallow-draft vessels ideal for operation inside and just outside the harbor. Each mounted a few guns and were in effect floating batteries. In all, the bashaw had about eighteen of them.

What Commodore Preble needed was his own fleet of gunboats, and that was why in the spring of 1804 he sailed to Naples, the capital of the Kingdom of the Two Sicilies (that city and the island of Sicily) to ask King Ferdinand IV to sell or loan him some Italian gunboats. He was greeted by Sir John Acton, a Briton whom Ferdinand had made his prime minister in gratitude for British protection. Because Ferdinand also was at war with Tripoli, Preble reasoned that he might be agreeable to his proposal—and he was. But all he could spare were eight gunboats and two bomb ketches, together with the necessary ammunition and seamen to handle them. Each twenty-five-ton gunboat mounted a long 24-pounder in its bow and the thirty-ton ketches were armed with a 13-inch* brass mortar, a high-angle-fire weapon that could hurl shells into the city.

These warships were far from seaworthy, having been built strictly for the defense of harbors, being heavy and flat bottomed and unable to sail or be rowed tolerably well at sea. They were best towed, and that was what Preble did with his flagship and the sloops *Nautilus* and *Enterprise*. To have pulled them safely across the open Mediterranean was a striking feat of seamanship, and it was a proud Edward Preble who finally arrived off Tripoli with them on July 25. He now had a formidable fleet: one frigate, three schooners, three brigs, six gunboats and two ketches. On July 28 he prepared to attack Murad Reis's gunboat flotilla, awaiting him in line just outside the harbor's rocky barrier. If the heavier American ships menaced him, he could easily slip inside.

But it was the wind, not the bashaw's son-in-law, that turned out to be Preble's most formidable foe. It veered to the northwest, instead of the milder southwest, and it came on with gale force. To avoid being

---

* Naval ordnance is now generally measured in inches, the diameter of the missile fired.

blown upon the rocks, Preble took his fleet seaward. His ships were cruelly buffeted for three days, and by another miracle of seamanship not a vessel was lost. On August 3, a beautifully clear and calm day, the Americans returned to the attack.

Preble divided his ships into two divisions: one under Decatur and the other commanded by Lieutenant Richard Somers, each of them to take on one of Murad Reis's two divisions. Meanwhile the bomb ketches would plow into the outer harbor to lob shells into the city, while the brigs and schooners would trail the gunboats to protect them by raking the shore batteries. At 1:30 P.M. as his vessels moved toward the Tripolitan gunboats again in line to repel the Americans, Preble could see that the city's rooftops were black with spectators eager to watch the gunboat battle and confident that their pirates—so skilled in boarding—would quickly prevail. At 2:30, Preble raised the signal to attack.

At once the bomb ketches began their bombardment. Their mortar shells rose humming in a high, looping arc to come plunging down on the waterfront buildings, chiefly on the bashaw's castle. Almost at once the rooftops were emptied of the enemy audience, an event that may have caused the mirthless Preble to indulge in one of those rare twitchings of his lips that passed for a smile. Now the shore batteries began firing with customary inaccuracy, their shells splashing short of the approaching gunboats and bringing down upon their heads the cannonballs of the American brigs and schooners. Without hesitation, Murad Reis's gunboats came wallowing forward to meet the Yankees.

This, of course, was the sort of sea-fighting the brigands favored: grappling and boarding, hand-to-hand fighting with scimitar and saber, cutlass and pike. Thus they were disarmingly surprised when the Americans came at them with the same tactics. Decatur's division struck first, with Decatur himself in Gunboat Four singling out the nearest pirate and spraying her stem-to-stern with grapeshot and musketry, killing her captain and sending her crew scurrying for cover. With the gunwales left undefended, and the Tripolitans firing pistols and muskets from cover, a screeching, screaming swarm of Americans came pouring onto her decks brandishing swords, cutlasses and tomahawks. The enemy, caught while attempting to reload and without their trusty blades in their hands, were completely overwhelmed. Most of them were cut down, while the rest dived overboard or surrendered. The fight had lasted only ten minutes.

Next Decatur took the captured prize in tow and came at another corsair gunboat to leeward. But a similar slashing attack met spirited resistance, led by a huge Turkish captain. Decatur lunged at him with his pike, but the Turk seized it and tore it away. Drawing his cutlass, the American now struck at his own pike, menacing him, but his blade broke at the hilt. Unsheathing his scimitar, the big Turk now slashed at his disarmed opponent, but Decatur deflected the stroke with his arm—receiving a deep wound there. The two men now grappled and fell wrestling to the deck with Decatur on top. At this point another Tripolitan swung his scimitar down at the American's neck, hoping to decapitate him. But an American sailor named Daniel Frazier, though wounded in both arms, lunged between the blade and Decatur so that it merely glanced off his head, cutting his scalp. Upon this noble intervention another American shot the pirate dead.

Now Decatur and the Turk continued to struggle, thrashing around as each sought to gain the upper hand. Finally, it was the big Turk who straddled the American while yanking a huge dagger from his waistband. Decatur seized his wrist, and for a moment an arm-wrestling contest ensued seemingly certain to end in the giant Turk's favor—until Decatur with his free hand dragged a pistol from his jacket and fired it into his adversary's back. Falling suddenly still, the Turk rolled away—and at the death of their captain the rest of the brigands surrendered.

Like all warriors since Agamemnon, Decatur went souvernir hunting, pulling the Turk's dirk—a foot-long poniard with elaborate chasing on the blade and a rhinoceros-tusk handle—from his lifeless fingers. He next stooped to extract a leather-bound Koran from another dead enemy. He and his men had killed or wounded fifty-two Tripolitans, taken eight prisoners and sent uncounted others swimming for safety, against only a half dozen of their own wounded. Just as the American lieutenant prepared to take his two prizes back to Preble, another U.S. gunboat pulled alongside.

It was the one commanded by Decatur's younger brother, James, but James was not at the helm. Rather the boat was steered by a young midshipman named Brown, who told Decatur that his brother had attacked an enemy gunboat which lowered its flag in surrender. When James stepped aboard, its treacherous captain shot him in the head.

Stephen Decatur went berserk. He sent Brown's gunboat with the dying James aboard back to *Constitution*, put skeleton crews aboard his prizes, and then, with eleven volunteers aboard, went hunting for the cowardly captain. He caught him trying to slip behind some rocks, and bore down on him like an avenging fury. Though heavily outnumbered, the Americans leaped aboard the enemy boat with the ardor born of vengeance, and while Decatur cornered and killed the captain, they subdued his crew or compelled them to surrender.

Overtaking his other two prizes, Decatur brought the three of them under Preble's flagship, where, his face and hands still smeared with blood and black with powder, he saluted Preble on the quarterdeck to report proudly: "I have brought you three of the enemy's gunboats, sir."

"*Three*, sir?" the indignant commodore roared. "Where are the rest of them."

Momentarily dismayed, Decatur soon learned the explanation of his chief's seeming ingratitude. Things had not gone well with the other gunboats. Lieutenant Somers was raked with heavy shore battery fire as he attacked Murad Reis's other division. His boat was repeatedly holed and would have sunk had not a lucky shot from a bomb-ketch mortar knocked out the enemy guns. Even so, Somers did damage five Tripolitan boats but was able to capture none. Elsewhere Lieutenant Joseph Bainbridge (Captain William's younger brother) ran onto the rocks and was put out of action. When a signalman mistakenly hoisted the recall flag, Lieutenant Joshua Blake returned to *Constitution* and was thereafter unable to re-enter the battle.

Nevertheless Lieutenant John Trippe redeemed these failures by boarding one of the enemy's biggest gunboats. Its captain—another huge Turk—struck at the much-shorter Trippe with his scimitar, cutting him on the head and chest and driving him to his knees. Just as the Turk sprang forward for the final blow, Trippe lunged upward with his pike in a lucky thrust that entered his assailant's groin and lifted him off the deck. When he fell back screaming, his men surrendered.

Constitution was also active. Preble at first had kept her out of the range of the shore batteries, but then he took her to within a mile of the nearest blockhouse and delivered two broadsides. Almost immediately Tripolitan cannonballs came shrieking back. They tore through the flagship's rigging, cracked her mainmast and carried her main yard away; otherwise the only damage done was by iron fragments tearing Preble's uniform and scratching the elbow of a Marine standing next to him. In exchange, a Muslim minaret came crashing down, to the cheers of the flagship's crew.

Eventually the black-powder smoke drifting over the harbor reduced visibility to near zero, and the American ships withdrew to the protection of *Constitution*, while Murad Reis's ships crawled inside the rocks for safety. The battle had ended, and the final score in no way justified Commodore Preble's furious dismay. His man had captured three enemy gunboats and sunk three more, while inflicting casualties of forty-four dead and twenty-six wounded, fifty-two taken prisoner, at a loss of only fourteen Americans wounded. Many of the bashaw's gunboats were smashed almost beyond repair, while all the American gunboats had survived the fighting and, with the three captured enemy craft, would serve their country again.

That night a grieving Stephen Decatur sat at the bedside of his stricken brother, who died at sunset of the following day. "I would rather see him thus," Decatur said quietly, "than living with any cloud on his conduct." His brother was buried at sea, with Preble acting as chaplain. Afterward, the commodore took his fleet offshore for repairs.

Commodore Preble had learned from a French privateer captain who had been in the harbor during the gunboat battle that the bashaw's flotilla had been badly damaged and many of his ships at anchor wrecked as well. The Frenchman also agreed to take fourteen wounded Tripolitan prisoners ashore as a humane gesture from Preble, together with a note asking a reciprocal gesture from the bashaw and an offer of $50,000 ransom for the American prisoners. Back came the defiant reply: "I would rather bury myself under the ruins of my country than basely yield to the wishes of the enemy." Upon this retort, Edward Preble decided to oblige Yusuf Karmanli.

At 9 A.M. August 7, Preble ordered his gunboats and bomb ketches into battle again, the ketches to take station west of the city, the boats toward the harbor's northern approaches. Support would come again from the brigs and schooners: *Argus*, *Nautilus*, *Enterprise* and *Vixen*. At 2:30 P.M. all opened up with a deafening bombardment that reverberated around the harbor. The bomb ketches pounded waterfront buildings and the bashaw's castle, and the gunboats struck at the shore batteries and the harbor ships. Once again the Tripolitans fought back, sinking one American gunboat along with its captain and most of its crew, while the fire from the ketches was so devastating that a division of enemy gunboats sought to steal up on one of them to sink her. But Preble quickly detected their attempt and brought *Constitution* bearing down on them so rapidly that they turned and scurried for the safety of the rocks once more.

By 5 P.M. most of the shore batteries had been silenced, but as the wind hauled to the northeast, Preble, fearing that his vessels would be blown too close to shore, ordered a withdrawal. That night the doughty commodore received news that was both good and bad.

• • •

The frigate *John Adams* had arrived unexpectedly. It was commanded by one of Preble's Boys: Master Commandant Isaac Chauncey. The good news that he gave the commodore was that President Jefferson, deeply dismayed at the report of the loss of the *Philadelphia,* had decided to strengthen the Mediterranean squadron by sending no less than five frigates there: *John Adams, President, Congress, Constellation* and *Essex.* The bad news was that he was relieving Preble as squadron commander and replacing him with Samuel Barron.

Preble was shocked. He knew, of course that he was junior to the available captains on the sacroscanct U.S. Navy seniority list, and that Jefferson had jumped him over the head of such doughty seamen as John Rodgers; and he also realized that Jefferson, probably impelled to this decision by news of the *Philadelphia* disaster, had been unaware of his recent successes. But even Secretary Smith's assurance that there was "no want of confidence in you" was no consolation for being removed from command of what would now be a mighty naval power indeed with which to crush and overthrow the bashaw.

Though understandably indignant and resentful, Edward Preble kept his own counsel and also withheld the information from his valiant boys such as Decatur, Somers and Hull lest they become infuriated and do something rash like handing in their resignations. He also decided to strike at Yusuf Karamanli one more time, hastily beginning to repair the damage done to his fleet during the latest battle. He need not have hurried, for it would not be until September 9 that the sails of *Constellation* and *President* would be seen over the horizon. In the meantime, Preble counted on *John Adams's* armament as a powerful augmentation of his strength—and here he was again shocked.

John Adams had almost no firepower. She had been selected in effect to be the supply ship of the new squadron, and her gun decks had been cleared to make room for the stores she carried. All but a few of her big guns were stored in tallow belowdecks to help serve as ballast. Here was a masterpiece of bureaucratic stupidity: the supply ship to be sent to the war zone *before the warships.* Nor was the ever-resourceful Preble able to overcome this monstrous mistake by bringing the guns back up on deck because the frigate's gun carriages were coming over in the holds of *Congress* and *Constellation. John Adams's* firepower, then, was all but nonexistent. In anguish and in anger, Preble wrote in his journal: "Had the *John Adams* brought out her gun carriages, I . . . can have no doubt that the next attack would make the arrival of more ships unnecessary for the termination of the Tripoline war."

Yet this indomitable sailor did not abandon his plan to assault

Tripoli once more. Having supposedly departed their ports only five days after Chauncey's frigate, the absent quartet could reasonably be expected to arrive any day. So Preble asked Chauncey to delay his departure for Syracuse so that he—or Barron, if he arrived in time—could use *John Adams*'s guns on *Constitution*'s carriages should any of the flagship's cannon be disabled in the coming battle. He also borrowed some of Chauncey's boats and a few of his officers and men. With days of an empty horizon turning into weeks, Preble decided to judge the effects of his attacks on Tripoli by making a final offer for *Philadelphia*'s prisoners.

Richard O'Brien was still aboard *Constitution*, his pregnant wife Betsy having decided to postpone an Atlantic crossing until her baby was born. Preble sent O'Brien to Bashaw Yusuf with an offer of $80,000 plus a personal gift of $10,000 for Yusuf. O'Brien returned with the bashaw's counter offer of $150,000. Even though Consul General Lear had authorized payment of that amount, Preble thought it was still too high and countered with a proposal of $100,000 plus that $10,000 "gift." This was indeed his final offer, because he believed that when Barron arrived with the powerful new frigates, the bashaw could be forced to return his captives. But Yusuf would not budge, and Preble immediately prepared for battle. Summer was waning and the customary autumn storms could scatter his fleet.

In one of his many invisible-ink messages, Captain Bainbridge had suggested that a nocturnal bombardment would be most likely to shake the bashaw's resolve. In the sea dark Preble's moving ships would be difficult targets for the shore batteries, while Tripoli itself and especially the bashaw's palace would be large, lighted and immobile—thus eminently visible to the American gunners. At eight P.M. on August 24 Preble assembled his fleet off the harbor once more. At midnight he signaled the attack, and the sloops and schooners began towing the bomb ketches inside the harbor, followed by the gunboats under both sail and oars. Two hours later a rocket from the flagship ordered the bombardment to begin.

For more than two hours Tripoli quivered and shook beneath the American bombardment. Terrified Tripolitans fled into the countryside with their hands over their ears, and most of the foreign consuls and personnel also evacuated the city. Preble's fleet fired upwards of three hundred round shot, besides grape and cannister, into the shore batteries, waterfront buildings and the bashaw's castle. All the castle guns and two batteries were knocked out of action. From the gunboats came another four hundred round shot, with more grape and cannister, inflicting heavy casualties and damage on the Tripolitan galleys and gunboats. It was not until six A.M. that the bombardment lifted and the schooners and brigs returned to tow the gunships out of firing range of the burning city.

If Bashaw Yusuf and those of his subjects remaining in the city, as well as the seamen of Murad Reis's battered navy, rejoiced to see the departing sails of the hated *Americani,* their jubilation was premature—for this had been merely a preliminary softening-up for the main bombardment scheduled to come. On August 27—giving the Tripolitans two days in which to return to their shattered city—Preble brought his squadron back. Moving with slow majesty—*Constitution* in the lead, followed by *Siren, Argus, Vixen, Nautilus, Enterprise* and the gunboats, with *John Adams* standing offshore as though with supporting firepower on call—it was a procession calculated to strike renewed terror into the hearts of those ashore, and inspiring to the Yankee seamen at their stations.

Shortly after midnight August 28 the fleet began to move to its firing stations. Three hours later another rocket flashed skyward from *Constitution* and another bombardment commenced. Once again, the shore batteries and ships in the harbor replied, but with the same inaccuracy so that the battery on the mole was soon silenced and a galliot and galley in the harbor smashed and sunk. Cannon flashes flickered over the harbor's rippling black wavelets, silhouetting the bashaw's castle and burning buildings. As dawn crept out of the sky to port of *Constitution,* Murad Reis sought to silence the Americans' thundering guns, sending a detachment of gunboats plowing out of the inner harbor. Preble saw them and quickly ordered his flagship's gun crews into action. As he came winging down with "a bone in her teeth"—white water boiling off her prow—sails taut and round with the wind, Preble signaled to his gunboats to retire. They backed off with cheering crews as the great vessel swept past with the sound of swishing water. "It was the most elegant sight I ever saw," one gunboat sailor wrote. "She had her tompions out, matches lit and batteries lighted up, all hands at quarters—standing right under the fort." A mere four hundred yards from the mole, *Constitution* began bellowing. In a single broadside she sank one gunboat and sent the rest dashing behind the mole, some of them with burning sails. Taking a heavy fire from shore that did no more then shred a few sails and smash some yards, the flagship poured 225 rounds of broadsides into the city. Each one sent showers of mortar flying from the burning buildings, and all eventually silenced the bashaw's shore guns. Only then did the American squadron withdraw.

But by September 2 Preble was planning another assault, after a Spanish vessel emerged from the harbor to speak *Constitution* with the report that the last bombardment had inflicted massive destruction in the city, wrecking much of the bashaw's navy and killing "a vast number of people." Encouraged, the commodore sallied into the harbor a third time, again delivering broadsides—eleven of them—into Yusuf's castle while his gunboats and ketches scourged the enemy ships. Only a wind change in the north compelled Preble to withdraw. And now he planned what he hoped would be the most devastating stroke of all: a fireship assault.

The fireship was among the most dreaded weapons during the age of fighting sail, especially if it were launched upon vessels caught in narrow waters, such as a river basin or a harbor. It was a ship stripped-down and loaded with gunpowder and combustibles, her guns double-shotted and aimed at the enemy—then set afire with her helm secured and the wind at her back to descend upon the immobile foe with all cannon firing, roaring, spitting, belching like a fiery monster from Hades. Preble planned something even more devastating, a floating bomb that would set alight or sink everything in the harbor within a half-mile of her.

Under Preble the Shipbuilder's supervision, *Intrepid*—the *Mastico* that Decatur had used to burn *Philadelphia*—was almost entirely rebuilt. Her forward hold was planked over and crammed with five tons of black powder. On top of the planks were placed several tons of shot and pig iron normally used for ballast, together with a hundred 13-inch mortar shells and fifty 9-inch shells. From this a small tunnel aft was built to a section stuffed with pitch, powder, lint soaked in turpentine and other flammables. A powder train would be laid between these two compartments.

Two fuses slipped through two musket barrels were to be lighted eleven minutes before *Intrepid* was cast off and the crew began rowing madly for safety. The fuses would ignite the combustibles amidships turning the vessel into a roaring inferno, and as she approached her target the sparks flashing along the powder trail into the forward hold loaded with powder and shells would set off a titanic explosion.

Almost every officer and man in Preble's fleet volunteered for this most dangerous mission. Preble chose Master Commandant Richard Somers—who had been so disappointed at missing the glory won by Decatur in the *Philadelphia* burning—as commander, and carefully selected a crew of ten. Somers would sail *Intrepid*—now called *Infernal* by some cynical forecastle wags—into the harbor in darkness, slipping past the gunboats and making for the castle walls. Each man had been carefully rehearsed in his assignment and given his place at the oars.

As night began to fall on September 3 the harbor conditions were ideal for such a surprise attack. A thin haze had settled over the water, reducing horizontal visibility to a few hundred yards, although the stars could be seen above it and the tallest minarets in the city were in view. A drifting fog obscured the harbor.

At eight o'clock *Intrepid* slipped away from *Constitution*, entering the harbor's western entrance trailing her two escape boats. *Argus*, *Vixen* and *Nautilus* followed, taking up station just outside the rocks to cover Somers's returning boats.

At exactly 9:47 P.M. the harbor, the shore, the city and even the desert and the sea were illuminated by a single, terrifying, flashing light, followed by a monstrous roar and shock waves felt in the city and as far away as the decks of *Constitution* a mile offshore. In light as brilliant as day Midshipman Charles Ridgely aboard *Nautilus* could see *Intrepid*'s mast spiraling skyward, next exploding shells, and then a shower of debris striking the water—and finally silence and darkness. It was a brooding silence. Lookouts aboard the three vessels outside the harbor peered into the darkness with slowly diminishing hope of sighting the escape boats—until, at dawn, with no trace of *Intrepid* visible either in the harbor or the surface of the blue Mediterranean, there was no longer any hope.

Speculation as to what had actually happened to the ill-fated fireship persists to this day. Commodore Preble firmly believed that *Intrepid* had been detected and that Murad Reis had detached four gunboats to intercept her, a maneuver unconfirmed by any known reports and based on the belief that one of them had boarded the fireship and gone up with her, while the remaining trio were badly damaged. In his report to Secretary Smith, Preble wrote: "The gallant Somers and heroes of his party, observing the other three boats surrounding them, and no prospect of escape, determined at once *to prefer death and the destruction of the enemy to captivity and torturing slavery*, put a match to the train leading directly to the magazine, which at once blew the whole into air and terminated their existence." The italics here are Preble's and were probably used to emphasize what could have been nothing more than conjecture, and also take another swipe at Captain Bainbridge for having surrendered *Philadelphia* so easily.

But Preble's deduction is based on not a shred of evidence, supported only by a naive belief that the Tripolitans could board an American vessel unopposed on a dark night, while ignoring the fact that no one in Tripoli—not the American prisoners with their Italian companions, or those from Malta, Greece, Israel, or even disaffected Turks, together with all the Christian consuls—ever heard of the bashaw's navy suffering any such losses. The perceptive William Ray offered a far more plausible explanation, claiming that if no Tripolitans were destroyed, "is it not fully as evident that the train communicated to the magazine sooner than was expected, and that the explosion happened before our men could possibly avoid a catastrophe so much to be lamented?" Dr. Jonathan Cowdery, the captive surgeon's mate impressed as the bashaw's physician, also observed that the explosion did Tripoli so little harm that Yusuf gave a banquet of thanksgiving to Muhammed, which he surely would not have done if he had lost ships and a few hundred seamen.

Thus the gallant Commodore Edward Preble's bold campaign against Bashaw Yusuf Karamanli ended in frustration, for on September 9 Commodore Samuel Barron aboard *President* arrived off Tripoli accompanied by *Constellation*. Although plagued by head winds in the Atlantic, but nevertheless in no great hurry, Barron had taken more than a month to reach Gibraltar. In that interval Edward Preble had struck so furiously at Bashaw Yusuf that even the loss of *Intrepid* could not have prevented him from destroying him; especially if he—not Barron—were in command of what was now the most formidable fleet ever arrayed off the Barbary Coast. But Barron had been appointed before news of Preble's triumphs reached Washington, so that on September 9 the retiring commodore was like a boxer who has his opponent on the ropes, his right arm raised for the knockout blow, only to have his manager throw in the towel!

Dismayed but still undaunted, Edward Preble returned to the United States, pleasantly astonished to be greeted by a hero's welcome. He was congratulated by Secretaries Smith and Madison and invited to the White House for dinner with President Jefferson. The president might have been having second thoughts about relieving his only fighting commodore simply because he was junior to the other captains. But there was nothing he could do now, except to have Congress authorize a resolution thanking the commodore and his men for their gallant service against Yusuf, as well as a special medal for Preble. Probably, Preble was pleased more by a glowing letter praising "the Old Man" from fifty-three of his officers—Preble's Boys—with the signature of Captain Stephen Decatur at the top of the list. Retiring, Edward Preble did not long survive, still stricken with his prison-ship illnesses, recurrent malaria, ulcers and tuberculosis. On August 25, 1807, the Old Man died. He was forty-six.

12

To the Shores of Tripoli

〜 COMMODORE SAMUEL BARRON, WHO REPLACED EDWARD PREBLE, WAS the oldest son in a famous Virginia seagoing family. His father was Captain James Barron, commander of the Virginia Commonwealth Navy during the Revolutionary War. It was Captain Barron who intercepted a letter from Lord George Germain, then directing the British military effort, revealing the plan to capture Charleston, South Carolina—intelligence that enabled the Americans to prepare for and repel Sir Peter Parker's invasion.

Samuel Barron had distinguished himself in the Naval War with France, but, like the indolent Commodore Dale, the fires of his erstwhile ardor seemed to be burning low. This might have been due to an infected liver, which regularly caused him, unlike the indomitable Preble with all his afflictions, to take to his bed or seek surcease in some hospital ashore. Indeed, just as the caustic fo'c'sle wits of the Mediterranean Squadron had pinned the derisive nickname of the Commodoress on the lady whose apron strings seemed to have hobbled Commodore Morris, they might also have sent Samuel Barron into history under the sobriquet "Sick-Bay Sam." Never in American military history has a single human organ had as frustrating an effect on a naval force at war than Commodore Barron's liver. Fortunately for America, there was an antidote to this liability in another human organ: the fighting heart of William Eaton, the new Navy Agent for the United States for the Several Barbary Regencies, who returned to the Mediterranean as a passenger on Barron's flagship, *President*.

William Eaton was born in Woodstock, Connecticut, on February 23, 1764, the second son of a farmer and schoolteacher who had thirteen children. Raised on a farm, he found in his youth, like Edward Preble whom he much admired, an aversion to the hoe; but unlike Preble he also discovered a love of learning so deep that he could often be found beneath a tree reading, when he should have been wielding that detestable instrument lying unused at his feet. At the age of sixteen, William "eloped from home" to enlist in the Nutmeg State militia during the Revolutionary War. He wielded neither musket nor bayonet, but rather knife and fork in his despicable duty as waiter on the major's table, or soap and dishrag as a battalion dishwasher. Coming home sick at the end of his year of service, he quickly recovered and re-enlisted to rise to the rank of sergeant before being discharged in 1783.

Now nineteen and still avid for learning, he walked from his home in northeastern Connecticut to Hanover, New Hampshire, to enroll in the thriving little college that Eleazar Wheelock had begun as a school for Indian boys. Self-taught in Greek and Latin, he was taken in hand by John Wheelock, son of the founder of what is now known as Dartmouth College, who introduced him to the classics while filling the voids and filing off the burrs usually accumulated through the shortcuts followed by most self-educated men. After being graduated, Eaton taught school in Vermont and became clerk of the House of Delegates there, seemingly embarked on a satisfactory career that could culminate in membership in that august body or a seat on a judicial bench. But his fondness for military history renewed his ardor for military service, and when disaster struck General St. Clair and his army on the Northwestern Frontier, he obtained a commission as an army captain and hastened to join the forces being assembled by General Anthony Wayne in Pittsburgh. Eaton was with Wayne when he routed the warriors of Blue Jacket at Fallen Timbers, and forever he revered that general's name.

But he had nothing but contempt when, after leaving Ohio for Georgia, he came into conflict with Lieutenant Colonel Henry Gaither of Maryland, described by one of Eaton's supporters as "an ignorant, debauched, unprincipled old bachelor" who would "sacrifice the purest character to gratify the spleen of his soul." It was a personality clash pure and simple: the all-but-illiterate Gaither resenting

Eaton's erudition, the spidery, little captain with the sharp tongue and sharper claws unable to conceal his contempt for this vintage blusterer with the brass-bound brains. As is usually true of such enmities the quarrel could be reduced to a petty disagreement: Eaton insisting on writing voluminous reports, his chief trying to limit them so as to keep the War Department in the dark about his conduct—not an unusual desire in a commander. In the end, Gaither had Eaton arrested and court-martialed. He was convicted of disobeying orders. There was no specific evidence if only because Gaither always issued oral orders, which were much easier to deny than the written variety. After Eaton was sentenced to two-months suspension from the service, the vindictive Gaither ordered him confined in Fort Pickering for a month, evidently to blacken his record. But after his release, Eaton went to Philadelphia where he was overjoyed to learn that the War Department had refused to confirm the findings of his court-martial. Now reluctant to continue to serve in an army in which Colonel Blimps such as Gaither then abounded, he was looking around for other employment when Secretary of State Timothy Pickering—impressed by his defiant spirit—appointed him consul to Tunis.

Thus began the diplomatic career of "the most undiplomatic diplomat" in the annals of American diplomacy. Haughty, acerbic, arrogant, domineering, frenetic, opinionated, caustic, yet genuinely, deeply, and intensely patriotic, this human dynamo landed on the Barbary Coast with all the ungentle critical fury of a northwestern Mediterranean gale. To have chosen this irascible man for a diplomatic assignment was error enough, but to have compounded it by dispatching him to serve among a people and a religion that he abominated was to join cardinal mistake to unforgiveable blunder. It was in October 1800 that the Barbary rulers realized what kind of representative had been sent to Tunis. At that time, he accompanied Consul-General Cathcart to the palace of Dey Bobba Mustapha of Algiers to protest his seizure of an American ship. Here is William Eaton at his best:

> We were shown to a huge, shaggy beast, sitting on his rump upon a low bench covered with a cushion of embroidered velvet, with his hind legs gathered up like a tailor, or a bear. On our approach to him, he reached out his forepaw as if to receive something to eat. Our guide exclaimed, "Kiss the Dey's hand!" The consul general bowed very elegantly, and kissed it, and we followed his example in succession. The animal seemed at that moment to be in a harmless mood. He grinned several times but made very little noise. . . . Can

any man believe that this elevated brute has seven kings of Europe, two republics and a continent tributary to him when his whole naval force is not equal to two line-of-battle ships? It is so.

During nearly three years of service at the court of Bey Hamouda of Tunis it was obvious that William Eaton, who, with his proclivity for learning languages, may have spoken better Arabic than his host, could not resist baiting His Royal Highness. He seemed to delight in provoking him into choleric, hair-curling rages, and once when the bey threatened to throw him into his dungeons, Eaton replied: "I came here expressly to be put in chains." To this, according to Eaton, Hamouda made the mild response: "You are a hard little fellow." But this continuing quarrel and exchange of insults—in which the bey usually came off second-best—could not long endure, and it ended in February 1803, when the indolent Commodore Morris made his first visit to Tunis after nine months in the Mediterranean. At once Hamouda announced that Morris was under arrest until Eaton paid his prime minister the $34,000 he owed him to finance one of Eaton's numerous and unsuccessful business speculations. Astonished and indignant, Morris wheeled on Eaton to accuse him of luring him to Tunis to pay Eaton's debts. Eaton protested that this was untrue, and in another interview claimed that the prime minister had "robbed me of my property." Shouting, "You are mad!" the prime minister was joined by a furious Hamouda, who yelled, "Yes, yes, he is mad! I will turn him out of my kingdom!" Turning to Morris, he snarled: "This man is mad. . . . I will not permit him to remain here. Take him away!"

"I thank you!" Eaton bellowed. "I long wanted to go away."

And he did, departing Tunis with Morris and from thence back to the United States where, for all of his peculiarities, he impressed President Jefferson. Having read enough history to realize that eccentric men often make good generals, refusing to abandon his policy of ending Barbary tribute by force of arms, the president approved Eaton's plan to replace Bashaw Yusuf with his usurped brother Hamet. With Hamet by his side, Eaton would lead an army from Egypt to Derna, capturing that second most important Tripolitan port for a final landward assault on Tripoli while Barron's squadron prevented any seagoing relieving force either from the other Barbary potentates or the sultan himself from coming to Yusuf's rescue. To do this, Eaton was given money, wide authority and the ambiguous and ponderous title of Navy Agent of the United States for the several Barbary Regencies, which was actually a cover designed to conceal the fact that the assault on Tripoli was now a land-sea operation.

• • •

Commodore Samuel Barron commanded the most powerful naval squadron the United States had ever sent to sea. Besides the flagship *President,* 44, it included the frigates *Congress,* 36, Captain Stephen Decatur; *Essex,* 32, Captain James Barron, the commodore's younger brother; *Constellation,* 36, Captain Hugh Campbell; and *John Adams,* 36, Master Commandant Chauncey; as well as 44-gun *Constitution* and half a dozen brigs and schooners. But the new commodore did not renew his predecessor's headlong assault upon Bashaw Yusuf's stronghold, even though his diseased liver could never rival his predecessor's many afflictions. Whenever this mighty armada did take to sea in a body, its quarterdeck was usually empty of its commodore, abed in a naval hospital. So there were no more bombardments of Tripoli, and no more gunboat assaults, for King Ferdinand had retrieved those he had loaned Preble, and Commodore Barron apparently was indisposed to ask for replacements. Thus the only operations against Yusuf to continue was a half-hearted blockade and William Eaton's expedition.

Because he distrusted Eaton, like all timid men in the presence of human fire, Barron was reluctant to give the Derna operation his approval. Finally, at a conference with Eaton and Master Commandant Isaac Hull of *Argus* he consented. Hull agreed to send Eaton Marine Lieutenant Presley Neville O'Bannon and seven Leathernecks to train Eaton's army.

O'Bannon was about twenty-nine at the time. A surviving portrait of him shows a handsome, husky, clean-shaven young man with the ebony hair of a black Celt combed forward in the style of the day. His features were almost delicate, but he was a tough veteran of the American frontier, the fourth generation of an Irish family that had settled in Virginia nearly a century earlier. Even in those nascent days of this cocky little corps, the Marines attracted American Irishmen, as they still do. O'Bannon was durable and resourceful, good-humored, unflinchingly brave and almost adoringly loyal to Eaton. "Wherever General Eaton leads, we will follow," he declared in the heroic style typical of his time. "If he wants us to march to hell, we'll gladly go there. . . . He is the great military genius of our era."

So anointed, the "general"—he had indeed claimed that rank—now clad in an Arab robe with a scimitar at his belt and a turban around his head, boarded *Argus* on November 14, 1804, along with O'Bannon and his Leathernecks, and with Isaac Hull at the helm set sail from Syracuse for Alexandria. It was a pleasant voyage under a light breeze, with *Argus*'s delighted seamen dancing jigs and hornpipes to the tunes issuing from Lieutenant O'Bannon's beloved violin, or "fiddle" as he called it. From Alexandria Eaton and the Marines continued on to Cairo, where Eaton discovered that Hamet had joined a group of three thousand Mamelukes besieged by eight thousand Turks at a town called Minyeh 120 miles up the Nile. Next, befriending the Turkish viceroy, Eaton was horrified to hear him say that he would send his soldiers to Minyeh to bring Hamet back to Cairo. Eaton was shocked because, familiar as he was with the Levant—where treachery and double-dealing were highly prized skills—he realized that if Turkish soldiers tried to rescue Hamet, the Mamelukes would certainly kill him, suspecting some motive inimical to themselves. Also, the viceroy might have an ulterior motive, not exactly friendly. Aghast, he dejectedly considered his cherished enterprise as already doomed.

But then William Eaton was approached by a man whose career was a picaresque study in the art of deception and survival, to whom, in comparison, Eaton's life would have been a model of mildness and rectitude. The name he gave was Eugene Leitensdorfer, an alias he always used when dealing with Americans. He had been born Gervasso Prodasio Santuari in the Tyrol in October 1772. His family was well-to-do and devoutly Catholic, hoping that Gervasso would become a priest. Instead he quit his theological studies, got married and immersed himself in literature, mechanics and agriculture, thereby laying the basis for an astonishing versatility, later increased by work as a surveyor. Next he joined the Austrian Army, fighting the Turks at Belgrade and the French at Mantua. When Mantua fell, he deserted, later rallying to the French again under Napoleon with the assumed name of Carlo Hossondo. Suspected of being a spy—which this absolutely amoral man might well have been—he was confined to a stockade, from which he escaped by poisoning his guards with opium. Successfully appealing to his family for funds, he became an intinerant peddler of watches (it is to be hoped that they actually told time) throughout France and Spain.

Next Carlo or Eugene rejoined the French army in Egypt, where he again deserted to open a coffee shop for British officers there and to make a Coptic maiden his Number Two wife. Upon the departure of his British customers, leaving Number Two behind, he recrossed the Med to Messina in Italy, where he took refuge in a Capuchin monastery, piously telling his beads while practicing card tricks that served him well when, his venturesome spirit refreshed, he left the monks and sailed to Constantinople. There he joined the Turkish Army and was sent back to Egypt. Defeat of the sultan's forces provided the opportunity for his fourth desertion, followed by his flight into the desert to seek sanctuary among a tribe of Bedouins. Disdaining a second return to Christianity, with theological feet as nimble as his prestidigitating fingers, he became a Muslim—convincing his doubting Beduoin hosts of his sincerity by circumcising himself in their presence.

A copy of the Koran under his arm and under his third alias of Murat Aga, he landed in Trebizond on the shores of the Black Sea as a self-proclaimed healer. At once he was taken to the aging bashaw, who was going blind. Murat Aga "the healer" quickly saw that he faced an either/or situation: either cure the bashaw or become a corpse. Chanting incantations, dancing a few dervish steps, and raising his eyes heavenward in supplication, he had caustic lime blown into the old man's eyes "to eat the films away," and washed them out with milk—after which he left the palace loaded with gifts and eager to put many miles between himself and the old man, whom he had filled with warm liquids and wrapped in blankets to produce salutary sweat. Joining a caravan to Persia, he and his companions were attacked by robbers. As he prepared to surrender his newfound wealth in exchange for his life, Murat Aga overheard one of the brigands marveling at how a wandering dervish had cured the blindness of the bashaw of Trebizond. Returning to the city to claim his reward, he was again loaded down with presents.

Wandering on and on, satisfied with nothing, he eventually returned to Cairo where he heard that an American named Eaton was in Cairo looking for a confidential agent, and so, this soldier-of-fortune par excellence went to meet him. Eaton knew that he had found his man the moment he heard Leitensdorfer shift fluently from language to language and give a brief résumé of his travels. Would he be interested in rescuing Hamet? Leitensdorfer's eyes gleamed. Indeed, he would, if he could just have $50 in advance.

It was the most productive investment that the failed entrepreneur William Eaton ever made, for Leitensdorfer immediately set out for Minyeh with one companion. Riding their camels night and day they quickly outdistanced the Turkish soldiers, and when they reached Minyeh the smooth-talking Leitensdorfer had no difficulty ingratiating himself with the Mameluke chief. Meeting Hamet, he took him aside and identified himself as Eaton's emissary, quietly proposing that Hamet steal into the desert with him. It would not be difficult. All he had to do was to go out one night with about forty Tripolitans on a routine desert reconnaissance and simply head for the Nile and a southward journey to meet Eaton. It was done, and on February 5, 1805, the two men met and embraced at a place called Damanhûr. Eaton was so delighted with Leitensdorfer's exploit that he made him his adjutant on the spot. Then he and Hamet entered a compact that he, Eaton, "shall be recognized as General, and Commander-in-Chief," and that Hamet "engages that his own subjects shall respect and obey him as such." Hamet remained in the Damanhûr area, safe from the Turkish viceroy who now threatened to arrest him, gathering to his cause, meanwhile, Tripolitan horsemen. Eaton rode on to Arab's Tower, a place eleven miles outside of Alexandria, where they set up camp and awaited the arrival of O'Bannon still aboard *Argus*. He arrived on February 19, bringing with him seven Marines and Midshipman Paoli Peck. With Eaton, O'Bannon went into the city to recruit soldiers.

What an "army" it was that they raised, if not actually unique, then one of the strangest in history. With some amusement Eaton called it his "Christian Army," meaning only that its members were not of the Muslim faith, though they might be of every racial strain assembled under the common name of Europe. There were perhaps seventy of them, dark-skinned Greeks, swarthy Italians and fierce-eyed Spaniards, stolid Germans who had drifted up from the Cameroons, saucy-tongued British cockneys from Cairo and Port Said, and silent, black-eyed Levantines whose olive-hued flesh seemed least tormented by the brassy sun and burning sands. Among this motley moved Lieutenant Presley O'Bannon and his Marines, shouting orders, straightening muskets, while the sweat streamed down their faces and bodies baking inside stiff woolen uniform cloth.

"Right shouldeh, ahms! Ordeh, ahms! Oh, you mother's mistakes! No, no, curse you, you there, the fellow with the black beard—careful of that bayonet before you cut your buddy's head off."

They had not come cheaply, these mercenaries. William Eaton had already spent $100,000 of his country's money, and was down to just $53. Only that day he had discovered that Richard Farquhar, the Britisher from Malta whom he had hired to handle supplies, had pocketed $1,350. Farquhar claimed that he had spent that amount on recruits, but Eaton knew better and had dismissed him. His disposition soured by endless haggling, he watched morosely from his tent while O'Bannon and his Marines tried to hammer some uniformity into this polyglot army. They could do nothing, of course, about their weapons. Some had rifles, some had muskets, some had swords or cutlasses stuck through their belts or the bright sashes affected by the Levantines. There was a sprinkling of Arabian daggers. Although Eaton was pleased with the conduct of O'Bannon and his Leathernecks, he was disappointed that Barron had ignored his request for a hundred of them and sent him only eight. Would he be as niggardly with his ships? He had promised *Argus, Nautilus* and *Hornet,* all under Isaac Hull. They were to bring supplies and money and rendezvous with Eaton's army at Bomba 400 miles west of Alexandria. After that it was only another hundred miles march to Derna—and the assault. So much depended on that trio of warships. Without them to bombard the fortress city, the attack could not succeed. There were so many variables! If Hamet lost heart, if Hull's squadron ran into bad weather, if the water ran out, if those "Christian" ruffians that O'Bannon was trying to train should mutiny, if that treacherous camel driver of an El Tahib tried to squeeze a few extra gold pieces out of him . . .

William Eaton shielded his eyes, squinting into the fierce whiteness and shimmering waves of heat rising against the horizon. He approached the commander of his "army."

"How are your eyes, Mr. O'Bannon?"

"Better than my nose, sir," O'Bannon replied, wryly pointing to the blister covering most of that organ. "You couldn't get a blister like this one if you walked from one end of Virginia to the other."

"You'll get used to it. Tell me, is that a caravan heading this way?"

Now it was O'Bannon who squinted. "Seems so, sir."

Eaton nodded. "That will be Sheikh Tahib," he muttered, and turned to reenter his tent. An hour later, he heard a growing commotion outside: the yells of the camel drivers—"*Walloo, Walloo, Walloo*"—the squeals of the beasts and the calls and curses of scores of voices babbling in a dozen different tongues and dialects. Eaton rushed outside to see a tall, powerfully built Arab dismounting from his horse. He came toward him, smiling, the hem of his long white burnoose dragging in the sand. At his waist was a dagger with a jeweled hilt thrust into an embroidered leather sheath. His dark face was hawkish, with the shrewd look of a man accustomed to bargaining.

"How dost thou, Sahib Eaton," he said, bowing.

"Well, Tahib—I am glad to see you. Come into my tent."

Inside the tent both men sat cross-legged on camel hides. "As we agree, Sheikh Tahib, I will pay eleven dollars a head for the service of your camels. That's eleven hundred and seventy-seven dollars for one hundred and seven of them. Agreed?"

The Arab arose, smiling again, and nodded. "May Allah bless our enterprise," he said, bowed again, and went outside with a soft swishing of his burnoose.

O'Bannon came inside. "I don't trust that fellow Tahib, sir."

"Nor do I—but we need his camels. He'll be loyal as long as he can smell money, but I'll be grateful, Mr. O'Bannon, if you keep an eye on him."

"Aye, aye, sir," O'Bannon replied, and stretched himself out on a cot. Even though the air was stifling, it was a refuge from the brazen ball of fire now high in the Tripolitan sky.

Hamet arrived before nightfall, and with a typical Arab flourish. A few hundred yards from the camp, his horsemen drew rein. Then with shrill shrieks of the Muhammadan war cry—"*Allāhu akbar!* God is great!"—they came pounding toward the camp in a colorful charge. Standing high in the stirrups, bandishing their rifles over-head, they urged their mounts forward with wild yells, before plowing up the sand in a sudden, rearing halt accompanied by a volley of musketry.

O'Bannon, standing beside Eaton outside the tent, quickly dropped a hand to his sword.

"It's all right, Mr. O'Bannon," Eaton murmured reassuringly. "It's the custom."

Hamet dismounted and strode toward them, his short legs and chubby body not exactly the physique of a fierce warrior. "All is well, Sahib Eaton?" he asked.

"Yes, Emir, we march tomorrow."

Hamet nodded. "Allah be thanked," he said, and returned to his troopers to lead them to their billet and to perform the ritual washing of the face and hands before he and his cavalrymen turned their faces to Mecca for the sunset prayers.

At almost the same moment that William Eaton prepared to march on Derna from the Egyptian border, Consul-General Tobias Lear in Malta had begun his campaign to sabotage the operation.

Lear was an experienced diplomat with impeccable social, aca-demic and political credentials. He had been born the son of a ship-master in Portsmouth, New Hampshire, and was graduated with hon-ors from Harvard College before studying in Europe. At twenty-three he had become George Washington's private secretary before the Revolution and continued in that position during the war with the rank of colonel, a title that he cherished in spite of his disdain for "men of blood," as he was prone to describe soldiers. Lear had also been Washington's presidential secretary, in which capacity he had impressed Secretary of State Thomas Jefferson. He had remained with Washington after he retired to Mount Vernon, and it was his hand that the Father of His Country had clasped with his dying breath. Despite his distrust and dislike of military men, Tobias Lear had idolized Washington to the absurd point of fancying that they resembled each other. He arrived in the Mediterranean as Jefferson's consul-general replacing Richard O'Brien, and brought his new wife—his third—supposedly distantly related to Washington.

He had hoped to persuade Edward Preble to employ the carrot of diplomacy rather than the stick of violence to bring the bashaw to terms, but had failed utterly—as one searching look at the commodore might have suggested. Lear was immensely relieved when Barron replaced Preble. Now, with Barron so enervated by illness and so often confined to his hospital bed in Syracuse, and assuming he was invested by Jefferson with full authority to negotiate a treaty—as he certainly was not, else why the five new frigates on station off Tripoli?—Tobias Lear believed that the moment of opportunity had arrived. To this irenic gentleman it was clear that the American purpose in the Barbary regions was to negotiate a peace not to win one, and, if necessary, to purchase it.

For the Eaton-Hamet expedition Lear had unreserved contempt. The French and Danish consuls in Tripoli had informed him that Hamet was a weakling and a coward, and in his own estimation, William Eaton was a romantic saber-rattler. Yet, he might just succeed and thus bring about that detestable conclusion: a military solution. To prevent it, Lear had to convince the ailing Barron to withdraw the approval he had reluctantly granted to Eaton. Barron was the key, for Secretary Smith had given him full authority to support or cancel the landward operation. And with the commodore so weak "as to disqualify him from transacting any business," Lear had to act immediately before he either died or resigned, leaving the squadron under the command of the fiery John Rodgers.

So he began an unremitting campaign to turn Barron against the operation. During October 1804, he spent ten days in Syracuse arguing deftly against it. A born intriguer, Lear sought out informants whom he knew to be against Hamet for self-serving reasons, or haters of Eaton such as the dismissed embezzler Richard Farquhar, who swore that Eaton was insane. With their testimony in hand, Lear bombarded the mind of the sick and distracted commodore. One of his favorite arguments was that Hamet would prove to be a more intractable bashaw than Yusuf, or that if Yusuf were supplanted, he would counterattack to regain his throne and take a fearsome revenge on his brother's American ally. But then in the spring of 1805, Barron's health improved, and Isaac Hull reported to him that the overland expedition was underway. Barron then agreed to the rendezvous at Bomba and naval support of the attack on Derna.

Consul-General Tobias Lear was dismayed, even close to despair. His only comfort was that Barron had no plans to renew the bombardment of Tripoli, and his only hope was that the Hamet-Eaton expedition would be defeated. Here, if ever it was needed, was proof that irenic gentlemen have no place in diplomacy: for it never seems to have occurred to Tobias Lear that if Tripoli were not bombarded and Hamet-Eaton routed, Bashaw Yusuf Karamanli would become so jubilant and defiant that his price for peace would sky-rocket.

To the west of the Hamet-Eaton encampment at Arab's Tower stretched a desert of sand reaching to Tripoli that one traveler described as "a journey more dreadful than can be conceived." It could not be undertaken without the aid of astronomy and the use of a compass, for the landscape was constantly changing under the impact of wind and blowing sand. Thus, as it says in the song, "Every valley shall be exalted, and the high places plain." On the morning of March 8, 1805, the march to Derna over this formidable terrain began.

13

Victory at Derna/
Sellout at Home

~ BEFORE DAWN, THE CAMP WAS ASTIR. THE SUN HAD NOT YET RISEN IN
the sky and the sands were still cool from the chill of the night.
Hamet's men had said their prayers and were swinging into their saddles. O'Bannon's army was drawn up, ready to move out. But from the
camp of the camel drivers came no sound of bustling confusion, no
high-pitched babble that usually arose when the drivers forced their
stiff-legged ships of the deserts to kneel so that casks of water and
sacks of rice might be hoisted onto their backs. There was only an
ominous quiet.

Lieutenant O'Bannon came quickly into Eaton's tent. "The camel
drivers are demanding their pay in advance, Mr. Eaton. They refuse to
move without it."

"Bring Tahib here."

"He's coming, sir. . . . Here he is now."

O'Bannon moved aside to permit the sheikh to enter. Tahib made a
profound bow. His face was impassive, as he said: "It was agreed, Sahib
Eaton, that my men were to be paid before the march."

Eaton's face was black. "It was not, Sheikh Tahib. You are to be paid
when we reach Bomba."

Tahib shrugged. "I can do nothing with them. They will not move."

Eaton hesitated. "I will speak to the Bashaw Hamet," he said stiffly.

Tahib gave a mocking bow and left.

Instead of consulting the bashaw, Eaton ordered O'Bannon to cow the camel drivers. Followed by his seven Marines and his motley "army," O'Bannon strode straight toward the Arabs, standing beside their beasts in sullen silence. O'Bannon halted his men. He ran them through the manual of arms, and the sounds of their hands slapping their muskets caused the cameleers to stir uneasily. He marched them backward and forward, as at a parade, all the while searching the ranks of the camel drivers until his eyes found those of Sheikh Tahib, leaning slightly forward on his purebred Arabian horse, one hand on the pommel of his saddle, the other on his dagger hilt. O'Bannon's eyes never left the face of Tahib until, at last, with a face-saving shrug, the sheikh called angrily to his men in Arabic—and they, grumbling, began to beat the camels with sticks until they had gone awkwardly to their knees and the provisions placed aboard. The march to Derna had begun.

For seven days they marched, Hamet's cavalrymen walking their horses before and after the columns of men on foot, the baggage train plodding along at the center, and the men of O'Bannon's army dispersed as scouts, as flank guards and as observers of the fretful cameleers—each detachment under the command of one of O'Bannon's seven Marines. They passed over the border into Tripoli, while a pitiless sun blazed down on them. The sands beneath their feet were like enormous beds of tiny coals. But they had not yet left human habitation behind them, there was plenty of water, the first few days of agonizing discomfort were over—and after the seventh day it began to rain.

It rained for ten days. The desert became a bog. The hooves of the camels and the horses sank deep into a gritty quagmire. The feet of the marching men were caked with mud, weighing every step, forcing them to pause at intervals to scrape the clinging burden free. Their muscles, high up in the calves of their legs, were sore from the constant effort of pulling feet free from the sucking slop. But at least the rain falling in torrents could be trapped and given to the camels and horses or poured into the casks to replenish their supply. And it could not rain forever in the desert.

It stopped, but when it did, so did the sheikh El Tahib and his disgruntled cameleers.

"My camel drivers will go no further, Sahib Eaton," he said.

With a bow and a friendly smile, he had upped his price in the middle of the Libyan desert. Eaton fumed. He had a few hundred dollars on his person, but that wouldn't be enough to grease the sheikh's greedy palm. There would be money waiting aboard the ships at Bomba, but Bomba was still a few weeks march away. Lieutenant O'Bannon proposed passing the hat among the Americans.

"I have a few dollars, sir. I'll see what my Marine lads can scrape together."

"Excellent, Mr. O'Bannon—and tell the men that Congress will repay them."

"The devil take Congress!" O'Bannon burst out furiously. "No, Mr. Eaton, we'll not worry about the money—though I must confess it pains me to think of knuckling under to that smooth-tongued scoundrel, Tahib. Better to pay him his wages at the end of a bayonet, I say!"

Scowling, O'Bannon strode off to speak to his men. Within a few hours, the sum of $673 had been raised and presented to El Tahib, but the sheikh refused to move on until his men had taken a three-day rest. Eaton agreed, and the march was resumed after that interval.

On the next day, a company of eighty Arab horsemen was recruited by Hamet from a large encampment of nomad families encountered on the desert. Two days later, at a similar bivouac, 150 Arab foot soldiers were added to the motley of O'Bannon's army. The force moving against Derna now numbered six hundred.

But on the evening of that day, as the keening cry of the Muslim worshipers rose from the desert stillness, a speck of life appeared far out in the west. It grew larger, caught in the last rays of light from the sun dropping out of sight behind the distant, flat horizon. It was an Arab horseman, coming at a gallop toward where Eaton and O'Bannon stood. His mount was exhausted and covered with a thin paste of flying sand that had clung to its perspiring hide.

He dismounted, and Eaton said to him, "Thou hast ridden hard. What news dost thou bring?"

"Ay, *wellah*, I have ridden," the horseman said. "For the Bashaw Yusuf has sent guns and men to Derna."

"Reinforcements, my God!" O'Bannon swore. "The Bashaw Yusuf means to fight us at Derna, and by God, we'll not disappoint him!"

"We will not, Mr. O'Bannon," Eaton said. "But I fear that the Bashaw Hamet will not think kindly of this news."

Eaton knew his man well. Once Hamet heard of his brother's move to strengthen the Derna garrison, he hurried to Eaton's tent. He came directly to the point. "Thou hadst assured me, Sahib Eaton, that there would be no bloodshed. By the life of my neck, I do not like this news."

"But, Bashaw," O'Bannon interrupted. "We have enough men,

now—and we will have support from the American warships. Surely you do not fear your brother?"

"Ay, *billah,*" Hamet said. "Thou dost not know him, that *jabbara,* that villain. Thy youth and ignorance of my people hast made thee fierce—but, *billah,* by the life of this fire I swear to you he will give you to the knives of his women."

O'Bannon laughed. "Perhaps, after we have beaten him, he will give his women to me."

Eaton frowned a reproach at his young gamecock and said gravely to the bashaw, "Wilt thou not march with us?" Hamet shook his head sadly, and Eaton rasped, "Then we will march without thee. Mr. O'Bannon, you may inform your men to be ready to move out at dawn."

A spasm of anger flickered across Hamet's dark face and he arose without a word, bowed stiffly and left the tent.

In the morning, Lieutenant O'Bannon assembled his "Christian" army and marched out of the encampment, leaving all the Arabs behind. Hamet and El Tahib watched them go with sullen eyes. Hardly had Eaton and O'Bannon been walking an hour, before they saw the straggling lines of beast and men hurrying after them.

"Carry on, Mr. O'Bannon," Eaton said, with a grim smile. "Our friends seem to be undergoing a change of heart."

Though the Arabs reluctantly rejoined the march, they did so with bad grace, and now the desert was the adversary, a malignant devil rising up to blind them, to torture them with a choking thirst, to slow the progress of panting horses and camels, to roast them in a hell compounded of scorching sands beneath and brazen sun above.

Water began to run out. Frequently, the marchers passed twenty-four hours without water; once forty-seven hours expired before they could moisten swelling tongues that seemed to fill their mouths, making speech an agony. The horses went three days without water. The supply of rice began to dwindle. They began to slaughter camels, to be gobbled half-cooked without salt or bread. When Eaton forbade the killing of any more beasts, they had nothing to eat for twenty days except a few grains of rice and whatever tiny roots they could pluck out of the sand.

Before this ordeal was done, Bashaw Hamet rose in open rebellion. On April 8, he ordered his men to halt after they had gone about five miles. He pitched camp. Eaton commanded him to strike his tents. Hamet countered by telling his followers to mount their horses. He was leaving.

"Mr. O'Bannon!" Eaton roared. "Get your men into battle line!"

Again Lieutenant O'Bannon called upon his Marines. They formed the "Christians" into battle array beside the remaining provisions and supplies. Briskly, O'Bannon put them through their gun drill. Hamet's Arabs drew up in a line of charge. Hamet lifted his hand. In a moment, the Arabs would fill the air with yells of "*Allāhu akbar!*"—and the expanse of sand between the two opposing forces would shudder beneath the pounding hooves of charging horses. In that moment, O'Bannon gave the order to aim. The Marines and their soldiers knelt in the sands, muskets leveled. Thus, they confronted one another, and in that second in which time seemed to stretch out—when a trigger-happy Christian or a rearing Arab horse might have plunged both sides into bloody battle—William Eaton calmly strode across the sand to speak to Bashaw Hamet.

The bashaw let his hand fall. He had been awed by O'Bannon's unwavering muskets. "*Billah,*" he growled irritably to himself. "By my oath, would that I had such a son as this." He spoke to Eaton. "By the beard of the Prophet, Sahib Eaton, wouldst thou murder thy friend?"

"Let us not quarrel, Bashaw," Eaton said evenly. "Perhaps we have misunderstood each other, and it is well that there be no enmity between us. Let us move on. . . . we are but a few days march from Bomba."

Hamet bowed and called to his men and the march of these thirsty, hungry, suffering skeletons was again resumed. Two days later, it stopped again. The "Christians" mutinied this time. There was no food at all, now, and there had been no water for two days. All of them—Spaniards, Italians, Greeks, Germans, Levantines and Britishers—lay in despairing immobility on the sands. They said they could not move, and some of them stared in speechless misery at the sky, as though searching for the vultures that would come to pick their bones. O'Bannon sent his Marines among them, but it was no use.

"Ere," one of the Cockneys panted, "why don't you just kill us, matey? Send us off to 'ell, Yank, and be thankful to you for a cool billet."

O'Bannon saw that force would be of no avail, so he strode among them and began to plead with them. Only the Britishers could understand him, but as he spoke, mentioning Bomba and holding up two fingers to show that the port lay only that many days march away, they began to stir, to push themselves to their feet with groans and curses and sharp cries of pain, and finally they set their faces into the merciless sun once more and began to walk. Two days later they saw the sea at Bomba—and no ships.

Despair was so black no one had the spirit to protest or revolt. All that long, silent, chilly night, Lieutenant O'Bannon went with his men to forage for brushwood, to strip camels and horses of combustible materials and even to use precious powder to set signal fires alight and burning. In the morning, it seemed that the march to Tripoli had ended in failure. The army was breaking up. But, then, against the bright blue of the Mediterranean sky appeared the twin masts and square sails of a ship. It was the brig *Argus*.

Two days later, *Hornet* hove into view. Water, food and ammunition (and, secretly, money) streamed ashore in small boats. A camp was established. But William Eaton began to fume again. Commodore Barron was still withholding the one hundred Marines he had asked for, and he had sent only $7,000 instead of the $11,000 that had been promised. To make matters worse, Captain Hull aboard *Argus* requested that O'Bannon return to his duties aboard ship.

O'Bannon angrily refused to leave, and Eaton smiled in pleasure.

On April 23, forty-six days after Eaton and O'Bannon had left Arab's Tower, the march was resumed. In two days, the refreshed and reinvigorated men covered forty miles. But on the evening of the second day, another horseman of bad tidings rode into camp bringing news of further reinforcement of Derna. Bashaw Hamet again prepared to go into his disappearing act. But Eaton gave him $2,000 to continue. On April 25, the attacking force of six hundred men arrived before Derna.

They took up positions on hills two hundred feet above the sea. They learned that the Bey of Derna had not received reinforcements, that he had only his original force of eight hundred men with which to defend the town. Bashaw Hamet was happy, doubly so, for he still held Eaton's $2,000.

Eaton sat down and wrote out a demand that Derna surrender. An Arab horseman rode into town under a flag of truce to deliver the message. He came back with a reply indicative of the fearful loyalty that the Bashaw of Tripoli could command among his lieutenants. It said: "My head or yours."

In that afternoon, *Nautilus* appeared off Derna. In the morning, *Argus* and *Hornet* sailed into view. A heavy cannon from *Nautilus* was brought ashore and hauled up the face of a cliff. Eaton placed Lieutenant O'Bannon in command of the Christians and ordered Hamet to take his cavalry around the town, to attack from the south and to cut off the garrison's flight to Tripoli on the west or to intercept possible reinforcements.

The cannon on the cliff opened up on Derna below. Out on the water, white sails gleaming in the bright sun, *Nautilus, Argus,* and *Hornet* began to hammer the town. Tiny balls of white puffed into view alongside their hulls, and from over the water came the sound of cannonading.

But then there came a cry of dismay from the gunners on the cliff.

"The ramrod's shot away!" one of them shouted. "We're out of action!"

Eaton turned to O'Bannon, standing with drawn sword alongside his Marines and soldiers, who were lying on the cliff peppering away at the parapets and houses of Derna. "We must charge, Mr. O'Bannon," Eaton said, and as he said it, a Tripolitan musket ball pierced his wrist and the American flag he held by a staff fell from his hand.

O'Bannon caught it, waved it high in the air in his left hand, and with his right, swung his sword and cried, "At them, my lads." He turned and dashed down the hill, with his seven Leathernecks and his strange army pelting after him. They sprinted across the level space that was alive and whistling with a shower of musketry from the men stationed by the Bey of Derna in an old castle. As he ran, O'Bannon saw one of his Marines stumble and pitch forward—dead. Another had fallen, wounded, before they reached the gates. In the scuffle around the steps leading to the bey's artillery atop the parapets, a third Marine was mortally wounded.

But O'Bannon fought on, thrusting with his sword, carrying the flag high above him as a rallying point, forcing a passage up the steps and finally bursting upon the gunners with a savage cry that sent them scurrying off in frightened retreat. He turned the guns on the town and the retreating garrison. "Quick, now, pepper their backsides," he called to his remaining Marines. The guns roared and the stricken garrison, plunging down the stairs and tumbling out of houses, were forced into the direct fire of *Nautilus*, *Argus* and *Hornet*.

With a shout of glee, Lieutenant Presley O'Bannon planted the American flag firmly on the battlement of Derna. For the first time in history, Old Glory waved above an Old World fortress.

The Bashaw Yusuf had no intentions of letting Derna slip from his grasp. On May 13, his troops appeared outside the town and launched a counterattack. It was repulsed, and Hamet's men fought bravely alongside O'Bannon's army, suffering the greater number of casualties. Another assault was launched at the end of May, and was again driven off with heavy losses—and this time, Eaton and O'Bannon led a sally that forced the attackers to abandon the livestock they had seized from surrounding Arabs. They were still in the field, though, and on June 2, O'Bannon led a feint that frightened them off. They marched back to their infuriated bashaw in disgrace.

Eaton was jubilant. He could not praise O'Bannon enough. He turned to the rejoicing Hamet and said, "We shall march on Tripoli and crush the Bashaw Yusuf."

"Allah be praised," Hamet said, and embraced O'Bannon.

Commodore Barron had suffered a relapse that Consul-General Lear considered a renewed opportunity for negotiation, and he beseiged the sick commodore's distracted brain with a drumfire of arguments. First, along with Captain Bainbridge, he was convinced that Bashaw Yusuf, in Bainbridge's invisible-ink phrase, "is very anxious for peace." This was true, for Yusuf saw everywhere about him evidence of Preble's destructive attacks, and was also feeling the pinch of Captain Rodgers's tight blockade. Next, Lear argued that rather than submit to force, the bashaw would retreat into a desert redoubt bringing with him his three hundred American prisoners to use as human shields; or, in the last extremity, to slaughter. Lear also claimed that the Hamet-Eaton expedition could also endanger the captives, a point in which he was seconded by the ever-helpful Bainbridge. But then came the dispatches from Derna, and Tobias Lear, who had sought for six months to sabotage this campaign, braced for the bad news of an American-led victory.

But it was actually good news. By an immense irony, the report to Yusuf from Bey Mustapha, governor of Derna, sought to save his face by vastly inflating the numbers and armament of the attackers. To the bashaw, this meant that large numbers of his subjects were deserting to his brother. The war with the United States was now escalating from one over tribute money to his very throne itself. Now, Yusuf saw the necessity of negotiating the release of the American prisoners, lest his despised brother replace him. With this information, Lear again hurried to Syracuse to extract from Barron a decisive decision to negotiate for ransom of the *Philadelphia* captives. Barron also sent Lear in *Essex* to join the blockade force off Tripoli and bearing a letter from the commodore appointing Captain Rodgers as his replacement. *Essex* arrived on May 26, and a few days later Don Joseph de Souza, the Spanish consul in Tripoli, came out to *President* under a white flag bearing the bashaw's proposal of a ransom of $200,000 for the prisoners.

This, Commodore Rodgers rejected out of hand, for he considered it much too high and regarded de Souza as a toady of the bashaw. Lear was infuriated, and he successfully asserted his authority over Rodgers and sent the Spaniard back to Tripoli with a counter-offer of $60,000. Back came Yusuf's reduced demand of $130,000. Such a sharp drop convinced Lear that he had the bashaw hooked, and he coldly sent de Souza back again with his $60,000 ultimatum—which was only to compensate for the difference in Tripolitans held captive by the Americans—or else expect renewed bombardment of the capital.

Bashaw Yusuf accepted Lear's final offer, and on June 10, 1805, the treaty was ratified and the *Philadelphia* prisoners freed. Six of them had died during that long nineteen-month ordeal of captivity, and one had "turned Turk." Four others who had embraced Islam only to secure better food and privileges now apostasized, and an infuriated Yusuf banished them to the countryside where they were probably executed. For only six Americans to have expired during that durance so vile was a remarkable record indeed, but when the Yanks were marched down to the docks they did not look so invincible. They had celebrated their impending release the night before, and now though washed and clean-shaven and wearing new clothes, their bloodshot eyes and palled cheeks suggested the kind of hangover that "goes out only by prayer and fasting." But when they were rowed back to freedom and heard the welcoming cheers of their erstwhile shipmates, they brightened and recovered their Yankee exuberance.

The same could not be said of Hamet and Eaton when *Constellation* appeared off Derna with news of the treaty. To both of them it was betrayal. After that dreadful march of six hundred miles through the desert's alternating hells of heat and cold, through thirst and hunger, mutiny and treachery; after four battles and America's first victory on foreign soil; with Commodore John Rodgers yearning to send his formidable squadron of eighteen ships, five of them first-rate frigates, to the culminating bombardment of Tripoli; with Yusuf's soldiers and supporters threatening to desert him and Hamet-Eaton-O'Bannon poised to deliver the crusher—Bashaw Yusuf had been rescued by the combined timidity of a sick commodore and a scheming consul-general, neither of whom considered their country's obligation or honor as more than a tactic.

Hamet, the legitimate ruler of Tripoli, was thrown to the wolves, with a pitiful allowance of $200 to sustain him and his retinue, and with even this sinking to $1.50 a day before disappearing altogether. Hamet's wife and family were never restored to his bosom, for his evil brother used them as hostages compelling Hamet's abandonment of Derna and eventual surrender of his right to rule. And the dishonorable peace that Lear had purchased failed to last for very long. Within a few years, under one pretext or another, the Barbary pirates resumed their predatory ways. None of them, of course, resorted to outright war with the United States, for the memories of how Edward Preble had roughed up Yusuf and of John Rodgers's later intimidation of a cringing Bey Hamouda of Tunis made the pirates reluctant to try conclusions again.

William Eaton returned to the United States determined to avenge himself on "this Machiavellian minister" Tobias Lear. Because he received a hero's welcome, there were many ears in high places willing to listen to his hymn of vilification, so that Tobias Lear became probably the most unpopular man in America. Eaton's skill in denunciation was also a great embarrassment to Jefferson and Madison, and it helped to get him elected to the Massachusetts legislature and to gain him a grant of ten thousand acres from the Bay State. But his ceaseless diatribes and his habit of flouncing about in Bedouin robes with a scimitar at his belt so wearied and disenchanted his fellow townsmen that they did not re-elect him; and in the end his indiscriminate flirtation with Aaron Burr in his conspiracy to seize for himself a huge chunk of the Louisiana Purchase so discredited Eaton that he sank into near-obscurity, a drink-addicted invalid who died on June 1, 1811, at the age of forty-seven.

Although the passage of nearly two centuries has not been kind to William Eaton's fame, it has only made the glory of Lieutenant Presley Neville O'Bannon glow more brilliantly in the unrivaled annals of his beloved corps. Hailed by Hamet Karamanli as "my brave American friend," he received from the grateful emir a Mameluke saber with a bejeweled hilt that has become the model for all blades carried by Marine officers to this day. The exploits of O'Bannon and his hardy little band of Leathernecks are forever enshrined in the phrase "To the shores of Tripoli," in the first line of that immortal battle hymn bellowed "in every clime and place" the world over.

Finally, the War with the Barbary Pirates—strange, shifting, squally, even bizarre little conflict that it was—acted like a military midwife assisting at the battle birth of those two incomparable fighting forces: the United States Navy and the United States Marines.

~III~

THE WAR
OF 1812

Free Trade and Sailors' Rights!

14

Impressments/Embargo Boomerangs

〜 THE WAR WITH THE BARBARY PIRATES WAS A SUCCESS, THOUGH A LIM-
ited one: for Bashaw Yusuf was neither humbled nor his fortress-castle
leveled. But because the thrones of the Barbary rulers soon were
awash with fratricidal blood, and even the Turkish sultan sought to
regain his dominion there, and because the renewal of the Anglo-
French struggle known as the Napoleonic Wars so distracted American shipping that fewer Yankee vessels sailed to the Mediterranean,
there was a corresponding decrease in the number of them taken by
the corsairs.

In the meantime the magnetic train of events that would draw the
young American nation into its second war with Great Britain had
already begun in 1803. That was when Napoleon broke the Peace of
Amiens and by a series of victories was poised in 1805 to invade
Britain. However, in that year Lord Nelson won the great sea battle of
Trafalgar, reasserting British supremacy at sea and ending Napoleon's
hopes of invasion. Instead, like Louis XIV before him, the Corsican
conqueror turned inward on Europe. After a series of lightning con-
quests he was supreme there.

Once again France, all-conquering on land, confronted Britain,
invincible at sea.

Both sides tried to strangle each other economically. Britain issued

Orders in Council proclaiming a blockade of Europe and the right to capture ships that did not submit to her regulations, while Napoleon countered with decrees closing European ports to Britain and stating his right to seize any ship dealing with the British.

The United States, largest neutral carrier in the world, was caught in an economic crossfire. But she suffered more at the hands of the British, who sailed right up to the shores of America to enforce their blockade, seizing ships and impressing American seamen. Very quickly impressment became a cause célèbre in America, rapidly escalating to become one of the two *casus belli*.

To defend itself against Napoleon, Great Britain depended on the Royal Navy and the 150,000 enlisted men necessary to keep its warships afloat. Because of the constant vigilance required to maintain the European blockade, and the slow speed of wooden sailing vessels, British sailors were kept away from home indefinitely, and were usually "recruited" for life. Under the low pay, poor food and brutal discipline of the Royal Navy, it was just not possible to supply the naval crews by voluntary enlistment. Thus loyal British subjects were seized by press gangs, a legal institution dating back to the Plantagenets. It was a detestable practice but was accepted because it was believed that the life of the nation depended on those "wooden ships and iron men." So the press gangs roaming the waterfront of port cities—not always in Britain—as well as judges and tavern keepers became the principal "recruiters" for the Royal Navy. A husky or agile man being treated to drinks by a friendly fellow who was actually a naval officer, or even one who got drunk on his own and was sold into seagoing slavery by the jolly bartender, would awake in the morning in the hold of one of the king's warships. Beggars or men charged with crime would be confronted by merciless judges who gave them the choice of a British jail or a British forecastle, and since prison food and life in general and no pay at all was even more horrid than service aboard one of His Majesty's ships, there was actually no choice at all.

Such reluctant sailors were understandably always on the alert for a chance to jump ship, which usually came in a foreign port and the opportunity to swim ashore, where they could pose as Americans. If the port were American it was even easier because then they could obtain naturalization papers. But Great Britain along with other European powers claimed the right of seeking these deserters and reclaiming them for the king's service.

In the American seaport towns there was actually little sympathy for the British deserters because their willingness to work for less money depressed wages for American-born seamen. But shipmasters were eager to employ them because they were trained sailors willing to work for as little as seven dollars a month—compared to an American sailor's monthly wage of $24 to $30—and delighted with the better food and easier life of an American vessel. Because the American merchant marine had nearly doubled during the first decade of the nineteenth century there was a desperate need for seamen which could not be filled by the American-born alone. Thus, to the ship-owners and skippers, the British deserter was indeed welcome, if not to their new shipmates.

Probably the basic difficulty of the growing controversy over impressment was the diametrically different naturalization laws of the two countries. Britain proclaimed the principle: "Once a Britisher, always a Britisher." This meant that for the purposes of impressment any able male but the highborn of England, Ireland, Scotland or Wales was an irrevocable subject of the king liable to be forced to serve him at sea. His Majesty owned them just as surely as he owned his dogs and horses or the wild animals of his forests. Only the Crown—never the person—could terminate this subservience.

In America by the most recent laws of 1805 an alien could become a naturalized citizen after five years' residence. A few of these deserters did become Americans by this legal process, but most of the new "Yankees" merely obtained "protection" papers for as little as a dollar paid to the customs collectors who issued them. The Royal Navy by act of Parliament recognized "no rights of citizenship conferred on British-born subjects by a foreign power" and certainly did not respect those spurious protection papers. British investigators claimed that it was "by no means uncommon for a man with blue eyes and sandy hair to carry about with him a 'collector's certificate' describing a mulatto."

Thus as the American merchant fleet doubled and Britain found itself locked in a duel to the death with Napoleon, the problem of deserters was serious enough to scuttle the Royal Navy. Those storied "wooden walls" that were the first defense of "this jewel set in a silver sea" would be left barren of seamen. There were various estimates of the number of British deserters serving on American vessels—both merchant and naval—and it would seem that the number varied according to the objectives of the calculator seeking to maximize or minimize the problem. The most extravagant British estimate was that at least one hundred thousand British deserters carrying protection papers served aboard American ships, but a more likely number was about forty thousand. Loss of a hundred thousand sailors, two-thirds of its enlisted strength—could have sunk the Royal Navy; and even forty thousand, a little less than one-third, would eventually have been crippling.

Since George Washington first took office, American administrations seemed to be sympathetic toward British efforts to plug this dreadful leakage. Washington and John Adams, Anglophile Federalists, had no desire to weaken John Bull in his duel with Napoleon. Even such an avowed enemy of Great Britain as the Republican and Francophilic Thomas Jefferson would not have wished to see an America left defenseless against the Corsican adventurer. So the impressment problem was never considered an immediate cause for war with the former mother country—until the British began stopping American ships and impressing native-born Americans.

In reply to official American complaints against this growing practice, the British replied that seizure of bonafide Yankee sailors was the result of occasional errors. It was easy for a British naval officer to recognize British deserters serving on French, Italian or Spanish ships or those of other non-English-speaking nations, but very difficult to distinguish between British and American sailors whose language and dress were so similar, if not identical. But this was solemn nonsense! How could a London Cockney without "'is 'aitches" or a Yorkshireman speaking as though with a mouth full of Yorkshire pudding be mistaken for a New Englander with his Yankee twang or a Southerner with his soft drawl? Or could an American sailor's relaxed and easy manner in the presence of his officers be confused with a British seaman standing rigidly at attention as though impaled? The truth was that the British officers searching American ships were arrogant and bullying. If an American's name and birthplace did not correspond exactly to the list that by American law was carried on each Yankee vessel, he was summarily declared a British deserter and hauled aboard a British warship—especially if he appeared to be unusually strong or agile. Thus estimates of the number of native-born Americans compelled to serve aboard British warships varied from a low of about one thousand to a high of seven thousand—and none of these were ever repatriated.

Impressment of native Americans as much as any other dispute escalated the mutual hatreds culminating in the War of 1812 and outraged the growing sense of "national honor" that America, like all young nations, possessed in supersensitive degree; and the inevitable blow-off came on June 22, 1807, in the infamous Chesapeake Incident.

Captain James Barron, who had brought his ailing older brother home from the Mediterranean, had been appointed commodore of what was left of the Mediterranean squadron in May of 1807. Hurrying to Norfolk he found his 38-gun flagship *Chesapeake* about as ready for the open sea as a railroad barge. None of her crews had been assigned to stations; her decks were cluttered with unstowed gear; most of her guns were unmounted and her cannonballs, rammers, sponges and other firing gear were scattered about the ship. Still Barron was eager to sail, so that on June 22 he gave orders to up anchor, planning to make *Chesapeake* shipshape while at sea.

Aboard Barron's flagship were four deserters from the British frigate *Melampus:* an American black, an American Indian and a native of Maryland, all with obvious proof of the land of their birth, and a fourth named John Wilson who swore he had been born in America. All claimed that they had been impressed into the Royal Navy from a U.S. merchant ship.

About fifty miles out of Norfolk the British frigate *Leopard,* 50 guns, commanded by an arrogant, supercilious captain with the superciliously British name of Salisbury Pryce Humphreys, hailed *Chesapeake* and asked if she would carry some dispatches to Europe. Barron consented and a boat put out from *Leopard* and a Royal Navy officer climbed aboard *Chesapeake.* What he brought was not a package of dispatches but an order from the commander of Britain's North American Station directing all his warships to stop *Chesapeake* and search her for deserters. Barron courteously replied that his government did not permit such unwarranted searches, and the officer was rowed back to *Leopard* while *Chesapeake* resumed course.

Now Captain Humphreys personally hailed the American frigate, but Barron could not make out what he said. At once *Leopard* fired a round shot across *Chesapeake*'s bow, the signal for combat—and Barron immediately ordered the crew beat to quarters. It was, unfortunately, a call to confusion: few of them knew their stations, unmounted guns lay on the decks and nowhere were there powder, wads, and slow matches to be found. With officers and men dashing frantically about like ants on an anthill, *Leopard* closed to within two hundred feet and opened fire. Broadside after broadside crashed into the stricken *American.* She was hulled twenty-one times, her masts smashed and her sails shredded. Three seamen were killed, eight lay dying, and ten—including Barron—were wounded. The rest of her men were cowering below, except for Lieutenant William Allen, who ran to the galley to seize a live coal in his bare hands, juggling it as he sprinted back to one of the few mounted guns to fire *Chesapeake*'s only answering shot. Barron now had no recourse but to haul down his flag. Immediately more boats put out from *Leopard* bringing a boarding party and two lieutenants, who found the four alleged deserters and dragged them back to *Leopard.* Eventually John Wilson, who had no proof of American birth, was hanged in Halifax; and the three Americans sentenced to death, but finally reprieved: an exemplary way to encourage loyalty in enlisted men.

News of the unprovoked attack upon *Chesapeake* so infuriated the American public that it almost catapulted a nation as unready for battle as Barron himself, into war with the greatest naval power on the seas. John Quincy Adams, son of the second president, quit the Federalists to become a Republican; and Winfield Scott dropped his law practice to join the army.

Commodore Barron himself became a casualty to the rage that seized the general public. Court-martialed for neglect of duty, he was convicted and sentenced to suspension from command for five years—a slap on the wrist if there ever was one. Barron was not, of course, guilty of cowardice in pulling down his flag, as was also charged by some overheated superpatriots. Rather, his offense was to go to sea unprepared when the Royal Navy was manifestly patroling the waters off Virginia in search of deserters. It was only because of his own neglect and monstrous indifference to a dangerous situation that he had no alternative but to surrender.

Jefferson was also nearly another casualty. Irate calls for war everywhere were mingled by gleeful Federalist demands for his head. Fortunately, he quickly ordered a quarantine against British officers and crews and closed the coast to the Royal Navy. By this immediate action, Jefferson was able to avoid being drawn into a war that could never be won by the pitifully weak American forces then available: the result of this economy-minded pacifist president's own reduction of military strength.

Even the British were shaken, the government disavowing the attack and recalling both Captain Humphreys and Vice Admiral Sir George Berkeley, the Halifax commander who had ordered the deserters seized. Jefferson demanded reparations and an apology, but Britain pretended that the affair had been settled amicably, allowing it to drag on unsettled.

One unfortunate result of the *Chesapeake* Incident was that Thomas Jefferson began to rethink his position on war itself. Although he has gone into history as a pacifist, this judgment is not exactly correct. Like all rational men, he did indeed abhor war. But he had shown by his action against the Barbary pirates that he would fight if necessary, especially if by fighting he could put an end to the dishonorable and increasingly costly policy of paying tribute to the Barbary extortionists. He could never say with Woodrow Wilson: "There is such a thing as a man's being too proud to fight." The absolutism of doctrinal pacifism just never could appeal to a mind as balanced as Jefferson's. But in 1807 during the *Chesapeake* uproar that threatened to drag America into the Napoleonic Wars, he realized that wars were becoming too total, too destructive to be embarked upon with emotion—outrage or revenge— that allows the heart to overpower the head. In modern wars there were no winners, only losers. Thus he developed a policy of "peaceful coercion," culminating in the Embargo Act of December 1807.

In essence, the embargo declared that if Britain and France continued to regard the Atlantic as their private pond, restricting commerce at will and refusing to accept the American principle that "Free ships make free goods," then the United States would not trade with them or any other country. Actually, the embargo was aimed chiefly at Britain. The United States was Britain's chief customer, and also the largest neutral carrier of goods to England. Jefferson believed that if he could cut off Britain's chief market and reduce the flow of its imports, he would bring Britannia to terms. Thus, under the embargo no U.S. ship could sail from a U.S. port for any foreign port.

How such a boomeranging, unbalanced, destructive policy could have issued from the balanced mind of Thomas Jefferson still baffles historians. All enterprise—business, retail trade, transportation, agricultural export, shipping—was crippled in America. Instead of humbling Britain and after her Napoleon, it enriched the Mistress of the Seas at the expense of maritime America and played into the hands of the French emperor, while coming close to provoking the secession of mercantile New England. Thus Jefferson's noble experiment was a notable failure, and the Embargo Act was repealed on March 1, 1809—three days before Thomas Jefferson handed over the reins of his government to his friend and protégé James Madison.

15

James Madison/
British Defiant

〜 IN 1652, FORTY-FIVE YEARS AFTER THE FOUNDING OF THE FIRST COLONY at Jamestown, an English ship's carpenter named James Maddison came ashore at an unknown Virginia port. He had paid the passage money for twelve immigrants, including himself, and thus earned "head rights" entitling him to six hundred acres of unalloted lands. He chose a site on the Mattapony River. There he cleared and cultivated a farm, and augmented his income by building small vessels. One of Maddison's sons, also named James, rose to become county sheriff; but as he grew older his heart turned toward the Blue Ridge Mountain wilderness. In 1714 he and a neighbor patented two thousand acres along the upper Mattapony. Ambrose Madison (the second *d* in the name had been dropped), James's second son, moved still farther west, taking title to about two thousand acres on the Blue Ridge overlooking the broad Shenandoah Valley. He died in 1731 with his cleared land still raw with stumps and slashes. His widow, thirty-two-year-old Frances Taylor Madison, was left with three children and twenty-nine slaves to work the tobacco farm that her husband had planted. She did so with intelligence and diligence, prospering. Her oldest child, James, then nine, joined her in operating the plantation and as he grew older regularly carried the tobacco to Francis Conway's warehouse on the Rappahannock. He was attracted by pretty little Nelly Conway, nine years his junior, and when she reached seventeen he married her. Their oldest son, James, Jr., destined to become the fourth President of the United States, was born on March 16, 1751.

Very little is known of the childhood of James Madison, except that he began life as a sickly baby for whom there had been little hope. Of James and Nelly Madison's twelve children, only five survived, and it was feared that the firstborn, James, Jr., would expire very quickly. But he did not, although afflicted with illness throughout his life of eighty-five years, proof of his college friend William Bradford's assurance that sickly people have a way of outliving their stronger brethren. He was probably taught to read and write by his sturdy grandmother, Frances, and the one childhood event that remained engraved upon his memory was her death on November 25, 1761. It was about then that the Madison family moved into Montpelier, the fine new brick mansion that James Madison, Sr., had built a half mile from the old farmhouse. In later years James Madison, Jr., recalled how he helped carry furniture from the old home to the new.

At Montpelier he played with the slave children his age, as was the custom, or with the numerous cousins and friends within a fifteen-mile radius always referred to as "the family." Boys then rode horses before they were strong enough to lift a saddle, and "Little Jemmy," or "Little Jamie" as he was variously called, proved himself an extremely dexterous horseman, a skill in which he continued to excel almost to his death. The fact that he weighed so little might have helped him to win the horse races that the Blue Ridge gentry were so fond of holding. At maturity James Madison was but five feet six inches tall and probably of slight build, and if the repeated references to him as "Little Jemmy" or "Little Jamie" or just plain "little" or "frail" or "spindle-shanked" with a "little round tummy" are any indication, he might not have weighed much more than 125 or 130 pounds, if that. A portrait of him as president—painted seated, as is usually the preference of smaller men—shows the outstanding characteristic of a bulging fore-head, along with large, wide-set eyes, a long nose and a full mouth. It is not a fighting face, but rather a shy, even timid one; but it is alive with intelligence and is extraordinarily gentle.

James's unusually intuitive mind became apparent the day he began formal education in June of 1762, three months after his eleventh birthday, in the boarding school operated by Donald Robertson, a Scots intellectual educated at Aberdeen and Edinburgh universities. James studied for five years under this remarkable educator, his instruction in Greek and Latin sounding like a parade of the great minds of classical antiquity. Among medieval writers he explored Montaigne and read such contemporary political thinkers as Montesquieu and John Locke. James also acquired a reading knowledge of French and Spanish, speaking French with the broad Scots burr he had absorbed from Robertson so that years later he horrified one of those Frenchmen who are as supersensitive to the niceties of their own tongue as they are indifferent to those of others. Logic, geography and history, as well as "natural philosophy," rounded out his studies so that when he entered Princeton (then the College of New Jersey) in June 1769, at the age of eighteen his tutelage under that "man of great learning" had given him an academic preparation years in advance of most of his classmates.

James's choice of Princeton, rather than William and Mary in the capital at Williamsburg, the traditional source of higher learning for well-born young Virginians such as Thomas Jefferson, the Lees and Randolphs and Patrick Henry, was due to the influence of both his tutor, Thomas Martin, and his father. Madison, Senior, was bitterly opposed to British control of the established Anglican Church in Virginia, and Martin, who had studied at Princeton, was eloquent in his praise of his alma mater. Young Madison was also by then appalled at the arrogance of the Anglican clergy and their custom of jailing any non-Anglican Protestants who dared to attempt to propagate their faith in the colony. So James chose the Presbyterian college in New Jersey, riding three hundred miles by horseback in a wearying journey that did his health no good. But he was delighted by the town of Princeton itself and the twenty-three-year-old college. Here he came under the influence of another Scots scholar (there were so many in those days of early America!): President John Witherspoon. James would always remember his canny admonitions, especially this rule of oratory: "Lads, ne'er do ye speak unless ye ha' something to say, and when ye are done, leave off."

James Madison would always be fond of aphorisms, those insights into human conduct that would fall from his own lips so easily in later years; and an indication of the range of his catholic tastes and studies may be found in his adoption of two of them from the 124 laid down by Cardinal de Retz of France.

A man shows himself greater by being capable of owning a fault than by being incapable of committing it.

Patience works greater effects than activity.

Both of these applied to Madison's political career: on the first, he

could never confess a failing; on the second he was patience incarnate.

At Princeton James Madison distinguished himself by needing only
two rather than four years to be graduated with honors. But he studied so hard that his sleep "was reduced for some weeks to less [*sic*]
than five hours in the twenty-four." He was so weakened that recovery
took five years, and he was unable to endure the homeward journey,
staying at Princeton throughout the winter. Upon his return to Montpelier in the spring of 1773, he replaced Thomas Martin, who had
died, as tutor for his two younger sisters and two brothers. He also
began to read in public law, drifting steadily in religion toward the
stance of the English deists. He did not actually—and certainly not
actively—oppose revealed religion; but he did come to detest established faiths with such a depth of loathing that Americans can be forever grateful to him for his part in framing the First Amendment to
the Constitution providing religious freedom to all citizens everywhere.

Most Americans also do not realize that in those pre-Revolutionary
days every colony except Maryland had an established religion, that is, a
faith supported by the political authority to the exclusion of all others.
New Hampshire, Massachusetts and Connecticut were Congregational;
Rhode Island was Baptist, although the organizer of that faith, Roger
Williams, granted religious freedom to all other Protestant sects; New
York and New Jersey were Dutch Reformed; Delaware was Lutheran;
Pennsylvania was Quaker, though the nonviolent Friends persecuted no
one; the South—Virginia, the Carolinas and Georgia—was Anglican
(modern Episcopal), with the southernmost three more likely to toler-
ate other Protestants. Maryland under the Catholic Lord Baltimore was
the first to grant universal religious freedom, but that ended when the
Virginia Anglicans invaded their northern neighbor to impose their
establishment there and put Catholicism to the ban.

Also at this time Madison became liable to sudden seizures that
might have been epileptic, although physicians of the period were
unable to diagnose them accurately. Because the attacks came at his
mature age and eventually disappeared, later medical science was able
to identify the affliction as epileptiform hysteria. Apparently it did him
no serious harm, but it did disqualify him from serving in the Revolutionary War. Upon his recovery James Madison plunged eagerly into
the exciting movement for independence then engulfing Virginia
almost as completely as it was Massachusetts. He also entered public
life, standing for the Virginia legislature and losing in his first campaign because—unlike George Washington and Thomas Jefferson—
he refused to ply his guests at a political picnic with whisky punch. It

was not that he was a prohibitionist—he could never be an absolutist anywhere when rights were at stake—but he considered buying votes with whisky unethical and debasing. Next time, however, he won— serving at Williamsburg from 1776 to 1780.

His fellow legislators were deeply impressed by his erudition, especially in political theory and constitutional law, but amazed by his shyness. During his first session at Williamsburg he sat silently in his chair without uttering a single word. Yet, when he would discourse in the corridors, he would be surrounded by a throng of eager listeners.

Madison's voice was also a political liability, nothing like Patrick Henry's sonorous organ, but rather so soft and low that when he arose to speak as Speaker of the First House of Representatives under Washington, the members would playfully cup their hands to their ears. Madison also served as Jefferson's secretary of state, carrying on a voluminous correspondence that kept him at his desk ten or twelve hours a day. The sight of "Tall Tawm" and "Little Jemmy" strolling together on the grounds of the President's House, locked in conversation, was a source of great mirth in Federal City. Obviously, Jefferson was the senior partner of the duo that founded "the Virginia Dynasty," and Madison never resented his junior status. He was fond of telling humorous anecdotes about Jefferson, especially one illustrating his equanimity, which was so unshakable that "no man could put him in a passion." At a dinner party in Jefferson's honor, the president was trapped by one of those stupifying bores who, like a leech, cannot be shaken without drawing blood. He was discoursing on the superiority of hereditary government, to which Jefferson with a wan smile and tired voice replied: "Yes, I have heard there was a university some place where the chair of mathematics was hereditary."

There are so many conflicting descriptions of James Madison. Washington Irving called him a "withered little applejohn," but his neighbor Richard W. Thompson felt that "I had rarely seen a face in which more benignity and quiet composure was [sic] expressed. It was a complete personification of gentleness and benevolence." Probably the most intuitive description of the fourth president came from one of his slaves.

I was always with Mr. Madison until he died, and shaved him every other day for sixteen years. I never saw him in a passion, and never knew him to strike a slave, although he had at times over a hundred. Neither would he allow an overseer to do it. I don't think he drank a quart of brandy in his whole life. When he had hard drinkers at the table, who had put away his choice Madeira pretty freely, he would just touch his glass to his lips, or dilute it with water, as they pushed the decanters. He always dressed wholly in black. He never had but one suit at a time. He had some poor relatives he had to help, and wished to set them an example of economy.

Here in strikingly simple language is a portrait of a gentle ascetic suggesting that James Madison, far from being fitted for leadership of a struggling new nation, would have been happier in a monastery toiling among his manuscripts in blissful quiet, finding peace in Gregorian chant at vespers and contentment in a mug of cool beer or cider drunk in the refectory before retiring to his cell. It has been well said that no man in the world knew more about government than Madison, and none less about governing. And yet it is truly amazing that such a reticent man could take to wife a woman seventeen years his junior who was as fun-loving, outgoing, worldly, and nonconforming as Dolley Payne Todd.

Dorothy Payne was born in 1768 in Guilford County, North Carolina, the daughter of Quaker parents. Called Dolley or Dolly for unknown reasons, she matured as a beautiful though slightly plump young woman with a gorgeous head of dark brown hair. Her fondness for fine French clothes, dancing, horse racing, and other worldly activities shocked her parents, so that early in life she chose to ignore—though not formally abandon—their reclusive creed. In 1790 she married John Todd, Jr., a wealthy Philadelphia Quaker who three years later succumbed to the yellow-fever epidemic then scourging the City of Brotherly Love. Less than a year after his death, Dolley, with the unconventional haste typical of this original woman, met and married the little speaker from Virginia. A widow at twenty-six Dolley was introduced to Madison by Aaron Burr at the boardinghouse conducted by her mother. Because she had wed a member of "the world's people," she was read out of meeting. People who knew the newlyweds wondered what she saw in her husband, or how this fun-loving lady would get along with this careful, reticent gentleman of forty-three who, though wealthy from tobacco plantation revenues, lived so conspicuously beneath his means. But Dolley Madison astounded all her critics by becoming a devoted wife.

She did not, of course, renounce her fondness for riding in an opulent coach worth $1,500 behind four gaily caparisoned and prancing thoroughbreds, or of using rouge. Under the newfound freedom of American women she dipped snuff in public—to some less liberated ladies a disgusting habit—or led parties of her friends into the Senate or House galleries, even invading the forbidding and sacrosanct premises of the Supreme Court in the basement below. Probably her most attractive quality was her absolute absence of hauteur or affectation. Henry Clay remembered meeting her at a state function and remarking on the beauty of a delicately traced laced handkerchief she held. At once Dolley drew from the folds of her dress a huge bandanna. Pointing to it, she said, "This is for business," and then to the dainty bit of lace, "And this, is my polisher."

Dolley began her "reign" in social Washington when the widowed Jefferson was still in office and had no First Lady to act as his hostess; and then, when her husband was elected, with great zest and glee she moved into the President's House as the capital's "Queen Mother," while proving to be her husband's greatest political ally.

When President Madison took office on March 4, 1809, he was already convinced that a milder form of economic persuasion than the disastrous Embargo Act would be more likely to obtain repeal of the odious Orders in Council and Napoleonic decrees. Accordingly, he turned to the Nonintercourse Act, also passed in Jefferson's second term and due to expire in 1810. Under it Congress offered to resume trade with whichever nation was first to remove its restrictions, and that if the abstaining nation did not three months later also repeal its own, the Nonintercourse Act would be proclaimed against it. In other words, the trade boycott would be maintained.

With this piece of legislation the Madison Administration played directly into the hands of Napoleon. After the shattering defeat of Trafalgar, the French emperor's blockade of Britain sank into desuetude while his enemy's blockade of Continental ports turned the economic screws tighter and tighter. So Napoleon decided that if he rescinded—or pretended to rescind—his decrees, Britain would have to repeal its Orders in Council and his Continental system would then be free to receive imports. If Britain refused, then it would be subjected to the ravages of an American embargo, and perhaps also the wrath of an American war. Madison naively believed that Napoleon was serious when he notified the president of his *intention* to revoke the decrees, and after receiving Napoleon's message to that effect, Madison immediately put Great Britain on notice that he expected it to do the same with its Orders.

That was in the late summer of 1810, and by late November no reply had come from London. Madison then ordered his new secretary of state, James Monroe, to notify the British Foreign Office that unless compliance was adopted by February, he would reinstate the

Nonintercourse Act with Britain—meaning an embargo on exports to her. Foreign Minister Lord Wellesley refused to budge. He said there was no proof of Napoleon's sincerity—indeed, he was still seizing American ships and cargoes—and that his stance was merely a ruse to remove the strangling lasso of the British blockade from around his empire. Finally, said His Lordship, this was now a war that his country was winning, and to end the blockade would be to renounce Britannia's naval superiority.

This was not only true but also a logical conclusion: for there was no doubt that Napoleon was losing, nor any proof that he had really renounced his decrees. By July 6, 1812, a report to Congress showed that during and after 1807, Britain had seized 389 American vessels, while France, Denmark and Naples under the rule of Napoleon had seized 434, and the Dutch, Spanish and other dominions had added to this a large but unknown number of unreported seizures. Moreover, about half of the British captures had been declared by the admiralty courts to be illegal and restoration ordered. During the same period, Napoleon had freed only about one-quarter of his total. He had also imprisoned all captured sailors who spoke English with any kind of accent.

Napoleon was not only still seizing American ships and cargoes while pretending to have ceased to do so, he evolved an absurdly casuistic defense of the practice. This was that any ship that had been stopped by a British warship, or had entered a British port, or been searched for British deserters, was in fact a *British* ship and therefore an enemy subject to seizure. To this was added the disingenuous disclaimer that they had not really been seized, but only "sequestered"— an infuriating consolation for the owners who had lost both ship and cargo.

Nevertheless, Madison—not to break good news to the American public as the Federalists claimed, but believing that Napoleon was acting in good faith and perhaps also that Britain's indifference to American outrage over the Chesapeake Incident still rankled—proclaimed the Nonintercourse Act against Britain. Another reason for Madison's move was that Secretary Monroe was an arch Anglophobe and an ardent Francophile. Washington during the Revolutionary War had described his fiery aide as perhaps too fond of France. Monroe's eldest daughter had studied in Paris and been the intimate friend of her classmate Hortense de Beauharnais, Napoleon's stepdaughter and later the wife of Napoleon's brother Louis. James Monroe also carried in his shoulder a British musket ball reminding him of his implacable enmity for the former mother country. So the embargo went into effect, was rigidly enforced—and brought Britain to the brink of economic disaster. Almost immediately American grain shipments to Britain ceased, and cotton—the lifeblood of Britain's new and rapidly expanding textile industry—vanished from all the seaport warehouses. Unemployment skyrocketed, and soon big-city merchants facing ruin with their shelves loaded with unsaleable goods were petitioning Parliament to repeal the Orders in Council. Actually the Orders were regulations drawn by the Privy Council, a body of advisers chosen by the king, and approved by His Majesty, in this case with George III then permanently insane, his son the Prince Regent who would in 1820 ascend the throne as George IV. The only way the British public could have them withdrawn was to persuade Parliament to repeal them, and this process was not begun until imported commodities disappeared from British factories and markets, hunger stalked the industrial towns, war with America loomed and public clamor no longer could be ignored.

Nevertheless, at the beginning of the embargo Great Britain obstinately refused to annul the offending Orders, and just as stubbornly Secretary of State James Monroe continued to ignore French ship-seizures and to insist that Napoleon had indeed abrogated his decrees.

But in those early days of the Madison administration the issue of impressment caused by the Orders, though explosive, was not nearly as infuriating to the American public as continued British support of the Northwest Indian tribes in their bloody raids upon the settlers of the Northwest Frontier.

16

Tecumseh and
William Henry Harrison

〜 ALTHOUGH IT IS GENERALLY BELIEVED THAT THE AMERICAN BATTLE CRY of "Free Trade and Sailors' Rights!" was but a cover for the true objective of conquering Canada, the fact is that the British did indeed intend to create in the Northwest an Indian buffer state that would halt westward expansion by the United States. Even though General Wayne had won the Battle of Fallen Timbers in 1794, the Indian menace on the frontier had not subsided. Neither had Britain yet withdrawn from its seven Northwest posts as promised, and she still supplied the tribes from her bases at Fort Niagara on the American side of the border and Fort Malden across the Detroit River from the American outpost of Fort Detroit.

The British plan was to settle the Indians on the southern shores of the Great Lakes, now the greatest industrial area in the world; and if the American settlers' desire to block that objective, though sincere and born of bloody experience with the British-supported red men, became corrupted into greed for the possession of all of Upper Canada itself, the movement was still at its inception a genuine yearning for security. There was no doubt that the settlers actually believed that Britain was inciting the Indians against them and was paying bounties for their scalps. William Henry Harrison, governor of Indiana Territory, informed Washington that the settlers there were so terrified that they were abandoning their farms to take sanctuary in blockhouses. Even if it does seem unlikely that the British wanted to pursue a policy certain to embroil them in another war with America across a supply line three thousand miles long while she was locked in a life-or-death struggle with Napoleon, the settlers were convinced that the Crown sought creation of the Indian buffer state more passionately than a victory over Napoleon in the Peninsular War. If this were not an actual fact, it was a psychological fact—which is just as persuasive. Frontiersmen simply could not forget the bloody Indian incursions from Canada during the Revolutionary War, and the Western press fueled their fear of the former mother country by printing such inflammatory documents as a letter from Major James Crawford to Governor Haldimand at Quebec, dated Fiago, January 3, 1782, which said:

May it please your excellency: at the request of the Seneca Chiefs, I send herewith to your excellency under the care of James Boyd eight packs of scalps cured, dried, hooped and painted with all the Indian triumphal marks of which the following is an invoice and explanation.

No. 1. Containing 43 scalps of congress soldiers, killed in different skirmishes; these are stretched on black hoops, 4 inches in diameter; the inside of the skin painted red with a small black spot to denote their being killed with bullets; also 62 farmers killed in their houses, the hoops red, the skin painted brown and marked with a hoe, a black circle all around to denote their being surprised in the night and a black hatchet in the middle to denote their being killed with that weapon.

No. 2. Containing 93 farmers killed in their houses . . . white circles and suns shew that they were surprised in daytime. Black bullet on some, hatchet on others.

No. 3. 97 farmers, hoops green to shew working in fields.

No. 4. 102 farmers. 18 marked with yellow flame to shew that they were burned alive after being scalped. Most farmers appear by hair to be young or middle aged.

No. 5. 81 women, long hair; those braided to shew they were mothers.

No. 6. 193 boy's scalps various ages, white ground on the skin red tear in middle.

No. 7. 211 girls scalps, big and little, small yellow hoops marked hatchet, club, knife etc.

No. 8. Mixture 122 with box of birch bark containing 29 infant scalps small white hoops. Only little black knife in middle to shew they were ripped out of mothers body.

Note of Seneca to Governor Haldemond [*sic*]

Father: We wish to send these over the water to the great king that he may regard them and see our faithfulness in destroying his enemies, and know that his presents have not been made to an ungrateful people.

Father: The king's enemies were formerly like young panthers, they could neither bite nor scratch; we could play with them safely; we feared nothing that they could do to us. But now their bodies are becoming as the elk, and strong as the buffalo; they have also got great and sharp claws. They have driven us out of our country for taking part in your quarrel. We expect the great king to give us another country.

How could the settlers fail to shudder while reading such a blood-curdling but business-like invoice of the grisly, ghoulish trade in the lives of their ancestors or predecessors? Nor were their fears allayed when they learned that the British commander at Kingston in 1812 was offering "the same price for the bringing in of a prisoner as that given for a scalp." At the same time Harrison reported that the British in Malden had in one year issued to the Indians goods valued at £20,000, commenting: "All the peltries [furs] collected on the waters of the Wabash in one year, if sold in the London market, would not pay the freight of the goods which have been issued to the Indians." Most frightening of all was the report that Tecumseh, the great sachem of the Shawnee who sought to form an Indian confederation exactly conforming to the British plan, had gone to Malden to offer his services to the king.

Tecumseh, the greatest of Indian chiefs, was born and bred to hatred of the white man. He was a Shawnee, one of twelve loosely united nomadic Algonquian tribes of that name, and he reveled in the Shawnee boast that no other tribe in the New World had killed as many "Long Knives," as the white men were called. The Shawnee, who first entered history in Georgia and the Carolinas—the name means "Southern"—had a peculiar legend of their origin. Where most Indians believed that they had emerged from the center of the earth, clambering out of caves and holes, the proud Shawnee, like the Children of Israel passing through the Red Sea to escape Egyptian bondage, insisted that they were led by their Turtle tribe down to the ocean, where the waters parted and they walked safely along the ocean floor until they reached the American continent.

Because they were arrogant and warlike they came to be hated by their neighbors—the Cherokee, Creek, and Choctaw—who combined against them and would have exterminated them had they not agreed to migrate north to the Wabash River in Indiana, the Wyoming Valley in Pennsylvania or the three towns of Piqua, Xenia and Chillicothe in Ohio. It was in Ohio along the Mad River in 1768 that Tecumseh was born, the fourth of eight children of the warrior chief Puckeshinowan. Because Indian women were not nearly as fecund as their white sisters—rarely giving birth to more than one or two children—the size of Puckeshinowan's family was always a source of wonder to his people; and his wife, Methoatske—a fierce Muskogee squaw—was believed to possess magical powers.

Tecumseh proved to be the handsomest, strongest, bravest and most intelligent of this unusual brood, and it was he whom Methoatske infected with her foaming hatred of the Long Knives, especially after her husband was foully murdered in 1774 by a hunting band of whites along the Mad River. When he did not return to the village, she took Tecumseh with her in search of him, finding him dying beside a trail and gasping his last words: "Behold the faith of white men!"

Heartbroken, Methoatske fell upon her husband's body with loud lamentations, arising to scream at the trembling little boy beside her a message of doom for the Long Knives. Tecumseh—or Shooting Star—would be a great warrior, "a whirlwind and a storm" that would "scatter desolation and death" among the whites.

"Tecumseh," she cried, "you shall avenge the death of your father and appease the spirits of his slaughtered brethren. Already you are elected chief of many tribes. . . . Your feet shall be swift as the forked lightning, your arm shall be as the thunderbolt and your soul fearless as the cataract that dashes from the mountain precipice."

The youth never forgot that bitter requiem for his father or the splendor of his mother's command of the Algonquian dialect, which he would one day surpass. As his great friend Shabbona would say in later years, "His enmity was the most bitter of any Indian I ever knew," and he himself would declare that he "could not look upon the face of a white man without feeling the flesh crawl on my bones."

A few months after the death of Puckeshinowa, Methoataske gave birth to another son, seven years younger than Tecumseh, who because of his endless boasting would be called Laulewasika, or "Loud Mouth." Then she went south to rejoin her people and vanished from the pages of history. Behind her Tecumseh and Laulewasika were entrusted to the care of their older brother Cheeseekau under the guidance of Cornstalk, the great Shawnee chieftain.

It was Cornstalk who opposed Lord Dunmore of Virginia when he invaded Ohio in 1774 seeking Shawnee lands. Assisted by braves from the Delaware, Mingo and Wyandot tribes, Cornstalk's Shawnee met Dunmore's militia at Point Pleasant on October 10. Although compelled to retreat, they inflicted upon the Long Knives twice as many casualties as they received, an affront so humiliating to the white men that three years later they brutally murdered Cornstalk along with his son, the handsome young sachem Red Hawk and other aides. With this they created in the hearts of the red men a horrible ache for revenge, and in the soul of nine-year-old Tecumseh there burned such a deep distrust of whites that he would never believe a word they said.

The death of both his father and his guardian, two noble chiefs from whom Tecumseh had learned idealism and compassion, had left the young Shawnee youth disconsolate—until he was adopted by Black-fish, chief of the Shawnee sister village of Chillicothe not far from Tecumseh's Piqua. Blackfish was a big, hearty warrior who never fought a major battle, relying more on ambush and bushwhacking than on the fierce engagements that made his contemporaries Blue Jacket and Little Turtle more famous. From Blackfish Tecumseh learned the art of guerrilla warfare that would one day make his name more dreaded than that of all other Shawnee chiefs combined. Like Blackfish he would train his braves in a deep understanding of the forests: of their flora and fauna, how to use them to beguile the Long Knives by simulating the cry of birds and four-footed creatures for signaling, to elude pursuit by hiding in caves or inside rotten trees. Small-party actions were the most successful in the forest, especially if they were based upon the twin tactics of speed and surprise: the sudden strike, the war whoop, the tomahawk in the brain followed by the swift withdrawal.

According to Shawnee custom the young sons of chiefs received instruction in handcrafts and hunting, as well as in oratory, history and personal conduct. Because none of the Indian tribes had a written language all the instruction was oral, traditions passed on by word of mouth along with admonitions to respect one's elders and honor their dead. The Shawnee had their own Golden Rule, strikingly similar to the injunction of Jesus Christ to "love thy neighbor as thyself":

> Do not kill or injure your neighbor, for it is not he that you injure, you injure yourself. But do good to him, therefore add to his days of happiness as you add to your own.

Tecumseh quickly became known for his kindness to the weaker or infirm members of the tribe, supplying them with game and skins for warmth during the cold winter months, never attempting to ingratiate himself with Shawnee of rank and authority. Usually good-natured and modest, he had a ferocious temper that could explode like tinder struck by a spark. Once, though hardly more than a boy, he stopped a mature brave from beating his wife, angrily crying that only a coward could strike a woman. He was also a fine athlete excelling at the Indian game of baggataway, the forerunner of modern lacrosse. As a hunter, he not only excelled but simply outclassed all others. On a three-day hunt of deer some of his companions came back with three or four skins, one had twelve—but Tecumseh brought in thirty! Because he was so accurate with the bow and arrow and with throwing the tomahawk, he regarded the white man's firearms with contempt, complaining to his brother Cheeseekau, who tried to teach him how to handle guns, that the sound of exploding powder only frightened the animals from the hunting grounds.

Tecumseh's instruction in the bitter, bloody reality of racial border warfare began when he was only twelve. In that year of 1780 George Rogers Clark, leading mounted riflemen and armed with artillery, destroyed the youth's beloved towns of Chillicothe and Piqua, doing such a thorough job that no trace of them appeared thereafter. But in the heart of this boy warrior their ashes still burned like embers. Yet, in his first battle along the Mad River near Dayton, he was so frightened that he ran away in terror. But he came back in time to join a party of braves that captured a flatboat on the Ohio. To his enduring horror he saw one of the white passengers burned to death, secretly vowing that he would never allow torture or murder practiced in his presence again—and he never did.

For a year this mere strip of a boy out in the world on his own vanished completely beyond the west bank of the Mississippi. On his return he was reunited with his oldest brother Cheeseekau to make a long trip down the Mississippi Valley to visit the Creek tribes along the Gulf Coast, forging friendships that would be of value in later years. To his deep sorrow he saw Cheeseekau receive his death wounds in an attack on a white settlement. Here was another loss to be avenged, and it would seem that there would be no more room in his boyish heart for more hatred. But the chance for revenge came quickly: in 1790 when he joined the Miami chief Little Turtle in the series of stinging defeats he inflicted on General Josiah Harmar's invading force of Americans along the Maumee River. Tecumseh also helped Little Turtle deliver that disastrous defeat to St. Clair, and was at Fallen Timbers hiding among the scattered trees with a party of scouts who opened fire on Wayne's advance guard to begin the battle. But the dreaded Black Snake became the Rattler and struck back fiercely, and the bullet that ended the life of Tecumseh's next-to-last surviving brother Sauwaseekau also pierced the young chief's heart with a new sorrow. Perhaps even more to his grief was the Treaty of Greenville negotiated by Wayne a year later. Having broken the power of the Indian alliance in Ohio and Indiana, Black Snake now extended the peace pipe—baited with a little gold and a lot of whisky. After feasting and drinking for two days, the chiefs of twelve tribes signed the pact by which they ceded twenty-five thousand square miles of territory— an area the size of modern West Virginia—in exchange for $20,000 and the promise of $9,500 in annuities. Tecumseh, implacable as ever, refused to sign the treaty and excoriated those who did as treacherous "village chiefs."

Tecumseh was by then twenty-five and was by all accounts from those who knew him perhaps the most handsome Indian they had ever seen. He stood five feet ten inches tall, but because he did not slouch like most red men but walked proudly erect with a graceful, athletic stride, he seemed taller. His hazel eyes were large and in repose friendly. His teeth were beautifully regular and white in his long, aristocratic face, gleaming against his coppery skin. Too much an Indian to adorn himself in the absurd top hats and other trinkets given to other chiefs by traders, all of his garments were of deerskin tanned by black oak bark. A plain hunting shirt hung almost to his knees over deerskin pantaloons, and his moccasins were modestly ornamented with porcupine quills. A single eagle's feather adorned his straight black hair. A British colonel who saw Tecumseh in Canada remembered him as being "in his appearance and noble bearing one of the finest-looking men I have ever seen."

Beautiful Rebecca Galloway was also impressed. Blue-eyed and golden-haired, Rebecca was the daughter of a Scots farmer named James Galloway who had settled near Xenia, the town rising on the ruins of Chillicothe and not far from Lake Erie. Galloway was an unusually cultivated man for a frontiersman, and his incredible collection of three hundred books in an area where those who were literate read only the Bible was sufficient to stock the library of a small wilderness college. He had seen to it that his lovely daughter not only was educated in her own history and literature but spoke fluent Algonquin as well.

The poetic Tecumseh fell deeply in love with Rebecca almost the moment he beheld her beauty and listened to her speak. He called her "the Star of the Lake." She taught him English and corrected his pronunciation. She read the Bible to him, and he was fascinated to learn how the Children of Israel had escaped Egypt in the way his ancestors had discovered America. She taught him Shakespeare's plays and he became fond of *Hamlet*, in which the tragic prince of Denmark was charged like himself with avenging his father. Most of all he exulted in the campaigns of Alexander the Great, the great white sachem who wept just as Tecumseh would have if his own father had left him no worlds to conquer. Rebecca was moved by the humaneness she discovered in this noble Indian, and she aroused in him the most tender feelings. Whenever he visited the Galloways he brought her presents: a silver comb for her gleaming yellow hair, choice furs and meats from the hunt, a birchbark canoe for them to paddle beneath the canopy of trees arching over the idyllic Little Miami. Eventually, he asked her to marry him.

Here was no easy decision for this perceptive and sensitive young beauty. Although she understood his enmity toward her own race, and could sympathize with his thirst to avenge the wrongs dealt himself and his people, she realized that noblest of savages that he might be he was still a savage and that she could never adopt his ways. Neither could Tecumseh abandon his carefree and nomadic life as an Indian, as she asked him to do. He could never accept the white man's fixed and unexciting life, clad in his woolens and cooped up in his house and barns, yoked to his cattle and his crops. With great sorrow he told Rebecca he could not accede to her request, and he never saw her again. But his love for this golden-hearted as well as golden-haired girl, so different from his preconception of white women, may explain his humane treatment of those who came into his power, even more than his horror at the burning of the flatboat captive. Thus the seeds of compassion planted in his soul by his father and by Cornstalk were nourished and cultivated by Rebecca so that this vengeful scourge of her race never harmed any white woman, child, or prisoner who came under his protection.

It is likely that Tecumseh's passionate desire to be the savior of his people was stronger than his love for Rebecca. Certainly after his farewell to her he pursued no other course. All around him in the Northwest Territory he saw nothing but a flood of white settlers since the establishment of Indiana Territory and the emergence of Ohio as the seventeenth state. Farmers from the original thirteen colonies, having exhausted their soil, flowed into the Western Reserve along Lake Erie. Old soldiers settled the Virginia pension lands in Ohio. Fertile valleys blossomed with grain, new cities were laid out. Everywhere, it seemed to a grieving and dismayed Tecumseh, the white men were as numerous as the leaves upon the trees. Inevitably, conflicts arose and there were murders on both sides. So a conference between them was held near Urbana, Ohio. It was there that Tecumseh emerged as the leader of the Northwest tribes.

The power of his oratory would have sufficed to achieve this end, for everyone in attendance—both red and white—agreed that the Algonquin language had never before been spoken with such eloquence and force. Rather it was this youthful chieftain's astonishing grasp of history. He knew every detail of not only Wayne's disastrous Treaty of Greenville and all the other Ohio pacts, but of hundreds upon hundreds of treaties since the Pilgrims of Plymouth got old Massasoit drunk to swindle him of lands he had not the authority to convey. He cited chapter and verse to show how every one of them had been violated by the white men, and after holding his audience in the hollow of his hand for three hours, not a single voice was raised to challenge him. After Urbana, the older sachems, electrified by his presentation, recognized him as their solitary spokesman.

It was in this capacity then that Tecumseh secretly began his campaign to weld not only the northern tribes but those of the Mississippi Valley into a confederation strong enough to halt the white man's western advance and keep him at bay. In this he was assisted by his younger brother Loud Mouth.

Loud Mouth began drinking in his early teens, and very rapidly became addicted to the bottle. In this he was not unusual, for it was a rare Indian such as Tecumseh who could resist the temptations of firewater. Indians did not drink to relax or be merry like most white men but rather simply to get drunk. If there were not enough whisky or rum for all, lots were drawn and the lucky ones consumed what there was, while their terrified squaws and children sought sanctuary in the woods. Too often these orgies ended in bloody brawls in which men were killed or maimed. For almost a decade Loud Mouth was regarded as a drunken loafer by most of his fellow tribesmen. He lost half his sight when the arrow he was drawing on his bow splintered and entered his eye, and the handkerchief he wore over the empty socket gave him a rakish or piratical look that he found useful after his incredible conversion.

It is possible that Loud Mouth had learned the story of the conversion of St. Paul from the Shaker missionaries who preached among the Shawnee. On the road to Damascus Paul had a vision of Christ rebuking him for his merciless persecution of the Christians, becoming thereafter the great apostle to the Gentiles. Similarly, Loud Mouth upon hearing of the death in 1805 of the old prophet Penagashega fell upon the ground in a deep faint. About to be carried off for burial he arose to declare that he had passed a marvelous sojourn in "the Land of the Blessed." En route he had passed through hell to behold thousands of drunkards spouting flame from their mouths. The Great Spirit whose messenger he had become told him that the Indians would never see the Happy Hunting Ground if they did not renounce firewater.

Loud Mouth assumed the new name of Tenskwautawa, meaning the "Open Door" and implying divine inspiration, but because of his insistence that he was now the spokesman of the Master of Life he was called simply the Prophet. He did indeed renounce what he now called crazywater and launched a campaign of abstinence among the tribes and also, probably at the instance of Tecumseh, advocated complete isolation from the contaminating whites. Any imitation of the sinful paleface was repugnant to the Great Spirit, his divine preceptor. The Prophet also introduced the simple life-style and wild dancing by which the Shakers expressed their spiritual devotion, and which, for their constant jerking and shaking, had earned them their peculiar nickname.

Although the whites regarded the Prophet as a faker, he seems to have been in dead earnest. He never again drank and by his total conversion from crazywater and the earnestness of his preaching he gradually commanded great respect among the Northwest tribes. He was a big man of great physical strength, and when he clothed himself in flowing colorful robes with a great headdress of eagle or raven feathers on his brow he seemed immense. A gold ring in his nose and that raffish handkerchief over his missing eye completed the impression of a great medicine man sent by the Great Spirit to save the Indian tribes. The Prophet also promulgated a code peculiarly adapted to his own Shawnee but also acceptable to the other tribes. It was borrowed from the Shakers, a millenarian sect that had migrated to America from England in 1774. They emphasized a life of celibacy, but allowed for the weakness of the flesh by creating a lower order of faithful allowed to have sexual relations but only to reproduce. In this, and much else of their creed, they were the spiritual descendants of the Albigensians of southern France who, six centuries earlier, issued such a shattering challenge to all authority—civil as well as religious—that it was not until two centuries later that a military crusade and an inquisition could destroy them. The Shakers, also like the early Christians preached the simple life and condemned all forms of dishonesty or deceit. The Prophet's code accepted all these tenents but celibacy, and grafted onto it the Shawnee belief that the Master of Life created the Indians first of all and the white people last. But because the Indians fell upon evil ways he transferred their superior learning to the whites. It would not be restored until the Indians overcame their corruption and regained their purity. His weeping, pleading style of oratory was also helpful, as well as his frequent retreats into the woods to commune in solitude with the Master of Life, and thus, in a sense, recharge his spiritual batteries.

Tecumseh, though doubtful at first of the authenticity of his brother's conversion, gradually came to accept it as genuine, and also, with the incisive insight of a born leader, to realize what a splendid instrument of propagation the Great Spirit had placed in his hand. Tecumseh began to look upon their relationship as a partnership between church and state, if such terms are permissible. With his concept of a great, free Indian confederation holding the fertile middle of the continent, Tecumseh felt he was the embodiment of the state; and his brother, with his ability to persuade the Indians to reject the white man with his firewater and other evil contaminations, was in a sense his pope.

In expectation of great numbers of converts to their cause, Tecumseh and the Prophet settled with their early followers on a tongue of land between two creeks near Greenville. To this center of religious and racial propaganda there flowed a steadily thickening stream of recruits that within six months of the Prophet's conversion so alarmed Governor William Henry Harrison of Indiana Territory that he unwisely sought to discredit the Prophet—whom he mistakenly believed to be the true leader at Greenville—by challenging him to produce a miracle. To the Delaware in April 1806, he sent this message:

Who is this pretended Prophet who dares to speak in the name of the Great Creator? Demand of him some proof, at least, of his being the messenger of the Deity. If God really employed him, He has doubtless authorized him to perform miracles that he may be known as a prophet. If he is really a prophet, ask him to cause the sun to stand still, the moon to alter its course, the rivers to cease to flow, or the dead to rise from their graves. If he does these things, you may then believe that he has been sent from God.

To the governor's amazement an incredibly confident Prophet calmly announced that on June 16, 1806, he would perform the requested miracle. It was typical of Harrison with his simplistic, inflexible mind that the announced date did not arouse his suspicions. He certainly must have known that on June 16 there was to be a much-heralded total eclipse of the sun. But he made no move to discredit the "miracle" in advance—and that was just what Tecumseh and the Prophet wanted him to do.

No event in the Northwest—as the modern Midwest was then known—had received such advance publicity as the approaching eclipse. Observation stations were everywhere and staffed by scientists from universities, private life and the federal government. The latter had nine professors stationed at Burlington, Iowa, and there was another observatory at Des Moines. Shelbyville, Kentucky, had an important station, and perhaps the best equipped of all was Harvard University's post at Springfield, Illinois, directly in the path of the eclipse.

It was here in early spring that Tecumseh on one of his westward journeys is believed to have learned of the impending solar eclipse. He had first surprised the scientists there by his ability to speak English, and next by his penetrating questions. How large an area would be darkened by the moon? When would it begin? How long would it last? Elated, Tecumseh turned his horse around and rode rapidly back to Greenville. The Prophet was also overjoyed, taking personal charge of staging the miracle. Couriers were sent far and wide to report that upon the Prophet's command the Great Spirit would turn day into night, and a great crowd of Indians assembled on the tongue of land between the two creeks.

June 16, 1806, dawned bright and clear in the Mississippi basin. A blue sky sparkled above the Prophet's center, and a great throng of Indians assembled there. Just an hour before the moon was to move between the sun and the earth, the Prophet stepped solemnly from his wigwam. A flowing jet black robe covered his great body from face to feet and on his head was a crown of raven's feathers. Over his missing eye a black handkerchief was drawn. He might have been King Arthur's wizard Merlin stepping out of the Dark Ages, and gasps of awe rippled through the encircling crowd of warriors. Slowly, majestically, the Prophet lifted a summoning hand toward the sun and the moon. Gradually, deliberately, the outer rim of the moon crossed the inner curve of the sun. An unearthly, ashen hue began to descend from the heavens. Wood thrushes trilled their evening serenade and then fell silent. Clucking chickens slipped into sleep, and cows lay down in the fields. All was silent and dark upon the earth, and in the heavens above, Venus and Mars shone brilliantly, the stars Sirius and Capella were visible, and three bright bodies could be seen in the belt of Orion.

Then the Prophet cried out to the Great Spirit in a deep, supplicating voice, entreating him to take his divine hand from the face of the sun—and it was done. Light gradually reclaimed the area, and as the roaring, whooping Indians began to dance in a frenzy of exaltation, the sleeping animals awoke and resumed their daylight rounds.

Thus the "miracle" at Greenville, and it seems safe to say that no other event since the white man first appeared west of the mountains had the effect upon the tribes of the Northwest that this marvel produced. News of the Prophet's miracle spread across the prairies like wildfire, reaching as far north and west as the Canadian province of Saskatchewan. Everywhere, in a ceremony designed by the Prophet himself to exploit the childlike credulity of the Indians, there were thousands of converts to the religion of Tenskwautawa, as well as recruits to Tecumseh's great crusade against the white men.

Nothing is known of Governor Harrison's reaction to this "miraculous" discomfiture of the great white father in Vincennes. He could not really object to it, for the incidence of drunkenness among the red men sank to an unheard-of low in the half dozen years between the eclipse and the outbreak of the War of 1812, and the lakes and streams of the Northwest were covered with the medicine bags and carcasses of murdered dogs thrown there by the Prophet's converts obeying his inexplicable order to destroy them. Yet, William Henry Harrison had been publicly tricked and humiliated by a pair of red aborigines, and this could not have been to the liking of a Virginia patrician.

William Henry Harrison was the son of Benjamin Harrison, one of the Virginia signers of the Declaration of Independence. As a young man he decided to study medicine, and was en route to Philadelphia to become a student of the famous Dr. Benjamin Rush when he received word of his father's death. Because the family estate of three thousand acres was just sufficient to support his older brother and not a medical education as well, Harrison decided to pursue a military career, probably because of his passionate interest in Roman military history. He had served under Wayne at Fallen Timbers, where Tecumseh had seen him, had married the daughter of Judge John Cleves Symmes, and had begun a steady though unspectacular climb up the military chain of command. Judge Symmes, who had opposed the match, apparently was unimpressed by his son-in-law, observing: "He can neither bleed, plead nor preach, and if he could plow I would be satisfied. His best prospect is in the army; he has talents, and if he can dodge well a few years, it is probable he may become conspicuous."

Conspicuous he was not, for William Henry Harrison was one of those thin, wiry men who live frugally, eat and drink sparingly and almost never get sick. He was the essential bureaucrat, always able to do a creditable job, but without vision, unable to rise above himself, to innovate or change. He did have integrity, although it did not always conform to any abstract concepts of such and seldom got in the way of his ambition. His record as a moral, sober citizen was impeccable, and in the bitter presidential campaign of 1840, as he prepared to ride his military glory into the White House, his enemies went over his career with a magnifying glass searching for the merest blemish that could be blown into a blimp, and finding only that he occasionally drank whisky or hard cider, had once owned a distillery, and in a U.S. Army in which the *S* often stood for *sot*, he remained a moderate drinker.

His ambition was much like Abraham Lincoln's—insatiable but concealed—and he successfully deceived the electorate with such disclaimers as this: ". . . some folks are silly as to want to make a President out of this clerk and clodhopper." But they did, and another insight into his character was granted when, having consulted his beloved Roman classics for material to compose his inaugural address, he called upon Daniel Webster, his apointee for secretary of state, to trim his massive manuscript. Webster wore a few pencils down to stubs reducing it to a mere nine thousand words—about a third of its original length—and in so doing "killed seventeen consuls and twelve proconsuls as dead as dried smelts."

But William Henry Harrison did possess one superb skill: as a negotiator for Indian lands. From thirteen treaties with the red men he secured no less than sixty million acres of what was probably then the richest land in the world. His tactics were simple: get them drunk and promise the chiefs annuities if they signed. He did not even need the annuities. As one of the Northwest chiefs arriving at a treaty site was to remark: "Father, we care not for the money, nor the land, nor the goods. We want the whisky. Give us the whisky." Harrison never doubted his own integrity, least of all in his masterpiece, the Treaty of Fort Wayne signed on September 30, 1809. By this he obtained three million acres covering the west central portion of Indiana for $8,200 in cash and $2,350 in annuities: a paltry $10,550, or three and a half mills an acre—35 percent of one penny—for land that settlers would buy for $2 an acre, thus enriching the U.S. treasury by $6 million. Ten thousand dollars spent to earn six million! Here was legal larceny on a scale unrivaled anywhere in the world, but William Henry Harrison regarded it as just another good deal. In his heart Harrison believed in the concept that another age would describe as "Manifest Destiny," a stirring phrase meant to justify the divinely ordained mission of the American nation to occupy the whole of the North American continent. He agreed absolutely with John Quincy Adams, who deified the "rights" of the many dispossessing the few in an 1802 speech declaring: "What is the right of a huntsman to the thousand miles over which he has accidentally ranged in quest of prey? Shall the liberal bounties of Providence to the race of man be monopolized by one or two thousand. . . ?"

Tecumseh and the Prophet could not have disagreed more emphatically with this illogical defense of the law of the jungle, and they were so outraged by the Fort Wayne swindle, which violated the Indian concept of common ownership of land, that they vowed to kill every chief who countenanced it. Dismayed by this threat, William Henry Harrison finally realized that in the Shawnee brothers he had a real problem, and he sent a messenger to the Prophet's Town to invite the Prophet to discuss the treaty with him at Vincennes.

17

Tecumseh
Challenges Harrison

WHEN HARRISON'S MESSENGER ARRIVED AT THE PROPHET'S TOWN, the Prophet was so angered by the governor's summary order to appear before him that he wanted to kill the courier as a spy. But Tecumseh intervened and told the man to tell Harrison that he would come to the capital personally. On August 12, 1810, at the head of four hundred hand-picked warriors, all in full war paint and feathers, Tecumseh departed the Tippecanoe for Vincennes. On his arrival he pitched camp outside the town and made for Grouseland, the governor's home, accompanied by a bodyguard of thirty armed braves. On the veranda sat Harrison surrounded by all the officers of Indiana, together with their ladies, as well as the chief dignitaries of Vincennes. A guard of a platoon of soldiers with pistols at their belts stood behind them.

Tecumseh was displeased by the arrangement and when the governor's interpreter invited him onto the veranda he declined. "Houses are made for white men to hold councils in," he said, shaking his head. "Indians hold theirs in the open air."

"Your father," the interpreter insisted, "requests you to sit by his side."

"My *father!*" Tecumseh snorted in derision. "The Great Spirit is my father! The earth is my mother, and on her bosom I will recline." With that, he sat cross-legged on the ground with his warriors squatting behind him. Outmaneuvered, Harrison had no alternative but to move the council outside to a grove, where it was halted by a heavy rain. It was not until August 20 that it was resumed.

It was not truly a council but a confrontation. Here two mutually contradictory societies stood face to face: the one complicated and civilized, national, standing on the shoulders of Greece and Rome and motivated by the Judaeo-Christian traditon, counting itself superior in its language and learning, religion and race, in its commerce, technocracy, political organization, and above all in its organization for war; the other simple and primitive, tribal, its population growth either checked or reduced by barren women or fratricidal warfare, actually a Stone Age people, food gatherers and hunters depending on berries, the fruits of the trees and animals for food, dress, shelter and weapons, yet proud and also believing in a creator God called the Great Spirit, and driven by a deeply moral sense of justice. Here was the intruder menacing the indigenous; gunpowder against the arrow and the tomahawk; the surveyor's chain marking off huge, unmeasured hunting grounds in individual homesteads and the fence and plow enclosing them in farm and pasture. Here, in essence, was the irreconcilable conflict between the *owner* of land and the *user* of land, as expressed in the very person of these antagonists: Harrison the Virginia patrician in silks and satins, soldier and scholar, smooth and artful trader surrounded by the full panoply of his government; and opposite him stood Tecumseh, child of nature, educated by the forest, experience and observation, unlettered primitive chief in buckskin at the head of his guard of half-naked braves. If the collision between these two societies came to war, there could be no doubt as to its outcome; and yet, the moment that Tecumseh opened his mouth there was no doubt in the minds of everyone present as to whom would be the personal victor.

"Brothers," he began, "I have made myself what I am. I would that I could make the red people as great as the conceptions of my own mind. When I think of the Great Spirit that rules over all, I would not then come to Governor Harrison to beg of him to tear this treaty into pieces, but I would say to him: 'Brother, you have liberty to return to your own country.'

"Once there was not a white man in all this country. Then it all belonged to the red man, children of the same parents, placed on it by the Great Spirit, to keep it, to travel over it, to eat its fruits and fill it with the same race. Once they were a happy people, but now are made miserable by the white people, who are never satisfied and are always encroaching on our land. They have driven us from the great salt water, forced us over the mountains, and would shortly push us into the lakes. But we are determined to go no farther. The only way to stop this evil is for all red men to unite in claiming a common right in the soil, as it was at the first, and should be now, for it never was divided but belonged to all. No one tribe has a right to sell even to one another, much less to strangers, who demand all and will take no less."

Tecumseh paused, trembling, his face twisted in contempt. "Sell a *country!*" he cried in disdain. "Why not sell the air, the clouds and the great sea, as well as the earth? Did not the Great Spirit make them all for the use of his children?" He paused, recovering his composure, and then concluded his oration by repeating his threat to kill the Fort Wayne chiefs unless the treaty were repudiated.

Harrison arose to make his reply, speaking for about a quarter hour while Tecumseh listened in silence. When the governor sought to justify his dealings with the Indians as just and fair, Tecumseh, falling victim once again to his quick temper, leaped to his feet shouting: "It is false! He lies!" Advancing toward Harrison he let loose a wrathful storm of abuse that stunned the interpreter. An Indiana official who understood Shawnee quickly drew his pistol and ordered a squad of riflemen to the front on the double. Harrison unsheathed his sword and as a Methodist minister rushed into Grouseland to seize a musket to defend Harrison's family, Tecumseh's braves jumped erect with their hands on their tomahawks and their eyes on their leader. At this, Harrison declared the council adjourned, and led his party back into his house, while Tecumseh at the head of his warriors returned to camp. When the council was renewed, nothing came of it, or from a second one held in July 1811. Like Harrison, Tecumseh knew then that war between the British and the Long Knives was practically inevitable. If he wished to serve on the British side, as he did, he realized that he must be stronger; and so, he sent most of his 400 warriors back to the Prophet's Town, and then, with two dozen chosen braves, he began paddling down the Wabash toward the Mississippi and the southern Indians he had not seen since his boyhood.

Tecumseh's mission to the southern tribes—chiefly the Choctaw and Creek—did not begin auspiciously. Almost from the moment he stood on Chickasaw Bluffs from which de Soto had first gazed in awe upon the Father of Waters coiling and uncoiling south, he encountered opposition. His chief opponent was Pushmataha, greatest of the Choctaw mingoes or chiefs who, like Tecumseh, had been a great warrior in his youth, fighting west of the Mississippi and even into Mexico, but always against Indians rather than white men. When the great chief from the north seemed to be gaining recruits among the fire-eating young Choctaw braves, Pushmataha followed him from village to village in what can only be described as a continuing, traveling debate over whether or not the Choctaw should lift the tomahawk against the Long Knives.

Pushmataha's message was simple: the Indians—all of them, not just the Shawnee and Choctaw—were too few and the whites too many. They were not organized for war like the Long Knives were and their weapons were toys in comparison. Such a war, he concluded in every speech, could only end "in the total destruction of our race," and if it erupted, "I shall join your friends, the Americans. . . ." Thus, in every village, whenever the rival chiefs called for a show of tomahawks, many of the young hot bloods opted for Tecumseh, but the great majority of the braves acclaimed Pushmataha.

Though discouraged, Tecumseh and his entourage of splendid warriors pushed farther south into the country of the Creeks.

As Tecumseh came closer to the land of the Creeks he was seized by a sense of exultation. The Muskogee! His mother's people! Founders of the Creek Confederacy! Reaching the ancient Muskogee town of Tuckabatche on the Tallapoosa River he was delighted to behold the entire grand council of the tribe assembled there: no fewer than five thousand braves. The sight of them rekindled his old passion for revenge. Here the murdered father that he had idolized had married his mother . . . here his slain brother Cheeseekau had passed his boyhood . . . here, Tecumseh thought, he would not fail. . . .

A week after his arrival, Tecumseh led his guard of warriors into the great square before the entire council. It was night, and the flames of many fires flickered upon the copper-hued bodies of the Creek audience. Tecumseh and his warriors were naked except for breech clouts, their bodies painted black, symbolic of a state between peace and war. Pouches containing tobacco and sumac leaves dangled from their loins and buffalo tails trailed from their buttocks. In their hands were war clubs painted red and at their belt scalping knives. As though unheeding of the thousands of eyes of Creek warriors fixed upon them, they paraded silently around the square, scattering their pouch leaves upon the ground.

"Purify this ground, O Great Spirit," Tecumseh cried. "Drive out the evil spirits, we beseech thee."

Three times the Shawnee paraded around the square, and at the end of the third the contents of the pouches were emptied into a fire at the base of a pole, and Tecumseh opened his mouth in a shrieking war whoop. It was a piercing, diabolical yell issuing from the Shawnee chief's undying hatred of the Long Knives. It startled the Creeks, and then the Shawnee war dance began.

It was the enactment of a surprise attack. Crouching low, Tecumseh and his braves silently crept up on the unsuspecting enemy. Howling, they rushed upon them with glittering scalp knives held high. Slashing down they came, lifted high once more and shaken wildly as though each blade held a scalp. Now the screeching Shawnee began a bobbing, weaving dance, flitting and whirling among their own shadows and beating their mouths with their hands to produce terrifying staccato cries. The tempo rose to a frenzy. Firelight glinted off their glistening painted flesh. They stamped the earth as though they sought to collapse it. Then, instantly, it was over. Only Tecumseh stood before the ceremonial fire.

"Accursed be the race that has seized on our country and made women of our warriors," he cried in a voice of anguish. His eyes flashed and his body trembled. His audience, entranced, leaned forward. "Our fathers from their graves reproach us as slaves and cowards. I hear them now in the wailing wind. . . .

"I have seen twice twenty and two summers come and go again, and during all that time the want of union has brought disaster and ruin to many Indian tribes." His voice turned sorrowful again, sinking to a whisper, before rising to a shout and becoming charged with passion. His words and phrases broke upon his hushed audience like waves of meaning, and yet they were almost unnecessary, for his expressive features were able to convey all of his swiftly changing emotions—hatred, defiance, friendship, grief, tenderness, revenge, the dire necessity for unity—so that if they had all been deaf, by his gestures, the mobility of his face, and his eloquent, trembling body they would have been able to grasp his message. And that was: "Kill the old chiefs, friends of peace!" he shouted, his defiant eyes falling upon Big Warrior, supreme chief of the Creek Confederacy. "Kill the white man's cattle, his hogs and fowls. Do not work—destroy their wheels and looms. Throw away the plows and everything used by the Americans. Sing the song of the Indians of the northern lakes and dance their dance. Shake your war clubs and shake yourselves, and you will frighten the Americans. Their guns will drop from their hands. The ground will become a bog and mire them, and you may knock them on the head." He paused, his voice and hazel eyes turning pleading. "I will be with you, my Shawnee and I, as soon as our friends the British are ready for us."

Growls of approval among the Creek braves—especially the younger ones—rose to a swelling roar. Tecumseh's face flushed with pleasure, and as he paused a handsome young half-breed chief named Billy Weatherford, but called Red Eagle, asked him why the Indians of the lakes did not themselves hurl back the white man.

"All the Indians must work in the same yoke," Tecumseh replied. "They must show the white man that they are in earnest, not for booty, not for scalps—no! no!—but for all the country they were born in, and all the country the bones of their fathers lie in."

Again came the roars of "*Sequoyah!*" or "Amen!" from that excited throng, and once more the Shawnee chief's features softened in a smile. But he scowled when Big Warrior arose clutching a bundle of red sticks that Tecumseh had given him. His huge coppery body was spotted with white sores, giving him the look of a two-legged leopard. Fixing his eyes on Tecumseh, he called him "a bad man" and said: "Tecumseh has said that when he gives the signal, we should throw away one of these sticks each day until they are gone, and then attack the Americans. He has given bundles of sticks to other tribes. This is his way of coordinating his attack on the Americans. Big Warrior will have no part of this. The Creeks will never attack their friends!" Raising himself to his full height to tower over Tecumseh, he hurled the bundle at him. The Shawnee caught it deftly, handing it to Billy Weatherford.

"Big Warrior's blood is white," he said, sneering, "but Red Eagle's blood is as red as his name. He will fight, and he will use my sticks." Whirling on Big Warrior, Tecumseh cried in a threatening voice: "You do not believe the Great Spirit has sent me! You shall know! When I return to Tippecanoe, I shall stamp my foot—and the earth will tremble!"

Two days later, Tecumseh and his braves set out for Georgia and northern Florida, where he made easy converts among the Seminole. But they were too remote from the Great Lakes to be of any use to Tecumseh, and so were the Osage across the Mississippi in modern Arkansas. Ending his mission on a note of failure, he sorrowfully turned his face toward home. As he neared Tippecanoe, beginning on the night of December 16, 1811, a monstrous earthquake shook the Mississippi Valley. There has never been a greater one. Remembering Tecumseh's threat, the Creeks were awestruck. Even Big Warrior wondered if the great Shawnee chief did not possess supernatural powers.

But when Tecumseh reached the Prophet's Town he was heartbroken to find that a man-made disaster had devastated his headquarters.

18

Battle of Tippecanoe

∾ ALMOST IMMEDIATELY AFTER TECUMSEH AND HIS GUARD OF BRAVES began paddling down the Wabash toward the Mississippi, Governor William Henry Harrison eagerly seized upon his absence to begin his preparations to destroy the Prophet's Town. He had no definite authorization for such an illegal invasion, the Tippecanoe being well inside Indian territory, but he did have the pretext of British incitement of the Indians against white settlers in two resolutions from alarmed American settlements in both Indiana and Illinois.

The British in Canada had no wish to turn the Northwest tribes against the United States. Locked with Napoleon in a fight to the finish they could hardly wish to begin another war in the interior of far-off North America. Because they feared that a French army might attack the Americans supported and supplied by their old Indian allies who had not lost their affection for France, Crown officials in Canada did all possible to restrain Tecumseh. It was not the British who urged the Shawnee chief to war, but Tecumseh who incited the British. And it was also not President Madison or Secretary of War Eustis who unleashed Harrison against the Prophet's Town, but Harrison himself who decided that that school for sedition must be wiped out. He could always quote from Eustis's letter of July 17, 1811: "If the Prophet should commence or seriously threaten hostilities he ought to be attacked, provided the force under your command is sufficient to ensure success."

Even though Eustis three days later repudiated that instruction with a letter declaring that hostilities "should be avoided," Harrison preferred to listen to the earlier order. It is also probable that he took those resolutions from alarmed settlers as his warrant to invade Indian land, even though Tecumseh had warned him that the boundary line was inviolable. "Should you cross it, I assure you that it will be productive of bad consequences." Harrison certainly was aware that Madison, a punctilious observer of the letter of the Constitution he had done the most to bring into being, would not violate its plain provision that a declaration of war could only be made by Congress. Yet, Madison had sent him about 250 regulars from the U.S. 4th Infantry Regiment under the colorful Colonel John Parker Boyd, a soldier who had fought other Indians on the other side of the world when he served the Nizam of Hyderabad in an army that had five hundred elephants. What were these troops for, Harrison might well have asked.

Actually both sides were beating the war drums. In Lexington, Kentucky, where Major Joseph Daveiss, the brother-in-law of Chief Justice Marshall and the district attorney who had prosecuted Aaron Burr, was raising volunteers to join Harrison's army, newspapers ran banner headlines blaring: "WAR! WAR!" At Tippecanoe a Potawatomi chief warned that if Harrison crossed the Wabash, the whites would then overrun tribal lands in Illinois. Shawnee braves boasted: "If they cross . . . we will take their scalps or drive them into the river. . . . The fish will eat their bodies." Thus the powder keg had been stuffed in the customary exchange of threats and insults, needing only some provocation—actual or pretended—to send the spark flashing into it. For Harrison that came after he left Vincennes on September 26, 1811, with an army of 910 men: the army regulars, sixty Kentucky volunteers and six hundred Indiana militiamen. Near the site of modern Terre Haute on the east bank of the Wabash, he built a fort. When Shawnee scouts fired on it, they gave him his excuse to cross.

Tecumseh had explicitly ordered his brother not to fight the white man. He tried to obey. As the Americans approached, emerging from the exhausting terrain of tangled trees, creepers, and vines to gaze in delight on beautifully tall grasslands sweeping majestically toward the lakes, the Prophet sent them a delegation asking for a suspension of hostilities until a council could be held on November 6. Harrison agreed and asked the Indians to recommend a campsite. Here was a strange request, akin to a commander of a city inviting the besieging enemy to roll a Trojan Horse within its walls. Yet the delegates actually suggested an almost impregnable position, and Harrison accepted. It was an anvil-shaped piece of high ground with a swamp and the Wabash to its rear and Burnet's Creek to the front. The one feature that gave the careful Harrison misgivings was a forest of oaks to his left rear flank. Indians could creep unobserved through it in a night attack. However, he also understood that the oaks gave protection to his men stationed there, and that there was an ample supply of wood and water necessary to any camp. So he laid out his position in the shape of a triangle near the anvil's pointed end. The critical point was its southern salient held by Captain Spier Spencer, a tavern keeper commanding a militia company called "the Yellow Jackets" because of the color of their short coatees. Along the three sides of the triangle the regulars of the 4th Infantry were mingled with the Kentucky volunteers and the Indiana militia. The veteran Indian fighter Major Samuel Wells commanded Harrison's riflemen while the mounted troops were under Major Daveiss. Satisfied that his position was sound, Harrison went to bed early.

It is possible that the Indian delegation recommended such a highly defensible campsite because they were familiar with the terrain and believed that the key to the position was that wood of thick oaks at its northern end. Harrison saw this but was not overly concerned because he had great faith in Captain Robert Barton, who commanded a company at the critical point. Another reason for this strange Indian cooperation was that the Prophet was sincerely trying to avoid battle as his brother had ordered. He also was afraid that Harrison was out to destroy his town and burn his corn crop. But the Prophet was no warrior, and his counsel of peace was ignored by the warlike chiefs White Loon, Steve Easter and Winnemac, who had pretended to be Harrison's friend. The Winnebago were especially hot for war. So the Prophet cooked up a "hell brew" that he read—like a medium reading tea leaves—and found that it called for battle. Then he retired to climb a rock from which, when the fighting began, he chanted incantations supposedly designed to make his braves bullet-proof. This, of course, was the sort of derisive myth typical of white frontiersmen always eager to portray Indians as superstitious savages. The Prophet did indeed maintain a steady chanting from his height, but actually only as a form of encouragement. Moreover, the three chiefs in charge of the attack prepared for it intelligently.

Scouts had reported that Harrison rode a light gray horse, which would be tethered outside his tent. The plan was for a hundred braves to creep into position undetected, and then, with all but the American sentinels asleep, to charge into the center of the camp and kill Harrison. If he had somehow become alerted and mounted his gray to ride to the battlefront, they would shoot him off his horse. This band of assassins, crawling "half a mile on their bellies like snakes," actually did reach their jump-off position a few hours before daylight.

But shortly before four o'clock on the morning of November 7, the 4th Infantry bugler—a soldier named Adam Walker—stepped into the general's tent to ask him if he should sound reveille. Harrison was at the moment pulling on his boots and before he could reply, he heard shooting in the vicinity of the left flank where Barton was stationed. At once he ran outside to mount his gray, finding to his dismay that it had wandered off. But there was a bay tethered in its place, and he leaped aboard it at once to gallop toward the threatened area.

What Harrison did not know at the time was that an alert young sentinel—Private Stephen Mars of Kentucky—had saved his army. Wise in the ways of Indians, he had heard the sound of drumming deer hoofs, which he realized at once was signaling. Next he heard the sound of Indians crawling through the brush and fired at the sound. This was the shot Harrison had heard, and it also luckily struck an Indian who screamed, when, according to the disgusted Shabbona, "he should have lain still and died." His comrades also unwisely arose whooping and made for Harrison's tent, an outburst that brought the entire American army to arms. In the ensuing exchange, Private Mars tried to return to camp and was cut down. A few minutes later Colonel Abraham Owen, Harrison's ranking aide, came running out of his tent to find his bay mount gone. Searching for another horse, he found Harrison's gray, vaulted aboard, and as he rode toward the firing was killed by whooping Indians who mistakenly thought they had despatched Harrison.

That worthy, however, had already arrived at his left flank where the Indians had penetrated the oak wood and were launching a heavy attack on Barton's company and Colonel Frederick Geiger's to his right. The Indians struck hardest at the point where both companies were joined, and Geiger's left was broken. But both he and Barton hung on while the quick-thinking Harrison rushed two more companies into the breech. It was a risky move and could have been fatal had the red men suspected that it had left a hole in the line along Burnet's Creek. But they did not and were gradually forced back into the wood from which they had attacked.

Simultaneous with the end of combat on the northwest corner of camp, fierce fighting broke out at the northeast salient held by regulars and three companies of Indiana militia under Colonel Joseph Bartholomew with Major Daviess and the cavalry to his left. Harrison spurred his bay and galloped to the threatened salient. From the intensity of Indian fire he deduced that they were concentrated in a clump of trees immediately to Daveiss's front, and ordered the gallant soldier-lawyer to clear it. At once he charged forward, but with not enough troopers to keep the Indians from gnawing at his flanks. They killed Daveiss, and his scattered dragoons withdrew. Harrison had seen Daveiss's mistake and ordered Captain Josiah Snelling to charge the enemy with his company of 4th Infantry soldiers, and their accurate rifle fire cleared the wood. Then, as though in the third maneuver of a rolling attack but actually only by coincidence, the defeat of the second assault was almost instantly followed by the third—and strongest—Indian charge.

It came against the other, or southern, extremity of Harrison's defensive triangle held by Captain Spier Spencer and his mounted riflemen. Harrison quickly rode toward the sound of battle, dismayed to hear the red men whooping wildly as though about to prevail. He came upon Ensign John Tipton and asked: "Where is Captain Spencer?"

"Dead," Tipton replied.

"Where are the lieutenants?"

"All dead."

"Where is the ensign?"

"Here," Tipton replied.

"Good," said Harrison. "Hold your position and I will relieve you in a minute."

He did, quickly commandeering a company under a Captain Robb and sending it on the double to Tipton's relief, after which he ordered a company of regulars to plug the hole left by Robb's movement. Now the Indians were striking hard at both ends of the triangle, and Harrison moved from point to point searching for any gaps in his line. There were none, and Harrison was content to hold until dawn, when he could determine the enemy's strength. When it came, he saw that both flanks were still under heavy fire and was planning to send Daveiss's remaining dragoons forward on a change at the north end. But by the time he issued the order, the ancient Major Wells was already attacking with his infantry, putting the Indians to flight with their bayonets—those "Long Knives" that they dreaded. Now the dragoons did sweep forward to pick off the stragglers, but their mounts moved slowly over swampy ground. A similar charge was launched at the other flank, where the red men were routed.

General Harrison was now content to hold his position throughout

November 7. Careful as ever, he wanted to be sure that the report of the arrival of Tecumseh with reinforcements was not in fact a rumor. It was. Tecumseh was still far away, while his brother had fled, hiding with a band of Wyandot on Wildcat Creek, complaining endlessly that his incantations did not work because his squaw had carelessly touched and defiled his sacred vessels. On November 8 the Americans moved cautiously into the Prophet's Town. Finding it deserted, they set all buildings afire and also destroyed the corn harvest. They found British rifles and muskets, which they seized.

Harrison's losses were 61 killed and 127 wounded, while the Indians lost from 25 to 40 dead and an unknown number of wounded, whom, as was their custom, they had carried off to safety. As battles go, Tippecanoe was not much, but it was received with great jubilation all over the Northwest and even in the original states of the Northeast and South. And it was explosive enough to propel William Henry Harrison into the White House.

Tecumseh did not reach the Tippecanoe until late February or early March of 1812. When he beheld the desolation of his headquarters he was stricken with grief. "I stood upon the ashes of my own home, where my own wigwam sent up its fire to the Great Spirit, and there I summoned the spirits of the braves who had fallen in their vain attempt to protect their homes from the grasping invader, and as I snuffed up the smell of their blood from the ground I swore once more eternal hatred—the hatred of an avenger."

Tecumseh almost murdered the Prophet when he found him. His mumbled excuses, his attempt to shift the blame on to the Winnebago, only fueled his brother's anger so that in a rage Tecumseh seized him by the hair and threatened to kill him. The Prophet slunk away to the upper waters of the Mississippi, where open tent flaps gave him a sympathetic welcome. But he never saw his brother again, for Tippecanoe had the adverse effect of sending the grieving Shawnee chief flying into the arms of Great Britain.

He would show himself to be a great commander in His Majesty's service, so able that it may be conjectured that if William Henry Harrison had not been so greedy for Indian land, and if Rebecca Galloway at sixteen had been patient and persevering, willing to spend a few years teaching Tecumseh to read and write as well as speak English, gentling him, taming him, with sweet subtlety drawing from his valiant heart the venom of his hatred for her people, and then turning him loose in her father's library to immerse himself in military history before marrying him as an American citizen—there might not be today a Dominion of Canada.

19

The War Hawks

⟋ WAR HAWKS WAS A DERISIVE NICKNAME PINNED ON THE FEDERALISTS BY Thomas Jefferson during the Naval War with France and was transferred after the mid-term election of 1810—one of the most momentous political upheavals in American history—to that band of young, boisterous and belligerent Republicans who successfully seized control of the House of Representatives by expelling scores of older, veteran members.

In this Twelfth Congress there were 142 representatives in the House, of whom sixty-one were newly elected members. Nine of these were faithful Federalists, a few were peace Republicans, and a dozen or so others were uncommitted on the question of war. About thirty were aggressive advocates of another war with Great Britain. Because they were unified and knew exactly what they wanted—in the way of Lenin and his Bolsheviki during the Russian Revolution—they were able to dominate the Republican Party, and were as contemptuous of the prerogatives of the old lieutenants of Jefferson and Madison as they were of the supposed seniority of the Senate. Ardently Jeffersonian in policy, sharing Madison's deep distrust of the Federalists and Britain, they were to a man the product of the frontier spirit of the southern and western districts. Many of them had not yet passed the age of thirty-five years. Born after the liberating victory at Yorktown, they were a new generation of politicians impatient with the dominance of Revolutionary War veterans. Above all, they would not truckle to any European powers, either by appeasement or a false humility, preferring instead outright hostility if that alone would preserve that highly developed sense of honor that was the legacy of their birth and life on the frontier, where men looked each other in the eye and stood ready to defend their sacred names with rifle, pistol or fists.

When they gathered at their "war messes"—the big round tables at the boardinghouses on New Jersey Avenue—they were as exuberant as a team of college football players, rising with war whoops when they heard of a particularly satisfying victory over the Federalists, circling the table in a bobbing, weaving Shawnee war dance with right arms raised as though grasping tomahawks and the left hand striking their open mouths to produce sharp staccato battle cries.

They were not exactly novices in parliamentary maneuver, for many like Henry Clay of Lexington, Kentucky, were veterans of state legislatures, and they perceived at once that the power they coveted resided in the post of Speaker of the House, and that the route to that eminence ran through the Republican congressional caucases. When the Twelfth Congress was convened by Madison on March 4, 1811, a month in advance of the prescribed date, they were ready with Clay as their candidate and the votes to elect him. On the very first ballot this thirty-four-year-old lawyer was elected by a vote of seventy-five to thirty-eight for William Wyatt Bibb, a Georgia physician who came forward as a peace candidate.

Although there is a popular misconception—shared by some capable historians—that Henry Clay was born into a Kentucky frontier family of nineteen children, his small gray eyes actually first saw daylight in a Virginia homestead fifteen miles north of Richmond on April 12, 1777. He was the seventh of nine children born to the Reverend John Clay, sometimes called "Sir John" for unknown reasons, and Elizabeth Hudson Clay. Although Henry Clay in later years was guilty of pandering to the American public's fondness for politicians reared in poverty, born in a log cabin and pretending to have been "reared in homespun and fed on hoecake," his father was anything but a pauper. When Henry was born Clay, Senior, possessed four hundred acres of land willed to him by his father in Henrico County about ten miles above Richmond, plus the homestead of 464 acres brought to him by his wife. He possessed at his death twenty-nine slaves.

The Reverend Sir John was the descendant of British ancestors supposed to have migrated to Virginia in the early part of the 1600s. He also may have been a dancing master before abandoning that frivolous pursuit for the more serious career of Baptist minister celebrated for sonorous sermons atop a rock on the South Anna River before leading his candidates for baptism into the stream below.

Elizabeth Clay was still in her thirties when her husband died, and she was still most attractive with her dark hair and dark eyes and a beautiful figure that child-bearing had not disfigured. She caught the eye of Captain Henry Watkins, ten years her junior, and became his wife, giving birth to seven more children: if not a record in those child-bearing days of a country whose prolificacy astonished the world, her productivity is at least noteworthy.

Henry Clay's early education—the other side of the Abe Lincoln coin—was indeed scanty. "The Slashes," as the infertile district where he was born was called, offered little opportunity for study. At best, young Henry had about three years of schooling under a schoolmaster named Peter Deacon, who, in the tradition common to those days, was both intemperate and itinerant. Probably Clay also had some instruction from his parents, for his mother was extremely intelligent and his stepfather, quick to see that the youngster was precocious, also encouraged him to read.

Henry was too young to remember the exciting and sometimes frightening era of his birth. But his mother could not forget 1781 when "Butcher" Banastre Tarleton came raiding, arriving at her home the day after her husband John was buried. She had just sent the only white man in the homestead out the back door when Tarleton's riders burst through the front entrance. They ripped open her beds, scattering their feathers out the window, stole her white satin wedding dress, seized some of the slaves and then, suspecting that Sir John's grave might actually contain buried treasure, either threatened to plunge or actually did thrust their swords into it. When Tarleton himself came inside, the story goes, the indignant widow Clay turned her tongue upon him, and to placate her the abashed Green Dragoon emptied a sack of coins on the table. A Rebel to the core, Mrs. Clay seized the Judas treasure and hurled it into the fire. Here the legend ends, but it is to be hoped that once the sound of departing whoops and hoof-beats had subsided and the fire cooled, this gallant and sensible lady retrieved the hard cash so rare and so necessary to life in those days.

The next decade of Henry Clay's life was a compound of his brief exposure to the drudgery of learning the three R's in the log-cabin schoolhouse and the fun of growing up barefoot on a farm. True, there was hoeing and digging to be done, but there were also pony rides, frog hunts in the marshes, traps to be set along the creek bank or the fence rows for mink, muskrats and skunk, with the occasional mind-boggling catch of a beautiful red fox. When the wealthy Samuel Watkins came to visit his brother, there was fun and games with his children. Best of all to young Henry, thrilled by reports of the speeches of the great men of Virginia meeting in Richmond in 1788 to debate ratification of the Constitution, was the chance to slip away into the woods, the cornfield or behind the barn to practice the art of speaking, that "art of all arts" as he later called it. Whenever he could he would wander barefoot into the capital, where he would be taken for just another backcountry yokel. No one, of course, would suspect the monstrous ambition burning in his breast.

But it became apparent in 1792 after his family—drawn by relatives' glowing reports of the opportunities in Kentucky—decided to move to the Blue Grass. Henry for some unknown reason was left behind in Richmond, at first as a fifteen-year-old grocery clerk, and then—probably because of his clear and legible handwriting—as a deputy clerk in the High Court of Chancery. That was where the celebrated legist Judge George Wythe found him. Wythe's right hand was so crippled by rheumatism or gout that he could no longer write. He needed an amanuensis, and young Henry Clay's beautiful hand got him the job.

Wythe at once saw the promise in his young clerk, opening his library to him and even—without success—encouraging him to study the classics. But Henry Clay's mind, though retentive, was chiefly for the world around him: for people and profits, for prestige and place, not for dead languages and legal precedents, or the profound and stultifying pages of Coke, Blackstone and Grotius. Yet, he was perceptive enough to realize that if he were to satisfy his ambition he must sit down and study enough to grasp the principles of law and the standards of admission to the bar. This he did under Wythe's direction and for about a year under a Richmond lawyer who would become a Virginia attorney general. In November 1797, he was examined and licensed to practice law in the Old Dominion.

Henry Clay was then sixteen and physically mature, standing six feet and one inch tall, his yellow hair prematurely white. His carriage, though no longer awkward, was rather nonchalant suggesting not grace but confidence. He was not handsome, with his small gray eyes, a long slightly hooked nose with a high, sloping forehead and his mouth "a long and deep horizontal cut" so wide that he still complained that he had not learned to spit. It was a pallid face indeed, but most expressive and sensitive. With this there went a melodious voice and oratorical style, which with years of practice would develop into a marvelous political instrument. In fine, Henry Clay was an actor. In voice and manner he covered the range of human emotions from the majestic to the tender. His friendly manner won him instant loyalties and his warm firm handshake was legendary.

These were the gifts that Henry Clay took with him when he decided to follow so many other Virginia lawyers over the dangerous trail leading across the mountains through Cumberland Gap and up the Wilderness Road that Daniel Boone had blazed in 1775 and down into Lexington, Kentucky, and prosperity.

Henry Clay did prosper in Kentucky, his prowess at winning so many of the land lawsuits that abounded in the frontiers was rivaled only by his reputation for drinking, dancing and gambling. At one merry dinner party he delighted his comrades by mounting the sixty-foot-long table bottle in hand to dance its length back and forth, laughing uproariously as the clamor of his audience counterpointed the tinkle and crash of smashed crystal and china. Next day when the innkeeper presented a bill of $120 lost in shattered tableware he promptly paid it. At the close of a card game, when his friend John Bradford owed him $40,000, he generously agreed to settle for a note of $500. At a later game Clay was Bradford's debtor for $60,000, and the $500 note was returned.

Clay was quick to sow these wild oats, for at the age of twenty-two he married eighteen-year-old Lucretia Hart. Though neither beautiful nor bright, Lucretia had the attraction of being the daughter of wealthy and influential Thomas Hart. She was also a devoted wife, bearing eleven children. Now well-connected, Clay's rise in politics was meteoric. At the age of twenty-nine, before he had reached the constitutional age of thirty necessary for service in the Senate, he had been elected to the senior chamber, where he served two partial terms. Before coming to the House in 1811, he had been speaker of the Kentucky assembly, making himself famous for his opposition to some unremembered member's resolution to outlaw British legal precedents in Blue Grass courts. Despite the widespread anti-British feeling in Kentucky, and a poll predicting that the vindictive measure would pass by a five-to-one vote, Clay left the speaker's chair to declare that such a ridiculous law "would wantonly make a wreck of a system fraught with the intellectual wealth of centuries," succeeding in preventing adoption of the law by amending it to make it apply only to British decisions made after the Fourth of July 1776.

For Clay to have taken this responsible and moral stand in the face of such a popular measure discredited those who charged that he was a complete opportunist—as though a politician could ever survive without at least a touch of that useful if not-always lovable trait—and demonstrated that he was balanced enough to find value in despised Old Mother England. Thus the man the War Hawks chose to lead their drive to obtain respect for America throughout the world, cleanse the frontier of the Indian menace and expel Great Britain from North America. He was bold, disarming, candid, calculating, dominating with his growing power of oratory so completely that when he was "up"—like Winston Churchill—the Senate adjourned so that its members might go over to the junior chamber to hear him speak. He might also have been the perfect caricature of his boisterous followers whom Josiah Quincy derisively described as "Young politicians with their pin-feathers yet unshed, the shell still sticking upon them—perfectly unfledged, though they fluttered and cackled on the floor."

20

Madison Yields: War!

~ PRESIDENT JAMES MADISON AT FIRST REGARDED THE WAR HAWKS AND especially their leader, Henry Clay, as adversaries. Precise and restrained as he was, he had no sympathy for Clay's bluff and rhetoric or the exuberant style of his followers. Madison was quite aware that the outcry for war with Britain was regional, coming almost exclusively from the frontier, with little but lukewarm support to be found in New England and such northeastern states as New York and New Jersey. In mercantile Massachusetts he might find open opposition. Neither did he underestimate the military power of Great Britain. In the Royal Navy were no less than 180 ships-of-the-line, supported by a huge fleet of smaller warships as well as a formidable merchant marine. British armies under the Duke of Wellington were obviously winning the Peninsular War in Spain. Should Britain ultimately triumph on the Continent, all these ships and men would be free to attack America. At that moment in November 1811, when the War Hawks came to Washington, such an eventuality seemed unlikely, but it could happen. And if the war to conquer Canada did not end in quick and easy victory as Clay and his cohorts obviously anticipated, what then?

The United States simply could not endure a prolonged war. Madison's friend and mentor Jefferson had so thoroughly meat-axed the armed forces that the army was hardly more than a ceremonial guard and the American coast was protected by a "mosquito fleet" of gunboats. Although Jefferson after the Chesapeake Incident did indeed obtain authorization in February 1808 to recruit six thousand soldiers forming eight new regiments, the U.S. Army was still a military pygmy compared to the British giant. The gunboats were a farce. Having heard of how they could maneuver in the harbors of the Barbary Coast, the economy-minded Jefferson had seized upon them as a cheap replacement for expensive sea-going warships. They were about sixty feet long with guns fore and aft, able to sail only in tranquil harbor waters but bound to sink in heavy seas. Even harbor storms could sink them, and when they occurred the guns had to be stowed below for ballast. But they were cheap—only $10,000 apiece—and Jefferson built over a hundred of them, of which about sixty were still in commission. When one of them was torn from its moorings by a spring tide and heavy gale, it was found perched in a cornfield, causing a Federalist wit to propose the toast: "To Gunboat Number Three: If our gunboats are no use on the water, may they at least be the best on earth!"

These were the realities that the War Hawks in their naive enthusiasm for war were scornfully brushing aside as the bleats of a timorous president. Speaker Clay was bumptiously asserting that there was no need for soldiers of the regular army to invade Canada: Kentucky backwoodsmen could conquer the northern neighbor by themselves! Here was an absurd optimism that was the unfortunate consequence of William Henry Harrison's victory at Tippecanoe: militia alone could lay Canada at the feet of the House of Representatives. They expected "Little Jemmy" to bow to their will. Indeed they regarded him by his retiring nature as unfit to govern in such tumultuous days. John C. Calhoun of South Carolina, one of Clay's most trusted lieutenants, openly declared that Madison lacked "the commanding talents to control those about him."

But James Madison was no truckler, and certainly not the man to make deals with youthful first-termers with "their pin-feathers still unshed." Nevertheless, much as he might not resemble a wild-eyed warrior in the mode of Andrew Jackson, he was a man of the highest principles who would absolutely not bend.

Madison was not going to ask Congress for a possibly disastrous war with Britain just to satisfy these rude frontiersmen. James Madison, "the father of the U.S. Constitution," and probably its strictest constructionist, would not give executive approval of a war unless he was convinced that there was no other course consistent with his country's honor, well-being and self-respect.

Gradually this stand became clear to the War Hawks, especially after they realized that their own objectives were secondary to those of the northeastern and central Atlantic states, whose votes would be needed if a war resolution were to be rammed through Congress. So Henry Clay, a landlubber whose constituents wore buckskin and never saw or smelled salt water, turned to the sea. If these badly needed allies regarded "Free Trade and Sailors' Rights" as their battle cry, then it would also be trumpeted by the War Hawks. Newspapers in the seaport cities of Boston, Newport, New York and Norfolk had great fun with these frontiersmen in homespun whose hearts bled so freely for shippers and sailors. Yet, if they could impute duplicity to a Speaker who had never seen the ocean, they could not refute his reasoned advocacy of the rights of the sea when he said:

> We were but yesterday contending for the indirect trade—the right to export to Europe the coffee and sugar of the West Indies. Today we are asserting our claim to the direct trade—the right to export our cotton, tobacco and other domestic products to market. Yield this point, and tomorrow intercourse between New Orleans and New York, between the planters on the James River and Richmond, will be interdicted. For, sir, the career of encroachment is never arrested by submission.

It is unfair to suggest that Clay and his War Hawks cynically adopted the sea as a cover for their true purpose. The Speaker did feel a genuine compassion for impressed American seamen. He was a true patriot with a clear vision of America's great destiny, and he could not bear to see his country humbled at sea by Britain or Napoleon or both. So he was willing to employ the slogan of "Free Trade and Sailors' Rights" if it would help to secure the frontier and expel Britain from North America.

On the subject of annexation of Canada the War Hawks were less subtle. They openly advocated it, not as a reason for going to war, but to seize it if war came. William Armisted Burwell of Virginia, who had been Jefferson's secretary, arose during Congressional debate on the subject to declare: "The expulsion of the British from Canada has always been deemed an object of the first importance to the peace of the United States." There was, of course, some subtlety in this remark, for the British could only be expelled by force—war—and a conquering army in Canada could become an army of occupation. Clay was more direct: "I am not for stopping at Quebec or anywhere else. I would take the entire continent."

The eloquent John Randolph of Virginia, who had left the Republicans to form a peace party called Quids, or others, bitterly charged without reservation that if war came, it would be because of American aggression, declaring with biting sarcasm: "Agrarian cupidity, not maritime right, urges this war . . . we have heard but one word—like the whippoorwill, but one eternal, monotonous tone: Canada! Canada! Canada!"

But the War Hawks had the votes, and when Peter Porter of New York, Clay's reliable chairman of the House Foreign Relations Committee, brought in his report on American preparedness, the full Congress went even further than his recommendations. An increase in the regular army of twenty-five thousand men was authorized, instead of the ten thousand suggested by Porter. As an inducement to enlist there would be a bounty of $16.00 per man and a bonus of three-months' extra pay upon discharge, plus 160 acres of land. Two major generals were to be appointed.

Tragically, the Navy got next to nothing: a meager $300,000 to repair three frigates. The Senate rejected a motion to build thirty new frigates, and the House ignored a proposal for twenty-five ships-of-the-line and forty frigates. In a Congress dominated by frontier landlubbers bellowing "Free Trade and Sailors' Rights" the means of securing them—a powerful navy—were ignored. So was the big-navy advocates' argument that "protection of commerce is the protection of agriculture." Although Madison would later be denounced for having failed to provide for a navy, it was the War Hawks who were at fault. Because they simply could not comprehend the importance of sea power, they could not realize that Napoleon was losing the struggle with the British-organized Allies because his navy could not match Britannia's. Neither could Madison or Jefferson, both planters and both landlubbers with soil not salt water in their souls.

If the United States had begun construction in 1811 and 1812 of a powerful new navy, the British then would have listened more respectfully to American complaints. As was to be demonstrated during the War of 1812, warships could be built in three or four months. Why, then, this unseemly haste toward war? Even then in that fateful spring of 1812 Napoleon was manifestly preparing to invade Russia to enforce the Treaty of Tilsit, and though he would encounter disaster there at the hands of General Winter, no one could have suspected that. Moreover, it would not be until April 1814 that Napoleon would abdicate and be exiled to Elba, and thus it would be two years before Britain would actually be disengaged and able to punish their former colonies for what they believed to have been their "stab in the back." Surely by mid-1813 the United States would have possessed a respectable army *and* navy.

By then the U.S. Navy would have been steam-powered!

Robert Fulton's steamboat *Clermont* had been in regular service since 1807, and by 1810 Fulton had completed his shipyard in Pittsburgh and was building his steamboats for the western rivers. Steam applied to naval vessels not only would have revolutionized sea warfare but would have brought the Mistress of the Seas to her knees, or at least kept her at bay off the American coast. British wind-driven warships becalmed in American coastal waters truly would have been sitting ducks—there is no better phrase!—for self-propelled American warships armed with long-range guns. Just as the welding of guns to internal-combustion engines—tanks and airplanes—gave Hitler his tremendous early advantage in World War II until America outproduced him, the introduction of steam-powered warships in 1813 would have made the Royal Navy obsolete. One such shattering naval victory of steam over sail would have made a war-weary Britannia much more anxious for parley than revenge. This, of course, never happened, and was never even considered. That was because it was and still is not in the character of the American people to be patient. Quick fixes and ready solutions, these are the foolish Yankee panaceas. George Troup of Georgia, a not-always-manageable War Hawk, put his finger on this failing when he cautioned his fellow Republicans:

> Sir, if the people are to be reasoned into a war, it is too soon, much too soon, to begin it. If their representatives are to be led into it by the flowers of rhetoric, it is too soon, much too soon, to begin it. Contrary to the practice of all nations, we declare war first and make preparations afterward. More magnanimous than wise, we tell the enemy when we will strike, where we will strike and how we will strike.

The gentleman was a true prophet.

One of the great mysteries—and tragedies—of this war that neither side really wanted was why President James Madison eventually yielded to the pressure of the War Hawks. One of the most plausible yet the least acceptable of these explanations is that Madison traded a war for four more years in the White House. This cynical and simplistic theory is based on nothing more than the fact that Henry Clay called on Madison in the critical spring of the election year of 1812 at the head of a delegation of War Hawks. At that time, presidential nominations were not made as now at national party conventions attended either by delegates chosen at state preferential primaries or by an elite group of them composed of former presidents and active Congressmen. Rather they were nominated at party caucuses or by state legislatures.

At this White House meeting the Speaker is supposed to have given the president an ultimatum: either support the war faction or lose the nomination, and the president acquiesced. Clay denied that any such deal was made, although Representative James Fisk of Vermont insisted that it had been. Madison, an inveterate diarist, left no record of such an arrangement. Neither was Clay the kingmaker that the story suggests. One of those first-termers that Madison distrusted, Clay had not yet acquired the power to make or break presidents. Furthermore, there were no other candidates in the field against Madison. To whom would Clay have turned? Himself? If he had, he would have wrecked the party. Obviously, the Republicans had to run on the Jefferson-Madison record. Certainly there was nothing in James Madison's character to suggest that he would consent to such a contemptible deal, either in the interest of a second term for him or of party solidarity. His position on war was compatible: he would not start one, but if Congress declared one he would approve it. This was eminently consistent in a man who had written into the Constitution a provision that only Congress should have the power to declare war. A president could only recommend that it do so.

Contemporary analysts have suggested that Madison was not as pacifist as his predecessor. But this is not true, because, as has already been shown, Jefferson was not a doctrinal pacifist and had fought a war without a Congressional declaration; and Madison as secretary of state under him fully agreed with his policy of avoiding involvement in the Napoleonic Wars. Again it was not in keeping with the character of Madison to have been a secret warmonger, and he could certainly not have deceived his mentor Jefferson on that point. What seems to have happened actually was that Madison only yielded to the War Hawks gradually, step-by-step, as each attempt to negotiate with the British failed; and these rebuffed appeals and British wrongs were fully described in his "war message" to Congress of June 1, 1812. He issued it only because he had become convinced that there was no longer any possibility of persuading Britannia to revoke these arbitrary and infuriating Orders in Council that were the root cause of the dispute between the two nations.

It was an eminently reasonable and unemotional conclusion, but the great tragedy of the War of 1812 was that even as Madison's message was read to a hushed Congress, to be followed on June 18 by his signature on a declaration of war itself, the movement to revoke the offending Orders was in full progress in Great Britain.

If the British minister to the United States had posted home complete reports of the seven-month-long war debate in Congress, it is possible that his country would not have been so bewildered by American truculence. Whitehall might then have realized that the Orders in

Council were not the only cause of Yankee belligerence and that there were indeed two others: weapons and whisky flowing to the Indians on the frontier and the presence of the Royal Army on American soil and in Canada. Whether or not the War Hawk program for securing that vulnerable frontier and expelling Britain from North America would have changed the unbending defense of the Orders by Prime Minister Spencer Perceval or, conversely, angered both them and the British public is not known. Nor is it really worthy of speculation.

But it is known that Spencer was almost universally despised as "an industrious mediocrity of the narrowest type," hated by merchants facing ruin under pressure of the American embargo and members of the House of Commons, whose demands for repeal of the Orders he steadily ignored. That is why, when he was assassinated on May 11 by a disgruntled and maniacal merchant named John Bellingham, everyone who was worried about the approaching and unwelcome war cheered. Then when his cabinet, buffeted by a rising clamor for their heads, obligingly resigned en masse, the applause, as theater critics say, "was thunderous." Finally, when Robert Banks Jenkinson, second Earl of Liverpool, formed a new government and promised immediate re-examination of the odious Orders, the entire nation was relieved.

Generally Lord Liverpool has been credited by historians as having conducted a sound but unimaginative administration during his service as Britain's prime minister from 1812 to 1827. Unfortunately for his reputation he had somehow provoked the wrath of the caustic Benjamin Disraeli, who would himself one day be at the helm of Britain's ship of state. Christening him "the Arch-Mediocrity," Disraeli described him thus:

> The Arch-Mediocrity had himself some glimmering traditions of political science. He was sprung from a laborious stock, had received some training, and though not a statesman, might be classed among those whom the Lord Keeper Williams used to call "statemongers." In a subordinate position his meager diligence and his frigid method might not have been without value; but the qualities that he possessed were misplaced, nor can any character be conceived less invested with the happy properties of a leader. In the conduct of public affairs his disposition was exactly the reverse of that which is the characteristic of great men. He was peremptory in little questions, and great ones he left open.

This is Disraeli at his peevish best, but an unbiased judgment comes from Sir George Trevelyan, the famous historian who believed that

Liverpool was unjustly blamed for Tory policies producing a country that could "organize herself for no social purpose, and allowed her millions to become the economic prey of the blind forces of war and of the unguided Industrial Revolution." Others have claimed that he was "pilloried . . . for the faults of mill-owners and justices." In essence he seems to have been a colorless plodder, but nevertheless "a man of good will."

At the very outset of his administration, however, Liverpool's attempt to inquire into the origin of the Orders in Council provoked a storm of outrage when it was learned that the House of Commons could not find a single member willing to support them.

Rage turned almost to apoplexy after the lone witness defending the Orders pooh-poohed reports that the embargo was causing famine in Britain with the obtuse remark: "Oatmeal and water are good enough for Englishmen." But John Bull recovered his sense of humor when it was suddenly realized that no one knew who had authored the Orders. Their supposed father, Sir James Stephen, declined an invitation to testify, and so on June 23, 1812, after five years of provocation of the Americans, Liverpool announced their repeal.

The London *Times* said: "May all the expected good follow this act," and all concerned British people began to breathe freely again. It seemed to them that war had been averted, and that once President Madison and Congress learned of the revocation they would rescind the declaration. This was the attitude expressed by the *Times:* "As the hostilities of America have been built on a foundation which is now withdrawn, the hostilities must fall to the ground also."

But they did not, and the suggestion of some historians that if there had been a trans-Atlantic cable in those days, news of Liverpool's intention to repeal the Orders would have preceded Madison's war message to Congress and thus averted a war, ignores the existence of the other two *casus belli* as completely as the British did. So did the Earl Bathurst, the secretary for war and the colonies, as late as February 19, 1813, when he arose in the House of Lords to ask of America:

Was there any country in Europe that had in the same time made the same advances in population, commerce, products of industry? And to what did she owe this very commerce of which she was so jealous, but to the superiority and protection of the British Navy? (Prolonged applause.) And was it not reasonable to have expected this might be felt by her and that if there were any casual irritation it would be passed over—any little object of dispute, it would be left to the decision of sober and friendly argument?

Thus spake Colonel Blimp, in Robert Browning's phrase, "a man jumping to his feet with his mouth full of bread and cheese and spluttering that he wasn't going to listen to any more damned nonsense!"

Casual irritation? Little object of dispute? Sober, friendly argument? Really, my Lord?

21

Baltimore Riot/
Disaster at Detroit

~ BY A VOTE OF SEVENTY-NINE TO FORTY-NINE IN THE HOUSE AND NINE-
teen to thirteen in the Senate—far from being the unanimous-but-one
votes that would put America into World Wars One and Two—a
pathetically prepared United States of America was at war with Great
Britain, the most powerful nation on earth. War had come chiefly
because of the vainglorious oratory and the naive belligerence of that
band of freshman Congressmen, who even at the outset were leaping
whooping to their feet in their war messes and circling the tables in
their ridiculous Shawnee caper. Like all amateurs in armed conflict,
they did not know but would soon learn that the war dance always
ends in a dirge.

Nevertheless, it cannot be denied that their timing was perfect,
Britain, engaged against Napoleon in Spain, could spare only about
four thousand regulars—reinforced by about three thousand trustworthy Canadians—to defend an open border running about 1,700 miles.
Moreover, British North America numbered fewer than 500,000 souls,
most of whom were French-Canadians indifferent to the cause of
British arms, as opposed to about 7,500,000 Americans. If ever the
time for attack was ripe, this was it.

America, however, was incredibly unprepared. Her Navy was in comparatively good shape, but her ground forces were a marching mock-

ery of the war whoops raised by Henry Clay and his War Hawks the day war began. There were fewer than seven thousand men in the regular army. True, Congress had voted an increase of fifty thousand men, but in the first six months of hostilities only five thousand men volunteered to serve in "Mr. Madison's War." To this could be added about fifty thousand militia, available for use only as the loyalty and politics of the state governors might dictate.

Commanding this force were ranking officers who seemed to be prodigies of senility or incompetence.

Henry Dearborn, the senior major general, had fought with John Stark at Bunker Hill and marched to Quebec with Benedict Arnold. He had also served as secretary of war, in which office he distinguished himself for his reluctance to apprehend Aaron Burr. Latterly, whatever ardor he possessed had been smothered in the soft life of the Boston customhouse. Taking the field again at the age of sixty-one, he was nicknamed "Granny" by his troops.

Thomas Pinckney, another Revolutionary War veteran, was sixty-two, and, in the words of a ranking Congressman, "as fit for his place as the Indian Prophet would be for Emperor of Europe."

The senior brigadier was James Wilkinson: Wilkinson of the Conway Cabal, the friend of the author of the Newburgh Addresses, secret agent of Spain, treacherous accomplice of Aaron Burr, and, at the age of fifty-five, an officer renowned for never having won a battle or lost a court-martial. After Wilkinson came four more brigadiers about sixty years of age, all sharing the distinction of never having commanded a regiment in battle, and chosen on the basis of family, wealth, politics or service in the Revolution. These were the top commanders who, together with officers of field rank whom young Captain Winfield Scott scorned as drunkards or drones, were to lead the lightning war envisioned by President Madison and penny-pinching Secretary of War William Eustis.

Eustis had been a military surgeon during the Revolutionary War. He was at West Point the day Benedict Arnold learned that Washington had learned of his treachery, and as Arnold fled down the Hudson to a British warship, his wife, Peggy Shippen Arnold, was feigning a frenzied fit of hysteria to divert any suspicion of complicity from herself, and also to gain time for her husband's escape. She completely deceived Eustis, who gave her medicine and put her to bed with orders that she was not to be disturbed. During Shays's Rebellion he was again a military surgeon marching with an army, later switching to politics, and was rewarded by Madison with the War Department. He was openly disliked by the other cabinet members and hated by Madison's

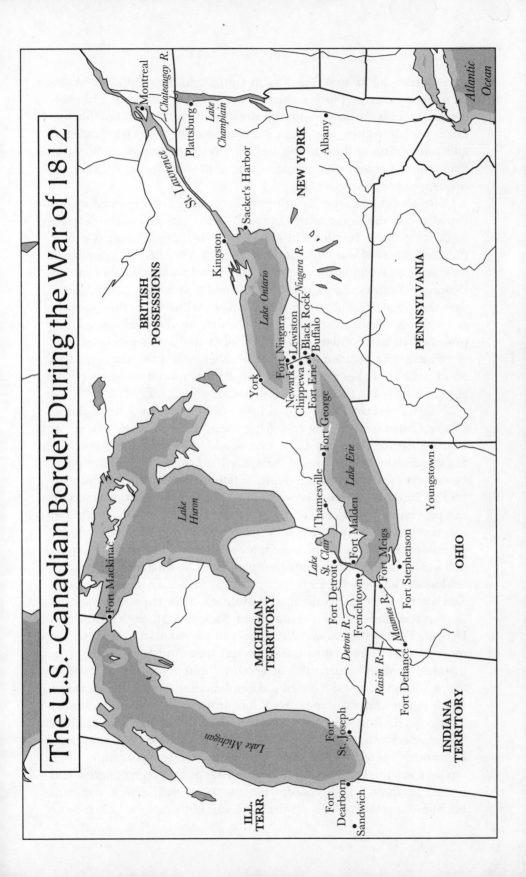

The U.S.–Canadian Border During the War of 1812

Montreal
Chateaugay R.
Plattsburg
Lake Champlain
Atlantic Ocean
St. Lawrence
Sacket's Harbor
NEW YORK
Albany
Kingston
Lake Ontario
PENNSYLVANIA
York
Fort Niagara
Lewiston
Black Rock
Niagara R.
Buffalo
BRITISH POSSESSIONS
Newark
Chippewa
Fort Erie
Fort George
Lake Erie
Fort Malden
Thamesville
Lake Huron
Youngstown
Lake St. Clair
Fort Detroit
Fort Meigs
OHIO
Fort Mackinac
Frenchtown
Fort Stephenson
MICHIGAN TERRITORY
Detroit R.
Raisin R.
Maumee R.
Sandwich
Fort St. Joseph
Lake Michigan
Fort Dearborn
ILL. TERR.
Fort Defiance
INDIANA TERRITORY

slaves, whom he treated like dogs in contrast to the gentle president. As secretary of war, Eustis's chief pleasure came in writing advertisements for bids on army supplies detailed down to the last biscuit. Eustis probably knew less about war than the shy, scholarly Madison, and between them they dribbled along a series of "proposals" for the conquest of Canada that, in retrospect, appear to be the negation of prudence erected into a plan.

Detroit, in the heart of hostile Indian country, and menaced by the British across the Detroit River in Fort Malden, was vital to the defense of the Northwest Territory. In February of 1812, four months before the declaration of war, William Hull, the governor of Michigan Territory, came to Washington to discuss Detroit's defenses. So did General Dearborn. Both Hull and Dearborn insisted that the key to the Northwest was naval control of the Great Lakes. At the time, this was possessed by the British. Britain, also according to the pessimistic Hull, possessed in her regulars and Indian allies the power to subdue the Northwest. The problem, then, was whether or not there was time to build a Great Lakes fleet before the British moved. And then the gloomy Hull made an enigmatic about-face.

He assured Eustis that the British could be forced to abandon Upper Canada merely by menacing them with an army placed in Detroit. British ships on Lake Erie would then fall into American hands and the nation would be spared the expense of building a Great Lakes fleet. From what depth of fatuous optimism Hull dredged up this fantastic proposal is not known, but the prospect of getting a vast province and a lakes fleet free-for-nothing was certainly appealing, especially to the parsimonious Eustis. Madison, accordingly, made no provisions for building an American fleet. Worse, out of these purely defensive considerations came the "plan" for Canadian conquest.

Madison approved Dearborn's proposal to launch a major operation down Lake Champlain against Montreal while supporting thrusts were made into Upper Canada from Sackets Harbor, Niagara and Detroit. Thus an army was not merely to garrison Detroit; it was to move across the river into Canadian territory. And Hull would command it, though reluctantly. Silver-haired and venerable at sixty, "a short, corpulent, good-natured old gentleman who bore the marks of good eating and drinking," Hull had insisted that a younger man should lead. But Madison persuaded him to accept the rank of brigadier general, and in April he went out to Ohio to take command. Dearborn went to Albany to prepare for the Montreal operation.

There was no detailed plan for either Hull or Dearborn. There could not be any time set for coordinated attacks, as such a plan required, because Congress had not yet declared war. Democracies, unlike dictatorships, cannot set invasion dates beforehand and then calmly go about faking "incidents" to justify them. Democracies are given to that debate which precludes timetables and guarantees late starts. They are not always united, either, as President Madison discovered when, on April 15, he asked for the Massachusetts militia for use against Montreal.

Massachusetts refused. Governor Caleb Strong coldly informed Madison that militia were for federal use only to suppress insurrection or repel invasion, and since neither exigency was imminent, Yankee Doodle was staying home. So were the Connecticut militia, and the message to Madison was clear: westerners wanted this war, let them fight it. Westerners, however, were too far from the Lake Champlain region to be of immediate use, as were the regular troops scattered in garrisons across the country. Therefore the major stroke against Montreal was blunted at the outset.

Opposition to the war also arose elsewhere, particularly in Baltimore where perhaps the most savage riot in the history of the United States occurred. The outburst was the result of a feud between two newspapers, the pro-war *Whig* and the anti-war *Federal Republican* published by twenty-six-year-old Alexander Hanson, scion of one of Maryland's leading families. Hanson was supported by the famous "Light-Horse Harry" Lee of Revolutionary War fame—Washington's favorite officer who had praised his chief in the immortal phrase: "First in war, first in peace and first in the hearts of his countrymen"—along with the elderly General James Lingan, another Revolutionary War hero. These three and twenty others were gathered in Hanson's home in July 1812, after the *Whig* inflamed a mob by describing them as murderous traitors. Most of the mobsters were working-class people, many of them excited by the kind of patriotism that comes in bottles. They were led by a brutal butcher named Mumma. They surrounded Hanson's house, hurling stones and spouting foul epithets.

From the cowardly Mayor Edward Johnson came an assurance that he would protect Hanson's group. A company of about forty infantrymen did appear, but did nothing. As the mob grew angrier and more menacing, Johnson persuaded Hanson and his associates to take sanctuary in the city jail. As they filed toward the jail under the escort of soldiers they were stoned, struck at and spat upon. They were called "Damned Tories!"—a strange epithet to bestow on Light-Horse Harry Lee, father of the great Confederate General Robert E. Lee. Inside this "refuge" the jailer, named Bentley, booked them as common criminals and put them in cells—a foreshadowing of what awaited them.

At dark, it was realized that the protecting company of infantry had vanished. There was no one to defend them, should the mobsters appear again. They did, in much larger numbers—and drunker.

When they rushed the front door, it swung open. There stood Jailer Bentley, proffering the keys. Mumma seized them with a demoniac laugh, and the "Tories" were dragged out of their cells. Eleven of them were fearfully beaten with the utmost sadism. The head of seventy-four-year-old General Lingan was smashed like an eggshell. Candle grease was poured into General Lee's eyes and penknives thrust into his body. Each groan of pain issuing from Lee's bleeding mouth provoked paroxysms of fiendish laughter. Lee was so mercilessly battered that his death was reported in Washington. It was only because of his splendid physique that he survived, but for the final six years of his life he was a physical wreck. Lingan died. His funeral oration was delivered by the playwright George Washington Parke Custis, grandson of Martha Custis Washington. He concluded:

> The liberty of the press is one of the noblest rights a freeman can boast. When the rights of opinion, the liberty of speech and the liberty of the press, are prostrated under the feet of lawless power, the citadel of freedom must soon surrender. Yes, my friends, and that power which destroys these attributes of liberty, is the pioneer which precedes the march of despotism.

Nevertheless the rioters had the last say. Although Mumma and three other ringleaders were indicted, the state attorney general repeatedly declared that they could never be convicted—not in that atmosphere of hatred for "Tories." Only one man was found guilty, and he escaped with an absurdly small fine. A deposition made by a witness named William Smith explained this miscarriage of justice by quoting one of the jurors "that the affray originated with them Tories, and that they all ought to have been killed, and that he would rather starve than find a verdict of guilty against the rioters."

Meanwhile, two other events helped to unnerve Hull further: the first was that the formidable Canadian war chief General Isaac Brock was hurrying to the defense of Fort Malden, and the second that Michilimackinac Island commanding the entrance into Lake Michigan had surrendered to the British. Fort Mackinac, built to defend the island, was garrisoned by forty-seven American regulars under Lieutenant Porter Hanks. At Fort St. Joseph forty miles away were forty-six British regulars under Captain Charles Roberts, plus almost four hundred Indians and about two hundred Canadian *voyageurs,* or transport workers, employed by the Northwest Trading Company. Brock ordered Roberts to take Mackinac, and in the early morning of July 17 he landed on the island, quickly emplacing artillery aimed at the fort.

Lieutenant Hanks, intimidated by those guns, called a council of war. As usually happens at such conferences, the frightened officers were more forceful than the fearless ones, and Hanks accepted their advice to surrender. A report to Brock from a storekeeper named John Askew spoke glowingly of the behavior of the Indians. "Since the capitulation they have not drunk a single drop of liquor, nor even killed a fowl belonging to any person (a thing never known before.)" But if the fort had resisted, he said: "I firmly believe not a soul of them would have been saved."

William Hull would have agreed, and he had indeed been terrified by the loss of Michilimackinac, fearing that it would send a huge throng of Indians howling into the Northwest, as well as 1,600 more of those warlike employes of the Northwest Company.

Nevertheless the golden opportunity to seize Malden before Brock could arrive with reinforcements still existed. Along the entire British front from Sandwich to Malden there were not five hundred men, of whom only one hundred were regulars. Now was the time to storm Malden, but the timorous Hull marked time. He sent off letters to Governor Meigs of Ohio pleading for supplies, but the supply convoy was halted by a band of Indians under Tecumseh, and when Hull sent out a relieving force commanded by Major Thomas Van Horne, Tecumseh ambushed him and routed his soldiers, and the provisions were left undelivered at Frenchtown. Hull pleaded again and again for a diversion out of Niagara, but Granny Dearborn was dragging his feet. At last criticism from Hull's angry colonels stiffened the commander's spine and he ordered an attack on Fort Malden. The men were to draw three days' rations and build scaling ladders. But then Hull changed his mind. On the night of August seventh and the morning of the eighth, he led his cursing and humiliated soldiers back across the river to take up a defensive stance in Detroit. Sandwich had been the high point of a campaign repulsed by the mere report that Brock and his reinforcements were already flying to the defense of Fort Malden.

When Hull crossed the river to Sandwich in Canada he fired off a bombastic proclamation promising Canadians who came to his side "the invaluable blessings of civil, political and religious liberty." He also warned them that any white man captured fighting with Indians would be immediately executed. Some Canadians did turn their coats—and were heartlessly abandoned when Hull recrossed the river to Detroit—but in the main the proclamation only angered the large majority who remained loyal. In Quebec the invasion and proclamation were described as the second and less subtle Yankee attempt to seduce Canada, referring to the failed Franklin commission of 1775. One newspaper advised Americans "when fabricating their next address, to apply to the people of Baltimore for a paragraph on 'liberty,' and to the horse swindlers and counterfeiters who have occasionally visited us from the United States for an article on 'property.'"

General Brock was delighted by this reaction, for he had already informed Sir George Prevost, governor-general of Canada, that the population generally seemed to believe that resistance was useless. Hull's presence near Fort Malden also disabused Brock of his belief that the main American thrust would come along the Niagara Frontier. But Fort Malden, he now realized, was the danger point—and he ordered Colonel Henry Procter with sixty regulars to that threatened outpost. Next Brock addressed the Canadian legislature in the capital at York (now Toronto), and by his confident manner lifted the members' hearts and secured from them the necessary supply bills, after which he wisely dismissed them. Finally, he issued a call for militia volunteers and, when they came forward, boated them on the north shore of Lake Erie in bateaux (flat-bottomed boats) and farmers' canoes. After a rough passage of about two hundred miles, he had his first meeting with Tecumseh.

Isaac Brock was seated in his office when the door opened, and an aide said: "This is Tecumseh, sir." The Shawnee chief stepped forward eagerly, his steady hazel eyes studying the British general. Brock was a big man, six feet three inches tall, possessed of great physical strength. Blond and blue-eyed, he was dressed in a tight-fitting scarlet coat with white breeches, with his cocked black hat on the table beside him, and his long legs were shod in gleaming, tasseled Hessian riding boots. So attired, Brock was in sharp contrast to the copper-skinned, black-haired Indian standing before him in buckskin and with a lone eagle's feather rising from his shining hair. It was as though a famous line from Kipling's "Ballad of East and West" had become embodied in this confrontation inside a rude frontier fort:

> For there is neither East nor West
> Nor border nor breed nor birth
> When two strong men stand face to face
> Though they come from the ends of the earth.

From Tecumseh came an explanation of delight, and he whirled upon his boyhood friend Shabbona standing behind him. "This, is a man!" he cried, and Shabbona nodded approvingly, grunting: "Ho, ho, ho."

"And so are you, Tecumseh," Brock said with a smile, extending his hand.

The door opened again and Brock's senior officers filed into the room. Brock asked each of them their estimate of the situation. All were for attacking Detroit, except Colonel Proctor, who vigorously opposed an offensive.

"We do not have the forces, sir," Proctor said, his fleshy, dewlapped face with its needle nose screwed into his customary expression of disdain. "I am aware that Tecumseh has with him many warriors," he continued in a haughty tone, one plump hand resting on his protruding stomach. "But I have never known Indians to be reliable in a pitched battle. Nor militia either, sir. Only British regulars can be counted upon. And we do not have enough regulars."

Tecumseh took a step toward Proctor, his face flushing angrily. "My father," he said, spitting out the word with no attempt to conceal his contempt, "we *must* attack. Hull is a fool and a coward. The tooth of time has chewed him to a pulp. He lives only to drink whiskey and chew tobacco. He could have taken Malden easily, but he moved backward instead—like a crawfish." Tecumseh angrily upbraided Proctor for his remarks about his Indians, sarcastically observing that it was the regulars who ran away in the battle with Van Horne, where, he said, pointing to his bandaged leg, he himself had been wounded. He also pointed to the captured American correspondence on Brock's desk and said the letters proved the Long Knives had begun to despair. Brock nodded, and the Shawnee sachem's face brightened. He grasped a piece of elm bark handed him by Shabbona and drew his scalping knife to draw a map of the Detroit area on it. Brock studied it approvingly and reiterated his intention to attack. Tecumseh's eyes shone, and he promised to parade his Indians in front of Fort Detroit so many times that Hull would think they were as numerous as the waves of the Great Water. Brock nodded in approval again and told his militia officers to dress their troops in scarlet coats to give the impression that they were regulars. Thus, the Canadian force of about six hundred Indians and about seven hundred whites—only one hundred of whom were regulars—would appear to be about two thousand braves and seven hundred British redcoats.

At Fort Detroit General William Hull had at last plucked up what remained of his courage, ordering Colonel James Miller to take the 4th Regiment and supporting troops to Frenchtown to bring the supply train back to the fort under guard. At the Indian village of Monguaga fourteen miles downstream, the Americans were ambushed by about two hundred British and Canadians and about the same number of Indians under Tecumseh. Upon hearing the volley that struck his advance guard, Miller hurried forward with the main body and put the regulars to rout—probably to the immense satisfaction of Tecumseh, who rallied his Indians and engaged the Yankees in a sharp firefight. But when the Shawnee saw the British boarding boats to row for the Canadian shore, they, too, fled.

Miller was the victor, although he had lost eighteen killed and fifty-seven wounded, against British losses of one dead and twenty-four wounded. However, the Americans counted forty dead Indians on the field, suggesting that Tecumseh's wounded, who had been carried off the field, might have been three times that figure.

To Miller's astonishment and anger, he received an order from the cowed General Hull to return to the fort without the supply train. Now Hull's four colonels—the three Ohio militiamen Cass, James Findlay, and Duncan McArthur along with the regular James Miller—were openly contemptuous of their general. Stung, morose, wishing that at his age he had never accepted this unwelcome command, Hull withdrew to his tent, accessible to no one except through his son and aide, Captain A. F. Hull. Now the colonels were on the verge of mutiny, and the three militia officers asked Miller to seize command. He declined, suggesting that McArthur take the lead. But, he, too, refused—and the recommendation of a group of junior officers that Hull be arrested was also rejected. Instead, a letter was sent to Governor Meigs asking him to come to Detroit with the next convoy. It said: "Believe all the bearer will tell you. Believe it, however it may astonish you, as much as if told by one of us. Even a c— is talked of by the —." The bearer was to fill in the blanks orally with "capitulation" and "commanding general." It was signed by the three Ohioans, but it never reached Meigs in time.

At Detroit General William Hull had begun to wilt in the presence of his men. On August 14 he notified the supply convoy at Frenchtown that he could send no help, and ordered its commander to try to follow a circuitous route to the fort through the upcountry. Then he changed his mind and allowed Cass and McArthur to try again to save the supplies. During their absence Brock sent Hull an ultimatum demanding his surrender and warning that if he did not, he could not be responsible for the conduct of his Indians—a message calculated to frighten Hull. It did, and so did a "captured" letter Brock planted on him alluding to "5,000 Indians" hurrying to Brock's side. That night Hull learned that Tecumseh with six hundred braves had also crossed the Detroit and taken up a position to prevent an American escape from the fort and to cut off the Cass-McArthur relief column now lost in the woods.

On August 15 Brock had his artillery in position and began battering the fort from across the river. Hull gave his next-to-last order, directing his troops to crowd inside the narrow confines of the fort, which could then become a slaughter pen. Some American batteries replied, but their spirit did not reflect their commander's mood, for he refused to allow guns to be emplaced at the waterfront to repel an attempted landing. On August 16 Brock crossed the river with his seven hundred troops all clad in regular red. As he did, Colonel Findlay approached Colonel Miller to suggest that they put Hull under arrest. Miller replied: "Colonel Findlay, I am a soldier. I shall obey my superior officer." That remark sealed the fate of Fort Detroit, for Findlay could not have been expected to act on his own. The sight of all those "regulars" also destroyed whatever fight was left in the heart of William Hull.

He sat on a folded old tent with his back against the rampart. His voice trembled. He avoided the contemptuous eyes of those officers who wanted to fight. In his agitation he stuffed quid after quid of chewing tobacco into his mouth until the brown spittle began to spill out and run down his beard and vest. Hull could think of nothing but the safety of the cut-off relief column or of an Indian massacre that would include his own daughter and grandchildren. Cannon shot still shook his fort, four men fell, the militia began to desert, and so William Hull sent his son to signal the surrender.

For the first and only time an American city unfurled a white flag to a foreign foe, and it was seen with incredulous delight by Isaac Brock and his soldiers as they came marching up the hill.

An hour after the white flag fluttered up the American flagpole, Isaac Brock sat on an empty American powder barrel and reported to Governor-General Prevost that with seven hundred regulars and militia and about six hundred Indians he had captured a Yankee army of about 2,500 men, thirty-three guns and the town and fort of Detroit. "When I detail my good fortune," he wrote, "Your Excellency will be astonished."

He was, and would have been more astounded if Brock had detailed what he later discovered: that the fort had plenty of provisions and ammunition and that a herd of about three hundred cattle plus several hundred head of sheep were grazing in its environs.

When the brave Colonels McArthur and Cass were informed that the surrender terms included themselves and their troops and the Frenchtown convoy, they were so infuriated that Cass broke his sword over his knee rather than yield it to the British. Detroit remains the most humiliating capitulation in American history, not even exceeded by the loss of Charleston during the Revolution, or the much greater surrender of the Philippines 130 years later, for there the Americans had fought bravely to the end.

Britain was delighted with the news, and the *Times* printed a parody of "Yankee Doodle" that went:

> Brother Ephraim sold his cow
> And bought him a commission;
> And now he's gone to Canada
> To fi-ight for his nation.

> Brother Ephraim he's come back
> Proved an arrant coward,
> Afraid to fight the enemy
> Afeared he'd be devoured.

Like all men who lose their nerve, William Hull at his court-martial two years later sought to justify his surrender of his post. He had already written Secretary Eustis from prison that he hauled down his flag because he was short of ammunition and food and could not be supplied across the wilderness. In fact, besides his livestock and fifteen days' provisions, he had forty barrels of powder and a hundred thousand rounds of ammunition as well as four hundred rounds of twenty-four-pound shot. His complaint about the difficulty of supply was seized upon by some contemporaries as justification of his conduct. Without control of Lake Erie, they argued, his position was impossible. His court-martial thought differently, convicting him of cowardice and sentencing him to dismissal from the service and execution by firing squad. President Madison, however, spared him, and the disgraced old gentleman spent the remaining years of his life defending his "honor" in print and pulpit.

In fact, Hull had been inept in the beginning and cowardly at the end. Upon his arrival in Fort Detroit he immediately should have sent all women and children—including his daughter and her family, the presence of whom so unnerved him—downriver to safety, along with any aged men who might be more of a liability than an asset. Having crossed the river to Sandwich, he should have struck at Malden at once with his overwhelming superiority in men and guns, seizing it and fortifying it to be ready for Brock upon his arrival with reinforcements. Failing this, if he actually did consider Detroit a more defensible position, he should have burned Malden to the ground and returned to the American fort. Hull's vacillation had the inevitable effect of demoralizing his troops, a fact that became known to Brock by Tecumseh's capture of their correspondence. These two valiant and able warriors had worked skillfully on his fears, and Hull had not once confided in any of his four colonels or asked their advice. All of these men would have scoffed at "5,000 Indians," knowing full well that never in the history of Indian warfare had there been as many as two thousand braves fighting together in the Northwest. Colonel Miller was indeed technically correct in refusing to depose his chief, but absolutely wrong in taking refuge in "regulations," the sanctuary of all officers too fearful of a court-martial. Finally, President Madison must share some of the blame for having ignored Hull's plea that he was too old to command in this critical operation.

Hull had been right then: he was too old and soft. To paraphrase the Bible—"The spirit is willing but the flesh is weak"—at Detroit both the flesh and spirit of William Hull were indeed too weak.

22

Ignominy on the Niagara

〜 THE SURRENDER OF DETROIT WAS NOT ONLY THE MOST DISGRACEFUL episode in the annals of American arms, it was the first of a series of Western defeats sufficient to shake even Henry Clay's faith in the invincibility of Western frontiersmen. Hull, stunned by the news of the fall of Fort Michilimackinac, had sent orders for the evacuation of Fort Dearborn, the site of modern Chicago. Captain William Wells arrived with these instructions on August 12. However, a friendly Indian chief warned the Americans not to leave the safety of the fort, explaining that "leaden birds had been singing in his ears." He was ignored. The soldiers, with their women and children, left the fort on August 15. Less than an hour later they were overwhelmed by five hundred red men who killed half of them and imprisoned the others.

Captain Wells was beheaded, after which the Indians cut out his heart and ate it.

Now, with the entire frontier laid open to Indian incursion, two thousand Kentucky militia were called out to punish Indians in the Illinois country. With typical bombast their general, Congressman Samuel Hopkins, described his army as the best he had seen "in the western country or anywhere else." The closer Hopkins's army came to the Indians, however, the more unruly it became. After the red men set the prairies on fire, the "flower of Kentucky" wilted and went home.

The Northwest frontier now lay wide open to invasion, the British were over the border at Detroit, and hundreds of frightened Western settlers began leaving their homes.

America's military weaknesses and internal divisions were never so naked as during the storm of reproach and recrimination that followed the Northwest disasters. Federalists could not conceal their delight at the dismay of the War Hawks, while these thwarted conquerers screamed in concert for the head of William Hull. Even Thomas Jefferson went so far as to say: "The treachery of Hull, like that of Arnold, cannot be a matter of blame for our government." However, as Henry Adams has observed, if any man was responsible for Hull's failure it was Thomas Jefferson, whose unyielding pacifism excluded military efficiency and unity from the American system. Even then, while Jefferson's protégé Madison yearned for the military victory that might retrieve his political fortunes in the election of 1812, the American military posture was a chaos of conflicts and confusions.

Madison wanted to raise a second Northwestern Army to retake Detroit. He thought of naming James Monroe, his secretary of state, to command this and all other northern armies. But the people of the West took the matter out of his hands. They thought of William Henry Harrison, the thirty-nine-year-old hero of Tippecanoe, and a Kentucky caucus elected Harrison major general of militia.

Harrison hastened toward Fort Wayne, then besieged by Indians. Meanwhile, the federal government decided to make him a brigadier general junior to James Winchester, who at sixty-one seemed to satisfy the Federalist preference for silver hair. But Winchester was a Tennessee aristocrat who was not loved in the West, as Harrison informed Madison. And so, under pressure of a state's action, Madison on September 17 gave Harrison the Northwestern command.

Harrison was to have an army of ten thousand men and to recapture Detroit in a rapid autumn campaign. But he could not traverse the road cut by Hull's army because his own force was five times as big and the autumn rains had made an impassable quagmire of it. So Harrison decided to wait until winter had frozen the lakes and rivers and made them passable. Winter, however, was slow in arriving that year, and Harrison was frustrated in his hopes of striking at Detroit before 1813.

In the meantime, the focus of the fighting shifted to the northeastern front.

After the fall of Detroit, General Brock hastened back to the Niagara Frontier. En route, he discovered that Prevost and Dearborn had agreed to an armistice! Prevost, hearing of the suspension of the Orders in Council, had at once sent an emissary to Dearborn in Albany. Dearborn, distracted and disorganized, looked upon a truce as a godsend. Although the armistice did not include Detroit, Dearborn assured Eustis that "it will not probably have any effect on General Hull or his movements." In other words, the left arm did not need the right arm. Madison angrily repudiated the agreement, but not before Brock had organized his meager force of 1,600 soldiers and three hundred Indians in mutually supporting positions along the forty-mile Niagara River.

By October some six thousand Americans had gathered across the Niagara from Brock's two thousand. Most of them were militia, undisciplined, poorly fed and supplied. But they had at last received a commander, General Stephen Van Rensselaer, a distinguished Federalist whom the Republicans appointed to give the campaign a nonpartisan coloring. Unfortunately, he had no military experience whatsoever. To compensate for this deficiency, Colonel Solomon Van Rensselaer, a relative and a Revolutionary War veteran, was named as his aide.

The new general's militiamen were eager to fight, threatening to go home unless the shooting started soon. So General Van Rensselaer drew up a plan for a double crossing of the Niagara. General Alexander Smyth with 1,650 regulars was supposed to move out onto Lake Ontario and come in on the rear of Fort George, located at the point where the river empties into Ontario. Van Rensselaer's own force would cross opposite Queenston, about ten miles upriver.

Smyth, however, did not wish to cross the river below Niagara Falls. He wanted to cross above the cataract at a point in the neighborhood of Buffalo, at the southern end of the Niagara, where he was based. Smyth, therefore, sat still.

Van Rensselaer went ahead. On the morning of October 11 all was in readiness—except that an American officer, either from ignorance or treachery, rowed across the river in a boat containing all the oars and left it there. Undaunted, Van Rensselaer made another attempt on the rain-swept night of October 12–13.

Colonel Van Rensselaer led about two hundred men across the river. They landed successfully but were discovered about four o'clock in the morning. The British-Canadians opened fire, and the Americans charged and scattered them. Down at Fort George, General Brock was awakened in surprise. He had expected the main blow to come from Fort Niagara almost directly opposite George. Instructing his gunners to open a restraining fire on Niagara, he hurried upriver to Queenston.

There the Americans had ascended the heights under Captain John Wool, who took charge after Van Rensselaer was severely wounded. And as Brock hurried to the battle scene, Lieutenant Colonel Winfield Scott, twenty-six years old and six feet five inches of muscle and righteous insubordination, came galloping down from Buffalo without so much as a by-your-leave from the uncooperative General Smyth.

Brock, meanwhile, had reached Queenston just as the Americans on the heights began firing down on a British gun. Charging down the hill, the Americans took the piece. Brock led a countercharge and was shot in the breast and killed.

Now, at about two o'clock in the afternoon, the towering Scott had come over to Queenston and taken command from Wool. He had between seven hundred and eight hundred Americans to hold off a British force that had swelled to about one thousand. Brock's system of supporting positions had gone rapidly into effect. Obviously, the Americans needed reinforcements.

But not a man of the militia so bold to fight would come to the side of their embattled comrades. They said there were no boats, but only half had been swamped or carried off by the Niagara's swift currents. They were asked to cross in detachments, but they still refused. The distraught General Van Rensselaer rode among them and pleaded with them to cross. One well-equipped militia company consented, but just as the men began stepping into the boats the sound of firing was heard from Queenston Heights and they changed their minds.

Not a soldier crossed the river, and Scott's outnumbered force braced for the enemy's assault. It was begun by the Indians, who charged splendidly. Then the British-Canadians crashed out a single volley and followed with the bayonet. The Americans gave way and broke. Many of them tried to hide along the steep banks of the river, but they were caught and killed. Others attempted to swim the turbulent Niagara and were drowned. Most of them surrendered, including Colonel Scott.

Once again a small but able British force had humbled an American military mob; but this time, with the death of General Brock, the Crown had won a Pyrrhic victory. No soldier of Brock's stature appeared on the British side for the remainder of the war. Meanwhile, the American cause passed from the tragicomedy of Queenston Heights to the travesty of Black Rock.

Alexander Smyth had replaced Van Rensselaer, who had resigned in chagrin. Smyth, more writer than fighter, spent much of his time composing ringing declarations. "Friends of your country!" he told his soldiers. "Ye who have 'the will to do, the heart to dare!' The moment ye have wished for has arrived! Think on your country's honors torn! Her rights trampled on! Her sons enslaved! Her infants perishing by the hatchet! Be strong! Be brave! And let the ruffian power of the British king cease on this continent!"

Thus, hurling his exclamation points like spears, Smyth rallied a force once again grown to six thousand men for another assault on Canada. In the early morning of November 28 a small advance guard crossed the river from the vicinity of Black Rock. The Americans seized two enemy batteries near Red House. As daylight approached, two thousand men climbed into waiting boats. Barely out on the river, Smyth suddenly and unaccountably called off the entire expedition.

Smyth's soldiers were so enraged, however, that their general was forced to reschedule the assault for December 1. Before that date Smyth told his troops: "The general will be on board. Neither rain, snow or frost will prevent the embarkation . . . While embarking the music will play martial airs. 'Yankee Doodle' will be the signal to get under way." The general's officers, however, objected to sending Yankee Doodle across a river in broad daylight into the mouths of enemy guns. General Smyth promptly called a council of war at which his officers vetoed his proposal. Seeing a chance to get off the hook, General Smyth agreed and climbed down.

Now his men were so infuriated that they began shooting off their muskets, some of them in the general direction of General Smyth's tent. And that was the end of the Niagara fiasco.

Meanwhile, at Sackets Harbor on the eastern end of Lake Ontario, there was simply no invasion whatever.

At Lake Champlain, General Dearborn had at last moved north, taking some six thousand or eight thousand men up to Plattsburg on the lake. The Canadians countered by sending 1,900 men south from Montreal. On the night of November 19 the Americans and Canadians collided in a skirmish on the Lacolle River. The Americans captured a blockhouse, the Canadians fled, and then the Americans got lost and began firing on each other. After his militia suddenly remembered their constitutional rights and refused to cross the border, General Dearborn went into winter quarters.

Disgrace at Detroit, ignominy at Niagara, a blank at Sackets Harbor and a fizzle on Lake Champlain: thus had the 1812 campaign to conquer Canada concluded in the most inglorious chapter in American military history.

Nevertheless the fiascoes on the Niagara Frontier did have one happy result for the ever-fortunate United States of America: the death of Isaac Brock removed from the ranks of the enemy the most able and energetic general of the War of 1812, one who, if he had lived, could have served the Anglo-Canadian cause much more effectively than the timid Henry Proctor and Sir George Prevost. It is then not too much to suggest that if Brock had lived and been given the chief command that he deserved, the Great Lakes would have become Canadian ponds and the maple-leaf flag would fly over that vast territory along their southern shores stretching from northern New York to Wisconsin, and the northwestward expansion of American settlers would have been forever blocked.

23

Glory to "Preble's Boys"

~ BECAUSE OF ITS RELIANCE ON UNRULY MILITIA AND ANTIQUE GENERALS, the United States had failed miserably in its campaign to conquer Canada, the true War Hawk objective in this war for "free trade and sailors' rights." But at sea, where the nation was most woefully unprepared, the brash young U.S. Navy sailed forth to shiver the timbers of the old Queen of the Waves.

Britain then was a sea mammoth of 600 ships, of which 120 were ships-of-the-line and 116 were frigates. At the outbreak of hostilities the Royal Navy had only one 64-gun "liner" and seven frigates patrolling the American coast. To oppose them, America had about 18 seagoing vessels. Mr. Jefferson's 200 gunboats were available, of course, but useless for naval warfare, and most of them so deteriorated that they were not even capable of harbor defense. Of the seagoing ships only 12 were of value, but of these the 7 frigates were superb. That measly $300,000 authorized by Congress to repair them had been well spent, and the War with the Barbary Pirates had blooded their captains and crews. They were eager to challenge the British, those doughty but arrogant sea dogs they both respected and despised—especially Captain James Dacres of the captured French-built frigate *Guerrière,* who had repeatedly challenged the supposedly timid Yankees to come out and fight him.

Probably the most famous of these American frigates was Edward Preble's old flagship *Constitution,* now known to the American public as "Old Ironsides" because her hull had been built of fibrous live-oak planks that could be bent into place without use of the softening steam believed to weaken wood. She was commanded by Captain Isaac Hull, the rotund little skipper who had served with such distinction in the Mediterranean. Hull was the nephew and adopted son of William Hull. On the morning of July 18, 1812, just as his uncle-father was beginning to crumble at Malden, Hull's lookouts sighted a formidable British squadron: the battleship *Africa,* 64; and the frigates *Shannon,* 38; *Aeolus,* 32; *Belvidera,* 36; and *Guerrière,* 38.

Old Ironsides, rated at 44 guns but actually carrying 54, was capable of sinking any British frigate, but not four at a time and backed up by a battleship. As the British frigates began closing in, Hull decided to make a fighting withdrawal.

Cutting away part of his stern rail, he mounted a long 18- and 24-pounder aft, and then, by widening his cabin portholes, was able to poke more 24s through them. Because it was a windless day, he put out his boats to try and drag *Constitution* out of range. So did his pursuers, although they had the advantage of putting all their boats at the disposal of *Shannon.* Gradually, *Shannon* drew closer, and Hull decided to kedge. In this maneuver, a cutter carried an anchor forward and dropped it, so that all hands might haul on the anchor chain and thus pull their vessel through the water. The gap widened, and *Old Ironsides* began to crawl slowly ahead. But then *Shannon* put out two kedges, drawing again closer until the American's hastily mounted stern guns forced the Britisher's cutters to keep a safe distance. So it continued throughout the day while the cursing, sweating sailors of both nations alternately dragged or rowed their ships over a glassy sea. Only nightfall brought respite, and in the morning Hull was not pleased when he saw that the battleship *Africa* had joined the chase.

With daylight, towing and kedging were renewed until noon, when a breeze sprang up. At once Hull ordered his dog-tired seamen to swarm up the rigging and saturate the sails. About ten tons of drinking water went over the side to reduce the ship's weight and lessen her draft by an inch. Still the lighter Britisher gained ground. Hull then had skysails made and set. All other sails were set and trimmed to the greatest advantage: close by the wind, and with the freshening of the wind the beautiful Yankee frigate began to pull away from her vexed pursuers. Two hours later *Old Ironsides* was plunging toward Boston at thirteen knots and the British were dwindling specks astern.

• • •

Captain Hull and his gallant crew received a hero's welcome from the seagoing population of Boston. Almost as though a great naval victory had been won, the people of the city were thrilled by the details of how Hull's skillful seamanship had thwarted a formidable five-ship British squadron under the command of one of the Royal Navy's most celebrated sailors: Captain Philip Bowes Vere Broke. But the chubby little Yankee skipper did not bask long in the admiration of his countrymen. Having taught the enemy a sailing lesson, he now wanted to treat them to a demonstration of naval gunnery. On August 2, with *Constitution* refitted and reprovisioned, he put out to sea specifically searching for Captain Dacres and *Guerrière*. To sink that ship, he believed, would be a tonic for a depressed American public still mourning the loss of Detroit. But he found an empty sea and no foe in sight either in the Bay of Fundy, off Halifax or in the Gulf of St. Lawrence. Turning south, on August 19 he was two hundred miles off the coast of Maine when a lookout sighted what appeared to be a British frigate. It was *Guerrière*.

Both ships immediately began maneuvering for "the weather gauge," that is, to get to the windward of the enemy. Each wanted to be able to rake the other without being raked. But Hull and Dacres maneuvered with such skill that neither could gain the advantage. *Guerrière* opened fire at long range, blasting away in a starboard broadside that fell short. Dacres next wore ship, that is, turned in a half-circle so as to bring his portside guns to bear. This time his cannonballs went shrieking high over *Constitution*'s topsails.

Suddenly Hull set extra sail and closed quickly on the surprised Dacres. Hull waited until he was within half-pistol shot—fifty yards—and then cried to his crew: "Now, boys, pour it into them!"

Old Ironsides' forward guns, double-shotted with grape, roared and flamed. They riddled *Guerrière*'s rigging, ripped her sails and reddened her decks with blood. Hull leaned over the rail, eager for a closer look, and split his tight buff breeches down the rear seam. His men shouted with laughter and bent to the guns.

Running before the wind, nearly abreast of each other, both ships exchanged fire. Gradually the superior American guns and gunnery began to tell. After a quarter-hour *Guerrière* was a cripple. Her rear mast fell overboard just as her main yard gave way in the middle. Slowing with reduced sail power, she allowed *Old Ironsides* to steer across her bow into the coveted raking position. *Guerrière* now could fire only a few forward guns, while *Constitution* could bring all guns to bear to blast the Britisher lengthwise. Hull seized the opportunity. He raked

Dacres with his starboard guns, wore ship, and raked him with the port battery. Marine sharpshooters in *Old Ironsides'* tops poured musket fire into *Guerrière's* decks. Now the ships swung close and the Britisher's bowsprit caught in *Constitution's* rigging. Both captains cried: "Boarders away!"

Marine Lieutenant William Bush leaped to the rail to lead his men aboard the enemy. He was shot through the head, falling back on *Constitution's* deck just as the wind filled her sails and broke her free of *Guerrière.* Now *Ironsides'* sharpshooters took a toll of British seamen clearly visible on the enemy's decks. American gunfire cut away the Britisher's foremast and then the mainmast. Dacres, streaming blood, gallantly ran up a new Union Jack on his stump of foremast—but the battle was over. Her decks slippery with blood, her hull riddled, her masts and canvas gone, and her rigging shredded, *Guerrière* was a helpless hulk dipping and rolling in the sea. Dacres fired a surrender shot to leeward and pulled down his flag.

Although Hull was forced to burn his prize, his victory was indestructible. It shone like a lone beacon of hope throughout the military eclipse of the northern campaign. In one half-hour, says the historian Henry Adams, Hull and his men had raised the United States to the rank of a first-class power. Never before had a British frigate struck to an American, and in Britain the *Times* of London reported: "The loss of the *Guerrière* spread a degree of gloom through the town which it was painful to observe." The *Times* observed that *Guerrière* had fallen to "a new enemy, an enemy unaccustomed to such triumphs, and likely to be rendered insolent and confident by them."

True enough, for even the Federalists of New England joined the general rejoicing, and "the cautious Madison was dragged by the public excitement upon the element he most heartily disliked."

Tasting blood and eager for more, the navy's fiery young captains were granted a freedom of action rare in the usages of warfare, and they quickly put to sea in three squadrons of three ships apiece. As they did, the *Times* of London thundered: "But above all, there is one object to which our most strenuous efforts should be directed—the entire annihilation of the American Navy."

The Thunderer of Fleet Street was disappointed. On October 18 the American sloop *Wasp,* 18 guns, Master Commandant Jacob Jones, came upon the British sloop *Frolic,* 19, Captain Thomas Whinyates, as she escorted a convoy of six merchantment from Honduras to England. The seas ran high, and the merchant ships made safely off while the two sloops closed for broadside battle.

In such seas one ship would be now above the other on the crest of a wave, now below in a trough, and serving the guns was a difficult feat. Yet the Americans firing their port guns were able to catch *Frolic*'s starboard rising on the roll of the waves and put holes in her hull. *Frolic*'s starboard battery fired on the roll as *Wasp* dipped into the trough, went screaming over the American's head or through her rigging. Thus *Wasp* quickly gained the advantage. As the ships drew closer, an American seaman named Jack Lang leaped to the rail waving a cutlass and jumped down on *Frolic*'s deck. Lang had been an impressed seaman, he was thirsting for revenge, and his impetuous action touched off an American boarding rush that brought *Frolic*'s colors fluttering down.

Once again the Americans had shown their superiority with guns, although their exultation was to be short-lived. While they struggled to bring *Frolic* home as a prize, the big 74-gun ship of the line *Poictiers* came up to free *Frolic* and take *Wasp* as a prize. Nevertheless, *Wasp* had won another American victory, and twelve days later Captain Stephen Decatur made a third British warship dip her colors to Old Glory.

Apologists for the Royal Navy had sought to dismiss the loss of *Guerrière* as a fluke. After all, they argued, she was a French ship, built in a French shipyard to inferior specifications. Her timbers were rotten, her masts weak, her sails flimsy and her hull porous. Let those Yankee upstarts discover a true-blue British frigate, and they'd soon find out what naval battle was all about.

That was what the delighted eyes of the Hero of Tripoli beheld off Madeira at daybreak of Sunday, October 25. It was the British frigate *Macedonian*, 38 guns, commanded by Captain John Surman Carden, son of a British army officer who had lost his life in the American Revolution. Carden was a fine sailor, and he was astonished by the speed of the bigger and better-armed American as he tried to outrun her. But Decatur had the *United States*—sister to *Old Ironsides*—under heavy sail and by midmorning he was abreast of the enemy. For half an hour the two frigates traded shots at long range.

Almost immediately the superiority of American gunnery became apparent. Decatur, though gentler in manner than the crusty sea dog who had trained him, was nevertheless just as demanding as Commodore Preble had been, especially in teaching his men how to shoot. Even at long range his gunners were punishing *Macedonian*, holing her and shredding her sails. Carden decided to close to the customary half-pistol shot hoping to give his gun crews a better target. It was a disastrous decision, for the Yankees loaded and fired with such speed that they not only outshot the British two to one but fired so fast that *Macedonian*'s crew thought the enemy ship was on fire. When *United States* bore off slightly, they gave a loud cheer, thinking they had set her on fire and put her to flight. A popular American ditty celebrated this mistake:

> They thought they saw our ship in flame,
> Which made them all huzza, sirs;
> But when the second broadside came
> It made them hold their jaws, sirs.

That first broadside had made a floating wreck of *Macedonian*, and when Decatur brought *United States* around for the second blast, Carden wisely struck his colors. His ship was not only close to sinking, but he had also suffered grievous losses in its crew: thirty-six killed and sixty-eight wounded, compared to only five Americans killed and six wounded. *United States* herself received only slight damage to some of its spars.

When Stephen Decatur brought both *United States* and *Macedonian* into the harbor of Newport, Rhode Island, on December 6, 1812—the only British war prize ever brought into an American port—it was a great day for that seaport city. On another December 6, thirty-eight years before, Sir Peter Parker's fleet had sailed into Newport to take the town captive. President Madison was profoundly moved when *Macedonian*'s tattered ensign was laid at his feet, and it is possible that he reflected how much more decisive his re-election might have been if Decatur had only sighted the Britisher a few months sooner. But the gallant Decatur's victory did have the effect of silencing the Royal Navy's somewhat mendacious defenders.

If further confirmation of Yankee seagoing skills were needed it came on December 29 when *Constitution*, now commanded by Captain Bainbridge of *Philadelphia* notoriety, capped six months of glorious combat by the U.S. Navy when it won a ship-to-ship slugging match with the evenly matched British frigate *Java*. True, the Americans had gained only a handful of single-ship victories and had not even challenged a ship-of-the-line; yet the Yankee seamen with their beautiful swift ships had shown that they could sail just as well as Britannia's sea dogs and certainly shoot better. More, they had compelled the London *Times* to ask the unaskable question: "What is wrong with British sea power?"

24

Frenchtown:
Canada Stays Canadian

REELECTED FOR A SECOND TERM—CHIEFLY THROUGH THE SOLID SUP-
port of the western and southern states that approved the war—and
encouraged by a glittering string of naval victories, President James
Madison began the year 1813 still looking hopefully toward the Northwest, where William Henry Harrison stood poised to redeem American military fortunes.

Harrison's army had entered on the cruel ordeal of the northern
winter. The ranks had dwindled to 6,500 men. Some of them were
mutinous, especially the fiercely independent Kentucky Long Knives
who held down the army's left wing at Fort Defiance under General
Winchester. Nevertheless, Harrison decided to get closer to Detroit.
He ordered Winchester to move from Defiance up to the Maumee
Rapids. In early January, at the head of about 1,200 men, Winchester
moved out.

His soldiers marched through snow two feet deep, harnessing themselves to sledges to pull their gear. At the front of the column men
floundering through the drifts gradually packed them smooth, so that
men at the rear slipped and fell or flailed their arms to keep their balance. Then the temperature rose and it began to rain. The soldiers
slogged through slush and mud or splashed through water floating
atop the rotten ice of thawing streams and ponds. Living on half-
rations, soaked, their teeth chattering, lacking axes to fell firewood or

cooking utensils, they plodded on—reaching the rapids on January 10.

Winchester had begun building a fortified camp and gathering supplies, when he received an appeal from American settlers at Frenchtown (now Monroe, Michigan) on the Raisin River. The Americans said their lives were endangered by one hundred Indians who were inside the town with about fifty Canadian militia. Frenchtown was thirty-five miles north of the rapids, one hundred miles away from Harrison's main body and only eighteen miles south of Fort Malden. Thus it was within easy reach of the British. Nevertheless, Winchester decided to succor Frenchtown, persuaded, perhaps, by the fact that his men had reached that point of exasperation where they were eager to fight anyone.

On January 17 Colonel William Lewis and 550 men began marching north over frozen terrain and in bitter cold. On the next day they reached the little settlement of thirty families and attacked the Indians and Canadians. After a two-hour fight the Americans cleared the village. Two days later, General Winchester came up from the rapids with three hundred additional men. He set up a camp that was an invitation to disaster, leaving most of his force stationed on the north bank of the Raisin River while he himself set up headquarters a half-mile south of the river. The sight and smell of his ragged and half-mutinous Long Knives were too much for the elegant Winchester's sensitive senses. And so, to the folly of placing men with their backs to a stream, and then trying to command them from the other side, Winchester added the dereliction of ordering no night pickets or night patrols.

Up in Fort Malden, meanwhile, it was clear to General Henry Proctor, the successor to the fallen Brock, that the Americans were incredibly far off base, although he could never have imagined that they were also off their guard. Taking about 1,200 men—half of them Indians under Roundhead and Walk-in-the-Water—he began stealing south. On the night of January 21, under cover of a raging snowstorm, he came within reach of the Americans. He put his artillery and his regulars in his center and his Indians and militia on his right and left flanks. Opposite him the American left was protected by a picket fence, while the right was only partially guarded by a crude rail fence.

Two hours before daylight of January 22, 1813, with the snow still falling, Frenchtown was suddenly shaken by artillery fire and the rattle of musketry. War whoops were heard. Almost at once the American right was overwhelmed. Within a few minutes one hundred soldiers were scalped by Indians who had gotten into the rear. General Winchester, blundering to the front to rally his men, was taken prisoner.

On the left, however, about four hundred men under Major George Madison fought with bravery and skill. They repulsed charge after charge. Came a lull in the battle and they saw a white flag approaching. Their hearts soared, for they thought that it was a flag of truce. But it was rather a British officer bringing a message from Winchester to the effect that he had surrendered his entire army, themselves included.

Chagrined, Madison sent back the reply: "It has been customary for the Indians to massacre the wounded and prisoners after a surrender. I shall not agree to any capitulation which General Winchester may direct, unless the safety and protection of all the prisoners shall be stipulated." Proctor raged that he would not accept dictation, but in the end he agreed and Madison surrendered.

Proctor kept his word by stripping his prisoners of some of their clothing, robbing them of their money and forcing them to drag his sleds to rest his horses. His wounded prisoners were left behind without guards. An American who had asked for help for the wounded was told: "The Indians are excellent doctors." So Proctor deserted them on the grounds that he wished to flee the area before Harrison could come up and attack him. As soon as he departed, the Indians became drunk and began scalping the wounded. They set fire to one houseful of them, and as those able to rise rushed to the windows to escape, they beat them back into the flames with tomahawks.

Thus the allies of the noble Proctor, and as Proctor hurried north to regain the safety of Fort Malden, Harrison, from whom he fled, was also burning Winchester's post at the Maumee Rapids and hastening south. Thirty-six hours after the Battle of Frenchtown the two enemies were 60 miles apart. A week later Harrison returned to the rapids with two thousand men. He built a fortified camp on its south bank and named it Fort Meigs after the Governor of Ohio. Ordering up all troops in his rear, he collected a force of four thousand men, which he planned to hurl against Malden. February 11 was fixed as the day of advance, but on that day the roads were sheeted with ice and impassable, and the expedition to Malden was canceled.

So ended, in defeat, massacre and disgrace, the western movement against Upper Canada. Although his contemporaries were kinder to Harrison than to Hull, and would one day make him president, the fact is that William Henry Harrison had done less with more. He had not even gotten across the Maumee River. The men whom he led, and in whom he had great faith, were obviously superior to those who had followed Hull into Canada. A British officer has left a description of them:

Their appearance was miserable to the last degree. They had the air of men to whom cleanliness was a virtue unknown. . . . It was the depth of winter; but scarcely an individual was in possession of a great coat or cloak. . . . They still retained their summer dress, consisting of cotton stuff of various colors shaped into frocks, and descending to the knee. Their trousers were of the same material. They were covered with slouched hats, worn bare by constant use, beneath which their long hair fell matted and uncombed over their cheeks; and these, together with the dirty blankets wrapped round their loins to protect them against the inclemency of the season, and fastened by broad leathern belts into which were thrust axes and knives of an enormous length, gave them an air of wilderness and savageness.

They were neither pretty nor perfumed, but hard with the lean toughness of adversity, and such men, given the leader to inspire and organize them, have always been invincible. However, America had yet to find its leaders. The penny-pinching William Eustis had done his country the great kindness of resigning, but Madison had replaced him in the War Department with John Armstrong, a leading Republican politician from New York who was also the author of the mutinous Newburgh Addresses as well as the crony of the treacherous James Wilkinson.

Despite his record, Armstrong was not disloyal—just personally ambitious. Neither did he fail to see, as Hull and Harrison had also seen before closing their eyes to the fact, that naval control of the Great Lakes was the key to the western campaign. But as Armstrong assumed office on February 5, 1813, the lakes were still frozen—and out on the open Atlantic another of Preble's Boys began 1813 with the last American victory when the British brig *Peacock*, 16 guns, was conquered by the American brig *Hornet*, 18 guns, commanded by Lieutenant James Lawrence.

25

"Don't Give Up the Ship!"

～JAMES LAWRENCE WAS BORN OCTOBER 1, 1781, IN BURLINGTON, NEW Jersey, the son of a prominent lawyer. As a boy he was enchanted by the white sails moving up and down the broad Delaware River near his home and yearned for a career at sea. But his father wished him to follow in his footsteps, and James at an early age began studying for the bar in nearby Woodbury. But he found the smell of printer's ink stultifying when compared to the tangy scent of the great salt sea, and at the age of eighteen he exchanged classroom boredom for the romantic decks of a merchant ship, the *Ganges*. Eventually he joined the nascent U.S. Navy aboard *President Adams* and five years later was serving as a first lieutenant on *Enterprise* in Preble's Mediterranean squadron. The *Enterprise's* ship's bell which he rang so often as first officer, is now one of the most cherished possessions of the U.S. Naval Academy at Annapolis. Lawrence had also been second-in-command to Decatur aboard *Intrepid* during the stirring recapture and burning of *Philadelphia*. His bravery and leadership in subsequent attacks on Tripoli led Preble to make frequent mention of him in his despatches to Secretary Smith.

Ironically, James Lawrence's flaming courage and zest for battle could detract from his fighting prowess. Like Robert E. Lee, his extreme combativeness bordered on rashness and could have been seasoned with a dash of discretion. Like Decatur he was gentle and courteous, solicitous for the well-being of his men, legendary in his bravery and admired for his seamanship. But by the very ardor of his nature he was incapable of the meticulous planning and the rare attention for detail characteristic of a great admiral. But then again, in 1813, when he was thirty-one, James Lawrence's gallant soul and sailing skill were exactly what was required of a lieutenant of the U.S. Navy.

During the first eight months of the War of 1812, however, while his erstwhile shipmates of the Mediterranean were winning spectacular victories, Lawrence found no opportunities for glory. But then commanding *Hornet* he was attached to Captain William Bainbridge's squadron after he took command of *Constitution*. It seemed the moment of glory had arrived when *Old Ironsides* and *Hornet* began chasing the heavily-laden British brig *Bonne Citoyenne*—another French prize—carrying half a million pounds of specie to Britain. *Bonne Citoyenne* found sanctuary in the Brazilian harbor of San Salvador, and refused—quite understandably, granting the possibility of losing such a valuable cargo—Lawrence's challenges to come out and fight. After *Constitution* sailed away, *Hornet* remained outside the harbor until the 74-gun British battleship *Montague* appeared, when Lawrence discreetly crowded on all sail northward.

On February 24, 1813, *Hornet* was off the mouth of the Demerara River at Georgetown, British Guiana, when his lookouts sighted a British brig approaching. It was the *Peacock*. To James Lawrence, here at last was glory!

Closing to half-pistol shot the two ships traded broadsides, and then, swiftly wearing ship, Lawrence unleashed a second bombardment, battering *Peacock* so mercilessly that within a quarter hour her captain was dead, more than half her crew wounded and—with six feet of water in her hold—the brig was in danger of sinking. As *Peacock* struck her colors she signaled distress, and Lawrence sent aboard a rescue-repair party that brought the British survivors aboard *Hornet* and strove to keep the stricken vessel afloat by jettisoning her guns and ammunition and plugging the holes in her hull. But the brig went down suddenly, as though sinking into the sunset, taking with her nine of her own crew and three of the *Hornet*'s party.

As *Hornet* sailed homeward with her cargo of prisoners, James Lawrence endeared himself to these captives by his courtesy and outgoing friendliness. *Hornet* was a vessel of only 480 tons with no spare room. But the Americans shared their clothing with their prisoners and rationed their water so that no one went thirsty. When Lawrence reached New York his captive officers signed a statement thanking him for treating them with "everything that friendship could dictate."

Upon his arrival in that "Port of the Hero's Welcome," he found himself nationally acclaimed and raised to the rank of captain. In May 1813, he was given command of *Chesapeake*.

In the world of the sea there is much superstition about a "bad" or "unlucky" ship, and that had applied to the frigate *Chesapeake* ever since she was humiliated by HMS *Leopard*. When Lawrence arrived in Boston on May 20 to take command, he found that the two-year enlistments of *Chesapeake*'s old crew had expired, and no one was interested in shipping over. Along the waterfront civilian seamen were more interested in lucrative privateering service than in the lower pay and meager prize money of the U.S. Navy. Many of the old crewmen were angry because they had not yet been paid the prize money owing from the frigate's last cruise, skimpy though it was. By issuing prize-money checks and meeting old obligations, Lawrence was able to sign some of these reluctant sailors, but he still had to flesh out his crew with British and Portuguese seamen. Among the Portuguese, a boatswain's mate was a mutinous malingerer.

Within ten days, Lawrence had *Chesapeake* shipshape and had sufficient trained gunners to handle the ship's fifty guns, some of them with colorful names such as True Blue, Brother Jonathon, Mad Anthony, Liberty-or-Death and Willful Murder. By June 1 he was ready to carry out his mission of preying on British merchant shipping between Canada and Great Britain. But then the British frigate *Shannon* appeared off Boston harbor with the redoubtable Captain Broke aboard.

No sailor in the Royal Navy was more highly regarded than Philip Bowes Vere Broke. Reared in the Suffolk countryside, he had been trained in the Royal Naval Academy at Portsmouth. At thirty-seven he had distinguished himself on the American station, and it was his *Shannon* that almost overtook Isaac Hull in *Old Ironsides*. Like *Chesapeake*, *Shannon* was rated at 38 guns, but actually carried, two more than the American. Again like the American, *Shannon* also had a reputation for bad luck, for two ships of the same name had been lost during the past fourteen years. But Broke's stern yet considerate style soon overcame that superstition. His gunners were the equal of the American cannoneers, trained by daily practice with the heavy ordnance and twice weekly with firearms. This was almost a unique routine in the Royal Navy of the day when the Admiralty was so parsimonious with gunpowder that some skippers in despair abandoned gunnery practice altogether. But Broke, like all good commanders, was so resourceful in obtaining gunpowder that supply officers complained he drew enough for a squadron. Like Lawrence, Broke was chivalrous, and the battle impending between them was perhaps that last combat in which challenges were courteously exchanged and surprise or deception was disdained as cowardly or false.

In that mood, Broke wrote to Lawrence: "As *Chesapeake* appears now ready for sea, I request you will do me the favor to meet *Shannon* with her, ship to ship, to try the fortunes of our respective flags." He even promised to send other British ships away "beyond the power of inter-fering with us" and suggested an area of the ocean where Lawrence could choose the exact waters for combat, while providing the precise strength of his vessel and the location of other British ships.

Captain James Lawrence was delighted, writing to the secretary of the navy that he could see the enemy frigate from his quarterdeck and "I am in hopes to give a good account of her before night." That was on June 1, 1813, a foggy day in Boston. When the mists cleared at noon, James Lawrence with shining eyes fired a departing shot and sailed gracefully from the bay toward Broke, awaiting him at sea.

At one o'clock *Chesapeake* passed the Boston lighthouse. To encourage his crew, Lawrence hoisted the banner: FREE TRADE AND SAILORS' RIGHTS. It had about as much effect upon his sailors as a battle cry of "Long live two-plus-two!" The seditious Portuguese boatswain openly mocked it, wondering aloud who would want to die for such a crass cause. Two hours later *Chesapeake* approached *Shannon,* and for the next two and a half hours the two equally matched ships maneuvered to gain the advantage of the wind, the seamanship of Lawrence being slightly more skillful than Broke's. Their evolutions carried them out of sight of a flotilla of light craft crammed with spectators, as well as the crowds lining the shore as far away as Salem.

Chesapeake finally drew abreast of *Shannon*'s starboard side and the fiercest naval battle of the War of 1812 began. They battered each other with broadsides. Cannon roared mouth to mouth. Grapeshot and langrage swept the decks, iron balls burst wooden walls, cannister flamed with spreading death; heads, limbs and flesh flew through the air mingling with hammocks, splinters and pieces of wreckage, while the Marines of both nations swayed in the fighting tops pouring mus-ket shots into the enemy below. At first it appeared that *Chesapeake* was gaining the advantage, but after ten dreadful minutes that turned both ships "into charnel houses," the American's fire slackened—many of the foreign gunners having scurried below for safety—and *Shannon* was in command.

Lawrence, standing on the quarterdeck resplendent in his dress uniform, was wounded in the leg but continued to shout orders. Then a British hand grenade fell in an American powder chest with a terrifying explosion that staggered *Chesapeake*. Next her jibway was shot away, slowing the frigate at the most critical moment. She rolled against the side of *Shannon* and her mizzen rigging became tangled and the enemy's anchor was caught in her side chains, holding her fast and exposed to the rapid fire of British carronades shredding her rigging and sending more crewmen scurrying for safety below. With the ships alongside each other, Lawrence called for boarders. But the bugler was so frightened that his mouth was dry and he could not blow the call.

At that moment a British musket ball struck Lawrence full in the chest and he fell forward into the arms of the men who caught him. They carried him to the wardroom now serving as a surgery. His voice weakening and the fire fading from his eyes, he gasped his last order: "Don't give up the ship! Fight her till she sinks!"

Now it was Broke who called for boarders, and he led them personally, leaping aboard *Chesapeake* his gleaming cutlass raised on high. Twenty Marines came rushing after him, some of them wielding pikes, others armed with muskets and pistols. They dashed across the quarter-deck. With the guns of both ships still bellowing, Chesapeake's decks seemed strangely still and deserted. Broke did not know it, but every American deck officer above the rank of midshipman had been shot down. Wheeling, he led a charge on the forecastle, now the center of resistance. He reeled from the blow of a musket butt, and then a cutlass stroke opened a gash on his head. Bleeding profusely, he called for reinforcements—and sixty more Royal Marines came leaping into the melee.

By then most of *Chesapeake*'s gunners had taken refuge below and the ship's firing ceased. Rushing down a hatch opened for them by the treacherous Portuguese boatswain, the British boarding party ended all resistance. But *Chesapeake* never surrendered, nor did any American pull down her flag. That was done by a British lieutenant who replaced it with the Union Jack, falling dead on deck only moments later, struck by friendly fire from *Shannon*. Apparently the efficient Captain Broke had forgotten to train his gunners to cease fire once his boarders had overcome the enemy.

Broke himself became delirious from exhaustion and loss of blood. He had lost twenty-six men killed and fifty-six wounded, most of them felled by the fire of U.S. Marines in *Chesapeake*'s fighting tops. The Leathernecks also suffered grievously: of the forty-four aboard, thirty-two were either killed or wounded, raising the American frigate's total to forty-eight dead and ninety-eight wounded.

Both nations took comfort from the battle. To the British, Broke's victory had restored the Royal Navy's self-respect, while the Americans, believing that their ship was overmatched and too dependent on hastily recruited foreign seamen, would never forget James Lawrence's noble death. "Don't Give Up the Ship" became the immortal motto of the U.S. Navy and actually replaced "Free Trade and Sailor's Rights" as the battle cry of the war. In Halifax, where *Shannon* arrived with *Chesapeake* in tow as a prize, the British buried the fallen Lawrence and his slain shipmates with military honors and great respect. Six companies of the 64th British Infantry Regiment, together with their officers and leading Halifax citizens, accompanied the funeral cortege to the cemetery.

Shannon's triumph also marked the beginning of the end for America's deep-water fleet. Only two more victories remained for the graceful frigates that were the precursors of the beautiful Yankee Clippers, and then, one by one, the others were taken or bottled up in port, until in 1814 even the far-ranging *Essex* was caught and destroyed on a Pacific reef. It was not, however the end of the U.S. Navy.

Far away westward on the warming waters of Lake Erie the words of the dying Lawrence echoed in the heart of a young sailor named Oliver Hazard Perry.

26

Oliver Hazard Perry

~ OLIVER HAZARD PERRY'S FIRST AMERICAN ANCESTOR WAS EDWARD Perry, an obstinate Quaker so often in trouble in Oliver Cromwell's Puritan England that he migrated to Sandwich, Massachusetts, in 1650 to escape petty persecution. There he faced similar prejudice from the dominant Congregationalists, who liked his stubborn refusal to take the oath of fidelity to the government no better, hauling him into court and socking him with heavy fines with an astonishing regularity that at last exhausted them. With this, the triumphant Edward became one of the town's leading citizens, dying a wealthy man in 1694.

But the Congregationalist dislike of the Society of Friends did not wane, so that Edward's son Benjamin moved to Rhode Island, where Protestants of all sects were tolerated. Benjamin also prospered, leaving upon his death an estate valued at a whopping $16,000. His son Freeman married the daughter of Oliver Hazard, a descendant of the original Quaker settlers in the colony. Freeman's son Christopher Raymond Perry shocked his father by spurning the doctrinal pacifism of his Quaker forebears to serve in the Revolutionary War, first as a soldier, next as a seaman. Remaining at sea he became a merchant captain, amassing a fortune of his own. In 1784 he married the beautiful Sarah Wallace Alexander of Philadelphia. On August 23, 1785, Oliver Hazard Perry was born.

Four more sons and two daughters followed, to form with Oliver the most distinguished naval family in the history of the U.S. Navy. One of the brothers became the famous Commodore Matthew Perry who opened Japan to world trade in 1853, while all the others became naval officers and the sisters naval wives.

When Oliver was about thirteen, the Naval War with France began, and his father was given command of one of the twelve new ships authorized by Congress—taking young Oliver to sea with him as a midshipman. Upon the cessation of hostilities, President Jefferson—elected on a pacifist platform and a pledge to save money by dismantling the navy—reduced a force of forty-two ships to only thirteen. Captain Perry was one of thirty-three out of forty-two post captains who were axed, but his son, at fifteen, survived the budgetary blade as a midshipman. Despairing of a future serving in such a tiny navy, Oliver was overjoyed with the onset of the War with the Barbary Pirates. But instead of sea duty, glory and promotion he was posted to the inactive list—and he began to think seriously of coming ashore permanently. Once again—like the winds at sea—his fortunes changed in 1802 when he was assigned to the new 28-gun ship *Adams*. Oliver was then nearing seventeen. His slender tall frame had filled out, and he was now not only big but brawny. He was also brainy, proving such an excellent young officer that on his seventeenth birthday he received a commission as a lieutenant thus transferring from the fo'c'sle to the wardroom at an unusually young age.

When the Barbary conflict flared anew, Lieutenant Perry was assigned to *Constellation* in the four-ship squadron sent to the Mediterranean. Unfortunately, Commodore Barron's defensive tactics made for a very dull war indeed, enlivened only when *Constellation* sailed in support of William Eaton's expedition to Derna. Having had no active share in this operation, Perry was back in the doldrums again until he got his own ship.

It was only a 170-ton schooner named *Nautilus,* mounting fourteen guns, but it was *his!* Even the fact that it was used only as a dispatch boat failed to discourage him.

In 1806, after the quasi-war with the Barbary powers came to a peaceful end, Lieutenant Perry sailed back to Norfolk. At twenty-one he was considered one of the most promising young officers in the U.S. Navy. But he was back "on the beach," on a prolonged furlough that might be indefinite, granting Jefferson's dislike of military preparedness. But then came the *Chesapeake* Incident, and the president, with his near-disastrous Embargo Act and his decision to defend these shores with an absurd mosquito fleet of gunboats too frail to put to sea, made it abundantly clear how dangerous it is for any nation to rely upon an absolutist—bellicist or pacifist—as its commander-in-chief. For Oliver Hazard Perry, however, it had the effect of lifting him off the beach and sending him back to sea.

The "sea" was only New York Harbor, where he commanded a gunboat flotilla charged with blockading his own country: that is, to keep profit-hungry American chandlers and sailors from supplying British ships outside the harbor. It was a humdrum assignment and lasted for two years, until, in 1809, he was given another ship, the schooner *Revenge*, mounting fourteen guns.

Cruising off Charleston in July 1810, a boat drew alongside and a U.S. marshal came up the jacob's ladder. He gave Perry a warrant ordering him to seize the ship *Diana*. It had sailed from New England and when in Spanish waters its master had run up the British flag, refusing to return the vessel to its owners. Taking three gunboats with him, Perry in *Revenge* set sail for Amelia Island off north Florida. There the Spanish authorities offered no objection to his seizing *Diana*, but warned him that the ship was under the protection of two British warships. Perry did not hesitate. He boarded *Diana*, capturing its crew and captain and put his own aboard her to sail with him back to Charleston. Just then the big British sloop *Goree* appeared. Its captain sent an officer aboard *Revenge* to inquire what the American was doing with *Diana*. Perry refused to answer.

Still mindful of the *Chesapeake* disgrace, he decided to attack *Goree*, even though he knew his armament was no match for the much bigger Britisher. He would rely on a surprise boarding attack. But then his calm, deliberative nature gradually suppressed his fierce yearning for battle, and he decided instead to send an officer to *Goree* to explain the situation. His hope now was that the British skipper would be reasonable. He was, sailing away—and Perry continued north.

The *Diana* affair made him a hero in a young, self-conscious nation still smarting from the *Chesapeake* episode—but six months later near-disaster almost made him a heel. At midnight January 11, 1811, *Revenge* sailed from Newport bound south for New London, Connecticut. It was a clear, cold night with a slight wind. An hour later fog engulfed the ship and a fierce wind began to blow. Perry thought of turning back until the pilot aboard *Revenge* assured him he could make port safely. But at nine the next morning the fog was so thick that seamen on the port side could not see those at starboard—and then with a shuddering crash *Revenge* ran aground on a rocky ledge.

It was high tide, the wind was still strong and the current swift. Perry ordered boats away to try to pull the ship off the reef but with no success. Then eight heavy cannon were thrown overboard to lighten her. Even this failed to help, and pumping was of little use for the pounding against the ledge had opened many holes in *Revenge's* hull. In desperation Perry ordered the masts cut down to reduce resistance to the wind pinning the ship against the reef, but nothing could stop the inrushing sea. Without hesitation Perry next turned to saving his crew. Boats went ashore carrying the sick and the midshipmen and then able seamen and the officers. Perry was the last to leave, relieved upon coming ashore to find not a man lost. He then turned to saving the ship's equipment—sails, rigging, arms, anything of value and portable—and his crew worked through the cold dark until waves began breaking over *Revenge* and nothing more could be done.

Without hesitation Lieutenant Perry requested to be relieved until a court of inquiry could clear his name, and the court, instead of censuring him, bestowed the highest praise upon his conduct—holding that if there were anyone to be blamed it was the pilot. Even so Perry could not be returned to duty because Jefferson had so thoroughly dismantled the navy that there were then far more officers than there were ships to command. A practical New Englander, Perry thereupon decided that being on indefinite furlough was just the time to conclude his romance with Elizabeth Champlin Mason, daughter of a distinguished Newport physician. They were wed on May 5, 1811, and on their honeymoon made a leisurely tour of their native New England, even visiting Sandwich, where Perry's oldest American ancestor had settled. Returning home, he resumed his studies, confident that war with Britain was inevitable and determined to be ready for it.

When it did come, it was a deeply disappointed Oliver Hazard Perry, who found himself passed over again and again by officers junior to him, and he could not shed the nagging notion that his loss of the *Revenge* was being secretly held against him. At last he was reassigned to the Newport gunboat squadron he had helped to build while training its officers and men, but to Perry this was no promotion but rather a demotion, and it certainly was not a seagoing assignment. His twelve vessels might look formidable inside the harbor, but outside it they were useless. It was then—perhaps out of desperation—that Oliver Hazard Perry's gaze seaward shifted landward toward the Great Lakes.

He spent months studying maps of the Great Lakes and their vicinity, gradually becoming convinced that the key to control of these northern inland seas lay in the second smallest lake: Erie. He communicated his conviction that the decisive battle would be fought there to the Secretary of the Navy, who was impressed. Perry also wrote to

Commodore Isaac Chauncey, who commanded the lakes fleet from Sackets Harbor, located on Lake Ontario at the mouth of the mighty St. Lawrence River. He asked for transfer to Erie. But months passed with no reply, and Perry redirected his eyes seaward in the hope that he would be given command of *Hornet* after Captain James Lawrence was promoted to a larger ship. But Lawrence kept *Hornet* so long at sea that Perry despaired of ever leaving Newport, until to his great joy Commodore Chauncey wrote to him saying that he had requested that he be transferred to his command, adding: "You are the very person that I want for a particular service, in which you may gain reputation for yourself and honor for your country."

Particular service? It had to be Lake Erie! Perry was positive, and then, on February 17, 1813, like the blare of bugles sounding "General Quarters," came the order from the Navy Department: "Go with all the best men in your flotilla and join Commodore Chauncey in Sackett's Harbor."

Upon his arrival at Erie, Pennsylvania, Oliver Hazard Perry hurled himself into the task of building his flotilla and training the men to sail and fight it. He beat the bushes for carpenters, combed the wilderness for blacksmiths, scavenged for scrap iron to make the mouths for his guns, went to the foundries to observe the casting of his shot and sailed downriver to Pittsburgh to set up a supply line. By the end of May two 20-gun brigs were launched. Soon a trio of gunboats followed. Five ships, however, were not enough to wrest control of Lake Erie from British hands. If only the young commander could free five other ships then stationed at Black Rock on the Niagara River. Unfortunately, the enemy in Fort Erie stood between them and Perry.

Then there began a chain of events in which Perry not only participated but of which he became the chief beneficiary.

27

Canada Again

~ SOON AFTER JOHN ARMSTRONG ASSUMED OFFICE AS SECRETARY OF WAR he proposed a northeastern campaign aimed at Montreal. Yet when the orders were received by General Dearborn, Montreal, which was certainly his true objective, was not mentioned. Dearborn was told to take Kingston at the western end of the St. Lawrence River with alternate objectives at York (present-day Toronto) and Forts George and Erie.

Dearborn consulted with Chauncey and after both men grossly overestimated enemy strength at Kingston, that project was dropped and the northeastern campaign faced farther away westward to York and Fort George.

York was assaulted on April 27 when Chauncey's Ontario ships put ashore 1,600 men under the capable Brigadier General Zebulon Pike.* Pike's soldiers drove off a small force of British regulars and Canadians, and seized the harbor batteries and magazines. They burned a half-built, 30-gun frigate that would have been a valuable addition to the British Ontario fleet, and destroyed naval supplies destined for Lake Erie. And then one of the magazines blew up with a tremendous explosion, raising a deadly shower of stones, one of which

* He was also the explorer for whom Pike's Peak was named.

crushed the life out of General Pike. In all, 53 Americans were killed and 150 wounded, while 40 Canadians perished and 23 were wounded. The cause of the explosion was not known, but some of the Americans began to think that it was an enemy trick. They thought angrily of "retaliation," ignoring the Canadian deaths and their own status as invaders, and they began to plunder and loot. They carried off the mace and royal standard of Parliament, and then set fire to the Parliament buildings; and in so doing, even though they might have been aided by capricious Canadians, they created in Canadian hearts a thirst for retaliation in kind which would be satisfied all too soon. That was all there was to York: the wanton burning of the capitol of Upper Canada, the more profitable burning of a ship and naval stores.

At Fort George there was even less military gain. Here, General Dearborn had about 4,000 men against 1,300 under the command of Brigadier General John Vincent. His spearhead troops were led by Winfield Scott, who had been exchanged and promoted to colonel. On May 27 ships commanded by Oliver Hazard Perry bombarded the fort's crumbling wall while his seamen rowed Scott's spearheaders through a wild surf. Reaching the beaches, the Americans were momentarily checked by a handful of defenders. But then, gathering force, they burst through. Bringing artillery ashore, Scott put the fort under fire, and Vincent abandoned it.

Vincent's garrison, not moldering old Fort George, was the true objective. But the British got away, chiefly because Scott was wounded and could not pursue, and the vacillating Dearborn was not ashore to give the order. Vincent ordered his garrisons at Fort Erie, Queenston and Chippewa to join him, and withdrew westward along the lake to Burlington Heights.

Two days later the British struck at the American rear. General Sir George Prevost with eight hundred men appeared at Sackets Harbor and forced a landing, only to be repulsed by the resolute defense maintained by Brigadier General Jacob Brown. With his line of communications thus guaranteed, Dearborn tardily turned to the pursuit of the retreating Vincent.

About 3,000 men under Brigadier Generals William Winder and John Chandler tried to catch Vincent with 1,600. On the night of June 5 the Americans set up camp at Stoney Creek, ten miles from Vincent's bivouac. Early the following morning, 750 British regulars struck them in a surprise attack, scattered them and took Winder and Chandler prisoner. Next a force of 600 Americans under Lieutenant Colonel Charles Boerstler surrendered to 400 Indians and 50 regulars.

With this freshest of fiascoes along the Niagara frontier, the fumbling career of Granny Dearborn came to an end. President Madison requested, and received, his resignation.

With the coming of the spring of 1813 General Harrison's force in Fort Meigs had dwindled to about 1,000 men. Harrison appealed to Governor Shelby of Kentucky, who sent forward about 1,200 men under Brigadier General Green Clay. As the relief force approached Meigs, General Proctor moved out of Malden with 500 regulars, 500 militia and 1,200 Indians under Tecumseh and Roundhead.

The British force reached Fort Meigs on May 1, set up batteries on both sides of the Maumee River, and attempted to pound the fort into submission. Just before midnight of May 4, Harrison received word that Clay's relief force was coming down the Maumee on flatboats only two hours away. Harrison decided on a daring plan to raise the siege of Meigs.

Clay's troops were to destroy the British artillery on the north side of the river while Harrison's sallied out of Meigs to take the guns on the south side. About eight hundred of Clay's men were to land on the north bank, spike the cannon, and then fall back into their boats before the British could get into action. Then these men would join Clay, who with the remaining four hundred soldiers was to land on the south bank to cut his way into the fort.

On the south bank the plan worked to perfection. Harrison's men rushed out of Meigs to take the south battery, and General Clay got safely into the fort with his four hundred. On the north bank eight hundred men under Lieutenant Colonel William Dudley quickly carried the enemy battery and spiked the guns. But then too little leadership and too much zeal betrayed the American cause. One of Dudley's details had wandered off and became engaged with Indians. Instead of falling back to the boats as planned, Dudley went to the aid of the detail. His men charged the Indians, broke them and pursued them through the woods up to the British camp. With this the British counterattacked the American front while more Indians struck the flanks. About six hundred men were killed or captured. Dudley was taken and tomahawked as the Indians began to renew the horrors of the Raisin River while Proctor looked on indifferently.

But this time Tecumseh was present. He rushed in among his murdering warriors, who had already taken twenty scalps. He knocked one down with the flat of his sword, seized another by the throat and swung at a third. "Are there no men here?" he roared, and the slaughter stopped. Enraged, Tecumseh ran to Proctor to demand to know why his Indians had been allowed to kill prisoners. Proctor said, "Your Indians cannot be controlled. They cannot be commanded." Tecumseh's face twisted in contempt. "You are unfit to command," he told Proctor. "Go and put on petticoats!"

Despite the Dudley disaster, Fort Meigs had been saved. On May 9, with his Indians deserting and his militia clamoring to go home to plant crops, Proctor raised the seige and returned to Malden.

Two months later he came back, and failed again. Disgruntled, he dropped down the Maumee, reached Lake Erie and coasted east to the Sandusky River. He went up the Sandusky determined to take Fort Stephenson, an American outpost so vulnerable that Harrison ordered it abandoned. Its commander, Major George Croghan, thought otherwise. "We have determined to maintain this place, and by Heaven we will," he told Harrison. He did. As the British and Indians charged they were mowed down by his Kentucky sharpshooters and a single cannon, called "Old Betsey," spewing out grape and nails. Proctor thought that Croghan's fire was the severest he had ever seen, and he gave up his offensive to return to Malden.

The date was August 1, one day before Commodore Perry began taking his flotilla over the bar at Erie.

28

Battle of Lake Erie

～ IRONICALLY, OUT OF GRANNY DEARBORN'S MISMANAGEMENT OF WAR on the Niagara Frontier had come an unanticipated but enormous advantage. Merely by acting, he had compelled Vincent to use the garrison at Fort Erie as reinforcements for his own army, thus freeing Perry's ships at Black Rock to sail up the Niagara into Fort Erie.

Perry harnessed the vessels to oxen to tow them through the Niagara's swift current. Reaching the open waters of the lake, they spread sail and made for the sheltering long arm of land that formed the harbor at Erie. Now there were ten ships in Perry's flotilla, and the youthful commander was elated.

On July 12, however, he was saddened to hear of the death of James Lawrence, an officer whom he much admired. In tribute to the *Chesapeake*'s fallen captain, he named his own flagship *Lawrence*. Her sister ship was called *Niagara*.

Now Perry's problems were of a different order. He needed men. Again and again he wrote to Chauncey back at Sackets Harbor, imploring him to send men. Even as Chauncey procrastinated, or sent him the raked-over leavings of his own command, the Navy Department ordered Perry to do battle on the lake. Stung, Perry wrote Chauncey: "For God's sake, and yours and mine, send me men." Chauncey sent him sixty sickly sailors, and Perry turned to recruiting his own crews by offering farmers and woodsmen the princely pay of $10 monthly for four months' service or the duration of a battle, whichever was shorter.

Even so, by mid-July he had only three hundred men, and Perry was as nearly frantic as a man of his stability might become; for continued delay gave the enemy time to finish the powerful brig *Detroit*, still on the stocks near Fort Malden.

One last obstacle faced this resourceful young commodore: the bar outside the harbor at Erie. To cross it he used "camels." Floats were placed on either side of a ship, filled with water and sunk to a depth just below the ship's portholes. Then timbers were run through the portholes, coming to rest on the decks of the camels to either side, after which the water was pumped out of the camels and as they rose they lifted the ship with them and floated over the bar.

By August 5 Perry had his fleet out in open water, and he began searching the lake for the British. But the enemy fleet was still in Malden under Captain Robert Barclay, a veteran sailor who had lost an arm at Trafalgar. Perry returned to Erie, where he resumed his demands for more men. On August 10 he got ninety of them, headed by young Lieutenant Jesse Elliott, whom he placed in command of *Niagara*. Perry still needed Marines, however, and this shortage was eliminated when General Harrison sent him one hundred Kentucky marksmen. With their easy discipline, these sailors in buckskin might have turned out to be a new trial, but they turned-to like old salts after Perry explained the demands of shipboard life. Now all that the eager American commander needed was a battle, and he got it on the morning of September 10, 1813, when the one-armed Barclay brought the British fleet to Perry's new base at Put-in-Bay.

Because of so many variables in guns, number and tonnage, it is almost impossible to estimate which was the stronger fleet. Suffice it to say that Perry, with ten ships to Barclay's six, held a slight edge. Otherwise they were evenly matched, Barclay possessing superior long-range artillery, Perry being stronger at close range. Barclay planned to fight at a distance and defeat his enemy ships in detail; Perry was eager to close to bring his carronades into action.

Perry's plan was to sail his own ship, *Lawrence*, supported by *Caledonia, Scorpion*, and *Ariel*, against Barclay in *Detroit*—most powerful ship on the lake—and *Hunter* and tiny *Chippewa*. Elliott with *Niagara* would fight Barclay's second ship, *Queen Charlotte*, to which she was superior, while *Somers, Porcupine, Tigress*, and *Trippe* took on *Lady Prevost* and *Little Belt*.

Slowly the American ships beat their way out of the harbor. Their decks were strewn with sand to prevent them from becoming slippery with blood. Outside stood the British ships, freshly calked and painted, with their red hulls gleaming and their polished brass glittering in the autumn sun. At first the weather favored the British, but then the wind changed and Perry held the weather gauge. Suddenly an American cheer rolled toward the British ships. Perry had unfurled his standard, a nine-foot square of blue on which white letters a foot high proclaimed the words of the dying Lawrence: DON'T GIVE UP THE SHIP. Then the British cheered. Their bands had begun to play "Rule, Britannia"—and out of the mouths of *Detroit*'s cannon came the first shots of the battle.

Lawrence was *Detroit*'s target. She took a punishing fire as she sailed down the British line in an effort to reach her adversary. Then *Queen Charlotte* joined *Detroit*, and *Lawrence*'s ordeal was nearly redoubled. *Charlotte* was free to pound Perry's flagship because Elliott in *Niagara* was not closing as ordered. Elliott stood off at a distance firing only a few long-range guns.

For two hours the British pair blasted away at *Lawrence*. They took her apart, cannon by carronade, spar by sail, brace by bowline, and they shot her hull into a sieve. Undaunted, Perry fought on alone. Of 103 men who began the fight, 83 were either killed or wounded. Perry stood upon the blood-clotted sand and cried: "Can any of the wounded pull a rope?" A few crawled to his side to help put a dismounted gun in place. It was *Lawrence*'s last gun, and Perry fired it to let the fleet know that he was still in action. But Elliott in *Niagara* still stood at a distance. All seemed to be lost, except for Perry.

The American knew that he had given as well as taken punishment. He knew that with a fresh ship he could turn the tide of battle. Hauling down his blue banner, he leaped into a boat with his thirteen-year-old brother, Alexander, and four seamen. They began rowing toward *Niagara*. Perry stood in the stern until the seamen pushed him down. A British broadside went over their heads. The water around them was dimpled with musket shot, but the little boat passed miraculously through. Coming aboard *Niagara*, Perry took command. He ordered Elliott to bring up the three schooners that had also lagged behind. *Lawrence* was now drifting out of control, her flag pulled down, but before the British could move to possess her, Perry returned to the fight.

Swift and straight, *Niagara* burst the British line. On the port side her batteries battered *Chippewa, Little Belt,* and *Lady Prevost;* on the starboard they thundered and flamed at *Detroit* and *Queen Charlotte*. *Detroit* tried to turn and fouled *Queen Charlotte*. Perry's gunners took aim at the tangled ships and shot them both to pieces. With the first- and second-in-command on each of his vessels either killed or wounded, with his remaining arm shattered, Barclay surrendered *Detroit*. Eventually his other ships were overcome, and the battle was over before dusk.

Now the battered *Lawrence* had run up her flag again, and a feeble cheer rose from the living and wounded men aboard her who still had breath to spare. Aboard *Niagara*, Oliver Hazard Perry took an old envelope from his pocket. He held it against a navy cap and penciled a message to General Harrison, waiting anxiously ashore. Perry wrote: "We have met the enemy and they are ours."

29

The Thames:
Tecumseh's Last Battle

~ THE DEFEAT OF THE BRITISH FLEET ON LAKE ERIE HAD UNMASKED Proctor at Fort Malden, and that jittery general, fearing American revenge for the Raisin River massacre, quickly prepared to flee. Tecumseh soon realized that Proctor was about to withdraw and leave the Indians to shift for themselves. He confronted him and said: "We must compare our Father's conduct to a fat dog that carries its tail upon its back, but when affrightened drops it between its legs and runs off."

Nevertheless, Proctor would not stay, as he had promised the Indians, and Tecumseh realized that he would have to go with him. "We are now going to follow the British," he told his people glumly, "and I feel certain that we shall never return."

As Proctor began withdrawing, William Henry Harrison moved to the attack. Governor Shelby had come to Lake Erie with three thousand Kentucky volunteers. Harrison also had the services of Congressman Richard Mentor Johnson with one thousand mounted volunteers. But Proctor got away. Harrison found Fort Malden and the nearby town of Amherstburg still burning. On September 26 Detroit was reoccupied, after which the pursuit of Proctor began.

Johnson's horsemen crossed the Detroit River and gave chase by land while Perry's ships tried to sail through the river into Lake St.

Clair in an effort to cut off Proctor's rear. Neither was quick enough, for Proctor had reached the Thames River and was moving up its banks. On the night of October 4 he halted at the modern town of Thamesville and prepared for battle. Tecumseh gathered his warriors. He took off the sword denoting his rank as a brigadier general in the British Army and said, "When my son becomes a noted warrior, give him this." He forecast his own death, just as his elder brother Cheeseekau had done in the Carolinas when Tecumseh was a young boy. "Brother warriors," he said, "we are about to enter an engagement from which I shall not return. My body will remain on the field of battle."

In the morning Tecumseh was more cheerful. He hunted up Proctor and spoke to him in a forgiving mood. "Father, have a big heart! Tell your young men to be firm and all will be well." Proctor's conduct, however, was not likely to make many men stand firm. His army was aware that he was giving battle reluctantly, that he preferred flight to fighting. Yet his battle position was fairly strong.

It lay between the river on the left and a large swamp on the right. In its middle was a smaller swamp. Most of the British troops were between the river and the small swamp. Indians under Tecumseh were between the small and large swamp.

Harrison planned to make an infantry frontal assault against the British, but then, learning that the enemy regulars were drawn up in open rather than close order, he called on Richard Mentor Johnson's mounted Kentuckians. Just before the attack, Johnson decided on his own that the space was too narrow for one thousand horsemen. He divided his regiment in two, one battalion under his brother James to ride at the British, the other under himself to charge Tecumseh's Indians between the swamps. The bugle sounded and the homespun dragoons on their ragged mounts galloped forward crying, "Remember the Raisin! Remember the river Raisin!"

On the American right James Johnson's cavalrymen burst the British line. Leaning from their saddles, the Americans swung their tomahawks and scattered the regulars in terror. General Henry Proctor became so frightened that he jumped into his carriage and clattered away from the battlefield. The Americans pursued in delight. They did not catch Proctor, but they took hundreds of prisoners and captured about $1 million in supplies, including guns taken from Burgoyne in 1777, then lost at Detroit by Hull in 1812.

On the American left, Tecumseh's warriors waited until the American horsemen were within a few paces before pouring a heavy fire into them. Perhaps twenty saddles were emptied. Richard Johnson was among the wounded, but he stayed with his men as they seized their rifles and leaped from their horses to engage the Indians on foot. American infantry hurried forward in support, and the Indians charged.

One of them came at sixty-four-year-old Colonel William Whitley. Both men fired and both fell dead. Another Indian rushed with upraised tomahawk at the bleeding Johnson. Johnson shot him through the head and fell down unconscious. In one of these two encounters—probably the first—the gallant Tecumseh was killed. His fall did not decide the Battle of the Thames, for British defeat was already guaranteed with the American charge and Proctor's flight. But the death of this noble Indian leader was also the death of his vision of a confederacy of Indians hunting, as their fathers had hunted, across vast and untroubled stretches of American plains and forest.

Tecumseh's body was never found. It was believed to have been borne off in the night by his sorrowing warriors, and his final resting place remains as much a mystery as the man who killed him. Richard Johnson never claimed the credit, although his followers claimed it for him during the election of 1836 that made Johnson vice president. What is known, however, is that vengeful frontiersmen as barbarous as the butchers of the Raisin River stripped the skin from a body mistakenly believed to have been Tecumseh's and cut it into razor strops. "Tecumseh razor strops" eventually appeared in fashionable Washington.

Harrison's victory had ended British power in Upper Canada, crushed the Indians and redeemed the Northwest Territory. All this had been made possible by the earlier and more important victory that Perry had won on Lake Erie. Together the two battles raised the American flag for good over northern Ohio, Indiana and Illinois, and over the territory out of which Michigan, Minnesota, and Wisconsin were formed—in other words, most of the modern Midwest, that rich, thriving, clanging, fertile territory that is at once the breadbasket and the tool shop of America and the iron heart of the continent.

And the Midwest was won for America chiefly because an ardent young captain would not give up his ship.

30

Privateering/British Blockade

⁓ ALTHOUGH BRITANNIA AGAIN "RULED THE WAVES" LORD LIVERPOOL'S government was deeply shocked by the losses of merchant ships to American privateers and the U.S. Navy. Swarming out of ports from Maine to Georgia, hundreds of privateers took no less than 1,344 prizes while the navy's warships did even better percentage-wise with 22 of its warships capturing 165 British vessels. In all then, Britain during the War of 1812 lost no fewer than 1,509 ships by capture, to say nothing of an unknown number of vessels that resisted and were sunk.

It would seem, then, that American privateers—that is, civilian ships licensed by the government to prey on enemy merchant shipping—were a great asset of the United States Navy. Actually they were probably more of a liability. First and foremost, they skimmed off the cream of Yankee sailors preferring the rich prize money of privateering to the low pay and only occasional prize money of the regular navy. Able-bodied landsmen who could have served in the U.S. Army also chose to make money at sea instead. So did shipyard craftsmen drawn by the higher wages of building privateers. Stores and supplies needed by the navy were also consumed by these civilian sailing sharks.

Privateers sought profits alone. They were not interested in helping their country defeat Great Britain. Usually, they were built by companies or corporations financed by shareholders. Other privateers were competitors, not comrades in arms. A captain possessing "trade secrets," that is, a knowledge of enemy sea tactics gained in experience, had no intention of sharing them with his rivals in the way that naval commanders were quick to communicate the enemy combat tactics they had learned to their brethren. In a phrase, the U.S. Navy was at war with the Royal Navy, the privateers were at war for money.

It has been argued that if the privateers drained off the supply of able-bodied men, caused shortages or forced up prices, they also did great damage to the British merchant marine. This may be partially true, but it is also true that if a privateer captain had his choice of taking a British coasting brig loaded with clothing for Wellington's army in Spain, or a homeward-bound East Indiaman carrying highly salable cargo or, even beyond the dreams of avarice, a specie ship like that *Bonne Citoyenne* that James Lawrence was unable to capture—there is no question that the clothing brig would come in last, even though its loss would have much more effect on the British war effort than the other two.

Privateers rarely resisted capture. Like the xebecs of Bashaw Yushuf, they had no stomach for battle. Coming upon an unarmed merchantman all they had to do was fire a single shot across her bow and her flag would come fluttering down. If she were armed and fought back, the privateer almost certainly would haul off. Privateers hailed by British warships usually capitulated without a shot. Only in a few instances did they engage the enemy, but more than one British captain reported coming alongside a Yankee corsair to find its decks deserted and its crew cowering below. Finally, discipline was difficult to enforce aboard these vessels because their seamen shipped aboard for profit and would resent being subjected to the lash or the noose. Theirs was purely a commercial agreement, and if the life proved too demanding or too dangerous, they would leave it; unlike a sailor who enlists for a stated period of time and can't quit the first time he hears "the music" of those howling cannonballs. Nevertheless, if the privateers were unpopular at home—especially with the secretaries of war and the Navy—they were dreaded by the British government, much as Winston Churchill in World War II was terrified that Hitler's undersea warfare would cut the British lifeline to the United States and the Mediterranean.

To check them, the Admiralty ordered a blockade of the exits of the Delaware and the Chesapeake. Having already paid the Americans the ultimate compliment of building bigger frigates the equal of "Old Ironsides" and her sister furies, Britain realized that repeal of the Orders in Council had not brought peace. So she not only ordered

234 ~ The War of 1812

the blockade but later extended it south to the Mississippi and north to Long Island, carefully excluding New England for the purpose of encouraging anti war sentiment there.

Vice Admiral John Borlase Warren was charged with enforcing the blockade, and by February 1813, he had at his disposal seventeen ships of the line, two 50-gunners, twenty-seven frigates, and about fifty smaller vessels. With the years, as his fleet grew steadily larger, he turned the screws of the blockade tighter and tighter. The American economy was strangled. Exports, which had been as high as $130 million in 1807, fell to $25 million in 1813 and to $7 million the following year. Import duties, which had yielded $413 million in 1811, fell to less than half that amount in 1814.

The blockade also bottled up coastal shipping, with the result that a dreadful burden was placed on land transportation. It took forty-six days for a wagon to move from South Carolina to Philadelphia, and the poor roads were so thronged with wagons that on one occasion, no less than eight hundred of them were counted waiting in line before a Pennsylvania ferry. Prices soared. Sugar quoted at $9 a hundredweight in New Orleans sold for $21 in New York in August, 1813, and by December had risen to $40. A hundredweight of rice that sold for $3 in Savannah brought $12 in Philadelphia.

Meanwhile, the Admiralty ordered Warren, assisted by his second-in-command Admiral Sir George Cockburn, to bring the war home to the Americans by blocking the mouths of the Delaware and Chesapeake to prevent Yankee privateers from sortying into the Atlanitc to attack British shipping or return to the port with prizes..

Cockburn reached the Chesapeake in the early spring of 1813, engaging first in cleaning out the hen roosts and pigsties in the area around Lynnhaven Bay. Next he ravaged Frenchtown, Maryland, put Havre de Grace to the torch and sailed up the Susquehanna sixty miles to destroy a cannon foundry. Carrying plunder and pillage to other areas in the upper Chesapeake, he turned south in June to join Warren and three thousand regulars in an attack on Norfolk.

There were two objectives: the frigate *Constellation,* anchored near the town, and the Portsmouth Navy Yard. But an amphibious assault on Craney Island, which guarded Norfolk, was hurled back on June 20 by Americans fighting coolly and shooting accurately under the command of Brigadier General Robert Taylor. Frustrated, Warren and Cockburn vented their spite on the little village of Hampton. Here the British lost all restraint. As one officer who was later to command the British Army in India noted in his diary: "Every horror was perpetrated with impunity—rape, murder, pillage—*and not a man was punished.*" Warren tried to place all the blame for Hampton on a unit of French prisoners who had elected to serve with the British rather than languish in prisons, but Warren deceived no one.

Neither was Warren able to destroy the Chesapeake's privateering sanctuaries. Before the war ended there were 526 Yankee privateers swarming out of American coastal cities to strike British commercial shipping and to take that fearsome toll that so disturbed Lord Liverpool.

31

Armstrong-Monroe Rivalry

~ THIRTY-SEVEN YEARS AFTER THE BATTLE OF TRENTON IN WHICH SECRE-
tary of State James Monroe and Secretary of War John Armstrong
both fought as young comrades-in-arms, they confronted each other
as the two most powerful members of James Madison's cabinet, each
hungering for the presidency and each following a different road to
the President's House.

Armstrong was born in Carlisle, Pennsylvania, in 1755, the son of
Major General John Armstrong, a hero of the French and Indian Wars
who also served under Washington at the Brandywine and Schuylkill
during the Revolution, and testified in his chief's defense when the
treacherous Conway Cabal tried to replace Washington with the toady-
ing Horatio Gates.

When the first shots of the Revolutionary War were fired at Lexington in 1775, the nineteen-year-old Armstrong was a student at Princeton, but he left the classroom to become an officer in Washington's
army. While he was with Gates at Saratoga, Armstrong met and
befriended another expert in the sly art of betrayal, James Wilkinson.
It was Armstrong whom Gates ordered to overtake Benedict Arnold
after he disobeyed orders and rode to the front to win the tide-turning
Battle of Saratoga. Armstrong's mission was to convey Gates's order
for Arnold to return to his tent before he did something rash—like

defeating Burgoyne—but even though he was mounted on an unusually fast horse, he never reached Arnold until the general was wounded and the battle was over, suggesting that, like Wilkinson, he was not too fond of the impact area.

At Trenton, where eighteen-year-old Monroe was wounded in the shoulder, Armstrong was an aide to General Hugh Mercer, and a few days later carried his mortally wounded chief from the battlefield at Princeton. Blunt, rough and outspoken—traits usually associated with frankness, either consciously or otherwise—Armstrong actually had a devious mind, schooled to intrigue with Wilkinson as his tutor. In character assassination his favorite tactic was the anonymous letter dripping with the vilification of an acid pen. It was not until twenty years after Washington squelched the mutiny that might have ensued from Armstrong's Newburgh Addresses that he admitted being their author.

After the Revolution Armstrong became a lawyer, serving as attorney general of Pennsylvania and one of its representatives in the first Congress of 1787. In 1789 he became attached to the wealthy and influential Livingston family by marrying Alida, the sister of Chancellor Robert Livingston of New York State, a signer of the Declaration of Independence who administered the oath of office to George Washington. This association foreshadowed a promising career in the Federalist Party, but Armstrong astonished everyone who knew him by retiring from active life to a farm in Red Hook, New York. For eleven years he seemed content with farming, until the Federalists passed the Alien and Sedition Acts. Seizing his pen once again, he dipped it in vinegar and gall, to compose a vicious, slashing and anonymous attack on his Federalist friends who had authored these masterpieces of legal prejudice, calling for their repeal.

The letter was also his farewell to the Federalists, for John Armstrong became an ardent Republican and an instant admirer of Thomas Jefferson and James Madison. When the Federalists were defeated in the annihilating election of 1804, and Robert Livingston returned from his post as minister to Napoleonic Paris, he was replaced by his Republican brother-in-law. Though shifty and deceitful, Armstrong was also incredibly gullible, with a mind about as subtle as the cows and pigs of his Red Hook farm, and thus, as Napoleon complained, a kind of kiwi bird unable to fly in the rarified air of European diplomacy. After the emperor requested his recall, John Armstrong came home preening himself on his great diplomatic triumph—revocation of the edicts of Berlin and Milan—a stunning reversal that never happened.

In 1812 Armstrong was an ardent Madison supporter, for which loyalty he was rewarded with a commission of brigadier general entrusted with directing the defense of New York City. Almost immediately he began to emerge as an opponent of Madison and was accused by the administration of discouraging enlistments in the regular army in order to expand his own militia. He soon became one of his benefactor's bitterest critics. Loyal Republicans called him a double-traitor or a power-hungry politician who would stop at nothing, but Armstrong—like his friend Wilkinson again—was well served by an impenetrable thick skin. That was why, when Madison on the last day of 1812 dropped the inept Eustis, held responsible for six agonizing months of defeat and retreat, and eventually replaced him with John Armstrong, official Washington was incredulous.

How could the President entrust the War Department to one of his most implacable enemies? Ten years later Madison gave a lame explanation for his decision: "recommendations [of Armstrong] by esteemed friends; a belief that he possessed with known talents a degree of military information which might be useful. . . ." It is possible that Madison was grateful to Armstrong for his support during the 1812 canvass that renominated him for president, but even so, he spoke not a word about the New Yorker's incessant plotting and his detestation of "the Virginia Dynasty" launched by Jefferson and which would include Madison and Monroe. Armstrong was determined to destroy what he called "the planter's dynasty," even if it meant moving the capital from its proximity to the Old Dominion—so salutary to Jefferson and his protégés—to a safer place on the Delaware or the Hudson, or even to his hometown of Carlisle.

John Armstrong saw his appointment as secretary of war as a giant step toward the President's House. The range of his duties had never been defined. Indeed the president was the civilian commander-in-chief, which would mean one thing in a president such as Washington and quite another to one like Madison, who was the first to admit that he knew nothing of military matters—if he did not indeed abhor them—and was in no way a warlike man. Armstrong was quite content to leave to Madison the army's "civilian" problems such as procurement or recommendations to Congress on the size of the army and the amount of money it needed to operate, while he, Armstrong, would take the field as the *Herr Feldmarschall* of the armies.

Here he could achieve the military glory that has made so many war heroes presidents of the United States, and thus squelch the chances of the equally ambitious Secretary of State James Monroe.

• • •

Another Virginian, born in Westmoreland County in 1758, James Monroe was immensely proud of his Revolutionary War service, which propelled him into the Continental Congress in 1783, and then, in 1790, to the U.S. Senate, from Fredericksburg, where he had practiced law. Here was perhaps the most ardent and incorruptible republican in American history. As Glenn Tucker had said: "His guide, God and obsession was the Cause," meaning liberty as described in the Declaration of Independence, representative government as organized in the U.S. Constitution—and to royalty everywhere, the French solution of the guillotine.

Monroe was as different from Gouverneur Morris, the minister whom he replaced in 1794, as democracy differs from monarchy. Morris had been an ardent admirer of King Louis XVI, whose treasury, army and navy had helped so much to defeat the British, and he did his utmost to protect the Bourbons whenever and wherever he could. Monroe took the exact opposite stance when he went to Paris, throwing his arms around the president of the convention in the presence of cheering delegates and presenting the Stars and Stripes to the assembly. The French tricolor he received in exchange was promptly sent to President Washington, who had always thought Monroe too fond of the French and had, much to Monroe's indignation, done so little to further the democratic cause in Europe.

Monroe's biggest political error was to attempt to wrest the presidency from Madison in 1808. Although he was indeed one of Jefferson's many protégés, the man from Monticello thought he was much too young and decidedly too eager. Thus when John Randolph threw his support to Monroe, Jefferson came to Madison's side, and Virginia decided the nomination by rallying to Madison rather than his challenger. Thus rebuffed, Monroe retired to private life and the practice of law—neither of which could satisfy his boundless ambition.

In reflection he decided not to follow the traditional routes to the President's House: either service in combat during the war or afterward at the Constitutional Convention. Instead, he would build his power platform as governor of a great state, a path more often followed now than then. He had already been governor of Virginia, and in 1811 he returned to Williamsburg—still an implacable enemy of James Madison. But politicians are as apt at mending fences as busting them, and it was Madison of all people who offered *his* enemy the olive branch. To Little Jemmy's great credit he realized that he was contemplative rather than active, and he needed someone in his cabinet who could get things done. Monroe was an energetic doer, so

Madison brought him back to Washington as his secretary of state.

He was then a muscular, compact man who to advance himself had learned to control his quick temper and to be courteous to everyone at all times. Occasionally, of course, he would lose control and the scorching language he had picked up in the war came flaming forth. "Profanity?" one of his slaves asked. "Bless your soul, you ought to hear old massa!" Monroe's biggest draw-back politically was that he was not attractive, his nose being too long and his mouth too wide, and his stolid manner was accentuated by his somber, democratic dress.

As wartime secretary of state he had little to do, for the British ambassador had gone home and the interests of most European countries were handled by Napoleon's minister, J. M. P. Sérurier. Consequently, because he was indeed a dynamo, what is today called a workaholic, Monroe complained that he needed only one of his five clerks. Madison then was desperate for new and younger generals, having even suggested a star or two to Henry Clay. Excellent frontier shot that he was, Clay knew where his future lay—and he declined. Next Monroe, eager for action, asked Madison to make him a general. He had always been fond of military glamor—as president he would attend state functions with a pistol on his hip—and his friends called him "colonel" rather than "secretary." Madison liked the idea, but then, after dropping Secretary of War Eustis on December 31, 1812, he asked Monroe to handle both the State and War Departments.

Monroe obliged, until Madison—always sensitive to the "Virginia Dynasty" charge—realized that with himself as chief executive and Monroe holding two portfolios, his cabinet was a bit too "planterish." Even though he had come to rely heavily on Monroe for military counsel, he could not continue politically to endure opposition taunts that with the Swiss Jew Albert Gallatin also in his cabinet the U.S. government was being run by "two Virginians and a foreigner." So he withdrew Monroe's war portfolio and gave it to Armstrong.

That was how the erstwhile advocate of mutiny and military dictatorship came to command all American armies, much to the glee of the Federalists he had deserted—who made haste to publicize his unsavory past—and to the consternation of loyal Republicans who were also aware of Armstrong's Cromwellian tendencies; and Madison soon found that his move to strengthen his administration had rather been productive of criticism and divisiveness. Armstrong, meanwhile, had made a rather happier discovery: his arch rival Monroe wanted to be a general! Why not? He would be subordinate to Armstrong in the New York area where the new secretary of war planned to establish his headquarters, a "coincidence" that would offer many opportunities for decapitation; and so, when Armstrong's list of new major generals was forwarded to the president, the name of James Monroe was at its head.

Monroe was astute enough to realize why it was there, and he declined this invitation to the guillotine, while artfully suggesting to Mr. Madison that his new war chief apparently was planning to take direction of the war out of Washington. The president at once informed the secretary of war that he must remain in the capital, except when occasional visits to the front might be required. Madison had also begun to question the wisdom of his own appointment, finding that Armstrong's "degree of military information which might be useful" was indeed limited. As James Wilkinson, Armstrong's present friend and later enemy, would observe: "In military affairs he is a mere writer and talker, and not an actor." And whose name was at the head of Armstrong's list after Monroe had removed his own? James Wilkinson's, the man whom Winfield Scott had described as an "unprincipled imbecile," and who had become, during his lotus-eating sojourn in Louisiana, a heavy, self-pitying drinker who spent much of his time in bed. Nevertheless, a rejoicing John Armstrong immediately dashed off to him the following message: "Come to the North, and come quickly! If our cards be well played, we may renew the scene of Saratoga!"

3 2

James Wilkinson

~JAMES WILKINSON WAS BORN IN MARYLAND IN 1757 ON A PLANTATION about three miles northeast of the present village of Benedict on the south side of Hunting Creek. His parents—Joseph and Betty Heighe Wilkinson—were both the children of old, established English families that had migrated to the colony in the seventeenth century, drawn there by the policy of religious freedom instituted by its founder, Cecilius Calvert, a Catholic and the second Baron Baltimore. Joseph Wilkinson was a successful planter-merchant, owner of thousands of acres and scores of slaves to work them. When Joseph died in 1764, his seven-year-old son James was a wealthy boy.

By then it was obvious that James was bright and was going to be big. At maturity, he stood close to six feet, with a burly body that in later years would become obese. He could also be described as handsome, although his oval face with its regular features betrayed a certain slyness and silkiness that was not entirely masculine. At the age of seventeen, Wilkinson was sent to Philadelphia to study medicine. This great metropolis of the New World fascinated him. He loved to stroll along its paved and lighted streets, excited by the passage of gleaming coaches with heraldic devices on their doors or of elegant gentlemen on horseback. He was astonished to see so many beautifully dressed men and women, having anticipated seeing no one but Quakers in sober gray or black. Yet, he did not neglect the Quakers, for they were the rulers of Philadelphia and Pennsylvania. He was often a guest at their fine two-story mansions, mingling among the Biddles, Bonds and Shippens, deferential in his bows, the soul of friendship in his smiles. Surprisingly, even though he was one of "the World's People," as the Society of Friends, self-mortifying in everything but wealth and power, spoke of self-indulgent non-Quakers, he found himself warmly accepted by them. James Wilkinson liked everyone, and he liked everyone to like him.

Because he arrived in the City of Brotherly Love in 1773—the year of the Boston Tea Party—he quickly came under the spell of that "fierce spirit of independence" generated by the continuing quarrel with the mother country. He was fond of watching the various militia units drilling on the green. Though an instant Patriot, this did not deter him from befriending the officers of the 18th Royal Irish Infantry. James Wilkinson would never withhold the warmth of his personality from anyone who might some day be of service to him, even if he were the enemy. Having friends in both camps would always seem to him a wise policy. Moreover, the Irish on parade in their gorgeous uniforms thrilled him. He would love to strut like that and wear such colorful clothes.

Unfortunately, in the spring of 1775 the call of medicine drew him out of Philadelphia to Monocacy, Maryland, about thirty miles up the Potomac from Georgetown. He was now beyond the stirring sound of bugle calls and rattling drums. So he missed the Battle of Lexington-Concord where "the shot heard round the world" was fired, and also the Battle of Bunker Hill. But after these famous fights were fought, he became a volunteer in a rifle corps and joined the Rebel army forming around Boston. Somehow James Wilkinson would usually be too late for a battle, or too far behind the lines to engage in one. Somehow he seemed to prefer the sound of martial music, or the sight of military marching to the smell of gunpowder. And he somehow always seemed to seek and find some superior officer of great influence, attaching himself to them with customary charm and deference in hopes of rapid promotion. This was what he did in Boston after Howe evacuated the city, quickly joining Colonels John Stark and Joseph Reed on a tour of the Bunker Hill battlefield, asking questions calculated to appeal to their pride and thus induce them to remember the name of this intuitive, affable young man. Wilkinson, though only eighteen, was even able to get himself appointed aide to General Nathanael Greene, Washington's finest general. And after Greene was transferred to New York, far from Washington's headquarters at

Boston—Promotion's Promised Land—he landed on Colonel Reed's staff.

Ingratiation with the mighty was not James Wilkinson's only skill. Though young, he did possess organizing ability and decisiveness. Thus he was able to lead a reinforcement of a hundred men north to Montreal on a march that was nearly the equal of Benedict Arnold's own nightmare trek into Canada. Reporting to Arnold on May 23, 1776, he was at once appointed to his staff. Again no action, although he did accompany General Arnold on his retreat from Montreal and was with him when they were the last two Americans to leave the northern land that a starry-eyed Continental Congress had hoped would become "the fourteenth American state." Captain Wilkinson's next mentor was Major General Horatio Gates, a most timid warrior but an able administrator and, best of all from Wilkinson's point of view, a master of intrigue.

Having sensed a kindred spirit in this charming young man, Gates promptly had him promoted to brigade major, but then typhoid fever temporarily halted Wilkinson's rapid ascent up the gold-braided ladder of promotion. Upon his recovery Wilkinson decided to seek out Major General Charles Lee, second in command of the Continental Army. Like Gates, Lee was a former British officer and an eccentric who was surrounded everywhere he went by a pack of yapping poodles. Between the two there was a growing conspiracy to bring down Washington. Wilkinson found Lee at an inn in Basking Ridge, New Jersey, but only in time to see him led away as a British captive. But he did possess a letter Lee had just written to Gates in which he hinted that "a certain great man is damnably deficient." "Wilkie," as he was known by the younger officers, hastened to deliver it to "Granny," Gates's troops' derisive name for their commander, becoming once again attached to him.

With Lee gone, Granny Gates was now Number One in the conspiracy to discredit Washington. It was known as the "Conway Cabal," after Brigadier General Thomas Conway, an Irishman who had served in the French Army and who publicly jeered at the commander-in-chief as a bungling amateur in buckskins. Through influential friends in Congress, including John Adams, the Conway conspirators hoped to replace Washington with Gates. For his part in the plot James Wilkinson was to become secretary of a revived board of war with the rank of brevet[*] brigadier general. At twenty a general! But not for long, if only because one night in his cups Wilkie's tongue wagged a bit too freely,

---

[*] A brevet commission is the rank without the pay.

revealing part of Conway's conspiratorial correspondence with Gates. When Washington learned of it, he boldly exposed the entire scheme, and the roar of outrage succeeding his revelation made Granny Gates scurry for cover like a cockroach running from the light, while silky Wilkie quickly resigned both his post and his star. When Gates tried to put the blame for the fiasco on Wilkinson's head, his dear young friend challenged him to a duel. Gates showed up, smiling, fatherly, putting his arm around Wilkie's shoulder, so that no shots were fired; which seems a pity, for now posterity will never know which of these treacherous toadies would have shot the other in the back.

Gates and Wilkinson were together again at the tide-turning Battle of Saratoga along the Hudson River in New York. Actually this struggle—probably the most momentous in the annals of American arms because it brought France into the war against Britain—was the result of the efforts of Benedict Arnold and Major General Philip Schuyler. But Gates, in an appearance before Congress, so throughly discredited Schuyler that he was able to replace him. With Colonel James Wilkinson as his adjutant general, Gates next went after Benedict Arnold. Between them they sought by insult and indignity so to goad Arnold that he would either resign or commit some indiscretion that would enable Gates to dismiss him. Arnold did resign, but remained in camp upon the plea of Gates's officer corps. Thus it was he, ignoring Gates's orders to remain in his tent, who went riding into battle like an avenging scourge, compelling John Burgoyne to surrender his army. Granny and Wilkie, who had been a safe two miles from the front, hastened to Congress to explain how cleverly they had won the battle.

But even Congress was appalled by Horatio Gates's disgraceful flight from the disastrous Battle of Camden, and no one objected after he retired from the service. James Wilkinson meanwhile, resilient as ever, used all of his ingratiating skills to persuade Washington to name him clothier general, a safe snuggery in which he remained for the duration of the war. By then Wilkinson had married, taking to wife Ann Biddle, the charming Quaker lady he had met in Philadelphia. For this heinous offense—marrying one of the "World's People"—she was read out of the Friends Meeting. While in Philadelphia, incidentally, Wilkinson sought to ingratiate himself with Joseph Reed, president of the supreme executive council of Pennsylvania—sworn enemy of Benedict Arnold and something of a skillful schemer in his own right—by offering him evidence of his former chief's dishonesty. But for some unknown reason, Reed demurred.

After the war James Wilkinson returned to civilian life, entering politics in Kentucky and going into business in New Orleans, where he obtained from the Spanish authorities there a secret annual pension of $2,000 a year for "advising" them on how to conduct themselves vis-à-vis the United States. But this was not enough to redeem his failing commercial ventures. To impress his Spanish contacts he resolved upon returning to the army to join the savage border warfare raging between the hostile Indians of the Northwest* and the United States. When a punitive expedition of about eight hundred one-month Kentucky volunteers under Brigadier General Charles Scott crossed the Ohio River in May 1791, Wilkinson went along as second-in-command. Entering the Wabash country, this force burned villages, destroyed crops, slaughtered Indians of all ages and both sexes, and took captives. Scott wrote proudly of the campaign and of Wilkinson's part in it, while Wilkinson had a kind word or two to write of himself. He did the same in August of that year when he personally led about five hundred militia against the village of L'Anguille, burning, killing, and destroying crops. Actually, the raid had no effect but to nourish in the hearts of the Indians a horrible ache for revenge; but it did serve Wilkinson's primary purpose of expanding his reputation. Secretary of War Henry Knox commended him, and in October of that year President Washington made him a lieutenant colonel. When Wilkinson took his oath of allegiance to the United States of America, he was well aware that he was still a secret agent in the pay of Spain. He had no intention of terminating this treacherous alliance, for James Wilkinson was a man fond of luxury, just like Benedict Arnold, and again like Arnold he was as a result always short of money. Wilkinson also confidently expected to become a brigadier and second in command of the United States Army after the retirement of General Arthur St. Clair. Actually, it was the Miami Indians under Little Turtle who "retired" St. Clair, ambushing his force of about 2,000 men along the Maumee River in 1791. Nearly two-thirds of the American army—1,320 soldiers—were casualties, and of these 900 perished, against Indian losses of only 150 killed and wounded. Unluckiest of all were those Americans who fell into the hands of the savages. Whether unharmed or immobilized by wounds, they were torn to pieces and scalped by their frenzied captors, while their women had huge stakes driven through their writhing, defiled bodies. Next day Little Turtle and his sachems ate the heart of Brigadier General Richard Butler. Thus the most disastrous and disgraceful defeat in the annals of American arms had the effect of getting rid of St. Clair while making James Wilkinson's useless August excursions shine like the silver star they placed on his shoulders.

* The Northwest of the 1790s is today's Midwest.

His fame now extended beyond his country's borders into the ears of the Spanish authorities in New Orleans. Baron Francisco Luis Héctor de Carondelet, governor of Spanish Louisiana, had heard that Wilkinson was a man with whom one might do business, and so on January 28, 1792, General Wilkinson accepted his kind offer of a pension of $2,000 annually retroactive to 1789 for his "advice" to the Spanish crown. Such counsel included how Spain might detach Kentucky and perhaps Tennessee as well from the country to which he had made an oath of allegiance, or how Spain should seize the opportunity offered by an "incompetent Secretary of War," "an ignorant commander in chief [Washington]" and a "contemptible" Union. In all, General Facing-Both-Ways received from Spain about $32,000 in bribes, usually shipped to him concealed in barrels of sugar or tobacco, of which he kept $26,000. Correspondence between Wilkinson and Carondelet and other Spanish officials was carried on in code. Unlike Benedict Arnold, the smooth General Wilkinson was adept at covering his tracks. No one suspected him of treachery until he joined Major General Anthony Wayne just prior to Wayne's victory at the Battle of Fallen Timbers on August 20, 1794.

While Wayne in his report spoke glowingly of "Brigadier General Wilkinson . . . whose brave example inspired the troops," Wilkinson was writing to a friend vilifying his chief as "a liar, a drunkard, a fool, the associate of the lowest order of society, and the companion of their vices, of desperate fortunes, my rancorous enemy, a coward, a hypocrite and the contempt of every man of sense and virtue." He also tried to have Henry Knox—that "incompetent Secretary of War"—summon Wayne before a court of inquiry, but without any specific charges and with only vituperation to offer, he got nowhere.

It was then that the aroused Wayne became acquainted with Wilkinson's treachery. Wayne may have decided that it would be wiser to wait until he could come up with specifics, but before he could he was dead of gout—and General Wilkinson was free to pursue his career of treason. He continued to do so until 1804, a year after President Jefferson purchased the Louisiana Territory—a vast region of 828,000 square miles stretching from the Gulf of Mexico to the Canadian border—from Napoleon for about $15 million. (In 1800 Spain by a secret treaty had ceded Louisiana back to France.) Wilkinson made hay in 1804 by contacting Caso Calvo, Spain's gullible boundary commissioner, to extract from him another $12,000 for his "reflections" on how Spain could still help herself in the New World. It took Wilkinson twenty days to compose this perfectly useless document, but even so, six hundred dollars a day was not bad in a time when his general's pay amounted to exactly four dollars daily. And he was now the senior brigadier general in the United States Army.

From his treasonous dealings with foreigners, Wilkinson turned to conspiracy with perhaps the most hated American of his time: Aaron Burr. Wilkinson met Burr during Benedict Arnold's expedition to Quebec. They became friends, as men of disparate size and personality often do: Burr, short and slight, fiery and impetuous; Wilkinson, tall and burly, silken and calculating. They met again in 1805, after Wilkinson's friend Jefferson sent him to New Orleans as military governor. Burr, on the run, charged with murder after the duel with Hamilton, universally despised, was anxious to obtain a diplomatic post. Wilkinson's attempt to help him failed, after which Burr spoke vaguely of carving out a personal empire in "the Southwest"—meaning Mexico. Such enterprises were not unusual in those days, and Wilkinson listened intently, accepting Burr's invitation to join the conspiracy. He thus began a balancing act between such bitter enemies as Thomas Jefferson and Aaron Burr—enjoying the friendship of the president and the confidence of the former vice president—that testifies to his mastery of the art of deception.

By late 1806 all was in readiness: Burr, with his barges loaded with troops, was ready to float down the Cumberland bound for the Mississippi. The night of October 8 Wilkinson received a letter from Burr in cipher detailing the entire plan. He sweated through the night decoding it. When he had finished he was trembling. *It was conspiracy!* Naked, bald, unmitigated conspiracy! Perhaps even treason! There was no way to twist it, conceal it, or camouflage it, in the tried-and-true Wilkinson way. Why should he risk his neck for it? He wasn't wanted for murder like Burr . . . he wasn't desperate. . . . He was James Wilkinson, general in chief of the United States Army, admired and trusted everywhere. So he sat down to polish up Burr's decoded missive with the necessary particulars to make it more damning—eliminating the use of his own name, of course—and then called upon a Lieutenant Smith, an officer as "trustworthy" as himself, who for five hundred dollars agreed to "resign" and secretly carry this communication to President Jefferson. It reached the president on November 25 and two days later he issued a proclamation warning against "unlawful enterprises." Before the year was out Burr had been taken captive near Natchez, Mississippi, never realizing that Wilkinson had betrayed him until he was charged with treason.

After Burr's acquittal, Wilkinson was surprised and aggrieved to find himself almost as thoroughly discredited as Burr. James Wilkinson, patriot and war hero, to be tarred with the same brush as Aaron

Burr, murderer and traitor! What an ungrateful people Americans were! And yet, he still had the temerity to demand of the Spanish viceroy in Mexico a payment of $200,000 for having saved the colony from Burr's raid! And he was furious when the demand was coldly refused. When this became known, and the truth about his Spanish pension leaked out, James Wilkinson on December 18, 1809, was ordered to resign his command of the army and report to Maryland to await a court-martial on charges of having accepted bribes from a foreign government. The trial did not begin until September 2, 1811, time enough for a man as clever as Wilkinson to learn that potentially hostile witnesses such as Carondelet and Casa Calvo and their agents were either dead, back in Spain or transferred elsewhere, and to fabricate a balance sheet showing that the money he received came from secret tobacco sales in New Orleans. With no real evidence against him, he was acquitted and restored to command in New Orleans.

Within a year, Madison had declared war on Great Britain, and Wilkinson's old friend John Armstrong had succeeded Eustis as secretary of war.

33

Two Old Cronies in

Frontier Farce

~ FEW GENERALS IN AMERICAN MILITARY HISTORY HAVE BEEN ABLE TO answer a summons to "come quickly" more slowly than Major General James Wilkinson. He received Armstrong's letter on May 19 and by July 31—a journey of eighty-three days—he was already in Washington. To have chosen this odious officer for the third attempt to conquer Canada disgusted every decent commander in the U.S. Army. Armstrong deepened this general repugnanace by placing Wilkinson over Major General Wade Hampton, his archenemy. For years these two men had led rival factions in the army. To exalt one over the other would be certain to divide the service, but to prefer the scheming and unscrupulous Wilkinson to the honorable though harsh Hampton was to give a kiss to vice and a kick to virtue.

At the outset Hampton refused to command at Lake Champlain unless his orders came directly from the War Department. Only when his and Wilkinson's commands were combined would he take orders from the crony of Aaron Burr. Armstrong agreed. Wilkinson, however, did not. He wrote Armstrong: ". . . if I am authorized to command he is bound to obey; and if he will not respect the obligation, he should be turned out of the service." Armstrong did not agree with this, but neither did he tell Wilkinson that he did not.

Thus another American attempt on Montreal was begun with its two chief commanders cooperating like a mongoose and a cobra, after which the secretary of war made his contribution to unity by getting into a wrangle over strategy with his own general in chief.

Armstrong had moved the War Department to Wilkinson's base at Sackets Harbor! It is said that he did so to slip the tight reins held on him by Madison. It is also said that he wanted to ride herd on Wilkinson. Whatever the cause for this unusual move on the part of a civilian war chief, Armstrong quickly found that Wilkinson was already unfit to command. By October he had fallen ill of fever. "He was so much indisposed in mind and body," according to General John Boyd, "that in any other service he would have perhaps been superseded in his command." But Wilkinson was never so sick as to stop giving orders or to forbear from quarreling with Armstrong.

Wilkinson, apparently thinking little of Harrison, had originally wanted to clean out the Niagara frontier and attack Malden. Armstrong vetoed this with the remark that a movement west "but wounds the tail of the beast." Montreal was the beast's true heart. But the louder Armstrong spoke for Montreal, the more Wilkinson veered toward Kingston. In the end Wilkinson demanded written directions to abandon Kingston, and it was agreed to take Montreal first and then come back and seize Kingston: in other words, the beast's heart first and then its hindquarters.

Actually, neither man expected to capture either Kingston or Montreal. Wilkinson went so far as to ask for authorization to surrender should disaster threaten, and Armstrong secretly ordered Hampton to provide winter quarters for the army at a point eighty miles short of Montreal. In other words, he intended no serious movement on Montreal.

Unfortunately for some ten thousand Americans who had put their trust in this perfidious pair, the farce was to be played out. Wilkinson with about six thousand men was to descend the St. Lawrence, where he was to meet Hampton with about four thousand men, and together they would move on to Montreal. As was the custom set by their colonial forebears of a century before, the Americans did not get started until autumn plumed the woods in red and gold and the nights were chill with the breath of approaching winter. On October 17 about three hundred boats carrying Wilkinson's men sailed north for the mouth of the St. Lawrence. Heavy gales scattered them, and it was not until November 5 that they regrouped and began sailing downriver. Behind them Commodore Chauncey's gunboats bottled up Kingston to prevent the British from following on Wilkinson's rear. To the left of the American flotilla, British guns on the northern bank made their passage difficult. But they faltered on, and as they did, Secretary Armstrong returned to Washington.

Meanwhile, Hampton had begun moving westward from his base at Lake Champlain. He reached Four Corners (New York) on the Chateaugay River and took up a position from which he could either join Wilkinson, cut the British communications to Upper Canada or move against Montreal. Appreciating this, Sir George Prevost sent about 1,500 French-Canadians against Hampton. Prevost had not always been sure of the loyalty of these Gallic troops, but in the Battle of Chateaugay on October 25–26 they fought Hampton's men with enough enthusiasm to dispel Prevost's doubts and to force Hampton to fall back. It was then that Hampton received Armstrong's orders to build winter quarters for the army. "This paper sank my hopes," said the disillusioned Hampton.

As Hampton's part in the campaign came to an end, about a thousand boated British troops slipped out of Kingston to follow Wilkinson's flotilla. They snapped at his heels, even as the artillery on the riverbanks struck his left flank. At last General Jacob Brown was landed with an advance guard to clear the north bank of the St. Lawrence, and a flanking movement was ordered. But the rear was left open until, on November 11, 1813, General Boyd took two thousand men ashore and deployed them at a place known as Chrysler's Farm.

Here, in alternating snow and drizzle, while his troops attacked bravely across a field of mud and slush, Boyd attempted to crush the British force from Kingston. But he was defeated, and that was the end of the campaign. Wilkinson, learning that Hampton was not moving to meet him, flew into a rage and ordered Hampton's arrest. Then he changed his mind and decided to throw the responsibility on Armstrong. In the meantime he turned south, ascended the Salmon River and went into winter quarters in New York.

Never again did American arms menace Montreal, if, indeed, this monstrously mismanaged expedition had ever actually endangered the city. Why, it may be asked, was it ordered? Did Armstrong, as Wilkinson and Hampton both insisted, deliberately order an impossible campaign so as to bring the blame of failure on their heads? History does not know, although it has been maintained that Armstrong's motive was to rid himself of his decrepit generals so as to take the field himself as the American general in chief. If he did—and it is difficult to place any other interpretation upon his actions—then he was eminently successful, for the Montreal fiasco disposed of the last of the graybeards: Wilkinson, Hampton and Morgan Lewis. But field command never did devolve upon John Armstrong. He was already in odium in the White House, and by stripping the entire northern border of troops so that not a regiment stood guard between Detroit and Sackets Harbor, he invited disaster along the Niagara frontier.

The British did not have to fight to recover Fort George, held by about five hundred men under the militia general George McClure. Most of McClure's men were near the expiration of their enlistments, and as the holiday season neared they began going home. McClure could neither restrain them nor persuade them to re-enlist, and so he moved his remaining force of one hundred men across the river to Fort Niagara. But before he did he wantonly burnt the town of Newark, leaving its residents homeless in the frightful northern winter. McClure said he wanted to deny the British winter quarters, but the truth was that the only building left standing was the army barracks.

Retaliation for this American atrocity, together with the burning of the capitol at York, was quick and dreadful. As the Americans in Niagara prepared to observe Christmas, a British force including six hundred Indians slipped across the river. Someone had left Fort Niagara's front gate open. Yelling for revenge, the British stormed inside and bayoneted sixty-seven Americans dead before they accepted a surrender.

Then the Indians were turned loose. By New Year's Day of 1814 Buffalo was a cinder smoking in the snow, and Black Rock, Lewiston, Youngstown, Manchester, Schlosser and Tuscarora village were black heaps of rubbish. An area twelve miles wide and thirty-six miles long had been devastated, and as the cold and hungry survivors mourned their slain, the country was treated to the spectacle of Wilkinson and Armstrong engaged in public acrimony, which ended with Wilkinson making his customary demand for a court-martial that would fix the blame elsewhere.

It would have been hard for Wilkinson to find a clean scapegoat. At the time, a New York newspaper printed the names of thirteen discredited generals, headed by Granny Dearborn, along with a refrain that became popular during the court-martial of General Hull:

Pray, General Dearborn, be impartial,
When President of a Court-Martial;
Since Canada has not been taken,
Say General Hull was much mistaken.

Dearborn himself, as records say,
Mistaken was the self-same way.
And Wilkinson, and Hampton, too.
And Harrison, and all the crew.
Strange to relate, the self-same way
Have all mist-taken Canaday.

Only one general of reputation remained. He was in the south, and his name was Andrew Jackson.

34

Andrew Jackson

～ANDREW JACKSON'S FAMILY WERE COMPARATIVE LATECOMERS TO AMER-
ica, migrating from the port of Carrickfergus in Northern Ireland in
1765. His father, also named Andrew, was one of four sons of Hugh
Jackson, a well-to-do linen weaver. All were farmers exploited by the
ruinous rack-rents imposed upon them by avaracious landlords, usually local Anglo-Irish nobility. No longer willing to pay two-thirds the
value of his farm's annual produce in rent, Andrew and his wife, Elizabeth Hutchinson Jackson, sailed for America with their sons, Hugh
and Robert, probably landing somewhere in Pennsylvania. Eventually
they settled on the South Carolina side of the Waxhaws District strad-
dling the Carolinas. The area gained its name from Waxhaws Creek, a
branch of the Catawba River, but it was along Twelve-Mile Creek that
Jackson actually began his new life.

It was not an easy one, but at least the land was his—or so he
thought—for Jackson may have been an inadvertent squatter, for after
his death of overwork in March 1767, his wife found herself compelled to pay fourteen pounds to one Thomas Ewing for the deed to
the two hundred acres cleared by her late husband. In the middle of
that month she gave birth to her third son: Andrew.

With Hugh, six; Robert four; and newborn Andrew to care for, Elizabeth Jackson wisely decided that it would be best to abandon the bar-

ren farm that had killed her husband and with her sons took up permanent residence with the family of her semi-invalid sister, Jane Hutchinson Crawford. Elizabeth very quickly became mistress of the household, caring for the eight Crawford children as well as her three boys: knitting, spinning, weaving, cooking and counseling out of a deep insight into the realities of human nature. And almost from the outset of Andrew's birth this pious woman prayed and hoped that he would become a Presbyterian minister.

Thus little Andrew must attend the finest academies, much superior to those "common country schools" to which his older brothers were sent. Probably these select schools were all run by clergymen, for Andrew in later life spoke of studying "the dead languages," meaning Greek and Latin, the classical studies forming the basis of curricula where youths were prepared for college or the seminary. Not much of Latin or Greek seems to have stuck to Andrew, although he would become fond of quoting some Latin cliché—*e pluribus unum, sine qua non,* or *de gustibus non est disputandum*—to suggest the depth of his learning. Actually, it was no deeper than his brothers'. His writings are prodigies of bad English. His grammar was so faulty, his syntax so atrocious, his punctuation so erratic and his spelling so varied and unclear, even in an age yet to come under the regularizing influence of Noah Webster's dictionaries and spelling books, that he must be considered to have had the most abominable command of written English of any occupant of the White House. Yet, because of his passionate nature and quick, lively intelligence, his spoken language would be eloquent and moving—as well as frequently terrifying.

To believe as some biographers suggest that Jackson was ignorant and almost illiterate is not true, neither is it quite correct as others maintain that he was "a genuine intellectual power." Rather it would be safer to say that he was a creature of instinct and intuition rather than of reflection, knowledge and intellection. In a word, he was an incredibly complex human being driven by insatiable ambition. Just as Justice Holmes could say of President Franklin Roosevelt that he was not "a first-class mind" but rather "a first-class temperament" it could be said of Jackson that he was a first-class personality.

Thus very early on his mother ruefully realized that he was in no way bound for the pulpit. His vocabulary was such a marvel of oaths blue and blazing that his companions would often wonder where and how such a strip of a boy came to possess it. His anger was explosive, and those who knew him came to believe that he often used it—like his flow of expletives—to cow those who disagreed with him. Nowhere within him, it seemed to them, was there a spark of that religious fervor that his disillusioned mother had sought to fan into the service of the Almighty.

Almost as soon as he could walk and talk Andrew Jackson became known as a "wild, frolicsome, willful, mischievous, daring, reckless boy." He loved foot races and jumping matches. He was fond of wrestling as well, but because he was of slender build and more agile than strong, he could not compete as successfully in a ring. One of his classmates said: "I could throw him three times out of four. But he would never *stay throwed.* He was dead game, even then, and never would give up." His lust to dominate others came quickly to the fore and his overbearing manners and quickness to take offense marked him as a bully early in life. Yet, he was gracious and protective to smaller or younger boys—so long as they deferred to his leadership. Woe to those who sought to ridicule or mock him, as his companions learned the day they stuffed a musket to the muzzle with powder, daring him to fire it in hopes that it would send him sprawling. It did, but he jumped instantly erect, blue eyes blazing and crying: "By God, if one of you laughs, I'll kill him!" Needless to say, no one laughed.

Andrew Jackson was only nine years old when the Declaration of Independence was signed in Philadelphia in 1776. For four long years the Revolutionary War was fought almost exclusively in the north. But then in 1780 Savannah and Charleston fell, and the Redcoats surged into the Palmetto State like a scourge. By then Andrew was a slender youth of thirteen who at maturity would stand six feet one inch, extremely tall for the times. He had a long head with a shock of reddish-sandy hair rising from his scalp almost like coils of electricity, but his outstanding feature was his dark blue Irish eyes—"Put in with a sooty finger"—that could turn black and blazing when he was aroused. His classmates knew him to be "remarkably athletic," impulsive, passionate, "ambitious, courageous and persevering in his undertakings." He was also familiar with the militia, attending drills with his older brothers Hugh and Robert, learning the manual of arms while discovering the social and political advantages to be gained from membership.

In those days only the church rivaled the militia as a center of social life. There were no others, and young men probably found greater pleasure in wearing uniforms and parading on the green with musket or sword than in carrying a bible to Sunday meeting. The militia was the only national organization existing then, and membership in it was a kinship found nowhere else. It was also a nursery for future generals, for there were as yet no military schools in the United States. Because the officers were elected it was actually a politico-military institution, which emphasized popularity rather than leadership, as Jackson came to realize after the War of 1812 erupted.

So Andrew was a full-fledged militiaman when in the spring of 1780 the dreaded Lieutenant Colonel Banastre "Butcher" Tarleton rode into the Waxhaws at the head of nearly eight hundred British horsemen. They fell upon a formation of Patriot soldiers half as large, killing 113 and wounding 150, and so mangling the bodies of the helpless with their sabers that the action became rightly known as a deliberate massacre. Because Tarleton made no effort to restrain his berserk troops, the slaughter became known as "Tarleton's quarter," and created in the hearts of the Waxhaws settlers a horrible hatred of the British. Among the Jackson boys, it merely magnified an animosity born of many a night before a crackling fire listening to their mother's tales of oppression at the hands of the British upper classes.

There was one more score to settle after the death of Hugh at the Battle of Stono Ferry. He did not die of wounds but from the "excessive heat of the weather and the fatigues of the day." Nevertheless, Hugh was gone—and then Robert and Andrew were captured by British troops sent by Lord Francis Rawdon to help the Waxhaws Tories ravage their Patriot neighbors. The two youths had taken refuge in the Crawford house where they had grown up, and they watched in horror while the detested Lobster-backs systematically wrecked everything inside it and then set it all ablaze. At that point a British dragoon officer ordered Andrew to clean his boots. "Sir," Andrew proudly replied, "I am a prisoner of war and claim to be treated as such." Infuriated, the officer aimed a sword stroke at the youth's head and might have killed him had not Andrew instinctively thrown up an arm to deflect it. He still received a deep gash on his head and slashes on his fingers, the scars of which would ever remind him of his gracious captors.

With other prisoners, the Jackson boys were thrown into a primitive prison fit to hold perhaps 100 men but actually crammed with 250. A tenth of them died of smallpox, and Andrew and Robert might also have perished but for the arrival of their mother, whose eloquence born of anguish persuaded the prison commander to include them in an exchange of captives. But by then Robert was dying, and his mother placed him across one of the two horses she had somehow acquired, and with Andrew trailing in barefoot agony, covered the forty-five miles back to the Waxhaws where Robert died and Andrew arrived delirious and in mortal danger.

Shortly after the surrender of Cornwallis at Yorktown, Elizabeth Jackson died, desolated by grief and worn out by her splendid sacrifices as a nurse among the floating hells of the British prison ships in Charleston Harbor.

At the age of fifteen Andrew Jackson was a veteran of war and a victim of tragedy, all alone in the world with nothing but his indomitable soul to sustain him.

•••

For many months after the death of his mother, Andrew Jackson was prey to fits of deep depression as well as malaria and other recurrent fevers resulting from his imprisonment. Mentally and physically he was a pitifully sick young man. Fortunately for him an opportunity arose to go and live with Joseph White, an uncle of Mrs. Crawford who kept a saddler's shop.

Work in the shop was like a catharsis for Andrew. With customary zeal he became a skillful craftsman in saddle-making, and this welcome distraction relieved him of his depression and eventually his illnesses. Then there came another distraction not so welcome, at least not to Andrew's friends and relatives. He became the darling of many wild Charleston youths his own age who had fled their charming city to the Waxhaws settlements. Now it was in drinking, gambling, cockfighting and mischief-making that he excelled. Never very close to his surviving relatives, a mutual alienation soon ensued, and after the British evacuated Charleston in December 1782, and his rakish pals returned to their hometown, Andrew followed—vowing never to return to the Waxhaws.

Eventually he tired of "burning up the town." Forsaking his vow, he returned to the Waxhaws and resumed his studies. Completing them, he taught school for a year, but then, realizing that teaching for a man of his ambition was only slightly less pedestrian than the saddler's shop, he began to dream of studying law. The legal profession in 1784 was far and away the most attractive profession in this new American nation, with its need for political leadership, and a lack of lawyers caused by a prolific birth rate and the flight of the Tory attorneys. So, in December of that year at the age of seventeen, Andrew gathered his belongings and rode his fine mare seventy-five miles north to Salisbury, the seat of Rowan County, North Carolina. There he was accepted as a student by an eminent lawyer named Spruce McCay.

Andrew was never a good student and even though he clerked for two years under McCay, diligently copying papers and reading the necessary books, it is doubtful that he ever made himself knowledgeable in the law, let alone erudite. His attitude was much like Abraham Lincoln's, who would advise an aspiring young law student: "Get the books, and study them till you understand them in their principal features, and that is the main thing. . . . Your own resolution to succeed is more than anything." This seems to be the course Andrew followed, although one of his friends wryly observed that he "was more in the stable than the office," and was regarded as "the most roaring, rollicking, game-cocking, horse-racing, card-playing, mischievous fellow that ever lived in Salisbury."

At twenty Andrew Jackson was not handsome, but because of his commanding figure and those expressive eyes, he attracted attention. His habit of staring intently into the eyes of others and of grasping their hand warmly as he spoke to them could "convey to strangers the impression that they [were] 'somebody.'" Regarded by his fellow law students as their leader in pranks and frolics, he was also gaining local fame as a serious leader in times of danger. If he were to join a party of travelers moving through Indian-infested woods, the moment war whoops were heard Andrew would without hesitation take command of the company. He was instinctively what is today called a "take-charge guy," and his companions knew it.

For about a year after his admission to the bar in 1787 Andrew Jackson was strangely indolent, practicing law only occasionally. Actually, he was bored, uncertain that eastern North Carolina was the place to begin his climb to the top. Then to his joy John McNairy, his old student friend and gaming chum, was elected by the legislature to be superior court judge for the western district of the Old North State—an immense area stretching all the way to the Mississippi. McNairy offered Jackson the post of public prosecutor for the district, and he promptly accepted. In the spring of 1788 Jackson and McNairy with four or five other comrades agreed to cross the mountains into east Tennessee and thence to Nashville in the west. They arrived in Jonesborough too late to push on to Nashville for the court session, deciding to stay there until the fall.

A few months later Jackson and his party, together with settlers and an armed escort, left Jonesborough for Nashville, moving through dangerous Indian country. One night with his comrades asleep and sentinels posted, Jackson sat with his back against a tree, smoking a corncob pipe. He began to doze off, his ears filled with the distant hooting of owls. The sound drew closer . . . louder. . . . Instantly he understood its meaning, seizing his rifle and crawling to the side of his friend Bennett Searcy.

"Searcy!" he hissed. "Raise your head and make no noise."

His friend obliged, whispering, "What's the matter?"

"The owls . . . Listen. There . . . There again. . . . Isn't that a little *too* natural."

"Do you think so?"

"I *know* it! There's Indians all around us. I've heard them in every direction. They mean to attack before daybreak."

Quickly awaking the other members of the party, Jackson urged that they break camp immediately and plunge deeper into the forest. They agreed—instantly accepting the young lawyer as their leader—and resumed their march. A few hours later a party of hunters stumbled upon the deserted camp, and deciding that it was a good place to stop, they bedded down for the night. At dawn the whooping red men attacked, killing and scalping all but one of them.

Faint on the wind Jackson and his fleeing friends heard the shots and screams of the victims, and they hurried on, reaching Nashville without further incident on October 26, 1788.

On the bluff above the mighty Cumberland River they beheld in awe the fertile valley that it watered, so rich in hardwood and game that the Indians had fought over it for decades. The town below had grown from a cluster of huts and cabins—fortified "stations" scattered along the river where the settlers could resist Indian raids—to a community of about three hundred persons gathered around a courthouse, two stores, two taverns, a distillery and a number of log houses, cabins, tents and shelters made of cloth and twigs. Jackson decided to stay in the blockhouse occupied by the widow Donelson and her family. She welcomed his request, for it meant another able-bodied man to help defend them against the still-menacing Indians. Here Jackson met John Overton, another young lawyer who became his fast friend. He also was introduced to Rachel Donelson Robards, a pretty and extremely vivacious young woman who had been married to Lewis Robards of Kentucky, an erratic and jealous husband, who suspected his wife of the same infidelities he committed in the slave cabins and quarreled with her constantly. In desperation he wrote to Mrs. Donelson asking her to take her daughter back. She did, but Robards soon found himself unable to live without Rachel, and they were reunited, Robards coming south to stay with her at her mother's blockhouse.

It was then that Andrew Jackson arrived at the Donelsons', his own personality a fitting match for this young woman described as the "best story-teller, the best dancer, the sprightliest companion, the most dashing horsewoman in the western country." He was immediately and deeply attracted to her, but because she was another man's wife he treated her with the utmost decorum. Robards thought otherwise, "catching" them in friendly chatter together too often to calm his insane jealousy. He made life at the Donelsons' intolerable for Jackson, so that eventually he moved elsewhere with his friend Overton. Before he did, Robards had complained publicly that Andrew Jackson was "too intimate with his wife," for which slur on his and Rachel's characters Jackson threatened to cut off his ears. When Robards had him arrested, Jackson borrowed a butcher knife from his guard and tested its edge and point while glancing at Robards with such a menacing mien that his frightened accuser ran off and hid in the canebrake. Without a plaintiff, the case was dropped. Next Robards practically accused Jackson of committing adultery with his wife and threatened—in the savage frontier custom—to obtain satisfaction by horsewhipping him. When he lifted his whip, Jackson challenged him to a duel. Cursing both Jackson and his wife, Robards returned to Kentucky prepared to sue for divorce.

In his absence, Andrew Jackson fell deeply and probably even passionately in love with Rachel. But he is not known to have compromised himself or her in any way, until the fall of 1790 when it was rumored that Robards was going to return to Nashville to reclaim his wife. Rachel became frightened and fled to Natchez—accompanied by Andrew Jackson! Why? Why did he so risk their reputations further and set all those malicious Nashville tongues wagging? Probably to give Robards all the evidence he needed to begin divorce proceedings so that Rachel would be free to marry Jackson. It was not a foolish move but rather a calculated one, in strict keeping with their characters. Rachel was not an immoral person, but a woman in distress: the gallant Jackson, so often throughout his life a rescuer rather than an exploiter, was rushing to her side. And that is what happened. Robards in 1791 apparently did get a divorce, or so it was believed in Nashville, and Andrew Jackson without bothering to investigate the report, immediately rushed south to Natchez to marry Rachel—or at least to inform close friends such as Overton that he had.

But no record of the marriage exists. It is doubtful that any such ceremony was held. Natchez then was under the rule of Catholic Spain, and all marriages were performed by duly ordained Catholic priests. Even if the partners were Protestant—as Rachel and Jackson certainly were—the minister planning to marry them was required to apply to Spanish authorities for approval. Usually, it was granted; but it was also scrupulously recorded, and there is extant no record of such a ceremony. Nevertheless, the "married" couple in the fall of 1791 did return to Nashville without any hint of embarrassment on their part, taking up residence there and leading a blameless life that won the admiration of their neighbors.

Two years later—in September 1793—they learned the awful truth: Robards did not receive his divorce until a Virginia jury held that "Rachel Robards, hath deserted the plaintiff, Lewis Robards, and hath and doth still live in adultery with another man." Rachel was crushed and Jackson infuriated, telling Overton that he would not under any circumstances go through another marriage because it would be tantamount to admitting the charge of living in sin. But the patient Overton explained that a court of law had already established that they "hath and doth still live in adultery." Even though he and Rachel were morally innocent, as they professed to be, they were technically guilty with no chance of escaping that imputation. Thus, with great reluctance, Rachel and Andrew were married January 18, 1794, by Justice of the Peace Robert Hays, Rachel's brother-in-law.

These were the facts presented to the American public in 1828 when Andrew Jackson, after his defeat in 1824, ran again for president—this time successfully—and it appears that they are probably true to an extent. The only flaw in this argument is that Andrew Jackson made no attempt to validate the first report of Robards's "divorce." In his defense it may be suggested that he was so in love with Rachel that he believed—or pretended to believe—this rumor, and immediately rushed south to claim his heart's desire. In a phrase, his heart had conquered his head.

Unfortunately, forever afterward throughout Andrew Jackson's career the epithet "adulterer" or the charge of "wife stealer" would be hurled at him by his enemies: and if there were indeed no legal way to refute them, they could only be disproved in a nobler way by the mutual devotion of their marriage and the rectitude of their lives.

After being licensed to practice law in Nashville, his friend Judge McNairy appointed Jackson attorney for the three-county Mero District. It was an opportune selection, for the businessmen of the area were near bankruptcy because of unpaid debts. Having banded together, the debtors refused to pay their legitimate obligations and bribed the only public attorney in west Tennessee not to prosecute. Jackson, an engine of energy, immediately obliged the swarms of creditors appealing to him for help. He even pursued debtors who had moved away in order to evade payment. One of them was so enraged when Jackson cornered him that he stepped on his foot, whereupon Jackson calmly picked up a loose fence post and knocked him unconscious.

As Jackson's popularity as public attorney soared, so too did his private practice. During a single court session in Davidson County in April 1789, a total of thirteen lawsuits were argued, and Jackson was a counsel in every one of them. He also at that time served as a rifleman during the numerous counterattacks against the Indians launched by the frontiersmen. His comrades found him "bold, dashing, fearless and *mad upon his enemies.*" He was said to tremble with "a great ambi-

tion for encounters with the savages." Thus, when Tennessee became
a state on March 28, 1796, it was no surprise that this 29-year-old warrior of both courtroom and forest should be chosen as its first member of the House of Representatives. His service in Philadelphia was
distinguished, especially when he was defending or advancing Tennessee's interests. It reached its apex when he delivered a passionate
and moving speech supporting a petition to pay Tenessee frontiersmen for their service against the Indians in a 1793 expedition led by
Revolutionary War hero John ("Nollichucky Jack") Sevier. President
Washington had repeatedly rejected this appeal, but Jackson's powerful speech drew to his cause such powerful House members as James
Madison of Virginia and the petition was approved.

But then exposure of William Blount's conspiracy to seize Florida
and Louisiana with the help of Great Britain ended his Senate career.
He was not expelled or even impeached but simply allowed to absent
himself from the Senate until his term expired. In Tennessee, however, Blount was still influential, and when a candidate was needed to
oppose Senator William Cocke—the "traitor" who had voted for
Blount's expulsion—he chose Jackson. By a vote of twenty to thirteen,
the Tennessee legislature in 1797 sent Jackson to Philadelphia for a
six-year term.

His tenure there was brief and unhappy. He seemed to be a victim
of his own passion, which he had formerly brought under such strict
control. Vice President Thomas Jefferson, who did not like Jackson,
said of him: "His passions are terrible. When I was President of the
Senate, he was a Senator, and he could never speak on account of the
rashness of his feelings. I have seen him attempt it repeatedly, and as
often choke with rage. His passions are, no doubt, cooler now; he has
been much tried since I knew him, but he is a dangerous man."

Jefferson was right, and the danger he perceived in those dark blue
blazing eyes would erupt one day on—of all places!—the Tennessee
Supreme Court.

Having quit the U.S. Senate, Andrew Jackson had not jettisoned his
political career, for upon his return to Nashville he assiduously sought
appointment to the state supreme court. He did so because it would
keep him active in Tennessee affairs, would pay more than any other
state office except governor—$600 a year compared to the governor's
$750—meanwhile advancing both his military and political ambitions
by enabling him to meet influential people from every corner of Tennessee. With both Blount and Governor Sevier—with whom Jackson
had buried the hatchet—both pulling strings, Jackson at the age of

thirty-one was chosen by the legislature to sit on the state's highest court.

He served there for six years, considered by his colleagues and the legal fraternity to be an excellent judge, a man of the highest integrity whose fierce sense of justice guided him to impartial decisions made swiftly and without prejudice or discrimination. His courage—both moral and physical—was legendary, and because it is physical bravery that men revere most, the most popular story about Jackson as a justice came in a contest with a big, wild-eyed brute of a man that even a sheriff and full posse could not subdue.

It took place in a rural village and the man was named Russell Bean, nicknamed "Hoss" for his size and indicted on a charge of having cut off the ears of his infant child during "a drunken frolic." Brought into court he began pacing up and down between judge and jury bellowing like a caged lion, cursing everyone in sight before marching straight out the door. "Sheriff," Jackson snapped, "arrest that man for contempt of court and confine him." Nodding, the sheriff went out the door, returning empty-handed and sheepishly explaining that the man was armed and could not be subdued.

"Summon a posse then," Jackson replied, "and bring him before me."

Again the sheriff returned without a prisoner, this time with the excuse that Bean had threatened to shoot the "first skunk that came within ten feet of him."

"Mr. Sheriff," Jackson said with icy contempt, "since you cannot obey my orders, summon me! Yes, sir! Summon *me!*"

"Well, Judge, if you say so—though I don't like to do it. But if you will try, why I suppose I must summon you."

"Very well," Jackson said calmly, rising to walk toward the door. "I adjourn this court for ten minutes."

Followed by sheriff, jury and spectators, he walked toward Bean, standing a short distance from the courthouse, flourishing a pair of pistols and cowing the crowd gathered around him. With leveled pistols in his own hands Jackson without hesitation walked up to him and roared: "Now, surrender, you infernal villain, this very instant—or I'll blow you through!"

Bean fell silent, standing still and staring wonderingly into those blazing blue-black eyes. Quietly, meekly, he handed over his weapons, and said: "There, Jedge, it's no use—I give in."

Asked later why he had so tamely surrendered to a single man when he had earlier defied a sheriff and an entire posse, he explained: "Why, when he came up, I looked him in the eye, and I saw 'shoot' and there wasn't shoot in nary other eye in the crowd. And so I says to myself, says I, Hoss, it's about time to sing small, and so I did."

The "shoot" that Hoss Bean had seen made Jackson's name a byword among all the militiamen throughout the state, and thus it was that in February of 1802, he challenged Nolichucky Jack Sevier himself for the post of major general. Sevier was no longer governor, having served the limited two terms. In his place was Jackson's close friend Archibald Roane. Under militia election rules all field officers of the three military districts, plus the three brigadier generals, elected their chief. When the results ended in a seventeen to seventeen tie between Jackson and Sevier, Roane broke it by casting the deciding vote for his friend.

Sevier was furious. That poor, pitiful, pettifogging lawyer with no military command experience whatever had inflicted a humiliating defeat on one of the heroes of the Battle of King's Mountain. Insults were exchanged, and then, inevitably, these two firebrands met in the Knoxville public square. By then, Sevier was again the governor. With a string of smoking frontier oaths, he slashed at Jackson's "pretensions" to exercise chief command. Momentarily shaken, Jackson meekly cited his many "services" to the state.

"*Services?*" Sevier repeated with a mocking laugh. "I know of no great service you have rendered the country, except taking a trip to Natchez with another man's wife."

Jackson turned white and went almost berserk. The "shoot" that Bean and Jefferson had seen now blazed in his eyes, and he screamed: "Great God! Do you mention *her sacred name?*"

Both men drew pistols and fired, but only a bystander was grazed. Friends rushed to separate the antagonists. But the damage had been done. Neither man would accept anything less than that "satisfaction" due to a Tennessee frontiersman's supersensitive "sacred honor." After an exchange of published insults and letters spiced with such friendly epithets as "coward," "poltroon," "polluted" and "base," they finally agreed to meet outside of Knoxville. Jackson hurried to the appointed field of honor only to wait fuming for days for the governor to appear. Convinced that he had sunk into a cowardly funk, Jackson started riding to Knoxville to confront him, but as he did he saw Sevier and a company of mounted men approaching. Jackson drew a pistol, dismounted, and drew another. Sevier leaped from his horse brandishing a pair of pistols. Both men glared at each other, and both, virtuosos in the frontier art of profanity and obscenity, cursed and swore at each other so furiously that they put away their weapons to free their hands for fisticuffs. Straining at tiptoe, shaking their fists, face-to-face, showering each other with a fine spray of spittle, they screamed and shouted until Jackson broke the impasse by lunging at Sevier with his cane. Sevier drew his sword, a movement that "frightened his horse and he ran away with the governor's pistols." Seizing his opportunity, Jackson again drew a pistol and the disarmed Sevier quickly ducked behind a tree. Next Sevier's son drew on Jackson and Jackson's second drew on him.

Except for the fact that the pistols were loaded and held by men intending to fire them, here was comic opera at its most clownish: Jackson's second was aiming at Sevier's son who was aiming at Jackson who was aiming at Sevier hiding behind a tree. The only participant in this fiasco retaining any dignity was Sevier's horse. There is no record that anyone burst into laughter, but the absurdity of the situation could not have failed to embarrass the antagonists. Finally Sevier's friends intervened, and Sevier and Jackson, breathless but still cursing each other, again sheathed their pistols and allowed themselves to be persuaded to end their vendetta. All concerned rode back to Knoxville together in peace. Although Jackson and Sevier never became reconciled, they did not allow their mutual hatred to explode once more in public.

Because of debts accumulated by his land speculations, Jackson in 1804 resigned his judgeship and committed himself full-time to his business interests, moving with his wife and slaves to a 420-acre site on which he would one day build a handsome mansion, calling the entire estate the Hermitage. He prospered, making enough money from the sale of his cotton and rental of his cotton gin, as well as prizes won by his great horse Truxtun, to pay off his debts and regain financial prosperity.

Horse racing was the passion of Andrew Jackson's life, indeed of most of the well-to-do in the Nashville area. In the autumn of 1805 the match of the century had been arranged between Truxtun and another mighty stallion named Plowboy, owned by Captain Joseph Ervin and trained by his son-in-law, the clever, witty twenty-seven-year-old Charles Dickinson. The stakes were "2,000, with an $800 forefeit should either side cancel the race." That was what Captain Ervin was compelled to do when Plowboy came up lame.

A quarrel arose between Ervin-Dickinson and Jackson over the method of paying the race forfeit. It was a trivial matter and would have been settled amicably but for the proud frontiersman's chronic refusal to treat almost any slight as trifling. As this molehill of a dispute became magnified into a mountain, Dickinson published a challenge to Jackson so scurrilous that he could not fail to accept it, even though he was well aware that his young challenger was easily the best shot in Tennessee—able to cut a string in two at twenty-four feet. The duel was to be held May 30, 1806, across the border in Kentucky. The day before, Dickinson kissed his pretty and tearful young wife farewell with the cheerful remark: "Good-bye, darling, I shall be *sure* to be home tomorrow night." Off he rode with his seconds, enjoying himself and amusing them at intervals by shooting strings in two. He left one with an innkeeper. "If General Jackson comes along this road," he said, laughing, "show him *that!*"

Jackson's journey north accompanied by General Thomas Overton, his friend's younger brother, was not quite so merry. They quietly discussed tactics. Both agreed that Dickinson could not miss. If Jackson tried to fire first, it was almost certain that Dickinson's shot would ruin his aim. Thus there was no other course but to await his opponent's shot calmly, and then—if he were still alive!—squeeze his own trigger. The incredibly indomitable Andrew Jackson simply would not discuss the possibility of being killed.

He was just as calm next morning when he and his party—which included a surgeon—arrived first in a poplar forest. "How do you feel about it now, General?" one of his seconds asked.

"Oh, all right," Jackson replied easily. "I shall wing him, never fear."

Dickinson and his party arrived, the distance was measured, and the antagonists took their positions with lowered pistols by their side. Came the count and the command.

"One . . . two . . . fire!"

Dickinson quickly raised his pistol and fired. The ball struck Jackson in the chest, raising a puff of dust from his coat.

Jackson was staggered, but straightened—slowly lifting his left arm and pressing it against his punctured chest. He stood still, his teeth clenched, Dickinson drew back a step, horrified to see his opponent still standing. "Great God!" he cried. "Have I missed him?"

"Back to the mark, sir!" General Overton shouted, leveling his pistol.

Dickinson stepped back to the mark and Jackson lifted his weapon. He could have been merciful, either refusing to shoot or firing into the air. But Dickinson, so superior as a shot, quite evidently had tried to kill him. For all Jackson knew he might at that moment be dying. "I should have hit him," he would say later, "if he had shot me through the brain." And he fired. . . . Came a click. . . . The hammer had stopped at half cock. . . . Jackson recocked his hammer and fired again. . . .

His bullet struck Charles Dickinson just below his ribs, and as he reeled his friends rushed forward to catch him as he fell. But there was nothing they or Jackson's surgeon could do, for the ball had passed clear through his body below his ribs, leaving a ragged hole through which his life's blood quickly poured. Within a few minutes he was dead.

General Overton led Jackson away with the remark, "He won't want anything more of you, General." Jackson nodded, saying nothing of his own wound. But his surgeon saw that his shoes were full of blood, and cried out in alarm: "My, God! General Jackson, are you hit?"

"Oh, I believe he pinked me," Jackson replied. "Let's look at it," he added, opening his coat.

It was a serious wound. The bullet had shattered two ribs and buried itself in his chest. Because it was so close to Jackson's heart, it could not be moved—and it remained there, the source of much pain, which could become excruciating when he moved the arm. More painful to Jackson was the damage Dickinson's death had done to his reputation. Because he had not spared his opponent—who had bet three hundred dollars that he would kill Jackson—it was wrongfully believed in Nashville he was a cold-blooded murderer. More justifiably, coming on the heels of his duel with Sevier, the Dickinson tragedy made Jackson a social outcast in western Tennessee, where he was shunned as a violent and vengeful man.

Surprisingly, Andrew Jackson's ostracism by the genteel folk of Nashville did not last much longer than a few months, chiefly because he and Rachel were a very social couple, given to lavish entertainment, with Jackson easy and graceful in conversation, and Rachel an ideal hostess able with her vivacious, outgoing personality to put her visitors instantly at their ease. Another reason was that Aaron Burr was again a guest at the Hermitage.

Burr was immensely popular in Tennessee because in his days in the U.S. Senate he had used his power to help the territory gain recognition as a state. When he appeared in Nashville, planters rode for many miles to see him. Parades were organized in his honor, flags flown, cannons fired. Dinners were given in his honor and everyone was charmed by Burr's suave manners, his cultivation and high intelligence. His five-day stay at the Hermitage also raised the Jacksons' social standing. During it he also disclosed a grandiose plan for carving out his own empire in the Southwest. He was never known to be specific about this plan to chastise the hated Spanish Dons by taking Florida and even Mexico away from them, but conveyed his meaning by hints and innuendos.

Burr was particularly adept at playing on the westerners' fondness for conspiracy: against the Spanish, against the French, against the British—even against their own government if it meant satisfaction of their almost insatiable dreams of expansion south and west. Any scheme or plot was acceptable, if it promised more land and trade. Thus Burr's western trip in 1805 was a great success. He met with the governor of the Mississippi Territory and also Governor Claiborne of the enormous Louisiana Territory, and was received with respect and cordiality. Upon his return to Nashville he contracted with Jackson to build boats and supply provisions for an expedition downriver aimed at nothing less than conquest of all Spanish North America! For this he paid Jackson $3,500.

Jackson was now an accomplice. In what, he was not exactly sure—except that it would be against the Spanish, which suited him fine. But he would not, like Burr and that other accomplice James Wilkinson, countenance treason. That he would never betray his country he made plain in a letter to Governor Claiborne: "I love my country and government. I hate the Dons. I would delight to see Mexico reduced, but I will die in the last ditch before I would yield a foot to the Dons or see the Union disunited."

But then, on November 10, 1806, a young associate of Burr's named Captain Fort called at the Hermitage and inadvertantly revealed his chief's plan to capture New Orleans with the assistance of Wilkinson. Jackson was stunned. *New Orleans! U.S. territory! Wilkinson! Spain's faithful spy!* Here was treason pure and simple. At once Jackson wrote to both Governor Claiborne and President Jefferson warning them of a conspiracy to seize the Southwest from New Orleans to Mexico City, but without mentioning Burr's name. With this he protected his own skin, but when Burr was arrested in January 1807 and charged with treason, he did not desert his former friend. Typically loyal and reckless, he even went to Richmond to testify in his behalf. But his speeches on the courthouse steps were so explosive and his language denouncing the triple traitor Wilkinson so violent—"Pity the sword at the traitor's belt, for its doubtless of honest steel!"—that defense attorney Henry Clay decided not to risk having him alienate the jury that eventually did acquit Burr.

Returning to the Hermitage, Jackson spent the ensuing five years living the life of a wealthy southern planter: tending his crops, dealing in land and slaves, collecting Truxtun's steady flow of prize money, and entertaining so frequently and lavishly that he became known as "the most public private man in the state." But then the War of 1812 erupted and the sound of bugles in the ears of Andrew Jackson suggested that at last he could pursue what had always been his heart's desire: military glory.

35

The March South/More Duels

∼As early as March 7, 1812—three and a half months before
Madison declared war on Great Britain—Major General Andrew Jackson issued a stirring call for fifty thousand Tennessee volunteers to follow him in a campaign to conquer "all the British dominions upon the continent of North America."

"Who are we?" he thundered rhetorically. "Are we the titled slaves of George the Third, the military conscripts of Napoleon the Great or the frozen peasants of the Russian Czars? No! We are the free-born sons of America; the citizens of the only republic now existing in the world; and the only people on earth who possess rights, liberties and property which they dare call their own."

The response was overwhelming, so great that it earned Tennessee the undying nickname of "the Volunteer State," although it is most doubtful that, as the legend goes, every able-bodied male in Tennessee seized his musket from over the fireplace and hurried to Jackson's side. Still, an overjoyed Jackson was able to offer Madison a small army of 2,500 hardy frontiersmen ready to march and fight under their beloved leader Andrew Jackson. Madison's reply did not exactly match Jackson's original joy at perceiving his long-awaited opportunity: it was polite and perfunctory—but no call to arms.

It was some time before Jackson realized that Washington had not much use for the friend of Aaron Burr, and as often as he appealed to Secretary of War Henry Dearborn for an active and immediate assignment, he received no reply. Understandably so, for Dearborn could hardly be expected to forget all those nasty Jacksonian sneers at him as the "oldest" of all those "old Grannies" in the capital.

It was not until October 1812 that the administration decided to reinforce General Wilkinson in New Orleans with 1,500 Tennessee volunteers provided by Governor Willie Blount, the half brother of the disgraced William Blount. Accompanying this instruction was a strong hint that it would not be wise to choose General Jackson—the bitter enemy of Wilkinson—to command the expedition. Blount deliberately ignored the nonbinding intimation and did select his friend Jackson. But the close friend who had proved so valuable politically to Blount in west Tennessee was incensed to be placed under the command of that "public villain" Wilkinson. Nevertheless, he was practical enough to realize that if this was the only way he could receive an active assignment—and it was—he had better accept it. In mid-December 1812, he hurled himself into the challenge of organizing and training a little army of about two thousand men, together with building a small fleet that would take the infantry and riflemen down the Cumberland to the Mississippi and thence to Natchez.

Jackson would rely heavily in the coming operation on his friend John Coffee. Easily the most commanding presence in this Tennessee army with his giant physique, thick shock of jet black hair and deep-set eyes the color of his chief's, Coffee was a brave and able soldier who was probably also a better tactician than Jackson. Fortunately, he was modest and devoted to the general. Jackson gave him command of the cavalry and mounted infantry and would proceed to Natchez by land. In early January 1813, the brigade of volunteers turned their faces south.

Coffee's horse had no difficulty reaching the rendezvous area, but the little fleet with Jackson aboard was delayed by ice on the Ohio River and a series of earthquakes along the Big Muddy that changed its course. Three men and a boat were also lost, but thirty-nine days and a thousand miles later the army reached Natchez.

Jackson was glad to join Coffee and his troopers, but most unhappy to read the letters from General Wilkinson awaiting him there. They had a single theme: stay where you are! Wilkinson was himself enraged to learn that the man who had insulted him so violently and publicly in Richmond was joining his command. But he spoke only of having no instructions from Washington on how to deploy Jackson's troops, had not enough provisions in New Orleans to feed Jackson's men and his own, and, if Florida were Jackson's objective, he should take up a position above New Orleans. But on one point he was quite definite: Jackson "should halt in the vicinity of Natchez."

He did, but with great misgivings; fearing the effect prolonged inactivity would have on his troops. "Indolence creates disquiet," he wrote. Weeks passed without further instructions from either Washington or Wilkinson, but on March 15 a letter arrived from John Armstrong, the new secretary of war, that transformed Jackson's irritation into a towering rage. It ordered him to dismiss his men and to deliver to Wilkinson "all articles of public property" in his possession—meaning all but their own personal small arms, as well as the brigade's medicine, transport and payroll!

Always regarding any setback as aimed at him personally, Andrew Jackson saw the order to disband and disarm his men in the middle of hostile Indian country one thousand miles from home as a plot between Armstrong and Wilkinson to get rid of him and steal his troops. This suspicion was definitely confirmed in a later letter from Wilkinson asking him to encourage his men to enlist in the regular army—meaning his own forces. With this Jackson would be effectively humiliated and compelled to crawl home alone and in disgrace, crouching thereafter on the retirement shelf for the duration of the war.

This Andrew Jackson would not accept. Instead of dismissing his men, he turned them around and led them home himself.

Although the homeward march was a personal agony to Andrew Jackson, toward his men this normally stern disciplinarian showed the face of an angel of mercy. He was as gentle as a nun, especially to his 156 invalids, of whom 56 were too weak to sit upright or lift their heads from their pillows. To them he allotted all his eleven wagons, ordering his officers to surrender their horses for the sick, giving up his own three mounts for that purpose. Day after day he trudged alongside his men, always erect, never showing a trace of weariness or fatigue. When a delirious invalid sat up on a wagon to ask where he was, Jackson replied softly, "On your way *home!*" All who heard him cheered.

They cheered again and shouted with derisive laughter when Jackson found one of Wilkinson's recruiting officers slinking around their bivouack, threatening to drum the officer out of camp before his entire corps if the man did not immediately depart.

Under Jackson's urging the pace of the march gradually grew faster until it reached about eighteen miles a day. Soon the men began to look at their general in awe. He was indomitable, they told each other. He was "tough," tougher than anything they could name—until one of them said he was as tough as Tennessee hickory. The nickname Hickory stuck, and when it was preceded by the affectionate adjective "old," he became "Old Hickory" forever more.

Within a month Jackson had led his brigade back to Tennessee, and by the time his troops reached Nashville, word had gone ahead of Jackson's heroic leadership and how his soldiers actually had come to love him. And yet, within another month, he had by his terrible temper and inclination to violence, dissipated much of the reputation which his conduct on the march had regained for him.

The origins of the affair are rather obscure, although it did begin on the homeward march. The brigade inspector was a bright young man from Pennsylvania named Billy Carroll. Jackson found him very capable, destined, as he had been, to succeed both in the military and politics. Because of his passionate nature, the general became fond of Billy, showing him every favor and unconsciously exciting the jealousy of other junior officers from Tennessee.

One of these was a man named Littleton Johnston. At some point he and the unpopular Carroll quarreled, and Johnston challenged him to a duel. Carroll refused on the ground that Johnston was not a gentleman. But then Johnston's second—Jesse Benton—repeated the challenge and because he was Carroll's equal, Jackson's favorite had to accept the challenge.

Jesse Benton was the brother of Thomas Hart Benton, another favorite of Jackson's who had served him as aide-de-camp both to and from Natchez, and who would one day become a famous and powerful U.S. senator from Missouri. Jesse was conceited, believing himself his brother's equal. He was indeed: before God and the law. Otherwise, no; although he was a fine pistol shot. Carroll, who was not, rode out to the Hermitage to ask Jackson to act as his "friend."

"Why, Captain Carroll," Old Hickory replied, "I am not the man for such an affair. I am too old. The time has been when I should have gone out with pleasure. But, at my time of life, it would be extremely injudicious. You must get a man nearer your own age."

It was wise advice, and Jackson seemed to be adhering to it when he rode into Nashville to confront Jesse and speak soothing words that persuaded him to forget the entire affair. But the other junior officers still bitter against Carroll prevailed on Jesse to renew the quarrel. With this a disgusted Jackson agreed to be Carroll's second.

Benton and Carroll met at six in the morning of June 14, 1813. Because Carroll had the challenged duelist's right to set the distance, he specified ten feet—close enough to "equalize" Benton's advantage as a marksman. They stood back-to-back, stepping off the distance preparing to wheel upon the command, "Fire!"

Wheeling "with great quickness," a crouching Benton fired first. His bullet struck Carroll in the thumb just as he fired, hitting the squatting Benton and inflicting a long, raking wound across both cheeks of his buttocks. Jackson was enraged by Benton's squatting tactic, thus reducing himself as a target, and would have protested except that he believed him to be "mortally wounded" and advised Carroll to say nothing about it.

But the people of Nashville had much to say about it, most of them enjoying a hearty laugh at Benton's painful embarrassment. His brother Thomas—also a firebrand—was not amused after returning to Nashville from Washington where he had persuaded the War Department to pay the expenses of the expedition to Natchez. Bursting with his good news, he exploded in wrath instead when he learned of his brother's humiliation, and he turned like a tiger on his former patron. Insults were exchanged and then the customary "publication" of the other man's cowardice. Angered at Thomas Benton's charges, fearing to lose once again his fame and reputation, an infuriated Jackson made it known throughout west Tennessee that he would horsewhip him the moment he saw him. Although now repentant, but still stubbornly jealous of his own honor, Thomas and Jesse (now recovered) decided to avoid trouble by moving from the Old Nashville Inn favored by Jackson and his friends to the City Hotel.

In early September Old Hickory, accompanied by John Coffee and Jackson's nephew Stockley Hays—a man almost as gigantic as Coffee—rode into town and put up at the Old Nashville Inn. Next morning Jackson and Coffee walked to the post office to pick up their mail. Each man was armed and Jackson carried a horse whip. Passing the City Hotel they saw Thomas Benton in the doorway "looking daggers" at them.

Old Hickory made no move, continuing on to the post office, probably to gain time to plan his attack. Returning, he passed the City Hotel again. Both Bentons now awaited him. Each carried a pistol loaded with two shots apiece. Abreast of Thomas, Jackson brandished his whip and shouted, "Now, you damned rascal, I'm going to punish you! Defend yourself!"

Thomas dug his hand into his pocket as though fumbling for his pistol. With that Old Hickory drew and backed Thomas into the hotel. Jesse, meanwhile, darted from the barroom to the back porch from which he could see Jackson. He fired at him, hitting him with both a slug and ball in the shoulder and left arm. Jackson pitched forward, firing a wild shot at Thomas as he fell. Thomas next fired twice at his prostrate body, missing both times, while Jesse reloaded and prepared to fire again—until he was interrupted by a bystander.

Coffee now came charging into the hotel, leaping over Jackson lying in the doorway with blood spouting from his arm and shoulder. He fired at Thomas, but missed. He then clubbed his pistol and swung, but Thomas retreated—falling backward down a flight of stairs. Big Stockley Hays now joined the melee, lunging at Jesse with a sword cane. The point struck a button and the sword broke. Hays next seized Jesse and threw him, repeatedly stabbing him with a dirk. Squirming to avoid the dagger thrusts, Jesse groped for his second pistol—finding and firing it. But the charge fizzled, just as bystanders rushed into the hotel to pull the antagonists apart.

Still pouring blood, Jackson was carried to the Nashville Inn where he soaked two mattresses before doctors were able to staunch the flow. It was said that every physician in Nashville worked to save his life. They found his shoulder shattered by the slug and the ball embedded in the upper bone of his left arm, and all agreed that amputation was necessary.

"I'll keep my arm," Old Hickory muttered, before losing consciousness. No doctor dared to overrule him, and the metal remained in Jackson's arm for nearly twenty years. It was also three weeks before he could recover from his loss of blood and leave the inn. As he lay there in agony, the Bentons by parading through Nashville waving Jackson's broken sword and boasting of their triumph over Old Hickory so angered his many friends that they had to flee for their lives. It was not until 1823 when both Thomas Benton and Jackson became U.S. senators that they saw each other again. Like true politicians they saw that to forget their feud would work to their mutual benefit, and they shook hands. Jesse Benton, however, never forgot it—and went to his grave cursing his brother's "betrayal."

Thus the last of Andrew Jackson's gunfights. As he lay at the Hermitage recovering from his wounds under the faithful and tender eyes of Rachel, word reached Nashville that the Creek Indians led by Billy Weatherford—the same Chief Red Eagle who had so admired Tecumseh—had heeded the Shawnee chief's call to total war against the whites by attacking and massacring both settlers and soldiers in Fort Mims, Alabama.

36

The Creek War

~ WHEN TECUMSEH LEFT THE COUNTRY OF THE CREEKS HE BELIEVED THAT he had failed in his attempt to persuade them to join him in total war against the whites. In fact, however, he had been successful, for his fiery speeches had aroused the martial ardor of young Creeks such as Billy Weatherford and his scheduled "miracle"—the stamp of his foot when he reached home and the coincidence of the monster earthquake that shook the Mississippi Valley at about that time—both conspired to send them on the warpath.

Thus these two related events—the speeches and the "miracle"—may be considered to be the most momentous in Indian history. Rivaling even the arrival of the whites, these incidents led the Creek nation into a disastrous and utterly unnecessary war at a moment when they were living in comparative wealth and luxury and had absolutely no reason to challenge such an obviously superior foe.

No tribe in North America possessed the noble traditions of the Creek federation. Their story was preserved by a Frenchman named Le Clerc Milfort who lived among them for twenty years, returning to France to become a brigadier general and who, in 1802, wrote a book about them. The original Creeks were the Muskogee—the people of Tecumseh's mother—who had been allies of the Aztecs against Cortés. After the fall and death of Montezuma II, they migrated north where

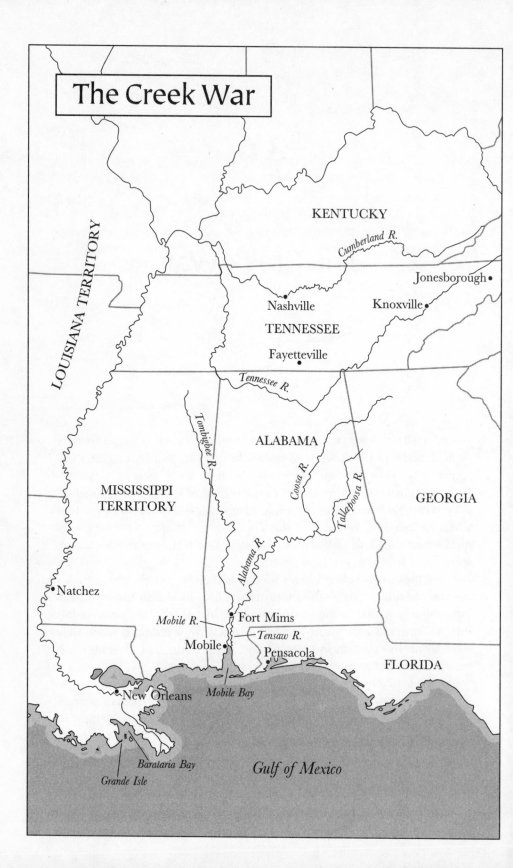

The Creek War

KENTUCKY

Cumberland R.

Jonesborough •

Nashville •

Knoxville •

TENNESSEE

Fayetteville •

LOUISIANA TERRITORY

Tennessee R.

Tombigbee R.

ALABAMA

Coosa R.

Tallapoosa R.

GEORGIA

MISSISSIPPI TERRITORY

Alabama R.

• Natchez

Mobile R.

• Fort Mims

Mobile • *Tensaw R.*

• Pensacola

FLORIDA

• New Orleans

Mobile Bay

Barataria Bay

Grande Isle

Gulf of Mexico

they encountered and fought the Alibamu (Alabama), until they buried the hatchet and decided to merge. Other tribes came under their protection, and a nation or confederation was formed in the region of the Coosa, Tombigbee and Alabama rivers. Because these Indians settled those numerous narrow waters flowing into the main streams—what the early whites called "the creek country"—they became known as Creeks.

Whites accustomed to the half-naked savages of the Northeast were astonished at the Creek civilization. Local self-government flourished among them, each town having its ruler selected from one of the leading families, people of rank similar to the nobility of Europe and named for forces of nature or animals such as "sun" or "deer." The Creeks were expert agriculturists as distinguished from the hunters or food gatherers who comprised the main body of Amerindians. Their laws were rigid and just, with regulations for marriage or divorce. They did not clothe themselves in animal skins but in fabrics woven by themselves from local fibers. They dwelt in buildings made of wood rather than in tepees, and there were also structures for the conducting of public business.

The Creeks received the early whites with friendship, often intermarrying among them while accepting their missionaries and sending their children to mission schools. Because of their system of military training and promotion, they often served as troops in the armies of Britain and Spain and were ably led by their mixed-breed chief Alexander McGillivray, a legendary warrior who held British and Spanish colonelcies and the rank and pay of brigadier general in Washington's U.S. Army. They also permitted private property, a concept diametrically different from Tecumseh's belief that all land should be owned communally. Thus it is surprising that these most sophisticated of Indians should have listened to Tecumseh's obscurantist vision of a vast confederation of simple hunters roaming an enormous primeval paradise provided for them by the Great Spirit. It is even more astonishing that his most ardent disciple was the young mixed-breed chief Red Eagle.

Not much is known of Red Eagle's early life except that his father was Charles Weatherford, a shrewd Scottish trader from Georgia who married the beautiful Sehoy of the tribe's leading Wind family and half-sister to Emperor McGillivray, as well as sister-in-law of the French general and historian Milfort. Charles Weatherford became McGillivray's secretary of state. He is supposed to have owned baronial estates on the sacred Hickory Ground at the confluence of the Coosa and Tallapoosa rivers. There he bred racehorses and built a racetrack where white settlers could place their bets. There also William Weatherford was born, probably, in 1780.

Besides his illustrious ancestry, Billy was also tutored by his two celebrated uncles: McGillivray and Milfort. But he resisted their every effort to teach him reading or writing, becoming fluent instead in conversational English and later only less so in French and Spanish. He was considered one of the finest horsemen and hunters in the entire Alabama region. It was said that when he was mounted on one of his father's blooded Arabian horses "the squaws all quit hoeing corn whenever he rode by the corn patch." Taking his place on the Creek council he rarely spoke until a divisive problem was under discussion, whereupon through the precision of his thinking and oratorical skill he would almost invariably convince his elders to accept his arguments. Wealthy beyond the dreams of most Indians, handsome, noble in bearing, eloquent and intelligent, he might have risen to leadership among his white relatives, yet he preferred to remain an Indian. Because he often visited the Spanish at Mobile and Pensacola, he learned from them to detest the Americans and would boast that "there is not one drop of Yankee blood in my veins."

After Red Eagle became a chief he was one of the first to complain that the white settlers from Georgia, Tennessee and Louisiana were encroaching on Creek lands from three sides while the Spanish controlled the gulf coast on the fourth. The Creeks were not only losing land to the whites, but also were facing a dwindling supply of game depleted by American hunters.

Thus Red Eagle's aversion to the Americans grew along with his resentment that they had become so numerous in a region once ruled by his ancestors in near-regal splendor. At thirty-one he was ripe for conversion to Tecumseh's cause of total war against the Americans, openly opposing Big Warrior's policy of continued friendship with them. Tecumseh also influenced Chief Little Warrior, who led a band of thirty Creeks north to the British headquarters at Malden in modern Canada. Welcomed with feasts and firewater they were also subjected to anti-American propaganda so effective that on their return south they massacred two white families near the mouth of the Ohio, and then, moving into Chickasaw country, slaughtered seven more families and carried off a woman. The enraged Chickasaw, who had rejected Tecumseh's message, appealed to the Indian agent to punish Little Warrior and his band. Lured from the swamp in which he had taken refuge, Little Warrior was shot down, another brave was burned to death in a house on the Hickory Ground, two more were tomahawked and still others mercilessly hunted down and killed by Creeks friendly to the Americans.

With these bloody incidents, the Creek nation began to divide: the larger and more warlike Upper Creeks wanted Little Warrior and his braves avenged, hunting down their killers and executing them; the Lower Creeks opposed war with the whites, resisting the war cries of their northern kinsmen. With this, the Upper Creeks began to attack white settlers and the Lower Creeks. When Big Warrior sent a message appealing for peace, they killed the messenger. Tecumseh deftly fanned the flames of war by advising the Upper Creeks to journey to Pensacola where they could obtain military supplies from a British fleet in the gulf. Through the cooperation of the Spanish, the British did land at Pensacola, setting up a base to distribute firearms to all Indians arrayed against the Americans.

Three chiefs—High Head Jim, Peter McQueen, and the prophet Josiah Francis, all mixed-breeds—loaded with loot collected during raids on southern settlers, immediately decided to take it to Pensacola and exchange it for guns and powder, food and whisky. Three hundred braves driving a herd of cattle before them attracted so much attention that the whites planned to intercept them on their return. Militia numbering about 180 men under Colonel James Caller and Captain Sam Dale surprised the Creeks at Burnt Corn Creek, attacking them while they were eating and scattering them. But the Americans did not pursue. Rather the undisciplined militia amused themselves plundering the Indian baggage, and as they did McQueen rallied his warriors and drove the whites from the battlefield.

Burnt Corn Creek assured the supremacy of the Creek war party, and after the British promised the Creeks that in the event of an American victory, they would be shipped to a sanctuary in Cuba, the voices of the peacemakers such as Big Warrior were ignored. The Creek nation then numbered about thirty thousand Indians, of whom seven thousand were warriors. Of these more than half—about four thousand—were for war. To Chief Red Eagle this was more than enough, and in the early fall of 1813 he led them onto the warpath.

The Battle of Burnt Corn Creek, like the Battle of Tippecanoe, had been the signal for the white settlers of the Creek country to move into forts. The chief post was at Fort Mims on Tensaw Lake in southern Alabama, about ten miles above the junction of the Alabama and Tombigbee rivers and forty miles north of Mobile on the Gulf. Here an elderly mixed-breed named Samuel Mims had built a trading post and plantation with a ferry across the Alabama.

When Creeks began attacking whites in the summer of 1813 he constructed a picket fence around about an acre of ground. At intervals he added buildings inside the compound. But when the veteran

Indian fighter Brigadier General Ferdinand Claiborne inspected the position, he found it weak and ordered blockhouses built at commanding points. A garrison of one hundred volunteers was raised under the mixed-breed Major Daniel Beasley. By the end of August 1813, there were 553 persons in Fort Mims, of whom 100 were children.

Beasley apparently had little fear of a Creek attack, even though there were frequent warnings that the fort was Red Eagle's chief objective. An escaped black slave of the Creeks arrived at Mims with information to that effect, but Beasley ignored him. Next two slaves sent out from the fort to round up beef cattle came running back inside in terror, stammering that they had seen Indians in warpaint skulking in the canebrake and swamp. When a scouting party found no trace of Creeks, Beasley ordered the slaves flogged for giving a false alarm. In a supreme demonstration of indifference to danger, he allowed the fort's heavy front gate to remain open, so that dirt and sand drifted against it and held it fast. But even this was exceeded by his failure to train and drill his troops, or to assign each man to a particular position. Instead, he permitted them to loaf about the fort all day, playing cards, smoking, chatting, even neglecting to complete the blockhouses. When a settler named Cornells suddenly and without explanation left the fort with his beautiful mixed-breed daughter—with whom Red Eagle was in love—he did not become suspicious. If he had, he might have learned that the Creek chief had secretly warned Cornells that Mims would be attacked.

On August 30 as the settlers and soldiers were sitting down to midday dinner, one of the slaves who had been whipped saw a vast throng of Indians gathering in the swamp. He gave no alarm, fearing to be flogged again. Screeching and whooping wildly, led by Red Eagle on a splendid black stallion, a thousand painted and befeathered Indians brandishing tomahawks and muskets broke from the swamp. At last Beasley took heed. With a few soldiers he dashed for the gate, and there with them became the victim of his own indolence—tomahawked to the earth by shrieking savages.

Within the fort the soldiers formed a defense behind a line of pickets, and a five-hour firefight ensued. Steadily, mercilessly the Creeks began a battle of extermination. They gradually forced the Americans back until they could breach the picket near an unfinished blockhouse. The whites led by Captain Dixon Bailey were forced from building to building. Gathering his diminishing remnants, Bailey formed a front in the last building standing, but the Indians set it afire with a flaming arrow and forced him to concentrate in a small enclosure called the bastion.

Now Red Eagle, appalled at the bloodbath that would begin if no surrender were requested, tried to persuade his maddened warriors to relent. But they had suffered heavy losses and were in a murderous fury. They would not listen, and Red Eagle rode away. Behind him, his whooping braves finished off Bailey and his gallant band, and then, like wolves having tasted blood, they fell in a howling frenzy on defenseless, screaming, supplicating women and children. "The children were seized by the legs, and killed by batting their heads against the stockade. The women were scalped, and those who were pregnant were opened, while they were alive, and the embryo infants let out of the womb." Of the 553 human beings who had been in the fort, only seventeen survived. Among them were a few blacks spared to serve the Creeks as slaves, a half-breed woman and her children saved by a warrior she had befriended, and about ten settlers and soldiers, led by Dr. Thomas Holmes, who fought their way to freedom.

At sunset the triumphant Creeks consumed the Americans' unfinished meal, and as darkness fell they lighted campfires, sitting around them chanting war songs, the flames glinting off their painted faces while they smoked their pipes and trimmed their scalps, brushing away the hordes of flies drawn to the puddles of Yankee blood and brains staining the soil of Fort Mims.

Nothing in the War of 1812—not even the later capture and burning of Washington—horrified the American people as much as news of the Fort Mims massacre. In the northern cities the report was doubly dismaying, for it broke in the middle of Perry's stimulating victory on Lake Erie, then in progress. A universal cry for vengeance arose, instant and insistent. In the Southwest a dread surpassing the first reaction of revulsion seized the people of Louisiana, Georgia and Tennessee. It was feared that Red Eagle would carry the tomahawk to the western settlers there. Even Mobile, then occupied by Americans, braced for the war whoop and flaming arrow, until the Spanish governor succeeded in deflecting Red Eagle farther north by reminding him that the homes and other properties there were owned by "true Spaniards."

News of the atrocities at Fort Mims was brought by a committee of public safety to Andrew Jackson, still bedridden in the Hermitage. In bitter self-reproach he listened to this dreadful litany of horror, conscious "that he had squandered in a paltry, puerile, private contest, the strength he needed for the defense of his country." Here also had come that long-awaited opportunity for military glory, and he was still too weak to seize it. But, no! He would *go*, even if he had to tie himself to his horse. Propped up against a pillow, he wrote out a ringing proclamation appealing for volunteers to rendezvous at Fayetteville in south-central Tennessee by October 4, 1813, and he concluded:

"The health of your general is restored. He will command in person."

By overwhelming a small outpost in Alabama and butchering its occupants, the Creeks—now often called Red Sticks with other tribes which had used Tecumseh's bundles of sticks as a timetable for "D-Day"—had awakened a sleeping giant. Because the Indian concept of war was and always would be local, they had no suspicion of the military strength of the people that they had aroused. Rapidly a powerful four-pronged operation against them was mounted. While Jackson marched down from the north, three other columns would converge on the Red Sticks from East Tennessee, Georgia and Mississippi Territory. It would seem that the campaign would not last three months, the period of service for which this mostly volunteer army had signed on.

It was true that the Creeks were not a formidable military force. At most there were about four thousand Red Stick braves of whom never more than one thousand could be assembled for a single battle. Opposing them was a force of nearly ten thousand Americans, many of them trained and armed with artillery. The Creeks had no cannon. Those who did have muskets only fired them at the commencement of combat, after which they relied on bows and arrows, war clubs and tomahawks. The difficulty, then, was not in fighting the Indians but in finding them. They dwelt within inaccessible strongholds in that nightrackless wilderness of mountain, swamp and river that was their homeland. The heart of the Creek country was at the sacred Hickory Ground where the Coosa and Tallapoosa rivers formed the Alabama— and it was 150 miles from the nearest American base.

Major General Thomas Pinckney commanding the Southern Department discovered these problems in forest logistics when two of his four columns failed to accomplish much, even though they passed over far easier routes than the terrain traversed by Jackson and his 2,500 Tennessee volunteers.

The difference was Jackson. His arm in a sling, weak, pale and emaciated by the painful recovery from Benton's bullet lodged in his left arm as a companion to Charles Dickinson's slug embedded near his heart, his appearance staggered his troops, many of them veterans of the march to Natchez and back. Old Hickory? they wondered: "Old, yes; Hickory, no!" But Jackson's indomitable will was now guided by a strategic concept so splendid that it would hardly seem to have been conceived by a militia general who had never commanded an army in battle. He would destroy the Creek nation by slicing straight through it and shredding it, while cutting a magnificent highway clear down to Mobile—one over which future settlers on land taken from the Creeks could migrate south—at the same time evicting the Spanish from the south and ending British influence there. With Spain and Britain gone, the Indian menace would die of supply starvation. Thus, though expansion in the north had been blocked by military failure up there, expansion in the south would continue.

Jackson had no doubt as to the outcome of his campaign, neither was he daunted by the terrain facing him. After all, he was leading Tennessee frontiersmen, hard-fighting, hard-drinking, straight-shooting "ring-tailed roarers, half horse and half alligator" who lived on "whisky and bear's meat salted in a hailstorm, peppered with buckshot and broiled in a flash of forked lightning." There were others like them, Ensign Sam Houston, for instance, and that legendary Indian fighter Davy Crockett "the merriest of the merry, keeping the camp alive with his quaint conceits and marvelous narratives." John Coffee, Jackson's closest friend and ablest lieutenant, had already advanced with the cavalry.

Coffee was an instinctively fine tactician. He gave Jackson his first victory at Tallushatchee on November 3, 1813. Like Daniel Morgan before him at Cowpens, Coffee executed a Cannae in miniature. He placed his men in a semicircle and sent forward a small body to lure the Indians into it. As the Red Sticks attacked, the advance force retreated, the end of the semicircle swung shut, and over 180 Creeks were killed. Coffee lost 5 dead and 14 wounded. Six days later Jackson tried the same tactic, but his lines failed to hold, and 400 of 700 Creeks escaped. Jackson's losses were 15 killed and 85 wounded.

Had Old Hickory been able to follow up these strokes, he might have ended the Creek War there and then. But he, too, was having his supply problems. As the year came to an end, the old American difficulty of short-term enlistments arose to plague him.

The men who had been to Natchez believed that their time expired December 10, 1813. They counted the months they had spent at home between Natchez and the Creek War as served time. Jackson disagreed. One stubborn company began marching home. Jackson, still unable to lift a musket because of the bullet in his back, rested his gun across the neck of his horse and threatened to shoot the first man who moved. The militiamen stood sullenly, glaring at him, but no man moved.

To everyone but Jackson the Creek War appeared hopeless. Governor Willie Blount wrote to him recommending a retreat. Jackson, who had dined on acorns at least once, flew into his customary passion at the perfidy of politicans. He composed a long letter to Blount, reminding him that he had "bawled aloud for permission to exterminate the Creeks," and asking: "And are you my Dear friend sitting with yr. arms folded . . . recommending me to retrograde to please the whims of the populace? . . . Let me tell you it imperiously lies upon both you and me to do our duty regardless of consequences or the opinion [of] these fireside patriots." Angrily sketching the consequences of a retreat that would send thousands of hitherto friendly but wavering Creeks, Choctaw, and Cherokee, flocking to the Red Stick cause, he concluded:

Arouse from yr. lethargy—despite fawning smiles or snarling frowns—with energy exercise yr. functions—the campaign must rapidly progress or . . . yr. country ruined. Call out the full quota—execute the orders of the Secy of War, arrest the officer who omits his duty . . . and let popularity perish for the present. . . . What, retrograde under these circumstances? I will perish first.

The letter together with a supporting thrust from the War Department stiffened Blount's spine. More troops came south. Although they were only sixty-day men, Jackson made good use of them in a pair of sharp but indecisive engagements at Emuckfaw and Enotachopco creeks. In February of 1814 Jackson's army rose to five thousand men, and the arrival of the 39th U.S. Infantry and the execution of a rebellious militiaman put steel into hitherto slouching ranks. Then Jackson learned that some eight hundred Red Sticks had fortified a position at Horseshoe Bend on the Tallapoosa River. They awaited an all-or-nothing battle, and Old Hickory marched at the head of two thousand men to give it to them.

The Horseshoe was a peninsula of about one hundred acres of brush and small timber furrowed by gullies. Across its neck the Indians had built a zigzag row of logs pierced with double gun ports. At its rear they had drawn up hundreds of canoes in the event they were forced to flee. Jackson arrayed his main body and artillery opposite the log breastwork and sent Coffee's cavalry across the river to cut off retreat.

Coffee's Cherokee scouts swam the river and stole the Creek canoes. Then the impetuous Coffee used them to cross and attack the Indian rear. To the front, Jackson's artillery plunged harmlessly into the breastwork's soft pine logs. Old Hickory called for a frontal assault.

Major Lemuel Montgomery, a relative of General Montgomery, who was killed with Arnold at Quebec in 1775, was the first on the works. The Red Sticks shot him dead. Next came tall Sam Houston, leaping onto the breastwork, waving his sword and jumping down. A fierce fight at the rampart followed. Gradually, the Red Sticks were pressed back. They fought on bravely. Their prophets had told them that the Great Spirit promised victory. The sign would be a cloud in the heavens, said the priests, moving among them, chanting their incantations, falling as the warriors fell.

In the middle of the afternoon the cloud appeared—just as Jackson's messenger arrived offering pardon to all who surrendered. The aroused Creeks nearly killed the messenger, and the battle was renewed with redoubled ferocity. At dusk one band held out in a fortress at the bottom of the ravine. Jackson called for volunteers to take it. Sam Houston stepped forward and was hit by two musket balls before he was carried from the field. After Jackson set the fort afire with flaming arrows, the battle came to an end. More than 550 Indians had fallen on the field, and perhaps 200 more had perished in the river. Jackson's losses were 49 killed and 157 wounded.

With the Battle of Horseshoe Bend the Creek War came to an end. Led by Red Eagle, the Red Sticks made their peace. Jackson summoned all the chiefs to the fort he had built at the confluence of the Coosa and Tallapoosa. They came, the friendly Creeks expecting rewards, the hostiles anticipating harsh punishment from "Sharp Knife," but none dreaming of such brutal terms as Jackson offered. Half of the Creek country, twenty-three million acres composing three-fifths of Alabama and one-fifth of Georgia, were to be ceded to the United States. The Creeks protested, and Jackson replied that through this territory led "the path that Tecumseh trod. That path must be stopped. Until this is done your nation cannot expect happiness, mine security."

On August 9, 1814, the sorrowing Creeks signed the Treaty of Fort Jackson. Andrew Jackson wrote to his wife, Rachel, back in the Hermitage that the "disagreeable business" was done and "I know your humanity would feel for" a fallen nation robbed of half its patrimony.

37

Winfield Scott

$\sim$ It is to John Armstrong's credit that in 1814 his graybeard generals at last gave way to young and vigorous men. Whereas in 1812 there had been eight senior generals averaging sixty years of age, in 1814 the ranking nine averaged only thirty-six. Among these was a fighting general named Winfield Scott, who was easily the most commanding presence in the U.S. Army, standing six feet five inches tall and weighing about 250 pounds of bone and muscle.

Scott was the grandson of James Scott, a member of the Lowland Scottish clan Buccleuch who, with an older brother, had hastened to the standard of rebellion raised by Bonnie Prince Charlie in his attempt to recover the British throne for the house of Stuart. James was at the fierce and bloody Battle of Culloden in 1745. He saw his brother fall there under the sabers of the Duke of Cumberland's dragoons, heard the wild bagpipes fall silent and joined the flight from the battlefield of the prince's weary warriors. But James did not flee north for the Highlands like most of these fugitives, there to be hunted down like rabbits in their hill warrens and caves by those extermination squads unleashed by the ruthless Cumberland. Instead he slipped stealthily south into the enemy's country, moving only by night, until he reached the busy port of Bristol where he took sanctuary in the home of a merchant relative. As quickly as possible, his uneasy host moved to rid himself of this dangerous guest, smuggling him aboard a ship bound for America. Before the end of 1746, James Scott was safe in Virginia, settling near Petersburg down in Dinwiddie County. He had no possessions, but he did have a thorough classical education and a knowledge of Scottish law, so that he was soon able to gain admittance to the Virginia bar. Prospering, he married—dying shortly after the birth of his only child: a son named William.

William served in a Virginia regiment during the Revolutionary War, rising to the rank of captain. During that conflict he married Ann Mason, the daughter of Daniel and Elizabeth Winfield Mason, both descendants of wealthy and distinguished Dinwiddie families. Ann Scott gave birth to four daughters and two sons, among them a boy born June 13, 1786, whom she named Winfield after her grandfather John Winfield, one of the wealthiest men in the Old Dominion.

Little is known of Winfield's early years except that he was an unusually big and bright boy, fond of listening to his father relate his exploits in the war against King George III or tell of his grandfather's loyalty to "the rightful heir" to the British throne in the war against King George II. These tales instilled in him a fierce hostility toward the house of Hanover. The youth's education was probably rudimentary because in those days the only adequate primary schools were in major cities such as Richmond or Norfolk. Even Petersburg, like the rural towns surrounding it, had to rely upon itinerant scholars to teach its children.

In 1798–99 Winfield, at the age of twelve, was enrolled in a nearby boarding school conducted by a Quaker named James Hargrave. This mild-mannered little schoolmaster—a doctrinal pacifist to the core—was appalled by his huge pupil's fiery temper and did his utmost to restrain his decidedly un-Quakerish pugnacity. Some years later when Winfield at eighteen had matured physically, Friend Hargrave could be thankful that the boy was both big and belligerent. Winfield had come home from Williamsburg, where he was attending the college of William and Mary, just in time to see a drunken bully assault his erstwhile preceptor. A cowed crowd of onlookers made no attempt to rescue him, so Winfield seized the bully's shoulder and knocked him down with a single blow to the jaw. Friend Hargrave was horrified: a former pupil had given way to the cardinal sin of physical violence! As the bully struggled erect, the little Quaker had seized Winfield's arms in an attempt to pinion them. As he did his own assailant began to pummel his protector. Stoically receiving these blows while gently detaching Hargrave's hands from his arms, Winfield had resumed the attack, beating the bully so badly that the cheering crowd joined him, and "it cost the Quaker and his pupil the greatest effort to save the bully from further punishment and perhaps death." (Many years later, after the War of 1812 was over and Scott was a national hero, he met Hargrave on a Petersburg street. "Friend Winfield," the little dominie said with an impish smile, "I always told thee not to fight, but since thou wouldst fight, I am glad that thou was not beaten!")

In 1804 Winfield transferred his pursuit of education to a high school in Richmond presided over by a Scots scholar named James Ogilvy. Many of Ogilvy's pupils were the scions of the city's most distinguished families; however, according to Winfield, the curriculum was so demanding— Greek and Latin classics, metaphysics, rhetoric, logic, mathematics and political economy, whatever that was—that quite a few of them, himself included, turned away from it in relief to the delights of Richmond. Exuberant and high-hearted though he was, Winfield Scott would always remain a lover of learning, especially literature, doing well enough at Master Ogilvy's school to be accepted at William and Mary. At this venerable institution—founded in 1693 and antedated by Harvard alone—he came under the spell of its energetic and wise president, James Madison, cousin of the American president-to-be of the same name and Bishop of the Episcopal Diocese of Virginia.

Under Madison's guidance he buckled down to his studies, combining courses in science with classes in philosophy and gradually gravitating toward the study of law. For his own pleasure he plunged into reading the plays of Shakespeare, the poetry of Dryden and Milton, the histories of Hume and Gibbon, and the economic theories of Adam Smith as well as the political insights of John Locke. He also tried to master the French language, but most of all he delighted in military history, being especially fascinated by Plutarch's lives of the Caesars and the careers of such Roman conquerors as Scipio Africanus and Julius Caesar.

Few men who ever lived have been as physical as Winfield Scott, yet he took no pleasure in the "he-man" diversions such as hunting and fishing, preferring instead chess and cards—in which he seems to have excelled—stimulating or controversial conversation, fine horses and politics and politicians. At William and Mary he became a fierce follower of Thomas Jefferson and his Republican party. He rejoiced in the abolition of the Alien and Sedition Acts and the distress of the Federalists, and applauded Bishop Madison when that devout Republican refused to describe heaven as a kingdom but rather "that great republic where there was no distinction of rank and where all men were free and equal." Yet, among all these far-ranging interests and pursuits, his first love was fine food and wine.

Normally a giant is not supposed to be a gourmet but rather is expected to nourish his great body with a side of beef and a barrel of beer; but Winfield Scott from his late teens until his venerable old age was a faithful devotee of grape and sauce. He learned a proper respect for both from an old French planter who had fled the horrors of the slave rebellion in Santo Domingo to settle near Scott's home. There in his little cottage he conducted a tiny restaurant that Scott frequented during vacation visits. All the meals were prepared by the old gentleman himself, who would exchange his apron for a frock coat green with age to sit at the head of his table and dispense both his kitchen creations and instructions in the culinary art. From him, Winfield learned to appreciate the great wines of France, what to look for in color, finish and bouquet that would announce a triumph of oenology. He learned to love Bordeaux, especially the growths of Saint-Julien in the Médoc, and was proud to learn that his idol, Thomas Jefferson, when he was the American ambassador to France, had also favored the same chateaux.

Scott was never so relaxed as when he could enter his kitchen wrapped in one of his specially sewn oversized aprons to bring out the perfect flavor of a Virginia ham or a wild turkey, or a dish of plump oysters from some secret Chesapeake Bay creek. He could cook a canvasback duck to perfection or roast a mouth-watering haunch of venison, but of all his culinary skills not even his mastery of the art of baking bread could approach his wizardry with baked Maryland terrapin. "This," he would say, a forkful of this favorite food poised below his lips, "is the finest food vouchsafed by God to man."

When in the field Scott would not scruple to approach the mess sergeant, recipe in hand, to tell him just how to prepare this succulent dish. It got so that mess sergeants dreaded Scott's approach, and he was not popular for his fondness of fine wine and soups. In those days the nectar of kings was regarded rather sourly by democrats fond of the free man's potion of corn whisky or beer. They also disapproved of cognac, even though it could be flavored with julep just like bourbon, and soup was the sup of those effeminate frog-eating French and was definitely not for American he-men.

Such a splendid physical specimen as Winfield Scott, it would seem, so congenial and handsome, with his massive head, light brown eyes, regular features, and wavy light brown hair, would have been a favorite with the ladies, yet little is known of any romance until his marriage to a great Richmond beauty named Maria Mayo in March 1817. Before then, the only hint of interest in women comes from Scott himself. On vacation at his home near Petersburg he went for a walk, stopping at a farmhouse to ask for a glass of milk. The farmer's wife, a "stout, buxom woman," cheerfully brought him the milk and fell into conversation with him as he drank it. "In a short time," Scott recalled, "the devil put it into my head to take manual liberties with her, but at my first motion she sprang away, seized a broom and came at me with a fury such as only an earnest female can display. The door being open, I shot through—cleared a high fence and ran with all speed across the fields until I got clear of her voice."

This encounter seems to have cured him of any future adventure in dalliance—or adultery—and he probably confessed his intended transgression to Bishop Madison in the confessional at Bruton Parish Church—for Winfield Scott was a lifelong devout Episcopalian. He did not share his contemporaries' scorn for revealed religion or their fondness for the works of atheistic or agnostic authors such as Voltaire, Helvétius or Hume, all proscribed by Bishop Madison with a ferocity calculated to do nothing other than to whet their appetites for them. But then, after a single year in Williamsburg, Winfield Scott surprised everyone by declaring himself bored beyond belief by classroom discipline, announcing that he would take a shortcut to the pinnacle of political success for which he yearned by becoming a lawyer.

In 1806 at the age of twenty Winfield Scott was admitted to the Virginia bar. A year later he joined the tide of lawyers flowing toward Richmond to witness the trial of former Vice President Aaron Burr on a charge of high treason. Wilkinson seems to have been despised by everyone in the courtroom. John Randolph, chairman of the grand jury, called him, "A mammoth of iniquity, the only man I ever saw who was from the bark to the very core a villian," and Winfield Scott instantly and instinctively despised Wilkinson the moment he set eyes on this fat, pompous and verbose double-crosser, who sought to send Burr to the noose to save his own skin. Scott had a marvelous view of the proceedings. Finding not even standing room available in the packed courtroom, he had climbed up on the heavy cast-iron lock of the main door. From this perch, he could study the great John Marshall, chief justice of the United States Supreme Court, who had come down from the capital to sit alongside the trial judge to make certain that only bonafide evidence—not presidential pressure and whim— would convict Burr. Scott could also see an obscure young reporter named Washington Irving scribbling notes, and hear every bitter word spoken by the fiery Andrew Jackson in his castigation of the president. Although Scott saw with his lawyer's mind that there was simply no proof that Burr was guilty of the Constitutional definition of treason—

"Giving aid and comfort to the enemy"—he still hoped for a conviction that would send a message to America "that playing at treason is a dangerous game." Already his young mind was forming in the doctrinaire belief that for disloyalty, cowardice or treason there would be only swift and condign punishment. And Aaron Burr was indeed acquitted, although the verdict had to give way to the sensation following the *Chesapeake* Incident and Jefferson's proclamation forbidding the blockading British ships from entering American territorial waters.

These events had so aroused the popular anger that Governor William Cabell of Virginia ordered a troop of volunteer cavalry from Petersburg to patrol the Chesapeake shore. Among the horsemen was big Winfield Scott, who had ridden all night from Richmond upon hearing the news, appearing in ranks as a private wearing a borrowed uniform and mounted on a newly purchased horse, with his father's saber—like the Irish minstrel boy's—hanging at his side. He soon rose to lance corporal in command of a squad guarding an inlet. One night, warned that a British boat loaded with supplies was returning to its ship, he saw it hugging the shore and called out:

"What boat is that?"

"It's His Majesty's ship *Leopard*," an indignant English boy's voice shrilled back, "and what the devil is that to you? Give way, my lads!"

Instead Scott, thrilled at the chance to do injury to the infamous *Leopard,* ordered his troopers to splash into the shallow water to surround the boat.

"I call on you to surrender!" Scott thundered, and two indignant boy midshipmen and six sailors did exactly that, while handing over a cargo of fresh vegetables and water. Washington throbbed once more with war hysteria, but the irenic Mr. Jefferson, perhaps at last aware of how his doctrinal pacifism had disarmed his country, had no desire to try conclusions with the British lion, instead ordering Scott to return his captives to their ship. So the minstrel boy was not to the war gone, but instead hung up his father's sword and returned his uniform to its owner.

It had been a bit too tight, anyway.

Although Winfield Scott resumed his law practice, he could not forget how splendid he had looked in a uniform. Thus, when President Jefferson in February 1808 asked Congress to expand the army by six thousand men forming eight new regiments, Scott hastened north to the capital to enlist the support of powerful Virginia congressmen in applying for a commission in one of these formations. To his intense joy the former lance corporal but twenty-two years old, received from Secretary of War Henry Dearborn a commission of captain in command of a company of light artillery. At once he quit the law forever, and then, not having forgotten his tight-fitting borrowed uniform, hastened to Richmond to order the finest military tailor in that metropolis to make him a uniform that would *fit*. When it arrived, he locked himself inside his bedroom and put it on. *It was gorgeous!* There was a short blue coat with tails, a high choker collar, and three rows of gold buttons down the front spaced far enough apart to permit insertion of the hand in a truly Napoleonic pose; a "tar bucket," or high glazed black hat over which there waved a white pompon tipped with red; white breeches worn with knee-high boots; a red sash for the waist; and gold epaulets for the shoulders. So attired, Winfield Scott dragged a pair of tall pier mirrors into place and spent two happy hours parading, posturing and posing before them. In truth, it would be hard to imagine a more imposing military presence than this gravely strutting twenty-two-year-old giant of a captain.

But there was bite as well as bark to this brand new war dog. He plunged into his new life with typical energy and dedication, riding back and forth between Petersburg and Richmond to recruit able youths for his command while steeping himself in the study of military history, tactics and ordnance. In those days light artillery was really "flying" artillery armed with four-, six- and eight-pounders, effective and extremely mobile little guns. Scott learned all about them in Kósciuszko's *The Manoeuvres of Horse Artillery,* imparting that knowledge to his sergeants who drilled it into his gunners. By the end of the year that had seen Madison elected president, Scott's company was ready, and on February 4, 1809, his guns and men went aboard a transport bound for New Orleans. After a horrible and debilitating two-month voyage aboard the leaking, listing and overcrowded old tub *Nancy,* Scott and his company arrived in the Crescent City—only to enter upon an even more miserable and actually deadly ordeal at what might have been the worst military encampment in the annals of American arms.

This was a campsite at Terre aux Boeufs thirteen miles down the Mississippi from New Orleans which General Wilkinson had chosen over Secretary of War Eustis's recommendation of Natchez. Scott and his company were among those troops sent forward to prepare the camp, and they found that their esteemed general was setting his army down in a swamp. Before they had time to clear the jungle and dig drainage ditches the entire army appeared, going under canvas in unfloored tents. They had arrived during the rainy season so that the spongy soil was converted into liquid mud, which, when the rains stopped, became a steaming, sweltering cauldron under the blazing Louisiana sun. As might be expected, dysentery, diarrhea and scurvy swept the camp, followed by malaria from the onslaught of clouds of horrible mosquitoes. With only limited medical supplies, men began to die by the dozen. Concerned, Wilkinson's officers signed a round-robin beseeching Wilkinson to move to the healthier location at Natchez. He refused on the ground that his mission was to defend New Orleans, which he could not do far above the city. Morale was not improved when he next began to withhold his soldiers' pay because of his fear that, armed with money, they would desert en masse.

Now Wilkinson's officers, many of whom had bought fresh food for the men out of their own pockets, became openly critical of their general—Captain Scott being among the most outspoken. Many of his remarks were heard by Dr. William Upshaw, a regimental surgeon and friend of Wilkinson, who reported them to his chief. Eventually reports of the unspeakable filth and suffering at Terre aux Boeufs began to appear in the newspapers. A national scandal ensued and Congress demanded an investigation, after which Secretary Eustis ordered Wilkinson to move up the Mississippi immediately. He did, this time losing three hundred more soldiers to malaria, malnutrition and the other ravaging diseases during a forty-day voyage aboard clumsy, open barges. With this Wilkinson was relieved of his command by Brigadier General Wade Hampton and directed to return to Washington to await a court-martial.

By then Captain Winfield Scott had had his fill of army life. Already disappointed by the gradual cooling of the fervor for war with Britain, he reasoned that if Terre aux Boeufs were typical of a career in uniform, he would rather return to the law. In June of 1810 he sent in his resignation, while obtaining a furlough to await acceptance of it. He had hardly returned to Petersburg, however, before fresh rumors of impending war changed his mind again and he went back the way he had come—only to face a court-martial.

Although it was brought by Dr. Upshaw, who had heard Scott say "I never saw but two traitors, General Wilkinson and Burr" and that Wilkinson was "a liar and a scoundrel," it was instigated by the general. Scott, expecting to be tried for libel or slander, was flabbergasted to find himself accused of embezzling enlisted men's money. In his defense, he explained that he had indeed withheld their pay, but that this had been only to repay himself for purchases of shoes, blankets and clothing he had made at his own expense. Several soldiers testified that this was true, but Scott was nevertheless convicted of this charge as well as his "unofficer-like" language and sentenced to be "suspended from all rank, pay and emoluments for the space of twelve months." Infuriated, Scott challenged Dr. Upshaw to a duel. When they confronted each other with raised pistols the huge young captain was so overwrought that he missed his opponent, whereupon Dr. Upshaw took deliberate aim to fire a bullet that plowed a furrow on Scott's skull, drawing blood and causing pain, but otherwise not harming him. Carefully concealing his bandaged head beneath his great tar-bucket hat, Scott again returned to Petersburg.

At home, Scott wisely accepted a lawyer friend's invitation to spend his unwanted twelve-month vacation inside his extensive library, immersing himself once again in martial lore, yet not neglecting to satisfy the exuberant side of his nature with evenings spent in congenial taprooms or in the handsome mansions of Petersburg. His reading was at least the equivalent of the military education available at the new United States Military Academy established by Congress at West Point in 1802 over the opposition of the pacifist Jefferson. Ten months after Scott began this course of self-instruction, the Twelfth Congress assembled in December 1811, under the influence of the bellicose War Hawks. By then he had returned to Louisiana, traveling in the fortuitous company of General Wade Hampton, who befriended him and became his patron.

After the War of 1812 erupted, Hampton again had Scott by his side when he hurried to Washington anxious not to be overlooked in the forthcoming appointments to major general; and Winfield Scott, no stranger to the art of climbing the rank ladder, through his powerful friends still in Congress, used that trip to jump two rungs and emerge with a lieutenant colonel's silver leaves on his shoulders, second in command of the newly formed 2nd Artillery. At his new headquarters in Philadelphia, Colonel Scott saw clearly that the plan of the campaign to capture Canada would entail fighting on the Niagara Frontier, and he wrote the War Department pleading for permission to lead at least two batteries to Buffalo. It came, and on September 3 the gigantic young lieutenant colonel with his guns and gunners crossed the Delaware to New Jersey and thence to New York where they took ship for Albany. Debarking there they marched westward through the beautiful Cherry Valley and the Finger Lakes in balmy weather and through hills riotous with autumn color, arriving in Buffalo on October 4 to join the command of Brigadier General Alexander Smyth.

38

Frontier Victories at Last

~ BESIDES WINFIELD SCOTT THE OTHER YOUNG OFFICERS COMMISSIONED as brigadier generals in 1814 were Peter B. Porter, the aggressive War Hawk Congressman whose saber-rattling so offended Lord Liverpool, and Eleazar Wheelock Ripley, one of many New Englanders whose loyalty during the War of 1812 helped to preserve the region's honor. All served in an army under Major General Jacob Brown, the soldier who had repulsed Prevost at Sackets Harbor the year before. Brown had orders to make a new invasion of Upper Canada. Speed was to be of the essence in this campaign, for Britain seemed to have brought the Napoleonic Wars to a triumphant conclusion. In April of 1814 Napoleon abdicated as emperor, thus freeing at least fourteen of Wellington's regiments to cross the ocean and thoroughly chastise "Brother Ephraim."

Opposing them was the energetic Lieutenant General Sir Gordon Drummond with about an equal number. But Drummond's force was spread thin over a vast frontier. About 1,000 men were kept in York to be rushed to any threatened point, while another 2,600 were strung out along the Niagara under Major General Phineas Riall. Obviously, to respond quickly to American movements would require hard marching from the British. However, the British had little fear of the Americans.

But this was a different Yankee army. Its soldiers saluted smartly and took pride in their uniforms and their brigade commanders. Scott the scientific had been particularly active drilling his troops. He put them in neat uniforms, albeit of militia gray, for Scott could not obtain cloth for regulars' blue.

On July 3, 1814, General Brown threw this force across the river and invested Fort Erie. It was surrendered in the afternoon, and Brown spent the Fourth of July moving north along the Niagara.

Riall, however, had moved swiftly. Gathering his garrisons, he came south with about two thousand men, halting at Chippewa eighteen miles above Fort Erie. Here, the next day, he attacked the American camp.

Porter's militia-Indian brigade drove off a Canadian force, but the British regulars routed Porter in turn. General Brown ordered Scott's brigade, fortunately already drawn up for evening parade, to give battle. With American and British guns already dueling counter-battery, Scott led his men over a creek and deployed. Marching steadily, tall in their trim gray uniforms and high hats, Scott's soldiers spread out in a concave line to put a converging fire into the redcoated British drawn up in column, two regiments abreast. The British opened fire. Americans toppled. But the gaps were quickly closed and the long gray line came on. Seventy yards apart the two forces halted and fired. Now there were gaps in the British line, and the Americans charged with the bayonet to break and rout Riall's redcoats.

British losses in the Battle of Chippewa were five hundred men, while the Americans lost three hundred. It was not an important victory, but its psychological effects were stunning and enduring. For the first and only time in the war, regulars of both sides had met and maneuvered on an open plain, and the Americans had won. At Chippewa the *esprit* of the United States Army was born, and the battle is commemorated in the gray uniforms worn by cadets at the U.S. Military Academy.

Brown followed up Scott's victory by pressing the British back to Fort George and Burlington Heights. Encamping at Queenston, he awaited the heavy guns needed to reduce the enemy forts. They were slow in coming from Chauncey at Sackets Harbor, and Brown was forced to return to Chippewa on July 24.

In the interval, General Drummond had hurried to the Niagara from Kingston. He now ordered his three thousand-man force out in pursuit of the Americans. While Riall followed Brown, another force crossed the river to menace Brown's supplies. Brown became worried. He sent Winfield Scott down the Canadian side of the river in hopes of forcing the enemy to recall his troops from the American side. Scott came upon Riall at Lundy's Lane, a point a mile below the falls, and immediately attacked.

Such was Scott's audacity that Riall was forced to retire. But just then Drummond came up with the rest of his army, ordering the cross-river detachment to rejoin him. Drummond put his artillery on a hill, with his infantry in line slightly to the rear.

Scott attacked again, directing his brigade against the British center and left. On the left, the Americans temporarily turned the British flank, capturing the wounded Riall while doing so. But the British eventually recovered there, while in the center they hurled back charge after charge. Still Scott hung on, until, at about five o'clock, Brown arrived with the rest of his army.

Brown ordered another attack. The lines swept forward in a darkness shimmering with the flashes of the British guns, but they could not seize the hill and the British battery blazed on. Brown ordered Colonel James Miller of the 21st Infantry to take the British works. While the enemy guns thundered at an American column moving along the river, Miller's regulars slipped forward through the darkened scrub. Coming to within a dozen yards of the enemy, they crashed out a close volley, charged with the bayonet and seized both hill and battery. Now Brown brought his entire army up to the hill, and the astonished Drummond counterattacked.

Three times the dark silhouettes of the British regulars swept upward, and three times the muzzles of American muskets and the captured guns flickered and flamed to drive them back again. Brown and Scott were both hit and evacuated. Around midnight, Brown ordered Ripley, now commanding on the hill, to withdraw for water and ammunition. He did, but he also left some of the enemy guns behind. With daylight Drummond quickly reoccupied the height and turned the guns around—restoring the situation of the preceding day except that both sides were battered and bleeding and each minus about nine hundred men.

In the Battle of Lundy's Lane the Americans might just possibly have won a tactical victory, but they suffered strategic defeat. Lundy's Lane put out the ardent flame enkindled by Chippewa and forced Brown to abandon all hope of conquering Upper Canada. He withdrew into Fort Erie. The energetic Drummond assaulted him there on August 15, but the American repulsed him. On September 17 Brown led a sally out of the fort to seize and spike the British guns. No less than five hundred men fell on both sides during this bitter flare-up, and now both Brown's and Drummond's armies were exhausted remnants. Drummond issued orders proclaiming a victory, and then fell back to Chippewa. Less than two months later the Americans acknowledged the futility of fighting on the Niagara Frontier by blowing up Fort Erie and recrossing the river to American soil.

All had not been in vain, however, if only for the gleam that Chippewa, Lundy's Lane and Fort Erie gave to a young but thus far lusterless military tradition. The cost had been high. James Miller, the hero of Lundy's Lane, wrote a friend: "Since I came into Canada this time every major save one, every lieutenant-colonel, every colonel that was here when I came and has remained here has been killed or wounded, and I am now the only general officer out of seven that has escaped."

But now the guns fell forever silent along the forty-mile strait separating New York and Ontario. For the focus of the war had long ago shifted east, where the weight of British arms flowing to the United States from victorious European battlefields was bearing the fledgling American eagle to the earth.

39

Hostages/Prince Regent

～WHEN WINFIELD SCOTT SURRENDERED HIMSELF AND HIS COMMAND AT Queenston in October 1814, the British seized twenty-three Irish-American soldiers and sent them home to Britain to stand trial for treason. It appeared that these soldiers would be convicted by British law maintaining that they were British subjects and could not change their nationality. On this point the Prince Regent could not be moved. Like his father he regarded his subjects as irrevocably his, just like his dogs and horses. He disdained to receive the Irish Americans' explanation that Ireland never had and never would accept British occupation, and that they had emigrated to America to escape the poverty and despair that were the twin malignancies of British oppression. There thus began an escalating policy of holding hostages on both sides of the Atlantic.

Enraged by the enemy's attitude, Winfield Scott held twenty-three British prisoners as hostages. In retaliation, the Prince Regent ordered forty-six native American commissioned and noncommissioned officers jailed.

In the United States the British attitude rankled like a bone in the craw. Most Americans had never heard of the citizenship precedents of the crowned heads of Europe. They believed, in their highly developed love of freedom, that all human beings had the right to emigrate and become citizens of the country of their choice. They demanded that President Madison adopt a policy of retaliation. If any American soldiers or sailors were hanged, the United States should hang the same number of British prisoners.

On October 27, 1813, Governor-General George Prevost of Canada published in Montreal newspapers orders from the Prince Regent not to yield to Americans on the point of hostages. This oldest son of King George III, who became Prince Regent upon the permanent derangement of his demented father, maintained that it was his royal prerogative to treat his subjects in his own way. Wherever or whenever they were found to have chosen another allegiance, he had the right to capture them and try them for treason. This right was incontestable.

Now thoroughly aroused, the American public demanded reprisals, and President Madison held forty-six British prisoners as hostages in response to the last batch of Americans held on the Prince Regent's orders. Britain then took sixteen American sailors alleged to be either British- or Irish-born hostage and imprisoned them in Halifax to await deportation to Britain. Madison replied with sixteen British sailors. Prevost countered with another forty-six, and upon this event all exchange of prisoners ceased. Each side refused to budge, and each waited nervously for the first hanging that would keep their gallows busy with the grotesque dance of death.

Soon virtually all prisoners of war became hostages, and during the standoff that ensued Secretary of State James Monroe evolved a cogent explanation of the American position. Every nation in Europe, he argued, naturalized citizens or subjects of other nations and employed them in their armies. He contended that citizenship was a temporary condition that could be terminated, and not a permanent relationship between a person and his government or ruler. It was in force only so long as the person remained in residence of that country or kingdom. The right to emigrate, recognized by all nations, implied the right to change allegiance.

This argument differed diametrically from the British position that the citizen was subject to the king's pleasure. His obligations to the state or monarch were inalienable. Monroe might have argued—though he did not—that Britain by its very recognition of the former colonies as a sovereign state also recognized its policy of the freedom of immigration, one which has generally been accepted by most nations.

While the United States seethed over the hostages—probably the first and only occasion of American solidarity during the entire war—

Governor-General Prevost angrily blamed General Dearborn for the impasse. Prevost had written to Dearborn asking about the status of his American prisoner-hostages, who were filling up his jails. When three months passed with no reply, he put every American officer imprisoned in Canada in close confinement, ended parol and denied the liberty of Quebec to any captive.

When these harsh measures were reported to Whitehall, they received the unreserved approval of the Prince Regent.

George Augustus Frederick of the house of Hanover, the oldest son of King George III, was born in 1762 in Saint James' Palace. Because of his demented father's maniacal family discipline, he passed from infancy to childhood to boyhood, cut off from all companions of his own age, although after he was able to speak he was given the sort of thorough education that no gentleman of that age could do without. His instructors were all hand-picked by the king, all distinguished in their specialities of Greek, Latin or French, history or mathematics, or English literature. Young George, unlike his father, who did not begin to learn to speak the language of his people until he was eleven, spoke English fluently. Despite his father's relentless efforts to compel his children to keep to the straight and narrow rather than follow the primrose path favored by his debauched and troublesome brothers or his nymphomaniacal sisters, the Prince of Wales gave him more pain and embarrassment than all these royal dukes and duchesses combined.

At the age of sixteen George became completely "acquainted" with the beautiful though aging Mrs. Mary Robinson, the darling of Drury Lane and better known as "Perdita" for the part she played in Shakespeare's *The Winter's Tale*. As soon as George was eighteen and had an establishment of his own, he set her up in Berkeley Square. But eventually Perdita, whose numerous adoring lovers included Banastre Tarleton of Revolutionary War ill-fame, proved too costly for the young prince and she passed into the keeping of the popular politician Charles James Fox. The union could not have been based on physical attraction, for Fox was fat, pig-faced and cross-eyed.

The Prince of Wales now embarked upon a career of debauchery that included not only wine, women and song, but cards, horses and a capricious delight in befriending his father's enemies while openly opposing his policies. King George's mental health was not improved by these incessant forays into immorality and disloyalty, but his disapproval was as nothing compared to his outrage when "Prinny"—as he was now called—secretly married Maria Fitzherbert, a twice-widowed, beautiful and amorous lady who was also a Roman Catholic. Other than a Frenchman, there was nothing that King George III hated more than Catholics. His detestation of that faith was reinforced by his ignorance of it and the probability that he had never in his life met a Catholic or even a Frenchman. Moreover, it was contrary to the Royal Marriage Act for a king's child to marry without his father's consent, and marriage with a Catholic was also a violation of the Act of Settlement on which Hanoverian possession of the throne of Britain was based. If the act could be contradicted, then the king of Britain was not George III in Windsor Castle but rather Charles III, the erstwhile Bonnie Prince Charlie in Florence. In Prinny's defense, he never really wanted marriage in the first place, but his true love made it the price of possession. It is possible that this scandal propelled George III more rapidly toward his second mental seizure of 1788–89, begun when, as he drove through Windsor Park, he ordered the carriage stopped, alighted and shook hands with the branch of a tree, addressing it as the King of Prussia.

Prinny repeatedly denied that he had married Mrs. Fitzherbert, but his enormous expenditures of £369,977 during the years 1784–86—about $2 million then, and probably fifteen or twenty times that now—showed that he had spent £54,000 on his new paramour. Eventually, as the lady might have expected, he became unfaithful to her and they separated: she to become the butt of cruel caricatures, the Prince of Wales to continue his wild extravagances to the embarrassment of his father and the dismay of Prime Minister Pitt. Pitt was then struggling to effect economies that would save the country from impending bankruptcy, and it was no help to have the royal family—George III had fourteen healthy children—acting as though the British treasury were the family piggy bank.

As the Prince of Wales grew older he began to slip into peculiar behavior, suggesting that the insanity that afflicted his father, grandfather and great-grandfather was also seizing him. These quirks became apparent after his father suffered his final attack in 1811, becoming permanently deranged and then blind, retiring to a few rooms in Windsor Castle where he sought solace in music, especially sad and sorrowing compositions connected with blindness or madness by his fellow German, Handel. In that year his son became Prince Regent, much to the joy of his new mistress, Lady Hertford. He celebrated the occasion by inviting the sheriffs of London to his dinner table, where he got them drunk and then in their inebriated condition presented them to his aged mother. The Duke of Wellington, as loyal a royalist as any man owing his peerage to the throne, said: "He speaks so like old Falstaff that damme if I was not afraid to walk into a room with him."

Prinny often pretended that he had campaigned with Wellington during the Peninsular War, claiming that he led the charge of the Heavy Dragoons at Salamanca. He fell victim to maudlin sentimentality, often weeping on the shoulders of his ministers or kissing Wellington on the cheek. Lady Bessborough gave this account of his amorous style: "Such a scene I never went through. I stared and he went on, and after a long tirade threw himself on his knees and clasping me round kissed my neck. Then vows of eternal love, entreaties and promises of what he would do. He would break with Mrs. Fitzherbert and Lady Hertford. I should make my own terms. I should be his sole confidant, sole adviser." From the amused tone of this account it would seem that her ladyship did not satisfy His Royal Highness.

George's loving and drinking did not stop after he married his cousin Caroline of Brunswick in April 1795, breaking off renewed relations with Mrs. Fitzherbert to do so. Upon meeting Caroline, he muttered a few words before ordering a servant to bring him a glass of brandy. He was quite drunk at his wedding, nearly keeling over as he knelt beside his bride. But the union did not last, probably because George was incapable of a stable life, and they separated. In 1803 he resumed his affair with Mrs. Fitzherbert.

After his father died in 1820, he ascended the throne as King George IV. His coronation in Westminster Abbey was the most splendid in memory, lasting four full hours, chiefly because His Majesty was slightly addled by frequent, tottering trips from his throne to the Chapel of St. Edward where the altar was covered with a sacriligious repast of wines and whiskies, caviar and cognac, and plates of sandwiches. He gradually withdrew from the public eye, sinking into indolence and rarely rising before six o'clock in the evening, usually receiving his ministers in his nightgown. When Viscount Goderich resigned as prime minister, and George summoned Wellington to form a new ministry, the duke found the king in bed: "dressed in a dirty silk jacket and a turban nightcap, one as greasy as the other; for, notwithstanding his coquetry about dress in public, he was extremely dirty and slovenly in private."

Thus the "First Gentleman of Europe," the most contemptible king to sit on the British throne. Certainly there have been crueler kings and despots than he, notably Henry VIII and Caligula, Hitler and Stalin, murderers of life and liberty, but this fourth German George who reigned over about ten million Britons was unrivaled as one of the most lecherous, drunken, petty, petulant and profligate rulers in the long sordid history of monarchy.

Nevertheless, it is to his credit that he never carried out his threat to execute his hostages, and that all those in captivity on both sides of the Atlantic who had not died of disease were repatriated during and after the war—including those twenty-three Irish-Americans.

40

Peace Feelers
Fail/British War Plan

∼ BY THE SUMMER OF 1814 THE BRITISH BLOCKADE, NORTHERN DEFEATS, internal dissension, a near-empty treasury and the certain prospect of an enemy invasion had so subdued Mr. Madison and the War Hawks— no longer whooping and war-dancing but cooing like the doves perched tamely on the Capitol steps—that any talk of peace would have been sweet indeed. But by then it was too late.

America's first opportunity appeared in 1812 after the British repealed the Orders in Council and ordered Admiral Warren to try to negotiate a cease-fire. But this feeler got nowhere when Secretary of State Monroe bluntly insisted that no talks could begin until after the practice of impressment was abandoned; and this was just not possible in an island kingdom depending on sea power for its safety.

Another chance seemed to have opened in March, when John Quincy Adams, the U.S. Minister to Russia, reported Czar Alexander's offer to mediate the Anglo-American quarrel. By then the Canadian reversals had so chastened the Americans that Madison quickly, without waiting for a British reaction to this proposal, appointed Secretary of the Treasury Gallatin and the Federalist James Bayard as peace commissioners. Bayard was an intellectual prodigy who had been graduated from Princeton at the age of seventeen. Becoming an eminent lawyer in Wilmington, Delaware, he had served three terms in the House plus one full and one partial term in the Senate. Madison chose him because of his reputation in international law, and because he had been a Federalist who opposed the war, but supported it completely once hostilities began.

Gallatin and Bayard were to join Adams in Moscow to conclude a peace that would still insist upon an end to impressment. After military success at York and along the Niagara Frontier, an incredibly over-confident Monroe wrote to Gallatin: "These successes ought to have a salutary influence on your negotiations, [and] it might be worthwhile to bring to view the advantage to both countries which is to be promised by a transfer of the upper parts and even the whole of Canada to the U.S."

Here was that Yankee bumptiousness that European diplomats found so infuriating. Here was the foundering U.S. ship of state about to go under, and Captain Monroe instead of shouting, "We are lost!" was instead jubilantly crying, "We're in port!" But the American commissioners soon found themselves faced with bleak realities: Czar Alexander was out of town fighting Napoleon and Britain was simply not interested in any settlement that would include dropping impressment. Yet Britannia did not slam the door of negotiation shut, and a still-hopeful Madison added Henry Clay and Jonathan Russell to the peace delegation. Gallatin and Bayard, meanwhile, had already left St. Petersburg for London, arriving there in April just as Napoleon fell from his imperial throne. Here was the loss of a powerful though accidental ally, freeing the British enemy to turn to the chastisement of the treacherous Americans who had struck her in her hour of peril. Both Madison and Monroe could not have been happy when they read Bayard's report from Britain: "The whole nation is delirious with joy, which was not indulged without bitter invectives against their remaining enemies: the Americans. They consider [the war] as an aid given to their great enemy at a moment when his power was most gigantic. . . . They thirst for a great revenge and the nation will not be satisfied without it." Gallatin wrote: "To use their own language, they mean to inflict on America a chastisement which will teach her that war is not to be declared against Great Britain with impunity." Gallatin urgently advised Madison to drop the impressment issue.

Madison did. While War Hawks still muttered darkly about maritime grievances and banners proclaiming FREE TRADE AND SAILORS' RIGHTS still fluttered from the masts of American ships, the issue which had called forth all the blood and bullets was quietly dropped in a Cabinet meeting of June 27. Instructions to that effect were sent to the peace commissioners gathered in Ghent to await the pleasure of their British counterparts. And while the Americans cooled their heels, Mother England raised the rod which was to despoil, as well as discipline, her runaway, impudent daughter.

•••

If successful, Great Britain's strategy for subduing the United States would have left her in possession of the Great Lakes and the American states and territories bordering their southern shores, New England, northwestern New York and the entire, vast Louisiana Territory stretching from the Gulf of Mexico to the lakes—in all an area three times the size of the seventeen states composing the American nation of 1814. Then if Britain decided to bargain at any peace conference she could claim *uti possidetis*, "the state of possession," recognized in international law. If she held most or all of these lands, she would no longer need that Indian buffer state she had hoped to establish to block further American expansion to the west, but could halt it herself.

Three operations were to be mounted for this purpose. The first and major force would invade New York State down Lake Champlain from Canada. In support, to distract the Americans from the Champlain thrust, an army-navy team would assault American coastal cities with particular emphasis on the vast Chesapeake Bay. Finally, an amphibious force would seize New Orleans, the gateway to the Louisiana Territory. None of these plans mentioned a campaign of revenge or reprisal, yet the first formation to move—the army-navy team under Admiral Sir Alexander Cochrane—went into action with retaliation as its objective.

That was because in July 1814, Cochrane in Bermuda received a letter from Sir George Prevost complaining of the burning of York and other depredations on Lake Erie by raiding American troops. Though neither of these expeditions nor the incineration of York were authorized, Prevost did not wait to receive the apology and American explanations and promise of reparations that actually did follow, but instead asked Cochrane to "assist in inflicting that measure of retaliation which shall deter the enemy from a repetition of similar outrages." Here was a marvelous excuse for making Yankee Doodle dance, and if there were any following letter from Prevost informing Cochrane of the American apology, there is no record of it. On July 18, Sir Alexander told his commanders: "You are hereby required and directed to destroy and lay waste such towns and districts upon the coasts as you may find assailable."

A few weeks later Cochrane sailed for Chesapeake Bay at the head of four ships-of-the-line, twenty frigates and sloops and more than four thousand of Wellington's regulars, those indomitable conquerers of Napoleon whom His Lordship so gallantly described as "the scum of the earth." Commanding these troops was Major General Robert Ross.

•••

Robert Ross, according to one of his American prisoners was, "the perfect model of an Irish gentleman . . . of easy and beautiful manners, humane and brave, and dignified in his deportment to every one." He was born at his home of Rosstrevor Estates in County Down, Northern Ireland. After he was graduated from Trinity College in Dublin, he joined the British Army and seldom thereafter gazed upon those bare green hills so dear to him in his boyhood. Though outwardly pleasant and urbane, he had an iron will and became known as a martinet.

Ross's rise in the British Army was rapid, and he eventually came to command the celebrated Lancaster Fusiliers, the immortal James Wolfe's old regiment. Britannia probably would have had much greater military success in North America if more professionals such as Brock and Ross and Wolfe, rather than the sons of the wealthy and influential, had been elevated to top command.

During the retreat of Sir John Moore to Coruña in Spain in 1809, Ross had the honor of commanding the rear guard. Wellington repeatedly mentioned him in his dispatches, making him a general. "General Ross's brigade distinguished themselves beyond all former precedents." At Sorauren, Ross had two horses shot from under him, and his division was praised again by the Iron Duke: "The gallant fourth division, which has so frequently been distinguished in this army, surpassed their former good conduct."

Even Wellington's oldest veterans had found the Peninsular campaigns full of hardship and danger, yet Ross's vivacious Irish wife accompanied him on the march, hovering on the edge of the battlefields when combat erupted. Yet she yearned for an end to war and a return to Rosstrevor and those sheep-covered hills. Life there would be so much more peaceful, once the anxiety of being married to a soldier was removed. She could remember the gaiety of the county fairs, with the horse racing, the games and the judging of livestock, the reels and jigs and step-dancing, and, of course, the whisky and the stout and the drunk tent for those unwary country lads taking too many sips too close together.

Because she could not accompany her husband to America due to the risks of long sea voyages and the possibility of sea fighting, she stood in August 1814 on the shore of the harbor at Bordeaux watching with tears in her eyes as Cochrane's great fleet sailed with slow majesty out to sea.

Her only comfort was that her husband had promised her that America would be his last campaign.

41

Ravaging the Chesapeake

∼WHILE ADMIRAL COCHRANE'S VENGEANCE-BOUND FLEET CROWDED ON all sail for the Chesapeake-Delaware area, the policy of retaliation for the Canadian raids was already in the capable hands of Admiral John Borlase Warren.

Admiral Warren was considered one of the best educated and most courteous officers in the Royal Navy, having been graduated from Cambridge and been called by his peers "the quintissential [*sic*] gentleman." He was also deeply religious, having had difficulty early in life in choosing between the altar and the quarterdeck. He finally abandoned both and went yachting in Bristol Channel seeking the peace of mind in which to choose. Napoleon, however, made that decision for him, for once the war with France erupted he hastened to join the Royal Navy. He remained devoutly religious, and when he arrived on the American station he became president of the Halifax Bible Society. His heroes were Moses and Joshua, and it is possible that he memorized the Mosaic prescription for war: "But if [thy enemy] will not make peace, and shall begin war against thee, thou shalt besiege [their] city. And when the Lord thy God shall deliver it into thy hands, thou shalt slay all that are therein of the male sex with the edge of the sword." Proving himself as quick with a torch as a text, Warren began his "blockade" of Delaware Bay by ordering Captain

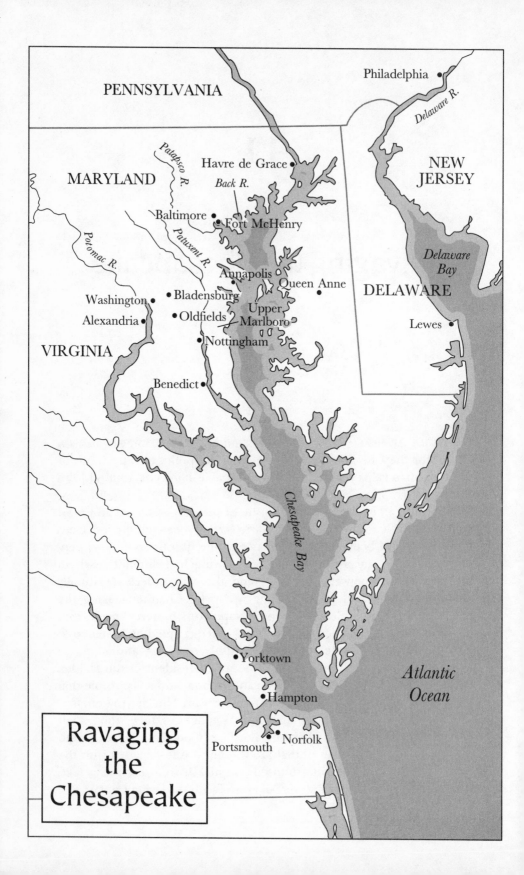

Ravaging
the
Chesapeake

John Boer Beresford to enter those waters with his 74-gun liner *Poictiers*. Appearing suddenly before the town of Lewes, Delaware, he sent ashore a requisition note demanding twenty-five live bullocks. In a spirited reply the mayor told him he would not surrender as much as a leg of lamb, and Beresford began to bombard Lewes. It is likely that Beresford was one of those skippers who, despairing of getting gunpowder for practice gunnery out of the Admiralty, had abandoned that drill altogether—for twenty-two hours of shelling did little damage and caused not a single casualty.

Meanwhile, the local militia had dragged Revolutionary War cannon from the common and begun to shoot back. They had no cannonballs, but they were able to use those fired from *Poictiers*, sending them spinning back with decidedly better aim than the British tars and disabling a British boat. Beresford eventually drew off. Whether or not he was frightened away is not known, but he did make a few feeble attempts to land elsewhere in search of those bullocks, but eventually he gave up in disgust and sailed back to Bermuda with the gums and teeth of his sailors sore from chewing on stale biscuits.

Lewes had been hardly more than a lark, and it did not turn Delaware against the war as Admiral Warren had hoped, but rather confirmed the state's support of it. Historically Lewes was important because it was the scene of a marriage between the U.S. Army and one of the world's industrial giants: du Pont de Nemours.

Pierre-Samuel du Pont de Nemours was a French economist and writer who supported the French Revolution, keeping his head during the Reign of Terror only because Robespierre had lost his first. He came to America with his two sons, returning to France while they established a small powder factory in Wilmington. They were not in the beginning chemists, but after their guns misfired on a hunting trip because of poor powder they decided to make their own. Jefferson and Madison, who had befriended their father, were among their customers. Hearing of the Lewes affair, the du Ponts filled a wagon with powder, arriving just as the militia's powder ran out. That was the beginning of the du Ponts' long association with American armed forces.

Back in Bermuda, Admiral Warren was not entirely pleased with Beresford's ineffectual cruise, and assigned direction of the Chesapeake-Delaware blockade to Rear Admiral Sir George Cockburn.

Sir George was a descendant of one of the oldest families in Britain, thought to have crossed the Scottish border from Northumbria in 1057 and been given lands by King Malcolm of Scotland for helping him to defeat Macbeth. One of his ancestors fought with Robert the

Bruce in 1314 when that legendary Scottish hero inflicted his annihilating victory on the English at Bannockburn, thus securing independence for Scotland. Four and a half centuries later George Cockburn was born on April 22, 1772, in a fashionable village for the well-to-do outside of London. Although his family no longer possessed those enormous estates owned by its original founders, they were still fairly wealthy and very influential. His brothers distinguished themselves in the church and diplomacy, one was a general, and George, of course, who succeeded to the family baronetcy in 1852, rose to the Royal Navy's highest rank of Admiral of the Fleet at the age of eighty-one.

Choosing a naval career almost as soon as he saw the sea for the first time, he was at a very early age introduced to a course of studies which, though it included the classics, emphasized mathematics and navigation, and was deliberately designed for service on the sea. When he was nine or ten* he came aboard HMS *Recourse* as a "captain's servant," or cabin boy. His family connections were undoubtedly helpful during his meteoric rise, but he was also a born sailor and an aggressive fighter. His ports of call in that astonishing career of seventy-one years read like the log of a tramp steamer, and the number of his sea fights like the roll call of Royal Navy battles during the long Anglo-French struggle for colonial supremacy. There is a painting of Sir George Cockburn as a vice admiral that depicts a tall, strongly built man with powerful, long legs encased in tight-fitting britches and a face as square as a frigate's sail. It is also disdainful, and the lifted chin suggests something of a swaggerer, a suspicion confirmed by the left hand resting arrogantly on the hilt of his sword. That blade was presented him by none other than Lord Horatio Nelson himself, and it is doubtful if there exists one more gorgeous. Its hilt and handle are of thick gold plate and it sparkles with jewels. Nelson gave it to him after Cockburn—with His Lordship aboard—captured a French convoy carrying cannon for Napoleon's siege of Mantua, together with maps, plans and orders for the Corsican's first Italian campaign. Such a loss would have immediately wrecked a veteran general's reputation, but the young Bonaparte survived it to convulse Europe.

Cockburn's career frequently coincided with Napoleon's. He was off Toulon when the young artillerist's guns battered Fort Mulgrave into submission and gave him the city. When Cockburn captured Martinique he raised the Union Jack over Empress Josephine's home. In 1815 after the emperor's escape from Elba and his decisive defeat at Waterloo, it was Admiral Cockburn who took him on the long voyage

---

* His biographers differ on the exact age.

to the final exile at St. Helena where he died at the age of fifty-one. Both men were vain and bombastic and took an instant dislike to each other. Whenever Napoleon appeared on deck—he was a late riser and remained in *deshabille* until midafternoon—all the officers and men aboard *Bellerophon* except Cockburn removed their hats. Cockburn angrily ordered an end to this mark of respect for the fallen emperor. Napoleon thought Cockburn was "not a man of bad heart; on the contrary, I believe him to be capable of a generous action. But he is rough, overbearing, vain, choleric and capricious." To which Cockburn might have replied: "Just like Napoleon." The admiral also sneered at his imperial passenger as "just an ordinary fellow." This rattled the conqueror, who retorted scornfully that if he were so insignificant, how was it that the crowned heads of Europe had spent so much in men and money to bring him down?

Upon entering the Chesapeake Cockburn was again mortified to find his campaign of spoliation interrupted by the attacks of a mosquito fleet of armed scows and barges commanded by the redoubtable Commodore Joshua Barney.

Commodore Joshua Barney was as colorful a sea captain as the forty-four-year-old Admiral Cockburn he was harassing, with a career nearly as various and tempestuous. He was born in Baltimore in 1762, going to sea on a pilot boat at the age of twelve. Two years later he was aboard the brig *Andrea Doria* off St. Eustatius in the Dutch West Indies. When her commander saluted the Dutch governor there, he returned the honor and Holland became the first foreign country to recognize the nascent United States. At twenty in 1782 he commanded the privateer *Hyder-Ally* with sixteen small six-pounders and 110 men and officers, challenging the much more powerful British sloop-of-war *General Monk* off the Delaware caps. In a fiercely fought action that James Fenimore Cooper in his *History of the U.S. Navy* called "one of the most brilliant that ever occurred under the American flag," he took the Britisher captive. For this feat Philadelphia awarded him a gold-hilted sword, while the populace sang:

> Come all ye lads that know no fear,
> To wealth and honor we will steer,
> In the *Hyder-Ally* privateer,
> Commanded by bold Barney.

Barney sailed his prize to France, and when the handsome, cocky, dapper American sea captain appeared at the court of King Louis

XVI, his pretty blond queen gave Barney a hearty hug-and-kiss in the presence of all her not-so-captivated courtiers. This Barney-like episode resulted this time in a full-length song entitled, "Barney, Leave the Girls Alone!"

Although the dashing young captain was in and out of British prisons three times—meaning that his constitution was strong enough to thrice survive what was often a passport to the graveyard—he came back to Baltimore as robust as ever and in time to be the first American to unfurl the Stars and Stripes there. When Baltimore celebrated adoption of the Federal Constitution, he disassembled a full-rigged brig, reassembling it on a float pulled down the street by a team of gaily-caparisoned horses and to the delightful roar of the sidewalk crowds.

Captain Joshua Barney was not so happy, however, when he was passed over in the selection of commodores for the six new frigates. Learning that the political sailor Richard Morris had been so honored, he sailed to France in a pique, seeing service with the Napoleonic Navy in the Santo Domingo expedition.

In 1812 as war with Britain erupted, Commodore Barney took his armed schooner *Rossie* down the Chesapeake in search of British prizes, capturing fifteen and sinking nine before he returned to Baltimore to fight a duel, and to accept on April 27, 1814, command of a Chesapeake flotilla consisting of fourteen old scows and barges and manned by 503 seamen. A ship-builder as well as a fighter, Barney turned them into gunboats more serviceable than Thomas Jefferson's "earthboats," and began to scourge the fleet of the honorable Admiral Sir George Cockburn.

Like all able commanders, Barney adjusted his tactics to his terrain and his strength, becoming a waterborne gadfly. Obviously he could not challenge Cockburn's heavyweights ship-for-ship. But he knew the Chesapeake: its deep water, its shoals, its numberous shallow creeks and estuaries into which he could fly for safety. So he buzzed, rather than assaulted, the enemy; waiting until a likely victim came too close to his watery sanctuaries, whereupon his flotilla, led by his appropriately named flagship *Scorpion*, mounting eight carronades and one long gun, plus a furnace for heating shot, would sally forth to inflict damage on them. He never hoped to sink them—a wise restraint—but he did make Sir George pay attention. A typical foray was against the British schooner *St. Lawrence*, which his flotilla pursued, firing away, until she came under the protection of the huge 74-gun liner *Dragon*. When *Dragon*'s big guns opened up, Barney's gunboats quickly put about and ran before the wind for shallow water with *Dragon* lumbering in futile pursuit. Because of Barney, Cockburn's hopes of renewing in 1814 the pillage of the previous year were frustrated, and instead of repeating such atrocities as Havre de Grace he was reduced to pig-sticking and tobacco-pilfering operations.

42

Bladensburg
"Races"/Washington Burns

〜On the morning of August 15, 1814, Admiral Cochrane's great fleet entered Chesapeake Bay propelled by a strong easterly wind blowing across the Virginia capes and up the Chesapeake. Residents of Yorktown stood onshore in undisguised dread as this symbol of British seapower paraded majestically past them. Some of them began counting: six liners, twenty-one frigates, six brigs and a flotilla of smaller vessels together with the larger troop transports—in all, more than fifty ships. In the center of this awesome armada was Cochrane's flagship *Tonnant*, a great double-decked liner flying his blue admiral's flag.

Many of those Chesapeake people were old enough to remember the war-ending Battle of Yorktown thirty-three years earlier, and how much Admiral de Grasse's French fleet contributed to Washington's great victory. They could comprehend sea power, and they were both terrified and indignant, for they knew that their area of the strategic Chesapeake was defended only by Barney's flotilla and two thousand militia—and not as much as a company of regulars. One irate resident wrote to the Virginia *Patriot* in Richmond bitterly blaming Madison for leaving his country and his capital open to invasion, concluding: "Thus we are about to taste the blessings of 'Free Trade and Sailors' Rights.'"

As Cochrane's fleet sailed north, General Ross's soldiers were lost in admiration of the rich and bountiful country that they beheld: a bay as spacious as no harbor in Europe, majestic rivers such as the York and Potomac, a country with "forests and rivers sublime beyond description." Probably if they had seen the lower Delaware and Hudson they would have been stupified. At the mouth of the Potomac next day the fleet dropped anchor to be joined by Admiral Cockburn with his own fleet of three liners, a dozen or so frigates, plus numerous gun brigs and sloops-of-war. Now there were close to a hundred British warships at the head of the Chesapeake, and Ross's ground troops were augmented by Cockburn's seven hundred Marines and about one hundred armed American blacks who could be deployed in combat as well as laborers. Cochrane's fleet carried even more Marines.

On August 16 Cockburn came aboard *Tonnant* for a council of war with Cochrane and Ross. Sir George was an excellent strategist as well as a fine tactician and knew full well that Baltimore should be the true objective of this mighty concourse of sea power. It was the third largest city in the United States as well as one of the greatest seaports in the New World. It was also home to hundreds of American privateers, destruction or capture of which would certainly be applauded by British shipowners and their insurers as well. But in his heart Admiral Cockburn yearned to seize and destroy the American capital, for Washington was the home of the *National Intelligencer* edited by that dastardly traitor Joseph Gales, an English-born gentleman who had made common cause with the Yankee scum. Gales also, Sir George believed, had dishonored the Cockburn name in his scurrilous articles, calling him every name permissible in print, so vilifying him that Attila or Genghis Khan would seem by comparison a veritable St. Francis of Assisi. That was why Cockburn—who was as thin-skinned as the French emperor he had derided as a monster of vanity—argued so forcibly for a feint at Baltimore and a descent on Washington.

In the end the plan adopted was an attack on Washington. The major portion of the fleet would enter the Patuxent, where the army would debark and stand as though in readiness for a march on Baltimore or Washington, or even Annapolis, thus compelling the Americans to divide their meager forces for defense of these three cities. The Patuxent was also chosen because it was Barney's base and would offer a plausible explanation of the fleet's presence, rather than arouse fears of an attack on Washington. The plan—and it was a good one—also called for a smaller force to sail up the Potomac to seize Alexandria and be in position to co-operate with Ross in front of

Washington. Cockburn was delighted when Cochrane ordered him to accompany Ross with his Marines. As supreme commander, Cochrane would remain aboard *Tonnant*.

Residents of southern Maryland and Washington were as fearful of the British amphibious force as they were furious with Secretary Armstrong and President Madison. One Marylander reported British seizures of black slaves, livestock and tobacco, complaining: "Will the people of the United States believe that a strong, regular force has been, for the past three weeks, within fifty miles of an enemy laying waste the whole country, and that the Secretary of War has not, although repeatedly solicited, ordered a solitary individual to our assistance?" Another wrote that the British had made Charles, St. Mary's and Calvert counties "unenviable places of residence," burning tobacco and destroying villages and houses.

Washingtonians were certain that they knew the explanation of Armstrong's indolence. It was not the stated excuse of his fixation on the northern border campaigns but rather his desire to destroy the capital and move it somewhere else. A correspondent to the New York *Post* wrote: "They think he wishes to have the seat of the government removed, that he may destroy the Virginia combination, which now stands in the way of his promotion to the Presidency." Another *Post* story claimed that Armstrong had already located a site for a new capital in his hometown of Carlisle. Armstrong, meanwhile, was more concerned with his epistolary battle with his former friend Wilkinson over who was responsible for "Mist-taking Canada," than with defending himself against these bitter attacks. When Major General John Van Ness, commander of the Washington militia, came to Armstrong's office to alert him to the fact that the enemy seemed to be preparing a powerful blow, the secretary replied: "Oh, yes, by God. They would not come with such a fleet without meaning to strike somewhere, but they certainly will not come here. What in the devil will they do here?"

Van Ness then observed that they might destroy the American capital, which would not tend to stimulate the war effort, and Armstrong said: "No, no! Baltimore is the place, sir. That is of much more consequence."

Upon the appearance of the British moving up the Patuxent, with Ross marching along its banks and Cockburn with his Marines on barges, Commodore Barney ordered about a hundred of his men to blow up his gunboats, and then to rejoin him and the remaining four hundred sailors at the Wood Yard. Hearing this, President Madison acted at last. Having rejected Wilkinson's ludicrous offer to take command of the District of Columbia if the charges against him could be lifted, he placed defense of the capital in the hands of Brigadier General William Henry Winder.

General Winder was a handsome, amiable man, celebrated for his fluent courtroom speeches. He had been graduated from the University of Pennsylvania and studied law in the office of his uncle John Henry, a delegate to the Continental Congress from Maryland during the Revolution. His knowledge of law and his speaking skills suggested politics, and he decided to migrate to Tennessee, the fabled state of political opportunity. Finding the frontier life too vigorous, he returned to Maryland where at twenty-three he was elected to the legislature as a representative from Somerset County. Moving to Baltimore four years later, he began what was to become an extremely successful law practice there. His pleasant, friendly manner was particularly effective with juries, but why President Madison should think that a man able to work a political picnic with handshakes, smiles and kisses was qualified to lead men in battle with bombs, bullets and bayonets moving both ways is not quite clear; nor is it known why he shut his eyes to Winder's disgraceful surrender at Stoney Creek in Canada after being defeated by a force half the size of his own. Perhaps he was chosen because he was the cousin of Levin Winder, governor of Maryland, upon whom most of the requisitions for militia would fall.

But now William Winder was back in Maryland, having been exchanged—much to the great misfortune of America—and discovered almost immediately that the several states were willing to defend themselves but not the capital. He called for three thousand men and got not three hundred. He asked for more, but Armstrong refused to approve his call. Winder, it appeared, commanded only himself and his horse—and he nearly killed that poor beast when, starting on July 5, he rode for nearly a month over the terrain he was to defend, returning to Washington on August 1 to proclaim the obvious: Washington was poorly defended.

Its only regular force was a half-trained district brigade. At Bladensburg on the Washington road, the obvious point to stop Ross and his four thousand, there were only 450 troops holding entrenchments voluntarily dug by the exasperated citizens of the capital. Alarmed at last, President Madison issued a call for more militia, and Brigadier General Tobias Stansbury began marching down from Baltimore to Bladensburg with about two thousand militia. As they did, Washington flew into a first-class flap.

Citizens and clerks fought each other for wagons to carry off private or governmental valuables. Families boarded up their homes and buried the silver under the shrubs. Dolley Madison, the president's charming and saucy wife, left off scolding her neighbors for foolish talk about evacuation and busied herself moving things from the residence of her friends, the Gallatins. And as General Winder rode everywhere at breakneck speed, Secretary of War Monroe, the only official who had constantly feared an attack on Washington, mounted his horse to ride to Benedict, where he spent two days personally scouting the enemy's movements.

On August 21 both Winder and Monroe joined the district brigade camped at the Wood Yard roughly midway between Bladensburg in the north and Benedict in the south. On August 22, the day Barney blew up his boats, Winder and his cavalry rode south toward the British at Nottingham. They came upon the enemy moving north to Upper Marlboro. For perhaps an hour the Americans sat their horses watching the perspiring redcoats marching through the fields. Then they galloped back to the Wood Yard and the entire force retreated out of Ross's way to Oldfields (now Forestville, Maryland). They were now about ten miles below Bladensburg. About half that distance east lay the British at Upper Marlboro. At Oldfields, meanwhile, Winder was joined by Barney with about 500 sailors and 150 Marines under Captain Samuel Miller. That evening President Madison and his cabinet rode out from Washington.

In the morning of August 23 the president reviewed Winder's troops and rode back to Washington. After he left, Winder rode north to Bladensburg. He had not gone far before a messenger overtook him to inform him that the British were marching on the army he had left. Wheeling, Winder galloped back to Oldfields in time to see Ross's columns approaching and to give the order for retreat.

It was not an orderly withdrawal. Winder's army simply turned tail and ran west to the capital. Ross, perhaps startled by his enemy's sudden disappearance, did not pursue. Instead, he marched south to the Wood Yard, and it was there that he decided to attack Washington on the following day.

Winder's retreat to Washington had brought him to the Navy Yard on the east branch of the Potomac. He went there, he said, because he believed the enemy might move on the city by the river. Winder had no thought of Bladensburg, the true avenue of approach. Neither, apparently, did Bladensburg's defender: General Tobias Stansbury. As the hot sun of August 24, 1814, rose in the Maryland sky, Stansbury pulled his troops out of that vital little village and began marching to join Winder at the Navy Yard.

President Madison and his cabinet had already reached Winder's camp. They spoke for fruitless hours with the distracted general, until, at ten o'clock, a scout came clattering over the bridge with news that the British had been marching for Bladensburg since dawn and were nearly halfway there.

Secretary of State James Monroe immediately mounted his horse and rode hard for Bladensburg, seven miles away. After him streamed President Madison and the rest of the cabinet, then Winder and his army, and then, after blowing the Navy Yard Bridge, came the resolute Barney with his sailors and big naval cannon.

Fortunately, the retiring General Stansbury was also alerted to the British approach. He turned and hastened back to block the Washington road west of Bladensburg. That road ran out from the town, crossed a bridge over the eastern branch, ran level through a marsh, and gradually ascended rolling hills. Stansbury certainly had time to destroy the bridge, but he did not. Instead, he placed artillery and about five hundred men in a position overlooking it. His main body was placed west of the marsh.

At about eleven o'clock Monroe came galloping down the hill. Without consulting Stansbury, he altered the general's dispositions—to their ultimate disadvantage. Some Maryland militia arrived at about the same time. Next came Madison and his cabinet, Secretary Armstrong repeatedly asking for command and being just as frequently refused. The president jogged through Stansbury's lines toward the bridge and inevitable capture, until a scout headed him off. Then Winder came puffing up, placing his men on a ridge too far behind Stansbury to assist him. Thus there were three lines consisting of perhaps six thousand men to oppose Ross's four thousand. But there was no real organization. The units had no understanding of their relations to each other, some were in excellent position to fire on their comrades, and everyone was exhausted and confused from days of marching.

At one o'clock British scarlet streamed into Bladensburg and Stansbury's artillery opened fire. Then the British light brigade rushed the bridge. Immediately, Stansbury's sharpshooters opened up. Redcoats fell, but most of them got across. Tearing off their knapsacks and tossing them into squad piles, the British formed files of skirmishers ten paces apart. They came on at the trot, and it was then that there was a gurgle, a screech and a whoosh overhead.

Ross had fired his Congreve rockets at Stansbury's second line. The first few sputtered harmlessly overhead. Then their trajectories were flattened out and the American men and mules seized with a mad, superstitious fright. There was little to be feared from the Congreves, a weapon so innocuous that it soon ceased to frighten even savage tribes. They were all bark and no bite, yet, without a single one falling among the Americans, they put Stansbury's left and center to rout. Soldiers threw away their guns and fled, and the only casualty was a captain who ran himself to death.

Not all the Americans fled so quickly. At one point, some of them even forced the redcoats back to the cover of the riverbank. But then Ross fed another regiment into the battle, and after this unit forded the stream and threatened to turn the American left, the rout became complete. The battle had not lasted a quarter hour. President Madison, watching the stampede from a hill, suggested to Secretary Armstrong that it would be wise "to take a position less exposed." Whereupon the American cabinet joined the American army in a flight that did not stop until it was at least sixteen miles beyond Washington.

Startled once again by his enemy's trick of vanishing, Ross regrouped and began marching west to Washington—and ran into Commodore Barney's sailors and Marines.

Barney had arrived on the field as Winder was being swept away. He set up his cannon and put his men into line about a mile west of Bladensburg. By his own account,

At length the enemy made his appearance on the main road in force and in front of my battery, and on seeing us made a halt. I reserved our fire. In a few minutes the enemy again advanced, when I ordered an 18-pounder to be fired, which completely cleared the road. Shortly after, a second and a third attempt was made by the enemy to come forward, but all were destroyed. They then crossed over into an open field, and attempted to flank our right. He was met there by three 12-pounders, and Marines under Captain Miller, and my men acting as infantry, and again was totally cut up. By this time not a vestige of the American army remained, except a body of five or six hundred posted on a height on my right, from which I expected much support from their fine situation.

But Barney got no such support. Even though his men actually counterattacked crying, "Board 'em! Board 'em!" to drive the world's finest troops before them, the militia on the height to his right broke and quit the field. Now the British got into Barney's rear. Barney was himself wounded. Even so, his men fought on. Some of them were bayoneted at their guns with fuses still in their hands. They would have stayed until the end had not Barney, lying in a pool of his own blood, ordered them to retreat.

It was a magnificent stand, and it cost Ross about 250 casualties against Barney's 26 killed and 51 wounded. The slightest follow-up of Barney's counterattack might have produced an American victory. As it was, the road to Washington now lay open, and Ross, accompanied by Admiral Cockburn, led two tired regiments down it into the heart of the American capital.

It was dark as Ross and Cockburn and their troops entered the deserted city. Yet bullets flew at them from the house once occupied by Gallatin, and Ross's horse fell dead beneath him. Angered, the perfect gentleman had the house burned. Under the urging of Cockburn, he next sent troops to the Capitol. Using gunpowder and rockets, the British set the symbol of American sovereignty blazing in the blackness. Now Ross and Cockburn and two hundred men marched through the eerily silent darkness to the President's House. No one was inside. Dolley Madison had long since fled with most of the plate and valuables, although the table was set for dinner for forty. Decanters of wine stood on the sideboards, and in the kitchen, spits loaded with joints stood untended over the fire, and the pots were filled with sauces and vegetables. Subaltern George Glieg, who was present, has written: "You will readily imagine that these preparations were beheld by a party of hungry soldiers with no indifferent eye. An elegant dinner . . . was a luxury to which few of them . . . had been accustomed." So they ate it, after which they disposed of the immemorial problem of cleaning up by setting fire to the President's House. Meanwhile, the Navy Yard and all the vessels in the eastern branch were put to the torch, along with the War and Treasury buildings. Before midnight the blazing city cast flickering red light over those Virginia and Maryland hills into which the American government and its army had crept. Then a violent thunderstorm sprang up to quench the flames and all fell dark again.

In the morning Dolley Madison hurried to meet her husband sixteen miles up the Potomac. En route she stopped off at what appeared to be a friendly farmhouse. She went upstairs while her attendants announced her presence to the housewife. Enraged, the woman ran to the stairs and shouted up them: "Mrs. Madison, if that is you, come down and get out. Your husband has got mine out fighting, and damn you, you shan't stay in my house! So get out!" Dolley went, her humiliation symbolizing the low estate into which the American presidency had fallen.

In Washington, meanwhile, the firebrands were up early to rekindle the dampened ruins, making certain this time that the Library of

Congress inside the Capitol was also destroyed. Admiral Cockburn was delighted. Riding an uncurried white brood mare with a black foal trotting by her side, he made for the office of the *National Intelligencer*. He ordered the newspaper's library heaped in the street and lent his own hands to the burning of the books. Then he ordered his men to scatter the type, shouting gleefully, "Be sure that all the *C*'s are destroyed so that the rascals cannot any longer abuse my name!"

At noon the sky darkened and a rare tornado struck the city with a dreadful howl. It increased the havoc, but it also put out the fires. Shortly afterward an explosion at the Navy Yard injured many of Ross's redcoats and placed a final check on "retaliation." At about nine o'clock that night, leaving their campfires burning and marching in extreme silence, the British departed the dishonored and disfigured capital.

43

Washington Aftermath

~ NEVER BEFORE HAD AMERICANS BEEN SO HUMILIATED AS BY THE NEWS OF the debacle at Washington. Not even the disaster at Pearl Harbor nearly 130 years later could rival the shock felt throughout the seventeen states when it became known that the District of Columbia, nearly three hundred miles from the ocean, had been captured and many of its public buildings set afire by an amphibious force of fewer than five thousand soldiers. Everyone in the capital blushed with shame, especially the keepers of the President's House and grounds. Unable to endure the rebuke of the blackened and charred walls of the chief executive's residence, they hastily smeared it all over with white paint—unaware that in so doing they were changing the building's name from President's House or President's Palace to "White House."

Eventually—again like Pearl Harbor—the sense of outrage gave way to the unifying emotion of indignation, begun in Vermont, once a seething antiwar center, when the governor declared that "the war had assumed an entirely different character," and must now be supported by everyone, Federalist and Republican alike. In New York thousands of civilians from the city and neighboring New Jersey flocked to Brooklyn Heights with picks and shovels to help build fortifications. Newspapers carried the story of a seventy-two-year-old woman found moving wheelbarrows filled with dirt. War fever also seized Philadelphia, Baltimore, Boston and Charleston.

An incident typical of American wounded pride occurred on a Hudson River steamboat where the writer Washington Irving heard a passenger declare in a sneering tone: "Well, I wonder what Jemmy Madison will do now?"

Irving at once swung at the scoffer, and after striking him only a glancing blow, subjected him to a tongue-lashing. "Sir, do you seize on such a disaster only for a sneer?" he shouted angrily. "Let me tell you, it is not now a question about Jamie Madison or Johnny Armstrong. The pride and honor of this nation are wounded. The country is insulted and disgraced by this barbarous success, and every loyal citizen should feel the ignominy and be eager to avenge it."

All over the country there were indeed men rushing to the colors to avenge "this barbarous success," but Irving was not quite right in insisting that the disaster was not the fault of Madison and Armstrong. The facts were that President Madison was so shaken by the Bladensburg defeat and his own shameful conduct there that he was on the verge of a nervous breakdown and had to turn the reins of government over to James Monroe, and with Monroe in charge it was clear that Armstrong would pay for his dereliction. All the old charges of deliberately neglecting Washington's defenses to satisfy his hopes of moving the capital elsewhere were renewed, as well as his former friendship with the odious Wilkinson. Everywhere officers and men were refusing to serve under his orders. The District of Columbia militia actually mutinied against the war secretary. Their officers told their commander, Brigadier General Walter Smith: "Here, sir, are our swords. We will not employ them if General Armstrong is to command us in his capacity as Secretary of War." Madison, who had recovered his composure by indulging in his favorite relaxing pastime of horseback riding, was loathe to dismiss Armstrong as Monroe insisted. But the president did advise Armstrong to leave Washington until the outcry against him subsided, and Armstrong did go to Baltimore, from which city he mailed Madison his letter of resignation.

John Armstrong's discomfiture was James Monroe's opportunity. Never a man to hesitate or minimize his talents, he promptly wrote to Madison asking for the war portfolio. Now it was Madison who was upset. To silence Armstrong's numerous supporters he had hoped to give the public the impression that Armstrong was not forced to resign but had stepped down of his own accord. But to make Armstrong's arch-enemy Monroe his successor would only set the political hounds to baying, so he wrote to Governor Tompkins of New York asking him if he would like the job. When Tompkins declined, the president reluctantly handed the War Department hat to Monroe. Madison was again dismayed when Monroe said he would run both State and War, for a Virginian running both departments might renew Armstrong's favorite criticism of "the Virginia cabinet." Actually, as Monroe explained once more, there was almost nothing to do at State, and he was not, therefore, biting off more than he could chew. So Madison acquiesced in what proved to be a wise decision, for Monroe was a diligent and energetic administrator whose arrival was a blessing for the U.S. Army. Under his leadership, American armies never suffered another defeat.

At Ghent, where the Anglo-American commissioners had reopened their peace negotiations, news of the Washington debacle did not arrive in time to influence either side. If the Americans had known that their capital had been contemptuously burnt like any stinking pirate's lair, they might not have been so firm in rejecting Britain's demand; but as it was, on August 24, the very date of the "Bladensburg Races," they flatly rejected them.

Britain had asked for an Indian buffer state to include one-third of Ohio, two-thirds of Indiana, and nearly the entire area from which Illinois, Wisconsin and Michigan were formed. They also demanded parts of Maine, control of the Great Lakes, forfeiture of American fishing rights in the north and other exactions equally humiliating. Asked what would be done with about a hundred thousand Americans then living within the area of the buffer state, the British shrugged and said that they would have to shift for themselves. So the Americans bluntly stated that the demands were inadmissible, and declared: "A treaty concluded on such terms would be but an armistice."

The American reply jolted the British. Prime Minister Lord Liverpool was afraid that if negotiations were broken off the British would be blamed and the war would become popular in America and unpopular in Britain. He wrote to the Duke of Wellington: "It is very material to throw the rupture of the negotiation, if it is to take place, upon the Americans." So the British, who had also not yet heard of Washington, retreated from their dictatorial stand. They did not change their demands, but neither did they reiterate them as sine qua nons. They also sought to adjourn rather than break off the negotiations. In the meantime, British arms would bring the "impudent" Yankees to heel. "If our commander does his duty," Liverpool wrote, "I am persuaded we shall have acquired by our arms every point on the Canadian frontier which we ought to insist on keeping."

Liverpool's policy of writing the peace with the point of a sword got off to an excellent start on September 1, when a British fleet entered Penobscot Bay and took Castine. At the cost of one man killed and eight wounded, all of Maine east of the Penobscot River gradually fell into British hands. One hundred miles of seacoast was restored to the dominion of the King of England, while all its male inhabitants meekly, often eagerly, took an oath of allegiance to him. To nail down these acquisitions and to tidy up the Canadian frontier in a southern direction, Sir George Prevost began moving down Lake Champlain.

44

Battle of Lake Champlain

∼ THIRTY-SEVEN YEARS AFTER THE DISASTROUS DEFEAT OF A BRITISH ARMY under General John Burgoyne at Saratoga in 1777, the British War Office was again mounting a grand offensive along the lake-and-river chain from Montreal to Albany. But this time the invasion was for different reasons and under different circumstances.

In 1777 Britannia sought nothing less than the subjugation of the rebellious colonies and restoration of their allegiance to King George III. To do this, those indifferent strategists Lord George Germain and King George accepted Burgoyne's plan to cut the colonies in two. Under it Sir William Howe in New York City was to unite with Burgoyne's army in Albany, thereby severing the northern from the southern region so that each could be defeated in detail or starved into submission. Unfortunately, Germain forgot to notify Howe of his part in the campaign and while he went hurrahing off to Philadelphia, Burgoyne was devoured piece-by-piece in northern New York.

During the War of 1812 Britain had different reasons for invading New York state again. These were simply to defend Canada—a desire achieved more by the disgrace of American arms courtesy of Eustis, Hull, Armstrong, Wilkinson et al., than to the glory of Britannia—and next to chivy off New York and New England because Canada badly needed a warm-water port. During the winter the St. Lawrence was

frozen and the only way to reach the mother country was a long journey by horseback or sled from Montreal or Quebec across the ice-
locked wildernesses of New Brunswick and Nova Scotia to the open
waters of Halifax. To avoid these hardships, Whitehall wanted either a
strip of the Maine coast or better still Massachusetts with its superb
port of Boston. She also wanted that Indian buffer state and absolute
control of the Great Lakes.

Just as in the Revolution when Germaine and King George never
shed their deluded conviction that the south was Toryland where redcoats would be kissed and coddled as liberating heroes and delirious
welcoming throngs would again sing "God Save the King!" Britain
believed that the antiwar sentiment in New England was pro-British
rather than Federalist hatred for both Jefferson and Madison. New
England did indeed discuss its "grievances," but not to join the British
Empire, rather to detach itself from the other states and set up
another independent republic—just as the South would do in 1861. In
1814, because Britain no longer held New York City from which Howe
was supposed to have moved north for a union with Burgoyne, the
conquest of northern New York and New England was to be accomplished by a single huge army of Wellington's veterans moving down
from Montreal to Albany. In this intention Whitehall was indeed
encouraged by the failures of American arms on the Canadian border.

In Washington, where the residents were still shocked by devastation
of the capital, there was a popular rumor, supposedly planted by Armstrong, that the Madison Administration actually did not want to capture Canada because that would mean the admission into the Union
of six huge provinces that would become free-soil states. This, so the
falsehood went, was unacceptable to the slave-holding south. To
achieve this underhanded purpose, the honorable Madison was supposed to have seen to it that none but southerners commanded on
the Canadian border: Smyth of Virginia, Hampton of South Carolina
and Louisiana, Wilkinson and Winder of Maryland, and George Izard
of South Carolina. It was said that the president had yielded to pressure from John Calhoun, and that he failed to reinforce Hull so that
Hull would fail.

To attempt to refute the charge by saying that the integrity of Madison and Monroe was unquestionable is to beg the question and to
ignore the truth that no human beings are fonder of "making deals"
than politicians; yet it seems enough to say that the first generals to
attempt to conquer Canada were Hull of Connecticut, Dearborn of
Massachusetts and Van Rensselaer of New York, while the best soldier

on the border was Winfield Scott of Virginia. Apparently these calumnies were published by Armstrong in a pamphlet that he later withdrew, and it is more to the point to ask why this devious war secretary at the time of his nation's greatest peril directed Major General George Izard commanding at Plattsburg—considered to be the first objective of the invading British army—to take almost all of his men to Sackets Harbor at the head of the St. Lawrence.

On August 11 Izard protested strongly that the enemy was approaching his front and that "we are all in hourly expectation of a serious conflict." But Armstrong insisted. On August 20 Izard told Armstrong he would not be responsible for what would happen if he obeyed orders to abandon his strong position at Plattsburg. Nine days later, not having heard from Armstrong, General Izard reluctantly obeyed his orders and took 4,000 men to Sackets Harbor, leaving behind him only 1,500 effectives to hold the Plattsburg forts.

Just as he had left the gates open at Washington, John Armstrong had stripped away most of the army defending the route down which this formidable Anglo-Canadian force was marching. Why? What was in Armstrong's devious mind when he gave this unbelievable order? Surely there was no danger at Sackets Harbor: Plattsburg was the place to defend. Was this accident or design? History does not know. Only from the record of this scheming, vengeful, ambitious man can an unworthy ulterior motive be suspected—but it can never be proven.

Lieutenant General Sir George Prevost was the son of a Swiss soldier who had also served the British Crown. He had shown himself to be an able administrator during service in the West Indies and in Canada, and Hull's ineptness at Detroit had for a while obscured his limitations as a commander in battle; but those who knew Prevost regarded him as a pedestrian general indeed. Nevertheless, the War Office had placed him at the head of the most splendid British army ever assembled in North America. In all of Canada he commanded some twenty-nine thousand regulars, and for the Lake Champlain expedition alone he had about eighteen thousand redcoats, not counting Canadian militia.

The problem of feeding this host might have been insuperable but for some of Prevost's friendly enemies to the south. "Two-thirds of the army are supplied with beef by American contractors, principally of Vermont and New York," Prevost reported. One commissary official noted on June 19, 1814: "I have contracted with a Yankee magistrate to furnish this post with fresh beef. A major came with him to make the agreement; but, as he was foreman of the grand jury of the court in which the Government prosecutes the magistrates for high treason and smuggling, he turned his back and would not see the paper signed." Major General George Izard, commanding at Plattsburg, reported: "On the eastern side of Lake Champlain the high roads are insufficient for the cattle pouring into Canada. Like herds of buffaloes they press through the forests, making paths for themselves. . . . Were it not for these supplies, the British forces in Canada would soon be suffering from famine."

Such complicity made it difficult for Prevost to decide whether to attack down the New York or Vermont side of Champlain. But then Vermont's ardor in its enemy's cause won him over, and he wrote: "Vermont has shown a disinclination to the war, and as it is sending in specie and provisions, I will confine offensive operations to the west side of Lake Champlain."

On August 31, 1814, two days after Izard led most of his army west, just as he had feared Sir George Prevost left a rear guard of about 4,000 men behind him and with 11,000 troops crossed the border into New York.

Awaiting him with 1,200 effectives was Brigadier General Alexander Macomb.

Alexander Macomb was a fighting soldier, proving his worth on the Niagara Frontier and moving up the promotion ladder along with Winfield Scott. He was the son of a Belfast fur dealer who had migrated from Northern Ireland to settle in Detroit. His father prospered and acquired 3,670,000 acres of land in Georgia, North Carolina and Kentucky. But his son did not emulate him, either as a dealer in furs or a land speculator, choosing instead a military career when war with France seemed likely in 1799. Commissioned a cornet of cavalry, he moved to the artillery and then to the engineers, always serving with distinction. It was fortunate for America that he was in command of the ground forces at Plattsburg after Izard made his reluctant march to the east.

Fortunately also, General Prevost's advance south was leisurely. As was customary he issued a proclamation inviting the Americans around him to switch their allegiance to King George, and requesting supplies. This delay lasted until September 6, giving the energetic Macomb eight days in which to improve Plattsburg's defenses and call in militia to increase his strength. Major General Benjamin Moorers commanding the New York militia brought him seven hundred men. These he put under the command of Major John Wool, the hero of Queenston Heights, with orders to harass Prevost's advance. Wool did an excellent job, striking the British with sudden volleys for ambush and quickly retiring, causing enough delay from Macomb to complete construction of two new forts named Scott and Brown after his Niagara comrades-in-arms. These were added to Fort Moreau, built by Izard. All of them commanded the Saranac River crossings and the flat land along Lake Champlain. Macomb also removed the planking from the two bridges over the Saranac. On September 6 Prevost appeared before Plattsburg and began probing actions, before moving into camp north of the river to await Captain George Downie's fleet.

Also awaiting Downie was another one of Preble's Boys, a sailor in the mode of Lawrence and Oliver Hazard Perry: Commodore Thomas Macdonough.

Unlike so many of his shipmates during the War with the Barbary Pirates and the second struggle with Old Mother England, Thomas Macdonough's ancestors were relatively late immigrants to the shores of the Land of the Free. Great-grandfather Thomas MacDonough (the family frequently changed the name's spelling) lived in County Kildare, Ireland, from which his son James McDonough migrated in 1730 to settle at Saint George's Hundred, New Castle County, Delaware.

Dr. James was an excellent physician; from both a profitable practice and a native business acumen he amassed quite a fortune, and his sons proved to be valiant, patriotic soldiers. Middle son James fought the Indians in 1791 and the eldest, Dr. Thomas, "threw away the lance and buckled on the sword" during the Revolutionary War, rising to the rank of major. He also served on Delaware's Privy Council and General Assembly and as a justice of the Court of Common Pleas. Dr. Thomas married Mary Vance, daughter of British parents and known as an "engaging and accomplished woman who inspired with respect all who approached her." On the historic date of December 23, 1783—the day George Washington returned his general's commission to Congress—she gave birth to the sixth of their ten children, who was named Thomas. His birthplace was a one-and-one-half-story log house, not exactly the sort of elegant dwelling worthy of the affluent Macdonoughs, but in the following year a handsome mansion built of bricks brought from Britain as ballast was constructed, and it was there—within "the Trapp Farm House" still standing in New Castle—that Thomas Macdonough grew up.

Because his father had been a doctor, soldier, politician and jurist, it is not too much to suggest that young Thomas grew to manhood in a sophisticated atmosphere, even though little is known of his childhood or youth. Probably under the influence of his oldest brother, Midshipman James, who lost a leg in the fighting tops of the frigate *Constellation* when she captured the French warship *L'Insurgente,* he became enamored of the sea early in life, receiving at the age of sixteen a warrant as a midshipman from President John Adams.

By then Macdonough had reached physical maturity: broadshouldered, lean in the hip and long in the leg, he was handsome with reddish hair worn combed high in the fashion of the day; large, wideset eyes of dark Irish blue, a long, straight nose, and a rather smallish mouth that, by its very firmness, suggested an iron self-control. Shipping aboard *Ganges* in 1800, he served in the West Indies during the Naval War with France, taking part in the capture of two Guineamen and a French privateer. He also came down with yellow fever, being sent to recuperate in a Havana hospital in which "nearly all the men and officers died and were taken out in carts as so many hogs would have been." A year later he joined *Constellation* off Tripoli, and was chosen by Stephen Decatur as one of two midshipmen—the other was James Lawrence—who sailed aboard *Intrepid* on the daring and decisive expedition to burn *Philadelphia.* He was again with Decatur during the Battle of the Gunboats, fighting hand-to-hand with a Tripolitan officer. When Macdonough's blade broke, he tore his opponent's pistol out of his hand and shot him dead.

Thomas Macdonough's coolness in combat, believed by shipmates to be born of his religious fervor, was legendary in the tiny navy that produced valorous seamen such as Decatur, Preble and Lawrence. He was patient with everyone down to cabin boy, but had nothing but contempt for officers such as James Barron of *Chesapeake* infamy who permitted arrogant British officers to search their ships and seize their seamen. As a young lieutenant aboard *Siren* in Gibraltar Harbor he saw a boat pull away from a British frigate and make for an American merchant brig to take off a seaman as an alleged British subject. At once he ordered a gig made ready and armed, putting out to overtake the Britisher just as it reached the frigate, liberating the American at gunpoint and returning him to his ship.

Soon a blustering British captain climbed aboard *Siren,* threatening to sink the Yankee unless the "deserter" were released in his custody.

"While she swims, you shall not have the man," Macdonough evenly replied. "He was under the protection of my country's flag."

Infuriated, the captain cried, "Would you interfere if I tried to impress men from that brig?"

"You have but to try," Macdonough replied, and the captain returned to his frigate without another word.

At twenty-eight a salty veteran of twelve years at sea, Thomas Macdonough in late 1813 was pleased to receive from Secretary of the Navy Paul Hamilton the following orders:

> Six vessels have been purchased by the War Department, and there are two gunboats built by the Navy Department on [Lake Champlain], the whole of which is to be under your direction and command.

The sailor who would soon be Commodore Macdonough was overjoyed. Independent command at last! What a wedding present for Ann! It was indeed, and as the icy hand of a northern winter closed its iron fingers around Lake Champlain, Macdonough hastened to Middletown, Connecticut, where he married the beautiful, vivacious and ingenuous Lucy Ann Shaler on Saturday, December 12. He had met her six years earlier in her hometown, where he had helped Captain Isaac Hull construct four of those Jefferson gunboats. She was only sixteen then, and he was twenty-one. Yet, sought-after princess though she had been, she had chosen Macdonough and had waited for him all those years. And when he resumed command of his Lake Champlain "fleet" after a two-week honeymoon, his bride went with him.

Macdonough did not build his fleet on Lake Champlain itself, but rather at a secure base at Otter Creek at Vergennes, Vermont. Here the narrow channel could be defended against British raids while his ships were being built, and it is a measure of the Madison Administration's unreal and starry-eyed management of the War of 1812 that he reported directly to Secretary Hamilton in Washington, while Hamilton believed that he was under Commodore Chauncey's command. Moreover, Macdonough was supposed to draw upon the faraway ports of Boston and New York for supplies, but he luckily discovered that the southern end of Lake Champlain actually had manufacturing resources upon which he could rely. Having seen at once that success in the campaign to drive the British from the lake depended on cooperation with the army, Macdonough found to his dismay and near-despair that he would have to appeal to Hamilton to use his influence with the president to order Monroe to give orders to the local generals—that odious triumvirate of Hampton, Wilkinson, and Dearborn—to come to his assistance. Just to mention those names is enough to suggest how little help Macdonough really could expect.

Eventually Macdonough sailed his fleet down Lake Champlain to the little basin of Plattsburg Bay. His ships, like Perry's, were built of green lumber and done at such urgent speed that not all of them were finished when he met Captain George Downie's squadron. Neither was Downie's fleet ready, rushed to completion while Prevost's army waited.

Macdonough commanded four ships and ten gunboats. His flagship *Saratoga* of 734 tons mounted twenty-six guns. The brig *Eagle,* 20 guns, weighed 500 tons and was commanded by Captain Robert Henley. The schooner *Ticonderoga,* 350 tons, 17 guns, and commanded by Lieutenant Commander Stephen Cassin, would have been the first steam-powered warship to fight in a naval battle, but her engines were so unreliable that Macdonough had her sail-rigged. *Preble,* 80 tons, seven guns, was skippered by Lieutenant Charles Budd. Six of the row galleys had two guns apiece and four mounted one each. *Saratoga* with 240 hands had by far the largest ship's crew, while *Preble* with 30 had the least.

Captain Downie's flagship *Confiance* was the largest vessel on Lake Champlain. Of frigate class but built for maneuver on Champlain, narrower and shallower in comparison to the Great Lakes, she weighed 1,200 tons or more, almost twice *Saratoga*'s weight, and carried thirty-seven guns. Downie swore that *Confiance* alone could destroy the Yankee fleet. Actually, he was far too confident, for his broadside weighed only 480 pounds against *Saratoga*'s 414 pounds. Downie's three smaller ships were lighter and had less armament than Macdonough's trio: *Linnet,* the second largest, weighed 350 tons, and mounted sixteen guns; *Chub,* 112 tons and *Finch,* 110 tons; were the captured American sloops, *Growler* and the old *Eagle.* Each had eleven guns. Five of Downie's gunboats had two guns each, and seven of them mounted only one. In all, fourteen American ships of 2,244 tons opposed sixteen British vessels of 2,400 tons, 882 Yankees against 937 British, while Macdonough's total broadside weighed 1,194 pounds compared to Downie's 1,192 pounds. The British had the advantage in long-range guns, the Americans in short-range cannon called carronades.

Rarely if ever before have two contending fleets been so evenly matched, even though their weight and armament were dwarfed by many of the seagoing liners and frigates of that age, and especially by the monsters that fought in the 1944 American-Japanese Battle of Leyte Gulf in the Philippines, the greatest naval battle of all time. The importance of a clash, however, is not always judged by its size. In this miniature Battle of Lake Champlain the very life of the new American nation was at stake, as was the success of the British plan to enlarge Canada at American expense and block Yankee expansion.

• • •

After Macdonough brought his fleet into Plattsburg Bay, he realized that he could not hope to meet Downie in long-range battle on open water. Rather he would try to lure the Britisher into a close-up fight with his own fleet at anchor. This was not exactly the soul of tactical wisdom, although there was one famous precedent for it: Lord Nelson's destruction of the French fleet at Abukir Bay, usually called the Battle of the Nile. But here the *anchored* fleet was defeated. Perhaps Macdonough chose this stratagem because, anchored alongside and protected by Crab Island at the mouth of the bay, his ships offered an extremely difficult target for the enemy at long range.

So Macdonough ranged *Saratoga, Eagle, Ticonderoga* and *Preble* across the mile-and-one-half-wide mouth of the bay, with his gunboats behind him to fill the gaps. Next he carefully rigged his ships for battle at anchor, preparing to use kedges and hawsers so that he could wind either of his broadsides to bear in the event that one or the other had lost too many guns. In effect, this tactic gave him double the firepower of his eighty-six guns against Downie's ninety. Downie could not attempt the same maneuver because, entering the bay for immediate battle, he simply would not have the time to rig his ships with kedges and hawsers. Thus for the British commander to give up his long-range superiority and close with Macdonough was like a boxer mixing it with a slugger. Yet, he did enter—because Sir George Prevost insisted on it.

In war there is nothing more destructive of success in battle than a soldier playing sailor, or vice versa. At Plattsburg, Prevost commanded the entire expedition, and though he knew nothing of naval warfare, he had already ordered *Confiance* to sail when she was still unfinished, so that Downie's flagship came down the lake with riggers and carpenters still at work on her. He had also wasted five days waiting for Downie to appear, and the moment that he arrived on September 11 he ordered him into battle with instructions to destroy the American fleet.

Early in the morning of September 11, 1814, under a clear blue sky, Commodore Thomas Macdonough conducted a religious service on the deck of *Saratoga*. Kneeling with his officers and men, he asked the Lord to bless his cause with victory and committed his officers and crew to His care. Onshore Sir George Prevost is supposed to have pulled out his watch to see how long it would take Downie to destroy the Americans. He predicted to his officers that he would not need more than forty minutes. The British were supremely confident that

Confiance alone would be too much for the Yankees, and the American spectators crowding the headlands of both the Vermont and New York shores were visibly anxious. At eight o'clock a great shout arose when all who were watching saw the ships of Downie's fleet rounding Cumberland Head. They were moving slowly in a light and baffling wind. Because they were coming bow-on with no opportunity to fire broadsides, they could be raked by Macdonough's carronades without an answering fire. This is probably what decided Downie to anchor his own fleet directly opposite the Yankees, but at a distance of three hundred yards. By this tactic he made most of Mcdonough's guns ineffective, for a carronade's thirty-two-pound ball is inaccurate at any distance above 250 yards.

Once his ships were secured, Downie poured a shattering broadside into *Saratoga*. Sixteen 24-pound balls and cannister staggered Macdonough's flagship. With that single blast one-fifth of *Saratoga*'s crewmen—forty-eight men—were either killed or wounded and the ship itself holed and her rigging torn. But *Saratoga* fought on, returning the broadside. Once again ball and cannister shook her, and as it did one ball struck a chicken coop on her deck, freeing the fighting cock that had become the crew's mascot. Aroused by the martial flame and thunder, the cock jumped on a gun to let out a defiant crow—and his delighted masters took his belligerence to be an augur of victory. Actually, the battle was going against the Americans—until a ball from *Saratoga* struck one of *Confiance*'s 24-pounders. The impact propelled the gun from its mount and it flew across the deck into the groin of Captain Downie, killing him almost instantly. Because his skin was bruised but unbroken, he probably died of shock.

If the Lord had failed to heed Macdonough's entreaty, Lady Luck— so often the true arbiter of battle—had waved her wand over the head of Thomas Macdonough, for from the moment of the British fleet commander's death, the advantage passed to the Americans and the battle became a melee.

Captain Henley aboard *Eagle* handled his vessel superbly in his fight with *Chub,* delivering broadsides that made her a floating wreck to be given the finishing shot from *Saratoga* that made her haul down her flag. But then *Linnet* struck at *Eagle,* and *Ticonderoga* and *Preble* found themselves reeling under the combined fire of *Finch* and all the gunboats. For the Americans, all depended on *Saratoga*'s duel with *Confiance.*

It was now a slugging match, and the air was filled with flying splinters and spars that were just as dangerous as cannonballs and cannistergrape. One of *Confiance*'s shots struck *Saratoga*'s spanker boom, splitting it in two and sending one half flying into Macdonough's head, knocking him unconscious. Revived, he returned to the fighting, but as he sighted a carronade himself another enemy shot struck it and sent him hurtling through the air, again knocked senseless. A rumor that the commodore was dead passed through the ship and there came a lull in her fire. But the indomitable Macdonough again recovered his senses and returned to the battle. Around him his officers and men had their uniforms torn by flying splinters, and they were often struck by heavy jagged pieces of oak that mangled and maimed.

Upon Macdonough's second return he realized that his guns on the engaged starboard side were being silenced one by one, for *Linnet* had driven *Eagle* to take refuge between *Preble* and *Ticonderoga,* and then joined *Confiance* in battering *Saratoga.* Although Downie's flagship had suffered hideously, she could still fire and appeared to be recovering the upper hand. At this point, Macdonough's forethought saved the American fleet. Ignoring the battle, he began to direct his men to wind their ship. Slowly, inexorably, the American's port guns were unmasked, opening fire the moment *Confiance* was visible through the gunport. Now it was the Britisher's guns that were falling silent. Whoever replaced Downie tried desperately to wind his own ship, but failed—and the queen of Lake Champlain struck her colors. Now her three smaller sisters could do nothing but surrender, although the oar-driven gunboats escaped because no ship in either fleet had a mast intact with a sail to pursue or join the fugitives.

Meanwhile, Prevost's redcoats had gotten over the Saranac at an upper ford. They were coming down on the forts when American shouts running upriver like a jubilant powder train proclaimed Downie's defeat. Prevost all but panicked. He could have, in the words of a subordinate, gone on to take Plattsburg in twenty minutes. But the news of the lake reverse so distressed him, as he explained later, that he decided to retire to the border to see what use the Americans would make of their naval superiority. Once launched on the retrograde, however, he did not stop until the last of his splendid troops crossed into Canada. Meanwhile, Thomas Macdonough reported to the secretary of the navy: "Sir: The Almighty has been pleased to grant us a signal victory on Lake Champlain."

It was indeed more significant than McDonough might imagine, and two days later an event more memorable though less momentous in American history was to be written in the red glare of rockets bursting over Fort McHenry.

45

The Star-Spangled Banner

~ WHILE ROSS'S VICTORIOUS ARMY MARCHED BACK TO THE SHIPS anchored off Benedict, many of his redcoats became stragglers. They were exhausted and hungry as they trudged down the Upper Marlboro Road, stopping at farmhouses to beg for food, or raiding henhouses and orchards. There were so many of them that Robert Bowie, the former governor of Maryland, feared that from being a mere nuisance they might become a menace. So he suggested to some friends that as a warning they should arrest and imprison a few of them. Dr. William Beanes, whose house on the Upper Marlboro had been seized by the British as a headquarters, heartily agreed. Others did not, and one of them spoke of "the dangerous consequences that might result with the enemy so near." But the plan was adopted and eventually six of these redcoated drifters were captured and taken to a jail at Queen Anne, nine miles away.

The speed with which the Upper Marlboro was cleared of enemy soldiers after imprisonment of their comrades might have suggested to Dr. Beanes and Bowie that they had been perhaps too successful. But apparently they thought nothing of it, until one o'clock in the morning of August 27 there came a thunderous knocking on Dr. Beanes' front door. Opening it the doctor confronted a party of mounted Royal Marines, who roughly seized him and his overnight guests, Dr. William Hill and a friend named Philip Weems, hustling them outside and forcing them to mount bareback on a trio of plow horses that carried them—on a jostling, painful ride—to the British camp at Benedict. There they were confronted by a stern General Robert Ross, who quickly discovered that Dr. Hill and Weems were innocent of detaining British soldiers and he courteously freed them. Dr. Beanes, however, was believed to be guilty, and Ross ordered him held for transfer to either Bermuda or Halifax where he would stand trial on an unknown charge having to do with unlawfully taking British soldiers prisoners. Because it was believed that Beanes had been born in Scotland, he might even be accused of treason, and if convicted, hanged.

Alarmed, many residents of Upper Marlboro petitioned Ross to release Dr. Beanes, citing his age and his status as a respected and beloved member of their community, but "the perfect model of an Irish gentleman" curtly refused. So did Admiral Sir George Cockburn, although somewhat more strenuously. When it became apparent that the British fleet was preparing to sail with the doctor aboard, a wealthy Marylander named Richard West appealed to his brother-in-law, the famous Georgetown attorney Francis Scott Key.

Key was an ardent pacifist who had openly vowed to be "reconciled to any defeat or disgrace of our arms." But the burning of Washington and the atrocities committed by the British during Cockburn's rape of Hampton had changed his mind. He was now, if not a fervent bellicist, at least a Patriot who could now agree that war might be necessary or even imperative to correct injustice. His first move was to call upon President Madison to receive his accreditation as an official emissary. Next, before he was rowed out to Cochrane's flagship *Tonnant*, he visited a hospital on Capitol Hill in which many of the redcoats injured in the monster Navy Yard explosion were being treated. All of them testified to their amazement at having received such humane care when, as invaders who had burnt their benefactor's capital, they might have expected somewhat less merciful attention. From a Sergeant Hutchinson he received a letter testifying to this compassion of their enemy.

Once aboard *Tonnant*, Key was pleased by the cordial reception given him by Cochrane, Ross and Cockburn, but once he had made his mission known, he was dismayed by the speed with which their manner changed from the pleasant to the cold and stubborn. Cockburn predictably flew into a petulant rage, pronouncing Key's request for Beanes's release the most preposterous and brazen suggestion he had ever heard. "The old man," he said, was entitled to no mercy, and ought to be hanged. When Key asked if he might give the doctor the change of underwear and soap he had brought with him, the admiral blew up. Such "luxuries" amounted to coddling a common criminal, he said, and insisted that the American commissioner should not even be allowed to see Beanes. Ross was not nearly as hostile, simply stating that the prisoner had been fairly treated. But when Key handed the general Sergeant Hutchinson's letter, his mood changed. He read it in silence, becoming thoughtful and abstracted, before fixing Key with a stern stare and saying: "Dr. Beanes deserves more punishment than he has received. But I felt myself bound to make a return for the kindness which has been shown to my wounded officers—and upon that ground, *and that only,* I release him."

Hearing this, Cockburn could not conceal his disgust; but Francis Scott Key beamed with pleasure. Sir George was also outraged when Admiral Cochrane permitted Key and Dr. Beanes to go on deck to watch the bombardment of Fort McHenry. If McHenry fell, then Ross's army would move on to the conquest of Baltimore. Throughout the night the two men watched in dread as British shells and rockets burst over and upon the fort. Key, who had a local celebrity as a poet, began to jot down his impressions: "rocket's red glare . . . " "bombs bursting mid-air . . . " Key was also thrilled by the sight of McHenry's huge flag illuminated by the explosions flashing around it. As dawn began to break, Dr. Beanes leaned forward to peer toward McHenry's rampart but his failing eyes caught no glimpse of Old Glory. Again and again he asked anxiously: "Is the flag still there?"

The question triggered in Key's poetic brain a theme for a poem, beginning, "O say, can you see, by the dawn's early light," and he began to convert his notes into verses. After he and Dr. Beanes were allowed to go ashore, he revised and expanded them and then took the completed poem to his brother-in-law, Judge J. H. Nicholson. The judge had been in Fort McHenry during those dreadful twenty-five hours. He had seen "the rockets' red glare" and had had his stomach squeezed by the shock of "bombs bursting in air." He had lived Key's poem, and he saw at once that it could be sung to the melody of a popular drinking song called "To Anacreon in Heaven." Nicholson suggested immediate publication, and a young printer's devil named Samuel Sands set it in type and it came forth anonymously in a handbill entitled "Defence of Fort M'Henry." It was published on September 20 in the Baltimore *Patriot;* soon soldiers began singing it, and it spread gradually—though not suddenly—across the country. But not until March 3, 1931, did the United States Congress adopt "The Star-Spangled Banner" as the American national anthem.

If the War of 1812 had not given Americans much to brag about, it had at least given them a song to sing.

46

Ross Killed/Baltimore Holds

～ BECAUSE THE VENGEFUL SIR GEORGE COCKBURN HAD PERSUADED ADMI-
ral Cochrane and General Ross to attack Washington when Baltimore
was their true military objective, the great port on the Chesapeake
had been granted precious time in which to strengthen its defenses.

At first General William Winder had ridden north from the fire-
blackened capital expecting to take command in Baltimore, only to be
rebuffed by Senator Samuel Smith, a militia major general who had
no intention of entrusting the fate of his beloved hometown into the
hands of the "starter" of the Bladensburg Races. Smith was a rarity in
this war of grandfather generals: although sixty-one years old, he was
still full of fight and had not forgotten the lessons he learned in the
Revolutionary War. Chief among these was his belief that on the
defensive the shovel can be of greater value than the musket; and so
he set the city's citizenry to work constructing formidable fortifications facing south toward an anticipated British approach. These positions were held by sixteen thousand men. A barrier of ships also was
sunk offshore to prevent the enemy from landing at Fort McHenry,
the key to the harbor.

Meanwhile both Ross and Cockburn sailed up the Chesapeake in
high spirits, determined to exterminate that "nest of pirates"—meaning its numerous privateers. The plan was for the fleet to bombard

McHenry into submission while Ross advanced overland with four thousand redcoats. On September 12, the fleet anchored off North Point at the tip of the peninsula between the Back and Patapsco rivers, and Ross's impatient redcoats went ashore.

Ross was confident and in high spirits. Breakfasting with Cockburn at a Maryland farmhouse, he toyed with the idea of making Baltimore his winter quarters. As he departed, the farmer asked him if he would be back for supper.

"No," Ross said, "I'll have supper tonight in Baltimore," and then, in afterthought, "or in Hell."

The first conjecture seemed more likely as Ross's eager redcoats swept briskly up the peninsula. But his scouts ran into a force of riflemen sent forward by Brigadier General John Stricker, who had marched out from Baltimore with about 3,200 raw militia. Shots were fired, the British spread out, flanked the Americans and drove them off.

General Ross hurried up with his advance guard. Two American marksmen who had not fled—Daniel Wells and Harry McComas—fired their last shots. One bullet hit Ross. He lurched back into the arms of his aide, calling his wife's name, and then he spoke no more. His body was laid under an oak tree, and the troops moving up to the attack saw it as they passed. "A groan came from the column," according to Subaltern Glieg, and it was obvious later when Colonel Arthur Brooke took command that "the army had lost its mainspring."

The Americans under Stricker made an unusually firm stand at Godly Wood. Musket fire blazed out from both lines in a battle that brought death to Wells and McComas, and that eventually ended in a British victory. But British casualties were three hundred against two hundred for the Americans, and on the next day, after Brooke saw the formidable entrenchments in front of Baltimore, he stopped short to await support from the fleet.

By then, midday of September 13, 1814, Admiral Cochrane's bombardment ships were at work battering Fort McHenry. For twenty-five hours the British ships rained shells and Congreve rockets upon the sturdy little bastion. The Americans fired back briefly, but could not make the range. Luckily, neither could the bigger British vessels because of the barrier of sunken ships. Some 1,800 projectiles fell upon the Americans, but they could not bring about the fort's surrender.

Ashore, Brooke feinted twice to no avail and a British landing party was driven away from Fort Covington. McHenry had held, along with the Baltimore defenses, and the British fleet eventually sailed back to Halifax and the troops returned to Jamaica.

47

British Seize
Pensacola/Jean Laffite

∽IN LATE JULY OF 1814 A SMALL BRITISH AMPHIBIOUS FORCE OF TWO sloops-of-war—*Hermes* and *Carron*—and no more than a hundred sailors and Royal Marines with two howitzers under Sir William Percy dropped anchor off the Spanish city of Pensacola in western Florida. Soon boats carrying the troops of Lieutenant Colonel Edward Nicholls, together with that pair of small cannon, came ashore to take the town from the docile Governor Manrique. Nicholls quickly ran up the British flag beside the orange-and-red Spanish colors. Because Spain was still a British ally, Nicholls considered this an extremely friendly gesture of good will. It is not known what Manrique thought of this rare concession from an arrogant British officer, but it was clear to him that Pensacola was practically defenseless.

Besides the troops he brought ashore, Nicholls also had with him one thousand stand of arms with which he intended to capture the south coast of America with the aid of its own inhabitants, be they white or Indian. Many of them were in fact Creeks, nursing the wounds inflicted on them by Andrew Jackson at the Horseshoe Bend. They had received sanctuary, brandy and arms from Governor Manrique, who had been gently urging them to avenge their defeat. The Creeks had no qualms about accepting the same assistance from Colonel Nicholls, although they privately preferred brandy to rum.

Having secured the allegiance of these Red Stick survivors, Nicholls turned to a second source of recruits: the populations of Kentucky and Louisiana. In a proclamation as impudent and inane as Hull's on the Canadian border, Nicholls urged the residents of New Orleans to protect themselves by flying a British, French or Spanish flag over their door. To the Blue Grass people he declared: "Inhabitants of Kentucky, you have too long borne with grievous impositions. The whole brunt of the war has fallen on your brave sons. Be imposed on no longer. Range yourself under the standard of your forefathers or remain neutral." Where he expected to post this appeal in Spanish-speaking Pensacola is not known. But the fact that Kentucky was more than a thousand miles away from the Gulf never seemed to trouble parochial British officers such as Nicholls, never able to comprehend the vastness of the New World.

Nicholls also thought of a third source of recruits in Barataria Bay near New Orleans: the lair of about one thousand smugglers and privateers, if not actually pirates, who had made the Gulf of Mexico their private pond. To gain their allegiance in the British plan to conquer New Orleans and then the entire Louisiana Territory, he sent his emissary Captain Charles Lockyer to their leaders, the brothers Laffite.

Jean and Pierre Laffite were born in Bordeaux. Both grew to be bold, shrewd, imaginative and intelligent men. Pierre was the elder. He served in the French Navy where he became expert in navigation and fencing. Jean was supposed to have been an army captain under Napoleon. By the time they arrived in New Orleans in 1803 by way of the West Indies they had knocked about the world long enough to gain a fluency in English, Spanish and Italian, as well as their own French. Jean was about twenty-four years old then, and Pierre about twenty-six.

They were strikingly different. Pierre was five feet ten and stocky. He was affable and even jolly. Jean was taller, handsome, so beautifully proportioned that he could be taken to be slender, when he actually had powerful shoulders and arms. He was also hot-tempered and seldom smiled. Both men had large dark eyes, but where Pierre's were friendly, Jean's were fierce and penetrating. Jean was also an expert duelist with either pistol or sword and is supposed to have killed a man in a duel in Charleston.

Upon their arrival in the Crescent City both men were fascinated by the opportunities in this bustling trilingual city commanding the vast Mississippi basin. Pierre set himself up as a fencing master, while Jean opened a blacksmithy at the corner of Bourbon and St. Philip streets.

They prospered, but not to the extent of their ambition. But in 1808—the year of Jefferson's boomeranging embargo, and the year that importation of slaves into the United States was to end—they saw that the main and golden chance had come: with no British goods being legally imported, they could buy and sell their own. At first they operated in New Orleans, where Jean Laffite could often be seen walking the streets. Elegantly dressed, gracious with impeccable manners, he quickly became a favorite among the upper class of New Orleans. People who saw him frequently strolling the city streets simply could not believe that he and his brother were pirates.

They weren't, at least not at first. They were privateers bearing letters of marque from the Colombian port city of Cartagena. A letter of marque is a document issued by one country authorizing a sea captain to attack its enemy's merchant marine, either to sink, capture, or loot its ships. In a sense, he was fighting for Colombia, then engaged with Spain in a war for independence, and as a former Frenchman was also serving France against her old enemy of Spain. Jean Laffite hated Spain, and would often say: "I will be at war with Spain all my life." It was a pleasant and profitable means of revenge, and as his fortune in captured or looted ships grew, he and his brother also became probably the most successful smugglers in the new Louisiana Territory.

Their headquarters were in Barataria Bay, a body of water separated from the Mississippi Delta by a peninsula remarkably similar in shape to the boot of Italy. For fifty years before the Lafittes arrived in New Orleans, these waters and swamplands had been populated by smugglers, as well as runaway slaves, escaped criminals and lawless men of all descriptions. Just as in the American colonies, smuggling, no more than privateering, was not looked upon with repugnance. When New Orleans was under Spanish rule, the tariffs on legally imported goods were so high that hardly anyone except the wealthy could afford them, and even they joined the flow of customers to Barataria where the smugglers sold goods at low prices and illegally auctioned off slaves.

At the beginning of their career in Barataria the brothers Laffite headed just another small band of privateers and smugglers. Although their power and wealth steadily increased, the other groups, refusing to accept Jean Laffite's leadership, gradually became organized into two rival camps. Civil war erupted between them when one gang raided the other's ships loaded with slaves, sank it and brought the captive bondsmen home to their "barracoon" at Barataria. Open warfare raged between them during the summer of 1810. They shot each other on sight or hunted each other in the marshes like beasts of prey. With men too busy killing each other to smuggle or sail the seas as privateers, the area's main source of revenue began to diminish. Jean Lafitte might have craftily waited until the rivals destroyed each other before taking over as king of Barataria; instead, he persuaded the leaders of the rival groups to attend a peace council supervised by him, and he showed such a remarkable skill in negotiation that the enemies not only agreed to bury the hatchet but accepted him as their chief.

By then, of course, Pierre Laffite, had also willingly acceded to his younger brother's rule. In 1810 he had suffered a stroke, and although he recovered, he was never again completely healthy. His eyes remained slightly crossed, giving him a fierce expression that did indeed make him look like a pirate.

By 1810 the Laffitte brothers were the undisputed rulers of Barataria, with all its waterways or bayous and the two large islands of Grande Terre and Grand Isle. Jean Laffite was now the unchallenged ruler of Barataria, living and ruling like a king over about a thousand privateer sailors, smugglers, trappers, and fishermen. With their families there might have been five thousand Baratarians. Most of them lived in cabins and huts on the two big islands or deeper in the swamps on islets called *chenieres*. Almost at a moment's notice the male Baratarians could be mustered in a fighting force of about a thousand men equipped with artillery and a fleet of armed ships. They could also, if pursued, take sanctuary in those same swamps, almost impenetrable green-blue-and-gold labyrinths populated by flashing, croaking tropical birds, water fowl, alligators and deadly water moccasins. Only the native Baratarians could follow those criss-crossing narrow streams twisting and turning among giant live oaks with trunks so thick they sometimes measured eight or ten feet in diameter, the gray beards of Spanish moss dangling from their grotesquely spreading branches. When the bayous joined they formed widening lakes flowing forth once more as narrow streams in a dozen different or hidden directions. A raid on any of these smuggling hideouts was almost impossible, for Jean Laffite—like Robin Hood—had devised a system of sentinels whose moaning horns gave ample warning of a posse on its way. Upon the first notes, merchandise was heaped upon the long trestle tables and the slaves on their auction platforms would be spirited into the swamps, so that the customs officials upon their arrival would find no one but Jean Laffite, chatting gaily with his "guests"—about a hundred or more merchants and planters assembled as though for a picnic.

Laffite was indeed often compared to Robin Hood. His kindness and generosity were legendary. Many of the tales about him were apocryphal, but there is one authentic and verified account of a Louisiana planter named Martin whose small ship was caught in one of those sudden storms that lash the Gulf of Mexico. Some of his friends were blown overboard, and although the winds subsided as quickly as they had risen, the ship was sinking fast until one of Lafitte's vessels came to the rescue. The survivors were taken ashore and brought to Laffite's magnificent mansion on Grand Terre. There they were fed and given new clothing, while Martin received money in recompense for what he had lost on the ship. A schooner was placed at his disposal, and among its provisions was a barrel of wine and pineapple cheese as special gifts to Martin's wife.

Laffite's remarkable hold on his men was due not only to such generosity, but to his fairness as well. Because he remained aloof, rarely joining in the camaraderie typical of men joined together in danger, he had no special friends or "pet" followers. He seemed to understand that a leader who wishes to be fair must give up all hope of friendship. When a ship arrived in the bay its booty was taken to Laffite's fine home and heaped on a table to be scrupulously divided among Laffitte, the ships' officers and seamen. A captain would receive a share; his officers a smaller share; and the seamen were awarded according to their rank, with the lowest entitled to one part each. Even the cooks received a part. Laffite also settled all quarrels among his men with the impartial wisdom of Solomon. If a man lost a limb or an eye in combat, he was paid an extra sum of money. If he was killed, Laffite took good care of his family.

Another reason for the success of Jean Laffite was the loyalty of the men who served as his lieutenants. There was Louis Chighizola, an old sea dog and an inveterate duelist whose face was covered with scars. He was seldom called by his real name, but rather his nickname, Nez Coupé, French for "Cut Nose," because he had lost most of that feature in a duel.

René Beluche, like Pierre Laffite, had served in Napoleon's army, later going to sea where he joined a privateering crew. Hearing of Jean Laffite's exploits, he entered his service at Barataria. Of all Laffite's men, the swarthy, hook-nosed Beluche looked most like a fierce pirate. He would live to become a commodore in the Venezualan navy. Dominique You was another veteran of the Napoleonic Wars. Short and swarthy, almost as broad as he was tall, he was called "the Ruffled Eagle." Dominique was exceptionally strong and was feared because of his explosive temper; but he was generally jolly, fond of jokes and laughter, and was devoted to Jean Laffite. Although Jean Baptiste Sauvinet was considered a Laffite lieutenant, he was not actively engaged in his activities, but was rather his banker and lived in New Orleans. So did Thiac the blacksmith.

Gambi was the oldest of Laffite's lieutenants and the least trusted.

He had been on Barataria before any of them. Small and wiry, burned black by the sun, a huge mustache curling beneath his hawkish nose, Gambi was contentious and evil. He openly proclaimed himself a pirate, and to look the part he kept his kinky black hair contained in a kerchief, with an earring in his ear and pistols on his hips. He loved to boast of his pirate past, the ships he had taken and sunk, and the men he had murdered.

Jean Laffite was most uncomfortable with Gambi, but dared not move against him because of the extraordinary loyalty of his men. One day Gambi sailed back to Grande Terre boasting that he had attacked and sunk an American ship in the Gulf of Mexico. Laffite was furious, but then, realizing that Gambi had probably chosen this moment to challenge his authority, calmly summoned his other lieutenants to a meeting to discuss Gambi's deliberate violation of Laffite's strictest order: never touch an American vessel.

They came trooping into Laffite's dining room: Beluche, Nez Coupé, Pierre Laffite, Dominique You. Laffite sat at the head of his table, Gambi at the foot. Between them were the lieutenants who would judge their chief's charge of piracy against Gambi.

"This can ruin us all," Laffite said to Gambi. "You have given the American authorities a chance to charge us all with piracy. They have been waiting for this for a long time."

"They will never know it!" Gambi shot back angrily.

"We can't be sure of that," Laffite said. "It must never happen again."

Enraged, Gambi refused to promise to refrain from harming American ships. "I am a pirate!" he cried. "We are all pirates! Why be a liar and a hypocrite?"

Laffite leaped from his chair and bounded toward Gambi, but Nez Coupé stopped him. "Let him go now if he wants to go," he said.

Whirling on Gambi, Laffite shouted, "Get out!" and the bristling little pirate went swaggering out the door, a glint in his fierce black eyes foretelling a mutiny. It came hours later when Gambi's men gathered outside Laffite's house, muttering and cursing him. He was not surprised and moved immediately to crush the mutiny by stepping onto the veranda with a pistol in his hand. When a tall young man jumped onto the steps brandishing a pistol and yelling, "Gambi is our leader!" and lowering his pistol—Laffite fired first.

Before the triumphant Laffite could reload his weapon, Gambi's mutineers had carried their fallen comrade away.

Although most of the people of New Orleans felt a warm affection for Laffite and refused to believe that he was a pirate, there were others who were not so sure. Piracy in the Gulf and the Caribbean Sea was then rampant. Ships of all nations were vanishing everywhere. In New Orleans people were afraid to leave the city by ship, or to send their children to France for their education. Pointed questions about Laffite were asked. Why were his ships armed? Where did his slaves come from, and where were the ships that brought them from Africa or the seamen who sailed them? Laffite repeatedly denied these charges. He hated the word pirate. "My men are privateers," he would insist. "They are corsairs, not pirates." As though to reassure citizens alarmed by horrible stories circulated by visitors from New York, Boston, Philadelphia or Charleston, he began to appear more frequently on the city's streets, strolling nonchalantly along, pausing to chat with friends, showing up at balls and cotillons in the mansions of the planters.

Many New Orleannais also admired Laffite for his boldness. They laughed when they saw his announcements of impending auctions nailed to the lampposts all over the city and inviting all residents to attend. Sometimes it appeared that many of them accepted. The biggest ones were held on Grand Terre in the Temple—so-called because of the legend that Indian tribes had once erected there an altar for human sacrifice. It was nothing more than a large level space surrounded by a circle of live oaks, but the mottled sunlight filtering through the leaves gave it a murky, mysterious sort of atmosphere. Nevertheless, on auction days it was invariably thronged with merchants and planters and their ladies, among whom Laffite mingled amiably, pausing with persuasive charm to assure a lady hesitantly fingering an imported silk that this was indeed France's finest, or else leading a planter to the auction platform where an unusually strong prime field hand was on the block. The Temple became so successful that a second smaller one called the Little Temple was added. In fact, Jean Laffite may have become too successful, living in regal splender in his fine mansion surrounded by all the accouterments of wealth and taste—servants in livery, exquisite china, fine French wines, heirloom silver, sparkling crystal, priceless paintings, carpeted floor, a library stocked with books in three languages—an elegance which, though calculated to excite the awe and envy of the less fortunate, created in the heart of Governor William C. C. Claiborne of Louisiana an utter contempt for this despicable pirate and smuggler as well as a horrible ache to bring him to justice.

Governor Claiborne was a conscientious civil servant, and he not only hated the Laffites for their hilarious flouting of his rigid concept of law and order, as well as their mockery of the U.S. Customs Service, but also feared them as potential betrayers of Louisiana to the British. With the War of 1812 going so badly, Detroit lost, defeat and retreat everywhere, and the conduct of the war in the hands of generals who were veritable prodigies of senility, New Orleans and the Louisiana Territory were in imminent danger of falling to the enemy. That was because these contemptible pirates—Claiborne would never call them privateers—had complete control of the mouth of the Mississippi River.

Claiborne did not know that Jean Laffite revered the American Declaration of Independence and Constitution as the two most sacred documents in the history of individual freedom. It was not that he loved or admired Americans themselves—few of the Spanish or French residents of New Orleans would confess to such feelings—but rather their institutions. As a youth he had seen how the French Revolution ended, in the bloodbath of the Reign of Terror and the arrival of a man on a horse—Napoleon Bonaparte—to ride roughshod over *Liberté, Egalité* and *Fraternité*. But as often as members of his official family—among them John Randolph Grymes, his district attorney who knew and respected Laffite—tried to persuade him that the Baratarian chief was a true democrat, Claiborne simply refused to listen. The Laffites were pirates, perhaps even murderers, evil and lawless leaders of a collection of outlaws and desperadoes best described as the scum of the earth. But when he appealed in 1811 to the Louisiana Legislature to raise a militia to invade and destroy Barataria he was refused on the ground that there were no funds for such an operation.

In 1812 he turned to the Customs Service for help, and was gratified when these enraged officials raised a local coast guard consisting of forty dragoons and a few small boats to patrol the lower Mississippi. It was placed under Captain Andrew Hunter Holmes, whose only order from Claiborne was: "Get the brothers Laffite!" When those objects of Claiborne's displeasure heard that Holmes's pitiful corporal's guard was on their trail they both pretended to be terrified, and then joined the general laughter. Throughout most of 1812 Laffite's warning system functioned smoothly, and Captain Holmes and his dragoons came back from every expedition with nothing but mosquito bites to show for their efforts. Then on November 16 they accidentally surprised the brothers and two dozen men loading pirogues—small, slender skiffs still in use on the bayous—with smuggled goods. Caught, outnumbered and outgunned, a smiling Jean Laffite surrendered. One of his men who tried to escape was shot dead, and the remainder with their smuggled merchandise were taken to

New Orleans and jailed. Claiborne was jubilant. He had the Laffites, and he had the evidence!

The Laffites and their men did not remain in jail long. Jean Baptiste Sauvinet, the brothers' financial adviser, put up the necessary bail bond and the prisoners went free, vanishing into the swamps and refusing to appear at their trial in April 1813, another in July and one more in October. Governor Claiborne was furious, aware that the entire territory was laughing at him behind his back. Nothing was more pleasing to these Creoles than the discomfiture of a high American official. Finally John Randolph Grymes did win a judgment against the Baratarians of $1,214.52—the worth of the seized merchandise—which Sauvinet was only too happy to pay.

But Claiborne had not been thwarted again, as so many Creoles believed; neither could he have been so naive as to expect the Laffites and their men actually to stand trial. Of their conviction there could have been no doubt, and they would have been sentenced to prison. This way, they were free—but definitely outlaws, subject to arrest when caught and facing additional charges. That was how they were publicly proclaimed by the governor, although he did not—for some unknown reason—mention their names. He did, however, redouble his efforts to capture Jean Laffite—and he nearly did. On October 14, 1813, a revenue officer named Walter Gilbert leading a company of dragoons surprised Laffite and some of his men in the swamps near the Temple. This time the Baratarians fought and drove off their pursuers.

A month later Claiborne dropped whatever reservations he still had and issued a proclamation naming Jean Laffite as the leader of the Baratarians who had fought Gilbert and wounded one of his men, offering a reward of $500 for his capture. Next day another proclamation was found nailed to all the lampposts in town. It offered $1,500 for the capture of William Charles Cole Claiborne and was signed: "Jean Laffite." Once again the Creoles had a good chuckle at the governor's expense, laughingly exclaiming: "That Laffite!"

As the year 1813 came to a close it may have seemed to Governor Claiborne that Laffite's clever riposte was a small scratch indeed compared to the crushing defeat that seemed imminent: loss of New Orleans and the entire Mississippi Valley to the British. An enemy fleet was already patrolling only a few miles off the Delta and Claiborne had been informed that he could expect no more than seven hundred soldiers to defend the city. That was only about half of what Laffite could offer the British—plus his fleet of a dozen ships—should he decide to join the enemy. And Claiborne, despite the assurances of officials such as Grymes that the Baratarian chief was loyal to America, was certain that was the course he would follow. Laffite simply had to be destroyed!

When in January of 1814 handbills appeared throughout the city advertising an auction at the Temple, the governor thought he saw his opportunity. He would capture the Laffites, both of them. And yet, he was so desperate, had so lost his balance, that he thought he could accomplish this with a pitiful force of a dozen armed men raised by the collector of customs and placed under a man named Stout. Inevitably, of course, they were routed by the Baratarians and Stout was killed. Next, he called on the Louisiana militia, all of whom were captured by Laffite and sent back to the city loaded with gifts, their laughter and jokes echoing in the governor's ears like catcalls from hell.

But then there came a little good news: Andrew Jackson's decisive defeat of the Creeks. With that war ended Old Hickory might well reach New Orleans in time to organize the defense of the Crescent City. Even better perhaps, Claiborne had persuaded a hand-picked grand jury to indict the Laffites, René Beluche and Dominique You for piracy. If convicted, they could be hung. Then—best of all—Pierre Laffite was captured! He had been strolling openly in the city to show that, like his brother, he did not fear the governor. Approaching St. Louis Cathedral he encountered a platoon of soldiers who immediately arrested him. Either they had recognized him or some enemy had tipped off the governor, it is not known which, but Pierre was quickly taken to the old calaboose, or jail, in the Cabildo, where Claiborn had his offices.

There was no way Jean Laffite could help his brother. Claiborne had denied him both bail and visitors. It was said that Pierre's health was deteriorating, but the examining physician reported no disease, only despondency, chained as Pierre was to the wall and without a friendly face to look upon. At times his jailers would taunt him, saying that the only way he could go free was if his brother joined the British and New Orleans fell. At this, Pierre would erupt in a healthy rage, bellowing: "We are not with the English! We have never been with the English. We are for Louisiana and the United States!"

Hearing of this, William C. C. Clairborne merely sighed and shook his head. He did not smile, as he might have, for the news was even worse: Washington had been captured and burned and the U.S. government put to flight. Almost as bad, there was no news of General Jackson. And then Jean Laffite moved again.

This time the privateer persuaded his friend Grymes and Grymes's law partner Edward Livingston to defend his brother. These two lawyers were the finest in New Orleans, and Laffite agreed to pay each of them twenty thousand dollars—a huge sum in those days—to represent Pierre. Claiborne was shocked when his district attorney resigned his post to "go over to the enemy." When Grymes and Livingston went to court in an effort to free Pierre, the new district attorney sneered at them as lawyers who had sold their honor for "the blood-stained gold of pirates." And Pierre remained in jail.

And then—almost miraculously—Pierre Laffite escaped.

One morning in August a jailer bringing him his food opened his door and found the cell empty. His chains had been cut, dangling empty from the wall, but the bars on his window were intact. There can be little doubt that one or more of Pierre's jailers had been bribed. Once again Governor Claiborne appears to have been somewhat naive. He must have known that his jailers were a rough breed, many of them illiterate and poorly paid. It would not take too much "pirate's gold" to persuade one of them to betray his trust. Aware of this, Claiborne should have insisted that J. H. Holland, the keeper of the prison, keep the key to Pierre's cell in his pocket.

Nevertheless, the escape of Pierre Laffite remains a mystery.

There was nothing mysterious about the bribe offered to Jean Laffite by the British. Like Claiborne, the British officers considered Jean an outlaw who would do anything for money, a buccaneer who could be bought. On the morning of September 3, 1814, just a short time before Pierre's escape, a British brig-of-war sailed into Barataria Bay, firing signal cannon to announce its presence. As a small boat put out from the vessel's side, Laffite went to meet it in a skiff of his own. He was greeted by Captain Lockyer, Colonel Nicholls's emissary, and a lieutenant of His Majesty's Navy and a scarlet-clad army officer, a Captain McWilliams. Courteous as ever, Laffite invited them to breakfast and they followed him ashore.

The British were astonished by their reception. Expecting a pirate like Gambi with a fierce mustache, rings in his ears, and a bandanna on his head, they encountered instead an elegant, educated gentleman. His air of easy authority also surprised them, for when they sat down at his table and they sought to get down to business immediately, he smiled and said that this was not done in Louisiana, where business and pleasure were never mixed. It was not until nearly noon, after the table was cleared and the finest cigars passed around, that Captain Lockyer handed Laffite a packet of four letters signed by the commander of His Britannic Majesty's forces in the area.

The first called upon all Louisianians of French, Spanish or British blood to join the war against the United States. If they did not, the Indians would be unleashed against them. The second letter asked the Baratarians to serve against the Americans, and if they did, Laffite would receive the rank of captain in the Royal Navy, together with more land than he now owned. The third required him to order his men to join the British, and the fourth threatened to destroy Barataria if they refused. Laffite put the letters aside and blew smoke. So that was it: either help destroy New Orleans or be destroyed. He did not like it at all, but he began to stall, passing around a bottle of vintage port. Captain Lockyer, suspecting a trick, quickly increased the bribe: if Laffite agreed to these proposals he would also receive $30,000 in cash once the Americans had been defeated. After all, Lockyer purred in sugary sympathy, how much more could he endure at the hands of the perfidious Americans? Laffite paused, as though pondering his answer. Then he arose, said he needed more time to decide, bowed, and left the room.

In his absence, the British officers talked among themselves exultantly. The pirate was obviously going to join them. How could he refuse? Now New Orleans would be destroyed and a British fleet would sail up the great river to conquer its valley and the war would be won. Suddenly they stopped and looked up in horror.

The room was filling with fierce-looking Baratarians, mustachioed and bearded, pistols in their sashes and cutlasses in their hands. They seized their chief's guests roughly and pushed them outside. On the beach were hundreds more of them.

"Kill the British spies!" they shouted. "Turn them over to the Americans."

Lifting a hand to silence them, Laffite led his guests—their splendid uniforms now soiled and torn—down to their waiting boat. They clambered aboard with downcast eyes, the stubborn look on their faces seeming to promise revenge.

"You see how my men feel," Laffite said with a gracious bow. "I must have more time to consider your offer."

There was no reply, for a shrill whistle had burst from the bo's'un's pipe and the sailors began pulling furiously at their oars.

In the fall of 1814, Governor William Claiborne was somewhat encouraged by the arrival of a few warships of the U.S. Navy at New Orleans and a promise that General Andrew Jackson was also on his way. Even so, this was far from being enough; and yet, the stubborn Claiborne actually refused Jean Laffite's offer to help defend the city. Laffite wrote: "This point of Louisiana that I occupy is of great importance in the present crisis. I tender my services to defend it." He added modestly, almost in supplication: "I am a stray sheep wising to return to the sheepfold." He also asked in exchange for his service a full pardon for himself and his men. But Claiborne, in his obstinate and obsessive conviction that the Baratarians were a band of murderous brigands, did not deign to reply. Instead he forwarded Laffite's letter to General Jackson with a covering note not exactly flattering to its author, and Old Hickory replied that he would have nothing to do with such "hellish banditti."

Meanwhile, Jean Laffite waited impatiently for Claiborne's reply. It came early one morning with hurricane force. A fleet of six American gunboats and the schooner *Carolina* loaded with soldiers under Colonel J. Y. Ross, all commanded by Commodore Patterson of the U.S. Navy, sailed into Barataria Bay. The Laffites, having been warned, had already ordered their men not to resist, but to take cover in the swamps. Then they vanished with them. Only about eighty men who had not gotten the word were at Grande Terre when the American soldiers went ashore. They destroyed everything above ground—including Laffite's warehouses and his splendid home—after stripping them of merchandise and precious possessions. Out on the water Laffite's fleet was captured, except for two ships burned by fugitive Baratarians.

If anything should have turned the Laffites and their men into merciless enemies of the United States, it was this wanton act of vandalism—and reverse piracy as well through unwarranted seizure of a half million dollars in money and merchandise, together with ten vessels—by an obtuse and vindictive politician. And yet, when a grieving Jean Laffite returned to the blackened ruins of his enclave, the first thing he did was to send a letter to his friend Grymes requesting a meeting with him and Livingston. They did meet and Laffite told the two lawyers that his ruination was the work of an individual American named Claiborne, not the settled policy of the United States. He repeated his offer to serve America, and when Jackson arrived in New Orleans, Grymes and Livingston—who had known the general for years—asked him to accept Laffite's offer. He refused. As often as they renewed his plea, it was refused.

And then Old Hickory changed his mind. Why he did is not known. There is a romantic legend that Jean Laffite slipped into his headquarters and that when Jackson beheld this splendid figure of a man— unarmed but sincere in his desire to serve the land of freedom that he could never regard as his enemy—the confrontation was much like the meeting between Tecumseh and Brock. Old Hickory, the legend suggests, could never resist such a brave and gallant man in the same mold as himself. Actually, it is more likely that Jackson, the practical commander on his tours of the city, realized that he could never defend it with the forces at his disposal. Willy-nilly—willingly or unwillingly—he would have to summon those "hellish banditti" to his side. So he sent for Jean Laffite, and Laffite came.

History does not know exactly where the two men met, except that it was somewhere in New Orleans. Some historians have suggested that Governor Claiborne was present. There is no proof of such an astonishing claim, except to say that desperate times require desperate solutions, and William Charles Cole Claiborne may have swallowed his pride to make common cause with the Baratarian chief if it would save his city and his country.

One of Old Hickory's most difficult problems was his lack of arms and ammunition—especially his shortage of flints. Without flints his soldiers' muskets would not fire. Laffite assured him that he could solve the problem: an abundance of cannon, cannonballs, muskets and flints—7,500 flints—was still hidden in the swamps. They were now General Jackson's. And so were his men: up to a thousand of them. If Claiborne was really there, one may suppose that Jean Laffite looked the governor in the eye and said: "Except for Dominique You and eighty other men of mine, still locked up in the Cabildo." If so, the governor would have had no recourse but to free them so they could join their countrymen in the defense of the city of New Orleans and the United States of America.

48

The Hartford Convention

~ BY THE FALL OF 1814 IT APPEARED THAT THE FEDERAL GOVERNMENT
had run out of both men and money.

All attempts to establish a dependable regular army seemed to have
failed. Although the paper strength of the U.S. Army was raised to
sixty-two thousand men, by the end of September the actual strength
was only thirty-four thousand men.

Secretary of State Monroe, who had taken over the War Department, boldly recommended conscription; but Congress had not the
courage to give the nation its first draft. Instead, it raised the land
bounty for enlistments, thereby encouraging desertion for the purpose of re-enlisting under another name to claim the bounty. At the
end of 1814 the country staggered along with thirty-four thousand
regulars and the six-month militia of the various states.

By then, however, even the despised militia could not be counted
upon to take the field, let alone remain there in the face of an enemy.
Led by Massachusetts—possessor of the finest militia, which she would
use only for her own defense—Connecticut, Pennsylvania, Maryland,
Virginia, South Carolina and Kentucky began to form or to plan the
formation of state armies.

Even more deplorable was the federal government's financial position, which was, in that fall of 1814, probably at its lowest point in the

history of the nation. Although Congress had doubled imports at the outset of the war, while reviving some excise taxes and imposing direct taxes on dwellings and slaves, it proposed to finance the war by borrowing money. After the first year of near-disaster the only way the Treasury could borrow money was by selling its stock at greater and greater discounts. It has been estimated that of $80 million borrowed between 1812 and 1816, the government actually received only $34 million in specie value.

While the national debt rose, a Congress afraid to draft soldiers was also too timid to levy the taxes that would cover expenditures. Moreover, the Treasury had no national administrative system. It was not even able to transfer its deposits from one section of the country to another. Millions of banknotes collected in middle and southern states' banks had to be left on deposit there while debts in Boston and New York remained unpaid.

Finally, the section of the country with the most cash was the center of opposition to the war. A variety of factors—not all of them so obvious or so culpable as the practice of playing quartermaster to the enemy—had enriched New England. Specie holdings in Massachusetts alone jumped from $1,709,000 in June of 1811 to $7,326,000 in June of 1814. Massachusetts, unalterably opposed to the war from the beginning, hoped to end it by withholding financial support.

When her war profits were shut off and British fleets menaced her shores, she called that quasi-secessionist assembly known as the Hartford Convention.

It is not fair to blame New England alone for the national government's shortages in men and money. Except New York, Kentucky, Tennessee, and perhaps Ohio, no state gave the war its full and earnest cooperation. Moreover, many Patriots from New England volunteered for the regular army and some of its finest regiments were recruited there. Nevertheless, the conduct of the Federalists who controlled New England is not to be admired. They gave the war the least support and made the largest profits. Shippers took advantage of Britain's licensing system to supply Britain and her allies in the Peninsular War against Napoleon, who, if he was not an American ally, was at least fighting the American enemy. Although these same ships later turned privateer to attack British shipping, their purpose was prizes not patriotism. Because of New England's antiwar spirit Britain had at first excluded her coasts from the blockade, enabling her to gain a monopoly of the import trade. Finally, New England so openly and effectively supplied the enemy in

Canada that Congress had to pass a law forbidding the coastal trade.

Outraged, New England came to a boil of town meetings, just as in the days of King George, only now it was the Republican "Jacobins" and "that little man in the Palace" who were denounced. Profiteering and smuggling were cloaked in the righteous mantle of assistance to the Lord's anointed—Britain—standing at Armageddon against the Napoleonic antichrist. However, after the devil incarnate had been defeated and exiled to Elba, there was still no lessening of opposition to the war. Even after Britain extended the blockade to New England—thereby cutting war profits—the Federalists could describe the British peace terms as "moderate" and recommend relying upon British magnanimity. But then, in September of 1814, those merciful cousins from across the sea seized one hundred miles of Maine seacoast and a British fleet prepared to descend upon Boston.

Massachusetts was not only dumbfounded but left to her own resources. Two years before, Governor Caleb Strong had refused to put the state militia under the War Department. Now, as the national government offered to maintain the militia so long as it was commanded by regular army officers, Strong replied that he would call out the militia only *to defend Boston,* providing the state retained control and the United States paid the bills. The answer, of course, was no. And so Massachusetts sent out an invitation to other New England states to confer at Hartford upon "their public grievances and concerns" and to concert plans for interstate defense.

The Hartford Convention met secretly in that Connecticut capital from December 15, 1814, to January 5, 1815. Full delegations from Massachusetts, Connecticut and Rhode Island attended, with only a smattering from Vermont and New Hampshire. Although the majority of these men were Federalists, the moderates rather than the firebreathers gained control at the outset, and the issues of a separate regional peace with Britain or outright secession never arose. Nevertheless, the Hartford Convention did point a pistol at the American Union. In simplest terms, New England proposed to defend itself with its own forces financed by federal taxes collected within its borders. Although the word "secession" was never uttered, the convention did declare that in case of "absolute necessity," any state could justify "severance from the Union." Seven amendments to the U.S. Constitution were recommended, which were:

1. Representation and direct taxes should be apportioned on the basis of the number of free persons. Thus, three-fifths of the slaves would not be included in the enumeration by which representation

from the slave states was calculated. Therefore the number of south-erners in [both] houses would be reduced.

2. A two-thirds vote of both houses would be required for the admission of new states.

3. No embargo by Congress would extend more than sixty days.

4. Two-thirds of both houses must consent to any interdiction of commerce with a foreign country.

5. Except in case of invasion, two-thirds of both houses would be required to declare war.

6. Only native-born citizens—excluding those already naturalized—would be permitted to serve in Congress or to hold civil office.

7. No president could be elected for more than one term, and no state could have two presidents in succession.

It has been said that there was "nothing subversive" in these ideas. Perhaps. But they were nevertheless the soul of bias and bigotry and so obviously designed to destroy Virginian and Republican influence while promoting that of the Federalists and New England, and to advance the interests of that party and region at the expense of all others, that to be honest the Hartford Convention should have listed its recommendations under the heading: "Prescription for Suicide for Republicans, and the Southern, Western and Middle States." Certainly counting three-fifths of the slave population as a basis for southern representation in Congress was wrong, but it was approved without any real opposition at the Constitutional Convention of 1787, attended by the ancestors of these Hartford delegates.

Because Virginia had held the presidency for twenty-two of the republic's twenty-six years, and Madison had two years to go with Monroe almost a certainty for four or eight more, the restriction on the presidency was not political wisdom but rather sheer Federalist spite. Only "native-born" to serve? Here was the ugly child of the unlovely Alien and Sedition Acts passed during the reign of His Rotundity John Adams of Massachusetts, the state that would become the happy home of Nativists and Know-Nothings.

Much as the Hartford delegates might maintain then and in years of debate afterward that they never envisioned secession, most Americans in the other states did believe that theirs was a treasonable gathering. Its secrecy was deeply distrusted. Indubitably the Continental Congress had often met thus, but that was to be expected in a revolutionary atmosphere: and Congress had declared the War of 1812 in executive (secret) session, but no Congress in history had ever kept a secret for more than a week. Proceedings of the Hartford Convention, however, remained unknown for nine years. Loyal Americans also despised such a divisive assembly during America's darkest hour when only a united people could avert disaster—and here was New England sowing the seeds of dissension. There can be no doubt that many Federalists with their hatred for Republicans and "the Virginia dynasty" nourished by the bitter waters of twenty-two despairing years did consider secession as the only solution. There were also Republicans present who had given up hope that there was any way to preserve the Union.

Nevertheless, it had to be clear to these delegates that what New England could do could be done by other regions and other states, and that would be the end of *e pluribus unum*. If Congress did not accept these recommendations to be carried to them by five "ambassadors," then New England would hold another convention at which, it was safe to infer, the final step of secession would be taken.

News had not yet reached America that the Ghent negotiations had been resumed with Britain softening its position. What was known at Hartford was that a large British force had invested New Orleans. Even Thomas Jefferson expected that city to fall and be held indefinitely by the British. And if New Orleans fell, then a federal government unable to pay its army or navy or even the interest on its national debt would topple too.

That supposedly was the cheerful expectation of the quintet of New England ambassadors making for Washington. But was it really? Or could it have been an ultimatum that they confidently believed would be rejected by the War Hawk Congress with its southern delegation and President James Madison, Father of the Constitution, so that the Hartford Convention could reconvene as planned and have this refusal as the excuse for outright secession? But before they arrived in the capital, two events—the Treaty of Ghent and the American victory at New Orleans—made a mockery of their mission. From their very dejection at this unwelcome news it may be suggested that they did indeed hope for rejection, and because they could not endure the War Hawks' barbs and caricatures, and especially not the national merriment occasioned by the realization that the war was over and their mission now as moot as their political careers and Federalist Party were dead, they turned gloomily around and headed home.

49

Jackson Clears Gulf Coast

∼ANDREW JACKSON WAS NOW A MAJOR GENERAL IN THE REGULAR ARMY commanding the Seventh Military District from his headquarters at Mobile, Alabama, to which he had come after signing the Creek Treaty. From Mobile he cast covetous eyes on Pensacola in western Florida. Jackson considered this Spanish coastal city to be the source of all the weapons and whisky that had caused such Indian uprisings as the massacre at Fort Mims. He wanted to seize it, and the fact that it was Spanish and the United States was not at war with Spain bothered him not at all. On June 27, 1814, he wrote to Secretary of War Armstrong asking permission to capture Pensacola, but Armstrong made no reply. Again that did not particularly upset Andrew Jackson, and he waited for some excuse to go on the offensive. It came when Captain Sir William Percy got there first and seized the town.

Jackson was now on fire to open the campaign, but before he could he had to wait until Tennessee could send him an army. In the meantime, hearing that the British in Pensacola were mounting an expedition to capture Mobile, he began to prepare to receive them. In all he had about 130 men to defend the town. They were in Fort Bowyer, a small earthen position about thirty miles below Mobile on a sandy point of Mobile Bay's eastern shore.

Bowyer's commander was Major William Lawrence, one of the few officers excepted from Winfield Scott's general condemnation of U.S. Army officers as drones and drunks. Lawrence had about twenty small Spanish pieces to defend the fort, plus a long 24-pounder. But he did dispose his meager garrison in well-chosen positions to repel a land-sea attack, and he did have courage—and determination—taking his battle cry from that other and immortal Lawrence: "Don't give up the fort!" With his officers, he made a compact never to surrender.

Captain Percy and Colonel Nicholls in Pensacola were disappointed when a rueful Captain Lockyer returned from his Baratarian mission empty-handed and embarrassed. Percy and Nicholls had hoped to employ the Laffites and their hellish banditti in the attack on Mobile. Nevertheless, they decided to persevere in that plan by attacking Fort Bowyer first. With 5 ships and 78 guns, 130 Royal Marines and 600 Creeks, the British fleet appeared off Mobile Bay on September 12, 1814. Almost at once Nicholls landed with the ground troops, waiting for the fleet to pulverize this insignificant little outpost before attacking. Nicholls was quite confident that Bowyer's defenders would be terrified, once they saw that an army of more than 700 British "regulars"—like Brock at Detroit, Nicholls had dressed his Indians in scarlet coats—was coming against them.

Three days later Percy had his ships in line, sailing to within musket range with his 24-gun flagship *Hermes* in the lead. Major Lawrence immediately opened up with his 24-pounder. *Hermes* replied, and Percy commenced a full-scale bombardment. When a British shot struck down the American colors, the enemy seamen cheered, and Nicholls's troops with huzzahs and Indian howls ran toward the fort to accept its surrender. But the flag was restored and a blast of grape drove off the British and scattered the Creeks.

Then *Hermes*'s flag was shot down, and Lawrence called for a cease-fire to be sure she was surrendering. A broadside from *Carron* suggested that she was not, so the Americans resumed their cannonading. Gradually, as was almost always true in these Anglo-American gunnery duels, the Yankees established their superiority. A lucky shot cut away *Hermes*'s anchor cable and she drifted toward the fort, where she was scourged by all of Bowyer's guns. Soon she blundered into shoal water and Percy set her afire, blowing her to bits. That was the end of the British attempt on Mobile, and the beginning of another period of humiliation for Britannia. Five ships, 78 guns, and 1,300 men could not conquer 130 of those faint-hearted Brother Ephraims armed with twenty puny and antiquated cannon and one lone 24-pounder. Worse, British losses totaled 232 men, of whom 162 were killed. Yankee losses were four killed and four wounded.

Like Captain Lockyer before them, Captain Percy and Colonel Nicholls sailed back to Pensacola in embarrassment.

In the mind of Andrew Jackson he now had his excuse to attack Pensacola. How he could translate a British fleet's seizure of that town and attack on Mobile into a Spanish insult, is an acrobatic feat of logic. But Old Hickory never allowed consistency to trouble him when he was standing at Gaugamela and battling for the Lord. By November 6, 1814, he was ready to march on Pensacola with an army of three thousand Tennessee volunteers. At dawn next day they were on the beach outside the town. Gradually, Jackson's gunners found the sand too soft to drag their pieces through, and Old Hickory ordered an infantry charge. A Spanish battery on the main street opened fire with two guns but was rushed and taken by an American charge. Snipers began firing from the houses, until Governor Manrique came out of the headquarters waving a white flag. Jackson granted his request to spare the town, and then moved against Fort St. Michael, which soon surrendered. Turning to Fort Barrancas on the other side of the bay, the Spaniards blew it up before he could reach it. Now Old Hickory watched with grim satisfaction as the British sailed away from Pensacola, never to return.

Fearing that Percy and Nicholls might try Mobile once more in his absence, he marched west again, arriving there on November 11. Awaiting him were instructions from Secretary Monroe dated September 24, 1814. Jackson was ordered to take command of a force being raised in Tennessee and Georgia for the defense of New Orleans. Ten days later Monroe informed him that the British invasion fleet was already at sea. On November 22, with John Coffee at the head of an army sailing down the Cumberland from Nashville, and Kentucky volunteers already bobbing down the Mississippi on flatboats, Major General Andrew Jackson began riding from Mobile to New Orleans.

50

Peace of Christmas Eve

~Although Macdonough's victory on Lake Champlain has often been described as the most important naval battle of the War of 1812, it was in its long-range effect not as decisive as the Battle of Lake Erie. If Perry had lost, the British would have been much more insistent on the principle of *status uti possidetis,* and no American army would ever have been able to wrest the Northwest from the grasp of Wellington's veterans. Macdonough's victory demonstrated that if the Americans could not conquer Canada, the British could not subdue the United States, which does not equal Perry's in ultimate importance.

Yet in its immediate effect it had a powerful influence on Lord Liverpool when, in October 1814, he received the bad news of Ross's death, the Baltimore repulse and the disaster at Plattsburg. His Lordship and his cabinet were badly shaken, although, with the southern invasion force already bound for New Orleans, they did not abandon their insistence on the state of possession at the end of hostilities. This, of course, included complete control of the Great Lakes; an Indian buffer state stretching from Sandusky, Ohio, to Kaskaskia, Illinois; cession of much of Maine; and dismantling of all American border forts, together with other lesser but equally humiliating demands.

The Americans, who had already firmly rejected these terms, still clinging to the *status quo ante bellum*—the state existing prior to hostilities—felt that news from America so stimulating that John Quincy Adams refused to believe it had immensely strengthened their position. They now scoffed at the London *Times's* earlier fire-breathing advice to Lord Liverpool reminding him of his sacred duty to punish the Yankees: "... oh, may no false liberality, no mistaken lenity, no weak and cowardly policy interpose to save them from the blow! Strike! Chastise the savages, for such they are!" The commissioners rejoiced when the *Times* now observed: "This is a lamentable event to the civilized world." Liverpool could not agree more, for "the civilized world" was in deep distress both at home and abroad.

At home the loss of the American market caused by the blockade was already being severely felt, and the success of American privateers in the Irish Sea had made shipping insurance rates three times higher than they were during the war with Napoleon. Prevost's defeat meant that the war would have to be continued another year, at an estimated cost of £10 million. To raise such a sum meant extension of the detested property tax, then due to expire in a few months. Liverpool knew that his ministry could not survive, much less obtain, continuation of a tax "for the purpose of securing a better frontier for Canada."

Abroad the coalition that had conquered Napoleon was coming apart at the seams. Western Europe was not only troubled by the perils of reconstruction, but also menaced by the new power of Russia. Diplomats at the Congress of Vienna, no longer impressed by British talk of the "contemptible Americans," would not fail to take note of the fact that some of Britain's finest regiments were beyond reach in far-off America. Czar Alexander's battalions were very close indeed.

Still, Liverpool faced up to the fact that the unpopular and unpleasant American war could yet be settled by a military decision. He asked the Duke of Wellington to assume command. Napoleon's nemesis replied: "That which appears to me to be wanting in America is not a general, or a general officer and troops, but a naval superiority on the Lakes." On the diplomatic side, Wellington said: "In regard to your negotiation, I confess that I think you have no right, from the state of the war, to demand any concession of territory. . . . Why stipulate for the *uti possidetis?* You can get no territory; indeed the state of your military operations, however creditable, does not entitle you to any."

The first soldier of Britain was not alone in his pessimism: all around Liverpool the country was giving way to a war weariness that quickly changed to outright opposition after the American cleverly made public Britain's outrageous territorial demands. Even the London *Times* was displeased, and liberals in Parliament bitterly castigated the Tory government for making demands it had no power to enforce.

What is not generally known is the deep dread of the power of the London mob in the hearts of Liverpool and his ministers. Though comparatively young men, they were not so young that they could not remember the horror of the Lord George Gordon Riots in London in 1780 during the Revolutionary War. A howling, drunken mob variously estimated at between 60,000 and 100,000 people erupted in a frenzy of murder, devastation, arson and general lawlessness that neither King George III nor Parliament could control. For almost a week they held Britain's capital city hostage in their successful attempt to block passage of the Catholic Emancipation Act ending persecution of Britons of that faith. This was their excuse for their rising, carefully cultivated by the execrable anti-Catholic Lord Gordon; but their actual grievance was against the government as the author of their status as second-class subjects and the misery of their lives.

During the War of 1812 the life of the oppressed British poor, most of them huddled together in cities, was even worse, so much so that King Louis XVIII of France compared it to the wretched existence of the French poor in 1789, the year of the French Revolution. What had happened was that under Tory rule in which—to use the battle cry of the American Democratic Party, "The rich got richer and the poor got poorer"—the yeomanry class of small independent land-holders, which had once been a bulwark of British liberties, was inexorably driven from the land into the cities. According to Sir Charles Petrie in his *Four Georges,* a study of the Hanoverian monarchy: "Between 1760 and 1797 there were no less than 1,539 private Enclosure Acts. In many cases the commons were enclosed without adequate compensation to those who had right of pasturage on them, and so were deprived of the means of keeping a cow or goose, or of cutting turf for fuel. Some received no allotment because they could not prove their claims, while others sold their allotments, and so became mere tenants, to be turned out at the whim of their landlord." The small farmer was given similar injustice: "If his holding was unaffected by enclosure, the loss of domestic industries rendered him less able to pay his rent; if it was to be enclosed, he found himself with a diminished income at the very time when he most needed money; if he managed to keep his land for a while, he was ruined by violent fluctuation in the price of corn. Sooner or later he sank into the laboring class."

Thus enclosure and the onset of a ruthlessly exploitative Industrial Revolution that the Tories made no attempt to guide or control combined to send vast hordes of uprooted and despairing people who had once been decent farmers and loyal Britons streaming into the cities, where they sank into an utterly wretched and bestial existence best illustrated by the painting of Sir William Hogarth, especially the famous "Gin Lane." This was the "mob" that Liverpool and his cabinet feared. They knew that these people hated the War of 1812 as fiercely as their parents had hated the first American war, and that they too could be misled by some rabble-rousing Pied Piper like Gordon. The Tories also feared the wrath of the merchants, so many of them facing ruin and likely to spawn another madman like Percival's assassin; or of the rising middle class unwilling to bear the burden of renewed taxation to finance a prolonged war.

Lord Liverpool, then, was indeed desperate. So he asked the American commission—now increased to five by Madison's appointment of Henry Clay and Jonathon Russell, a former *chargé d'affaires* in London and Paris—to draft a peace treaty. With the war over there would be no need for impressment, and without this *casus belli* there was really nothing for the Americans to do but settle an internal disagreement.

The Treaty of 1783 had given Britain the right to free navigation of the Mississippi. This was done because at that time it was believed that the Father of Waters rose in Canada rather than what is now Minnesota, and Canadians could rightfully claim free passage. Henry Clay was determined not to grant that right. Conversely John Quincy Adams was not ready to surrender the compensating right Americans gained to the fisheries off Labrador and Newfoundland. This was of great importance to New England, as Adams's father well knew when he helped to negotiate the treaty. Eventually Gallatin persuaded Clay to drop his opposition, and the commissioners of both sides agreed that if some dispute should arise later it would have to be resolved then. On Christmas Eve of 1814 the Treaty of Ghent was signed.

Since that date historians on both sides of the War of 1812 have argued over who actually won it, or whether it had not been indeed a standoff. Perhaps the best answer to that question was given by the reactions in the rival countries. In the United States there was the merriest jubilation, and for the first time since Cockburn and Ross put Washington to the torch President James Madison was seen to smile.

In Britain there also had to have been relief of some kind, although the daily press records no widespread rejoicing, either in London or anywhere else. Rather the London *Times* put the sourest face upon the treaty, sarcastically publishing an "Advertisement Extraordinary" that said:

> WANTED—The spirit that motivated the conduct of
> Elizabeth, Oliver and William.
> LOST—All idea of national Dignity and Honor.
> FOUND—That any insignificant state may insult that which used to
> call herself the Mistress of the Waves.

A week later the Thunderer of Fleet Street published the comment of the unhappy Prince Regent.

> If any of the powers who have received our subsidies or have been rescued from destruction by our courage and example, have had the baseness to turn against us, it is morally certain that the Treaty of Ghent will confirm them in their resolution. They will reflect that we have attempted to force our principles on Americans and have failed. Nay, that we have retired from combat with the stripes yet bleeding on our backs. . . .

The War of 1812 occurred because the United States of America, being the world's largest neutral sea carrier, could not avoid becoming involved in the Anglo-French struggle so dependent upon sea power. Impressment and ship seizures thus became powerful issues in America, so much so that the War Hawks, who had never smelled salt water or even seen the sea, made "Free Trade and Sailors' Rights" their battle cry in their crusade to capture Canada. Both the Royal Navy and Napoleon seized American merchant ships. To stop this piracy, America certainly could not fight both. Neither could she remain neutral. But Napoleon was not impressing Yankee sailors, and Britain was. So America fought Britannia. Moreover, Jefferson and Madison were both Anglophobes and Francophiles, positions that must have influenced Madison's choice, probably made after his customary conference with the man from Monticello. If John Adams who held exactly reverse loyalties—and who had come close to war with France in 1799—had been in the President's House, the choice might have been different; although it would have had to be made over the opposition of the War Hawks. Thus, when the Anglo-French conflict ended, the causes of ship seizure and impressment disappeared.

Most Americans realized this, and even the New England Federalists, although outwardly distressed by the early demise of their party, were secretly pleased at how the end of the war conferred upon their region a revival of shipping and manufacturing beyond the dreams of avarice. On the borders that sent the War Hawks to Congress, the withdrawal of British military might caused the Indians there to drop their tomahawks, much to the satisfaction of those areas that had agitated the war. Henry Clay, however, called the peace "a damned bad treaty." In this hasty judgment, the War Hawk leader who would one day be called the Great Pacificator was a bit too hawkish.

Ghent produced a lasting peace, a rarity in those days and even in our own. The British and American nations that fought the war became close friends and four times wartime allies. Ghent was unlike the vengeful Versailles Peace that spawned Adolf Hitler. It left no Alsace-Lorraine or Polish Corridor or those hyphenated, divided democracies carved out of the defunct Austro-Hungarian Empire. Neither did it create any Koreas or Vietnams dissected in the wake of World War II and victimized by the Cold War that succeeded it.

And yet, Ghent had not really ended the War of 1812, for across the Atlantic on that same December 24, 1812, that had seen the signing of the Peace of Christmas Eve, Major General Andrew Jackson had begun building his defenses along the old Rodriquez Canal, and Sir Edward Pakenham was hastening from Britain to take command of the great invasion force charged with the conquest of New Orleans.

51

Battle of New Orleans

⌖ IT HAS BEEN OFTEN ASSERTED THAT THE BATTLE OF NEW ORLEANS was indecisive and that the blood shed there would never have flowed had there been such a rapid means of communication as an Atlantic cable. New Orleans, it has been maintained, was a battle fought after the war was over. But this is not true, much as this version remains gospel truth in most history textbooks, because a treaty by itself does not end a war. It must be ratified by the legitimate governments then in power: in this case the British Crown and Parliament, and President Madison and the Twelfth Congress. Until this occurred, the Treaty of Ghent alone had no binding power. It had not the power to end hostilities, but only suggested certain conditions that, if endorsed by both governments, would end the War of 1812.

Judging from the orders issued by Lord Bathurst it is not idle conjecture to suggest that if Britain's southern invasion force had been victorious, the vast Louisiana Territory with Texas and the Southwest might have fallen to the Crown. If—and this is indeed a big IF—news of an American defeat at New Orleans had reached Whitehall prior to ratification of the treaty, it is possible and perhaps even likely, granting the mood of Crown and Parliament and the Foreign Office's infinite capacity for Double-Think and Newspeak, that the Ghent Treaty would have been ignored as a worthless scrap of paper and the business of organizing these new "British" lands begun.

The Battle of New Orleans, then, was one of the most decisive and significant in American history. Madison in his message to the Senate on February 15, 1815, made this clear when he declared that "the termination of hostilities depends on the time of the ratification of the treaty by both parties."

Meanwhile, on the morning of December 2, 1814, Major General Andrew Jackson rode into New Orleans.

Old Hickory did not impress a Creole populace accustomed to the mannered and elegant grandees of Castile and Aragon, or the perfumed and polished courtiers of the French monarchy who served their sovereign in the New World as governors or generals. Here was a tall, gaunt man in worn and travel-stained garments. His face was so emaciated that those who received him wondered if he were ill or merely undernourished. His short blue Spanish cloak was frayed, concealing the two stars of a major general loosely sewn to his shoulder straps, and his knee-high boots so muddy he might just have come from duck hunting in a Louisiana bayou. On his head was an absurd little schoolboy's leather cap, without plume, braid, ornament, or insignia. Indeed Major General Andrew Jackson seemed such an insignificant commander that a Creole woman, famed for her culinary skill, who had been asked to prepare his welcoming meal complained to the host:

"Ah! Mr. Smith ... you asked me to ... receive a great general. I make your house *comme il faut,* and prepare a splendid *déjeuner* ... all for ... an ugly old Kaintuck flatboatman."

Yet this first impression did not last, once Old Hickory took command in New Orleans. What was noticed thereafter was his almost demoniac energy, the way his blue eyes beneath that thick shock of iron-gray hair flashed and compelled. That thin body seeming hardly capable of sustaining life was able to surchage those around him with something of his own immense vitality. The day after his arrival Andrew Jackson threw himself headlong into organizing the city's defenses. One day's inspection shocked but did not horrify him. What he beheld has been described by Alexander Walker, one of his biographers familiar with the New Orleans of a century ago, who interviewed many of the survivors of the battle:

Indeed, never was a city so defenseless, so exposed, so weak, so prostrate, as New Orleans in the fall of 1814. There was not sufficient time to obtain aid from the West. There was no naval force in the port or adjacent waters; not a regiment of armed men in the city. The resources of the whole state were scarcely adequate to the production and organization of two militia regiments. The population of the city was a new and mixed one, composed of people of all nations and races, who had been too recently admitted into the Union to feel that strong attachment to the government and flag, which characterizes an old and homogeneous community. Besides, there was a vast amount of valuable property, merchandise and produce accumulated in the storehouses, which would be in danger of destruction in case of an attempt to repel an invader. To save this property would be a strong inducement to a surrender and capitulation of the city. Few, indeed, were there who could look these perils and difficulties in the face, and entertain the idea of a serious defense of the city against any well-organized and well-conducted expedition.

Yet the sense of despair and general expectation of disastrous defeat gave way almost instantly to a thrill of hope upon the arrival of Jackson. Throughout the city ran the exhilarating cry: "Jackson has come!" At once he began drilling the militia. Units with mostly French and colorful names—the Chasseurs, Louisiana Blues, Carabiniers d'Orleans, Hulans, Francs plus one with the impossible name of "Foot Dragoons"—formed in the past chiefly as social groups given to feasting and parading on holidays, now functioned as a battalion of 385 men under the Creole Major Jean Plauché. And of course there were those hellish banditti from Barataria Bay. Here were trained cannoneers who were a welcome reinforcement. Whether or not the story of Jackson and Lafitte meeting face-to-face is fact or fiction it is indubitably true that Jackson did concede that the Baratarians "could not fail of being very useful."

Jackson also appealed to all the engineers in the area to provide him with all available information on the local topography. He studied each approach likely to be exploited by an invading army. Numerous bayous or canals originating in the Mississippi flowed into surrounding lakes to provide watery approaches for the enemy. Jackson had Governor Claiborne organize details of citizens to block the mouths of these streams with fallen trees and earth. He inspected the forts, strengthening Fort St. Philip guarding the city from any approach upriver from the Gulf, arming it with the guns and gunners needed to repel any British squadron. On December 20, Old Hickory was delighted to hear the shouts of William Carroll's three thousand raucous Tennessee volunteers coming ashore from the flatboats that had brought them floating down the Mississippi. Soon he would hear the clattering hoofbeats of big John Coffee's dragoons, who were still five miles upriver after a ride through eight hundred miles of wilderness. By December 23 Jackson could write home: "All Well."

But it wasn't.

The New Orleans Expedition was formed after Lord Bathurst received Admiral Cochrane's wildly optimistic report that three thousand red-coats assisted by Spanards and Indians could seize the Gulf Coast from Mobile to New Orleans. Cochrane, of course, judged the American will to fight by the sight of all those Yankee heels fleeing for safety in the Bladensburg Races. But Bathhurst believed him, and began gathering veteran regiments at Plymouth while informing General Ross— of whose death His Lordship was unaware—that he was to proceed to Jamaica with his army and there, awaiting the arrival of reinforcements from Plymouth, to prepare to attack the American Gulf Coast. Ross had two missions: the first, to hold the mouth of the Mississippi to block American commerce down the great river; the second, to seize as much territory as possible to be claimed at the peace conference under the principle of the state of possession.

Ross was dead before these instructions reached America, and until a new chief could be named, temporary command fell to Major General John Keane. Like Ross, Keane was an Irishman, though younger. He had risen in Egypt from subaltern to a brigade commander. His disposition was not quite like Ross's, if it was not diametrically different. On the Peninsula under Wellington, one of Keane's brigade's regiments was the famous 17th Enniskillens. These were Irish troops whom the French had tried to talk into mutiny against their British officers. Keane learned of the attempt and approached the Frenchmen with a smiling face, suggesting a friendly little get-together with his Irish. When the French came forward to fraternize, Keane ordered the Enniskillens to charge them with the bayonet.

This was the man who on September 18, 1814, had led four thousand four hundred men aboard the transports at historic Plymouth, sailing for the New World out of the harbor from which Howard and Drake had sailed against the Spanish and Lord Nelson against the French.

News of Ross's death did not reach Lord Bathurst until late October, when he promptly named Sir Edward Pakenham as the new commander of the Louisiana expedition. Pakenham immediately sailed for the rendezvous area at Negril Bay, Jamaica, where Keane's army of 4,400 men joined the 3,100 troops Ross had led at the Chesapeake.

Pakenham was born in Ireland in 1778. He was the brother-in-law of the Duke of Wellington—another Irish soldier—who considered him one of his ablest lieutenants. Handsome and popular, he was highly respected for his military insights, although his service as commander of a large formation was brief. This was when he led Sir Thomas Picton's famous 3rd Division at the Battle of Salamanca, when Picton was too ill to mount his horse. During this engagement Wellington was maneuvering against Marshal Auguste Marmont when he suddenly found the Frenchman's left flank exposed and a gap in his center. At once the Iron Duke ordered his brother-in-law to attack the middle of Marmont's line, and Pakenham led the charge that "beat forty thousand Frenchmen in forty minutes."

Salamanca was the high point of Pakenham's career. Although as brave personally as any other British officer, he had never commanded his own army. Wellington did not recommend him for any American post, probably because he wished to escape a charge of nepotism. Yet there were other veteran generals accustomed to high command—notably Picton—and there were critics of the choice of Pakenham who thought aloud that the mistake with Prevost at Lake Champlain was about to be repeated. But the War Office, encouraged by the experiment with Ross, who did not command independently but under Cochrane, explained that it had decided to employ the same chain-of-command at New Orleans.

Pakenham had another distinction not exactly sought or cherished, having been wounded twice in the neck with astonishing results. At Santa Lucía a musket ball had struck him there, and when the wound healed it left his head leaning to one side. Ten years later in the attack on Martinique, another ball had lodged in the same place, restoring his head to its original, upright position.

On November 26, 1814, before Sir Edward could reach Jamaica, Admiral Sir Alexander Cochrane sailed from Negril Bay for New Orleans.

Cochrane's fleet of sixty ships carrying a force of about nine thousand men was a magnificent sight as it sailed with awesome majesty and spreading white sails onto the blue Caribbean. Some of his warships were among the most famous in the Royal Navy, including his flagship *Tonnant*, as well as *Bedford, Royal Oak, Norge, Ramillies,* and *Asia,* all 74, plus the lighter liners with fewer guns *Seahorse, Hydra, Annide, Diomede, Gorgon* and *Dictator,* all attended by a swarming host of frigates, sloops and gunboats, mounting a total of about a thousand guns.

Plodding along with the warships was a fleet of transports, carrying civilians as well as troops. By their presence these experts in civil affairs made it plain that Britannia had not come merely to punish the Yankee upstarts as in Washington, but to organize Louisiana as another colony of the Crown. As a reminder that Old Mother England had not abandoned her domineering mercantilist policy was a collector of revenue accompanied by a horde of tax collectors. There was also an editor present equipped with a complete printing press and fonts of type with which he would publish a slightly pro-Limey and anti-Yankee newspaper.

On December 10 the great fleet was poised outside Lake Borgne, the gateway to New Orleans. There they encountered two of the five-gunboat flotilla commanded by Lieutenant Thomas ap Catesby Jones. They had been stationed there by Jackson both as forward observers and the first line of American defense. Cochrane was profoundly disturbed at being sighted, for both he and his ranking officers believed that their destination was a secret, and he actually hoped to surprise New Orleans. Perhaps also hoping to crush these Americans before they could warn the city, he assembled an attack force of sixty barges, launches and gigs mounting carronades and long guns. Jones with twenty-three guns and about 180 men sought to lure the British fleet within range of coastal guns, but he soon became becalmed. Nevertheless, he put up a valiant fight, one that lasted an hour before his ships were sunk and he was wounded and taken captive. Surprisingly the British suffered three hundred casualties and lost quite a few barges, while American losses were only six killed and thirty-five wounded and those two gunboats sunk.

The watery road to New Orleans was now open to the British fleet.

Andrew Jackson was somewhat surprised when he learned of this skirmish at Lake Borgne. He found it hard to believe that a British fleet was actually coming against New Orleans by the direct route that he considered so easily defensible. While still in Mobile he had set that conviction down on paper, writing: "A real military man, with full knowledge of the geography of this country, would first possess himself of (Mobile), draw to his standard the Indians and march direct to the Walnut Hills (Vicksburg) . . . and being able to forage on the country, support himself, cut off all supplies from above and make this country an easy conquest." Old Hickory was right. New Orleans was indeed a hard nut to crack, but it could not survive if its communications with the back country were severed by a strong army above the city. But what Jackson probably did not understand, being a true soldier of democracy fighting the new ideological war introduced by the American Revolution, was that professional British generals and admirals were as mindful of private profit as public glory. Prize money could exert a powerful influence on their decisions, and Admiral Cochrane was very much aware of that $20 million in goods lying ready for the taking in Crescent City warehouses. It was he who decided to attack New Orleans directly, and he had sailed from Jamaica without waiting for Pakenham. The presence in his fleet of numerous barges and empty merchant ships sailing in ballast could be for no other purpose than carrying plunder back to Britain, loot of which he would receive a substantial share.

So Old Hickory, though startled at first, gradually recovered his confidence, pleased that Cochrane was playing into his hands—attacking when every bayou from Lake Borgne was blocked and guarded.

Brave, bold and indomitable general that Andrew Jackson was, he might have been an even better commander had he been a little less contemptuous of the value of "book larnin'"; for even the slightest acquaintance with military history might have warned him of the danger of relying upon passive defense in the face of a determined and resourceful enemy. In war the impregnable position is often penetrated and the fort usually falls. Troy was deceived and undone by the ruse of the wooden horse, Jericho was betrayed to Joshua by the harlot Rahab, Jerusalem crumbled under the catapults of Titus, Constantinople was stormed by Crusader and Saracen alike and Quebec was surprised by Wolfe.

At New Orleans in 1815 Admiral Cochrane was not playing into General Jackson's hands as he thought—attacking straight ahead into defenses that were indeed formidable—but relying like General Francisco Franco in the Spanish Civil War on an unsuspected "fifth column" inside New Orleans. This was the Spanish Creole population. Unhappy that their city had been secretly ceded to Napoleon and then angered that the Corsican conqueror had crassly sold it to the detestable Yanquis, loyal to Britain because Wellington had evicted the French from their homeland, they were, like the harlot Rahab, eager to serve the enemy. They told Cochrane how he could approach the city undetected by using shallow-draft craft loaded with soldiers. The route was across Lake Borgne to its extreme northwest shore, thence by the Bayou Bienvenu to within a short distance of the Mississippi. Cochrane sent two junior officers to explore this chink in Jackson's armor. They traveled up the bayou to a fishing village where sympathetic fishermen gave them their blue shirts and tarpaulins to wear as they passed through Villeré's Canal to its head. From there they walked to the banks of the Father of Waters, drinking from the great river at a point nine miles below the city. Returning to the fleet they informed a delighted Cochrane that New Orleans could indeed be surprised.

Because there were not enough small boats to transport the entire British army to Villeré Plantation eight miles below the city, Keane placed a picked force of 1,800 men under Colonel William Thornton, a master of assault who had led the attack on Washington. On the morning of December 22 they clambered into the waiting boats and set off in rain and cold winds across the lake. Cochrane and Keane were with them.

When the assault force came to the fishing village they found it empty of those sympathetic fishermen who had rented boats to them, but guarded by an American picket of eight Frenchmen. All but one was taken captive, and one of these, Joseph Rodolphe Ducros, a superb storyteller, shocked Cochrane and Keane with his tale of a city defended by a well-armed and well-trained army of between twelve and fifteen thousand men. Now the British chiefs began to doubt their Spanish spies who had spoken so encouragingly of Jackson's meager and porous defenses. Thus, when they emerged from the grotesque and gloomy cypress swamps into the level ground and orange groves of Villeré Plantation they decided to halt. If they had pressed on to New Orleans they might have struck the city at a time when Jackson could not organize effective resistance, when so many of his troops were still floating down the Mississippi on flatboats and so many others were patrolling the swamp trails and bayous leading into New Orleans.

But Cochrane and Keane did have the presence of mind to capture the Villeré brothers—Gabriel and Celestin—and put them in a room under guard. While the admiral and the general conferred, Gabriel Villeré leaped through an open window—racing through the swamps he knew so well, gaining the safety of the cypresses while the pursuing British soldiers with their customary poor marksmanship filled the air above his head with murmuring but missing musket balls. Hearing the shouting soldiers coming closer, Villeré hid among the great spreading limbs of a live oak tree, until to his horror he saw his favorite hunting dog approaching. When the dog stopped beneath the tree, his tail wagging joyfully and barking, Villeré climbed down to seize a fallen branch and beat his brains out lest he betray him. Climbing back into the tree he stayed there until he thought it was safe to move on to the Mississippi where he found a boat, rowing to the opposite shore. Obtaining a horse, he galloped up the riverbank to New Orleans.

At about noon of December 23—the day the British force emerged at Villeré Plantation—the young picket Augustin Rousseau who had escaped capture at the fishing village dismounted from his lathered horse outside Andrew Jackson's headquarters to burst upon the general with the report that the British had penetrated his defenses. Jackson was incredulous, retiring to a sofa to ponder such astounding and disturbing news. Just then a sentry rapped on his door to announce three gentlemen bearing "important intelligence." Jackson nodded and they rushed in, mud-stained and breathless. From the lips of Major Gabriel Villeré there fell a torrent of French, and from an interpreter came confirmation of young Rousseau's warning: "The British have arrived at Villeré Plantation! Major Villeré was captured by them and has escaped!"

Jackson listened to the details in renewed incredulity. The enemy had found the nonexistent hole in his defenses—an unblocked and unguarded bayou—and were in force only eight miles below the city! Blue eyes flashing, Jackson sprang erect, striking the table with his fist and crying: "By the Eternal, they shall not sleep on our soil!"

Regaining his composure as quickly as he had lost it, the general gave his informants wine to sip, calling his aides inside his office with the calm announcement: "Gentlemen, the British are below. We must fight them tonight!"

There is a temptation to criticize Andrew Jackson for having allowed the British to pierce his defenses so easily. But that is not exactly fair. He had done all possible to guard and block every watery route into the city—actually an impossibility in that labyrinth of lake, bayou and canal—and had been undone by the treachery of Spanish Creoles and those fishermen of unknown ancestry. Of all the multitudinous unknowns of war, treachery and sellout for gold are among the most difficult to defend against, and so far from harshly blaming Old Hickory it is more just to praise his quick and decisive reaction. He did not wait for the expected reinforcement of those 2,400 Kentuckians, but was counter-attacking! Immediately! To surprise, he was offering counter surprise. Certain that the enemy would pause before attacking, he would strike them unawares at night when British discipline would be the least effective.

Coffee was still five miles upstream, nothing had been heard from the Blue Grassmen, Plauché with his New Orleans militia, and Lacoste with his battalion of free blacks was miles away guarding the approaches. Only the 44th Infantry stationed at the city barracks was available. Yet a signal gun was fired calling for these farflung units to rally round their resolute commander. The drummer boys among Jackson's beloved Tennessee volunteers began beating the calls that had sounded at Talladega and Horseshoe Bend. Messengers on foot, horseback or by boat sped off in all directions. Gradually, probably the most polyglot army that ever fought beneath the Stars and Stripes was assembled. At three o'clock that afternoon—an hour after Major Villeré had rushed into Jackson's headquarters—some 2,050 men of the 4,000 then available to Old Hickory were marching south.

There were troops in leather jerkins and homespun, U.S. Army regulars in blue and a detachment of U.S. Marines in forest green, marching to the Celtic lilt of the fifes and drums. From Barataria Bay came the hellish banditti. Wearing red shirts with knives or pistols thrust into colorful silk sashes around their waists, their heads swathed in bright bandannas, laughing and singing French marching songs, their white teeth flashing in their swarthy, mustachioed faces, striding south with a sailor's rolling gait, they were a merry most unmilitary mass, looking like a moving flower garden. Not all of them were there, for the dandified little Captain Dominic You with eighty of Laffite's men were still locked up in Cabildo cells. There were men of every size and color—whites, mulattoes, free blacks, Creoles, Frenchmen, frontiersmen in buckskin, Dominicans, and sailors from as far away as the Levant—speaking in that great variety of tongues heard any given day on the docks of the Crescent City. There were mounted troops as well, for John Coffee had arrived with his dragoons, most of them walking beside their horses rather than weary them before the bugles sounded the charge.

These were the contemptible "Dirty Shirts" that the British redcoats expected to put to flight, making them run just as fast as their Bladensburg brothers. After all this was a rabble, at best a mob of militia—and when had militia ever stood up to British regulars? Here was a question that King George III and Lord George Germain had asked nearly forty years earlier, and the answer had come from Lexington-Concord to Yorktown. Now at New Orleans in 1814 it was being asked again, but a better question was: when had British regulars ever met a general like Andrew Jackson?

While Jackson moved, Keane dawdled. With a sinking heart he had witnessed Gabriel Villeré's flight through the swamp, realizing that he had lost the element of surprise. So he decided to wait for reinforcements. After another 400 troops arrived, raising his force to about 2,200 men, Colonel Thornton urged an immediate attack on the city. Keane overruled him. In his defense it should be remembered that December 23 was one of the shortest days of the year in America, with darkness falling about 4:30. It would be madness to move over unknown ground against an unfamiliar city at night. The assault would be made the next day.

Meanwhile, Keane formed a line on the northern edge of the Villeré Plantation. He put his three cannon into position at the Villeré sugar works. Two regiments—the 85th and 95th foot—faced toward the city and another, the 4th or King's Own, along the Villeré Canal connecting with the Bayou Bienvenu and thus maintained communication with the fleet at Lake Borgne.

With the coming of night, an eerie quiet seemed to settle on Villeré Plantation. A cold white moon flitted intermittently among racing clouds. Its flickering beams danced on the obsidian surface of the great river flowing silently to the sea. At about 7:30 a dark shape was seen drifting slowly downriver.

It was the American schooner *Carolina.*

Andrew Jackson had made good use of Jean Laffite's guns and gunners. He had placed many of them aboard *Carolina,* with emphasis on her port side, so that the schooner sank lower in the water with a slight list to port. In the gathering dusk, *Carolina*'s shadowy bulk began sliding gently downstream toward Villeré Plantation on her left. Captain Daniel Patterson would not need to search for targets. The British, drenched for days like swamp rats, had been busily gathering wood and lighting fires that blazed cheerfully in the darkness fallen on the Villeré flats. Patterson was to open fire at 7:30; a half-hour later, giving the enemy enough time to conclude that the main assault would come from the river, Jackson would attack.

A cold fog rising from the river closed in on *Carolina* as she floated away on the current. Mist dimmed the moon and enshrouded the enemy campfires. Suddenly, a great glob of red glowed through the fog, followed by the muted roar of *Carolina*'s guns. For a moment, Britain's veterans came close to panic as the earth bucked and roared and men screamed. Some of them tried to douse their fires, but most ran for the cover of the Mississippi levee. *Carolina* roared on, and then, at 8:00 exactly, the Americans attacked.

The higher voice of American 6-pounders joined the deeper-throated chorus of *Carolina*'s guns downstream. Then *Carolina* fell silent, not wishing to catch friend and foe alike in her raking fire. The Americans stumbled on against an enemy who had turned to fight, and the battle became a lieutenant's melee: squad by squad, platoon by platoon, men seeking each other in the darkness with clutching fingers or drawn knife, rifles twinkling and cannon muzzles gushing flame, and the cries of men mingling with the neighing of Coffee's horses. At one point the British threatened to capture the American 6-pounders. Jackson rushed into the fight, shouting, "Save the guns!"

Marines and a company of the 7th Infantry rallied around Jackson and saved the cannon.

"Charge! Charge!" yelled the Americans, and the Creoles cried, "*A la baïonnette!*"

At midnight the black battlefield became suddenly silent. Jackson, correctly suspecting that the enemy was being reinforced, decided to withdraw. Unknown to himself, he had dealt the British a blow from which they never completely recovered. British casualties of 46 killed, 167 wounded, and 64 captured did not seem very heavy, even though they exceeded American losses of 24 killed, 115 wounded, and 74 captured, but the very audacity of the American assault had shaken the redcoats' conviction that the "Dirty Shirts" at New Orleans were the wing-footed brothers of the Bladensburg speedsters. And so, as the dawn of December 24, 1814, disclosed his assault force safely drawn up behind the dry Rodriguez Canal, Old Hickory sent into the city for those lowly shovels which, more than rifles, bayonet or cannon, are the soul of every defensive stand.

Christmas Day in New Orleans began with a salvo of artillery from the British camp. Americans building their mud rampart behind the canal dropped their spades, seized their rifles and jumped to the firing platforms. Then they relaxed. The salvo was only a salute to Sir Edward Pakenham, who had arrived to take command from Keane.

Pakenham's presence gave a lift to his bedraggled redcoats. The boyish, brilliant hero of Salamanca was popular with the army. Moreover, he was confident and eager for a victory that would make him the royal governor of Louisiana with an earldom to match. His wife waited at sea, as did many other ladies accompanying a force "prepared to take over the civil administration of New Orleans, with appointments from tide-waiter to collector of customs already designated." Sir Edward apparently wanted to withdraw from the present poor position and land elsewhere. But Admiral Cochrane, perhaps panting for all that lovely plunder, wanted an immediate attack, vowing scornfully that his sailors alone could defeat the Dirty Shirts, and "The soldiers could then bring up the baggage." So Pakenham agreed to attack Jackson's fortifications.

On December 27 the British batteries opened on the American ships *Louisiana* and *Carolina*. *Louisiana* narrowly escaped but *Carolina* blew up with a roar that rattled windows in New Orleans. On the same day the Americans dragged their own artillery into position while Jackson began construction of a second line of defense two miles behind the first. Next day the British showered the American lines with rockets, and sent two columns forward in assault.

On the American left, the redcoats came very close to turning the sector held by Coffee's and Carroll's men standing almost waist deep in the swamp. On the right, the enemy column moving along the riverbank was raked dreadfully by the guns of *Louisiana*. Rampart guns, manned chiefly by Laffite's red-shirted pirates, thickened the fire from *Louisiana,* and the assault on the American right was dealt a bloody repulse. As it halted, so too did the threat to the left flank— and Pakenham's first attempt failed. Although he tried to excuse it as a "reconnaissance in force," one of his aides wrote later: "In spite of our sanguine expectation of sleeping that night in New Orleans, evening found us occupying our negro huts at Villere's, nor was I sorry that the shades of night concealed our mortification from the prisoners and slaves."

The last three days of 1814 were ones of back-breaking toil on both sides. The Americans fortified the other side of the river with three batteries of naval guns, and the mud line's cannon rose from five to twelve. Cotton bales were sunk into the mud flats and wooden platforms placed over them. The faces of the gun embrasures were protected by cotton bales stiffened with dried mud. As Jackson's defenses grew, he continued to send "hunting parties" into the British lines every night. His men lay still in the cane stubble between the lines, rising suddenly to shoot or tomahawk a careless sentry.

On the British side Cochrane's sailors had brought off an incredible feat of labor, bringing forward naval guns from the fleet seventy miles away. On New Year's Eve, a black and foggy night, these big pieces of ordnance were put into position seven hundred yards away from the Americans. Protected by mounds of earth and hogsheads of sugar, the British guns were to silence the American artillery and blast a breach in the rampart through which the redcoats, their bellies now pinched by hunger, might stream to victory.

New Year's Day, 1815, was still foggy. Nevertheless, General Andrew Jackson persisted in his intention to review his troops. Visitors from the city, among them ladies, streamed into the camp. A band played. Troops assigned to parade had cleaned up their uniforms. Suddenly the fog became suffused with scarlet, there came a thunder that was not the roll of drums, and as the mist became slashed with showers of rockets and civilians went scurrying frantically cityward while soldiers sprinted for the ramparts, the British bombardment began to work over the American camp.

One hundred balls struck and shattered Jackson's headquarters, a supply boat was crippled, cotton bales on the ramparts were set ablaze, a gun carriage was shattered, a 32- and a 12-pounder were knocked out, and a caisson loaded with ammunition was blown up. With that, the British infantry waiting to attack sent up a cheer, and their gunners, satisfied that they had silenced the enemy, suspended fire. To their astonishment, through clouds of billowing, pungent smoke that blotted out everything, came the American answering fire.

It began faintly at first and then rose with a gradually ascending roar. Converging from Jackson's line and the batteries across the river, fifteen guns in all answered Britain's twenty-four, and Subaltern Gleig has described their effect:

> The enemy's shot penetrated these sugar-hogsheads as if they had been so many empty casks, dismounting our guns and killing our artillery-men in the very centre of their works. There could be small doubt, as soon as these facts were established, how the cannonading would end. Our fire slackened every moment; that of the Americans became every moment more terrible, till at length, after not more than two hours and a half of firing, our batteries were all silenced. The American works, on the other hand, remained as little injured as ever, and we were completely foiled.

The Dirty Shirts had slugged toe to toe with the pride of the fleet and driven them to cover, and Andrew Jackson jubilantly wished his troops a Happy New Year with the message: "Watch Word: Fight On— The Contractor will issue half a gill of whiskey around."

A week passed during which both sides were reinforced: a brigade for the British, 2,400 Kentuckians for the Americans. Pakenham now had about 8,000 men and Jackson 5,700, although Old Hickory was startled to hear that most of his Kentuckians were unarmed.

"I don't believe it," he exclaimed. "I have never seen a Kentuckian without a gun and a pack of cards and a bottle of whiskey in my life."

Nevertheless, only one man in three had a firearm, so Jackson sent about 500 of them across the river to act as reserve for the 550 Louisiana militia who defended Patterson's batteries there under Brigadier General David Morgan. For a while Jackson was undecided about where to expect the enemy's next attack. News that the British were dragging boats from Lake Borgne to the Mississippi suggested that they might cross the river to strike Morgan. But then the sight of redcoats bundling cane stalks into fascines and making ladders made it clear that the enemy might try to cross the canal and scale the rampart of Jackson's main position.

In truth, Pakenham meant to do both. The boats were for Colonel William Thornton to take 1,400 men across the river to overwhelm Morgan, seize the guns and turn them on Jackson's rear. Meanwhile, three columns would hit the canal and rampart: General Keane on the British left by the river, Major General Sir Samuel Gibbs on the right by the swamp, and Major General John Lambert in the center to be rushed wherever needed. It was a good plan, especially the cross-river thrust for the American guns. Artillery playing on Jackson's rear could be decisive. However, British fear of Dirty Shirt marksmanship had dictated that the assault take place in the confusion of darkness.

At the outset Thornton got only half of his men into boats on time and was quickly swept downriver below his landing place. Then Gibbs on the right discovered that his men had forgotten their fascines and ladders. Before dawn broke, only Keane on the left was ready. Nevertheless, Pakenham fired a rocket, that *"fatal ever fatal rocket"* signaling the attack of January 8.

Andrew Jackson and his aides had been up since one o'clock in the morning inspecting the line. They came to one of the Baratarian batteries. It was commanded by Dominique You and manned by the eighty Laffite men who had been freed from jail to fight the British. Dominique's red-shirts were cooking coffee, and Jackson said, "That smells like better coffee than we get. Smuggle it?"

Dominique grinned. "Mebbe so, General," he replied, filling a cup for his commander.

"I wish I had five hundred such devils in the butts," Jackson muttered, passing on until he came to his Tennesseans under Coffee and Carroll on the left. He was there, standing on the parapet, when Pakenham's rocket burst in a bluish-silver shower overhead. Another from Keane answered from the riverbank, and Jackson peered intently into the opaque wall of mist before him. Then a providential breeze sprang up, opening patches in the fog through which Jackson could now see the British advancing.

They were coming through a cane stubble silvery with frost. They came on bravely, crossbelts forming a white X on scarlet tunics, and Jackson issued the order: "Aim above the cross plates."

American cannon spoke first, then the British answered, and the fog again glowed red. Soon smoke spoiled the aim of the American riflemen, and Jackson ordered two leftward batteries to cease firing. The air cleared and the British could be seen coming at a run three hundred yards away. American cannon to Jackson's right angled a scything fire into the British ranks. The red ranks shuddered, closed up, and came on. Now the gleaming cross plates were just a hair above the sights of American rifles.

"*Fire!*"

Flame and flash and single crack, and the first rank of riflemen stepped down to reload while the second took its place.

"*Fire!*"

The second rank gave way to the third.

"*Fire!*"

Scarlet coats lay crumpled among the stubble. Gibbs's oncoming column had been splayed out into skirmish line as though a giant hand had slapped it. Again and again the American fire ripped into them, until the foreranks turned to the rear. "Never before had British veterans quailed," an English officer wrote later. "The leaden torrent no man on earth could face."

Sir Edward Pakenham came galloping up to his shattered right flank, had his horse shot dead beneath him, and flung himself upon his aide's black pony. A second assault was formed, led by a "praying regiment" of Highlanders, every man six feet tall—coming on with swinging kilts, and going down among the silver stubble. Perhaps seventy of these brave men gained the bank of the canal, perhaps thirty got across it and clambered up the parapet. But none of them survived.

That was the end of Gibbs's attack. Gibbs himself was dying, Keane had been shot through the neck, and Pakenham had received his third and mortal wound. On the British left a splendid charge had carried through an American bastion, but penetrated no farther. In the center, General Lambert ignored Pakenham's dying orders to throw in the reserve and began withdrawing the stricken British army from the field.

In all, the British had suffered more than two thousand casualties against only eight Americans killed and thirteen wounded. At half-past eight it was all over at the Rodriguez Canal. "I never had so grand and awful an idea of the resurrection," said General Jackson, "as ... [when] I saw ... more than five hundred Britons emerging from the heaps of their dead comrades, all over the plain rising up, and ... coming forward ... as prisoners."

• • •

The battle was not entirely over. Across the river, Colonel Thornton drove steadily through Morgan's militia. Jackson's elation over the British failure at his main position changed to alarm as he saw the Americans across the river give way completely. Cross-river cannon fire still raking the British in front of Jackson suddenly ceased. Captain Patterson was spiking his guns. Night came and Jackson still held his breath. He had moved too late to counter Thornton, and now the British held an advantage that might easily be exploited. But in the morning Lambert recalled Thornton to the east bank. On the night of January 18, leaving their campfires burning, the British returned the way they had come. Ahead of them went the body of General Pakenham "in a casket of rum to be taken to London. What a sight for his wife who is aboard and who had hoped to be Governess of Louisiana."

The British War Office's experiment in allowing a sailor to command on land had ended this time in a bloody boomerang.

Three days later the majestic notes of the "Te Deum" reverberated around the stone walls of St. Louis cathedral in New Orleans.

On February 13, 1815, the news of the Treaty of Ghent reached a rejoicing Washington. Four days later President James Madison declared the War of 1812 at an end.

~IV~

THE WAR
WITH MEXICO

*Poor Mexico! So far from God,
and so close to the United States!*

52

Westward, Ho!

~ In February of 1815, a week after the War of 1812 came to an end, Napoleon Bonaparte escaped from Elba. Four months later he met the Duke of Wellington at Waterloo and went down to his last defeat.

Thus ended the Anglo-French duel that had extended over nearly two centuries. Six times—four times with the British, twice against them—the Americans had been drawn into that worldwide conflict; but now this new nation, hating war yet born and bred to battle, was at last free of "the broils of Europe."

America was free because Waterloo had conferred upon Britain an immense, worldwide prestige and had ushered in the Pax Britannica, that relatively peaceful century during which Britannica "controlled extra-European events and localized European wars." It is one of the great paradoxes of American history that the British navy, which had so insulted America by its insistence on the right to impress her seamen, would now by its mastery of the seas enable the United States to embark unmolested upon an era of territorial expansion and internal development.

The year 1815, then, was a great turning point. Relations with Great Britain became friendly, and the so-called Era of Good Feelings commenced with the election of James Monroe as president in 1816. So also began a spirit of nationalism, which seems to have sprung from the common experience through which Americans had just passed as well as from a reaction against the selfish sectional strife that had characterized the war. Albert Gallatin, returning from Ghent, said this of his countrymen: "They are more American; they feel and act more like a nation; and I hope that the permanency of the Union is thereby better secured."

Nationalism buried the states' rights Federalists in the grave dug by the Hartford Convention. Once nationalism had been the very soul of Federalism, as it was the *bête noire* of Republicanism, but the Federalists had since shifted to states' rights, and the Republicans, observing to what depth their rivals had been interred, quickly switched to nationalism. The movement's leaders, John Calhoun and Henry Clay, had a formula called "the American system," which included a protective tariff for the manufacturing industry developed during the war, a home market for national products and improved transportation.

Good transportation was vital to the new westward surge begun when American settlers flowed into the lands taken from Tecumseh and the Creeks. Four new states—Indiana (1816), Mississippi (1817), Illinois (1818) and Alabama (1819)—were admitted to the union. Unfortunately, territorial expansion raised the ghost of slavery extension. An even balance between slave and free states had been maintained by alternately admitting slave-soil and free-soil territories. After Alabama's entry there were eleven each. But then, in 1819, Missouri sought admission as a slave state, and this most divisive of sectional issues came alive with an acrimonious vigor that threatened to shatter the nationalist honeymoon.

Outraged Northerners insisted that the entry of Missouri, which lay north of the line then dividing slavery and freedom, was a Southern attempt to increase its voting power. Southerners, who had not yet come to defending slavery on moral grounds, claimed that they had the right to take their property, i.e., slaves, into Missouri. Both sides talked secession. Eventually the Missouri Compromise was agreed upon. Under its terms, Missouri was admitted as a slave-holding state, while Maine, which had detached itself from Massachusetts, was admitted as a free state. More important, slavery was prohibited in unorganized territory north of Missouri's southern boundary of 36°36'. Thus the South provided for the eventual admission of Florida and Arkansas as slave states, while the North guaranteed freedom in the huge unsettled stretches of U.S. territory.

Whatever the Missouri Compromise may have done in restoring a fatally deceptive tranquillity to the Era of Good Feelings, it had also driven home for the first time the fact that slavery was not a political or economic problem but a moral one. Thomas Jefferson saw this, and wrote: "This momentous question, like a fire bell in the night, awakened and filled me with terror. I considered it at once as the knell of the Union." John Quincy Adams, now secretary of state, informed his diary: "I take it for granted that the present question is a mere preamble—a title page to a great, tragic volume." Much of the dreadfully involved wrangle over Missouri was actually a struggle to control the trans-Mississippi West, an area finally delineated by Adams after Jackson tore Florida out of the hands of Spain.

In the fall of 1817 the first of the wars with the Seminole Indians broke out, and Andrew Jackson marched to battle again at the head of about 2,500 Tennessee militia. Breaking the power of the Seminoles, he kept marching south until he had taken Pensacola and ejected its Spanish governor, after which he went back to Tennessee a hero. In Washington, however, there were powerful men who remembered Julius Caesar and wished to have Jackson disgraced or at least reprimanded.

Adams was not one of them. He stood behind Old Hickory, insisting that Spain had long ago shown her inability to govern Florida. Spain seemed to agree, for negotiations to sell the troublesome province were begun. They concluded in the Transcontinental Treaty of February 1819, under which, in return for $5 million, Spain ceded all her lands east of the Mississippi together with her claims to the Oregon territory. The treaty also traced the boundary between the United States and Mexico, and because it recognized an American line to the Pacific running west from the Rockies along the forty-second parallel, it made the United States of America a continental power. Mexico, however, the last Spanish province in North America, remained enormous. It included not only its present-day lands but the modern American states of California, Nevada, Utah, Arizona, New Mexico, Texas and parts of Wyoming and Colorado. Mexico was roughly equal in size to the United States itself—bigger if the Oregon territory that America jointly claimed with Britain were excluded—and Mexico a few years later was herself a free republic.

Mexican independence climaxed a seven-year eruption of revolutions that convulsed Latin America after the fall of Napoleon. One by one, under the leadership of José de San Martín, Simón Bolívar and Bernardo O'Higgins, Spain's colonies in the New World renounced allegiance to the mother country and set themselves up as free republics. Unfortunately, they did not unite as the North American colonies had. Such a multiplicity of young and unsteady republics, all open to the intrigues as well as the commerce of the older powers, created a dangerously unstable situation. Britain took the lead in attempting to stabilize it by asking the United States to join her in a declaration barring France from South America. But the Americans went Mother England one better. They decided to bar *everyone* from South America, and on December 2, 1823, in his annual message to Congress, President Monroe laid down the Monroe Doctrine warning all European powers against attempting to interfere with nations in the "Western Hemisphere." The United States, of course, had no power to enforce such a declaration. Only British sea power was capable of patrolling the shores of both continents. Yet Britain was at that moment deeply interested in preserving the peace in South America, just as she was not interested in expanding at the expense of the new Latin republics. So the Monroe Doctrine stood up—propped up, as it were, by the British navy—gradually solidifying into one of the pillars of foreign policy as the U.S. grew in power and prestige.

On this note, the Era of Good Feelings came to an end.

53

Mexico and Santa Anna

∿ From the final destruction of the Aztec Empire by Hernando Cortés in 1521 to the successful revolt against Spain exactly three centuries later there are two words to describe the country now known as Mexico: *instability* and *chaos*.

In the beginning the Spanish colony of New Spain was a society of conflicting loyalties and interests and a fragmented culture. Unlike the eventual United States to the north, where British colonists replaced—or exterminated—the native Amerindians, the Spanish colonists, having brought with them few women, mingled and mixed with the Aztecs so that the new society was a blend of the two.

Mexicans of pure Spanish blood were a distinct minority. By 1846, the year in which the War with Mexico erupted, two million of Mexico's seven million people were Mestizos, that is, persons of mixed Spanish and Aztec (Amerindian) blood, and four million undiluted Amerindians—leaving only one million of pure Spanish blood. Incredible as it may seem to most Americans, race was of little importance in the Mexican society of that time, although the native Aztecs though converted in the main to Catholicism had no real standing. Place of origin was more important: whether one was of Spanish blood but born in Spain (Gapuchíne) or of the same race but born in Mexico (Creole). The Gapuchínes considered themselves socially superior to all, and therefore though willing to dirty their hands with filthy lucre did not deign to smear them with the muck of politics; and as a result, power gradually drifted away from them. After the revolution of 1821 every Mexican president came from the ranks of the Creole.

Before then political power had resided in the hands of the Spanish viceroy, and although he did provide a measure of stability, the royal rod of the Spanish crown was never fully accepted in Mexico, especially by the Amerindians. Because the viceroy's control was tenuous, there were revolts, and these were always put down by Creole generals at the head of an army of peasants and Amerindians. Thus Spain ruled Mexico by mercenaries in the pay of the Crown.

Inevitably, these Creole army officers became creatures of privilege, along with the hierarchy of the Roman Catholic Church, an almost exact copy of the Altar that supported the Throne in Spain. Both soldiers and priests enjoyed the *fuero*, an incredible privilege guaranteeing immunity from the courts. In defense of the Church, it may be said that it did try to serve the people, at least providing the oppressed with their only glimpse of beauty and splendor through their access to the great and ornate cathedrals. Even the small whitewashed chapels were centers of devotion with a sense of community and dignity, although they were seldom staffed by resident pastors. Usually they were visited at intervals as infrequent as a year apart, and the priest—a Franciscan or Dominican—who formally married a couple through the sacrament of matrimony might also confer the sacrament of baptism on their children. Latins were not then nor are they now quite as squeamish about these formalities as the Christian races of western and northern Europe. Thus it could be said of the lower-class Mexican that he had two homes: the hovel where he lived and the place where he worshiped and told his beads.

Though the cults of saints proliferated in Mexico, it cannot be said that many of them were drawn from the hierarchy, more preoccupied with preserving their own privileges and comforts than in defending the downtrodden or raising their living standards.

By the beginning of the nineteenth century the gulf between rich and poor, privileged and exploited, was so wide in Mexico that rebellion against the Gapuchínes—for they were the chief beneficiaries of every injustice—was inevitable. The first erupted in 1810 when a poor parish priest named Miguel Hidalgo y Castillo was induced to join a group of revolutionary officers plotting against the viceroy. Father Hidalgo was a man of great personal charm, though naive politically. He did not understand the depth of the hatred of the Amerindians for all whites, believing that when they rose they would only kill

Gapuchínes while sparing the Creoles. But after he seized Guanajuato his Amerindians slaughtered every white in the city. This so shocked Hidalgo that he lost control of his followers and also—it seemed—of his mind. Captured in Chihuahua in 1811 he was executed and his head displayed on a post in Guanajuato for ten years.

Next came Father José María Morelos y Pavón. More realistic and practical, Morelos turned his followers against Spain and defined his objectives, thus managing to last until his own capture and execution in 1815. Six years later the revolution finally succeeded, not as a revolt of the masses but from the disenchantment of the privileged, who, feeling that a new and less oppressive government in Spain might deprive them of their "rights," turned against the viceroy. General Agustín de Iturbide simply changed sides, taking his soldiers with him, and proclaiming the Plan of Iguala: recognition of the Catholic Church, independence from Spain and union of Gapuchínes and Creoles. He also called for a constitutional monarchy, but when he could not find a suitable Spanish nobleman willing to serve him as the puppet king, he proclaimed himself emperor.

The United States was first to recognize Mexico as a sovereign state, but Iturbide's absurd imperial posture did not keep him long in power. Within a year he was ousted and when he foolishly returned to Mexico in 1824, he was captured and executed. Unfortunately for America's unhappy neighbor to the south, the procession of revolts and civil wars fought among Creole generals anxious to obtain the title of *El Presidente* had already begun. Most successful of them all, as well as the most frequent occupant of the presidential chair, was a military Creole adventurer named Antonio Lopez de Santa Anna.

Antonio López de Santa Anna is believed to have been born in 1795 in the white-washed, sun-bathed little city of Jalapa northwest of Veracruz on the Gulf of Mexico. Eventually he would own much of the land surrounding this paradise perched among steep green hills, and when fortune turned against him as it frequently did, he would retire there to nurse his wounded soul; but in his youth this arrogant schoolboy despised Jalapa and yearned "to leave heaven for earth." He was especially outraged when his father suggested that he enter the employ of a merchant as a clerk, and he vowed that he would never be a "counter jumper" in a village store. Instead, he wanted to see the world—preferably as an officer in the Royal Spanish Army. In 1810 with his father's permission he enrolled in the elite military academy in Vera Cruz.

At fifteen Antonio was approaching maturity and would grow into a man of great physical presence, broad-shouldered and muscular, much taller than the average Mexican, with fine, dark eyes that were soft or penetrating by turns. His voice was deep and melodious, and in repose his handsome face touched with melancholy.

It was in 1813 that Santa Anna first encountered American soldiers. They were not truly trained regulars but rather filibusters, or freebooters from the Dutch word *vrijbuiter*—land pirates marching and fighting for gain, willing to rent their muskets to the highest bidder. They had been recruited by the Mexican rebel Bernardo Gutierrez de Lara, who had escaped from Mexico and gone to Washington to plead with Secretary of State Monroe for aid. Monroe could not give him much, the United States being then reeling under a string of early defeats in the War of 1812. Yet, being the republican par excellence, Monroe could not turn the Mexican rebel away empty-handed. So he supplied him with money and munitions, plus American officers to lead his ragtag motley of military mercenaries and Mexican rebels. Gutierrez became a figurehead, merely tagging along "to give a Mexican character to the army," and thus not anger Spain. But the Spanish viceroy in Mexico City was not deceived, and after the invaders captured Goliad and San Antonio, inflicting horrible atrocities on their enemies, he sent General Joaquín de Arredondo north to crush them. With Arredondo rode the nineteen-year-old Lieutenant Antonio Santa Anna.

By April 1814 Gutierrez's army had swelled to 1,500 men, including 850 Americans—almost all of them irregulars notorious for their dedicated debauchery. In August this force collided with Arredondo's army near the Medina River and were all but annihilated. Of the 250 Americans still alive another 150 were massacred while in flight, "cut . . . in quarters, and suspended on poles and limbs of trees, like beef or pork for the packer. . . ." From the Medina, Lieutenant Santa Anna earned an *escudo* (decoration) for bravery, but more important for his military career he learned valuable lessons: how to conduct a major campaign hundreds of miles from base, how to guard against ambush or to deceive the enemy with feints or false retreats, how the bayonet and the lance in the warfare of the day were the true arbiters of battle. The bayonet and the lance . . . burned deep into the back of his brain was the sight of those screaming, terrified, American filibusters being overtaken by Mexican infantry and lancers and spitted from behind like so many fleeing pigs. From this, Santa Anna became convinced that Americans were a contemptible rabble and could never stand up to regular troops.

After the Medina, Santa Anna demonstrated that no officer in Mexico could match the astonishing agility with which he could change sides. His career became an incredible checkerboard of blacks and whites; black when he barely escaped conviction on a charge of forging his commander's name to a bank draft to cover gambling debts; white one morning in March 1821, when the Spanish promoted him from captain to lieutenant colonel for having crushed a rebel force; and whiter still that afternoon when he joined the rebel Iturbide and was promoted by him to full colonel. After Iturbide proclaimed himself emperor, he promoted the twenty-eight-year-old Santa Anna to brigadier general. It was not really a great honor, inasmuch as every officer or NCO in either the loyalist or rebel army had no more than two privates to command; and the army of the later republic would have twenty-four-thousand officers and only twenty-thousand enlisted men, and the phrase "Like a Mexican army" would describe armed forces topheavy with rank. But Santa Anna sought higher rank, celebrating Iturbide's ascension to the imperial crown in 1822 by writing him a letter of congratulations packed with no less than seven hundred superlatives. Iturbide liked that, but when his fawning young admirer begged for the hand of his sister Doña Nicolosa—a sixty-year-old hag—His Imperial Majesty choked and with splendid sarcasm replied that he could not permit her to marry a commoner. Unblushing, Santa Anna solemnly swore: "I am and will be throughout life and till death your loyal Defender and Subject." Such a splendid protestation of loyalty should have warned the emperor: a few months later his ever-faithful subject and dauntless defender led a successful revolt against him.

During the next decade Santa Anna was either leading a revolt or repulsing one, his dexterity unchallenged in a land where political agility was regarded as the premier skill and few generals were ever guilty of obeying an order. Between April 1829 and December 1844, fourteen different men held the presidency, which changed hands twenty times while the national treasury had exactly double that number of chiefs. The average life of an administration was seven and one-half months.

In 1832 Santa Anna was again on top: a patriotic Cincinnatus loath to leave his plow at Jalapa, but deeply mindful of his responsibility to lead his country out of chaos. Clothed in a liberal toga, he solemnly promised: "My whole ambition is restricted to beating my sword into a plowshare." To the conservative generals and clergy who denounced his liberal new policies, he issued the warning: "I swear to you that I oppose all efforts aimed at destruction of the Constitution and that I would die before accepting any other power than that designated by it." The soldiers and the priests exchanged winks, for they knew that *El Caudillo* (the leader) was already dickering with them to do the opposite. Two years later in 1834—scenting no new rebellion on the political winds, convinced that he was firmly in the saddle—he reversed course, scrapping his liberal program, annulling the Constitution of 1824 with its emphasis on state's rights, and remodeling the government along "centralist" lines: meaning that he was now the dictator and all power resided in the capital.

As a general, Santa Anna was at least the equal of any commander in Mexico, and probably better than most. His boldness and presence lifted the hearts of an army accustomed to corrupt show-offs. His resonant voice thrilled his soldiers and his marvelous sense of timing not only improved his skill as a military leader but also made of him an adroit politican. When out of power he would retire to Jalapa patiently waiting until whomever ousted him had so thoroughly alienated the population that all Mexico would be begging him to return to the capital. Back in command, he cultivated the adulation of the poor and oppressed, for he had learned when he built eight villages for them during a seven-year stint at Veracruz how grateful they could be. But he did not seek their company or share their misery like a true missionary, rather appearing among them as though he were the reincarnation of El Cid, mounted on a splendid horse and always accompanied by an escort of thirty dragoons, their bright helmet plumes waving and their bared sabers and breastplates gleaming in the sun. For his own relaxation Santa Anna preferred the company of the wealthy and the privileged, for excitement the flying feathers and blood of the cockpit from which his unrivaled collection of fighting cocks usually emerged cocka-doodle-dooing in triumph, and for pleasure the charms of beautiful and obliging young ladies.

Showman that he was, he was also a monster of vanity. The equipage of his stable of thoroughbreds was heavy with precious metal and stones, and the frogging and epaulets of his uniform so plastered with silver that they could be melted down for a complete service of flatware. Because he had himself toadied his way to the top, he was susceptible to flattery. Subordinates eager for promotion competed with one another in reminding him how much he resembled Napoleon or in presenting him with statuettes of the Corsican conqueror suitably clothed in Mexican colors. Yet, it was a mistake to deride or underestimate this complicated man. His energy was boundless, and his power of organization something entirely new in the annals of Mexican arms.

Santa Anna's resourcefulness as a commander was legendary. During one siege he dressed in women's clothing to spy on the enemy, and when his army ran short of cash—not a rare occurrence during Mexican civil wars—he dressed a company of soldiers in monk's clothes and ordered them to rob a churchful of enemy soldiers, stealing alms intended for the holy places of Jerusalem. His escapes were not only legion but sometimes laughable: defeated in 1832, he trailed the victorious enemy up a road, stopping at the home of a local mayor to claim that he had triumphed and was pursuing the routed enemy.

Like so many other Mexican generals, Santa Anna was as ardent in the boudoir as on the battlefield, as the numerous Mestizos born of the Aztec girls around his country estate might testify. He acknowledged none of them and also rejected the "afflicted" child among the five born to him by his tall and thin wife Inés García de Santa Anna, a woman beloved throughout Mexico.

Such was the man who was in power when the American settlers in Texas rose in rebellion against Mexico.

54

"Go-Aheads" and "GTTs"

〜 MEXICO AND THE UNITED STATES WERE SISTER REPUBLICS IN NAME
only. A better term is neighboring republics: they bordered each other
from the Pacific to the Gulf, that was all.

One spoke English, the other Spanish; one was Protestant, the
other Catholic; one, colonized on British lines, was organized by a
strong federal government, was energetic, proliferating and expanding; and the other, colonized in the Roman way, had little unity, was
torpid, thinly populated, and already weakened by an oppressive
clergy and upper class and by the immemorial Latin custom of celebrating today's revolution by toasting tomorrow's. Such differences
were not disputes, and none was a valid reason for going to war. But
the two republics were neighbors—one strong, the other weak—and it
is only in recent times, under the Sign of the Mushroom Cloud, that
strong neighbors have acted as though they thought they should feed
rather than eat the weak. In a sense, Mexico was to America what Ireland was to England. Again, it was a geographical fact, sheer proximity; Americans had yearned for Canada, and now, in the two decades
(1825–45) following Monroe's administration, they turned their eyes
from their northeastern border to the southwestern one.

This desire was never so conscious or deliberate as the War-Hawk
raid on Upper Canada. Neither was the American government—at
least not before President Polk—actually its instrument. Its agents—it

might almost be said its advance guard or fifth column—were the frontiersmen and backwoodsmen who crossed the Mississippi hungering for land and came upon the outposts of Mexico.

The Mexican provinces of New Mexico, Upper California,* and Coahuila-Tejas† (Texas) were sparsely populated and bound to the federal government in Mexico City by the most distant and tenuous ties. Neither California nor New Mexico encouraged immigration, but in Texas immigrants were not only welcomed but actually imported from the neighboring United States. Why, it is difficult to determine. Even if it were imperative for Mexico to populate its vast and empty lands, it would seem that the place to recruit immigrants would be in southern Europe, where in France, Spain and Italy they would find people more nearly Mexican in customs, race and religion. But the only Europeans so encouraged were a few Germans. In the main it was *los Yanquis* who poured into Texas.

In the half century since the vast territory called Louisiana came under Spanish rule in 1763, the viceroys of New Spain allowed the northernmost provinces to sink into desuetude and decay. There were so few people in Coahuila and Texas that they were joined into one with a capital at Saltillo. In Texas missions and settlements were abandoned and the population declined until only a handful of native-born Tejanos were living in the tiny towns of San Antonia de Baxar (now plain San Antonio), La Bahia (now Goliad) and Nacogdoches. It was not until 1821, when the last viceroy was driven from Mexico, that any attempt was made to revivify Texas. In that year one of the last acts of the last viceroy was to grant colonization right to a series of *empresarios,* or immigrant recruiters. The first of these was Moses Austin, a Connecticut-born entrepreneur from Missouri. Two years later, after Moses Austin died, these rights passed to his son, Stephen, the man for whom the modern capital of Texas is named.

Under the leadership of Stephen Austin and the other *empresarios* who followed him the settlement of Texas experienced an astonishing growth, so much so that it became a bone of contention between the Abolitionists and the so-called "Slavocracy" in the great propaganda struggle culminating in the American Civil War. Because the American colonists brought slaves with them in violation of the Mexican laws prohibiting bondage, Abolitionists in the Northern free states maintained that colonization of Texas by American slaveholders was a plot of "the slave power" to extend its influence into new cotton-growing territory.

---

* There were two Californias, Lower and Upper, the latter being the modern American state.
† *Tejas* is a native word for "friend" or "ally."

If anything, however, it is much more likely that the existence of slavery in the South retarded rather than hastened expansion in the Southwest. Settlement of Texas was simply another step in the westward march of America from the eastern seaboard to the western ocean. It occurred in the free-soil North as well as in the slave-soil South, and the lure in both cases was simply land and the motivation was individual. Settlers in Texas were no more agents of the Slavocracy than those in Missouri were the advance guards of Abolition. Throughout the history of Texas—in its colonization, its brief independence, and its longer life as an American state—there were few, if any, planters in the ducal Southern style, living on vast plantations worked by hundreds of slaves. Actually, slavery on such a scale never would have worked in Texas for material reasons; the shortage of wood needed for fencing such vast holdings (barbed wire had not yet been invented), the fear of droughts and the absence of railroads. Texas, then, was a frontier—settled by frontiersmen in individualist style.

Certainly most of them were Southerners who came pouring over the Sabine River dividing Louisiana from Texas, or the Red River as it flowed through Arkansas or down the Gulf Coast from New Orleans; and it is also true that all of the emissaries to Mexico City prior to the outbreak of hostilities were Southerners, a fact that acted like an abrasive on the super-sensitivities of those self-righteous Abolitionists; but there is also no doubt that the settlers who crossed the Mississippi into Missouri and Iowa and beyond were indubitable free-soilers from the north. The explanation, then, is proximity, not conspiracy.

Nevertheless, no area in North America filled up as rapidly as Texas. By 1834 Stephen Austin's colony numbered twenty-thousand Americans and two-thousand slaves and outnumbered the native Tejanos by four to one. Two years later there would be thirty-thousand Americans in Texas. Few of these pioneers fulfilled their pledge to become Catholics once they became Mexican citizens to obtain land, or abided by the Mexican prohibition of slavery. If reproached for this dual duplicity, they complained that as much as they tried to adhere to the laws of their new home, they were forever changing in the wake of the latest revolution. This, of course, was sophistry pure and simple. The true explanation of their indifference to the criticism of their adopted countrymen was that, much as they might admire, say, their skillful horsemanship—unrivaled anywhere else in the world—they had the Anglo-Saxon's deep-seated faith in the superiority of the fair-skinned races, and soon came to despise their darker brethren as "greasers"—"Squeeze a Mexican, we need the oil!"—a lazy, light-fingered, superstitious, priest-ridden people who didn't deserve and couldn't exploit the bountiful land they lived in. Such were the caricatures printed in the newspapers north of the border, along with this disparaging estimate of the Tejano made by a Mexican critic: "The character of the people is carefree. They are enthusiastic dancers, very fond of luxury, and the worst punishment that can be inflicted on them is work."

For their part, the Hispanic estimate of their unwelcome Anglo-Saxon visitors was that they were the descendants of Godless plunderers, subjects of the Pirate Queen (Elizabeth), who robbed Spanish bullion ships on the high seas and roamed the Gulf Coast sacking peaceful villages, pillaging and desecrating Catholic churches, raping pious women, carrying off cattle with their sea bags stuffed and clanking with gold and silver chalices and candlesticks stolen from church altars.

Within the United States there were many Americans who actually believed that Texas by right belonged to America. In 1805 when Jefferson was president the government contemplated an invasion of the department. The plan was for a U.S. Army invading force to make a surprise crossing of the Sabine, destroying Spanish forts and scattering their garrisons, and then quickly returning whence they came. It would be nothing less than a punitive expedition aimed at frightening Spain into a quick cession of Texas. Fortunately, Secretary of State Madison working quietly behind the scenes—and also having the friendly and familiar ear of his close friend Jefferson—scuttled the proposal. Nevertheless there were still plenty of those "expansionists"—who today would be called super-patriots—who insisted that the "natural border" of the United States reached clear to the Isthmus of Panama.

After John Quincy Adams was elected president in 1824 he offered to buy the province. So did Andrew Jackson following his election in 1828. Both times Mexico angrily rejected the offer, although Old Hickory to his dying day still firmly believed—without a shred of evidence in maps, titles or treaties—that the Louisiana Purchase extended all the way to the Rio Grande. Meanwhile, *empresarios* such as Stephen Austin were still diligently and quietly recruiting American immigrants to colonize the land. At first they were peaceful pioneers eager to acquire grants of that fantastic virgin soil of the river valleys, chocolate-brown bottomland ideal for growing cotton. But then they were joined by their unsavory migratory twins, those hard-drinking, straight-shooting, land-grabbing, fork-tongued younger brothers of those "ring-tailed roarers, half-horse and half-alligator" who had fought under Jackson at Talladega, Horseshoe Bend and New Orleans. They were called "Go-Aheads" and "GTTs" and it was they—not their decent, hard-working, God-fearing forerunners—who were to tear the great state of Texas out of the bleeding side of the Republic of Mexico.

• • •

It was the jolly Tennessee frontiersman Davey Crockett who coined the phrase "Go Ahead," when he arrived in Washington to take his seat in the U.S. House of Representatives where his mentor and benefactor Andrew Jackson had placed him. Rosy-cheeked but respectable—not clothed in the linsey-woolsey hunting shirt or fringed buckskin jacket of legend—but wearing a sober, dark, high-necked frock coat like any other congressman, Crockett gave the frontiersmen their motto when he wrote: "I leave this rule for others when I am dead/Be sure you are always right, then go ahead."

Go Ahead! It was like a spiritual summons, the sort of call from on high that had led Moses up the slopes of Mount Sinai. To them it meant simply, "Take all you can get!" Their forebears had shaken off the rule of Old Mother England and made the eastern seaboard of North America their own, and now they would flow toward the setting sun and the western ocean to make that coast and everything in-between America.

Land-fever was the consuming disease of the eighteenth century in America: first there was Kentucky Fever and then Ohio Fever, which was followed by Illinois Fever and Missouri Fever. But the greatest delirium of all was Texas Fever.

Following the Go-Aheads were the GTTs, an acronym for "Gone to Texas," a farewell to a wife or a life of boredom chalked on cabin doors or scrawled across scraps of paper in unsteady hands more familiar with bridle reins or pistol butts than pen or pencil. GTT—it was like an obituary read by sobbing wives, infuriated lawyers, white-faced bankers closing out unpaid loans, frustrated sheriffs, bilked bail-bondsmen or preachers puzzled to find that the charming young fellow who had admitted to being the sire of the baby in the womb of his distressed young parishioner had no intention of "doing the right thing" by her. Those who were not fugitives from every sort of responsibility or crime were sly lawyers and greedy land-speculators who saw instinctively that a "free" Texas could be for them a gold-plated Texas. So they helped to organize these Go-Aheads and GTTs into what they called the War Party, but which was excoriated by disgusted early settlers as a group of War Dogs or Crazy-orians.

But they were not crazy in the sense of being aimless or not knowing what they were doing: they were just crazy for land. There was so much of it, millions of acres of fabulously fertile soil, selling at something like $12\frac{1}{2}$¢ an acre compared to the U.S. price of $1.25, and not in measly 80-acre lots but in whole leagues of 4,428 acres or more. To get it, all they had to do was turn Mexican: swear an oath to the young republic and promise to become a Catholic and obey Mexican laws against slavery. It was so easy for these basically dishonest and lawless men, these hard-bitten Celts from the Western Islands—English, Welsh, Scots and Irish—still mistakenly referred to as Anglo-Saxons. That was another great attraction about Texas: there was actually no law to restrain them, no nosy *alcaldes* sneaking around to make sure they went to Mass or freed their niggers. Here was an ideal climate for Go-Aheads, men on the run and looking for a fresh start. Moreover, it would not be land regulated by the latest government in far-off Mexico City, it would be *their* land and they would run it. They had a precedent and a model: Hernándo Cortés and his *conquistadores,* who had landed on these shores to wrest the country away from the Aztecs, claiming it for the kingdoms of Aragon and Castile. And they, the new breed of invader, would do the same to these feckless, fainéant descendants of those mighty warriors into whose feeble keeping the land had fallen, claiming it for themselves and the United States of America.

That was the unspoken ulterior motive dwelling in the hearts and minds of these War Dogs, these Crazy-orians—men like Jim Bowie of Louisiana and his brothers John and Rezin, Jr. Jim was the most famous of the trio, probably because of his invention of the Bowie knife. Actually it was a short sword, about ten to fifteen inches long, and was probably modeled on the Celtic *gladius,* the blade adopted by the Roman army. It had a tip about three inches long curving to a sharp point. No better blade for hand-to-hand fighting ever existed, although against a soldier's bayonet, a sailor's cutlass or a trooper's saber, it would be too short.

The Bowies led a wild youth in their native Georgia, roping deer, trapping bear and even riding alligators. Jim was six when the family moved to Louisiana, probably after his father was jailed for killing a squatter in a land dispute. Freed by his wife and an armed slave, Bowie, Senior, took his boys down to the bayou country. There they met the slave-smuggling Laffite brothers Jean and Pierre. The Lafittes' slaves would arrive in east Texas where the Bowies bought them at a dollar a pound, fattening these poor emaciated scarecrows like any drover "watering" his cattle so that upon delivery in Louisiana they averaged 140 pounds. Once across the border, the Bowies turned themselves into the authorities, a clever ploy by which they could claim the reward for their own incarceration: half the auction price of the confiscated slaves. This gave them a 50 percent advantage over rival bidders. Moreover, by buying their slaves back they received legal title to them, thus freeing them to sell the bondsmen on the legal market, showing an incredible profit of about a thousand dollars per slave.

Jim Bowie was a handsome man with thick jet-black hair and sideburns, regular features and hard gray eyes. He stood about six feet tall and weighed a muscular 180 pounds. Not powerful like Sam Houston, he was nevertheless extremely agile, tough and possessed of an incredible stamina. He was probably one of the most feared duelists in the South and Southwest and was even more accurate with a shoulder weapon—rifle or musket—than with a pistol. In 1828 he migrated to Texas, choosing San Antonio de Bexar as his theater of operations. There he ingratiated himself with Don Juan Martín de Veramendi, one of the wealthiest and most respected men in the department. With customary charm Jim pretended to be an American gentleman of great wealth, so successful in his protestations of love for Mexico that Veramendi and his wife stood as sponsors when Jim was baptized a Catholic. Next the artful Bowie met and mesmerized Veramendi's beautiful teenage daughter, Ursula. They were married in 1831.

Shortly afterward, Jim borrowed enough money from Ursula's father—then vice governor of Texas—to buy nearly fifty thousand acres of land at a nickle an acre. Irresistibly suave, he persuaded Veramendi's friends to apply for eleven-league grants also, selling him the titles, which he probably bought with his slave profits. In record time, Jim Bowie now owned 750,000 acres of Texas land. Obviously, he had neither the money nor the time nor the slaves available to work such an enormous holding. But Jim Bowie was not a planter at heart, but rather a shrewd speculator. If the thirty-thousand Americans then in Texas could shake off Mexican rule, there would be a great flood of settlers streaming over the border to whom he could sell land at profits beyond the dreams of avarice. If an independent Texas chose to join the American union, the land's value would at least double.

However, the restless James—who really had no money of his own then—could not wait for that to happen. Instead, using his father-in-law's estate as a base and his money as a stake, he spent the eighteen months following his marriage scurrying across the face of Mexico in search of abandoned Spanish gold and silver mines. If Jim were suave and deceitful, the defect of that unlovely talent was his gullibility. He actually believed that such treasures existed, as though the Spaniards would abandon a mine before exhausting it. Even so, he showed his gratitude to both his wife and his in-laws by drawing up a will leaving them exactly nothing—and that was hardly less than the "fortune" of seventy-seven dollars that he acquired after all his frantic pursuit of easy money. Just before Veramendi, his wife and the lovely Ursula died of cholera within three days of each other, the obliging señor replied in kind by disinheriting Bowie. So now Jim was left with what he had had in the beginning: nothing. Resourceful as ever, he sued the Veramendi estate for the sixty thousand acres of Arkansas land that supposedly had been his dowry from Ursula. No one in Mexico grieved when the court ruled against him.

Jim Bowie's only hope now lay with the War Dogs: successful rebellion would not only make him solvent again, it would spin his fortune in a 180-degree turn. So he became one of the arch-agitators at Washington-on-Brazos, a super-patriot wrapped in the Stars-and-Stripes and singing "The Star-Spangled Banner."

But the established American colonists of Texas had nothing but contempt for what seemed to them to be a new breed of *filibustero*. They knew what the Spanish had done to the swaggering, unvaliant freebooters of 1813, and if they had not witnessed their massacre, they at least had seen their skeletons as a reminder of what could happen should they too challenge established authority. Risk their splendid estates and their necks as well to satisfy the delusions of this latest crowd of greedy gallows-bait? *De nada.* Frustrated, many members of the War Party began to turn to the War Dog whose soaring ambition was matched only by the depth of his degradation: William Barret "Buck" Travis.

Buck Travis was a young, tall, good-looking lawyer essentially shallow and perhaps even somewhat effeminate, if he can be judged by his bergamot and lavender perfumes and his custom of coiling his red hair in equally fragrant ointment. He was born in 1809 in "Pandemonium," or "Home of the Devils," a nickname that religious revivalists bestowed on Edgefield County, South Carolina. In 1818 his family migrated to Alabama, settling in a wild wood inhabited by Creeks until the arrival of Andrew Jackson. Here they pitched a "pole shack" made of saplings with one side open to the weather, and a wagon canvas protecting the top and one side. Travis's parents planted corn in a clearing and with the money earned from a cash crop of cotton bought livestock for meat and milk. It was an existence hardly less primitive than the life of the Creeks who had preceded them, and it was far from satisfying to young Buck, who seems to have learned of a better world beyond the howling wilderness at the Sparta Academy kept by his Uncle Alex. There he absorbed the basics, plus a smattering of Greek and Latin. Next he became a schoolteacher at nearby Claiborne and then studied law under a local judge, being admitted to the bar before he was twenty.

Travis married one of his students, Rosanna Cato, daughter of a prosperous farmer. After the arrival of the first child, Buck Travis seemed happy and content. He joined the Masons and wangled a commission as adjutant of the local militia, while publishing a small newspaper called the Claiborne *Herald*. Its mast-head carried the strange motto *Thou Shalt Not Muzzle the Ox That Treadeth the Corn.* Here apparently was the typical careerist on his way. His next step should have been to announce his candidacy for the South Carolina legislature. Instead he became a GTT.

In 1831, with Rosanna in her fifth month with the second child and the first-born a toddler, with no explanation whatever, Travis went to Texas, traveling west in a wagon. Behind him in Claiborne, a flurry of rumors arose: Rosanna had been unfaithful; Buck had killed her lover, pinning the crime on an innocent slave; he had fled to avoid prosecution. Whatever the reason for his flight, Travis was a true GTT: a man without a past.

He arrived in east Texas in May 1831, promptly applying for a land grant. He listed himself as "single," and then later as "widower," perhaps to obtain another grant illegally. Settling first in the little port of Anahuac, he later moved to the larger town of San Felipe de Austin, center of Stephen Austin's colony. He hung out a law shingle and began to prosper, willing to take any case: recovering a stolen rifle . . . blocking the sale of a blind horse . . . drawing wills . . . No case was too trivial, no payment too small.

Living at a boardinghouse, he drank a little and gambled a lot, carefully cultivating the image of a new Buck Travis: an inveterate and fearless duelist (which he was not), a lady's man (which he definitely was), a gentleman and a dandy and an ardent devotee of the cause of an independent Texas. Although there were ten men for every woman in Texas, Travis was fondest of his portrait as the local Don Juan, recording every sexual conquest in his diary so that at the age of twenty-three he was able to post Number 56. Nevertheless he was a dashing figure in San Felipe, mounted on his black Spanish mare in his red pantaloons and affecting a big white sombrero to make himself appear taller. With a wide, sweeping, lordly gesture he would scatter small change among the barefoot Mexican children who ran yelling in his wake. In the evenings he usually trotted off to a rendezvous with some sloe-eyed señorita, bringing gifts of cologne or cinnamon—as well as venereal disease.

It is not generally known that many of the frontiersmen of the day were often victims of syphilis or gonorrhea, usually contracted during their relationships with Indian women. Bones of pre-Columbian Indians of the Southwest have been found to bear evidence of syphilis believed to have been introduced by the practice of bestiality: sexual intercourse with animals. When the infected explorers and their men returned to the Old World in the sixteenth century the affliction ravaged Europe. So too did it torment the frontiersmen. Treatment of either illness was usually by calomel (mercurous chloride)—the

"Sampson of the Drug Store"—a white powder taken internally, but with such disastrous results that the cure seemed worse than the cause. The effects of mercury poisoning include extreme abdominal pain, cramps, trembling, kidney failure, bloody diarrhea, derangement and death. Its psychological effects are loss of sleep, memory, confidence or sensory perception, confusion or emotional instability. These symptoms, so often confused with insanity, explain the phrase "Mad as a hatter"; for the fumes of mercury used in treating beaver pelts to make hats also caused mental disturbance. This was the powder that Travis and some of his fellow GTTs were swallowing.

Although Travis dreamed of military glory, he was, like almost all lovers, no fighter. In a case opposing another lawyer named Ephraim Roddy, he lost his temper and pulled a Bowie knife on him. Roddy grinned, drawing from his pocket a small, broken penknife he used to trim goose-quill pens.

"Your honor," Roddy told the judge, "owing to the discrepancy of our weapons, I cannot do opposing counsel much bodily harm, but if he insists upon it, I will try."

Blushing furiously at the ensuing laughter, Travis put away his butcher knife.

Nevertheless, Travis was welcomed by the War Party because of his seeming sophistication and because his constant reading had gained him the reputation of an intellectual, a habit of mind so rare on the frontier that most GTT did not know what the word meant. He read voraciously—Herodotus, Disraeli, Addison, Steele, Sir Walter Scott—and probably bought more candles to illuminate his pages than half the population of San Felipe combined. His favorite writer was Scott, the author of those Waverley novels then so popular in the South. It was from these romances that the Dixie planters found the threads with which to weave the "Moonlight and Magnolias" myth of a Southern aristocracy descended from those dashing Cavaliers who fought for King Charles I of England against the boorish and bloody-handed Roundheads of Oliver Cromwell. All the South's fondest themes were there: the glory of arms, sacred war, honor and the code duello, chivalrous knights wearing the colors of the purest ladies as they contended with the forces of evil; and, of course, undying loyalty to the Great Cause. In a sense Travis's propaganda for an independent Texas, which he wrote with a messianic fervor, knighted the rude frontiersmen: though he might ride in buckskin, his heart still beat with the high purpose of those champions who jousted in Arthurian armor. Thus enobled, the War Dogs needed only a dragon to slay, and this was provided by the Mexican government when it issued its draconic Law of April 6.

55

Texas Rebels!

~ THE LAW OF APRIL 6 WAS PROMULGATED AS THE RESULT OF A SCIEN-
tific expedition into Texas led by General Manuel de Mier y Terán in
1828. It was intended to assess the wealth and potential of the area,
but instead General Terán had returned to Mexico City deeply
shocked at what he saw among the growing population and power of
the American colonists there.

First, he realized that for the most part they absolutely ignored the
authority of the faraway federal government and were motivated by
the same fierce spirit of independence that had led their ancestors to
break away from Britain. Terán and his scientists were appalled by the
Americans' introduction of slaves into Texas, and indignant at their
arrogance. The town council of La Bahia informed him: "Let us be
honest with ourselves, Sir, the foreign *empresarios* are nothing more
than money-changing speculators caring for their own well-being and
hesitating not in their unbecoming methods." Even worse was the general immorality of the frontiersmen: in Nacogdoches some of the
Anglo-Americans were peddling their wives' charms to the Mexican
soldiers stationed there. The few native Mexicans still remaining had
been completely corrupted by the Yanquis, and Terán admitted that if
he were to judge his countrymen by these debased people he would

look down on them all. "Either the government occupies Texas now," he warned, "or it is lost forever...."

The new laws passed on April 6, 1830, stipulated a military occupation of Texas, an opening of Texas coastal trade, an introduction of European and Mexican colonists and finally the complete prohibition of further American immigration.

With these measures, the Texans realized that if they did not rebel, the days of wine and roses were over. They had found in the department not only access to huge tracts of cheap fertile land but a haven from U.S. tariffs, unrestricted passage between both countries and a lawless atmosphere in which *they* were the law. Now, no foreigners could cross the border without a passport and a Mexican visa and there would be no further importation of slaves. Moreover, the seven-year period free of tariffs on imported goods was about to expire, and there would be no renewal.

Of all these provisions the payment of duties was resented most deeply, even by the most decent and least hot-headed settlers. Although the War Dogs had magnified such complaints as the fact that the capital of Saltillo in Coahuila was hundreds of miles away, that legislative business was conducted solely in Spanish, that there was no trial by jury, and that there were no schools for their children, the imposition of tariffs with the consequent disappearance of cheaper smuggled goods was their most powerful issue. They succeeded in identifying it with the Stamp Act and other unpopular British taxes that provoked the American Revolution. The sending of troops to Texas to enforce the tariffs was considered perhaps an even greater grievance, much like the Coercive Acts imposed on Boston that brought the final break with Mother England.

No one was more enraged by the Law of April 6 than William Barret Travis. When in May of 1832 Colonel Juan Bradburn, the Mexican commander at Anahuac, launched a vigorous campaign against smuggling, Travis considered that the time had come for action. With his friend Patrick Jack he confronted Bradburn face-to-face to warn him that a hundred armed colonists would rise against him. Frightened, the colonel stayed up all night awaiting the attack. When it never came he learned that the threat was an empty one—or, worse, a practical joke—and he arrested both Travis and Jack. Now the colonists really rose. Hundreds of them converged on Bradburn's headquarters demanding the release of the two Texans. Bradburn pointed to Travis and Jack pinioned to the ground and threatened to kill them both if anyone fired a shot. Here was the dramatic moment that Travis cherished: he pleaded with his countrymen to open fire, for he would rather die a thousand deaths than see this tyrant live.

Instead the cooler-headed colonists laid siege to Anahuac. Soon similar groups were rising all over east Texas. War seemed imminent, but then Travis and Jack were released, Bradburn was replaced and an uneasy truce ensued. The explanation was that the latest revolution in Mexico City had ousted the fierce, American-hating Presidente Anastasio Bustamante and replaced him with the apparently milder General Santa Anna, a professed liberal and supposed friend of the Texans. As a sign of good faith, the tariff was abolished for two years.

Travis was disappointed. Worse, a person far more powerful and influential than he among the colonists had stepped forward: the *empresario* Stephen Austin. He had always believed in cooperating with the Mexican government and had signed his letters to the capital *Esteban* Austin, rather than Stephen. He believed that the real cause of discontent was the faraway and corrupt provincial government in Saltillo, which always blocked statehood for Texas. So he decided to go to Mexico City to talk to this refreshingly open-minded new president. In the summer of 1833 he set out for the capital. For five months he cooled his heels in various bureaucratic reception rooms waiting to see Santa Anna. Discouraged, Austin wrote to the San Antonio *ayuntamiento* (combination town council and county commission) recommending that Texas take its own steps toward state government. But then to his joyous surprise *El Presidente* received him. He had been busy making himself virtual dictator of Mexico, but now—courteous and friendly—he would talk to the aging *Yanqui empresario*. Briskly rejecting statehood for Texas, Santa Anna did agree to trial by jury as well as repeal of the tariff and anti-immigration laws.

Satisfied with what seemed to be a successful mission, Austin saddled up and headed northeast. But before he reached the Texas border, Mexican officials armed with a copy of his obviously seditious letter to San Antonio, overtook and arrested him, returning him to Mexico City where he was placed in three-months' solitary confinement. All of the sober colonists of Texas were dismayed when they heard the dreadful news—but not Buck Travis and the other War Dogs. They were actually ecstatic when in 1835 Santa Anna turned savage, ordering Mexican coastal garrisons to intensify their war on smuggling, slapping import duties back on the Texans, and sending Captan Antonio Tenorio to the reopened Customs House at Anahuac to make sure the Yanquis paid the tariffs.

Travis considered that conditions for rebellion had never been better. In late June he raised a company of twenty-five armed volunteers and led them to Tenorio's headquarters, where he gave the astonished capitan fifteen minutes to surrender or "be put to the sword." Tenorio with no real garrison to defend his post quickly capitulated to the exultant Travis. But those moderate colonists were shocked rather than overjoyed. Negotiation was one thing, seizing a Mexican *presidio* (fort) was quite another, just as Ethan Allen's capture of Fort Ticonderoga had dismayed the cautious members of the Continental Congress. As these moderate Texans well knew, in 1775 King George III had been a huge ocean and three thousand miles away, but in 1835 Santa Anna's soldiers in San Antonio were somewhat closer. So they compelled Travis to apologize, which he did with unbecoming blubber.

Santa Anna now miscalculated. Guided as he always would be by his mistaken conviction that Americans were cowards, he decided that now was the time to crush the Texan discontent before it could swell into open rebellion. During August he poured more troops into Texas and sent his inept brother-in-law, General Martín Perfecto de Cós, to San Antonio to command them. If he had been a little less severe with Stephen Austin and listened more to the reliable Texans who wanted no revolution but only to continue their comfortable way of life without outside interference, he might have averted armed conflict. But by threat of martial law, and military occupation, by making a martyr of Austin and the arrest of decent people, he had played into the hands of the War Dogs. All of the people of Texas turned solidly against Santa Anna. Sober settlers joined hands with Go Aheads and GTTs, the drunken, lice-ridden refuse of southern America that they had always despised. As in the American Revolution, committees of public safety sprang up everywhere, while throughout east Texas the settlers reached for the guns above the fireplace.

Buck Travis was ecstatic. Quotation after quotation from Tom Paine's *Common Sense* fell from his lips: "Now is the time that will try men's souls." "Oh, ye, that love mankind! Ye that dare oppose not only tyranny but the tyrant!" But his delirium was as nothing in comparison to the general rejoicing erupting in September 1835 when it became known that Stephen Austin had reappeared in Texas. He had been freed as part of a general amnesty for political prisoners and criminals. His release was neither a pardon nor the result of a completed sentence, for he was really never indicted, and it might have happened by mistake. Certainly it is hard to believe that Santa Anna would have condoned the return to Texas of the one man who could set the hearts of these rebellious Texans ablaze with patriotic fervor.

A thousand people jammed the banquet given in Austin's honor in Brazoria. A roar like a Texas tornado burst from their lips when the frail and sickly little *empresario* rose to speak, his hand flying to his lips to smother his frequent coughs. Without hesitation he banished all doubts about his devotion to moderation: it was gone! A General Consultation must be held, he declared: in effect calling for a provisional government. And as for the Mexican army: the people "would not unite with any armed force sent against this country; on the contrary, it would resist and repel it, and ought to do so. . . ." Another storm of approval saluted this remark tantamount to a declaration of war; and in the third week of September, Austin did declare war against Mexico with the appeal: "Every man in Texas is called upon to take up arms in defense of his country and his rights. . . . It is expected that each man will supply himself with provision, arms and ammunition to march with." A week later General Cós landed at Copano with four-hundred soldiers, immediately marching for San Antonio, and Austin trumpeted: "WAR is our only recourse."

It came on September 29 when a party of soldiers from San Antonio under a Lieutenant Castaneda entered Gonzales to seize a small Texas cannon believed to be hidden there. Castaneda found no gun but rather a group of eighteen armed Texans who taunted him "to come and take it." Meanwhile, volunteers poured into Gonzales until there were nearly 170 there, vastly outnumbering Castaneda's little patrol. On October 2 a battle began, and after the Texas 6-pounder—dug up from a peach orchard—spouted a charge of nails and horse-shoes at the enemy, the Mexicans broke and ran for San Antonio.

The revolution had begun, and on October 9 a party of Texans captured Goliad, along with two cannon and two hundred muskets. On October 13 the Texas "army" five-hundred strong marched on San Antonio. Their 6-pounder mounted on two slices of tree-trunk and drawn by oxen preceded them. They now had a banner and a slogan, too: a white sheet and in black paint a lone star at the top, then a cannon barrel and underneath the words: "COME AND TAKE IT!" Stephen Austin marched at his army's head, looking more worried than warlike. Awaiting them was General Cós. He had built barricades in the streets, stationed sharpshooters in the houses—even placed a small cannon in the bell tower of the church. He had also fortified a structure that he considered easily defended. It was an abandoned old mission across the San Antonio River from the town. It had occasionally been used as a barracks, and once sheltered a Spanish company from Alamo del Parras in Mexico. It was now called the Alamo.

Although a flood of aroused volunteers from the States was flowing south toward San Antonio—among them Davy Crockett—they would not arrive in time for the battle. Still, by November 1, the Texas army had General Cos bottled up in both the town and the Alamo. But there was really nothing menacing or very military about the loose, sprawling circle of Texans winding around the Mexicans, chiefly because there was nothing very military about the besiegers. They were hardly more than a body of undisciplined hunters given to constant but harmless pop-pop-popping of musket shots against the Mexicans.

Of leadership there was little. Stephen Austin had departed to rally support in the United States, where the entire population went wild with enthusiasm for their gallant countrymen in Texas. Jim Bowie, though devoted to the cause and the victor in a brief skirmish at Concepción, seemed to have lost much of his old ardor; and might have been sick, constantly coughing with a nasty, rasping sound that his more perceptive comrades-in-arms were reluctant to identify as what was then called consumption. Bowie tried to resign twice. Lieutenant Colonel Buck Travis galloped about aimlessly on his black mare, much like General Winder outside Washington in the War of 1812. On November 6 Travis also tried to resign, explaining that because of "complaints being made" he felt he could no longer be useful; probably meaning that he was getting in everyone's way. Later in the month he did depart, riding to San Felipe where the General Consultation was busy setting up the provisional government of Texas, and also debating whether to declare for outright independence, or, as the cautious members still sought, for reestablishment of the Federal Constitution of 1824.

General Edward Burleson, who had replaced Austin, was an elderly soldier much on the model of those same silver-haired commanders of 1812. His reluctance to fight was made manifest by his practice of convening councils-of-war composed of officers animated by the same unmartial spirit; while in the way of all sieges disease and desertion began to whittle the army's strength. Then on December 2 the camp was electrified by the arrival of two American residents of San Antonio—Sam Maverick and John Smith—who had escaped from the town. They reported that the morale of General Cós's troops was low and his food and ammunition were also meager. Maverick and Smith urged immediate attack, producing maps of the enemy's positions.

Burleson called his customary council-of-war. For two days its members procrastinated until an old frontiersman with a weather-beaten face named Ben Milam burst from the general's tent shouting angrily: "Boys, who will come with old Ben Milam into San Antonio?" Nearly 250 Americans gathered around the old Indian-fighter with yells of delight, and shortly before dawn of December 4 they attacked the town and Alamo. For four days they fought house-to-house, street war-fare at its most savage. Mexican sniper fire was extremely effective, in spite of the enemy's poor reputation as marksmen. Old Ben Milam fell dead in the arms of Sam Maverick. Still the Texans drove relent-lessly forward, taking Cos's strong points one by one: the Navarro house, the Sambraso row, the priest's house.

At half-past six in the morning of December 9, Cós ran up a white flag and began surrender negotiations. On the following morning he agreed to terms, promising to retire above the Rio Grande on parole, never to return south of it until after the war. He and his officers would "not in any way oppose the re-establishment of the Federal Constitution of 1824." In the words of Captain José Juan Sánchez Navarro, named by Cós to sign the surrender document: "All is lost, save honor."

56

Santa Anna Marches North

∿ SANTA ANNA WAS DEEPLY SHOCKED AT NEWS OF HIS BROTHER-IN-LAW'S defeat, and he hurled himself with customary energy into assembling a punitive force to crush the rebellion. The Tamaulipas *Gazette* reported proudly: "Don Santa Anna, feeling as every true Mexican ought, the disgrace thus suffered by the Republic, is making every preparation to wipe out the stain in the blood of those perfidious foreigners."

The *Gazette* was one of those superpatriotic papers that believed that those "perfidious foreigners" in Texas were the agents of the United States government, which planned to take over the entire department. Santa Anna also shared—or pretended to share—this conviction. It was a plot typical of the land-greedy neighbor to the north, he swore; and he told the British ambassador that if the Gringos tried to prevent him from stamping out the revolt, he wouldn't stop until he had planted the Mexican tricolor at the White House door.

Santa Anna's first problem was money. Revolt and counter-revolt had impoverished Mexico. At first, he turned to the church—but received only a measly 1,000 pesos from the Monterey cathedral. So he went to the money lenders, specifically Messrs. Rubio and Errazu, who, always intensely patriotic in such crises, cheerfully supplied him with 400,000 pesos at interest of only 4 percent—a month—plus certain customs-house duties, the right to import specific military supplies free of tariffs and the entire proceeds of a forced loan on four Mexican departments. Not to be outdone in love of country, they volunteered to provide troop rations on credit—at double the customary price. Santa Anna pretended to be outraged but signed on the dotted line, anyway. As he well knew, profiteering among Mexican businessmen was as common as graft among his generals. During the march north, General Antonio Gaona would corner the market for the necessary supplies, selling them back to El Caudillo at 100 percent profit, while the master purveryor Colonel Ricardo Dromundo would not even bother to account for the money given him to purchase provisions.

Such speculation was common in the Mexican army, although there were many honest and brave professionals among the officers of lower grade. Among its 130 generals it would be difficult to find one that could be trusted. So Santa Anna buckled on his gold sword valued at $7,000, mounted his horse and began to ride northward—having ordered his various formations to assemble by the end of December 1835, either at San Luis Potosí or higher north at Saltillo in Coahuila—the starting point for San Antonio 365 miles farther north.

General Santa Anna arrived at Saltillo on January 7, 1836—and immediately fell ill of a stomach ailment. He was bedridden for two weeks, during which he agonized over having forgotten to provide for a medical corps. Recovered, he plunged into training his army of about six thousand men. Captain Sánchez Navarro, the officer who had signed the surrender document at San Antonio, marveled at his thoroughness. "His Excellency himself attends to all matters whether important or most trivial," he said. One somewhat important military detail was overlooked: teaching his soldiers how to shoot. They were almost deathly afraid of the ferocious recoil of their heavy muskets which for some inexplicable reason they overloaded with powder and which could actually break their shoulder or collar bones. Instead, they fired them from the hip, meaning that they were not aimed and probably would send their missile whispering harmlessly over the enemy's head. Still, Minister of War Tornel calmly assured the Mexican nation: "The superiority of the Mexican soldier over the mountaineers of Kentucky and the hunters of Missouri is well known. Veterans seasoned by twenty years of war can't be intimidated by the presence of an army ignorant of the art of war, incapable of discipline and renowned for insubordination."

Insubordination, it is true, is the enemy of that discipline that keeps a soldier at his post, and the American frontiersman was notoriously susceptible to it. But if "the art of war" almost exclusively consists in the skill of killing enemy soldiers, it would seem that to teach one's foot soldiers and artillerists to shoot accurately would be no small achievement. Again on this "minor point" ignored by Senor Tornel: the Kentucky rifleman could put a bullet into a six-inch square at two hundred yards, while the Mexican musketeer's unaimed ball fell to the ground at seventy. Still, as Minister Tornel insisted, "tactics," not firepower, would win in the end, for the Americans were woefully "ignorant of maneuvers on a large scale." But there was nary an officer in the Mexican army—including *El Caudillo*—who had *ever* brought off a maneuver in the face of an enemy. The blare of bugles and the pounding hooves of a cavalry charge were the only tactics they knew.

On January 25, 1836, the grand review was held at Saltillo. While Santa Anna in gold and silver watched from his similarly clad horse, the army of about four thousand men and a dozen cannon paraded past him in fairly good order. They made a colorful martial spectacle: the officers in blue uniforms with scarlet fronts, the dragoons in gleaming cuirasses, lancers with glittering uplifted spears, the main body of infantry in white cotton fatigue suits, on their heads tall black shakos with pompons and small visors. The Generalissimo was obviously satisfied and the march began.

It was not long before Señor Tornel's vaunted discipline became dissolved by the ordeal of marching en masse through a land hostile in both terrain and climate, for the bare, dry hills of Coahuila offered neither sustenance nor sanctuary. Behind Santa Anna's brilliant entourage crawled the infantry, their white uniforms grimy with dust. It settled upon them in clouds, especially those troops following *El Caudillo*'s mounted staff and the cavalry. Behind the infantry raising even heavier clouds was the supply train struggling along the narrow track: 1800 mules loaded with saddle bags of hardtack, 33 huge four-wheeled wagons, 200 two-wheel carts drawn by oxen, and then either more carts or hand-trundled wagons, the property of the sutlers and loaded with the tobacco, wine, bread or preserves that they sold to the troops. None of the vehicles, military or civilian, were held together by metal but rather by pegs and thongs of rawhide, and the seven-foot wheels of the big land barges made a hideous screeching as they rolled slowly north.

Finally to the farthest rear except for a mounted rear guard trudged an army of camp followers about three thousand strong—the *sol-daderas* of the men, women with their children—chattering and yelling with a consistent buzz and shriek that appalled Italian-born General Vicente Filisola, Santa Anna's second-in-command. In Europe camp followers had been practically eliminated by the efficient service of supply introduced by Frederick the Great of Prussia. Filisola had never seen or heard anything like it, and when he complained of the "distraction" to his chief, Santa Anna courteously explained that without the women half the army would desert. They not only cooked for their men, who were not always their husbands, but mended and washed their clothes as well. They also foraged for them, for Santa Anna, having neglected to form a medical corps, also had no formal quartermaster or commissary.

So the columns clattered or shuffled on, moving ever higher into northern Mexico, where the cold especially affected the Mayan Indians of the Yucatán Battalion, who had never been out of the tropics. On the night of February 13 their worst fears were realized when a cold white blizzard struck with a dreadful howl. It caught General Andrade's cavalry moving through mesquite thickets, blinding both men and mounts. Horses thrashed against each other and fell crashing to the ground, sometimes crushing the troopers who rode them. A hundred oxen were lost. Without tents Santa Anna's soldiers were buffeted about by the wailing wind, clinging to each other for stability and warmth. Worst of all were the stunned and terrified Mayans, covering their ears against the shrieking of what in their superstitious dread seemed to be an evil northern god. They died by the dozen, dust-gray bundles of flesh stiffening among pure white drifts. In the spring the wolves would find them.

Once out of the blizzard—a rarity that dry winter—the marchers found neither grass for animal fodder nor water. Horses and draft animals perished from thirst or fever caused by stagnant water. Soon soldiers were falling, unable to continue without sustenance. Santa Anna put his starving men on half rations. In desperation they foraged for berries or nuts in the field—some of which poisoned them—or unripe fruits that gave them dysentery. Eventually the wagons of the artillery were draped with exhausted infantrymen. When they began to die, the absence of doctors and priests became evident. In desperation many men tried to desert, but there was little habitation along the way and no place to hide. Most of them were caught, flogged, and thrown back into ranks. Execution for desertion was not permitted in the Mexican army: if it were, there would have been no army. Instead they were sentenced to longer periods of service. A shoemaker from

Durango named Juan Basquez was twice caught trying to run away and was sentenced to ten more years of service without pay. Such was the encouragement to enlist in the army.

Yet with the immemorial stoicism of soldiers everywhere, they stumbled on—while Antonio López de Santa Anna with his entourage of aides and dragoons pranced ahead on well-fed horses. Behind the general was his ornate carriage and perhaps a round little lady or two wearing a soldier's uniform—a common dodge in the annals of arms, and one that has fooled nobody—and then his baggage train, so incredibly complete that it would have made Gentleman Johnny Burgoyne gasp in envy: the striped marquee to protect His Excellency from the scorching southern sun . . . the exquisite silverware and monogrammed china . . . the crystal decanters with their solid gold stoppers . . . the silver tea caddy and cream pitcher . . . the silver chamber pot . . .

At last the broad and gleaming Rio Grande was visible. Santa Anna rejoiced along with his soldiers, for awaiting them there was General Joaquin Ramírez y Sesma supposedly with about 1,500 troops and 8 guns. He had originally gone north to reinforce Cos. Arriving too late he halted on the river's south bank to await *El Caudillo* and his avenging army. Sesma, of course, granting the desertion and disease that whittles every army, had nothing like 1,500 soldiers. Nor did Santa Anna have the 6,000 he was supposed to have led when he departed the capital. When he crossed the Rio Grande into Texas he probably had upwards of 2,500, and when he reached San Antonio de Bexar at the end of February 1836, he had 2,400 fit for duty.

57

Anarchy at the Alamo

∼ IT IS DOUBTFUL THAT THOSE AMERICANS WHO CELEBRATED THE DEFEAT of General Cós with torchlight parades and victory picnics would have been quite so exuberant and proud if they had known the true character of the "gallant soldiers" of Austin's "army" who had sent General Cós hastening south across the Rio Grande.

They were almost to a man volunteers from the states, lured to Texas by the promise of land. There was nary a regular among them, and the only officer with the slightest acquaintance with formal military training was a mercenary slave trader from Georgia named James Walker Fannin, who had spent seventeen months at West Point. They had joined the Texas rebellion because of propaganda written by Texas leaders such as Sam Houston, who had cried:

> If volunteers from the United States will join their brethren in this section [Texas], they will receive liberal grants of land. We have millions of acres of our best lands unchosen and unappropriated.
>
> Let each man come with a good rifle and one hundred rounds of ammunition and come soon.

They did indeed. Those who remained until the end of the fighting were to receive 1,280 acres apiece, while a six-month tour earned 640 acres and three months 320. Although they thought of themselves as warriors invincible in battle, they were in reality militia who had never been in combat or even realized that there was such a calling as professional soldiers trained in the art of war. Frontiersmen and hunters who were indeed skilled riflemen, when organized into companies and battalions they were nothing more than armed mobs, which both Houston and William Barret Travis did not hesitate to call them.

Militia then was almost exclusively an institution of the South and the western frontiers. Because West Point was still a novel institution detested by these very same people as a school for snobs, and the national army as yet a tiny force incapable of defending the vast territory of the United States, it was the militia in the main who had "pacified" the Indian tribes of the south. Once this menace had disappeared, there was little for the "milishy" to do but strut about in the county seats on muster days or to fire off their field pieces on the Fourth of July.

Musters held every few months were actually more social than military events, except for the election of officers and a few hours of "drill," which can only be called the negation of precision marching. During this time the militia wives and sweethearts would be busy preparing food and drink for the afternoon picnic, which was really what had brought everyone "to taown." There were rarely two uniforms or weapons alike: men dressed in calico, linsey-woolsey or buckskin, wearing moccasins or barefoot, brandishing weapons ranging from ancient firelocks to fowling pieces, hunting rifles to Brown Besses to horse pistols. Sometimes, fearing to damage their precious firearms in "practice war," they wielded sticks or cornstalks, causing the troops of the regular army to deride them as "cornstalk soldiers."

Hardy frontiersmen they were indeed, but toughness and durability are no substitutes for military discipline. A man who can shoot accurately is just as liable to panic as a man who can't the first time an enemy shell explodes among them. Yet, they hooted in derision at the suggestion that trained regulars could ever defeat a force of American frontiersmen. They believed in the myth of the New England Minuteman able to rout British redcoats just by getting his dander up. As proof of their invincibility they cited the Battle of New Orleans, unaware of how easy it is for entrenched sharpshooters to riddle massed regulars in bright uniforms marching over the battlefield in parade-ground precision, or of Pakenham's obtuseness in ordering such a murderous frontal assault.

These, then, were the volunteers who flowed into Bexar under the pretext of noble anger at the massacre of their countrymen by hordes

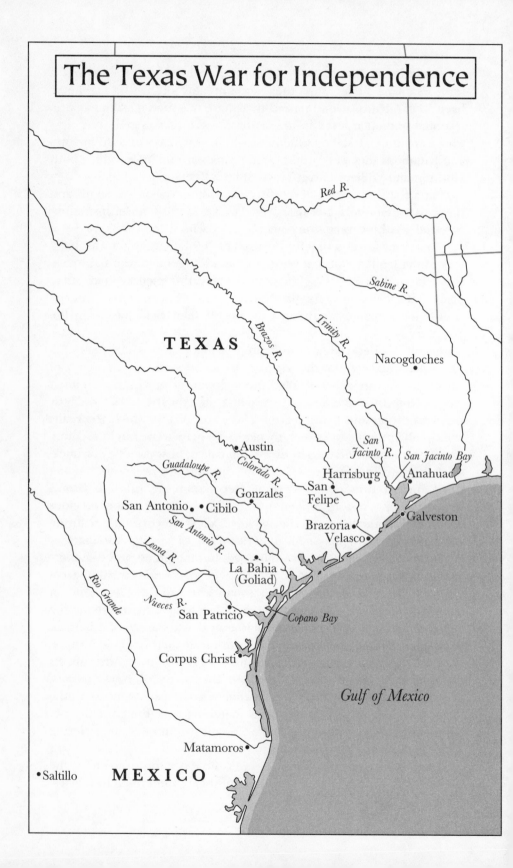

The Texas War for Independence

TEXAS

Red R.

Sabine R.

Trinity R.

Brazos R.

Nacogdoches •

San Jacinto R.

Guadaloupe R.

Austin •

Colorado R.

San • Jacinto Bay

Harrisburg •

San Felipe •

Anahuac •

San Antonio • • Cibilo

Gonzales •

San Antonio R.

Brazoria •

Galveston •

Leona R.

Velasco •

La Bahia
(Goliad) •

Rio Grande

Nueces R.

San Patricio •

Copano Bay

Corpus Christi •

Gulf of Mexico

Matamoros •

• Saltillo   **MEXICO**

of savage Mexicans, but actually drawn there by the lure of land. Once the Mexicans under Cos had been defeated, their true character emerged. Creed Taylor, one of the earliest and most dedicated rebels, has described them:

> For two weeks after the fall of Bexar the soldiers who garrisoned the town enjoyed a season of almost utter abandon. They were mostly volunteers from the states—nearly all Texans having gone to their homes—and being disappointed in not having their promised rewards, they soon learned to regard the property belonging to Mexican citizens as lawful prey and so acted accordingly. . . . When a Mexican appeared in town with a good horse, ownership of the animal was promptly transferred to a needy *American.*

In Goliad drunken American volunteers went on a rampage, breaking into Tejano homes to loot and rape. From a population of one thousand, Goliad fell to exactly ten persons as everyone else fled the lust and larceny of these drunken Gringos. Sam Houston called these unsavory soldiers exactly what Santa Anna called them: pirates. When the aforementioned West Point dropout Colonel Fannin suggested that the volunteers should be paid by despoiling the Mexican population, Houston rebuked him angrily with the disclaimer: "This in my opinion . . . divests the campaign of any character save that of a piratical or predatory war."

Fortunately for the honor of America many of these disgruntled mercenaries began to return to their homes, waving mocking good-byes with the banners bearing the noble motto: "Liberty or Death." Then upon the proposal of what was nothing less than a pirate raid upon the Rio Grande city of Matamoros three hundred miles due south of San Antonio, the mercenaries prepared to abandon Bexar en masse. A greedy land speculator named Dr. James Grant had cunningly convinced most of them that Matamoros was the key to all of Mexico. Grant had amassed huge tracts of land through bribing the Coahuila-Texas legislature. When that corrupt body disappeared under the Law of April 6, he had lost his titles and been arrested by Santa Anna. Escaping, he made his way to Bexar. Aware that an independent Texas would nullify his land titles just as surely as Santa Anna had, he had schemed to revise the old federal system, which would honor them. He believed he could set all federalist Mexico afire by seizing Matamoros. Assisted by Colonel Fannin, he stripped the Alamo of supplies, arms, medicines and all but a hundred men and at the head of a force of from five hundred to six hundred mercenaries began marching south.

General Sam Houston was convinced that they were parading to disaster. Even if they conquered Matamoros, they would be hundreds of miles beyond reinforcement or supply. Should they overcome that difficulty and secure a successful federalist revolution in Mexico, Texas would be compelled to resume its old standing as a mere Mexican state. At the very worst, if the American rebels were defeated at Matamoros, Texas would be left without an army to defend it and would become Mexican again—this time in the humble role of a conquered province. No matter what the outcome, then, Matamoros would be disaster unmitigated. To prevent it, Houston hastened to southwestern Texas where the volunteers were massing in early January 1836.

"Comrades! Citizens of Texas!" he cried, in an impassioned appeal to them to return to Bexar, now menaced by the approaching Santa Anna. "Two different tribes on the same hunting ground will never get together. The tomahawk will ever fly and the scalping knife will never rest until the last of either one tribe or the other is either destroyed or is a slave. And I ask, comrades, will we ever bend our necks as slaves . . . ? NO! NEVER!"

But all the eloquence of this handsome, charismatic giant, so revered and respected among the older settlers of Texas, could not move these mercenaries inflamed with dreams of loot and lusting for the charms of dark-eyed señoritas. They had not endured journeys of unspeakable hardship and the blaze of battle to become despised regular soldiers on garrison duty. From this dismaying confrontation Houston learned what the Mexican government already knew: the stateside volunteers had come for profit, not patriotism. In a word, they were filibusters. In dejection, Houston rode east again to inform Governor Henry Smith that unless the Constitutional Convention set for March 1 could establish a solidly based government, "the country must be lost."

On January 16 Houston also received bad news from the Alamo, a dispatch from Lieutenant Colonel James Clinton Neill the commander there, which said: "The men all under my command have been in the field for the last four months. They are almost naked, and this day they were to have received pay for the first month of their last enlistment, and almost every one of them speaks of going home, and not less than twenty will leave tomorrow, and leave here only about eighty officers and men. . . . We are in a torpid, defenseless condition, and have not and cannot get from all the citizens here horses enough to send out a patrol or spy company. . . . I hope we will be reinforced in eight days, or we will be over-run by the enemy, but, if I have only 100 men, I will fight 1,000 as long as I can and then not surrender...."

News from Goliad was just as grim. The fort there had been stripped of all men, munitions and transport for the Grant-Fannin expedition to Matamoros, and the interior of Texas was thus completely exposed to Santa Anna. Houston had always thought that San Antonio and the Alamo were too far away from the capital at San Felipe de Austin to be successfully defended. He did not believe the volunteers under Neill were disciplined enough to stand up against Santa Anna's regulars. Dreadful marksmen that they might be, these mostly peon and Indian troops were trained enough to obey orders. Rather than conventional warfare, Houston preferred guerrilla tactics, the sort of combat that Santa Anna with his disciplined but unimaginative troops feared most. Houston agreed with the sage advice given to Austin by a planter-colonist named Eli Mercer, who warned: "I think the only chance in our situation is to fight them from the brush, fight them from the brush all the time; never take our boys to an open fight. Our situation will not admit of it. All must be disciplined before we can fight in the open field."

With Grant-Fannin about to march south to Matamoros and the Alamo-Bexar and Goliad practically defenseless, the Texan commander decided to concentrate what forces he had left at Gonzales, about sixty miles east of San Antonio. To this end he sent Jim Bowie, now a militia colonel, with about thirty men to the Alamo to inform Neill that he wanted his position abandoned and destroyed. After this General Sam Houston inexplicably put himself "on furlough" to "negotiate" with his beloved Indians.

The Texas army was in effect leaderless and anarchy reigned at the Alamo.

58

The Alamo Prepares

∼ DURING THAT FATEFUL JANUARY OF 1836 THREE MEN WHOSE NAMES would live in the annals of American arms rode south toward Bexar-Alamo: Colonel Jim Bowie, Lieutenant Colonel William Barret Travis and Colonel Davy Crockett.

Bowie was not at all enthused at the melancholy mission entrusted to him by General Houston. Defense of Bexar-Alamo—not destruction of that position—would have been much more to his liking. To a man of Bowie's combative nature, such an assignment was not conducive to the military glory that he sought even more ardently than money or beautiful women. It smacked of cowardice. Yet Houston had seized his hand, fixed him with that famous confidential gaze, and said: "There is no man on whose forecast, prudence and valor I place a higher estimate." Later, the general had added: "Much is referred to your discretion." During the two-day ride to San Antonio by Bowie and his companions—among them the gallant young firebrand James Bonham of South Carolina and the aging Napoleonic veteran Louis Rose, with whom Bowie had struck up a strange friendship—the phrase "your discretion" seemed to crowd from Bowie's mind all other instructions from the commander in chief.

When Bowie arrived at the Alamo on January 19 he silently handed Houston's letter to Colonel Neill, and then, with his entourage, conducted his own inspection of the fort. At once he saw that San Antonio was not defensible, but the Alamo might be made so. It had been a Catholic monastery or mission built by the Franciscans in 1718, becoming after its abandonment a military outpost with a parade ground and barracks for small outposts of the Spanish army before housing the headquarters of that trading company that gave the entire complex its name.

This large sprawling compound across the San Antonio River from the town of that name occupied three acres. Its center was a rough rectangle of bare ground grandiloquently called "the Plaza." It was about the size of a city block and was bordered by various walls and buildings. An empty church was the strongest building, and although it had stone walls four feet thick, its roof had fallen in and there were no firing slits. What came to be called the fort was a large, rectangular enclosure 154 yards north-south and 54 yards east-west. It had no watch towers, redoubts, slits bastions, or even a firing step. Its walls were made of dirt nearly three feet thick and nine to twelve feet high and had been designed only to protect settlers and their livestock from the attacks of marauding Indians. The walls could swallow an arrow and perhaps even a bullet but cannon balls would quickly shred them.

Bowie realized that the Alamo was also no stronghold, and was disappointed—for that phrase "your discretion" actually had been eroding whatever small measure of caution that he had ever possessed. In its place the urge for battle and glory was growing larger. Why, the Alamo had twenty-five guns—probably the heaviest armament between Mexico City and New Orleans! Certainly, morale was low. The troops refused to drill, or even go out on a patrol. Roll call was a joke. Some of the volunteers from the newly arrived New Orleans Greys were living independently in the rubble of the Alamo church—refusing all orders. But these were frontiersmen! Bowie's own people! They chafed at discipline and hated "biggety" officers who tried to enforce it. But show them a real sockdolaging fight and they'd be in the middle of it, right to the end with the enemy high-tailing it like a striped-assed ape.

For days Bowie hesitated, actually pleased when the indecisive Colonel Neill did nothing but moan and wring his hands. He hesitated to obey Houston's orders while Bowie began to insist that the Alamo was too vital to be abandoned, that it was the one outpost standing between Santa Anna and the independence of Texas. Bowie was also gratified when Green Jameson, a Kentucky lawyer who was one of the first GTTs to arrive in Texas, echoed his confidence in the band of volunteers at the Alamo. Jameson said that though resentful and discouraged at the moment, these were the men who had beaten General Cós and refused to join the Matamoros filibuster. That showed they had a sense of responsibility, didn't it? Jameson had said that if properly supported these men would "do duty and fight better than fresh men, they have all been tried and have confidence in themselves."

Colonel Bowie now began to employ his redoubtable energy in pursuits more useful for defense than retreat. Still popular in this region of his dead wife's girlhood—the beautiful Ursula Veramendi, whom he had disinherited—he obtained from his Mexican friends fresh horses for long-range scouting. On January 22 he heard from the Navarro family that Santa Anna was near with about four thousand men. From the local padre he received a report that the Mexican cavalry was headed straight for Bexar, intelligence suggesting to Colonel Neill that the time had come to visit his family. Bowie ignored his reticence, for everyone in Bexar-Alamo now realized that the de facto commander was Jim Bowie.

Bowie's growing determination to hold the position inflamed the ardor of his heretofore listless men. Some of them suddenly discovered that they had useful skills. Captain Almeron Dickinson, a blacksmith from Gonzales, found that his calling had given him an understanding of artillery. The Virginian John Baugh's officious nature so disliked by many volunteers made him an excellent adjutant. Because Hiram Williamson of Philadelphia liked bellowing parade-ground orders and counting cadence, he became a good drill master. Even Jameson surprised himself with engineering insights. He built palisades to close the chinks in the Alamo's armor, erected platforms of earth and timber for parapets and gun mounts, emplaced the heavy 18-pounder to command Bexar, and actually began sketching plans for moats and aqueducts to bring in water, as well as "a contemplated drawbridge across a contemplated ditch inside a contemplated half-moon battery."

All the while supplies began flowing into the fort: forty-two beeves, priceless ammunition for the 18-pounder, one hundred bushels of corn. Bowie suddenly remembered his own skill and negotiated a $500 loan, from whom is not known, but Bowie must have been fairly persuasive to borrow money on nonexistent credit and zero security. Unfortunately, though Bowie's spirit did not flag, his flesh had begun to weaken. The old mysterious sickness with the rasping, nagging cough had returned, and Bowie had need of frequent rests. Neither of the two physicians at the Alamo could diagnose the ailment. Dr. John Sutherland of Alabama spoke vaguely of an illness "of a peculiar nature, not to be cured by an ordinary course of treatment." It might have been pneumonia, but this affliction even then could be diagnosed and treated; but Sutherland's imprecise language suggests some socially censurable sickness such as venereal disease. During those waning days of January 1836, it had not yet put Bowie on his back—and he carried on grimly.

On January 27 the scout Señor José Cassiano rode into headquarters to report the strength of Sesma's force that he had been shadowing: about 1,600 infantry and 400 cavalry plus what appeared to be a half-dozen 12-pounders. Both Neill and Bowie doubted that Sesma was that strong, for he had had only 1,500 to begin with. Then on February 2 another scout reported Santa Anna's army of 5,000 men, another exaggeration, still farther back. Now Neill and Bowie had no doubt that the Mexican dictator intended "to make a descent on this place," and Bowie wrote Governor Smith: "Colonel Neill and myself have come to the solemn resolution that we will rather die in these ditches then give it up to the enemy."

Next day there arrived at Bexar-Alamo a welcome reinforcement: about thirty cavalrymen under Lieutenant Colonel William Barret Travis.

Nearly four months earlier when Bowie was a full colonel of militia, Buck Travis was but a lieutenant courtesy of Stephen Austin. By the end of October he had climbed up to captain and was sent to join the force besieging San Antonio. Cutting a fine figure on his black horse and wearing a tall white sombrero, he dashed about on scouting missions, setting fire to the praries to deny the Mexicans fodder and cover, even capturing a string of three hundred enemy horses. But somehow he never seemed to get the recognition that he believed he deserved. He was not popular with his troops, who seemed to regard him as a somewhat ridiculous figure, a soldier in a comic opera, a man of little talent obviously searching for the main chance. He was discouraged, especially by the growing number of desertions in his command. His offer to resign was rejected, and he was briefly mollified; but he later left camp to resume his law practice in San Felipe and join the General Consultation then setting up the provisional government of Texas.

But he still thirsted for military glory, the path to high political office. After Cós surrendered Bexar, he proposed to Governor Smith and the Provisional Council that a regular Texas army of three infantry battalions and one of cavalry be authorized. With becoming modesty this model patriot did not specify who should command what, especially the dashing mounted unit likely to gain the most glory. But he did promote his idea of a regular army with such ardor and diligence that when it was adopted, he could hardly be denied higher rank. Thus, the council was pleased to inform him that he had been granted a commission as a major of regulars—but in artillery, not cavalry. Artillery! Travis was furious. What artillerist besides Napoleon had ever become famous? So he declined, explaining with icy courtesy that he did not believe he could be "so useful" behind the lines pulling lanyards. But he did not give up, laying siege to the governor's office, and on Christmas Eve, 1835, Governor Smith appointed him a lieutenant colonel of regular cavalry.

He promptly ordered himself a gorgeous colonel's uniform from New Orleans, and designed an even gaudier soldier's suit for his legion of cavalry—the expense to be borne by the wearer. This meant that his formation would be filled out by the sons of the wealthy, a not unwelcome condition to a man on the make. Unfortunately, none of the uniforms arrived before Smith in late January ordered Travis to take his command to beleaguered Bexar-Alamo. Travis was crushed, not so much at being compelled to ride into history clad in blue jeans, but because so far, having been told to raise a force of only one hundred troopers when he wanted three hundred, he had been able to recruit only thirty-nine. He had also been spending his own money to buy messware, twine and a five-dollar Texas flag, and would spend more for blankets, coffee, sugar and then more blankets. Morale plummeted, and on the first or second day of the march nine men deserted. Worse, one of them rode off with his horse, saddle, blanket and gunpowder.

"Volunteers can no longer be relied upon," Travis wrote despairingly to Smith, and offered to resign his high rank to allow junior officers to carry on. Smith, by then probably weary of reading Travis's third letter of resignation since November, made no reply. Travis in deep gloom led his disillusioned men onward to Bexar-Alamo arriving there on February 3. Travis was not pleased when Colonel Neill informed him that his command would be engaged in harassing the approaching enemy, cutting off their supplies, chopping down the bridges over the Leona and Nueces rivers, savaging their rear, setting the prairie on fire. . . . *Burning grass again?* Buck Travis, a light colonel with silver leaves on his shoulders, doing the work of a lieutenant wearing a single bar? Travis was indignant.

But then, on February 8 he forgot his resentment and joined the general jubilation when Colonel Davy Crockett of Tennessee rode into camp.

Colonel David Crockett, lately a Democratic Congressmen from Tennessee, was in a sense the prince of backwoodsmen who by his merry nature, rude dress, colorful but horribly mutilated language, and wildly exaggerated stories of hunting and fishing made bumpkinism in America a badge of honor. He was born in Tennessee in 1786, the son of a frontier couple whose parents had been murdered in 1777 by the Creeks. In his youth he was a mild-mannered, likeable young man from whom everyone who knew him expected very little. At first it seemed that Davy, as he called himself, would not disappoint them, but then in 1813–14 he served as a volunteer scout under Andrew Jackson during the Creek War, and had the distinct pleasure of seeing his grandparents avenged at the horrible massacre of the Creek village of Tallushatchee. "We shot them down like dogs," he wrote with obvious relish. They also burned many of them alive.

Thereafter Crockett's life appeared to be one long, unbreakable string of misfortune and bad luck: his first love married another man, his first wife died, his mills were flooded out and his barrel-stave venture literally sank on the Mississippi River. For thirteen years he dwelt in the back woods—in what he called "the harricane"—from which he made his hunting forays in both forest and politics. Eventually his eloquent rifle more than compensated for his murder of the English language, and his deliberate creation of the backwoods ignoramus clothed in buckskin shirt, coonskin cap, and Indian moccasins made his name a household word in an age that cared little for punctuation and syntax and very much for a "man of the people." He was also the Mighty Hunter who had actually killed forty-seven bears in a single month, six bucks in a day and supposedly rode alligators for fun. As the epitome of the shrewd backwoodsmen who could outwit any fifty Yankee slickers, Crockett could "wade the Mississippi, leap over the Ohio, ride upon a streak of lightning, and slip without a scratch down a honey locust." Of his supposed illiteracy, he said: "When a man can grin and fight, flag a steamboat or whip his weight in wildcats, what's the use of reading and writing?" Unfortunately, all this bluster and bombast, this pretense of ignorance, was a facade and a cover for a man who knew instinctively that when he started swimming in treacherous political waters he was far, far beyond his depth.

Crockett as backwoodsman was not a sham or a fraud, but a genuine frontiersman in the mold of Daniel Boone. He was also a warm, good-hearted man whose merry jokes and thigh-slapping guffaws were a natural expression of his desire to please. Nor was he stupid but rather just naive, if that is not actually something worse. His instincts were sure and his morals irreproachable, but he was just too shallow and never tried to deepen himself to qualify in the battle of wits that can be politics. It was so much easier to respond to every dilemma or hurdle every impasse with a joke; and because he was lazy, he made no effort to write his many publications himself—which he certainly could have done—but relied on ghostwriters.

At first Crockett's formula—cheek the swells, deride the dandies, ridicule respectability—worked very well. In 1817 he was appointed a magistrate in western Tennessee, where he earned a reputation for fairness and honesty. Not for wisdom, of course, or legal perception, for cases dealing almost exclusively with boundary disputes or wolf-scalp bounties required neither. In fact, his own prowess at exterminating wolves earned him enough money to buy enough corn liquor at militia picnics to be elected a colonel.

From this triumph he advanced to the Tennessee legislature in 1820, where his self-cast role of man of the people, his mastery of rough-and-tumble politics, and his frontiersman's love of practical jokes—during a joint-stumping tour in 1823 he delighted his audiences by repeating his opponent's speeches word-for-word—attracted the interest of the world's champion lover-of-the-masses and perhaps even the inventor of such homey tactics: Andrew Jackson. Inevitably, he became one of Old Hickory's many protégés and in 1827 he moved from the statehouse to the U.S. House. It was there that his true and better nature got the better of him. He ignored most issues and made no secret of his detestation of authority or privilege. He repeatedly called for the abolition of West Point, which he regarded as a school for snobs where a "snot-nose kid" was paid to be "eddicated" and to spend the rest of his life feeding at the public trough. His genuine compassion for the poor led him to demand that the people of the frontier be allowed to keep the land they were squatting on.

This was exactly the opposite of the intentions of the state and federal governments, which wanted to raise revenue by selling land. This brought Crockett into rebellion with Jackson, who saw to it that Crockett narrowly lost his bid for re-election in 1831. Nevertheless, he squeaked back into the House again in 1833, to renew his empassioned defense of the underprivileged. In his simplistic mind all issues could be reduced to a conflict between the selfish rich and the honest poor. Andrew Jackson and the Democrats who opposed free land were the devil's disciples. Anyone who shared his own defense of it was an honest man and dedicated public servant. On this question there could be no compromise, no retreat.

To the opposition Whigs the popular figure of Davy Crockett was a godsend. They had been too thoroughly excoriated by Jackson as the party of the rich and privileged. They needed their own man-of-the-people to challenge the reigning King Andrew. Who better than Davy Crockett, Robin Hood in Buckskin? Who was easier to seduce with his love of fame, his vanity, gullibility and deepening estrangement from Jackson? Had he not begun to boast that he would never wear a collar marked, "My Dog, Andrew Jackson?" Why could not they, these clever, sly, scheming politicians with their perverse priorities of party and personal power, why couldn't they make lovable Davy the best-trained stalking dog in Washington?

So they wined him and dined him . . . laughed at his jokes . . . sponsored his public appearances . . . Whig publishers pushed his books. Whig ghosts wrote his speeches. Whig clubs packed his rallies. The Young Whigs of Philadelphia gave him a handsome chased hunting rifle called "Sweet Betsey" and the Whig angel Du Pont furnished some powder, just as his ancestors had done in the Revolution. When they could, they whispered in his ear that he might become their candidate for president, smiling to themselves at how those guileless blue eyes brightened at the suggestion. They also commissioned five artists to paint his portrait, and the kindly Nicholas Biddle, president of the second Bank of the United States, loaned him money and then generously forgave the debt. Crockett was so thoroughly duped that he recited a canned Whig speech denouncing Jackson as "a greater tyrant than Cromwell, Caesar and Bonaparte"—with whom he probably had a doubtful familiarity only less dubious than Old Hickory's.

As might be expected his erstwhile patron fought back with the hellish fury of a woman scorned. No man in America could love or hate harder than Old Hickory, and in August 1835, his hand-picked candidate turned Davy Crockett out of office by the slim margin of 230 votes. With this Crockett returned to Tennessee an embittered man who told the constituents who had rejected him, "You may all go to hell, and I will go to Texas."

He did, in the jolly company of eight Tennessee volunteers, and he quickly recovered his irrepressible high spirits. Though approaching fifty with the weight of his once-hard, muscular body redistributed by six years of dissipation and indolence in Washington, he was again the Davy Crockett of old. He was moving on, as he always did when fortune turned against him: as a twelve-year-old after four days in a stuffy school, when a flash flood wrecked his little mill in 1817. But now he was telling jokes again, guffawing, his trusty rifle, old Betsey—not that gaudy Whig weapon Sweet Betsey—safely in its sheath beside him, in a saddlebag his beloved fiddle for strumming those gay Celtic reels and hornpipes, and in another, of course, to make the dance go faster, a jug of corn whisky. It was invigorating, this tonic of moving on, discovering new places ... riding, hunting, joking, the love and laughter of gay companions. ... Davy Crockett was Texas-bound, but at that point he said nothing of the Texas rebellion or fighting for freedom. He even spoke of returning to Tennessee. Yet, when he reached Arkansas—his party had grown to about a dozen—his journey was not unlike the royal progress of a king.

Frontier villages turned out to welcome him en masse. Shooting matches were held, and the people shouted with glee when tall Davy knelt to cradle Betsey under his chin to put a second bullet through the bull's-eye pierced by the first one. Then the banquets ... even Davy gasped at the provender of the far west frontiers. On banquet tables sometimes 150 feet long there might lay an entire black bear, skinned and roasted, redolent and dripping, mouth watering, in its claws the Texan lone-star flag and fixed in its jaws the Red-White-and-Blue ... To either side of this mountainous, sizzling viand stretched roasted raccoons, rabbits, squirrels, and turkeys, the hindquarters of roasted oxen and every kind of waterfowl fricasseed, stewed or baked. There would be, of course, no tablecloth, and yet, sometimes fine china and even sparkling crystal. But when Davy noticed that there was nary a knife, fork or spoon he would tell his hosts how he was the guest of honor at a fancy banquet in Washington and stirred whiskey into his finger bowl and drank it. Howls of derisive laughter would greet such delightful disdain for the decadent, dandified East. To honor Crockett there would be cannon salutes and military music, dancing, toasts innumerable enough even to challenge Colonel Crockett's legendary capacity for drink. Wherever he stopped, cheers and adulation, and the chance to tell everyone again how he'd told everybody back home to go to hell; how he was fast becoming a born-again Texan—so that when he crossed the Sabine and entered Nacogdoches on January 5, he could declare: "I had rather be in my present situation than to be elected to a seat in Congress for life." As proof of his rising enthusiasm for Texan independence, this former congressman who had renounced politics forever added: "I have but little doubt of being elected a member to form a constitution for this province." He also wanted to be sworn in as a Texas citizen and join the fighting. But when the judge administered the oath of allegiance, Crockett stopped him to protest that the phrase to uphold "any future government" could mean a dictatorship. His Honor changed it to "any future *republican* government," and Davy repeated the oath in front of a cheering courtroom.

In Nacogdoches Crockett was able to recruit many of the excited volunteers gathered there for his own Tennessee Company of Mounted Volunteers. Then followed by about two dozen companions, he set out for Bexar-Alamo.

News that the great man from Tennessee had arrived at the Bexar-Alamo flashed through the area with hurricane speed. Soldiers, citizens of the town, Bowie, Travis, and Neill and all the other officers gathered on the plaza with wild yells of delight. Someone found a packing case and Crockett mounted it. He gave probably the best performance of his career, exhausting his repertoire of jokes, boasts and exaggerations—including that charming little confection about the finger bowl. It was not true of course, being the invention of a Whig writer ghosting one of Davy's books. At first the congressman from Tennessee had resented it, but when he remembered it on his triumphant progress from Tennessee to Texas, he saw that it could be the showpiece of his entire spiel. Then, to everyone's surprise, he concluded quietly: "I have come to your country, though not, I hope, through any selfish motive whatever. I have come to aid you all that I can in your noble cause." Though a colonel of Tennessee militia, Crockett informed his hushed audience that he would serve in the ranks as a private with Betsey in his hands. A storm of applause arose, and among the most vigorous shouters of approval were the three colonels.

A dispute of sorts had arisen among Neill, Bowie and Travis. Travis had told Neill that because his was a "regular" commission, he outranked him. Neill refused even to consider this preposterous claim, for he had been in command at Bexar-Alamo since November, when Travis was still a civilian in San Felipe. Neither of them appealed to Bowie, for that would have been to signify their approval of his status as the de facto commander. Nor would either of them dare to challenge the authority expressed in those cold gray eyes and that firm calm manner. Thus, a fourth colonel in the person of Crockett could only have aggravated the situation.

But Davy, with becoming modesty, had demurred, and in gratitude the three colonels organized a *fandango* for the night of the tenth celebrating the arrival of him and his companions. It was a gay event, with the leading citizens of San Antonio who had not fled—and, of course, their daughters—in attendance. Corn whiskey and beer flowed in abundance, and Crockett with his fiddle and John McGregor with his bagpipes staged a rollicking Celtic musical duel that had even the Mexicans shouting with laughter. At about one o'clock in the morning a courier arrived with a report that Santa Anna was close at hand. At once Bowie, Travis and Crockett—ignoring the official commander Neill—went into conference and decided that the warning was not really urgent, and the party continued until the wee hours.

But Neill, who was not stupid, realized that the snub may have been intended, and that he was being shunted aside. In the morning, he placed himself on "twenty days' leave," and rode away from Bexar-Alamo. Neill had lame explanations for this decision: sickness in his family, the need to raise funds, but Travis was certain he would not return. That was fine with him, for Neill had appointed Travis in his place "because he was a regular." Unhappily for eager Buck, his troops "didn't truck" with such Yankee nonsense. Jim Bowie was their man, the best-known fighter in Texas. They had put up with the indecisive Neill because he had been in charge from the start, but Travis had been around for only a week. Moreover, he was a baby, only twenty-six with no combat experience, and Bowie was a dozen years older, battle-scarred and battle-wise. He was a legend in the Southwest and Travis was but a legend in his own mind. They had not spoken the word yet, but Travis could deduce that they were ready to mutiny. So he ordered an election. Bowie won big, and that made the proud and moody Travis even more sulky, unwilling to endure further humiliation.

But then Bowie unintentionally lifted Travis off the horns of his dilemma. His illness had worsened and he had turned to whisky as a pain-killer. Unfortunately, his resistance had been lowered and he quickly became roaring drunk, bursting into town bellowing that the garrison was his to command. He rudely accosted private citizens, and ordered Bexar officials to open the calaboose and free all the prisoners. When one of them was thrown back in jail, Bowie erupted in an insane fury, calling his men into town from the Alamo to cow the populace. They were soon drunk as well, marching back and forth on the Main Plaza, screaming and brandishing their weapons. Eventually these unruly Americans staggered back to the Alamo and to Bowie, who was mortified when he awoke the following morning with a monster hangover. He sheepishly came to an agreement with the indignant Travis: they would keep their separate commands, but take all major steps together. Amazingly, it worked—and by late February all but three of the Alamo's twenty-five guns were in place, and a shortage of cannonballs was being overcome by the ingenious device of chopping up horseshoes for shrapnel.

In the early morning of February 23 a Santa Anna courier on a mud-spattered horse rode into darkened San Antonio de Bexar shouting that the town would soon be attacked and everyone should leave. Immediately lights flashed all over town. Residents rubbing the sleep from their eyes piled their belongings on horse carts or buried the family savings in the dirt floor and hurried creaking, rattling, bumping into the open country. An infuriated Colonel Travis attempted to stop them but they paid him no heed, murmuring that they were going into the country to do a little planting. "In *February?*" Travis cried in disbelief, and they merely shrugged silently and flicked the reins on their horses' backs. Soon Travis and Bowie agreed that they too should evacuate the town, and all troops—in the end there would be 182 of them—were ordered to their posts in the Alamo.

An all-but-empty little city silently awaited the appearance of His Excellency *El Presidente* Antonio López de Santa Anna. In mid-afternoon he rode at the head of his cavalry into the Campo Santo burial ground, watching in supercilious pleasure while a little knot of pro-Texan Mexicans lowered their flag proclaiming the 1824 constitution and retired into the Alamo. It would be 1813 all over again. The "perfidious foreigners" were already routed. Now, just as in 1813, they would beg for mercy. But there would be none. By three o'clock his troops—his lancers in gleaming breastplates, his infantry in dusty white—were pouring into the military plaza. Then came the marching bands—excellent musical groups—followed by standard-bearers carrying the massed battle flags of Mexico.

Soon another flag—huge and blood red—was thrown to the wind from the squat bell tower of San Fernando Church. It was the traditional Mexican symbol of massacre: no quarter—no surrender—no mercy. Next from the bands formed beneath it rose the stirring notes of the "Degüello," a hymn of hate and merciless death carrying the same grim message.

About eight-hundred yards away the Americans and their Mexican friends who had followed them into the sanctuary of the abandoned old mission saw that flag and heard that music—and they understood.

59

The Battle

∿ IN THE ALAMO A RUMOR AROSE THAT SANTA ANNA WAS EAGER FOR A
parley, and Colonel Bowie decided that defiance of such a powerful
force might not be the best policy if negotiation were possible. So he
sent Green Jameson into town to find out if this were possible, handing him a note ending "God and Texas."

This so angered the Napoleon of the West that he refused to see
Jameson or even to read the note himself, scornfully ordering an aide
to give it the contemptuous reply that it deserved. This was that if the
Americans wished to live, they must immediately and unconditionally
surrender.

Bowie's proposal was a departure from his agreement with Travis to
undertake all major decisions together, and it apparently angered the
proud and supersensitive young rebel from Pandemonium, and he
sent Albert Martin to a footbridge over the river under a flag of truce.
Martin brought back the same uncompromising answer given to
Bowie, and the infuriated Travis ordered the big 18-pounder to open
fire on the town, proudly reporting to Houston: "I answered them
with a cannon shot."

Nevertheless, for each commander to have acted so independently
did not auger well for the joint command, and there seemed no way
to put it together again, until on the following day—February 24—Jim

Bowie solved the impasse by collapsing. Ill for weeks, his incredible stamina being steadily eroded by pain and his magnificent spirit dissipated by the whisky he drank to assuage it, he simply could not continue. Too weak to walk, he was placed on a litter, from which, with the gallantry that was probably his finest quality, he called to his dead wife's adopted sister, Juana Alsbury: "Sister, do not be afraid. I leave you with Colonel Travis, Colonel Crockett and other friends. They are gentlemen and will treat you kindly." Then he was carried to a small room and laid upon a cot where he began to cough his life away.

Now in complete command, Buck Travis was buoyant. With the sound of bugles in his ears he sat down to compose a message to the provisional council at Brazoria, a note that as much as any other event at the Alamo was to immortalize the American stand there. It said:

Commandancy of the Alamo
Bejar, Feby. 24th, 1836

To the People of Texas & All Americans in the World:
FELLOW CITIZENS AND COMPATRIOTS—I am besieged, by a thousand or more Mexicans under Santa Anna—I have sustained a continued bombardment and cannonade for 24 hours and have not lost a man—the enemy has demanded a surrender at discretion, otherwise, the garrison are to be put to the sword, if the fort is taken—I have answered the demand with a cannon shot, and our flag still waves proudly from the walls—I shall *never* surrender or retreat. Then, I call on you in the name of Liberty, of patriotism, and everything dear to the American character, to come to our aid, with all dispatch—The enemy is receiving reinforcements daily and will no doubt increase to three or four thousand in four or five days. If this call is neglected, I am determined to sustain myself as long as possible and die like a soldier who never forgets what is due to his honor and that of his country—VICTORY OR DEATH.

William Barret Travis
Lt. Col. Comdt.

Here was Buck Travis at his egotistical best. Not a word about Colonel Bowie or Colonel Crockett, or the gallant Texans or the brave volunteers from the States, or their Mexican friends—women and children among them—but just a steady parade of pronouns in the first person singular. Not until the appearance of Douglas MacArthur would another American soldier display such insufferable and arrogant self-esteem, and yet, when the communiqúe was published in America it set off a paroxysm of patriotism equally as self-exalting and made of Travis's name—as he undoubtedly hoped—a household word. But it never brought to the Alamo a single soldier, biscuit or bullet. Nevertheless it did reach its destination, carried by Albert Martin, the soldier who had been Travis's emissary for that fruitless parley with the enemy.

Martin left after dark, when the Mexican bombardment had ended and the Alamo defenders discovered to their incredulous delight that the enemy's furious cannonade had harmed no one. It was true, they told each other with joyous frontier disdain: "the Mexicans can't hit a bull in the ass with a bass fiddle!"

February 25 dawned in a gray drizzle and the men in the Alamo saw another earthwork going up on their side of the river. At about 10 A.M. there came a cannonade of solid shot, grape and cannister and the Americans peering through the smoke saw tiny figures swarming across the river to take possession of a cluster of adobe huts and wooden shacks known as La Villita. In Spanish days it had been a place where soldiers lived with their common-law wives, who, with professional prostitutes, sometimes serviced the various Bexar garrisons. Now the Mexican soldiers were flitting from hut to shack, coming ever closer until they were only about ninety yards away from the fort. At once, Travis ordered a foray. The Alamo gates swung open and about a half dozen men carrying torches emerged running toward La Villita. Volley after volley was fired at them with the customary high trajectory, and then they hurled their firebrands atop the thatched roofs, turned, and sped back to safety. Smoke and flames engulfed La Villita's closest buildings, and they burned to the ground, while American cannon and small arms scourged the occupants. The Texans had opened a new field of fire and the Mexicans had lost their cover. At noon they withdrew, dragging their casualties with them. Once again no Americans had been harmed.

At nine o'clock that night a northern wind suddenly lashed the area, followed by drenching rains. But the storm did not halt construction of Mexican fortifications. Throughout the day General Sesma's rear echelons had been arriving, and they were put to work. Two new artillery batteries were built across the river, one about three hundred yards to the south, or right, of the Alamo, another one thousand yards southeast by the powder house. In the Alamo the defenders could hear the Mexicans drawing the encircling ring tighter. It was now quite clear that the Alamo was surrounded, and that melancholy conclusion compelled Travis to compose still another appeal for help, this time directly to Sam Houston himself. It said:

> Do hasten aid to me as rapidly as possible, as from the superior number of the enemy it will be impossible for us to keep them out much longer. If they overpower us, we fall a sacrifice at the shrine of our country, and we hope posterity and our country will do our memory justice. Give us help, oh my Country!

Unknown to the Alamo, relief was indeed on the way. One of Travis's messages to Goliad ninety-five miles to the southeast had been received by Colonel Fannin, who commanded about four hundred men from the Matamoros expedition. They had never come close to that objective, and after Dr. Grant disappeared, Fannin took complete command. Fannin—a timid man—was positive that a march to the relief of the Alamo was ill-advised but "simply had to be done" because of the gallantry of the defenders there. On the afternoon of February 26 with 320 men and four cannon, and the norther blowing directly into their faces, the relief force set out.

Upon reaching the San Antonio River, a wagon broke down. The entire caravan paused. Then two more wagons came apart, and it became clear that the single yokes of oxen were not strong enough to drag the guns across the stream. Double teams were employed, but to get the artillery across the swift-flowing river was still a slow and wearying process. The men were discouraged, and Fannin decided to let them rest. They stacked their arms while the oxen were freed to graze in the grass. The north wind was still blowing when dawn revealed a prarie empty of oxen. More time was lost while search parties were sent out to retrieve them. Then, to Fannin's concealed relief a council of war was called. Someone asked if this expedition was really a wise move. Most of the firebrands were shocked and indignant, but Fannin was not dismayed. Speaking precisely like his old West Point professors, he detailed a dismal situation. Their food supply was down to half a barrel of rice and some dried beef. The closest supply depot was at the Seguin ranch seventy miles away (which Santa Anna had already stripped bare).

Militarily their prospects were hopeless. Could 320 men with four cannon and little ammunition really hope to overwhelm a well-led, well-fed and well-armed force of thousands? Could they leave Goliad defended by only a small rear guard. If the town fell, it would expose

Texas's entire left flank and make a present of Dimitt's Landing supply depot to Santa Anna. To *abandon* the men in the Alamo might smack of cowardice, but to attempt to *relieve* the fort was not sound strategy.

That was the advice that carried the council, and the entire expedition recrossed the river and returned to the old stone compound called Fort Defiance. "I have about 420 men here," Fannin wrote to a friend on the 28th, "and if I can get provisions in tomorrow or next day, can maintain myself against any force."

But on that same 28th of February Fannin's confidence was again shaken when a courier rode into Goliad to report that General José Urrea with a large force had just fallen on the garrison at San Patricio fifty miles south. Most of the men there were the remnants of the once-carefree Matamoros expedition, and all were executed—except Colonel Frank Johnson and a few others, who escaped. When Johnson arrived at Goliad with the bad news, Fannin's resolve was more than somewhat shaken.

Antonio López de Santa Anna was beside himself. He had surrounded the Gringos, yes, but he still had not enough men to rush the Alamo as he had planned. Where was that great grafter General Antonio Gaona, or Santa Anna's second-in-command General Filisola? The answer was that they were still on the Rio Grande dragging their feet, leading their grumbling divisions through the debris left by Santa Anna's own march: the carcasses of mules and oxen starved to death, smashed packing cases, wrecked carts. There was hardly any water available, and Filisola, who was charged with organizing a supply train, realized with a sinking heart that *El Presidente* would never even try to understand his situation. Filisola hated to see cavalrymen stumbling under the weight of their saddles. Rather than ride their underfed mounts to death, they had unsaddled them and were themselves in danger of starvation—only because among other neglected necessities, the Napoleon of the West had forgotten to provide fodder wagons.

But Santa Anna was pleased the night of February 27 when a forage expedition sent to plunder the Seguin and Florez ranchos returned loaded with corn, hogs and beef. Such good news should be celebrated, the general thought—turning to the comfort of the beautiful San Antonio ladies he had enrolled in his entourage. Sergeant Francisco Becerra—a most unreliable reporter—in his lurid account of the Alamo campaign has exaggerated the influence of these desirable companions upon *El Presidente*, but there is no doubt that there was a beautiful young lady available. She was supposed to have been wed to Santa Anna by an unscrupulous aide posing as a priest. She must have had charms, because before the battle exploded, Santa Anna had her sent back to San Luis Potosí for safety, riding in his own carriage and clutching a clinking little gift of two thousand pesos.

But this dalliance was rudely shattered on February 28 when word of Fannin's approach reached Santa Anna. Irked at having to weaken his forces surrounding those defiant Texans, he sent General Sesma with a battalion of infantry, cavalry and guns to block the Texans' approach, reminding Sesma: "In this war, you know, there ought to be no prisoners."

Nevertheless, for all of *El Presidente*'s precautions, a relief force did enter the Alamo.

On the afternoon of February 24, Dr. Sutherland and John Smith from the Alamo galloped into the little town of Gonzales seventy miles to the east, bringing news of the Mexican attack. To their surprise it seemed that the entire town rallied to the cause, calling themselves the Gonzales Ranging Company of Mounted Volunteers. In the end there were twenty-five of them, counting Sutherland and Smith: men from a dozen states, fathers and grandfathers and teenage youths; a hatter from New York and a Carolina farm boy on the make for "a rich old widow," a former sheriff and a surveyor and a shoemaker from England and the richest man in town whose pretty young wife had been stolen from him by a dashing nineteen-year-old rogue who had also joined up.

At two o'clock in the afternoon of February 27, leaving weeping wives and cheering children behind, they pounded out of town. Waiting for them was a fifteen-year-old boy who begged to go in his father's place. After all, there were nine children to feed and he wasn't up to it. Reluctantly the father dismounted and handed his horse's reins to his son. By nightfall they had crossed the Guadalupe River ford and next day had reached Cibolo, where they added seven more recruits. Thirty-two strong, they trotted west over the prairie to Bexar. On the twenty-ninth they rested just short of their objective, and as night fell a cultivated English voice came out of the darkness.

"Do you wish to go into the fort, gentlemen?"

In the dusk the Gonzalistas beheld a man sitting his horse calmly, and someone answered, "Yes." Without a word the man turned and trotted off, the Gonzalistas following. But John Smith did not like it. The stranger spoke good English and was obviously not a Mexican, but yet. . . . Smith was a veteran scout who when puzzled always trusted his intuition—and so he blurted: "Boys, it's time to be after shootin' that feller!"

Instantly, before any of the Texans could aim a weapon, the stranger kicked his mount hard and bolted out of sight. Warned that they were in enemy territory, the Gonzales men moved ahead cautiously—very cautiously—until the silent bulk of the Alamo rose before them. They drew rein and a horse whinnied and a rifle on the Alamo wall blazed and a Gonzales man shot in the foot screamed and cursed.

"By God," the Alamo sentinel swore, "that's an *American* cussin'!" At once the fort's gate swung open and the Gonzalistas went thundering inside the Alamo, to be greeted with the whoops and the high yipping cries of the Southern hunter. There would have been fireworks from their rifles and pistols, too, except that Travis to conserve ammunition had issued strict orders against firing weapons except to repel an attack. Later in the bitter cold of the 1st of March he ordered a more practical means of celebrating the fact that there were now 182 men in the Alamo: two cannon shots delivered by a 12-pounder against a house on Bexar's Main Plaza believed to be Santa Anna's headquarters. One missed but the other crashed right on target, sending stones, timbers and Mexicans flying. But Santa Anna was not there. He was out scouting. His Excellency was disturbed. Sesma had not found Fannin and that snail Gaona was still crawling north . . . and his eastern flank was far too weak.

Santa Anna might have been more disturbed if he had learned how Texas, stung by Travis's ringing calls for help, at last began to shake itself out of its lethargy. In San Felipe the militia was notified to stand by to march, and in Brazoria on March 1 Sam Houston made an electrifying appearance before the convention. Next day the hysterical delegates proclaimed the independence of Texas and were later thrown into another tumult of joy when they learned of the Gonzales reinforcement of the Alamo.

Antonio López de Santa Anna, though unaware of the tide of Texan patriotism running against him, still had enough sense to perceive that this first small reinforcement of the Alamo might be the opening trickle of a wave of perfidious foreigners flowing to the enemy's side. After all, were there not thirty thousand of them in Texas?

Two days after the Gonzales men galloped into the Alamo, another reinforcement arrived: one man, James Butler Bonham, the bold battler from South Carolina and Travis's most dependable courier, if not actually now his best friend. There were now 183 men in the abandoned mission, but Bonham's arrival—though welcomed with cheers and shouts—sobered Travis when he heard that Fannin had retreated into the safety of Fort Defiance and had no intention of coming out. He would have been even more depressed to learn that on that very same day Colonel Fannin had shelved all plans for another march to the Alamo's rescue. Dismayed by Johnson's San Patricio report, Fannin was again filled with fear to learn that Urrea had next caught Dr. Grant leading fifteen men on a horse-hunting foray along the Rio Grande and killed them all.

On March 3 Colonel Travis, so far from being discouraged by Urrea's victories, was actually writing to Brazoria requesting "at least 500 pounds of cannon powder, 200 rounds of six, nine, twelve and eighteen-pound balls, ten kegs of rifle powder. . . ." He also called upon the convention to declare Texas's independence (which it had already done). "If independence is not declared," he wrote, "I shall lay down my arms, and so will the men under my command. But under the flag of Independence we are ready to peril our lives a hundred times a day." The veteran scout John Smith was to carry these messages, and many others from Alamo men writing last letters to their loved ones. Travis also told Smith that any reinforcements should bring ten days' rations with them, that he planned to fire the 18-pounder three times a day to show everyone—Santa Anna included— that he was still fighting. Smith nodded, eager to be off, but forced to wait until a party of Texans sallied forth to distract the enemy by random firing. When the Mexican guns erupted in reply, the Alamo gate swung open and Smith galloped through, turned east—and vanished.

On the morning of March 4 dawn seemed to burst from the gun tubes of a new Mexican battery to the north. Its cannonade was followed by Sesma's howitzers beginning to lob shells into the compound. Some of the men began to feel discouraged, even Davy Crockett, who said: "I think we had better march out and die in the open air. I don't like to be hemmed up."

Many of the "friendly" Mexicans also had misgivings. It seemed to them now that Santa Anna was going to win, and they did not like to be on the losing side with His Excellency's enemies. They began to complain that they would be second-class citizens under a Yankee government. Men with familiar names such as Garza, Silvero, Rodriguez and Flores simply vanished. One Mexican woman deserted the night of March 4, going directly to Santa Anna's headquarters to inform him that the Alamo defenses were crumbling . . . the men were weak and discouraged . . . ammunition was low . . . the place could be taken easily.

In the clear, warm dawn of March 5 the garrison could see that during the night the northern battery had moved closer. It was now only two hundred yards away. Perhaps worse, the Mexican gunners were showing unusual respect for the American sharpshooters. Ever since a marksman who was probably Crockett had killed a Mexican engineer at two hundred yards, the "Greasers" had kept their heads down. On that same day Travis summoned the entire garrison to the open plaza. He told them that he was determined to fight to the end, but if any of them wished to leave they could do so now. For emphasis he drew a line in the ground with his sword, inviting all who would remain to cross it. All but one man crossed. Louis Rose, the Napoleonic veteran whom Bowie had befriended, stood alone. Patriotism, the ideal of dying for one's country, these are not the themes that move mercenaries. They fight for pay or plunder, and when defeat looms—they leave. Jim Bowie had been brought to the plaza. Lying on his cot, pale and emaciated, racked by his cough, Bowie pleaded with his friend not to leave, but by nightfall he was gone.

The day before—the 4th—Antonio López de Santa Anna made a decision rare or even unique for him: he called a council of war to ask if the Alamo should be stormed. In response the officers raised such a babble of conflicting advice that he wished he had kept to his policy of consulting no one. Only Sesma and the smooth but brave Colonel Juan Almonte, Santa Anna's chief aide, were for immediate assault. General Cós, who knew the Alamo well, argued that the light Mexican howitzers and 8-pounders were not heavy enough to batter its walls. Why not wait for Gaona's pair of 12-pounders due on the 7th? The veteran from Spanish days, General Manuel Fernandez Castrillon, agreed. So did Colonel Romero whose Matamoros battalion had been badly battered. Another officer claimed that the army was still short of doctors and medical supplies, to which the sarcastic *El Presidente* replied that this would make the men realize that it was "not as bad to die as to come out wounded."

In the midst of all this indecision, Santa Anna abruptly dismissed the council. On reflection he realized that the 12-pounders really could be decisive. But there were other considerations. The Alamo's defenses grew stronger daily. Those wretched Gonzalistas had easily gotten inside the fort. More might follow. Siege warfare was always debilitating and his own men were weary. He needed them for subsequent operations, decisive strokes that would crush the rebellion. It was much better to strike now before more troops could reinforce the enemy, and he was certain that Fannin was on his way. That night when the female deserter came to him to describe the Alamo's weaknesses, he knew that he was right—and the assault was scheduled for four A.M. March 6. Four columns would strike the fort simultaneously. Cós would hit the northwest corner . . . Francisco Duque the northeast . . . José Maria Romero the east . . . Juan Morales the south . . . Sesma's cavalry would patrol the east ready to cut down any Texans attempting to escape. Santa Anna himself would command the reserve at the new battery north of the Alamo. Counting Sesma's troopers, the entire assault force would consist of 1,800 men, about three-quarters of Santa Anna's army.

Throughout the night of the 5th and into the early morning darkness of the 6th, the Mexican troops moved into position, sinking shivering into the cold wet grass to await the bugle call sounding the assault. It did not come at exactly 4 A.M. because His Excellency wanted a little daylight before attacking. At five the first faint streaks of dawn appeared in the eastern sky. Even then *El Presidente* hesitated, until one of the 1,800 Mexicans surrounding the fort could stand the tension no longer and yelled, "*Viva Santa Anna!*" Others took up the cry and Santa Anna, now certain that the Alamo had been warned, ordered Bugler Gonzalez to sound the charge.

It came, high and strident, and General Cós shouted, "*Arriba!* Up!"—and the men of his spearhead crouching in the grass two hundred yards from the Alamo jumped to their feet, grabbing their scaling ladders and pikes and surging toward the silent fort with a mighty shout. On the Alamo wall the adjutant Captain John Baugh heard them. Turning, he raced for the barracks, shouting: "Colonel Travis! The Mexicans are coming!"

Travis threw aside his blanket and grabbed his homespun jacket. Buckling on his sword and seizing his double-barreled shotgun, he yelled to his black slave Joe to follow him—and ran across the plaza to mount the north battery wall where two guns were already manned. The enemy in their white jumpers were not yet in sight but the tumult—yells, bugle calls, massed battalion bands playing the chilling notes of "Degüello," and then rockets exploding above him—told him the assault was on.

"Come on boys!" Travis yelled. "The Mexicans are upon us and we'll give them Hell!"

All over the Alamo the Americans were scrambling for their battle stations, muskets or rifles in their hands. A long 12-pounder spoke with a roar and twelve-year-old Enrique Esparza in the church shrank from the tongue of flame flashing from its mouth.

Travis remained at the north battery, shouting over and over, "Hurrah, my boys." Still holding his jacket, he slung it over a peg and called out to the men of the pro-Texan Captain Juan Seguin's company: "*No rendirse, muchachos!* No surrender, boys!" Because Santa Anna's hoped-for surprise had been complete, the Mexicans assaulting the north battery were already at its protective ditch—too close for the Alamo cannon to be depressed to scatter them. Soon planks and ladders rose against the outer wall. Travis sensed the threat and fired both barrels of his shotgun down into them. An answering volley of musketry rose upward. Travis spun, shot in the head. Dropping his shotgun among the Mexicans climbing upward, he fell backward fatally wounded. His slave Joe, horrified, fled back to the barracks.

Other noncombatants crouched in terror within the sacristy of the church. Mrs. Susannah Dickinson, wife of the artillerist, put her hand to her trembling lips as she listened to the horrible hymn of battle: the screams of the stricken, yells, cheers, explosions, thuds of falling timber, the sound of running feet. Her little daughter Angelina buried her head in her mother's apron. A teen-age Gonzalista burst into the sacristy, blood streaming from his shattered jaw. He tried to speak, but only gibberish came out.

Every artillery position was now besieged by Santa Anna's men, and the Texans who held them were firing with deadly efficiency. In support were sharpshooters lying prone with four or five rifles or muskets beside them. Firing them one after another, they waited until but one loaded weapon remained to be used in emergency, while reloading the others. All around the Alamo now the deadly American fire was taking a terrible toll. On the northwest a double blast of grape shot—those chopped-up horseshoes—struck down forty men. On the northeast another blast scythed half a company to the ground and shattered Colonel Duque's leg. His men trampled his crumpled body as they ran forward ducking low. These were the troops that killed Travis, but only a few reached the north battery wall. Struck by a withering fire they retreated, reformed—and came forward again, only to be driven off a second time.

A third advance was attempted. Shouting and yelling, cheering "*El Presidente y la republica,*" the Mexicans now clearly visible in the spreading daylight, were again hammered to the ground. Now the enemy troops were so confused by that steady hum of bullets and shriek of cannon balls—even the steady shrill notes of the no-quarter hymn of hate—that they gathered together beneath the walls, safe from artillery but imperiled by rifle fire.

Many of the Mexicans killed or wounded were victims of friendly fire. Shooting blindly—often with their eyes squeezed shut—the Mexicans inevitably fired high, and their bullets flew over the Alamo to scourge their own soldiers gathered on every side. Meanwhile, most of the scaling ladders had vanished, along with the troops detailed to bring them. They were either shot or in hiding.

Watching from his earthwork where the reserve was stationed, General Santa Anna was dismayed at the continued blaze of gunfire from the Alamo. It flashed and flashed unabated. Turning to Colonel Agustin Amat, he ordered him to send in the reserves. They went in with a rush, sometimes stumbling over the uneven ground, cheering and yelling wildly. But they were unable to turn the tide of battle.

But then Lady Luck, so often the arbiter of battle, waved her wand over the Mexicans. They accidentally stumbled upon a redoubt built by Green Jameson to mask a breach at the wall's east end. Because this rude and unfinished structure thrown up so hastily was full of voids and chinks, the Mexicans were able to find handholds while they clambered up it, sometimes stamping on each other's hands. Led by General Juan Amador, they scrambled onto the parapet just at the same time that General Cós changed front at the northwest corner to hurl a battalion against the north end, outflanking the Texan battery at the northwest angle.

Although there was no easily mountable structure there, the Mexicans were able to squirm through the numerous embrasures unwisely cut in the Alamo wall to give the Texan marksmen fields of fire. They did, taking a fearful toll, but there were simply too many Mexicans and too few sharpshooters, and from a trickle of white uniforms penetrating the Alamo, Cós's men poured inside in a flood.

Seeing this, Almeron Dickinson momentarily left his cannon to run below to the church sacristy where his wife and daughter clung to each other in terror, crying: "Great God, Sue, the Mexicans are inside our walls!" Embracing her, he shouted, "If they spare you, save my child," and turned to run back up to his guns. His men were already turning their cannon to aim them at the northern postern, while another squad mounted on a high platform on the plaza did the same. Their gun had the enemy perfectly in view and its blasts of grape sent many of them tumbling. But more came through, and then Colonel Morales led his battalion at the palisade at the south end held by Colonel Crockett and his Tennessee sharpshooters. A withering fire cut down the Mexican spearheads, and Morales was about to signal a retreat when the fierce battle at the other, northern end of the wall, gave him an opportunity to take Crockett's position in the rear.

Staying well out of the range of that deadly palisade, Morales's men seized a cluster of stone huts near the southwest corner. They were now in position to attack the 18-pounder that spread so much death and destruction among them. Racing across an open space between them and the gun, they climbed the barbette on which the gun was mounted and came in on the surprised Texan gunners with flashing bayonets that soon were red with blood. Simultaneously the northern defenses gave way completely. The columns of Romero and Duque now led by General Castrillon, poured unchecked over the wall, flowing over the plaza to join Morales's troops in the south. With the enemy in their rear, some of the men on the palisade leaped to the ground seeking to find refuge at Goliad or some other sanctuary in the east.

Instead they were ridden down by Sesma's cavalry waiting for just such an opportunity. Few of these fugitives escaped their flashing sabers or glittering lances. One Texan hid under a bush but was found and killed. Another wriggled under a small bridge, but was seen and reported by a local woman washing clothes. He was quickly found and executed.

Most of the Texans, however, went down fighting—and especially Crockett and his Tenneseans. They fought with a fury that astonished even their assailants. Man-for-man the Mexicans were no match for these taller, stronger Americans—especially in a hand-to-hand melee fought with fists, clubbed rifles and pistols, bayonets and Bowie knives. It was so close that firearms were of little use and certainly could not be reloaded. It was not exactly known when Davy Crockett went down, but Sergeant Felix Nuñez remembered one heroic fighter who might have been the legendary frontiersman:

> He was a tall American of rather dark complexion and had on a long buckskin coat and a round cap without any bill, made out of fox skin with the long tail hanging down his back. This man apparently had a charmed life. Of the many soldiers who took deliberate aim at him, not one ever hit him. On the contrary, he never missed a shot. He killed at least eight of our men, besides wounding many others. This being observed by a lieutenant who had come in over the wall, he sprang at him and dealt him a deadly blow with his sword, just above the right eye, which felled him to the ground, and in an instant he was pierced by not less than 20 bayonets.

Actually, Crockett and his men had been fighting an individual battle of their own, far from the general struggle on the plaza or around Texan gun emplacements on the wall. That was because their position was quite some distance from the barracks, where Captain Baugh had a bugler blow the rallying call. One by one, or in squads—riflemen, artillerists, dismounted cavalry—they dropped from the walls and headed for the barracks. They did not run but fought their way into them, opposed every step of the way by the crack *zapadores* battalion under Lieutenant Colonel José de la Peña.

Once safely inside the Texans turned to face their tormentor fighting from what could be described as a monster chunk of Swiss cheese full of holes. Every doorway was blocked by a parapet, semicircular mounds of earth pressed between stretched hides. They were just high enough for resting a rifle on them. In the rooms behind, holes had been bored, and there were even trenches dug in the bare earth. From these positions a steady, deadly fire raked the Mexicans so severely that they turned and ran for cover in the plaza. But there was no cover there, and Texan fire continued to strew bundles of white streaked with blood on that bare, open place.

On the north wall where Travis had fallen, General Amador was shocked by the carnage among the Mexicans, ordering his men to turn the guns around to blast the American barricades. To the south Colonel Morales seized upon the same tactic, and his men began firing the captured 18-pounder at the barricades of the long barracks. While fighting continued to rage in the plaza, Lieutenant José Maria Torres of the *zapadores* saw a blue flag waving atop the long barracks. It was the banner of the New Orleans Grays, but Torres thought it was the Texas flag, the symbol of rebellion and treason. Enraged he raced for the roof, dismayed to find three dead Mexican color sergeants lying beneath that hateful symbol. Ignoring enemy bullets whining around him, Torres ripped it down and ran up the Mexican colors. Now the Texan bullets sang like a horde of angry bees, killing young Lieutenant Damascus Martinez, who had rushed to help Torres, and in the next moment the gallant Torres as well.

With the Plaza now safely in Mexican possession, there was absolutely no hope of help for the Texans behind their barricades. The prime targets were the long barracks to the east, the low barracks on the south, and that collection of stone huts on the west wall. Against all of these positions the Mexicans used captured cannon to blast the barricades into shreds, then fired volleys of musketry to destroy the defenders, and finally wild bayonet charges—Santa Anna's favorite tactic. One by one these structures fell. In one of these rooms on the west Mrs. Horace Alsbury crouched with her baby, her sister Gertrudis Veramendi beside her. Why they were there alone is not known, although Bowie may have thought that it was the point of least danger. But it wasn't, when Gertrudis opened the door hoping to show the

Mexicans that there was no one but women inside, a *soldado* reached for her shawl. Terrified, Gertrudis slammed the door shut. But it was wrenched open and enemy troops came rushing inside. A young Texan tried to protect the women, but a Mexican drove his bayonet into him. Just as it appeared that his comrades would turn on the women, a Mexican officer came inside and ordered the yelling *soldados* to leave. "How did you come here?" he angrily asked the frightened women. "What are you doing here, anyhow?" Without waiting for an answer he ordered them outside to stand against a wall in comparative safety.

On the south Morales's men were mopping up. Coming to the small room occupied by Jim Bowie, they yanked the door open and drew back instantly. There was the legendary warrior erect on his cot, his back against a wall—a brace of pistols in both hands. He died, of course, but almost certainly not before he had taken two Mexicans with him.

Only the Alamo church remained in Texan hands. Dickinson's crew continued to fire their 12-pounder. Bonham had joined them so that there were eleven men altogether, including Robert Evans and Gregorio Esparza. Colonel Morales had the answer to this impasse: the captured 18-pounder. Rolled into position, the Mexicans began a point-blank fire that slowly but steadily took the church apart, timber by timber, and stone by stone. Dickinson fell . . . so did Esparza. . . . A great shout arose when the heavy double doors sagged on the hinges. Yelling wildly the Mexican soldiers raced into the smoke- and dust-filled church, eagerly seeking Gringos to bayonet. Robert Evans was wounded, yet he seized a torch and crawled for the powder room . . . He never reached it.

Even though it was all but over at the Alamo the frenzied Mexicans continued their bloodbath. Only the women and the two babies were spared. Before their eyes three twelve-year-old boys—two Texans and one Mexican—were mercilessly bayoneted. Gradually, the shots, shouts, and screams were fewer and the tumult subsided. Hope like the thrill of a tiny nerve began to rise in the breasts of those three horrified women in that tiny room. Would they be spared?

Suddenly Jacob Walker, the little gunner from Nacogdoches, burst into the room, his frightened eyes darting about for a hiding place. But before he could find one, four Mexican soldiers with outthrust bayonets rushed inside. They ignored Mrs. Dickinson, now on her knees in prayer, and killed Walker with musket shots. Then they drove their blades into his bleeding body and hoisted him high like a hunter's trophy to march yelling from the room.

By 6:30 A.M. it was quiet at the Alamo. All of its defenders—182 of them—were dead, and 600 men of General Antonio Santa Anna's assault force of 1,800 were dead or wounded. That was about a third of his attacking army, a terrible price to pay for a so-called indefensible compound and a broken-down church. It was, as William Barret Travis always insisted it would be, a Phyrric victory. It had not crushed the Texas revolt, but rather by its merciless massacre of its defenders had given that infant rebellious state and the United States as well a maniacal ache for revenge and a terrible rallying cry:

"Remember the Alamo!"

60

Massacre at Goliad

 UNLIKE THE ALAMO, FORT DEFIANCE AT GOLIAD WAS EMINENTLY defensible. No makeshift presidio, it had been built as a military stronghold atop a hill. Colonel Fannin was not boasting when he wrote, "I can maintain myself against any force." With thick walls that his troops had reinforced, more than four hundred men, ample and heavy artillery and abundant food supplies, he could withstand the most powerful besieger.

But Travis's defeat had unnerved Fannin, and he was upset when General Houston—still convinced that volunteers could not stand up to regulars—ordered him to destroy the fort and withdraw toward Victoria. Deciding to obey Houston's order, he prepared for retreat by burying a number of the fort's cannon, but then, in the confused and indecisive way that he had started and then stopped the relief of the Alamo, he ordered the guns dug up and remounted. On March 18 he was again prepared to retreat, with his oxen hitched to the guns he was taking with him. But then a party of Mexican cavalry was sighted outside the fort, and he postponed the withdrawal, ordering the cannon again buried; and then, once again, he ordered them dug up.

During the norther that lashed the area that night, Colonel Fannin seemed finally to have made up his mind: he would retreat. At about nine o'clock next morning, under cover of a thick fog, the withdrawal began. Goliad went up in flames and all surplus food was burned. Unfortunately, this column of about four hundred men was not traveling light, as it should have been, but rather with every cart loaded with personal possessions. At the first river crossing, the banks were so steep that all carts and wagons had to be partially unloaded before crossing, and then brought back empty to be reloaded. Not only the oxen but the men as well were already travel-weary—and a halt was called only a few miles outside Goliad!

Next day Fannin was shaken by scouting reports that a large Mexican force—General José Urrea's—was only four or five miles to the rear. Yet, toward the end of the second day, the oxen appeared on the verge of collapse. Within sight of a splendid sanctuary in the forest of Coleto Creek only two miles away, Fannin found it necessary to halt and pitch camp in an open field. It was a disastrous decision, probably made out of Fannin's contempt for Mexican fighting prowess, always a mistake by any commander no matter who the enemy might be. He also thought he was safe from surprise because of the four mounted scouts he had left behind to watch for Mexicans. Unknown to him, those observers had dismounted to take a siesta, and barely escaped capture by Urrea's cavalry. They were so frightened that three of them reaching Fannin's resting column did not stop but rather galloped even harder for safety. The fourth joined his comrades and reported the Mexican approach.

Now aware of his danger, Fannin resumed the march toward the water available at the creek and cover in the forest. About a half mile away from it, moving through a low meadow, his column was attacked by Mexican cavalry. It was the worst possible place to make a stand. It was a depression into which enemy artillery could deliver a plunging fire. But Fannin had no other choice, and the battle was joined. The Americans—none of these young men were Texans, but rather volunteers from Georgia, Alabama, Louisiana and Arkansas—fought very well at first, repulsing a succession of Mexican charges, either on horse or on foot, and punishing the enemy with grapeshot from cannon mounted at each corner of the square they had formed. They took casualties, but they gave as good as they got. In midafternoon, however, Urrea's entire army had come up, and before night fell Fannin's position was entirely surrounded. Dawn revealed Fannin's terrible losses in men and equipment. He was down to two hundred men with wrecked carts and dead oxen—killed by sharpshooters on Urrea's orders—lying everywhere. Grimly aware of his predicament, Fannin put the question of surrender or continued fighting to the vote. Although the New Orleans Greys and Alabama Red Rovers argued fiercely for fighting, the vote was for surrender—and Fannin ran up the white flag.

Urrea would accept no surrender other than "at discretion," meaning unconditional and based upon an old Spanish law declaring any foreigner who came into Mexico armed should be treated as a pirate: killed wherever and whenever found, executed if taken captive. Urrea even came into the enemy camp to explain the limits of his authority to Fannin and his men. "If you gentlemen wish to surrender at discretion, the matter is ended," he told Fannin, "otherwise I shall return to my camp and renew the attack."

Fannin capitulated much to the relief of those who voted for capitulation, and the humiliation and anger of those opposed it. At two o'clock that afternoon, about three hundred prisoners were herded back to Goliad and literally stuffed inside its burned-out little church, so small that at no time was it possible for more than a quarter of them to sit down. A few days later 90 of their wounded comrades were brought back to Goliad, while at the same time about 120 Matamoros filibusters were picked off by Urrea and also packed inside the church. Later 82 volunteers from Tennessee were somehow jammed among them. In all, there were between 425 and 445 Americans so imprisoned.

But they were not dismayed. At the parleying prior to their surrender they had been told that they would be shipped back to the United States. "Well, gentlemen," an English-speaking officer told them after they had surrendered their weapons, "in ten days liberty and home." Thus, as soldiers accustomed to privation, they made light of their plight and even began singing songs such as "Home, Sweet Home."

Saturday night, March 26, there came to Lieutenant Colonel José Nicolas de la Portilla—Urrea's temporary replacement at Goliad—a message from His Excellency Antonio López de Santa Anna. Here it was a week after the fight at Coleto Creek, and word had come to him that the prisoners had not been executed according to the Law of the Pirates. Let them be killed immediately.

Portilla was a decent man, as were many of the other Mexican officers in Goliad, but there was no way any of them could challenge an order from the Generalissimo. A few volunteers who could prove that they had carried no weapons were spared, along with two Gringo surgeons needed to care for wounded Mexicans. Some officers were given sanctuary by brave and compassionate Mexican women, but there were still more than four hundred prisoners who were awakened next morning and told to prepare to march.

They were separated into three columns, one starting in the direction of San Antonio, another toward San Patricio and the third to Copano on the coast. They were in double file, with armed Mexican infantry to either side of them, cavalry and lancers to front and rear.

"*Pobrecitos!*" many Mexican women murmured as they passed, anguish in their eyes. "Poor little ones!"

Knowing no Spanish, the Americans didn't understand, and it was thus that they marched out of Goliad singing. They were going home—going home on Palm Sunday.

About a mile outside of Goliad—far enough from the hospital so that the wounded Gringos would not hear anything—the three columns were halted. The soldiers on one side joined those on the other. They stepped back a pace and cocked their muskets.

"*My God!*" somebody screamed. "*They're going to shoot us!*"

Some of them fell flat on the ground, others knelt with outstretched arms begging for mercy, some ran away to be killed by the lancers, but most simply stood there huddled together frozen in disbelieving fear. It took several volleys to complete the slaughter, after which the Mexicans in their white jumpers went in with their bayonets, lunging at anything that moved. They heaped the bleeding bodies into piles and covered them with brushwood and oil and set them on fire, knowing full well that many of them could still be alive.

Colonel Fannin and his second-in-command, Lieutenant Colonel William Ward—both Georgians—were given the honor of a separate excution. Fannin behaved nobly. He handed his watch to the officer-in-charge and asked that it be sent to his wife. He also asked not to be shot in the head and to be given a decent Christian burial. They kept his watch, shot him in the head and threw his body on top of the others.

Ward was not so controlled. When they ordered him to kneel, he told them to go to hell and stood proudly erect, shaking his fists and cursing them when they cut him down.

Back in Goliad the wounded were being slaughtered, taken from their beds or shot or bayoneted inside the hospital, and their bodies were also set afire. But they did not burn too well, for next morning the *zapilotes*—the vultures—were feeding on them.

In San Antonio the Napoleon of the West read Portilla's report with satisfaction. The Alamo ... Goliad ... One more such massacre should crush the Texas Rebellion forever. All that stood between Santa Anna now was the tiny, demoralized army led by General Sam Houston of Tennessee.

61

Sam Houston Saves Texas

∾ THE CHILDHOOD AND EARLY LIFE OF SAMUEL HOUSTON, LIKE THOSE of almost all Go Aheads and GTTs, is not well documented, except that from his birth in 1793 in Rockbridge County, Virginia, he was never called anything but Sam. As a boy Sam migrated with his family to Tennessee, where his parents apprenticed him to a village store. But Sam rebelled and went to live in the forests with the Cherokee, protesting: "I would rather measure deer tracks than cloth." His Indian hosts welcomed him, for at maturity he was a splendid physical specimen, standing two to four inches above six feet, with shoulders as wide as live-oak trunks and arms as brawny as their limbs. He also exuded great personal charm and was a great favorite with the Indian girls, although none of them could understand why he would so often leave them to seek the solitude of the woods and there memorize Pope's translation of the *Iliad*.

Sam's large, wide-set eyes were a brilliant gray. They could blaze with anger or the excitement of battle or of the hunt, or make a life-long friend of a stranger simply by fixing him with their warmth followed by his simple "Howdy-do." That steady gaze was also calculated to melt female hearts, although more discerning ladies such as the perceptive Varina Davis, wife of the Confederacy's first and only president, found his studied salutations to the fairer sex something more like a grotesque mating dance. "When he met a lady," she recalled, "he took a step forward, then bowed very low, and in a deep voice said, 'Lady, I salute you.' It was an embarrassing kind of thing, and it was performed with the several motions of a fencing lesson."

There was, however, nothing studied or artificial about Sam Houston's prowess as a fighter, as he showed at Horseshoe Bend when he served under Andrew Jackson against the Creeks. Leading a charge at an enemy barricade with drawn sword, he vaulted onto the breastwork to capture the position by himself. But his men were tardy in following, and by the time they joined him big Sam was reeling and bleeding with a barbed arrow protruding from his thigh. Commanding an officer to yank it free at swordpoint, he sank to the ground in exquisite agony. That was where an admiring Old Hickory found him, sternly ordering him to risk no further harm.

Houston's response—like a dog ordered to stop barking—was to charge into the battle again on the following day, launching another solitary attack on a Creek breastwork, and being hammered to the earth by point-blank musketry that broke his right arm and shoulder and nearly killed him. As he lay there apparently dying, Jackson's soldiers finished the battle by setting the enemy fortifications afire—but Old Hickory never forgot the young giant's impetuous charges.

That, of course, was exactly the impression Houston sought to make. Like all exuberant young men playing for high stakes—he was then exactly twenty-one—he had deliberately exposed himself to enemy fire to catch his general's eye. He had indeed, and Jackson visited him frequently during his long and painful recuperation; so that young Sam wisely decided to study law and set up his practice in Nashville beneath the approving eye of the Old Hero of the Hermitage. Soon the childless Jackson—ever grieving at having no son and heir—treated Sam as though he were indeed of his own flesh and blood.

He guided him into the Tennessee legislature, the U.S. House of Representatives and finally into the Tennessee governor's chair. Throughout this meteoric rise, Houston comported himself with a self-advertising flamboyance, draping his splendid body in garish, theatrical styles of dress, ranging from the feathers-and-buckskin of the Cherokee, with whom he often sojourned, to the Mexican, Arab or European. Sometimes he appeared robed in silk like a Turkish sultan, or in a black velvet coat so heavy with gold embroidery that a Frenchman who saw him gasped that the garment must have been worth twelve hundred francs. In later years he delighted in flaunting the silver-studded saddle and huge sombrero of a Mexican vaquero, and even, as age and dissipation swelled his waistline, strapping on a corset or girdle. When running for governor in 1828, the year Jackson won the White House, he appeared frequently in a ruffled white silk shirt, black satin vest, "shining" black silk jacket and socks, silver-buckled dancing pumps and a bell-crowned black beaver hat—which, with his unfailing touch of the grotesque or anomalous, he sometimes complemented with a "gorgeous Indian hunting shirt and beaded red sash." Frequently his insatiable delight in shocking people would lead him to comb his hair forward over his forehead à la the Caesars or Napoleon; and then, as though in contempt for the scandalized faces around him to smear it with stinking bear grease and work it into some bizarre style of his own design. Inevitably this prince of caprice came to be widely regarded as a freak, and when Jackson was asked what he thought of his antics, the old man would reply with fierce and angry loyalty: "Thank God there is one man that was made by the Almighty and not by a tailor."

Jackson was not dismayed when Houston exploded in Congress like a bomb, caning a fellow member who insulted him; and then, brought to trial, delivering an hour-long oration on the subject of honor, finishing to a thunderous outburst of applause and a bouquet thrown to him by a woman in the gallery. Old Hickory also chuckled when he heard how his protégé had humiliated a posturing Frenchman who, fancying he looked like Napoleon, appeared at a costume ball flaunting a chestful of medals supposedly conferred upon him by the emperor. Houston, clad only in an Indian blanket, bared his battle-scarred torso, pounding his chest like any Cherokee brave with the remark: "Monsieur, a humbled republican soldier who wears his decorations here, salutes you." One of Houston's first acts as governor of Tennessee was to take to wife a wealthy and beautiful young plantation belle named Eliza Allen. With Old Hickory, other leading Democrats attending the splendid reception in the state house agreed that blond and blue-eyed Eliza would make a marvelous First Lady.

But then, four months after the wedding, Houston's teenage wife shocked the Volunteer State by fleeing from her distinguished husband's side to seek sanctuary in her parents' home. Nashville was scandalized. A fresh rumor explaining her inexplicable flight seemed to circulate every day. Eliza had another lover, she had been repelled by Houston's battle scars, he had physically abused her. A burning effigy of Houston was dragged through the capital's streets by a jeering mob.

Sam Houston confided to no one about the scandal—not even Jackson. His obstinate though gallant silence infuriated those Democrats who had hoped to ride to Washington on his coattails. One night, after burning all his letters, Houston went down to the riverfront and quietly sailed out of town aboard a Cumberland River packet. "I was in an agony of despair and strongly tempted to leap overboard and end my worthless life," he wrote later. "At that moment, however, an eagle swooped down near my head, and then, soaring aloft with wildest screams, was lost in the rays of the setting sun." Not even a Hollywood ending could match this vintage Sam Houston. Standing upon the steamer's deck, he recalled, he watched the great bird turn into the sunlight. "I knew then, that a great destiny waited for me in the west. . . ."

True, but it was still a few years away, even after he met the celebrated duelist Jim Bowie aboard a flatboat. Bowie had just returned from San Antonio de Bexar in the still-Mexican province of Texas. His eyes glowed as he spoke of the opportunities awaiting Go-Aheads south of the Rio Grande. Houston listened, his imagination—like Aaron Burr's—fired by the lure of the Southwest. Between regular swigs from the whisky bottle on the table he plied Bowie with questions. In a drink-thickened voice he vowed that a man of his abilities could make himself a millionaire in a few years. But not yet, not now when he was so dependent on the glass crutch at his elbow. So he bade Bowie good-bye and rejoined his beloved Cherokee in the forests, his saddlebags clinking with bottles.

For the ensuing few years Sam Houston was a victim of deep depression, disease—probably venereal, the gift of those sloe-eyed, copperskinned, obliging Indian girls—and an addiction to alcohol that would have finished a less robust man. He was, of course, not alone in the America of the mid-nineteenth century. In 1830 the annual per capita consumption of pure alcohol was estimated at an incredible ten gallons. The really serious drinkers such as Houston may have doubled that figure, once the non-drinkers and women were excluded. Whisky—rye in the East, Bourbon or corn in the West—sanctified every business or social event from contract negotiations to political picnics. "The way to men's hearts is *down their throats*," said one prominent Kentucky politican—for which read "votes" for "hearts"—while the U.S. Surgeon General made it clear that if drunks could not be recruited by the armed forces, they might dry up.

Even in this atmosphere big Sam Houston was a world-class drunkard, so much so that the Cherokee called him "*Oo-tse-tee-Ar-dee-tah-skee*"—Big Drunk. He also was an opium eater, an addiction that might have developed while recuperating from his painful wounds. Two such habits were inevitably drawing him closer to the graveyard, when suddenly—inexplicably—he began to struggle against them. He made his way to Texas—exactly when or how is not known—and as he reached

San Antonio he rejoiced to see an eagle flying overhead. Destiny was again beckoning!

But slowly, for his impact among the Americans there was hardly spectacular. For a few more years he operated on both sides of the border: speculating in land, arguing an occasional law case, impressing a friend as being "of excellent heart, but dissipated, eccentric— and vain." Traveling east to Washington, he tried to wangle government funds but failed; and his attempt to become an agent for land-speculation companies in Philadelphia, Baltimore and New York also foundered. Finally he appealed to his mentor Jackson for help, and was sent back to Texas with five-hundred dollars and a passport, supposedly on a "confidential mission" the nature of which is still unknown. Here is one of the difficulties in following the trail of this scheming giant, so visible, so popular—and so adept at covering his tracks while rising steadily toward his goal as the chief man in Texas.

After his failures back East, Houston deliberately became a Mexican to acquire land. He took the Mexican oath of citizenship, falsely promising to become a Catholic and hold no slaves—and promptly began cheating the Mexican government out of more land. In this, he was no different from the other Go Aheads practicing the same duplicity. Having taken a married man's grant of a league of land in Stephen Austin's colony, he then jumped over to another colony to take an unmarried man's grant. Houston need not be condemned too severely for such tactics, for they were common. One *Yanqui* swapped a dog for thousands of acres and both the Coahuila-Tejas governor and legislature authorized land grants as though that commodity were as vast as the oceans. But Houston and his like were pikers compared to Jim Bowie: when he was made "special land commissioner" he signed away an incredible half a million acres in the single month of September 1835.

Meanwhile, Houston was busy intriguing at the little Texas village of Washington-on-Brazos. A Britisher who passed that way in 1834 was astonished by the number of American conspirators gathered there under "the pretense of collecting government lands, but whose real purpose was to encourage the settlers of Texas to throw off their allegiance to the Mexican government."

Houston was one of the most active among them, successfully advancing himself as the only acceptable candidate for the rank of major general of militia and commander of the "Texas Army," if that as-yet unformed rabble may be so described. His war wounds and service against the Creeks, plus his friendship with Jackson, were probably his greatest assets.

History still does not know the nature of Houston's confidential mission from Andrew Jackson; but it is not too fantastic to suggest that Old Hickory—the Grand Sachem of American Land Grabbers—made one last desperate gamble to make Texas an American state by sending Houston there to foment and lead a revolution.

But by March of 1836 it appeared that Houston with his tiny army had come to Texas to join the martyrs of the Alamo and Goliad.

Major General Sam Houston arrived at Gonzales on March 11 hoping to organize an army to oppose Santa Anna. That night he heard a secondhand account of the Alamo massacre from two pro-Texan Mexicans, and canceled plans for a march on San Antonio while ordering Fannin to withdraw to the Colorado River. On the night of the 13th his reliable scout Erastes "Deaf" Smith came trotting into town escorting Mrs. Dickinson and her daughter and Travis's slave Joe. Santa Anna had thought it was a good idea to send them into Gonzales to spread panic with her terrible eyewitness tales of the Alamo's end. Houston held her hand as she spoke, weeping like a baby. Grief-stricken as he was to lose fighters such as Bowie, Crockett, Travis and the men they had led, the fall of the Alamo was in a sense reinforcement of his own conviction that his tiny army—half-trained or untrained—could not stand up to Santa Anna's in conventional warfare. He must put a stop to these costly sieges and adhere to his policy of holding his army together and retreating, drawing Santa Anna in pursuit, to be ready always, whenever the terrain or his enemy's position favored him, to turn and strike him.

"By falling back," Houston informed his jittery government in Brazoria, "Texas can rally and defeat any force that can come against her."

To give substance to his words, Houston ordered an immediate withdrawal from Gonzales, turning his own wagons over to those settlers who needed them and calling upon all families to leave first, followed by the army as a protecting shield. By 9:30 P.M. the exodus had begun, and with hardly a trace of panic among the civilians. By 11 o'clock they were all gone, with the army trailing as a shield and carrying all its rations, ammunition and artillery—minus two huge brass 24-pounders that had to be left lying at the bottom of the Guadalupe River. It was a dark night, until the sky to the west grew bright in a lurid glare that illuminated the column. Houston was leaving nothing for the enemy, burning Gonzales to the ground.

Meanwhile all over east Texas there had begun a flap or panic later called the "Runaway Scrape." "Head east!" the alarmed settlers told each other, piling belongings and families on wagons or oxen-drawn sledges, the mooing livestock trotting alongside. That night twenty of Houston's men deserted. They would be back, of course, but they were Texans who had families and it was their duty to hurry to them and move them out of harm's way. At San Felipe the editor of the *Telegraph and Texas Register* printed a front-page editorial warning his readers against panic, urging them to stay where they were, before he loaded his presses on a wagon and took off eastward himself. At Washington-on-Brazos the fledgling government cobbled together a constitution, elected an interim government and joined the exodus. The new President David Burnet expressed his "regret" at "the slightest indication of alarm among us," and was within a few hours bound for the tiny provisional capital at Harrisburg. Nothing less than a wild, pell-mell rush like lemmings headed for the sea was sweeping the entire civilian population toward the Gulf of Mexico.

Following this motley throng was Houston's little army, like a sheep dog protecting the flock from Santa Anna, the wolf supposedly in full pursuit. Actually, he had not yet set out from Bexar-Alamo. "It was but a small affair," His Excellency had told his generals with a lofty, condescending shrug. A mere frontier skirmish. Much larger battles remained to be fought, he assured them; and if he could have witnessed the Runaway Scrape, he would have added: "Gentlemen, it is 1813 all over again."

On March 17, Houston reached the Colorado, taking up a good defensive position there, hoping to blunt the Mexican advance, and also to await the arrival of Fannin and his men. On March 25 the shocking news of Fannin's surrender was received, ending Houston's hope to make a stand on the Colorado. The retreat was resumed, and on the thirty-first they reached Brazoria, spending two weeks drilling there, while their chief tapped out marching orders on a drum. At night he read Julius Caesar's *Commentaries*.

On April 12 word was received that Santa Anna was crossing the Brazos downstream, and the retreat began again. What Houston did not know, what would have filled him with rejoicing, was that Santa Anna had divided his forces! The Napoleon of the West was violating one of the real Napoleon's greatest maxims: "An army must have but one line of operations. This must be maintained with care and abandoned only for major reasons." On March 11 Sesma's troops left San Antonio for Gonzales and San Felipe. Other detachments followed: Morales to help reduce Goliad, General Eugenio Tolsa to support Sesma, Gaona to seize Nacogdoches. On March 31 Santa Anna himself set out to join Sesma, putting aside his eagerness to return to Mexico City on the plea of Filisola, obviously worried about this division of forces in the face of a still-unconquered enemy. But His Excellency's attitude was one of complete confidence. It was as though the final campaign to crush "the land thieves" was a holiday excursion.

Land thieves, incidentally, had replaced "perfidious foreigners" in *El Presidente*'s dictionary of insults. It was contained in a taunting message from him delivered to Houston on the morning of the 15th by a mysterious visitor who said: "He knew Mr. Houston was up there in the bushes, and so as soon as he whipped the land thieves out of the country, he would come up and smoke him out." Houston smiled, and said nothing. Clearly the Napoleon of the West was having fun. Perhaps his happy holiday mood might lead him into a mistake or two.

On April 14, the day after the little steamer *Yellow Stone* had put the last of Houston's eight hundred men across the Brazos, Santa Anna received an exhilarating report: President Burnet and his cabinet were at Harrisburg only thirty miles away! His Excellency was thrilled. Prompt action could end the rebellion with a single stroke. At three P.M. that afternoon Santa Anna was hurrying toward Harrisburg with seven hundred infantry, fifty horse and one 6-pounder, leaving the rest of his army—Sesma, Filisola and the others, perhaps 4,500 men—in the dark and wondering where he was going. Santa Anna's *soldados* murmured to each other in wonder: they flopped onto the earth in an unguarded camp without either wood or water, and were up at dawn next morning still hurrying eastward—pausing only in the languid Mexican manner to loot a small plantation. Dismayed at this delay, Santa Anna hurried on ahead with a force of dragoons, swooping down on Harrisburg just before midnight.

But Burnet and his government were gone! Only a few civilians and three printers turning out the latest issue of the *Telegraph and Texas Register* were caught. In disgust, Santa Anna pitched the presses into the Buffalo Bayou and jailed the printers. From them he learned that the government had fled to Galveston, and also that Houston was still up the Brazos with about eight hundred men. Stymied, Santa Anna sent Almonte with the cavalry farther eastward toward New Washington. Back came the stimulating report: Houston was retreating again! He was headed for safety east of the Trinity River, and would have to cross the San Jacinto at Lynch's Ferry to get there.

The *Generalissimo*'s dark eyes gleamed. Destiny was beckoning! Again the chance to crush the revolt with a single stroke! Get there first, cut Houston off, and it was all over! Just as he'd done in 1813. Off again eastward . . . driving . . . hurrying . . . New Washington on April 18 and Almonte waiting for him . . . eight hundred strong again. . . . On the 19th he rested his men. Next day he sent a scouting party toward Lynch's Ferry to search for the enemy. At 8 A.M. the following morning, they came pounding back, breathless. Houston was only eight miles away, facing *them*—not Lynch's Ferry.

His eyes gleaming again, Santa Anna mounted his horse and galloped to the head of his troops. They followed, marching "with joy and in the highest spirits." The *Generalissimo* was pleased that Filisola was not there. He would have counseled caution . . . wait for the main body . . . Urrea and Gaona and the others. . . . Then crush the Gringos. And share the glory with those *zapilotes?* What foolishness! The victory would be his and his alone! So *El Presidente* hurried east, unaware that his eagerness to capture the Texan government at Harrisburg and end the rebellion at a stroke had led him past Houston's little army, and that instead of him following the Texans, they were following him. Thus, the Napoleon of the West had ignored another of Bonaparte's favorite maxims: ". . . a general should say to himself many times a day: if the hostile army were to make its appearance on my front, on my right, on my left, what should I do?" Santa Anna realized that the battle then impending was not shaping up exactly as he had planned, but in his habitual contempt for Gringo soldiers, he remained completely confident of victory.

No such confidence had Sam Houston's normally irrepressible spirits soaring. When he reached Buffalo Bayou on April 18 just across from Harrisburg he paused in uncertainty. He really did not know where Santa Anna was, but unlike His Excellency, and with no familiarity with the maxims of Napoleon, he was asking himself what he would do if the enemy appeared before, to his right, his left or even behind him. Deaf Smith gave him his answer. Bursting into camp with his scouts just before dark, he reported that Santa Anna himself was leading an enemy force on his front—just a few miles ahead! Even better, he was now far east of Vince's Bridge coming down San Jacinto Bay. Houston was *between* him and his main body! He could cut Santa Anna off from reinforcement and annihilate him!

Exhilarated, Sam Houston still had to be sure. Where were Smith's prisoners to prove his report? Smith called for the courier and escort he had captured. Houston studied them dubiously, until Smith produced the courier's saddlebags marked: "W. B. Travis."

That was enough!

At daybreak reveille of the 19th General Sam Houston spoke to his troops, now a few dozen short of eight hundred. He told them that they had Santa Anna in a trap. To return to his main body he would have to go either by Lynch's Ferry to the east or by Vince's Bridge to the west—and they were smack-dab in between both points. Whichever way the enemy went, the Texans could get there first.

"Victory is certain!" Houston cried, with rising jubilation. "Trust in God and fear not! And remember the Alamo! Remember the Alamo!"

A mighty shout rose from the ranks, rushing to form marching order—the cavalry swinging aboard their mounts, the infantry falling into formation. With Houston at their head riding his beautiful white stallion Saracen—taking with them the pride of their little army, two new 6-pounders called the "Twin Sisters," the gift of the people of Cincinnati—they began marching eastward.

Next day—the 20th—they were up at dawn, ready to march after breakfast. But just before that meal Santa Anna's scouts were sighted, galloping madly south to warn their chief and to set him hurrying north. Breakfast was forgotten as the Texans hastily formed ranks and set off again. Reaching Buffalo Bayou, they halted and Houston laid out his position. On his right, or west, was the bayou, about three hundred feet wide and fifteen to thirty feet deep. On his left, or east, was the San Jacinto River. On his front or south was a marsh called Peggy Lake. His rear was an extenuation of the forest of live oaks made ghostly by the Spanish moss dripping from their limbs. Among them grew rhododendron, giant magnolia, and sprinkled along the ground were pink and purple hyacinths—called *jacintos* in Spanish—the flower that gave the river and battle its name. To his far right was his cavalry.

Some historians have called Houston's choice of a battleground suicidal. Perhaps, but only on a map. The terrain favored him completely. The bayous and river to either side made an enemy flanking movement impossible, and the forest's massive oaks gave his men protection from both bullets and cannonballs. Santa Anna could not maneuver, and with but a single 9-pounder available, neither could he launch a punishing bombardment before he struck. He could only mount a frontal attack, out of a marsh and across a prairie—like a man taking a flying jump from a bowlful of jelly. Besides, Houston's Rebels were in a frenzy. The battle cry "Remember the Alamo!" had sunk into their hearts, driven deeper when they passed through Harrisburg and seen how Santa Anna in his frustration had deliberately devastated the tiny makeshift capital. Moreover there were Goliad survivors in camp and their horror stories of the massacre had them panting for revenge. Finally, such a position, with unseen marksmen firing from unrivaled cover, could favor no one but the defense.

At one o'clock scouts came galloping back reporting the Mexicans in sight, coming fast. A half hour passed ... another ... Suddenly, there they were! A line of men in dusty white jumpers and tall black hats moving through the cat-tails toward the prairie, their cavalry on their right with the sun glinting on their sabers and lances. But there was no climactic clash, only a harmless artillery duel between the Twin Sisters and Santa Anna's lone 9-pounder, called *El Vulcan* after the Greek god of fire and inscribed: VIOLATI FULMINA REGIS, "The Strength of Royal Lightning"—which struck nothing and no one. Colonel Neill's hip was shattered by a musket ball, and a Mexican captain was wounded by grapeshot.

At the end of this exchange of spit balls, the Rebels remained hidden in the forest, and the Mexicans withdrew three-quarters of a mile into the marsh with their backs to Peggy Lake, and their chief officers despairing of having to fight in such a cul-de-sac. "What ground had we to retreat upon in case of a reverse?" Colonel Antonio Delgado asked himself. "I answered, 'None!'" When he spoke of the trap to Castrillon, the aging general shrugged and replied: "What can I do, my friend? I know it well, but I cannot help it. You know that nothing avails here against the caprice, arbitrary will and ignorance of that man [Santa Anna]."

But the Napoleon of the West actually was proud of his position, describing it with starry eyes: "A hill that gave me an advantageous position [no hill, but a marsh], with water on our rear [for drowning, not for drinking], heavy woods to our right as far as the banks of the San Jacinto [filled with Rebels], open plains to the left [full of cavalry] and a clear front [Houston]." During the late afternoon and night of April 20 the Mexican soldiers improved upon this marvelous position by building a "defensive line": on the right a barricade of branches, on the left a barrier of saddles, luggage and hardtack. Confident, Santa Anna went to sleep, not under his famous striped marquee, but beneath a live oak shielding him from the setting sun.

April 21, 1836, dawned a rosy, beautiful day, and the Mexicans prepared to repel the Rebels. But none came. Rather General Cós appeared with reinforcements of four hundred soldiers. They were received with cheers and rattling drums, although Santa Anna rebuked his brother-in-law for bringing him raw recruits when he had requested veterans (which he had not done).

In the Texan camp all was calm and readiness. Sam Houston, who had slept no more than three hours a night, had a good rest with his head propped on a coil of rope. To his men's surprise, he slept until the sun was high: "the Sun of Austerlitz," he remarked later, Napoleon's greatest victory. When he awoke he saw an eagle soaring overhead: his totem, like the one that flew screaming into the sun on the Cumberland. He arose, speaking encouragingly to some of his men upset at the arrival of enemy reinforcements. Instead of having to take two bites at the Mexican cherry, he joked, they could do it in one. To show his confidence, he sent Deaf Smith and a party of ax-men to chop down Vince's Bridge, thus blocking both armies' only path of retreat. It would be a fight to the finish.

El Presidente was perhaps even more confident than his enemy. When General Cós at noon suggested that the cavalry be permitted to eat and water their horses, he graciously consented. With the enemy still reluctant to appear, he decided to retire for a nap, again beneath that spacious oak with its pleasant shading limbs. His men also sought *siesta*, falling down upon beds of grass and boughs. There were no pickets out and the unsaddled horses were being slowly ridden bare-back to and from the river.

At three-thirty P.M. in the Rebel camp came the order: "Parade and prepare for action." With quick silent steps, the men formed into a column two abreast. They seemed sunk in thought. One of them, Alfonso Steele, who had deserted Travis on the march to the Alamo because he had not felt like fighting, felt differently now. At four o'clock Houston on his splendid white horse raised his sword and pointed to the enemy. Behind him the column of Go-Aheads fanned out into a long thin line moving rapidly through the tall prairie grass, serenaded by a fife and drum playing the lively but—for the age—risqué air, "Will You Come to the Bower, I Have Shaded for You?"

Will you come to the bow'r I Have shaded for you?
Our bed shall be roses all spangled with dew.
There under the bow'r on roses you'll lie
With a blush on your cheek but a smile in your eye.

Houston rode Saracen back and forth across the front of his advanc-ing line, brandishing his sword aloft. Two hundred yards from the still-silent Mexican camp, he ordered the Twin Sisters loaded with grape shot—the customary chopped horseshoes—and fired. Like so many razors the missiles went screaming and scything among the sleeping Mexicans. Cries of distress and pain were heard from across the prairie, acting like an electric shock on the Texans so that they slipped the halter of command and went rushing to the slaughter yelling, "Remember the Alamo! Remember Goliad!"

It was a massacre surpassing even those two combined, and remains the bloodiest in the annals of American arms.

Shouting and yelling and firing as they came, the Texans fell upon the Mexican breastwork already shredded by the Two Sisters like demons from hell. Screaming themselves, but in terror, the white-suited enemy ran wildly about like sheep in a fold filled with a pack of snarling wolves. "The utmost confusion prevailed," recalled Colonel Delgado, who stood upon an ammunition crate horrified at what he beheld. "General Castrillon shouted on one side; on another, Colonel Almonte was giving orders. Some cried out to commence firing, others to lie down and avoid grapeshot. Among the latter was His Excellency."

But orders meant nothing to these thoroughly demoralized men. Singly and in small groups they went flying in every direction, like ants scattering on their hill. "The evil was beyond remedy," Delgado concluded. "They were a bewildered and panic-stricken herd."

Some *soldados* tried to fight back, firing volleys from their breastwork. Five of these musket balls pierced the side of Saracen, and the stricken horse sank to the ground, its legs churning like an upended centipede, screaming hideously with its lips working over its big teeth. Houston was unharmed, swinging aboard a second steed. This mount also fell after a ball struck his rider in the achilles heel, shattering his right ankle. Undaunted, Houston hobbled toward a third riderless mount and clambered painfully aboard.

Now the Texans and Stateside volunteers were pouring through the enemy breastworks. One of them was an ancient warrior named Jimmie Curtice, whose son-in-law Wash Cottle was killed at the Alamo. Curtice had sworn to avenge him, and each time he cornered a terrified Mexican pleading for mercy he swung his clubbed rifle to brain him with the shout: "You killed Wash Cottle!"

Suddenly Santa Anna appeared near the breastwork. Disheveled, his hair flying, his fine silk shirt with the diamond buttons flying open and still wearing the blood-red bedroom slippers in which he had retired, he was awakened from his siesta by the tumult of the battle. As Delgado recalled: "His Excellency was running about in the utmost excitement, wringing his hands." But neither he nor any other officer exercised the slightest command over their thoroughly cowed soldiery. "It is a known fact," said Delgado, "that Mexican soldiers once demoralized cannot be controlled . . . " Delgado also added that most Mexican officers remaining faithful to their duty were either killed or wounded.

"General Castrillon was stretched on the ground, wounded in the leg. Colonel Trevino was killed and Colonel Marcial Aguirre was severely injured. . . ."

When the frantic Mexicans caught sight of Buffalo Bayou about a hundred yards away on their left, they rushed for it like a herd of bisons themselves, seeing in its blue waters a sanctuary from those bayonets, Bowie knives and bullets sinking into the bodies of their kneeling, supplicating comrades. But most of those who threw themselves into it drowned in its thirty-foot depths. Colonel Almonte escaped by swimming across, pulling with his right hand while holding his saber above his head with his left. On the shores of Buffalo Bayou, however, "the greatest carnage took place."

Witnessing it, the Napoleon of the West ordered Colonel Juan Gringas to dismount, and "accepted" his horse, on which he fled the battlefield with the precipitate speed which practice in this rare art had conferred upon him. Unknown to His Excellency he was escaping into a cul-de-sac, for Deaf Smith had destroyed Vince's Bridge with customary efficiency.

By Houston's own watch, the Battle of San Jacinto lasted exactly eighteen minutes, but the massacre of Mexicans trying to surrender lasted for hours afterward. It remains the greatest stain upon the honor of American arms, even though those who butchered terrified enemy soldiers trying to surrender might plead justifiable revenge in their defense. Nevertheless, "'Vengeance is mine,' sayeth the Lord." Most American officers did try to restrain the human wolves that their men had become, but among these mostly undisciplined troops there was no fear of lash or rope. In their unchecked passion for revenge they were simply insane, seized by a killing frenzy.

Colonel John Wharton sought to restrain one of them, and the man replied: "Colonel Wharton, if Jesus Christ were to come down from heaven and order me to quit shooting Santanistas, I wouldn't do it, sir." A man who saw this confrontation reported that when the defiant soldier stepped back and cocked his rifle aimed at his commander's chest, "Wharton very discreetly (I always thought) turned his horse and left."

Not even the aged were safe from assassination. When the wounded Castrillon struggled to his feet, one of his aides urged him to flee. "I've never showed my back," the general replied proudly, "I'm too old to do it now." Mounting an ammunition crate, he stood calmly with folded arms while a mob of Yankee riflemen howled around him. Texas Secretary of War Thomas Jefferson Rusk hastened to his side, ordering his men not to fire, even knocking up some rifle barrels. But the Rebels shot the old man down, the gallant Castrillon who had momentarily saved Davy Crockett from a similar mob.

As at the Alamo, young boys were not safe either. Moses Bryan, cousin of Stephen Austin, tried to stop a Kentucky riflemen from killing a drummer boy lying on his face with both legs broken. Instead, the man prodded the boy with a Bowie knife. Catching the man's ankle, the terrified boy sobbed: "*Ave María purisima! Per Dios, salva mi vida!* Hail Mary, most pure. For God's sake, save my life!" Bryan begged the man to spare him. But the man "put his hand on his pistol, so I passed on. Just as I did so, he blew out the boy's brains."

Probably the worst thing for any Mexican attempting to surrender to do was to kneel with supplicating arms outstretched, murmuring: "Me no Alamo." It brought merciless, instant death.

Even Sam Houston had no power over this berserk mob. Riding among them with his wounded leg draped over the pommel of his third horse, he pleaded with them repeatedly to stop. But they would not. He ordered the drummers to beat the retreat, but it had no effect. He bellowed, "Parade, men, parade!"—but they ignored him. "Gentlemen," he pleaded, "gentlemen, gentlemen!" Came a slight pause in the butchery. "Gentlemen, I applaud your bravery, but damn your manners!" They laughed in derision and resumed the bloodbath, and Houston rode away.

As he did he could hear one of his captains haranguing his men. "Boys, you know how to take prisoners, take them with the butt of your guns. Club your guns, and remember the Alamo! Remember Goliad! Club your guns right and left and knock their god damn brains out!"

They did indeed, killing more Mexicans than all the Texan-Americans who had died at both the Alamo and Goliad. Against only 9 Texan-Americans killed and 34 wounded, 630 Mexicans died, while another 200 were wounded and the remainder of Santa Anna's star-crossed army was taken prisoner. Only darkness ended this ghoulish sport, and the dishonorable Battle of San Jacinto came to an end.

That night a huge fire was lighted on the prairie. Fed by whole trees it lighted much of the battlefield, where on its darkened fringes howling wolves and coyotes feasted on the fallen. Prisoners who were led to the blaze approached it with trepidation, suspecting that this was to be their funeral pyre. But instead of being hurled on its crest, they were seated around it to dry their wet clothing while being interrogated by Spanish-speaking Gringos searching for that prisoner par excellence: Antonio López de Santa Anna. But he was not to be found.

Scouts sent out the next morning did discover a dismounted Mexican horseman in white linen pants and a blue trooper's jacket, but wearing suspiciously expensive-looking worsted red slippers and a fine silk shirt with diamond buttons. He was found crouching in a thicket of small pines.

Joel Robison, who spoke Spanish, questioned him. The man said he was a private cavalryman and that Santa Anna had swum to safety across the bayou heading for Thompson's Pass farther south. One of Robison's comrades wanted to finish the man off then and there, but Robison refused. At lance point the man was forced to walk two or three miles, and when he complained of exhaustion, Robison took him up behind him. Arriving at the campsite, the prisoner turned white at the grisly sight of all those red-and-white bundles strewn around the Mexican camp. After Robison pulled rein opposite the enemy prisoners, the man dismounted. At once all the Mexican officers saluted, and the enlisted men arose—all crying with one voice: *"El Presidente!"*

Santa Anna had rejoined his army.

Santa Anna was taken to Sam Houston, who was awakened from an opiated nap intended to assuage the extreme pain of his wound. "General Santa Anna," he said courteously, even warmly. "Ah, indeed! Take a seat, General. I am glad to see you. Take a seat." Santa Anna sat down on a box, obviously nervous. He asked for and was given some opium. Under the soothing influence of that drug, victor and vanquished discussed the situation.

Santa Anna was most mindful of those fierce-looking ruffians armed to the teeth crowding around him as though awaiting the order to take him outside and shoot him, and he wanted to live. Houston was also mindful that the civil and military chief of Mexico was in his power, and he wanted a free Texas. Eventually Santa Anna on May 14 did sign the Treaty of Velasco, recognizing the independence of Texas with a southern boundary at the Rio Grande, as well as ordering the withdrawal of Mexican troops. This agreement was immediately repudiated by the Mexican Congress, as Santa Anna certainly expected. He was a prisoner under duress when he signed, and international law recognizes no pact negotiated under constraint. As a lawyer, Houston had to have been aware of this; nevertheless the treaty was a powerful arguing point, and Texas immediately acted on it.

The new republic elected Houston as its first president, legalized slavery and sent an emissary to Washington to ask for recognition or annexation. It was a delicate question and the indelicate Andrew Jackson for once acted discreetly. Texas had become a political football. First, John Quincy Adams, with the help of Daniel Webster and Henry Clay, had formed the Whig Party, successor to the hapless Republicans. The Whigs, with their ears attuned to the cries of Northern Abolitionists that the Texas rebellion was a plot to extend the area of slavery, opposed recognition and especially annexation. By then Arkansas and Michigan had been admitted to the Union, making thirteen slave and thirteen free states. But Florida was the last slave state remaining to the South, with free-soil Minnesota, Wisconsin and Iowa waiting for admission. Obviously power would shift from the South to the North, and Dixie leaders such as John Calhoun began thundering for outright annexation.

In such an explosive situation Old Hickory had to be careful not to do anything that might prevent the election of Vice President Martin Van Buren of New York, his hand-picked candidate for the presidency. So he waited until his last day in office—March 2, 1837—to recognize the independence of the Lone Star Republic.

Van Buren though a Democrat had definite free-soil sympathies and did little about annexation of Texas. His successor, William Henry Harrison, had no time to do much about anything. With John Tyler of Virginia as his running mate ("Tippecanoe and Tyler, Too"), the old Whig general defeated Van Buren in 1840, but one month after "Tip and Ty" took office, Tip was dead of a cold caught at his inauguration, and Ty, a slaveholder from Virginia who was reluctantly accepted by the Whigs because he could "deliver" the South, was now the president. Tyler wanted Texas, but with the Lone Star Republic having become such a political football with all those unpredictable crazy bounces, he, like Jackson, had to wait until his last day in office before he could inform President Sam Houston that Texas had been invited to join the Union by a joint resolution of Congress.

In the meantime General Antonio López de Santa Anna, with that unrivaled capacity for changing his colors that had made him the undoubted prince of political chameleons, had returned to power in Mexico.

62

Re-enter Santa Anna,
Re-exit Same

〜 IT WAS IN THE PORT CITY OF VELASCO AT THE MOUTH OF THE BRAZOS
that Santa Anna signed the treaty of the city of that name with his
unspoken intention to repudiate it, after which he was placed aboard
the armed schooner *Invincible* for his return voyage to Vera Cruz. In
an effusive and somewhat sticky farewell to the soldiers of Texas who
had captured him, he concluded: "Rely with confidence on my sincerity, and you shall never have cause to regret the kindness shown
me . . ."

Unfortunately for the *Generalissimo,* a storm delayed the sail-rigged
Invincible's departure but did not deter the steamship *Oceana* arriving
from New Orleans with 250 American mercenaries upset at having
missed the bloodbath at San Jacinto. But once they learned that Santa
Anna was was aboard *Invincible* and would soon—with subsiding
winds—be sailing away to freedom, they set up a howl for his blood.
One of their leaders swore: "General Santa Anna had better be executed twenty times if it could be done that often." A group of them
boarded the schooner to take Santa Anna prisoner, whereupon the
Napoleon of the West tried to kill himself by swallowing an overdose
of opium. His captors found him raving and weeping by turns. He was
transferred to *Oceana* where he and Colonel Almonte—Santa Anna's
aide, and the future minister to the United States—were confined,

chained and treated with the utmost degradation. In despair the fallen *Caudillo* tried suicide again three times. Ultimately, an enraged Sam Houston, then in New Orleans for treatment of his wounded and infected ankle, had to use all his influence from that distance to set him free. But Houston thereafter could never expect Mexico to honor the Treaty of Velasco.

Neither did he dare forward Santa Anna to Vera Cruz, where his reception might be just as hostile, but instead sent him to the United States. Incredibly, he was treated as a visiting statesman. Though not exactly hailed as a hero, he was granted an interview with General Winfield Scott and, upon his arrival in Washington in January 1837, cordially welcomed by the newspapers there. He was even invited to the White House, where a friendly Andrew Jackson chose not to recall His Excellency's earlier threat to plant the Mexican tricolor at his front door. Instead, Old Hickory privately proposed $3.5 million in "hush money" if Santa Anna would use his influence to persuade Mexico to let Texas go. Evidently the Old Hero was not aware that at the moment the Soldier of the People was about as welcome south of the border as a bell-ringing leper. Nevertheless, he bade him an affectionate farewell and sent him home aboard the U.S. Navy frigate *Pioneer.*

Homecoming at Vera Cruz might have been another ugly experience for His Excellency if *Pioneer*'s commanding officer Lieutenant Josiah Tattnall had not donned full dress and escorted his passenger ashore. When the band on the wharf struck up the national anthem there was a scattering of feeble "Vivas!" from the soldiery massed there and a few flags were waved—but from the welcoming populace there issued a thunderous cold silence that might have erupted in violence had not the American officer been present. Tattnall stayed by Santa Anna's side all the way to his splendid hacienda at Jalapa.

In a national election that followed, the Soldier of the People got only a few votes. His old enemy Anastasio Bustamante won easily, but under this aging, slothful, gluttonous *presidente* the country seemed to sink deeper into chaos in exact proportion to the outward thrust of his enormous paunch. In Jalapa, among his fighting cocks, his children and his faithful, long-suffering wife, as well as his numerous female friends, Antonio López de Santa Anna bided his time. He had been through this before . . . he could wait . . . Mexico City had become a battleground between conservatives and liberals with innocent civilians the chief casualties . . . it could not continue . . . something would have to give. . . .

It did. Incredibly, this unbelievable buffoon whose farcical career and real-life antics make the raffish stage rascal Scaramouch seem by comparison a solemn ass indeed was at last freed from his self-imposed exile and restored to power—by what?

A Pastry War.

One Monsieur Remontel, the proprietor of a French restaurant near Mexico City, had been visited by a group of high-spirited Mexican Army officers just before they departed under Santa Anna for Texas and the Alamo. They had had a great time, laying hands on Remontel, locking him in a room while presuming to drink him dry, wrecking his establishment and staggering happily out his front door carrying all his pastry with them—for none of which they had paid a cent. Aware that Mexican justice was both venal and xenophobic, Remontel did not go to court with his claims but rather to the French minister, who had already assembled many such complaints totaling about $600,000. When he pressed Mexico for payment, he was ignored. It was not so much that Mexico had refused to pay but that it could not pay. The Mexican treasury was empty. A debt of 3 million pesos in 1835 had swollen into 17 million pesos by 1838. Moreover, France was a monarchy again, eager to chastise the upstart Mexican republic.

Thus in December 1838, a French fleet sailed into the harbor at Vera Cruz to take apart the venerable Fort San Juan de Ulúa—the Gibraltar of America—stone by ancient stone. At once General Santa Anna descended from his heavenly hacienda to organize a defense of the port. He did succeed in negotiating a brief cease-fire, but before he could conceive of anything more substantial, it occurred to Admiral Baudin commanding the French fleet that he might emulate General Sam Houston and seize the Santa Anna *corpus* to hold it for ransom: to wit, payment of the aforesaid 600,000 dollar claim. So he sent an armed kidnaping party ashore. Santa Anna eluded capture, fleeing, it is said, in stages of nakedness ranging from partial to mother, but nonetheless properly attired for the activity in which he had been engaged.

Pausing in a wood outside the city to reclothe himself in dignity and uniform, he mounted a horse to lead a counter-attack on the withdrawing French. Reaching the waterfront he was chagrined to see the enemy rowing to the sanctuary of their fleet. Once aboard ship, an 8-pounder was fired as though in parting contempt. Naval gunnery of the day being what it was, if the cannon had been aimed at Santa Anna he would have been the safest person on the wharf, but because it was dark and the shot a random one it struck both himself and his horse, killing his mount and shattering his lower left leg. The limb had to be amputated, and it was done so crudely that it left a painful two-inches of bone sticking from his flesh. Even though provided with a wooden leg, Antonio López de Santa Anna would limp in pain for the rest of his life.

But what was pain in comparison to the golden opportunity now beckoning, what was it to lose a leg and gain an empire? Invincible as always with pen and paper, Santa Anna composed a wildly exaggerated report of "the Battle of the Pastries," claiming to have killed well over a hundred Frenchmen, including Admiral Baudin. "We conquered, yes we conquered!" he wrote. "Mexican arms secured a glorious victory in the plaza and the flag of Mexico remained triumphant: I was wounded in this last effort and probably this will be the last victory that I will offer my native land. . . . May all Mexicans, forgetting my political mistakes, not deny me the only title which I wish to leave my children; that of a 'good Mexican.'"

Well might the exultant Napoleon of the West have cried: "Oh, lucky shot—to have returned me to the throne of Mexico!" And return he did, while the unfortunate Bustamante fled Mexico City. Seated in a gilded coach pulled by four magnificent white horses, Santa Anna drove through Mexico escorted by an immense body of cavalry. On October 7, 1841, he was carried on a litter into the palace at Tacubaya. Three days later the splendid but gloomy cathedral in Mexico City was ablaze with the glittering light of hundreds of candles. They illuminated the stained-glass windows, gleaming on golden crucifixes carried by dozens of black-robed priests, or on the silver chalices of the altar where the country's hierarchy knelt in silken miters and grasping the shepherd's crooks that were the badges of their office. The click of heels on stone announced the arrival of formations of soldiers in colorful uniforms, the gay military music of Mexico guiding them to their stations. At last a limping tall man in the ordinary uniform of a Mexican soldier entered the church, advancing to the splendid throne on which he seated himself. After him came the corps of generals in gold and crimson dress uniforms, after which the majestic notes of the "Te Deum" rose to the vaulted ceiling of the crowded nave, and when it had ended Antonio López de Santa Anna arose to proclaim the bases of Tacubaya that would eventually make him *El Dictador* of Mexico for the second time.

This time his hold was greedier and more grasping. As the historian Justin Smith wrote: "No coach wheel could turn without first paying a tax. Anybody with a promising scheme to get national funds could find a partner at the palace. Brokers and contractors took the place of politicians; wealthy merchants, able to loan great sums at great percentages, took the place of statesmen. Corruption was rampant everywhere."

By 1842 Santa Anna's unchallenged power was so complete that it turned his head, leading him to order his amputated leg to be dug up and given a state funeral in the capital. It was indeed a sacriligious act and it probably did not convulse Catholic Mexico with outrage because he had prefaced it by declaring on his honor as a soldier that—in spite of his undoubted promises to Andrew Jackson—he would stop at nothing to restore Texas to the Mexican fold. Not even the hierarchy objected to this attempt to make a portion of his own body a first-class relic in the way that remains of a saint are so venerated, but almost always years after their canonization, an event which itself usually only occurs decades after their deaths. Nevertheless, among scenes of pomp and circumstance rivaling those of his inauguration, the bone was installed in an urn atop a stone column in the cemetery of Santa Paula. Thereafter there appeared everywhere in Mexico City statues, busts and paintings of El Caudillo, including a huge bronze statue of him atop his new Gran Teatro de Santa Anna, with one summoning finger pointed north toward Texas (some wags said toward the Mint). Soon to his numerous titles of Soldier of the People, El Dictador, Napoleon of the West, El Caudillo, and Generalissimo was added the undesired appellation of "the Immortal Three-Fourths," a wry allusion to his missing limb. Gradually, Santa Anna became the embodiment of the perceptive Edmund Burke's observation: "An arbitrary system, indeed, must always be a corrupt one; there never was a man who thought he had no law but his own will, who did not soon find that he had no end but his own profit." He acted as though Mexico were his, absolutely ignoring the people he had professed to serve. He wasted his country's wealth on building his army, and when he thought it was strong enough to allow him to do as he pleased, he put in his place a puppet named Valentin Canalizo and turned full-time to gambling and cockfighting and wenching, out of sight of the populace and out of hearing of criticism.

Eventually, however, the insatiable greed and self-adoration of this amoral charlatan—for he was nothing better—was his own undoing, and he committed two unpardonable sins: one, he failed to reward the men who had put him in power; two, he showed disrespect to his wife, the beloved Doña Inés García de Santa Anna. As she lay dying of pneumonia, he chose her replacement: fifteen-year-old Doña María Dolores de Tosta, suspected by those who knew her of having turned into a witch before reaching the age of puberty. Six weeks after the death of Doña Inés, he married Doña María Dolores—and the Mexican people he had so contemptuously ignored exploded in wrath. It was not so much that this teenage witch had been his mistress while his wife lay dying, for in Mexico a general without a mistress was an anomaly. But to have married this strumpet who for some inexplicable reason could wind him around her little finger so soon after his wife's death was unforgivable.

Challenged on the field of battle by his sometime ally General Mariano Paredes, he left the capital in the hands of Canalizo and unsuccessfully sought to corner Paredes in the mountains northwest of Mexico City. Then he learned that the troops in the capital had rebelled against him and infuriated mobs were roaming the streets smashing every statue or bust or painting of him that they could find. They broke into the Teatro de Santa Anna threatening to wreck it until the manager saved it from destruction by changing its name, although the bronze statue above it was torn down. Most insulting of all, they desecrated the unholy sepulcher in which the Immodest One Quarter had been intombed to seize this self-anointed relic and kick it gleefully through the streets until, tiring of the sport, they left it lying in the gutter, where it was reverently retrieved by a soldier, who secretly cherished it for nearly three decades, when he presented it to a tearful Santa Anna.

Finally, toward the end of 1844 the Mexican Congress deposed both Santa Anna and Canalizo, replacing them with General José Joaquín Herrera. In January of 1845, the Napoleon of the West conceded defeat, hastening into exile in Cuba and taking with him his stable of fighting cocks, whatever gold and jewels he could carry—and, of course, his teenage vixen.

By the time Santa Anna reached Cuba there was a new occupant in the White House: James Knox Polk of Tennessee.

63

James Knox Polk

~ AMBITIOUS PEOPLE WHO SCOUR THE PAGES OF BIOGRAPHY AND HISTORY searching for guidelines to success might do well to study the life and career of James Knox Polk and there learn how far one may travel on unlimited ambition yoked to limited talent; for this eleventh president of the United States was indeed a marvel of tenacious mediocrity.

His ancestors were Scots-Irish immigrants who arrived in the New World at the end of the seventeenth century, settling along the broad creeks and estuaries of Maryland's Eastern Shore, where they became sturdy, steady and substantial farmers. Some time before 1740 one of these Maryland Polks—William by name—came under the spell of the lure of the frontier so common in those days and moved to western Pennsylvania, where he settled near modern Carlisle in the Cumberland Valley. William's children moved still farther west, into the Little Sugar Creek area of western North Carolina. Among these sons of William was little, six-year-old Ezekiel—a biological sport if there ever was one—who throughout his childhood, youth and into his old age would scandalize his sober brothers by refusing to become a proper Polk; that is, to accept without question the stern piety of these Scots-Irish Presbyterians including its bans on non-Sabbatical activities such as cooking, cutting firewood or cracking walnuts; or to refrain from his favorite sport of parson-baiting or his unseemly haste in taking a new wife upon the death of the last one; but especially for opening a tavern in Charlotte where whisky and rum—the drinks of the devil— were sold for sinful gain. His solid Patriot relatives were also ashamed of his record during the Revolutionary War as an indifferent soldier suspected of Tory sympathies, and they were puzzled by his unquench- able penchant for pioneering, leading him to migrate farther and far- ther west, founding new communities in Tennessee as easily as a farmer might clear a few acres to extend his pastureland, and just as quickly abandoning them to join the latest flow of settlers into the wilderness. Most of all Ezekiel Polk was remembered for the unbe- coming glee with which he joined his second son Samuel in a theolog- ical battle that shook the staid Sugar Creek community right down to its King James version of the Holy Bible.

The unwitting cause of the quarrel was little Jimmy Polk, born on November 2, 1795, as the first child of Samuel and Jane Knox Polk. Proud of a family name that could be traced all the way back to John Knox, the grim founder of Scots Presbyterianism, Jenny was as devout and canonical in her faith as her husband was indifferent to it. Yet, at the outset of their marriage he was amenable enough to drive her the seven miles to Providence for Sunday services. But his and his father's open contempt for the theocratic pretensions of the Presbyterian clergy earned them the enmity of the young Reverend James Wallis, who ruled his Providence congregation as a parson "strong, ardent and more dreaded [than] loved." Wallis's pointed pulpit barbs at these new Philistines, though they might amuse Grandfather Zeke, annoyed his son Sam, who saw nothing sinful in elevating material val- ues—i.e., the steady acquisition of land—above the spiritual. Never- theless, Sam did take baby Jimmy to Providence to be baptized as Jenny had requested. But he refused to make the profession of faith required of all Presbyterian parents, and Wallis just as adamantly refused to baptize the infant. So Little Jimmy returned home still an unbaptized pagan, and he would not receive that Christianizing sacra- ment until he lay on his deathbed fifty-three years later.

Even so, the dispute might have been smoothed over because Sam was not by nature a radical. But his wife and father were, and while Jenny allied herself with Parson Wallis, Grandfather Zeke formed a "deist"—more likely athiest—debating society for the purpose of sub- mitting biblical revelation to the light of reason, if not actually ridicule. Enraged, Wallis and the other pastors in Mecklenburg County counter-attacked from press and pulpit, and the battle raged in fury for five years, gradually simmering down thereafter but never actually ending until Grandfather Zeke died in August 1824, leaving behind him instructions for his burial and an epitaph from his own hand that went:

Here lies the dust of old E.P.
One instance of mortality;
Pennsylvania born, Carolina bred,
In Tennessee died on his bed.
His youthful days he spent in pleasure,
His latter days in gathering treasure;
From superstition liv'd quite free,
And practiced strict morality.
To holy cheats was never willing
To give one solitary shilling.
He can foresee, (and for forseeing
He equals most of men in being,)
That Church and State will join their power
And misery on this country shower;
The Methodists with their camp bawling,
Will be the cause of this down-falling;
   An error not destin'd to see
   He wails for poor posterity,
First fruits and tenths are odious things,
And so are Bishops, Tithes and Kings.

Grandfather Zeke was living in middle Tennessee when those lines were written. He had made his last migration in 1805–6, after the Chickasaw and Cherokee tribes signed a treaty relinquishing their rights to the area. Again accompanied by a host of children and grandchildren, he had settled on a tract of several thousand acres in the fertile Duck River country. Only Samuel had decided to remain in North Carolina, probably because his wife was only too happy to be rid of this inveterate parson-baiter of a father-in-law. But the "strange old man," as Sam described his frenetic father, artfully excited his second son's acquisitive instincts by writing glowing descriptions of the beautiful and productive land that was to be had almost for the asking, and Sam and his family also went west. In the fall of 1806, after the crops were in, as the appointed day of departure dawned, the family bade their neighbors a tearful farewell and began the long, arduous five hundred-mile journey across possibly the most rugged terrain in the eastern United States. It was mostly on foot, at a rate of about twenty miles a day, and it was not completed until a month and a half later.

Surprisingly, eleven-year-old Jim was excited by his new surroundings. As a child he had been an extremely quiet and reserved boy, small and sickly with neither the strength nor the inclination to perform the farm chores expected of frontier lads. But he joined the fun of "the cane-cutting," a literal carving out of a place among the canebrake in what some disappointed migrants found to be "a howling wilderness," which they quickly abandoned the following spring. Polk would always remember the pistol-like explosions of the dry cane as it was heaped on roaring fires. He loved the day after a homesite was cleared and the logs cut to the proper size and the neighbors gathered round for the rollicking fun of the roof-raising. There were also corn shuckings and quilting parties to be remembered.

Although the first years in the Duck River country were not easy, none of these frontier people doubted that they were happy. Almost everything they ate, wore or used they produced themselves, depending upon tobacco patches for the cash necessary to buy sugar, salt or iron for tools. Corn was the main staple, being ground at the neighborhood gristmill and then cooked into varieties of hoe-cake, cornbread or johnnycake. Whisky was also distilled from corn, and the still—that "never-failing sign of dawning civilization"—appeared almost simultaneously with the gristmill. Every family had a little cotton or flax patch—often both—providing the fabric for women's dresses and the men's summer clothing. Because Sam Polk eventually became the most prosperous settler in the area, Jim Polk probably wore a suit of dressed buckskin in the winter. It was soft and velvety. When new, its color was a rich buff, although constant wear could eventually turn it black and "almost as slick as glass." Because the frontier had outrun the Presbyterian preacher, most of the boys were happy not to be morose on Friday knowing that preparation for the endless Sabbath observances would begin then. Instead, the youngsters "literally ran wild" on Sunday. There were sports and marbles, trips to the creek to shoot fish with bows and arrows or to go splashing naked in the water, or excursions into the woods in quest of nuts, wild grapes and persimmons.

Strangely enough, Jim Polk, who had been so exhilarated by the freedom of the new life on the frontier, gradually seemed to lose interest in everything. He took no part in the vigorous sports that the farm boys loved: running, jumping, wrestling, swimming, as well as hunting and fishing and riding. He eventually came to be regarded as a weakling, much to his shame and his father's dismay. When Sam, a surveyor like almost all land speculators, took Jim with him on surveying trips into the forest, the boy usually had to remain in camp to watch the horses and prepare the evening meal, while everyone else was out in the wilderness running lines.

Gradually it became clear to Jim's father that his son's listlessness was due to physical causes. He became immobilized by frequent attacks of abdominal pain. Eventually, this affliction was diagnosed as gallstones; but to cure it required abdominal surgery, an almost nonexistent skill on the frontier. If such an operation were successfully attempted, it would have been given wide coverage in the western press—and it was in this way that the Polk family heard of the skills of Dr. Ephraim McDowell of Danville, Kentucky, who had removed a woman's tumorous ovary. Expensive though McDowell might be, Sam decided that nothing was too good for his son. In the fall of 1812, he and Jim swung aboard their horses for the 230-mile trip to Danville.

When they finally hitched their mounts to the post outside McDowell's simple white cottage that also served him as a surgery, Jim was so weak that the doctor immediately ordered two weeks of rest before he would attempt the operation. In those days anesthesia and antisepsis had not yet been developed, and Jim knew that he faced an ordeal of exquisite pain. Yet this feeble youth of seventeen had a powerful will, and so, fortified with brandy, he was strapped to a plain wooden table and held down by McDowell's assistants while the doctor's scalpel sank into his bladder. Incredibly, he survived; even more miraculously, as he recovered he seemed to get instantly better. By the time he reached home he was a different little Jimmy Polk, in high spirits that had not been seen in him in years, proudly showing the offending stone to admiring friends and relatives.

There can be no doubt that this ordeal lasting throughout James Knox Polk's formative years had a profound influence in shaping his character. Pain and shame at being mistaken for a weakling had been his constant companions, and he had endured both—especially the crueler psychological disgrace of being called a quitter, without a murmur. In this he was assisted by his devoutly religious mother. No matter how stern her faith might have been, she impressed upon her suffering son the necessity of facing adversity with courage and in maintaining unshakable fidelity to the Christian values of duty, self-reliance and devotion to the will of God. Polk was never robust, even after his operation he remained frail. But his struggle against the torments of his boyhood and youth had developed in his soul a fierce determination to succeed and an indomitable will, no matter how fragile his health might be. Of him, the words of Christ might well be quoted: "The spirit indeed is willing, but the flesh is weak." In a phrase, James Knox Polk's ordeal had led him to place his protesting body at the service of his unconquerable soul.

Thus, because he was not exceptionally intelligent, or gifted with the insights of genius and originality, he made the most effective use of his ordinarily good mind and could outdistance men of superior mental ability. Before his operation he had been acutely aware of his physical inferiority and been almost constantly frustrated in the natural aspirations of a frontier boyhood; but after the operation he was transformed into a rejuvenated human being driven by a fierce pride and almost insatiable ambition. Thus when his father upon their return from Kentucky, though overjoyed, had soberly concluded that his son would never be strong enough to live a demanding life, and had proposed a career in merchandising, he was proudly surprised to hear how quickly and curtly Jim could dismiss such a paltry ambition. Cutting calico and weighing salt was not for James Knox Polk. His life would not be passed in tepid tea rooms and quiet counters, but in storming ramparts. Even so, Sam insisted that Jim try clerking in a Columbia store, and though he obeyed, he made it so obvious that he would rather be in a classroom preparing himself for life's real challenges that his father relented and sent him to school.

At eighteen Jim Polk was barely better educated than Abraham Lincoln was at about the same age, when "all his schoolin' did not amount to one year." He wrote badly and spelled worse, an unintended emulation of his hero Andrew Jackson. He was equally unfamiliar with history or mathematics, and with such esoteric studies as classical languages or philosophy he had no acquaintance at all, if he had indeed even heard of the last two. Yet, when he entered the little Presbyterian academy in Columbia, he was stung to realize that his classmates four to two years younger than he were also much better educated. He did not—as he had done prior to his operation—accept an inferior role among his peers but reacted with a fierce inner drive not only to excel among them but to surpass them. And he did, by dint of a dedication to his books that astonished the Reverend Robert Anderson, the Maury County headmaster celebrated for his erudition and blistering marathon sermons, one of which denouncing the evils of cock-fighting was preached to a restive audience of gamecock gamblers that included General Jackson. Jim was also a model of obedience and rectitude—not in a pretentious, prissy way, but in an unconscious assumption that rules were made to be followed—and was probably the first student in the brief history of the school to escape the disciplinary switch.

Father Samuel was so pleased with Jim's first year of formal education that he transferred him to an academy in the new town of Murfreesboro with a better reputation and broader curriculum. Because Jim boarded with a nearby family, he avoided the distraction of farmyard chores and was thus able to dedicate more time to his books, emerging as "much the most promising young man in the school." In two brief years, then, James Polk had ceased to be a barely literate uncouth country yokel and had become instead a sophisticated scholar and urbane young gentleman socially acceptable in the finest homes of middle Tennessee. Samuel, prospering while his son studied, now decided that James was ready for college, choosing North Carolina State University at Chapel Hill. For Jim to study in his native state was not just a natural choice, for the calculating Samuel thus put his son under the benign influence of Sam's cousin and patron, Colonel William Polk, an active trustee at Chapel Hill.

Appearing before a board of professors, James performed so well under their scrutiny that he was accepted as a sophomore for admission in January 1816. In the spring of 1818, after two and a half years of study so intensive that his health was again threatened, yet adjudged the finest scholar in his class, Jim was awarded the top honor of delivering the Latin Salutatory. No evidence remains of what he said in a dead language absolutely foreign to him when, five years earlier, he had entered the little academy at Zion Church, bent only on learning something of English grammar and arithmetic. But the fact that he was selected to deliver this prestigious oration—to his doting father's great pride matched only by his total inability to understand a word of what his son was saying—gives eloquent testimony to the demonic desire to excel that drove this young man of twenty-three years.

Even before his graduation James Polk decided to follow in the footsteps of his idol Andrew Jackson by studying law with a political career his ultimate goal. He could not tarry in tiny Columbia, of course, with its minute population of three hundred, but rather in the metropolis of Nashville where there were three thousand inhabitants, paved streets, a college, two bookstores, three newspapers and an array of two-story and even three-story buildings. He shrewdly chose the celebrated Felix Grundy as his mentor, one of the leading War Hawks under Madison and middle Tennessee's outstanding criminal lawyer.

That he preferred Grundy, no legal expert but rather a masterful manipulator of juries, suggests that Polk was already an avid student of human nature, eager to play upon human emotions for votes just as Grundy did for verdicts.

Polk shared Grundy's office with another young barrister: Francis B. Fogg, a student of legal precedents and fine points of the law. Where political success was Polk's passion, Fogg's was abstract law. He was not interested when Grundy, now a state legislator, suggested in the summer of 1819 that he seek election as clerk of the senate, about to convene in Murfreesboro. Fogg told Grundy he would rather remain in Nashville increasing his legal knowledge. Polk heard this conversation, and after Grundy departed Polk told Fogg that he'd like the job himself, and asked his friend to put in a word for him with Mr. Grundy. Fogg did, and through Grundy's influence, Polk defeated his only competitor for a post that paid a princely six dollars daily—compared to only four for the members—but was even richer in a harvest of political friendships. Although the legislature sat for only a month, the $180 he received was more than enough to finance his law studies, so that in June of 1820 he easily passed the bar examination. He did not resign his senate clerkship, however, serving during three more sessions to expand his circle of political allies while building up his law practice and personal popularity in Maury County, especially in Columbia.

Soon his host of friends began to notice how frequently he made the fifty-mile trip from Columbia to Murfreesboro, and the belles in the Duck River country were dismayed that the object of his visits by this prime "catch" was Sarah Childress, daughter of Major Joel Childress, a wealthy merchant, tavern keeper and planter who, like Jim's father, was also a close friend of Old Hickory's. Sarah was not beautiful, but she was extremely well connected politically and a highly educated product of a genteel school for ladies operated by the Moravians of Salem, North Carolina. The courtship culminated in a wedding on New Year's Day, 1824. In middle Tennessee, a Polk-Childress marriage was a distinctive social event indeed, and carriages filled with the area's "quality folks" converged on the Childress plantation house on that date to see Parson Anderson make James and Sarah man and wife. Among the revelers was Andrew Jackson Donelson, the orphaned nephew of Old Hickory whom the childless Jackson had adopted. Still another rung had been fitted into Polk's ladder leaning against the slope of Mount Olympus.

The first had been inserted in 1819 when Polk chose Felix Grundy as his mentor and patron. That was the year of America's first financial panic, when the boom after the War of 1812 collapsed in a catastrophe that sent cotton prices tumbling, plunging merchants and planters into bankruptcy, drying up credit, and spreading despair and suffering through every level of society. In its fall the panic also buried the old system of politics based mainly upon the supremacy of wealth and privilege. From the ruins of the old oligarchy—if it may be so described—there arose debtor discontent, workingmen's parties, Thomas Jefferson's dreaded "fire bell in the night"—the rising and bitter regional conflicts over tariffs and slavery—all of these innovations making for political democracy and enfranchisement of the common man. Sweeping into the twenties under the name of Jacksonian Democracy it would make Old Hickory its standard bearer in an unsuccessful bid for the White House in 1824, and put him there in 1828 and 1832.

At its beginning in 1819, Felix Grundy seems to have been one of the first politicians to comprehend how popular discontent would destroy the old oligarchs, and he staked his political future on a novel technique of appealing—not to bankers, creditors and "men of substance,"—but to the common folk and their local prejudices. Announcing for the Tennessee lower house on a platform of relief for debtors, he triumphed over the bitter opposition of the Old Guard. That was when James Knox Polk entered his office. In 1823, a few months before his wedding, Polk inserted the second rung in the ladder to the skies: challenging a veteran legislator for his seat in the Tennessee lower house, appealing to the same voters who had chosen Grundy and running on the same platform. It was a close race, with the voting taking two days. Voters marched up to the polling place to make public choices of their favorites, always surrounded by a crowd of candidates and campaign managers trying to influence his decision either by flattery, cajolery, bribery, or intimidation. Meanwhile, liquor flowed freely. In one election district alone James Polk paid for twenty-three gallons of hard cider, brandy and whisky. As the lead changed hands, groans and shouts of jubilation arose—and of course there were fistfights. In the end James Knox Polk triumphed by a comfortable margin—and the upward climb into the rarefied atmosphere of political power was fully begun.

James Knox Polk was then but a few months short of his twenty-eighth birthday; and he was, of course, physically mature. He stood something under middle height: probably five feet seven or six inches. Although he was never strong, neither was he scrawny or skinny, but rather solidly built with a good thick torso. Introverted and unrelaxed, there was in his intense face no humor or suggestion of camaraderie in the manner of Henry Clay. Unlike Clay, he could never be "one of the boys"—drinking, dancing and playing cards until sunrise. But for the defect of his perpetual gravity and sober demeanor, he might have been called handsome. His deep-set, restless eyes were steel-gray and large, and his mop of unruly black hair was brushed straight back from a broad forehead. His nose was long and sharp, and his darkish skin stretched tight as a drumhead over high cheekbones. His lips were thin and compressed. In those two features—the constantly probing eyes and the narrowed mouth—his personality was betrayed: watchful, methodical, calculating. He did have a mind capable of mastering the law, but he knew in his soul that he did not have the personality to succeed in politics; for if any man accepted the dictum of the Oracle of Delphi—"Know thyself"—it was James Knox Polk. Neither a gay companion like Clay nor a fierce, enemy-hating fighter like Jackson, he chose instead to cultivate a certain artificial affability that would charm most people.

One of Polk's associates has described an incident throwing light on his passion for making friends; that is, allies who could be helpful. Outside a tavern one day a stranger rode up on a horse. Polk came up to him, "offered him his hand and with a smile looked him in the face" as though he knew him. The traveler replied that they were not acquainted, and at once Polk said: "I was in doubt, sir, until you spoke. But now I am sure that I know you. You are Colonel Holman, of Lincoln County." Holman gasped. "You must have a remarkable memory," he said, for the only time they had met was at a Fourth of July barbecue ten years earlier. Polk nodded. "Colonel Holman, I don't think I was ever introduced to a man and talked with him for ten minutes, that I ever afterwards forgot him." Such a calculated approach to "friendship," it would seem, could not fail to crush whatever spark of spontaneity remaining in James Polk's careful soul. Yet for all his contrived bonhomie, he was an extremely effective speaker.

Although he had no natural gifts of eloquence in the manner of Clay or Webster, he deliberately developed a style that he knew would please his Tennessee audiences, especially "the wool hat b'hoys," those coarse and simple-minded farmers who made up most of his constituency. He specialized in sly sallies, knowing winks and rude witticisms by which he could accuse his opponent of "making deals behind the barn." Like the modern Florida politician who in a voice of horror could shock the same sort of audiences by charging his rival with "living for years *in celibacy* with his sister," Polk did not hesitate to play upon the ignorance and credulity of his listeners. Nor did he forget to milk them with the customary bombastic obeisance before the Hero in the Hermitage: "That brave old Hero and Patriot, who stood like a wall of fire when England hurled her avalanche of brutal myrmidons upon the ramparts of New Orleans, yelling like demons their beastly watchword—'Beauty and Booty'—and when the lives of and honors of our fair women had no shelter from the storm but his gallant heart, his wise head, his strong arm and indomitable courage." This was putrid prose, indeed, and though it might produce superior and indulgent smiles among the handful of sophisticated townspeople in the crowd, it brought from the wool hats a great roar of delight.

Such loyalty was not lost upon Old Hickory and his supporters, and Polk had been barely two weeks in the state legislature before the Jacksonians began considering him as an ally to help drive the anti-Jackson men out of office as the campaign to place Old Hickory in the White House began to gather popular momentum. By the time the 1823 session ended, James Knox Polk was clearly the candidate for the national legislature. Although Jackson had the most votes in the presidential election of 1824, he did not have a clear majority, thus throwing choice of a chief executive into the House of Representatives, which selected John Quincy Adams. A year later Polk did indeed defeat the anti-Jackson candidate for the House, being re-elected for six more terms and in 1835 and 1837 he was its Speaker.

In 1839, with his gaze now fixed unwaveringly on the White House, seeking a power base and some administrative experience, Polk successfully ran for governor of Tennessee. He seemed on the verge of achieving even higher office when he was prominently mentioned as a possible running mate for Martin Van Buren in the presidential election of 1840. His political acumen was well known among Democratic party leaders, and his open and active support of the annexation of Texas might serve to soften criticism of van Buren's reluctance to do the same. Yet, Polk declined to offer himself for the Number Two spot, much to the gloating glee of his enemies in both parties. "HENCEFORTH," one political columnist wrote exultantly, "HIS CAREER WILL BE DOWNWARDS!"

Actually, James Knox Polk was a far more astute political analyst than this malignant gentleman. He foresaw clearly that the old Indian fighter William Henry Harrison—the Whig presidential candidate, almost as popular as Old Hickory—would defeat the Democrats in 1840. He realized that his own party was deeply divided North and South, with Calhoun in command in Dixie and "the Little Magician," as van Buren was called, in charge in Yankeeland. Polk would not accept the vice presidential nomination without the solid support of both these leaders. Without it, he declined to seek the honor, certain that Van Buren in his comeback attempt for the White House would never defeat "Tippecanoe and Tyler, too." That was what happened, and Polk, still young at forty-five—with no defeat to disqualify him for running for the White House in 1844, though still far from being the Democrats' Anointed One—had four more years in which to build an organization and make his name a household word nationally.

Until he ran twice again for governor of Tennessee and was twice rejected, for then it appeared that his career was truly headed "DOWNWARDS!" But then came the national political convention of 1844.

National conventions were new procedures by which the two parties nominated their candidates for president, although by the time both Whigs and Democrats convened in Baltimore in the spring of 1844, the techniques of "the smoke-filled room" were fairly well known to the delegates. However, there was little opportunity for wheeling and dealing at the Whig conclave, for Henry Clay's unrivaled popularity made him the standard-bearer by acclamation.

Among the Democrats, however, there were any number of horses entered in the race. Martin van Buren seemed to lead the field. The Whigs in 1840 might have chanted gloatingly, "Van, Van, is a used-up man," but the Little Magician arrived in Baltimore with seemingly enough delegates in his pocket to win the prize on the first ballot. But van Buren was extremely vulnerable on the issue of annexation of Texas. He had publicly declared that such a decision might divide the Union, North and South, over the slavery issue. The Little Magician had underestimated the annexation fever that had gripped the country, never realizing its depth until he went to Baltimore.

Lewis Cass of Michigan, a hero of the War of 1812 and considered van Buren's strongest challenger, was a fervent advocate of annexation. Little Van's other rivals were John Calhoun, the South's Ancient of Days and "the sleepless guardian of slavery"; Silas Wright of New York, popular but believed to be too free with the bottle; James Buchanan and Commodore Charles Steward of Pennsylvania, the former a veteran of both House and Senate and onetime minister to Russia, the latter a comparative unknown; and Richard Mentor Johnson of Kentucky, the only vice president ever elected by the House, whose followers still loved to do a War Hawk dance, brandishing Tecumseh razor straps and chanting, "Rumpsey-dumpsey, rumpsey-dumpsey, Colonel Johnson killed Tecumseh"—but-still, by his liaison with a mulatto woman who bore him two daughters, absolute anathema to the South.

James Knox Polk was also at Baltimore, but in the gallery. "James Who?" the delegates asked, for the affable gentleman from Tennessee was by then a phantom politician. Though he had been twice Speaker of the House, those two Tennessee defeats seemed to have erased all recollection of his name.

Van Buren seemed unbeatable, until the atmosphere in those smoke-filled rooms became murkier, deals were made and a "Stop Van" movement began to evolve. Of the convention's 266 votes, 177 were needed for the two-thirds vote required for nomination. Van Buren's floor managers realized that their hold on their delegates was being eroded, that they had to turn to steamroller tactics—try to stampede the convention on the first ballot. They didn't come close. Little Van received only 146 votes, his high point. Thereafter he slipped, while Cass crept closer. On the seventh ballot the man from Michigan's count was a little above 100. Obviously, a stalemate had ensued.

That night many of the delegates did not go to bed. Most active among them was the historian George Bancroft, a member of the Massachusetts delegation. He conferred with the New Yorkers, who were holding out for Governor Wright, if they could not get van Buren. But Wright was a close friend of the Little Magician, who was not even in Baltimore and probably would not turn on his friend. Someone— probably Bancroft—mentioned Polk. He had taken a step out of obscurity, being mentioned as a possible *vice* presidential candidate should the nomination go to a northeasterner such as Van Buren. Bancroft and the New Yorkers agreed to push Polk. Dark horse though he might be—the first in American political history—he was after all the protégé of Andrew Jackson. Moreover he was a fervent annexationist.

Next morning on the eighth ballot, van Buren sank to 104 and Cass rose to 114. The deadlock had deepened. But James Knox Polk had received 44 votes. That not only ended the stalemate, it started a stampede: on the tenth ballot the dour little man from Tennessee became the Democratic candidate for president.

Throughout the election week of November 1844, the contest between Henry Clay and James K. Polk had seesawed back and forth. It seemed to the Whigs that ultimate victory would be theirs when the tally from Tennessee arrived in Washington. Henry Clay had beaten the Democrat Polk! But by a mere 113 votes! Such had been the shock in Tennessee that the Old Hero dying in the Hermitage came close to weeping when he learned that the Volunteer State, which he had served so loyally, had left the Democratic camp. Candidate James K. Polk at home in Columbia was shocked, but not despairing. As his friend General Robert Armstrong, the postmaster in Nashville, forwarded to him the latest returns by mounted courier, he could see that the tally was so evenly balanced that all now depended on New York State.

On Saturday morning, Polk heard hoofbeats drumming down the road from Nashville. There came a rapid pounding on the front door. Polk flung it open and the courier cried: *"Glorious news!* New York is *yours!"* Polk took the man's proffered bulletin, put it carefully away in his waistcoat, nodded his thanks—and carefully closed the door.

James Knox Polk spent that momentous day walking cheerfully about his hometown, greeting his friends and neighbors, nodding, bowing, smiling—affable as ever—but never confiding in a single soul, secretly secretive man that he was, that he was now the President-elect of the United States of America.

64

Polk Tries to Buy the West

~ To understand why Mexico and the United States went to war in 1846 it is necessary to comprehend an egregious Mexican mistake and a flaw in the American character that can only be described as bumptious.

Mexico's error, already discussed, was to encourage migration from a neighboring people who were as different from the Mexican people as these two former colonies of Protestant Britain and Catholic Spain could possibly be. These mostly Southern Americans who migrated to Texas were drawn pure and simply by the lure of land and for no other reason. When they promised to become practicing Catholics and to obey the Mexican prohibition of slavery they had no intention of doing so. Worse, they were inflamed by a peculiarly American expansionist fever that came to be known as Manifest Destiny. The phrase is attributed to John O'Sullivan, editor of the expansionist *United States Magazine and Democratic Review,* who wrote of "our manifest destiny to overspread and to possess the whole of the continent which Providence has given us for the development of the great experiment of liberty and federated self-government."

Manifest destiny! It had a Godly as well as a golden ring to it. Not only was land to be had in Texas and—later—gold in California, but the will of God was to be executed there by his newly Chosen. Here again was the crusading spirit that had energized the American colonists against their French and Indian foes, to be emulated in 1812 by the land-greedy War Hawks. Here was what one Congressman called "the right of our Manifest Destiny," and even Abolitionists crying "slavocracy plot" could not resist the lure of that magical, mystical phrase. Their spokesman, the *American Whig Review,* could ask in 1845: "Why not extend the 'area of freedom' by the annexation of California? Why not plant the banner of liberty there?"

Why not do the same with Texas, most Americans were asking one another after the "miracle of San Jacinto." So were the Texans. They were free, but they wondered how long they would remain free. After all, Mexico was a nation of more than seven million people and the Republic of Texas was one of but fifty thousand. Mexico would not easily let the Lone Star go. Texas needed protection, and when it appealed to the United States for annexation, that was really what it was seeking: a powerful parent that Mexico would provoke only at its peril.

Apart from a few Europeans, Texans were Americans. When a Southerner scratched GTT on his front door he did not think of himself as abandoning his country but only as moving to another part of it. He was a Texan in the same way as a man living in Pennsylvania was a Pennsylvanian, but the nationality of both was American. Scratch every Texan in Texas and you would find a son of Uncle Sam (the nickname was relatively new, and Brother Jonathan was still widely used). If the United States were to remain neutral on the subject of annexation, what would happen to these Texans when the Mexicans reclaimed their land?

Among those early settlers annexation was actually taken for granted, and instead of discussing it as a *possibility,* they argued instead about whether it should be cut up into two or three large states—not the land giant that it was—each with two senators. New England was irrevocably opposed to such a proposal, believing that the South was already too strong. John Quincy Adams and twelve other members of the House issued a circular denouncing "the undue ascendancy of the slave power" and predicting that annexation of Texas would end in dissolution of the Union. Although they were ignored, in a sense they were not exactly false prophets: those luscious fruits of the Mexican victory would be already rotten with the seeds of Civil War.

Americans at home most ardent in the cause of annexation always spoke of *re-*annexation, for they firmly believed that the territory of Texas as far south as the Rio Grande had been part of the Louisiana Purchase. If the United States annexed Texas, they argued, it would not be seizing another nation's land but only taking back what had belonged to it all along. It made no difference to them that America had forsworn all land west of the Sabine River—the Louisiana-Texas border—when it bought the Floridas from Spain. If pressed, they would reply that the United States was now dealing with Mexico, not Spain, and the Florida treaty no longer had any standing. Zealots though they were, and mistaken as well, they still devoutly *believed* this; and if a psychological fact is not an actual one, it is nonetheless still as persuasive.

Usually Texas re-annexationists were also re-occupiers of the vast Oregon Territory over which both the United States and Britain were still in disagreement. They argued that although the British had explored Oregon along its sea edges, the Americans had *occupied* it and developed a thriving fur trade. Thus, to them, it could be *re*-occupied as far north as Russia's southern claims—the line of latitude 54 degrees 40 minutes—and the slogan "Fifty-four Forty or Fight!" was prominent in Polk's successful campaign in 1844. The Democratic platform then joined the "*re*'s" hoping to appeal to both Northerners and Southerners. The fact that to attempt to make both of them realities might provoke war with Mexico as well as Britain was conveniently ignored.

Andrew Jackson could not dare to sidestep such a real possibility. His recognition of Texas in March 1837, the day before he left office, was approved and followed by the entire civilized world, but *annexation* so soon after San Jacinto would make it appear to Mexico—and again the entire world—that, just as it had claimed, the United States had truly sent bands of armed men posing as immigrants into Texas for the purpose of rebellion and ultimate annexation of that department. Such a possible boomerang would not be helpful to his hand-picked successor van Buren.

Van Buren also sidestepped annexation, and Tyler, after the death of Harrison though eager for annexation, preferred to allow Secretary of State Daniel Webster—of whom he seems to have been wary—to concentrate on the Oregon dispute with Britain while ignoring Texas. The young republic, however, tired of standing at the altar for two years waiting for Uncle Sam to take her hand, began talks with Mexico about an armistice. But because Texas insisted on independence, to which Mexico was just as adamantly opposed, the conversations foundered. They had continued for two years, during which Tyler did not dare to reopen the subject of annexation for fear of angering his neighbor.

Eventually, after Webster stepped down at State and his replacement

Abel Upshur was killed in an ordnance accident, Tyler named John Calhoun to the vacant post. Like Tyler, the Pride of the South was a fervent annexationist. He also had presidential aspirations. He believed that if he could bring off annexation—opposed by the Whig leader Henry Clay and the Democrat van Buren—he would gain the White House. Tyler shared that conviction and hoped to prolong his stay there by pushing an annexation treaty through the Senate. Meantime, Calhoun, a man of splendid though calculated rages, pointed a trembling finger at Britain as the villain that sought to complicate the Mexican-American standoff.

Both France and Britain had extensive holdings in Mexico, and both therefore quite naturally claimed to have some say in what should happen to Texas, now a buffer state between Mexico and the United States. If either of these powers should gain control of Texas, the United States could expect an enormous increase of smuggling along a border already difficult to control. If Britain, which had just outlawed slavery throughout its empire, should emerge dominant in the young republic and put bondage to the ban, Texas would become one enormous escape hatch for fugitive slaves. To reach the sanctuary of Canada through the Underground Railroad, an escaped slave from, say, Georgia, would have to pass through as many as a dozen states, in any one of which he was subject to capture and return to his owner. But a slave escaping to a British Texas—especially so easily from the lower South—could thumb his nose at any pursuers. Such a prospect brought Calhoun to the customary boil, and he predicted a servile uprising and a racial war.

In those days, nothing too vile could be said about "Perfidious Albion." Much like Communism during the Cold War, the former Mother Country could be blamed for floods, hurricanes, droughts, crop failures, or the birth of a two-headed calf with a decidedly good chance of being believed. When a rumor circulated that Britain had offered Texas an enormous sum of money if it abolished slavery, the South seemed ready to ram Tyler's cherished annexation treaty through the Senate. But both Tyler and Calhoun erred: the president by warning of the dangers of abolition in Texas, the secretary by writing to the British minister defending the institution of slavery, and by so doing alienating senators heretofore indifferent to annexation. The Senate rejected the treaty by a vote of thirty-six to fifteen.

Undaunted, Tyler went to the entire Congress—thus obviating the necessity of a two-thirds vote in the Senate—and on his last day in office informed Anson Jones, the new president of Texas, that the Lone Star Republic would be welcome as an American state.

Next day, March 4, James Knox Polk entered the White House; and Polk not only wanted Texas, he wanted California, too—and New Mexico as well.

Some modern historians—especially Robert Selph Henry in *The Story of the Mexican War*—have argued that President Polk did not deliberately provoke Mexico into a war that expanded the United States by almost two million square miles—an area five times the size of France—while making it a two-ocean power. Henry and those sharing his conviction argue that there is no truth to the generally accepted judgment of the War with Mexico as one of the most shameful episodes in American history, rivaling even the extinction of the Indians: a criminal act by which a mighty, predatory nation raped its weaker neighbor. These beliefs, they maintain, are based on both Whig propaganda to discredit "Mr. Polk's War" and the groundless fears of Abolitionist agitators of the slavocracy plot to annex Texas and thus extend the area of bondage. They admit that Polk did indeed covet the northern outposts of Mexico, but as territory to be purchased, not seized.

Ever since the astonishing success of Thomas Jefferson's Louisiana Purchase, American presidents had been eager to buy Mexican land. John Quincy Adams offered $1 million for Texas and Andrew Jackson raised the price to $5 million. Both offers were angrily rejected. In the beginning Polk was more anxious to obtain California, especially after reading reports on the great strategic military value and potential for development of the San Francisco Bay area. He had nothing, of course, to do with the Texas rebellion, but it did happen to coincide with his purchase plans. He thought he could get all the northern Mexican territory as far west as the Pacific for somewhere between $15 and $40 million. These were fast slipping out of Mexico's grasp and would soon become fair game for the colonizing powers of Europe, especially Britain and France. Polk wanted to obtain them before they acted.

All this is true. So also is the claim that Polk's position was consistent with his oft-reiterated warning to the Europeans given in his first message to Congress on December 2, 1845, in which he declared: "Existing rights of every European nation should be respected [but] . . . it should be distinctly announced to the world as our settled policy that no future European colony or dominion shall . . . be planted or established on any part of the North American continent."

As early as his inaugural address in March 1845, he announced this policy as it applied to the disputed Oregon Territory, and though the British at first refused to accept his proposed boundary, they reversed course in June 1846 and agreed to the present line, which includes Oregon, Washington, Idaho and part of Montana.

In this, James Polk was only restating the Monroe Doctrine, even though, he, like Monroe, had almost no power to enforce it. It was his good fortune that Britain was still not interested in exploiting those new Latin American republics breaking away from Spain. Neither did she intend to intervene in the Mexican-American dispute. Nevertheless, a historian can only gasp at the temerity with which "Little Jimmy" Polk—with a tiny army and a puny navy at his back—chose to challenge the world's two foremost military powers.

Revisionists who seek to reverse the judgment of a war deliberately provoked and waged for land alone insist that those who advance this explanation are guilty of the logical fallacy of *post hoc; ergo propter hoc,* "after this; therefore on account of this." For example, if someone in a classroom were to cough and a student dropped dead, this would explain the cause of his death. Henry writes: "The argument runs that Polk desired California, that there was a war and that Polk got California: ergo, Polk wanted war." This is not so. Polk's sincere desire to buy these lands at a fair price is well known and undeniable.

It is, of course, inconceivable that Polk could have been thinking of war at that time. The U.S. Navy, although it had no Mexican Navy to fear, was hardly comparable to the navy that fought the British in 1812, and the U.S. Army consisted of only 7,000 officers and men, of whom only about 5,500 were effectives. Most of these troops were spread out so thin on frontier outposts so wild that most Americans of the interior could live and die without ever having seen a soldier. Could this tiny force actually defeat a supposedly better-trained and - armed Mexican army of 30,000 men? If Britain or France or both were to intervene on the Mexican side, would there be, instead of a glorious victory and extension of freedom from coast to coast, a disastrous defeat and a renewal of allegiance to the British Crown? It is not known if Polk actually asked himself these questions, but neither is it wise to assume that because the American David did slay the Mexican Goliath that he was positive this would happen.

Vis-à-vis Mexico, Polk was anything but a saber rattler. He actually did hope that he could make peaceful purchase of the land he sought, thereby misunderstanding both the proud Mexican character and their contempt for what was eventually to be known as Uncle Sam's "dollar diplomacy." Polk knew that widespread corruption and civil war kept Mexico almost permanently short of funds.

. But he miscalculated, for the offer of annexation made to Texas in March 1845 so angered Mexico that it broke off diplomatic relations.

Minister Juan Almonte, the same suave aide of Santa Anna's who had swum the Buffalo Bayou at San Jacinto, was instructed to ask for his passports. At the same time the Mexican Congress authorized an increase in the armed forces to resist any attempt to annex Texas forcibly. With this, on June 15, Polk ordered the "Army of Observation" stationed at Fort Jesup, Louisiana, to march to a point on "or near the Rio Grande" to defend Texas against possible invasion. This force of about 3,500 men—half the entire U.S. Army—was commanded by Brigadier General Zachary Taylor.

65

Zachary Taylor

~ ALTHOUGH ZACHARY TAYLOR BECAUSE OF HIS UNMILITARY SLOUCH
and dress and willingness to share the hardships of his men would one
day be known as "Ol' Rough 'n' Ready"—a sobriquet suggestive of
humble origins—he could in fact claim an ancestry as illustrious as
any other American in history. His English forebears settled on Virginia's Mattapony River in 1640 when that colony numbered only ten
thousand persons. His father was Lieutenant Colonel Richard Taylor,
who served with the 1st Virginia Continentals during the Revolutionary War, and his family was closely related to other patrician families
in the Old Dominion. President James Madison, under whom he
served in the War of 1812, was a distant cousin.

Zachary Taylor was born November 24, 1784, the third son of
Richard and Sally Taylor, about a year after his father had received
from Virginia his war bonus of some six thousand acres of land in
what is now Kentucky. In the spring of 1785 the entire family began
the long trek to the trans-Appalachian West, following the "easier" of
two routes because it allowed them to transport their household
goods and other heavy equipment, as well as the younger children
such as two-year-old Zachary. This took them over the Blue Ridge
Mountains down into the valley of the Shenandoah to descend that
river to the Potomac, swinging west along the famous trail followed by

George Washington and General Braddock, and then, reaching Pittsburgh, floating down the beautiful Ohio six hundred miles to the Falls where the frontier settlement of Louisville was located. It was a journey of about a thousand miles usually completed in about two months. Although the threat of marauding Indians always existed, none appeared to harrass the Taylors. Indeed, there was then a rush of settlers to the western lands discouraging such attacks, and by the end of 1785 Kentucky could boast of a population of twenty-five thousand. Although there were no great battles in the Louisville area—simply because there were no tribes located there—Colonel Taylor was a frequent volunteer for the expeditions against the red men of the northwest, gaining such a reputation as an Indian-fighter that Governor Scott said that "if he had to storm the gates of Hell, he should want Dick Taylor to lead the column."

Very little is known of the childhood of Zachary Taylor except that, even without local tribes, the fear of Indians was always a reality with the presence of the Indian alarm bell and the nightly barricade. Neither was he too young to remember friends of his father slain in the Indian wars. His boyhood was probably as comfortable as the frontier would permit, for his father was the fifth largest of the thirty-eight slave owners in the district, and Beargrass Plantation on the creek of that name with its four hundred planted acres and solid two-story mansion was as fine a home as could be found in the Blue Grass. Because Richard Taylor was extremely active in Kentucky politics, serving four terms in the state legislature and also acting as a presidential elector in four elections, his son Zachary probably learned the political facts of life at an early age. With two older brothers, three younger ones and three younger sisters, he certainly could not have wanted for playmates, although the great distances separating the plantations did not make for many friendships with boys his own age. His education was at best basic, and perhaps sketchy. He studied briefly under a well-known scholar named Kean O'Hara, and probably learned his three R's from his mother, who had been educated by European tutors, and possibly also from his father, believed to have attended William and Mary College in Virginia. Nevertheless it is doubtful that Zachary Taylor ever saw the inside of a classroom, and his correspondence in later years betrays a rather shallow acquaintance with either literature or history—though he did know politics—nor with literary composition.

At maturity Zachary Taylor was of medium height and probably would have seemed short but for his long head. His blue eyes were sunken and his prominent nose hooked and his mouth too large for his narrow face. Short-legged, he gained weight easily and in later years would be obese. By the time he was twenty-three he had yet to travel far from the family plantation, being apparently satisfied to accept more and more responsibility for supervision of the plantation, and to develop a fondness for farming that he never lost. But then, inexplicably, he decided to become a soldier.

The year was 1808 and the crowned heads of Europe were embroiled in that series of bloody military struggles that would enter history under the omnibus heading of the Napoleonic Wars. President Thomas Jefferson, avowed and active pacifist though he was, became upset by the *Chesapeake* Incident and other humiliations on the high seas, and began to think of how defenseless the United States was with its tiny army of three thousand men, and in April Congress approved his recommendation to authorize the secretary of war to triple its size. Immediately, young Taylor, perhaps motivated by a desire to emulate his gallant father, applied for a commission, and in May of that year he was appointed a first lieutenant in what was to become the famous 7th U.S. Infantry Regiment. It was then only a regiment on paper, and in the procedure of the day Lieutenant Taylor spent most of the following year in Kentucky recruiting the soldiers he would lead. In the spring of 1809 he led two companies aboard ship at Louisville, making for the Mississippi and the New Orleans area where General James Wilkinson with 2,000 men was charged with the defense of the vast Louisiana territory recently purchased by Jefferson. If Great Britain were to attack America, Jefferson thought, the blow would come there.

But there was no fighting, and the real enemies were the hot, humid climate, clouds of buzzing, biting mosquitoes, as well as the malarial swamp that the inept Wilkinson had chosen for a campground and the back-breaking task of draining and clearing it. Almost all the chronic and deadly diseases known to armies—malaria, yellow fever, diarrhea, dysentery, scurvy, and an amazing variety of unknown bilious fevers probably caused by the vermin infesting the men's thick wool uniforms—rapidly cut the defense force almost in half. In ten months, out of 2,000 men, 686 died of disease, 108 deserted and another 58 were discharged for various disabilities. Lieutenant Taylor was one of those afflicted, probably by dysentery, and was sent home to recuperate.

In November of 1810 Taylor was promoted to captain. About this time he was married to Margaret Mackall Smith of Maryland, daughter of a retired army officer and wealthy planter who had died a few years earlier. It was a happy marriage, for Mrs. Taylor was almost always with her husband except when expecting a baby. In all, the Taylors had six children, and Taylor, though ill-educated himself, did everything possible to see that they had a finer education.

On the subject of education, Zachary Taylor was somewhat ambivalent. He cherished it for his children, but apparently despised it for himself. Having had little formal schooling, he depended upon his native intelligence, practical good sense, and deep insights into human nature. He could be compared to the modern American homespun sage Will Rogers, who said: "I don't mind a man's being educated, just so long as it don't mess up his mind too much." Yet, if he did see through the conceits of the classroom mind, and if he tended to belittle book-taught soldiers and even learning itself—an unconscious defense mechanism—he nevertheless had enough common sense to accept the judgments of professional, trained officers. Occasionally, however, if he found his rough and ungrammatical speech insufficient to defend his opinions against the smoother criticism of his educated subordinates, he would take obstinate refuge in rank.

Taylor's indifference to learning was also matched by a contempt for sartorial elegance that horrified his trim West Pointers and greatly amused his men. His dress was not only unmilitary but actually slovenly. One day it might be a dusty green coat, on another a blue-checked gingham coat, then an old brown jacket or a linen waistcoat or even a soldier's light blue overalls. On his head was an old straw hat, and when mounted on "old Whitey" with one leg nonchalantly slung over the pommel, he looked about as military as a sack of flour. One of his soldiers even declared that "he looked like a toad." In the spring of 1812—with war clouds gathering—Taylor took command of Fort Harrison in Indiana Territory.

Learning that Tecumseh, now a British ally, was preparing to attack Harrison, Taylor with customary energy drove himself to make the fort defensible and its garrison battle worthy. But at the end of the summer a fever put him and many of his troops on their backs. By September Taylor was well again, but considerably weakened, and with only about fifteen able-bodied men at his command. The rest were either still sick or convalescing. Taylor's situation was also made more difficult by settlers seeking sanctuary in the fort with their families. Although the men were hardy frontiersmen familiar with firearms and thus were a welcome asset, the women and children were a distinct liability. Because Tecumseh had never sanctioned a massacre, the civilian men might very well counsel surrender to save their families. Taylor, however, was determined to give battle—and because Tecumseh struck at midnight on September 4 without warning, he was spared the divisive argument of a council of war.

Leaping out of bed upon hearing his sentries open fire and then the howling of hundreds of Indians, Taylor found to his dismay that Tecumseh's redmen had not only begun firing on the fort but had set fire to a lower blockhouse. The flames were spreading rapidly and now the cries of nine women and their children were proving just as unnerving to the soldiery and male civilians as the screeching of the Indians. Moreover the handful of men at Taylor's command were almost fatally slow in carrying out his orders. But he retained his presence of mind.

I saw [he wrote in his report], that by throwing off part of the roof that joined the blockhouse that was on fire, and keeping the end perfectly wet, the whole row of buildings might be saved, and leave only an entrance of 18 or 20 feet for the Indians to enter after the blockhouse was consumed. A temporary breastwork might be erected to prevent their entering there. I convinced the men that this could be done, and it appeared to inspire them with new life, and never did men act with more firmness and desperation.

That was what happened. Although the barracks also caught fire during the night, the fires were put out and the Indians' "heavy fire of ball and an innumerable quantity of arrows" had little effect on the garrison. At dawn, Tecumseh withdrew his attackers beyond range of the fort's cannon. Throughout the day the garrison—sick as well as healthy soldiers—labored with the male civilians to block the gap left by the burned-out blockhouse. With nightfall, Taylor prepared to repulse a fresh attack—but none came. Still, his efforts to warn Vincennes of his predicament were of no avail, his messengers finding the river and woods patrolled by Indians in war paint. Unknown to him, however, a party of mounted U.S. soldiers on a routine trip to Fort Harrison caught sight of Tecumseh's war party and hurried back to Vincennes, and a relief force was sent to the besieged fort. By September 12 the Indians were gone, and the Ohio Valley echoed to the praise of Captain Taylor's "brave defense" as "one bright ray amid the gloom of incompetency which has been shown in so many places." President Madison evidently felt the same way, for the promptly promoted his kinsman to the rank of major.

Fort Harrison was the extent of Zachary Taylor's participation in the second war against Great Britain, and he did not see action again until the eruption of the Black Hawk War in the spring of 1832. Black Hawk was the name of a Sauk and Fox chieftain whose followers were known as the British Band because they had chosen to fight the Americans during the War of 1812. Before then—in 1804—the Sauk had ceded to the United States the region lying east of the Mississippi between the Wisconsin and Illinois rivers. Inside this territory lay the seat of Sauk power: a town of some five hundred families including their burial ground and around this their cornfields. Cession had only been made with the proviso that the Sauk could continue to live and hunt upon it as long as it remained part of the public domain.

In the mid-1820's, however, American settlers began encroaching upon these lands, and Black Hawk in 1831 warned them that if they did not withdraw he would expel them by force of arms. When they appealed for protection to the Illinois governor, 1,600 mounted volunteers and ten companies of regulars were sent to the area. Confronted by this immensely superior foe, Black Hawk withdrew during the night to the west bank of the Mississippi where he joined other Sauk who had already yielded to white pressure and crossed to the Iowa shore. A few days later all of the Sauk agreed to forswear all lands east of the Mississippi.

In the spring of 1832, Black Hawk changed his mind and recrossed to the east bank with five hundred warriors and their squaws, children, and baggage. His intention, he said, was merely to replant corn in the abandoned fields; actually, he planned to take the warpath once the crops were harvested in the fall and his food supply was secure. Once again the settlers appealed for help and Brigadier General Henry Atkinson placed Major Taylor in command of a militia force charged with protecting settlers on the Illinois and Fox rivers. Before he could arrive Black Hawk struck, murdering three families and sparing only two young women carried off as future squaws. In late June of 1832 General Atkinson set out in pursuit of the Indians, who had taken refuge in the "almost impenetrable marshes and swamps at the head waters of the Rock River." From this sanctuary, Taylor wrote, they "commenced an indiscriminate massacre of men, women and children."

Taylor also described some of the nightmare marches made by Atkinson's regulars in pursuit of the wily Black Hawk, particularly a fight forty miles above Fort Crawford on the Mississippi, where the Americans caught the red men crossing the river, "killing I presume about one hundred, and making fifty or sixty prisoners, besides destroying a large portion of their baggage . . . with a loss on our part of some twenty-seven killed and wounded. . . ." He was also at the culminating defeat of the Indians at the Battle of the Bad Axe in which few of the Sauk survived, and those who did escape either drowned or reached the west bank of the Big Muddy only to be exterminated by their Sioux enemies.

Zachary Taylor saw action again during nearly two and a half years of service in the Seminole War (1835–42), being commander of U.S. forces in Florida during two of them. This was a longer period than his predecessors, even the illustrious Winfield Scott. But he did not contribute more to winning the war inasmuch as most of the fighting occurred before he took command. He did, however, face a more difficult mission, for the Seminoles who chose to remain in Florida, though much smaller in number than those who departed, were, in their determination to live or die in the land of their fathers, more difficult to subdue. Being fewer, they traveled in smaller parties and were thus harder to flush from their hideouts. But Taylor the Tenacious pursued them relentlessly, driving them from one sanctuary to another, making their lives so miserable that in despair they, too, decided to abandon their homeland.

The Seminole War, if this merciless pig-sticking operation may be so dignified, was one more shameful episode in the long and sorry saga of the deliberate extinction and dispossession of the southern Indians by the U.S. government. Its objectives were just as odious as the tactics employed to gain them: first, to crush the tribes or drive them west of the Mississippi; second, to recover runaway slaves who had found sanctuary—and sometimes wives—among the swamp-dwelling Seminoles. Nothing could have been more unconstitutional than to put U.S. armed forces at the service of Southern planters, but the gentlemen from Dixie who still controlled Congress and the White House had their way. Zachary Taylor, though a Southerner and slaveholder himself, nevertheless had little enthusiasm for such repugnant duty, repeatedly requesting to be relieved of his command, and just as steadily having his appeals denied.

The high point of Taylor's service in Florida came on Christmas Day, 1837, when he broke the Seminole power at the Battle of Lake Okeechobee, so that hundreds of the braves of that tribe surrendered to him during the ensuing months. Having tracked the foe over some of the most formidable terrain on the American continent, he had at last cornered them in the very heart of their wilderness retreat and there dealt them a defeat from which they never recovered. For this he was given a brevet commission as brigadier general, placing him among the first half-dozen officers in the U.S. Army. More important to Taylor, his victory had made his name known to President Tyler, who sent General Taylor to Fort Jesup, Louisiana, on the Texas border to command "a corps of observation" to be held "in readiness for service at any moment."

After the Texans called for a convention on the Fourth of July, 1845, to approve annexation, Secretary of War William Marcy ordered Taylor to advance without delay "to the mouth of the Sabine, or to such other point on the Gulf of Mexico . . . as in your judgement may be most convenient for an embarkation at the proper time for the western frontier of Texas."

General Zachary Taylor received these instructions on June 29, 1845, and immediately prepared to move his army to Corpus Christi on the south bank of the mouth of the Nueces River as it emptied into the Gulf. The Army of Observation would soon become the Army of Occupation, and Zachary Taylor was poised to come on center stage in the long drama of American military history.

66

Stuffing the Powder Keg

~ By moving into Texas itself on the south side of the Nueces as instructed, General Taylor unwittingly widened the growing split between his country and Mexico. Texas claimed the Rio Grande at its southern boundary, but Mexico, still refusing to recognize Texan independence, insisted that the southeastern limit of the territory had always been the north bank of the Nueces about 150 miles above the Rio Grande. As a Mexican department, Texas had never extended below the Nueces. Land south and west of that river belonged to the department of Tamaulipas. At best, Texas had a most doubtful claim to territory below the Nueces, yet an American army was encamped there. It was as though a Canadian army, to "defend" Ontario, had crossed the Niagara River into New York State.

After Texas accepted the terms of annexation to the United States, Mexico rocked with rage and resounded to cries for war with the United States. Polk replied to these threats with remarkable decisiveness and efficiency, alerting the Pacific Fleet to seize San Francisco Bay should war erupt and the Atlantic Fleet to stand by to establish a blockade of Mexican gulf ports. It was at this time that he also ordered Taylor to move into Texas to repel a possible invasion of the new American state.

But then, having reacted so firmly to the threat of war, Polk began to make diplomatic mistakes. Either naive or uniformed, he seemed not to comprehend how sensitive any young republic can be about "national honor." He believed a report in August that stated Mexico would be willing to resume talks, and was encouraged that the latest revolt that had ousted Santa Anna had put José Joaquín Herrera in the president's chair. Herrera had a reputation as a dove, an attitude almost unique among hawkish Mexican chiefs, and was also married to an American. He had secretly met Polk's representative, W. S. Parrott, a dentist who spoke Spanish, and Parrott had reported that Herrera was willing to receive an American minister to discuss the impasse between the two nations. It is more likely that Herrera said "commissioner," rather than "minister"—for to receive the latter would have been to recognize the annexation of Texas.

But Polk chose to designate his emissary as a "minister," and he chose for this secret mission John Slidell of Louisiana. Here was one more mistake: the assignment of yet another slaveholding Southerner, in an unbroken succession of such envoys, to slavery-hating Mexico. Slidell was born the son of a New York tallow chandler, who migrated to Louisiana to escape debt and prosecution for a duel with a theater manager over the affections of an actress. Making a fortune in sugar, he entered New Orleans society by taking a Creole wife. Slidell was also the brother-in-law of the Civil War general Pierre Beauregard, and he was well named. He looked sly, with his carrot nose and twisted little mouth. A British journalist wrote of him as a man "who loves the excitement of combinations, and who in his dungeon, or whatever else it may be, would conspire with the mice against the cat rather than not conspire at all." It is not always true that a talent for conspiracy is also one for diplomacy, and Slidell was probably chosen because he spoke both Spanish and French.

Slidell's mission—supposedly secret—was to offer to assume the debt of some $4.5 million owed to American citizens in damage claims if Mexico would be willing to accept the Rio Grande as Texas's southern boundary; another $5 million would be offered for New Mexico and for California "money would be no object." In all, unanimously supported by his cabinet, Polk was prepared to pay from $15 to $40 million. When it is recalled that Thomas Jefferson paid Napoleon only $15 million for the far greater territory of the Louisiana Purchase, it may be realized how desperately James Knox Polk wanted those southwestern and western lands.

But he had not a chance, for the moment President Herrera heard that Slidell had come to Mexico with the status of minister rather than a mere commissioner he refused to see him. If he had, he would not have lasted two hours in the president's chair, which had already, with the bellicose General Mariano Paredes breathing down his neck, begun to wobble beneath him. In fact, he lasted no more than two more weeks, and after both Britain and France rejected his appeal for help, he was replaced by the firebrand Paredes. On January 4, 1846, Paredes took over, and in ringing tones declared that he would never treat with the treacherous Colossus of the North and would defend to the death every inch of national territory, including Texas.

In Washington, learning that Slidell had been rebuffed and had retired to Jalapa to await developments, President Polk ordered General Taylor to move his little army down to the north bank of the Rio Grande. That was in January, but Taylor, mistakenly believing that torrential rains barred his path, did not move until two months later. On March 24, 1846, he reached a point on the Rio Grande opposite the Mexican port of Matamoros and thirty-three miles inland from Point Isabel, his eventual supply base on the Gulf. Taylor assured the local Mexicans that he had come only to protect Mexican property. They replied that his army was illegally on Mexican soil, a fact that automatically created a state of war. General Pedro de Ampudia demanded that Taylor withdraw to a point above the Nueces. Instead, Taylor built a fort and trained its guns on Matamoros, while blockading the mouth of the Rio Grande to cut off Mexican supplies.

Thus was the powder keg built and stuffed: Texas had seceded from Mexico making very doubtful claim to a southern boundary at the Rio Grande. Mexico recognized neither secession nor claim, while refusing to honor those American damage claims; and was now infuriated by American annexation of the Lone Star State and outraged by *Yanqui* attempts to buy New Mexico and California. American troops now stood on soil Mexico insisted belonged to her, and opposite them were Mexican soldiers poised to evict them. All that was needed now to ignite the powder keg was the spark of war: blood.

No one appreciated this more than President Polk, who was deeply dismayed by the failure of Slidell's mission and still unwilling to provoke a war—until he was informed by that emissary on May 8 that force was now the only means by which he could obtain his territorial objectives. Next day Polk met with his cabinet to put before them his proposal to ask Congress for a declaration of war. All but one supported him, and all agreed that the American position before the world would be much better if the first shots were fired by Mexico.

Aggression is never popular except at home. That very night Polk learned that Mexico had indeed taken that first fatal step.

On April 24 General Mariano Arista had taken command at Matamoros and promptly sent a force of 1,600 cavalrymen under General Anastasio Torrejón across the Rio Grande above Taylor's camp. Next day the Mexicans had ambushed a detail of sixty-three American dragoons under Captain Seth Thornton, killing eleven of them, wounding others and capturing most of the others. On April 26, Taylor had informed Polk that "hostilities may now be considered as commenced" and issued a call to Texas and Louisiana for volunteers.

Taylor's eleventh-hour message lifted James Knox Polk off the horns of a dilemma. He could not really declare war because a neighboring state had refused to sell him some of its land, or suggest that this same nation was an aggressor because it had proclaimed its intention to reclaim some of its territory illegally annexed by the United States. He *could* do it, of course, and to do so would be popular at home where that expansion fever called Manifest Destiny still raged unchecked. But in the outside world it would not be so easily swallowed. Britain and France might not agree that the refusal to honor American claims or to receive Slidell was such a monstrous insult, and so far from being true *casi belli* were actually an excuse for unprovoked aggression; and thus give them their own pretext for intervention and an eventual joint jackal's feast on the prostrate body of Mexico. Polk's position under such circumstances was fraught with unpleasant possibilities proceeding from the presence of a victorious Anglo-French army to the south of Texas. But now, he had a much more viable *casus belli:* an act of aggression, if one can actually be an "aggressor" on soil that one believes with undeniable truth to be one's own.

On May 10, a Sunday, Polk worked on his war message before and after church, piously regretting "the necessity . . . for me to spend the Sabbath in the manner I have." The following day he told Congress: "The cup of forebearance has been exhausted. After reiterated menaces, Mexico has passed the boundary of the United States, has invaded our territory and shed American blood upon the American soil." Congress then declared that "by the act of the Republic of Mexico, a state of war exists between that government and the United States" and authorized Polk to accept fifty thousand volunteers and appropriated $10 million for the conduct of the war. In the House the vote was 174 to 14, in the Senate 40 to 2—an amazingly solid stamp of approval, considering the later Whig opposition to "Mr. Polk's War" and an ultimate snowballing and widespread unpopularity, once it became clear to most Americans that James Knox Polk, frustrated in his attempt to make peaceful purchase of Mexico's northern outposts, had deliberately provoked a war to seize them. Only Vietnam, for far less defensible or justifiable reasons, would exceed Mexico in public disapproval.

On May 13, 1846, Polk signed the war bill into law.

67

War! The Rival Armies

∾ OUTNUMBERED BY THE UNITED STATES—20 MILLION TO 7 MILLION—
Mexico nonetheless was supremely confident of victory.

This was because most of her ranking officers, including General
Paredes, were European-trained and had been infected with the European contempt for American military prowess. Such unfounded confidence had led Paredes, who had come to power promising to chastise
the detested gringos* to order Arista to gain that small victory over
Captain Thornton's dragoons that was so big with consequence for
Polk's *casus belli:* Mexico had "shed American blood on the American
soil."

Paredes was not being vainglorious in predicting swift victory; he
merely mistook size for skill. In 1845 the Mexican Army numbered
about 32,000 compared to the ridiculously small effectives of 5,500 in
the regular United States Army. True enough, Polk had been authorized to call up 50,000 volunteers, but except for the Battle of New
Orleans—where the controlling factor was Jackson's decisiveness
opposed to Pakenham's fatal order to charge entrenched American
marksmen—volunteers have yet to write a glorious page in American
military history.

Mexico's soldiers were considered superior to America's: because of

---

* It is a derogatory Spanish word meaning "foreigner" but when applied to
Americans has a special connotation of contempt.

their country's numerous civil wars; and they were combat-wise because they were almost to a man stolid peasants, Indians or Mestizos, they fulfilled the Napoleonic maxim: "Adversity is the school of the good soldier." Stoical, durable and brave they were indeed, but they were also quite stupid, entirely incapable of original or innovative action; indeed, to show any sign of intelligence or independence was to provoke the wrath of their officers. Battle-trained they were not. In his Texas campaign, Santa Anna ridiculed such ideas. Lt. Col. José Enrique de la Peña, a perceptive observer and dedicated Mexican patriot, wrote of this enormous failing: "All the efforts of the brigade chiefs to instruct the recruits were useless because the commander-in-chief maintained that they would become accustomed to gunfire *during combat!*"

The infantry were armed with the famous—or infamous—British Brown Bess, a muzzle-loading smooth bore flintlock* that was both outmoded and condemned and which the foolish Mexican Army had bought by the thousands. It was supposed to have a killing range of about one-hundred yards, but usually fell harmlessly to the ground at seventy. The British never seemed to have thought of this weapon as a killing or maiming instrument; if they had they would have put a sight on it. Instead, it was a noise-and-smoke-making machine designed to demoralize the enemy and soften him up for the bayonet charge, the true arbiter of battle: wildly cheering redcoats bursting out of the smoke with gleaming blades outthrust. It was bad enough that the Brown Bess had no sight and the Mexican Army no order of "Aim!," but worse that the Mexican soldier had so inexplicably overloaded his musket with powder and then been so terrified of its severe recoil that he fired it wildly from the hip—and often with his eyes squeezed shut—rather than from his shoulder for fear it would break his collar or shoulder bones.

Mexican artillery was also outmoded and, conversely from the Mexican musket, so underloaded with poor powder to conserve same that "not one ball in a thousand" struck the enemy target.

Though outnumbering the American effectives by at least six to one, the Mexican Army because of its officers overpowering preoccupation with political power was not an efficient fighting force. Even its emphasis on its spectacular cavalry—no finer horsemen existed on earth—was intended chiefly for showy pageantry in Mexico City. Designed to impress the populace, these displays instead gave the people a false sense of security.

Many of its officers were trained in military schools such as the one

---

*A firearm's lock is its firing device.

at Vera Cruz attended by Santa Anna, or in the academies of higher military education of the leading European powers, usually in Spain. Because its formations were so heavy with rank—at one time in Mexican history there were twenty-four thousand officers commanding twenty thousand men—and its generals more celebrated for their dexterity in changing side than in matters military—no true spirit of professionalism ever emerged. Typical of these posturing generals was the inept Francisco Mejía, who could actually boast of the cannon fodder he commanded at Matamoros: "Those adventurers [the foreigners in the American Army] cannot withstand the bayonet charge of our foot, nor a cavalry charge with the lance."

From another observer, Waddy Thompson, the pro-Mexican American minister to Mexico in 1843, came a different estimate:

> There is not one in ten of these soldiers who has ever seen a gun, nor one in a hundred who has ever fired one before he was brought into the barracks.... Their arms, too, are worthless English muskets which have been condemned and thrown aside.... Their powder, too, is equally bad; in [one recent battle] which lasted the whole day, not one cannon ball in a thousand reached the enemy—they generally fell about half-way between the opposing armies.

If these remarks sound exaggerated, consider this first-person account from a young Mexican soldier describing his first encounter with a firearm. He was stuck in the rear rank behind a drugstore clerk, and when the orders to load and fire were given, "I closed my eyes . . . and said under my breath to the druggist, 'God help you.' When I opened my eyes, the druggist was getting up off the ground badly frightened and bruised. I had singed his bushy hair and he wished to devour me.... On returning to the barracks expecting arrest or some such thing I found I had been made a sergeant—so as to prevent me from firing any more guns. . . !"

Incredible as this may sound, accurate fire meant nothing in the Mexican Army. Foot soldiers were nothing but cannon fodder, trained in "volley firing." Infantry strode forward with lowered muskets and fired on command. It was believed that this made of, say, a company, a giant, moving shotgun. In actuality, it was a self-execution tactic, not only for the Mexican soldier's habit of firing from the hip, which would certainly devastate the forward ranks, but because to reload and fire again he would have to make eighteen motions executed on eleven commands. For how long this would make him a stationary target is not known, but it certainly would have taken at least two minutes—all within view of enemy marksmen and artillery. In the classic, two-deep, shoulder-to-shoulder formation of volley firing in which one unit would present a musket muzzle every twelve inches, it was believed the enemy would be riddled by devastating flights of musket balls. In reverse, like that poor drugstore clerk who could thank God for his countryman's horrible inaccuracy, the friendly first ranks would be shattered. This may explain why so many Mexican soldiers at the Alamo were killed by friendly fire. As proof that no one believed in such self-destructive tactics, nothing really mattered to a Mexican general except blaring bugles and a stirring cavalry charge with saber or the lance.

General Mejia was quite right when he spoke so contemptuously of the foreign "adventurers" in Zachary Taylor's little army. No less than 47 percent of the regulars of about 3,500 men were foreigners. Irish alone made up 24 percent of that force, 10 percent were Germans, 6 percent English, 3 percent Scots and a scattered 4 percent from Canada and western Europe. These were the warrior races of Europe, and most of the Americans who marched with them, though certainly almost all native-born, were also the descendants of immigrant parents or grandparents.

They shared the regular's pride in his calling, and to a man they had only one God: accuracy with firearms. In a nation that idolized such legendary marksmen as Davy Crockett, Jim Bowie and Daniel Boone, such an attitude was not surprising or unusual. Among the Americans especially it would be a rare soldier who had not grown up with a firearm in his hand.

Taylor's artillery probably had no peer anywhere else in the world. Three secretaries of war—the southerners Calhoun and Joel Poinsett and the Michigan frontiersmen Lewis Cass, who had been a hero of 1812—hunters all, had shaped this vital arm. In 1840 Poinsett made the greatest contribution by sending a board of officers to Europe to study the artillery there and bring back the cannon of the various armies for study by the Ordnance Department. As a result, a full family of American artillery pieces appeared in 1841, just in time for the Mexican War.

In those days a cannon's missile was measured by its weight rather than its diameter, as nowadays. There were also, as today, three different kinds of ordnance: the gun, howitzer and mortar, each differentiated by its angle of fire. A gun fires a low flat trajectory of the highest velocity; a howitzer, usually with a shorter barrel for the same size shot but with less powder and an elevated muzzle; and the mortar—then usually a heavy piece, but today of varying weights—firing at a steep angle usually of about forty-five degrees.

The American family of weapons, model 1840, included two light artillery pieces for field use: the 6-pounder gun and 12-pounder howitzer. Of these the 6-pounder gun with its range of 1,500 yards and weight of 880 pounds was the basic field piece. For siege purposes a collection of heavy howitzers was developed. They were the 18- and 24-pounder guns, 8-inch howitzers and 8- and 10-inch mortars. They were extremely heavy, some reaching 5,600 pounds, and therefore with little mobility in the field. Taylor had none of this heavy ordnance.

In 1844 the U.S. Army had four artillery regiments along with its eight infantry regiments. Each artillery regiment had ten companies of fifty men each—a sizeable formation. Only one company in each regiment, however, was designated "light" or fit for use with infantry. It was also called "flying" because of its speed. There were only four of these four-gun units in the entire U.S. Army, and Taylor had three of them. These were usually placed at the point of greatest danger so that the outcome of a battle sometimes did not depend on the conduct of a regimental colonel, but a lieutenant whose guns were supporting the infantry.

While at Corpus Christi Taylor had hammered these troops into a decidedly efficient fighting force, one of whom, young Lieutenant Ulysses S. "Sam" Grant, could write home that "a better army, man for man, probably never faced an enemy." Taylor's pride was those three companies of flying artillery under the innovating and daring Major Samuel Ringgold. Moreover, the entire American Army under statuesque Winfield Scott—the hero of Lundy's Lane—was fortunate in possessing what was then and probably still is the finest collection of junior officers in American military history. Most of them had been trained at West Point, and to read their names is like calling the roll of famous soldiers and sailors in the American Civil War. Not all of them were with Taylor, and some of them would not even be in Mexico but in New Mexico or California instead: Grant was one of the most outstanding, along with the matchless Robert E. Lee and Pierre Beauregard—who would be among Scott's favorite officers; George Thomas, the future "Rock of Chickamauga"; Joseph E. Johnston and the gallant Albert Sidney Johnston; "Fighting Joe" Hooker; Burnside and Bragg; both Kearnys, Phil and Stephen; Pope and Meade; McClellan; Irvin McDowell, notorious for having been thrown by his horse onto a giant cactus, which decorated the "family jewels" with inch-long thorns;

Stonewall Jackson and Jefferson Davis; Simon Bolivar Buckner; "Prince John" Magruder, already a consummate military actor; Longstreet; Pickett; Armistead; Hébert; Pemberton; Sherman and Halleck, both out of combat range in California; both Hills; Reynolds; Hancock; Buell and Ewell and Jubal Early; Ed Baker, the best friend of Abraham Lincoln; John Charles Frémont, whom modern historians now call the Path Follower rather than his own somewhat exaggerated sobriquet of the Pathfinder; the former West Point commandant C. F. Smith, already silver-haired but still pink-cheeked and blue-eyed with his great white mustache drooping on either side of his jaw, a strict disciplinarian and the terror of volunteer officers. And among the sailors DuPont, Buchanan, Raphael Semmes, and David Glasgow Farragut.

Not all of these officers were enthusiastic supporters of the War with Mexico. Young Sam Grant, already perceptive beyond his years, called it an "unholy" war. Before he joined Taylor at Corpus Christi he had considered resigning from the army in protest, but then, thinking that this might seem to be "showing the white feather," he had changed his mind. When Polk ordered Taylor to move 150 miles farther south opposite Matamoros, Grant wrote: "We were sent to provoke a fight, but it was essential that Mexico should commence it." He spoke for many of his comrades when he castigated the war that resulted as "one of the most unjust ever waged by a stronger against a weaker nation." Lieutenant George Deas said he saw no Americans or Texans south of the Nueces. "All were Mexicans, acknowledging none but Mexican laws. Yet we . . . drove those poor people away from their farms, and seized their custom house at Point Isabel."

Nevertheless, for all their disenchantment, none of these young officers left the service, and all obeyed every order given them.

The march south from Corpus Christi was a grueling ordeal of 150 miles made miserable by a blazing sun that "streamed upon us like a living fire." The light blue jackets and trousers of the infantrymen became caked with soft white powdery dust, and soon those stiff-necked cavalrymen who rode above the choking clouds were calling the foot-sloggers "adobies" after the white Mexican huts along the river. It was a short step to "dobies" and after this to "dough-boys," and thus the immortal nickname was born. And the floury dust that had christened the doughboys also coated their tongues and clogged their nostrils to aggravate a thirst that was terrible for both men and animals. A whole day's march often lay between ponds of potable water, and yet even the agony of thirst and sunburn might be forgotten in the universal delight to behold the wide blue sky filled with "mirages":

ships and islands reflected from the Gulf sixty or more miles away.

It was on this march that Zachary Taylor endeared himself to his troops. Ol' Rough 'n' Ready made no attempt to avoid the hardships suffered by his men. His hawkish nose was also white and peeling beneath his old straw hat, and he rode along on Old Whitey, often with one leg nonchalantly slung over the pommel.

At last, on March 23, Taylor's suffering doughboys formed into columns four abreast and went marching through a praire now thick with grass and red and gold with blossoming cactus. On March 28 they saw the blue mists of the Rio Grande ahead of them. At ten-thirty that morning they came to the riverbank and stared across the water at Matamoros.

They saw Mexicans standing in curious throngs atop the town's tiled rooftops. They saw red roses climbing snow-white walls. They heard bands blaring, bugles pealing, dogs barking and church bells ringing in a medley counterpointed by the liquid Spanish of excited civilians and drilling soldiers—but most of all they saw the cool blue waters of the Rio Grande and many of them stripped and went bathing in it.

That was when they saw the Mexican girls come laughing down to the opposite bank to step out of their skirts and chemises and go naked in the water, and with that a difficulty unforeseen by Zachary Taylor had begun.

"Efforts are continually [being made] to entice our men to desert," Taylor reported on April 6, "and, I regret to say, [they] have met with considerable success."

By then, thirty of Taylor's soldiers had crossed to Matamoros. Naked Mexican lasses splashing in the water had not been the only attraction, nor had the girls been official sirens but only local maidens following a Matamoros custom which happened to coincide with Mexican policy. The Mexicans had guessed that many of the foreigners in Taylor's army were Roman Catholics, and they made a powerful appeal to their religious loyalties. Nearly every day Matamoros celebrated a saint's day with masses, music, and processions. Taylor's troops were encouraged to desert to claim bounties starting at 320 acres. Old World allure was also complemented by the contempt and cruelty that too many American officers visited upon their foreign soldiers. And so, as sex, saints, and sadism began to whittle the army he had worked so hard to build, Old Rough 'n' Ready acted. He got tough and began shooting soldiers trying to desert, starting with a Frenchman and a Swiss. Such draconic measures—taken, incidentally, before the state of war which justifies such executions had begun—

plugged the leak at last. But desertions among regulars was a continuing problem for Taylor, and those who turned their coats at Matamoros were to form the nucleus of that San Patricio or Saint Patrick's Battalion which turned out to be Mexico's finest fighting unit.

In the meantime, both sides crowned the Rio Grande with fortifications, General Arista arrived to take command, to order the ambush which provided President Polk with his *casus belli,* and to cross the river downstream to cut Taylor's communications with Point Isabel.

68

Battle! Palo Alto,
Resaca de la Palma

⏳ In late April 1846, General Zachary Taylor was alarmed to receive word that a strong enemy force of three regiments was attacking his vital supply base at Point Isabel. Finding himself in the paradoxical position of a full depot with light defenses and at Matamoros an excellent defense but short supplies, he decided to move to the relief of Isabel with almost his entire army.

On May 1, he struck his tents at "Fort Texas," the bastion facing Matamoros across the river. Leaving five hundred men of the 7th Infantry there to hold the fort, he began marching northeast toward Isabel with his main body of about three thousand men, plus three hundred empty supply wagons with which he intended to resupply Fort Texas.

Taylor's army was in high spirits, actually spoiling for a fight. Neither officers nor men bore any hatred toward the enemy, but were indeed grateful to the Mexicans for their considerate treatment of Captain Thornton and the other soldiers taken prisoner in Torrejón's ambush. But they also realized that the way to end exposure to such whittling small actions was to defeat Arista's army in a major action. They wanted this to happen "quick and soon" because they knew that they would shortly be inundated by a flood of untrained volunteers upon whom the American press, still kneeling before the shrine of the

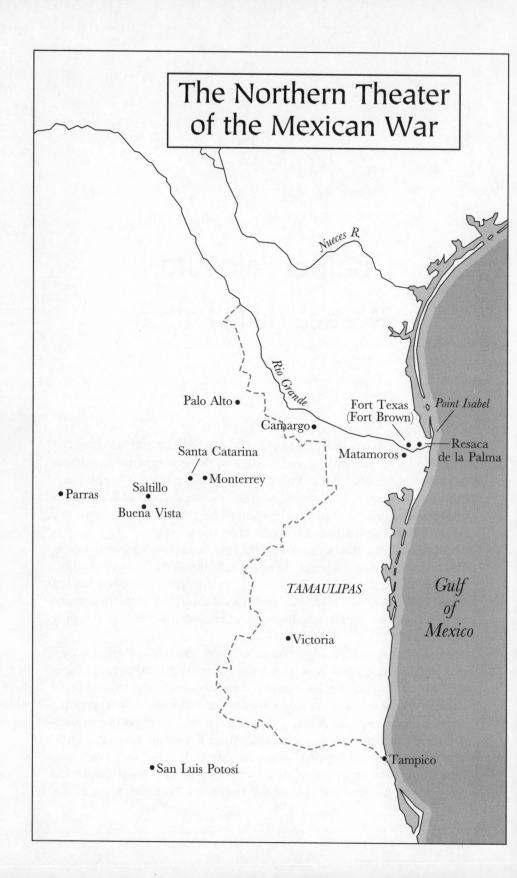

The Northern Theater of the Mexican War

Nueces R.

Rio Grande

Palo Alto •

Camargo •

Fort Texas
(Fort Brown)

Point Isabel

Santa Catarina

Matamoros •

Resaca
de la Palma

• Parras

Saltillo
•

• Monterrey

Buena Vista

TAMAULIPAS

Gulf
of
Mexico

• Victoria

• San Luis Potosí

• Tampico

mythically invincible Minuteman, would shower all its accolades.

This belief was shared by the 7th Infantry, disgruntled at being left behind and therefore out of the glory as well. Known as "the Cotton Balers" because of their heroic defense of New Orleans behind a defensive line of cotton bales, they were commanded by fifty-eight-year-old Major Jacob Brown, who thirty years earlier had joined the 7th as a private from Massachusetts and spent his entire career within its ranks. Taylor had wisely given Brown his heavy artillery—four powerful 18-pounders—plus three 6-pounders and a mortar. Fort Texas itself was a well-chosen and well-constructed position, designed by the veteran engineer Captain Joseph K. F. Mansfield, another future Civil War hero. It was only just completed, for Taylor delayed his march almost a week to be sure it was defensible—a decision that would be proved wise. Situated at a strategic point on the winding Rio Grande, it commanded the river both downstream and upstream. Three of its six redans (fortified artillery positions) dominated Matamoros to its front. Its eight-hundred-yard perimeter was protected by a wall fifteen feet thick at its base and over nine feet at its apex, surrounded by a ditch eight feet deep. Though the wall was earthen, it was considered too strong for the 12-pounders that were Matamoros's heaviest ordnance. Thus Taylor began his march to Point Isabel confident that his rear was safe.

On the same day that Taylor marched from Fort Texas, General Arista left Colonel Mejía in Matamoros with a small garrison and at the head of his main body moved downstream toward a place called Longoreno, where he planned to cross to the left bank. Torrejón, who was still upstream with his cavalry, was ordered to make a wide sweep around Taylor's army to join Arista at Longoreno. If all went went well, Arista would have a force of about 5,700 men—3,500 infantry, 1,100 regular cavalry plus 425 irregular horse, 175 artillerymen and 500 Matamoros guerrillas—concentrated in the rear of Taylor with about 3,000 and between him and Point Isabel. It was a good plan, but as so often happens with plans made on paper, it ignored the difficult terrain over which Torrejón must pass and the absence of boats to cross the Rio Grande. Arista's army was also divided by the constant bickering among its ranking officers. Backbiting and recrimination were rampant, and General Ampudia had not been enchanted to be superseded by Arista, either belittling him or predicting glorious victories impossible of attainment. Arista, meanwhile, was at odds with the Ministry of War in Mexico City.

Torrejón was slow in arriving at the juncture point, and when Arista reached it he found that his quartermaster, fearing to attract the attention of the Americans, had provided only two rickety boats to ferry the army across the river. It took an entire day to get the spearheads alone over to the east bank. By the time Arista had his army deployed, his scouts told him that Taylor—pressing his men forward with all his redoubtable energy—had already passed up the road to Point Isabel.

Taylor meanwhile was disturbed by conflicting reports from Major John Monroe in the supply depot and could not be sure if it would still be in friendly hands when he arrived there. He was also dismayed to hear that on the night of April 29 Captain Sam Walker's company of Texas Rangers lost ten men in a surprise ranchero raid. This suggested a rise in Mexican aggressiveness that worried Old Rough 'n' Ready. For all his outward nonchalance, he was a worrisome man—as no successful military man can fail to be. So he drove his troops unsparingly, and they responded with the toughness of regulars accustomed to adversity: little sleep, meager food, and no campfires, but they covered the thirty miles through rough country in less than twenty-one hours. As General John S. D. Eisenhower has observed, Stonewall Jackson's legendary "foot cavalry" would "never do better."

Sighting Point Isabel at about noon May 2, Taylor was relieved to see the Stars and Stripes flapping lazily above the fort and no sign of any "strong enemy force." With fierce energy he began loading his provision wagons, while detailing troops to work at improving Isabel's defenses, especially vulnerable on the mainland side. The morning after his arrival, Taylor heard the faint booming of artillery in the vicinity of Fort Texas, and was torn between the obvious necessity of improving Point Isabel's fortification and the urge to rush to the relief of Major Brown. But then his confidence in both Brown and his troops and Texas's defenses calmed him, and instead he sent Walker and a party of Texans back to the Rio Grande fort to report on its situation. In the meantime, the sound of guns rose and fell with the wind, and as Sam Grant was to recall: ". . . for myself, a young second lieutenant who had never heard a hostile gun before, I felt sorry that I had enlisted."

On the evening of May 2 the church bells at Matamoros began pealing, and the men in Fort Texas rushed to the ramparts to peer across the river. They saw a procession of colorfully vested priests and monks followed by altar boys in red cassocks and white surplices holding aloft golden crucifixes on long poles and a throng of worshippers singing hymns. They moved solemnly from one artillery post to another, the priests wielding silver aspergillums filled with holy water to bless every gun.

Next morning the guns opened fire with the bombardment heard in Point Isabel. As it continued Major Brown and Captain Mansfield grew steadily confident of its ultimate failure: Fort Texas was just too strong for the enemy's 12-pounders, those undercharged cannon that, as Waddy Thompson had observed, could not land one shot in a thousand on their targets. Conversely, Brown opened up with his own heavier 18-pounders and silenced the Mexican artillery one by one, except for a mortar sited too low to hit anything but the sky.

Zachary Taylor was a happy general when Sam Walker returned from a conference with Brown to report that the major was confident that he and his Cotton Balers could withstand a two-week siege. One seasoned regular, however, complained that he "would rather have fought twenty battles" than to have passed through another such bombardment. As of May 5 only one man in Fort Texas was killed: Sergeant Weigert was hit by a shell, and as he lay dying on the surgeon's table another struck him, and then as he lay buried, a third sent his "exhumed" and dismembered body flying through the air. A few other men were wounded, Walker reported, so General Taylor, his confidence renewed, continued to load his wagons while ignoring the frantic pleas of some of his officers wild to rush to Brown's relief, and still working to make Isabel stronger. On May 6 the first recruits from New Orleans arrived, together with five hundred sailors and Marines from Commodore David Conner's blockading squadron. That morning Brown received his mortal wound at the position that was henceforth to bear his name and become the city of Brownsville, Texas. Defense of Fort Brown continued under Captain Edgar Hawkins, who rejected a Mexican surrender demand by explaining that he could not speak Spanish, "But if I have understood you correctly, my reply is that I must respectfully decline to surrender."

At three o'clock that afternoon Taylor was ready to march. There was a moment of comedy when old Colonel William Whistler wrathfully rounded upon "a young officer of literary tastes" who had dared to put a case of books into a wagon.

"That will never do, Mr. Graham," he snapped. "We can't encumber our train with such rubbish as books."

At this point Lieutenant Charles Hoskins nervously admitted that, not being well, he had taken the liberty of inserting a keg of whiskey in the wagon, and the old colonel murmured: "Oh, that's all right, Mr. Hoskins. Anything in reason. But Graham wanted to carry a case of *books!*"

Those who heard this exchange chuckled, but they were less than mirthful when Old Zack's general order was read to all. If they met the enemy on the road, Taylor wrote, they would give him battle.

"[The General] wishes to enjoin upon the battalions of infantry that their main dependence must be in the bayonet!"

With the recruits and the seamen left behind to guard the base, whips snapped, pennants fluttered, wheels turned, feet fell—and wagons and men went swishing through waist-high grass. Throughout that day and the next the Americans saw no Mexicans. Then, through the shimmering heat of noon of May 8, 1846, they saw the enemy. At first they were only a line of gleaming metal drawn up on the plain of Palo Alto, the "Tall Timbers" which rose dramatically behind them. Then they were distinguishable: the sun danced on the needle points of lances in the grasp of mounted men, it burnished the brass of cannon drawn up between masses of tall-hatted infantrymen. They seemed an enormous host, but actually, having raised the siege of Fort Brown, General Arista had little more than four thousand men on the field.

Ol' Rough 'n' Ready commanded fewer than three thousand. But these men had an unshakable faith in their indomitable old general, sitting there on Old Whitey while he waited for his wagon train to close up. Then he advanced to within half a mile of the Mexicans, where he halted and ordered a platoon from each company to stack arms and collect their comrades' canteens and fill them from a nearby pond. The men relaxed and forgot their tension.

Taylor was somewhat surprised, not at finding Arista confronting him on the road but to be caught with the enemy in such a strong position and his own immense wagon train a distinct liability. Arista was content to assume the defensive, confident that the pressure was on Taylor, and Ol' Rough 'n' Ready realized that he had no choice but to attempt to break through a superior force before the Mexican cavalry could fall upon his precious supplies.

So he sent out two young engineers—Jacob Blake and Lloyd Tilghman, the latter to become another Confederate hero—to scout Arista's position. They reported that Arista's flanks were invulnerable, with a swamp on one side and a wooded knoll on the other. His center though flat was made only partially visible by high chaparral inside and behind it. Conversely, Taylor could neither conceal nor protect his wagons because they could not be moved into those dense woods. Because Arista's horse might ride around Taylor's position and scourge his lifeline, the American chief drew them up in a park protected by a squadron of dragoons—mounted troops that could have proved invaluable somewhere else.

Opposite the Americans the gallant General Arista rode across his lines waving his sword. The men shouted "Viva!" and lifted their banners. At three o'clock in the afternoon, the Mexican cannon began firing. At first the round brass balls came bounding through the tall grass so slowly that they could be easily sidestepped. As the Americans continued to advance, however, the missiles came faster and thicker. Lieutenant Grant gasped to see a ball knock off the under jaw of a captain standing next to him. Then General Taylor halted his advance and sent his own artillery into action.

Major Ringgold's battery went flying to the right, Captain James Duncan took his galloping to the left, and into the center went two bulky 18-pounders, each towed into place by ten yoke of oxen. Now the Americans had the range and their fire was devastating. Again and again American shot cut a swath through the massed Mexican infantrymen, and each time the enemy ranks closed up bravely. But the field artillery, which the Americans were using with a precision unrivaled since the time of Napoleon, prevented almost every Mexican effort to advance. The only attempt was a cavalry charge at the American right.

A thousand lancers with two guns came sweeping through the grass, but Taylor's flank regiments rapidly formed a square and cut the Mexican riders down with musket fire while Lieutenant Randolph Ridgeley led a section of Ringgold's battery to the rescue on the run, unlimbering and blasting the Mexican guns before they could fire a shot.

Palo Alto had become strictly an artillery duel, with the Americans holding the upper hand. American doughboys who had expected to charge with the bayonet merely stood at order arms, cheering as their artillery tore gaps in the enemy lines, or carefully watching for the Mexican solid shot so as to step out of its way. Then smoke obscured the battle. A flaming wad from one of Duncan's guns had set the grass on fire, and the breeze from the Gulf had swept the choking smoke toward the Mexican line. Under cover of the prairie fire, Taylor advanced his right. But Arista threw his own right forward, so that the relative position of the lines was little changed. However, Duncan's battery had also moved under cover of the smoke, swinging out to the left to take the enemy right under an enfilading fire.

It was the moment for the American foot soldiers to press forward with the bayonet, but the opportunity had come too late. Darkness veiled the field of Palo Alto, and both sides withdrew. Nine Americans had been killed—among them the invaluable Major Ringgold—and 44 had been wounded. But Mexican losses had totaled 250, and in the early morning darkness of May 9 Taylor gathered his leaders in a council of war and asked them if he should press the attack.

It is in councils of war that the cautious are most aggressive, and this one was no exception: seven of ten officers wanted to wait for reinforcements. But then Captain Duncan rode past, and Taylor called to him to ask his opinion.

"We whipped 'em today and we can whip 'em tomorrow!" Duncan snapped, and Taylor said, "That is my opinion, Captain Duncan. Gentlemen, you will prepare your commands to move forward. The council is dissolved."

The Mexican withdrawal from the field of Palo Alto began at sunup. Taylor did not pursue until he had arranged for the protection of his valuable—and distracting—wagon train. At noon his men plunged into the gloomy chaparral that had masked Arista's retreat.

Here the terrain differed sharply from the level plain of Palo Alto. Here were dense thickets broken by resacas, or remnants of riverbeds. Some were sunken lagoons and others were dry trenches, and as such they were excellent for defense. Two of them, the Resaca de la Palma across which the American attack was launched, and the Resaca de Guerrero inside which the Mexicans made their defense, have given their names to the same battle of May 9, 1846.

The Resaca de Guerrero, which Arista occupied, extended east and west across the road to Matamoros. It was about two hundred feet wide and of a depth of three to four feet at the banks. Within it were a few narrow ponds surrounded with bushes and small trees. To either flank and to its rear it was protected by thick chaparral. Arista put his infantry on each side of the road behind the resaca. To his right or east of the road he stationed three or four guns. Then the Mexican general went back to his headquarters tent to attend to paper work. He did not believe the Americans would attack.

They did, however, coming chiefly against the Mexican artillery. Here Taylor, slouching on his horse, was delighted by the spectacle of Lieutenant Ridgeley, now commanding Ringgold's battery, charging down the road with horse-drawn guns unprotected by infantry. Ridgeley deliberately drew the fire of Mexican infantry and artillery, blasting back at their smoke. Meanwhile, the battle had become a sergeant's war. Small parties of men stumbled through the chaparral and tore at each other shot for shot and blade for blade. The Americans went forward yelling like fiends, and the Mexicans, who had not eaten for twenty-four hours, fought them off bravely.

In all, however, possession of Arista's guns was to mean victory or defeat. Sensing this, Taylor called upon Charles May, a dashing captain of dragoons, to lead his squadron down the road. May went trotting off to form his troopers, but he soon found that the enemy artillery was better emplaced than he had thought. He rode back to General Taylor and asked for new orders.

"Charge, Captain!" Taylor roared. "Charge, *nolens volens!*"

May dashed off, his long black beard streaming in the wind. Ridgeley called to him: "Hold on a minute, Charley, till I draw their fire!" Again Ridgeley lured the Mexicans into giveaway fire, and May's dragoons, observing their position, went sweeping forward in four columns.

Down the road they clattered, down into the resaca, up its opposite bank, over the guns and beyond them—too far beyond them. Before they could stop their hard-bitted horses, the Mexican gunners came swarming out of the chaparral to reclaim their pieces and to cut up May's squadron as it returned to the American lines.

Taylor was furious. He called his infantry forward and roared: "Take those guns, and by God keep them!" Bayonets leveled, the infantry obeyed orders. Ridgeley's gunners followed in behind them to turn the captured cannon on the Mexicans—and it was then, with its flanks slowly giving way to stubborn Americans clawing through the chaparral and its center cracking, that the Mexican line broke. It snapped and flew backward like a broken bow. Even General Arista's tent and possessions were abandoned in the mad rush to the rear. En route to the Rio Grande and Matamoros, the fleeing Mexicans were taken under a bloody enfilade by the guns of Fort Brown. Within the river itself many of them drowned. A priest named Father Leary tried to calm a crowd of crazed fugitives aboard a big flatboat, but then a party of fleeing lancers spurred their horses aboard the boat and swamped it. The last sight the pursuing Americans saw was the priest's upheld crucifix slowly sinking beneath the water.

Now was the time for Taylor to cross the river and to crush the enemy army. He might have ended the war then and there. But Old Rough 'n' Ready was old in his ways. He told his younger officers that the enemy had taken all the boats to the other side, and because he was an "old 'un" he had little time for engineers clamoring for permission to build new ones. No, Zachary Taylor had won two fine fights. His casualties for both totaled 48 dead and 128 wounded, perhaps not one-sixth of Arista's losses. And so, on the evening of May 9, he retired to his tent to write his report.

Even as President Polk far to the northeast was working on his war message, Taylor set down the concluding words: "The enemy has recrossed the river, and I am sure will not again molest us on this bank." Arista not only failed to molest Taylor again; he eventually gave up Matamoros without a fight.

69

U.S. Volunteers: "Vandals Vomited from Hell!"

∼ THE LONG-RANGE EFFECT OF ZACHARY TAYLOR'S VICTORIES AT PALO Alto and Resaca de la Palma was to give to American arms a tradition of offensive success that has lasted to this day. Up until May of 1846, American troops had seldom sought and defeated an organized foe. Excepting Trenton, which was hardly more than a raid, and Yorktown, which could not have been won without the French, American victories had been gained in defensive stands or in retreats that averted disaster. But now Americans were attacking and winning, and the American nation, no less than the French placing the laurels on Napoleon's brow, was quick to idolize Ol' Rough 'n' Ready.

Cities and towns across the nation passed resolutions nominating Zachary Taylor for president. Toasts were raised everywhere to "Old Zack," and the fact that he had no known political preferences meant nothing to those delirious Whigs who at once embraced him as their own. No result could have been more abhorrent to James K. Polk. He realized immediately that he, a Democrat, might be waging war to make a Whig president. But there was nothing Polk could do. Even if he had wanted to recall Taylor, he could not have dared it, for it would have made Old Zack a martyr. And with whom would he replace Taylor? Certainly not Winfield Scott, with whom Polk had already quarreled and whom he had removed from field command, for Scott was an active Whig who had once tried to obtain his party's nomination. And so, in this era of extreme partisanship when a political general was a commonplace, Polk turned to making Democratic generals in the faint hope that one of them might outshine Old Rough 'n' Ready.

Meanwhile, a tidal wave of enthusiasm rolled across the country. Everywhere except in New England, where the annexation of Texas was still resented, volunteers rushed to the colors in the tens of thousands. In New York City walls were plastered with placards proclaiming MEXICO OR DEATH or HO, FOR THE HALLS OF THE MONTEZUMAS! America's streets reverberated to the roll of drums and the squeal of fife and the tramp of marching men roaring out such songs as

Come all ye gallant volunteers
Who fear not life to lose,
The martial drum invites ye come
And join the Hickory Blues.

In Indianapolis Lew Wallace raised a company in three days by parading the street with a four-sided sign inscribed FOR MEXICO: FALL IN! Ohio, unhappy with both annexation and the war itself, nonetheless sent 3,000 of her sons to war in less than two weeks. Illinois volunteered fourteen regiments instead of four, North Carolina tripled her quota, and Tennessee upheld her nickname of Volunteer State after 30,000 men responded to a call for 2,800 and the rejects angrily tried to buy their way in.

It was not only patriotism or a sense of Manifest Destiny that solved the manpower problem. Privately, recruiters excited almost every passion with promises of "roast beef, two dollars a day, plenty of whiskey, golden Jesuses, and pretty Mexican girls." The charming customs of the maids of Matamoros were presumably not excluded from such recitals. And so the highways were black with thousands hurrying off to the Halls of the Montezumas where life was lazy, lush and golden, and dark-eyed señoritas were obliging.

This time, however, the men were not diverted into those state militias that had been Washington's bane and Madison's mortification. This time the federal government avoided collisions with state authority by enlisting men in volunteer units separate from the regular army but still liable to foreign service. They were as yet untrained and still given to the pernicious practice of electing their own officers. A soldier in the Alton (Illinois) Guards has described how one such candidate for command recommended himself to the men:

Fellow Citizens! I am Peter Goff, the Butcher of Middletown. I am!
I am the man that shot that sneaking, white-livered Yankee abolitionist son of a bitch, Lovejoy! I did! I want to be your Captain, I
do; and I will serve the yellow-bellied Mexicans the same, I will! I
have treated you to fifty dollars worth of whiskey, I have, and when
elected Captain I will spend fifty more, I will!

He was elected, he was—and he and those raw volunteers whom he
and his ilk commanded soon became the personal hairshirt of America's latest hero: Old Zack.

Down on the Rio Grande General Zachary Taylor, though well aware
of his newfound popularity and secretly pleased by all those resolutions nominating him for president, had little time to savor his victories. At first, he had been jubilant to discover that General Arista had
evacuated Matamoros, leaving his sick and wounded behind him. At
once he crossed the river, carefully keeping both his troops and his
headquarters outside of town to conform to Polk's instructions to
treat the Mexican people as friends. He deliberately chose a light
guard to patrol this beautiful town of about four thousand Mexicans,
making it clear to these regulars that he expected them "to present a
model of discipline and correct deportment." Unwilling to comman-
deer supplies or to impose a financial burden of any weight upon the
populace, Taylor paid for all of his provisions on the barrelhead, even
though he was aware that these happy and eager farmers and merchants often inflated their prices. In another attempt to promote
mutual good will he established a Spanish-English newspaper. So a
miniature Era of Good Feelings seemed to have begun between Mexican conquered and American conquerors—until the U.S. volunteers
arrived.

On May 11, 1846, the first of eight thousand volunteers recruited by
General Edmund Gaines at New Orleans arrived at Point Isabel.
Thereafter they swamped Taylor in a steamboat flood—most of them
Southerners—chugging down the Mississippi, out onto the Gulf and
thence to Isabel or to Taylor's advanced base at Camargo about seventy air miles farther west. The first arrivals were useless. They had
been enlisted for six- or three-month terms, and by the time most of
them arrived it was time for them to go home. Then, in July and
August, 1846, the twelve-monthers came whooping into camp.

They murdered; they raped, robbed and rioted. A Texas colonel
thought the Tennessee men were worse than Russian cossacks; Taylor
himself thought the Texans "were too licentious to do much good";

testy little Lieutenant George Meade considered all volunteers to be "full of mutiny"; and the Mexican priests called them "Vandals vomited from Hell." When they did not attack Mexican civilians or fight each other, they fought the regulars. They defied their officers and helped their comrades escape from the guardhouse. They dressed as they pleased. The "Volunteers of Kentucky" wore full beards, three-cornered hats and hip boots faced with red morocco. Elsewhere the various "Guards," "Rifles," "Killers," "Gunmen," "Blues" and "Grays" who came crowding in on the long-suffering Taylor appeared in colors ranging through gray, green, blue and white with trimmings of red, yellow and pink. When their gorgeous going-away raiment wore out, they objected to putting on regulation blue. "Let 'em go to hell with their sky blue," swore an Indiana soldier. "I'll be blowed if they make a regular out of me." Volunteers who were slaveholders expected the despised "foreigners" among the regulars to wait on them, and many of them, bitter because they did not get more than regular pay of seven dollars a month, cursed themselves as "seven-dollar targets." Gradually, in the immemorial way of undisciplined troops, they fell sick.

Camargo, at which some fifteen thousand American troops were assembled by August, came to be known as a "Yawning Grave Yard." It was too far from the Gulf to be cooled by sea breezes, and the rocks rimming the encampment round made it a caldron in which men were baked and boiled to death. All day long the troops heard the crashing of three volleys over the grave of some soldier, and as one officer said: "The Dead March was played so often on the Rio Grande that the very birds knew it."

Such conduct, which so many of a handful of mostly prejudiced and parochial American historians of this "dirty little War" have attempted to brush off as merely "disorderly," remains the most dishonorable episode in the annals of American arms. It is true that the volunteers had ample cause for complaint, crammed into inadequate camps as they were, there to riot, sicken and die. But this was not Taylor's fault but rather the consequence of Secretary of War Marcy's policy of sending him far more troops than the five thousand he had requested. Both Marcy and Polk knew that General Gaines's eight thousand had been illegally recruited for six months, when obligated by the Constitution to serve only three, and they tried to solve the problem by instructing Taylor to "urge" them to enlist for a year. Taylor was furious, as well he might be, and he did nothing of the sort—glad as he was to see them go. But before they did, they pillaged, raped and murdered in a paroxysm of barbarity rivaling the merciless riders of

Genghis Khan or the cruel and bloody Nazi death squads and SS troops in World War II.

"How much they seemed to enjoy acts of violence too!" wrote a horrified Lieutenant Sam Grant. "I would not pretend to guess the number of murders that have been committed upon the persons of poor Mexicans and our [regular] soldiers . . . but the number would startle you."

In his letters home Lieutenant George Meade tried to minimize the depth of this maniacal racial and religious hatred resulting in merciless slaughter and torture of innocent Mexican civilians, yet he admitted that he had seen how these men of Manifest Destiny had "killed five or six innocent people walking in the streets, for no other object than their own amusement. . . . they rob and steal the cattle and corn of the poor farmers, and in fact act more like a body of hostile Indians than civilized whites."

The incredible insolence and insouciance of these volunteers toward their officers—even generals!—is simply impossible to exaggerate. Here's a sample from Trooper Samuel Chamberlain, a member of Colonel William Harney's regiment of regular dragoons, in his autobiography *My Confession:*

> One day I was on General [John] Wool's guard, he with his staff rode into town to dine. As we approached the guard line a "Sucker" on post was seated on the ground with a roguish looking Senorita, engaged in eating *frijoles* and *pan de maiz*. The sentinel coolly eyed the cavalcade, and with no thoughts of rising to salute, he remarked, "Good day General, hot riding out I reckon."
>
> The General thundered out, "Call the officer of the guard!"
>
> The man just raised himself on his elbow and drawled out, "Lieutenant Woodson, come here right quick, post nine, for the old General wants you!" He then turned to his companion with a self-satisfied air, as if he had discharged his duty in the most exemplary manner.
>
> The officer of the guard made his appearance without belt or sword, coat unbuttoned and a straw hat on. The General gave him a severe reprimand for his own appearance as well as the unsoldierlike conduct of the guard, whereupon the officer broke out, "Jake Strout, yer ain't worth shucks. If you don't git right up and salute the General, I'll drive yer gal away, doggone if I don't."
>
> The gallant sentinel riled up at this and replied "that if the General wanted saluting the Lieutenant might do it, he wan't a-going to do anything of the kind."

Worst of all were the Texas Rangers, as these volunteers from the Lone Star State came to be called. They were in three regiments commanded by the state's Governor J. Pinckney Henderson. There had been little time to furnish all of them with uniforms, so that they were on the whole a villainous-looking lot, long-haired, bearded and mustachioed in an age when most men—especially soldiers—cut their hair and were clean-shaven. They could be identified by the wide-brimmed slouch hats—akin to the Mexican sombrero—that they wore and the belt of pistols hanging at their waists. They were unwashed and lice-ridden, just like those poor Mexicans they despised, and like them also regarded frequent bathing as a foppish affectation and seemed to respect *el piojo*—the louse—as an endangered species. These Tejanos were not all frontiersmen who had been fighting both Indians and Mexicans since Texas won her independence in 1836, but included in their ranks doctors, lawyers, educators, engineers, and other professional men, as well as college students enlisted for a lark. Superb horsemen, their courage was of the highest degree, a virtue eroded by its vice of cruelty.

One of their most celebrated atrocities occurred when a company of these "packs of human bloodhounds" attacked a *ranchero* near Agua Fria. "The place was surrounded, the doors forced in and all the males capable of bearing arms were dragged out, tied to a post and shot! . . . Thirty-six Mexicans were shot at this place, a half hour given for the horrified survivors, women and children, to remove their little household goods, then the torch was applied to the houses and by the light of the conflagration the ferocious *Tejanos* rode off to fresh scenes of blood."

Even more hideous was the massacre perpetrated by volunteers of Colonel Archibald Yell's regiment of Arkansas cavalry witnessed and described by Trooper Chamberlain. One of a detail of nine men ordered by Brigadier General John Wool to ride toward the sound of rifle fire in the mountains near Saltillo—either to destroy or disperse the riflemen if they were Mexicans or arrest them if they were Americans—the dragoons were drawn to a cave by the sight of "a cloud of *zapilotes* or vultures" circling overhead and peeling off to plunge upon their prey, presumably carrion. Here is what they found:

> On reaching the place we found a "Greaser" shot and *scalped* but still breathing; the poor fellow held in his hands his Rosary and a medal of the "Virgin of Guadalupe," and only his feeble motions kept the fierce harpies from falling on him while yet alive. A Sabre thrust was given him in mercy, and on we went at a run. Soon

shouts and curses, cries of women and children reached our ears, coming apparently from a cave at the end of the ravine. Climbing over rocks we reached the entrance, and as soon as we could see in the comparative darkness a horrid sight was before us. The cave was full of our volunteers yelling like fiends, while on the rocky floor lay over twenty Mexicans, dead and dying in pools of blood. Women and children were clinging to the knees of the murderers and shrieking for mercy.

Sergeant Clifford ordered the volunteers, mostly from Yell's Cavalry, to come out and give themselves up as prisoners, which order was received with shouts of derision and threats of cleaning us out if we interfered. Clifford gave the command and we dropped behind rocks and took aim on the foremost ruffians, when our Sergeant again ordered them to file out or we would fire. They became silent, not knowing our strength. Soon a brutal looking Rackensacker advanced towards us brandishing a huge knife dripping with gore in one hand, and a bunch of reeking scalps in the other, and cried out:

"H'yer, you Regulars! I'm Bill stamps, I am! We don't a muss with you, we don't! I raised this 'ere hair from the damned yellow bellies that had on poor Arch's clothes. I did! Take me to 'Old Fussy' and I'll be responsible for the whole."

With this the savage cutthroat marched out with a swagger, gave a fancy Indian dance and subsided in tears. With curses and threats, more than a hundred volunteers filed out of the slaughter pen and with the muzzles of our carbines bearing on them they sullenly marched down the mountain. We soon met our Squadron, who took charge of our prisoners while the Officer of the Day ordered us back to the cave with several surgeons. On reaching the place we could hear the low groans of the dying mingled with the sobs of women and cries of children. A fire was burning on the rocky floor, and threw a faint flickering light on the horrors around. Most of the butchered Mexicans had been scalped; only three men were found unharmed. A rough crucifix was fastened to a rock, and some irreverent wretch had crowned the image with a bloody scalp. A sickening smell filled the place. The surviving women and children sent up loud screams on seeing us, thinking that we had returned to finish the work!

No one was punished for this outrage.

Such was the "friendship" of these missionaries of Manifest Destiny, these soldiers of democracy and apostles of freedom, and not a word of their barbaric behavior was published at home; indeed, the Texas Rangers openly sneered at the protests of Taylor and General in Chief Winfield Scott—fastening on Scott the derisive nickname of "Ol' Fuss 'n' Feathers." Taylor to his credit refused to accept any more Texas volunteers, although he continued to employ those infamous Rangers, now so revered in the fawning textbooks of superpatriotic historians. This was neither hypocrisy nor cringing submission to the pressure of those political generals foisted on Taylor by Polk either to reward party loyalty or as agents to spy on Old Zack. As an independent commander Taylor could hardly deprive himself of such a matchless corps of scouts and shock cavalry, even though as a professional soldier and a compassionate human being he despised them in his heart of hearts. Furthermore he had been impressed by the men of Sam Walker's company in his two actions against Arista, and now preparing for a much larger battle—an attack on Monterrey the capital of Nuevo León—he needed them more than ever.

70

"From Sea to Shining Sea"

◇ ONE REASON MEXICO WENT TO WAR WITH THE UNITED STATES WAS because its leaders hoped to have British military support, if not directly, at least in an Anglo-American war that would draw off Yankee arms to the Oregon Territory.

Since 1818 both America and Britain had jointly occupied this vast area. But then Britain made the same mistake as Mexico had by encouraging settlements in the area of their trading posts. Most of the settlers, of course, were hardy Yankees moving northwestward in the early 1840s over the rugged Oregon Trail. Inflamed by the Manifest Destiny fever, they began to clamor for assertion of U.S. territorial claims as far north as Russia's southern limit at the Alaskan Panhandle: the line 54°40' which gave rise to Polk's slogan "Fifty-four Forty or Fight!"

James Polk did not want to fight, but he still believed that "the only way to treat John Bull is to look him straight in the eye." Thus, after Britain rejected his offer to accept the forty-ninth parallel as a compromise line, Polk returned to the 54°40' claim and served notice of his intention to terminate joint occupation. John Bull, however, stared straight back. Aware that war between Mexico and the United States was imminent, conscious that Polk's extreme position might split his party, the British rattled the saber. Polk naturally did not want war on two fronts, and so he renewed his forty-ninth parallel offer and a conciliatory British government decided that this was an honorable compromise after all. On June 15, 1846, the Senate ratified the Oregon Treaty whereby the future states of Washington, Oregon and Idaho, as well as part of Montana and Wyoming, became American territory. Except for minor revisions made later on, the forty-ninth parallel became the permanent dividing line between the United States and Canada west of the Lake of the Woods.

Much as the apologists for President Polk may maintain that he did not pursue his expansionist policies by force of arms, the fact remains that a day or two after passage of the War Bill orders went out to Commodore David Conner, commanding the Home Squadron, instructing him to blockade Mexico's home ports; to Commodore John Sloat, commanding the Pacific Squadron, to do the same to enemy harbors on that coast; and to Colonel Stephen Watts Kearny at Fort Leavenworth on the faraway Missouri River frontier to invade and seize the vast and lightly defended Mexican province of New Mexico.

Colonel Kearny was a veteran of the War of 1812. He was fifty-two, a small man with graying hair and large pale blue eyes, of quiet demeanor but admired for his decisiveness while often feared for his iron discipline. He had served in the West for twenty-five years, the deep seams and furrows in his weather-beaten cheeks testifying to the rigors he had endured. Only a year earlier he had taken his First Dragoons on a march to the South Pass of the Oregon Trail, at a point where British intervention was then feared. When word of his orders reached the Rio Grande Zachary Taylor's newspaper, the Matamoros *American* printed an anecdote about how the straitlaced Kearny had rebuked a subordinate who addressed a gathering of officers as "gentlemen." "There are colonels, captains, lieutenants and soldiers in this command," Kearny had said. "But no such persons as gentlemen."

Kearny found the flow of volunteers that so annoyed Taylor at Matamoros more than gratifying at Leavenworth. His call for mounted Missouri frontiersmen to join him and his regulars in their march on the City of the Holy Faith—fabled in their minds as the great trading mecca of northern Mexico—that within two weeks of his call for volunteers three full companies of mounted riflemen had ridden into Leavenworth. In all, the First Regiment of Missouri Mounted Volunteers would include about a thousand men in eight companies and commanded by a Kentucky frontier lawyer named Alexander Doniphan. Soon Kearny's horse would be augmented by infantry and artillery, so that he had a force of something less than 1,700 men with sixteen small cannon when they began departing Leavenworth by detachment in late June of 1846.

Their first objective was Bent's Fort, a protected trading post 650 miles from Leavenworth. At first the going was rough, made even more difficult on the Fourth of July by a celebration of the nation's birthday with the sort of patriotism that comes in jugs and bottles. But Kearny the Driver had no intention of wasting a day while the men recovered from their hangovers, and they were up at dawn with an elephantine thirst and mouths that seemed to have been shaved and shampooed. About fifteen miles south of the Kansas River they hit the broad, well-marked Santa Fe Trail running to the southwest, and the going was easier. Once past Council Grove, the famous meeting place of both Amerindians and frontiersmen, they saw "nary a stick of timber." Although Kearny—aware of Napoleon's dictum: "An army marches on its stomach"—had not failed to provide ample supplies of food, without firewood it was difficult to cook it. Eventually as they entered buffalo-grazing country they could gather blankets full of "buffalo chips," what the French called *bois de vache,* in a word, dried dung—and with these cook their meals. But there was no way to overcome the desert's shortage of water. Many a tough frontiersman or trooper sickened from drinking filthy water that no horse would touch. Scorched by the southern sun, blinded by dust storms, tongues thickened with thirst, tormented by mosquitoes and buffalo gnats by day, and freezing in the desert cold by night, they plodded on—so tired they had not the strength to kick at the rattlesnakes and prairie dogs that crossed their path, so distracted by their ordeal that many of them seemed to have lost their minds, raving and cursing like maniacs in their blind fury. Yet, in one more demonstration of how the hardiest of animals cannot endure the punishment that mere men can survive, of Battery A's complement of one hundred fine horses, sixty perished—and were promptly butchered and cooked.

Mirages were common, much like those reflections of the Gulf waters on the blue sky seen by Taylor's soldiers as they advanced to the Rio Grande. But often these beckoning illusions of rest and sanctuary turned out to be true oases nourished by springs of cool fresh water, brilliant with carpets of wild flowers. Great herds of buffalo were everywhere, and almost always there were glimpses of Pike's Peak, the towering outpost of the Rockies. Moving over the desert and through the mountain passes like a great, glittering, undulating serpent, Kearny's army must have awed the Navajo and Apache scouts, almost certainly watching from a distance; and it is almost equally certain that their reports to their sachems discouraged even discussion of any attack on such a force, and may have encouraged the Navajo chiefs to agree to the Peace Treaty of Bear Spring negotiated by Colonel Doniphan in October.

Finally on July 29 Brigadier General Kearny (his star had overtaken him), escorted by Doniphan's regiment, reached the rendezvous area: a broad grassy meadow on the Arkansas about nine miles below Bent's Fort. Here Kearny learned that Mexico and the United States were at war, and here he also found a merchants' caravan that had left Independence in May and had stopped within the protection of Bent's when they learned that hostilities had commenced. Now with more than four hundred wagons and a million dollars worth of merchandise they came under the protection of the Army of the West as well. Pausing at Bent's to receive reinforcements, Kearny also granted his exhausted soldiers a respite in which to replenish both soul and body, letting out those belts that they had tightened again and again. Four and five days later the Army of the West was on the march again, bound for Santa Fe 250 miles away and now 2,000-men strong.

In Santa Fe Comandante General Manuel Armijo had begun to make preparations for defense of the province. He had been assured by the *comandante generals* of Chihuahua, Zacatecas and Durango that they would come to his assistance, and so had rejected the wise advice of Manuel Alvarez, the American consul in Santa Fe. He told Armijo that it would "be better for himself and the people under his government to capitulate, and far preferable" to become Americans than to be citizens of a country as divided, disordered and weak as Mexico. Armijo disagreed. Though held in contempt as a fat functionary who rose to power by shrewd shifts of allegiance, he was not so stupid as to believe that in any popular election his oppressed people would name him— the wolf—to be their shepherd. So he was resolved to resist the *Yanquis,* replying to a conciliatory message from Kearny with the warning that the populace would rise en masse to defend the province. In truth, the people were in an angry mood: resentful of the Gringo invasion and eager to fight. Moreover, Armijo told them that the Americans would take their land, rape their women, and outlaw their religion. Thus, several thousand men—Mexicans, Amerindians and Mestizos— armed with primitive weapons such as clubs, lariats and bows and arrows, were on their way to Apache Canyon, a formidable defile blocking the Santa Fe Trail in which a battalion could hold off an army ten times the size of Kearny's.

Gradually, however, their anger and ardor cooled. Remembering their old hatred of Armijo and contempt for the federal government, they listened to the anti-Mexican or pro-American voices among them. They heard also of the discipline of Kearny's troops, who paid for everything they seized and harmed no one. The general endeared himself to the people in the villages his army passed through. He would mount the roof of a house and declare, in effect:

> We are among you as friends, not as enemies; as protectors, not as conquerors; for your benefit, not your injury. I absolve you of all allegiance to the Mexican government and Armijo. They have not defended you against the Indians, but the United States will. All who remain peacably at home shall be safeguarded in person and in property. Their religion also shall be protected. A third of my army are Roman Catholics. I was not brought up in that faith myself, yet I respect your creed, and so does my government. But listen! If any one promises to be quiet and is found in arms against me, I will hang him!

Kearny then had all the village officials take the oath of allegiance to the United States.

By both deed and word then, the Americans demonstrated that they were not diabolical monsters, and when the people also became aware of their absolute military superiority, they drifted back to their homes and families. Thus, when the Army of the West approached Apache Canyon and Kearny sent out patrols to probe its defenses, fearing that instead of penetrating the pass he would have to make a difficult and dangerous swing to the west, a fat *alcalde* mounted on a mule came galloping toward him. Roaring with laughter, he bellowed: "Armijo and his troops have gone to hell and the canyon is all clear."

With delight modified by wariness against a trap, the Army of the West marched cautiously through the pass and on to Santa Fe twenty-eight miles away. There they found, not a glittering Mecca peopled with richly robed merchants, pretty girls and *vaqueros* mounted on beautiful horses, all promenading or prancing along wide, tree-lined boulevards decorated with splendid cathedrals, gleaming mansions and gorgeous gardens—but rather a straggling collection of abode hovels lying in the flat, sandy valley of a mountain stream, and rising among them a "palace" one story high with a leaky roof and earthern floor. Looking around them in dismayed disbelief, the Gringos burst into laughter and re-named the fabled city "Mudtown."

Nevertheless they were pleased by the warm reception and entertainment given them by Santa Fe's residents, like themselves now Americans. They found the town's ample supply of *aguardiente* just as agreeable as their own corn whisky, although their first mouthful of chili brought gasps and tears rolling down their cheeks, much to the amusement of their hosts. General Kearny was also pleased, immensely proud of his feat of having led an army of about two thousand men on a march of nearly one thousand miles to capture a vast province of eighty thousand inhabitants without firing a shot. But he still thirsted for more glory; and so, after sending Colonel Doniphan with his thousand-mounted Missourians into Chihuahua to join General John Wool as ordered, he began another march with his original regiment of three hundred dragoons, this time to California in pursuit of broader conquest and greater glory.

There were two Californias: *Baja* or Lower, just south of San Diego and *Alta* or Upper, stretching almost a thousand empty miles from San Diego to what is now the Oregon border and reaching back to the ranges of the Rocky Mountains. Today the home of about 25 million Americans, Upper California then was inhabited by only a few thousand Amerindians and still fewer thousands of *Californios* of Spanish descent with a sprinkling of perhaps a thousand foreign merchants and venturesome settlers from other countries. It was this beautiful land with its great seacoast and ports, its immensely productive soil and mineral-rich hills that had nourished the land-lust of President James Polk. After he heard an American sea captain describe the San Francisco Bay area, he had coveted California even more than Texas and was disappointed that his offers to buy Mexico's northernmost province were angrily rejected. As a result, when diplomatic relations between Mexico and the United States ceased in the spring of 1846, Secretary of the Navy George Bancroft cautioned Commodore John Sloat of the Pacific naval forces "to avoid any act which could be construed as aggression" but "to ascertain beyond a doubt that the Mexican government has declared war against us." At such a point, Sloat should "at once . . . blockade San Francisco and blockade or occupy such other ports" as his strength permitted. With the worsening of American-Mexican relations, these orders were repeated in October but did not reach Sloat at Mazatlán off the point of Lower California until February 1846. Marine Lieutenant Archibald Gillespie, who brought them, had required almost four months to reach the western ocean. Sloat—an "aging, ailing and anxious" man—did not sail north until early June of 1846, even though weeks before then he had received word of "the shedding of blood on American soil" as well as news of the battles of Palo Alto and Resaca de la Palma.

Meanwhile Lieutenant Gillespie had arrived at Monterey on California's northern coast to deliver similar instructions to Thomas Larkin, the U.S. Consul there. At Monterey, Gillespie met Brevet Captain John Charles Frémont of the U.S. Army Topographical Engineers. In May of 1845 Frémont had left Missouri to begin the explorations of the Oregon country that would, through self-praise flowing from his facile pen and the influence of his powerful father-in-law, Senator Thomas Hart Benton, confer upon him at home a widespread popularity and the nickname of "The Pathfinder." As the late historian Allan Nevins has astutely observed, Frémont in truth should have been called "The Path*marker*," for the trails that he claimed to have discovered and described in his glowing accounts of his explorations had been used for centuries by the tribes of the Northwest, and many of them were shown to him by that intrepid scout and hunter, Christopher "Kit" Carson.

Frémont had collected a private army of sixty-two armed frontiersmen, having brought them in December 1845 to the fortified ranch of Captain Johann August Sutter, a Swiss adventurer who had secured title to two hundred square miles of land from the California government. At *Nueva Helvetia*—Spanish for New Switzerland—Captain Sutter for a second time graciously outfitted Frémont with animals and supplies to continue his explorations. Frémont then ventured into the San Joaquin Valley, exchanging shots with Amerindians he described as "the Horsethief Tribes." With the onset of winter, leaving his men behind, he went to Monterey to obtain from José María Castro, *comandante general* of the province, permission to winter in the interior. But when Castro in early March found that Frémont had exceeded his permit by leading his party into the Salinas Valley only twenty-five miles from the capital at Monterey, he ordered the American to leave the province.

Frémont defied Castro. With typical bombast he wrote Consul Thomas Larkin that he would "fight to extremity and refuse quarter, trusting to our country to avenge us." Changing his mind, he retired "slowly and growlingly," making his way back to Sutter's Fort and from thence back to Oregon. That was where Lieutenant Gillespie found him, delivering to him a controversial letter from his father-in-law. In it, Frémont presumed to find Senator Benton's "confidential instructions" from President Polk "for taking possession of California." Frémont's claim was preposterous. Would James Polk through his implacable critic Thomas Benton convey to an unknown mere captain of engineers "confidential instructions" to do exactly the opposite of what he intended to do in California: buy, not conquer, the province? Never! Even Benton, the father of Frémont's wife, Jesse, possibly even more ambitious and belligerent than her flamboyant husband, stated flatly in a Senate speech: "Frémont had no orders from his government to commence hostilities."

Yet John Charles Frémont did indeed start a war. With the same willful recklessness that would lead him in 1861 as a major general commanding in Missouri to get into deep trouble with Abraham Lincoln by issuing his own unauthorized emancipation proclamation, he seized 170 horses being driven to Comandante Castro's headquarters. His excuse was that they were going to be used to raid American settlers north of the Sacramento River. To most of the native *Californios,* the seizure was undisguised horse thievery, and Frémont's excuse the sort of double-talk they had come to expect from the fork-tongued Gringos. But Frémont, always deaf to criticism, next sent a party of armed Americans into Sonoma, the last and most northerly Mexican settlement in California established to check the Russian advance south. They seized the post, carrying off cattle and military supplies and eighteen citizens as prisoners, among them Mariano Vallejo, founder of the post and former *comandante general* of the province. Meanwhile, a rear guard, emboldened by Vallejo's excellent brandy, replaced the Mexican flag with one of their own: the figure of a grizzly bear and the words CALIFORNIA REPUBLIC. On the same day, presumably after a few more sips of brandy, they proclaimed the government of the Bear Flag Republic.

Delighted, Frémont went to Sonoma in person to take charge of conquering California under the banner of the bear. Hostilities, however, were limited to a minor skirmish and the execution of a few captives by both sides; although Frémont did make himself famous by crossing San Francisco Bay to the *Presidio* just inside the Golden Gate (which he had himself named) to spike an ancient cannon of this abandoned fort. There followed a big Fourth of July celebration at Sonoma, where Vallejo's brandy was again freely imbibed, and at which Frémont was chosen by the settlers "to take direction of affairs" of the new republic.

But the Bear had only three weeks to live, for Frémont's uprising had so upset the hesitant Commodore Sloat that he at last acted decisively, unwittingly following in July the course enjoined upon him in the orders he would not receive until the end of August. He sailed into Monterey and on the morning of July 7 demanded from Comandante Mariano Silva surrender of the town. Silva quickly obliged, leaving the town "peaceful and without a soldier," whereupon a party of 250 sailors and Marines went ashore, and with "three hearty cheers" mingling with the booming of a 21-gun salute, replaced the Mexican flag with the Stars and Stripes. Hearing this news, Frémont hurried from Sonoma to Monterey with a force of 160 armed horsemen, partly his own followers, partly adventurous settlers. When on July 19 he put himself at the service of Sloat, his action had the undesired effect of unifying the rival *comandante generals* of California: Pío Pico in the south at Los Angeles and Castro, who had fled his headquarters at Monterey. Putting aside their feud over the location of the provincial capital, the custody of the customhouse and division of revenue, they joined forces in Los Angeles at the head of 800 men and ten cannon determined to uphold the sovereignty of Mexico.

On July 16 the triumphant Americans in Monterey had momentary qualms when Sir George Seymour entered the bay in the British line-of-battle ship *Collingwood*. About the same time the U.S. frigate *Congress*, commanded by Commodore Robert Stockton, arrived there. A naval battle and perhaps a third Anglo-American war seemed imminent as Stockton ordered his decks cleared for action. But Seymour upped anchor and sailed away July 23, and on the same day Commodore Sloat relinquished his command to Stockton, sailing home a few days later.

Stockton and Frémont were kindred spirits, both eager for glory and unwilling to accept a situation in which the American flag flew over most of northern California and the *Californios* themselves, no lovers of their federal government, seemed content. Neither man was willing to cooperate with the pacific Consul Larkin in his attempts to reach an accommodation with the *Californios*. So Stockton's first act as the commander in Monterey was to denounce Castro as a "usurper," guilty of keeping the province in a "constant state of revolt and misery," while Frémont was to organize the California Battalion of Mounted Riflemen with himself as major and Gillespie—the first "Horse Marine" in the history of his gallant corps—as second-in-command.

On July 25 the battalion boarded the sloop *Cyane* and sailed south for San Diego to do battle with Castro-Pico. A few days later Stockton followed in *Congress*, landing at San Pedro for the march with a "sailor army" of 350 men northeast on Los Angeles. En route he was met by a deputation from Los Angeles anxious for parley rather than battle. Stockton replied that he would not negotiate until Castro ran up the American flag. But Castro, informed that Frémont had come up from San Diego to join Stockton, promptly retired to Sonora commanding nothing but his horse and leaving "the City of the Angels" open and undefended against the American invaders.

Commodore Stockton quickly proclaimed all of California as territory of the United States, setting up a government with a code of laws drafted by himself, with himself as governor and Major Frémont commanding the north and Captain Gillespie the south and elections scheduled for September 15. Next, he sent off ships to blockade ports in Lower California, planning meanwhile to capture Acapulco and march on Mexico City, where he expected to shake hands with General Taylor.

Instead it was General Kearny with whom the commodore shook hands, and the sailor was only too happy to greet the soldier he needed to put down revolt in Southern California.

It is still not clear what caused the *Californios* of the south to rise against the government proclaimed by Commodore Stockton on August 17, 1846. One participant attributed it to "the patriotic fire which burned in the hearts of the majority of the citizens," and also to the "impolitic and despotic conduct of the military authorities." The first supposed reason is pure rhetoric, for the *Californios* thoroughly despised the federal government in Mexico City. The second is more likely, for Captain Gillespie, as the military commandant of the southern department, under Stockton's orders ordered a curfew and prohibition of bearing arms. Both men as officers had succumbed to the imperiousness that is the vice of the military virtue of discipline. This was the estimate of General Kearny, who had shown remarkable and admirable restraint in New Mexico, attributing the uprising to people who had been "most cruelly and shamefully abused by our own people," and even Fremont ascribed it in part to "police regulations."

Whatever the reasons, in the early morning hours of September 23—exactly one month and one week after Stockton's proclamation—a party of *Angelenos* under Auxiliary Captain Cerulvo Varela attacked Gillespie's tiny garrison in Los Angeles. They were easily repulsed, but next day Captain José María Flores of the regular army rallied a force of about five hundred men armed with weapons that had been in hiding to establish a camp about a mile or so outside Gillespie's position. Gillespie was now under siege and on September 30—surrounded—he felt compelled to surrender. With his men and their arms he retreated to San Pedro. In early October Stockton at San Francisco, still motivated by his vision of glory at the gates of Mexico City, sent Captain William Mervine in *Savannah* to San Pedro where he was joined by Gillespie and his men. Mervine then led a force of sailors and Marines ashore to challenge Flores's cavalry. They marched five miles inland but could not bring the elusive enemy horse to decisive battle. Instead Flores's jabbing tactics forced Mervine back to his ship after the loss of a dozen men. Elated, the native legislature on October 29 named Flores governor and *comandante general:* from San Diego north to San Luis Obispo—slightly more than half the province—California was again Mexican. It was into this situation that General Stephen Kearny and his handful of exhausted dragoons came stumbling.

Kearny's march to California with his regiment of mounted riflemen was the equal in agony to the *jornada* from Leavenworth to Santa Fe. Its one redeeming incident was the chance encounter on October 6 with Kit Carson. The legendary Mountain Man was riding east with a party of fifteen men, including six Delaware scouts, bearing the great news of the American occupation of California. Kearny was delighted to come upon this most famous of American frontiersmen, a small man like himself, quiet and soft-spoken with "a keen hazel eye." But Carson was not overjoyed at Kearny's insistence that he accompany him as guide. He did not wish to pass another year away from the wife he had left in Taos, but yielded after Kearny promised to place his letters to Washington in the hands of a reliable courier. Meanwhile, Kearny, jubilant at Carson's report that "California had surrendered and the American flag floated in every port," decided to send two hundred of his dragoons back to Santa Fe while pressing forward with the remaining hundred. But it was some time before the great beauty of California described by Carson became visible to these ragged, sunburned, footsore scarecrows, slaughtering their pack animals for food as they marched, sometimes struggling ninety scorching miles from water hole to water hole. Sometimes animals "sinking with thirst" would have to be left behind, and when the marchers heard a hideous howling behind them they knew that the wolves had found them.

At night Kearny and his staff would gather around the campfire with Carson and his party to discuss the next day's journey, and Carson, at the urging of his newfound comrades, would relate his adventures in the mountains. An officer who kept a diary recorded how Carson "remarked that he never knew how fine a weapon the bow-and-arrow was until he had them fired at him in the night." Eventually, on November 25, two months after leaving Santa Fe, General Kearny crossed the broad Colorado River into California. But it was not until December 2 while crossing the coastal range that he and his men beheld "the beautiful valley of the Agua Caliente, waving with yellow grass." On December 5 Kearny's party was joined by Captain Gillespie at the head of about forty men. At dawn next day, Kearny's dragoons, who had marched some two thousand tormented miles from Leavenworth to within forty miles of the Pacific without firing a shot, fought their first battle with the Mexicans. It was at the Indian village of San

Pascual, and the American charge, though brave and succeeding in driving the enemy off, was not worth the loss of eighteen men killed and thirteen wounded, among the latter Kearny and Gillespie. Six days later the Americans saw the Pacific—for most of them their first sight of the sea—and next day they came clip-clopping into the little village of San Diego. Riding at anchor in that beautiful broad blue bay were the U.S. frigate *Congress* and the sloop-of-war *Portsmouth*.

San Diego was then the only post held by the Americans in all of southern California. Kearny was dismayed to learn that the town had been held for five weeks with no attempt made to attack the *Californios*. At his urging, however, an advance on Los Angeles was begun with a column of about five hundred men and a few small cannon under Kearny's direct command but with Stockton directing the operation. Some twelve miles below the City of the Angels, the Mexicans under Flores met Kearny's Americans at the San Gabriel River. Flores sought to repel his enemy's crossing with the use of sharpshooters and small cannon. But the *Yanquis* splashed across the stream to form a square on the opposite side. After their own cannon were dragged across the river, they opened a bombardment followed by a charge. "New Orleans!" the Americans cried, remembering that memorable battle fought exactly thirty-two years earlier—and the Mexicans fled.

Next day the advance continued, halted momentarily by long-range but ineffectual artillery fire from the enemy and some cavalry skirmishing, after which the rebels again withdrew. Los Angeles was now undefended, and the next day—January 10, 1847—the jubilant men of Stockton and Kearny entered the city to raise once again the flag that Gillespie had lowered three months earlier. Nevertheless, the revolt had not yet ended until Frémont at last coming down from the north with his California Battalion encountered the enemy's scattered remnants under Andreas Pico in the San Fernando Valley north of Los Angeles. On January 13 Frémont negotiated the Treaty of Cahuenga, which granted to the insurgents the right to leave or stay in California, excused them from making an oath of allegiance while the war continued, protected them in person and property and granted them the same rights and privileges as all citizens of the United States. Thus the contention between the Americans and Mexicans in California came to an end, to be followed by perhaps even more bitter contentions among the conquerors.

Kearny claimed his instructions from the War Department gave him the right to form the new government of California; Stockton claimed the same right from his Navy Department orders. Neither would budge, but the general backed off because the commodore with his ships and their companies and the California Mounted Battalion had might to enforce his right. So he relieved Kearny of all command but his own dragoons and named Frémont governor of California. Unwilling to provoke a confrontation he could never win, Kearny left Los Angeles for San Diego. There to his delight he found Commodore W. Branford Shubrick, Stockton's replacement as the naval chief in the Pacific, who recognized the validity of the general's claims. Frémont protested but a succession of naval commanders remained loyal to Kearny, and in the end the fiery little general triumphed by replacing Frémont with Colonel Richard Mason, and taking that unchastened young firebrand back to Washington to face a court-martial on charges of mutiny, disobedience of orders and conduct prejudicial to the public service.

Frémont's trial was the most sensational in the brief history of the United States. Defended by his powerful father-in-law Senator Benton and his distinguished brother-in-law William Cary Jones, Frémont was nevertheless convicted of all three charges and sentenced to explusion from the army. There was, however, a majority recommendation for clemency, and President Polk sought to calm the unprecedented howling hurricane of political partisanship aroused by this unrivaled cause célèbre by dropping Frémont's mutiny conviction and pardoning him on the other two. Even this was too much for the proud and vainglorious John Charles Frémont, for he promptly resigned from the army while Senator Benton stepped down as chairman of the Senate Military Affairs Committee, a powerful post he had held for twenty years, to mount a vicious vendetta against the War Department.

By the time Polk made his decision—February 16, 1848—the Mexican War was over and the Frémont court-martial forgotten in a paroxysm of public ecstasy and a flood of wild-eyed fortune hunters sent surging westward to northern California, both caused by the news that the millwright James Marshall while repairing the mill race at Captain Sutter's fort had found the water filled with flakes of gold.

71

Return of Guess Who?

∼ IN THE SUMMER OF 1846 PRESIDENT POLK PLANNED TO SMUGGLE THE exiled General Santa Anna into Mexico on his promise to deal with the United States, asking Congress for a secret appropriation of $2 million to be used as a down payment on bribing Santa Anna to cede California. But then came an unforseen intervention of the slavery dispute already simmering and threatening to boil over at any moment into civil war. An obscure representative from Pennsylvania named David Wilmot attached to the appropriation measure a prohibition against bondage in any land acquired from Mexico. This provoked a debate far more bitter than the one ending in the Missouri Compromise, and although the House eventually approved what was called the Wilmot Proviso, the entire measure was filibustered to death in the Senate.

Polk was furious. He had been confident that he could stop the war and gain California by paying the Soldier of the People enough money to support an army strong enough to put down any public uproar certain to succeed any deal with Uncle Sam. It seemed to him that there was now no hope of achieving his objectives by peaceful means. But then President Mariano Paredes of Mexico inadvertently came to his rescue.

• • •

Paredes needed a scapegoat to save his tottering and impoverished government, and he found one in General Mariano Arista. Even though Arista's men had suffered cruelly on their retreat from Matamoros—so exhausted and hungry that some of them committed suicide or killed and ate their mounts and pack animals—they were treated like pariahs by Paredes when they staggered into the sanctuary of the Well of All Saints. Humiliated at every turn, they saw their general arrested and carried off to the capital to face a rigged court-martial, which convicted him of an unknown charge and dismissed him from the service.

To the dismay of Paredes the exile of the popular Arista to his beautiful hacienda in Monterrey did not calm the angry populace of Mexico City. They knew it was both a face-saving gesture and a base attempt to get rid of a rival, and they vilified Paredes as a dictatorial product of the army and an enemy of the people. When the president appealed to the Church for funds, he got neither a peso nor a blessing, while his own Monarchical party turned against him. Attacked for failing to protect the northern frontier against the Amerindians, he withdrew most of the army to the capital and was promptly accused of organizing his own bodyguard. One by one in the traditional Mexican way, his allies among the generals began to pronounce against him. At the end of July Paredes resigned and the reins of government fell to the figurehead Nicolás Bravo. In a few more days he too would resign, and the way was clear for the return of Antonio López de Santa Anna.

As long ago as February 1846, plotting had begun against Paredes. That was when Colonel A. J. Atocha, an agent of Santa Anna's, had visited President Polk. In the meantime Santa Anna had gained the support of a powerful ally: General Juan Almonte, *El Caudillo's* aide at San Jacinto and later Mexican minister to Washington, who had become Santa Anna's chief rival for the presidential chair. Once Almonte pronounced for the Soldier of the People, everything was downhill for Santa Anna. Through him and Atocha, Polk had supposedly learned that if Santa Anna were allowed to slip back into Mexico, he would seize power and sign the sort of treaty Polk wanted. For once the tough gray squirrel from Tennessee allowed his heart to get the better of his head, and he did something no sane Mexican general or politician would ever do: he believed the Napoleon of the West.

Thus on the night of August 8, still vigorous at the age of fifty-two, accompanied by his aging wife of seventeen, limping on his wooden leg, Antonio Santa Anna slipped aboard the British steamer *Arab* in

Havana Harbor and made for Vera Cruz. As instructed, the American blockading squadron under Commodore David Conner allowed *Arab* to enter Vera Cruz Harbor unchallenged. Santa Anna was greeted by a carefully staged military celebration in which "not one viva was heard." Then with his wife he retired to his villa, to await with hyena-like patience the slow demise of his rivals. Master of Mexican mob psychology that he was, he knew instinctively that he could not move immediately on Mexico City. The way had to be prepared by Almonte and Atocha. In September the moment to move seemed at hand, and he departed for the capital after an encouragingly cordial reception in Jalapa.

Ahead of him in Mexico City the National Theater resumed the name of the Santa Anna Theater. Statues and pictures of him were brought out of hiding. When it was suggested that his figure again adorn that northward-looking pedestal, he modestly declined, insisting rather that it become the base for the national colors. Happily for Santa Anna, no one mentioned rebuilding another shrine for his desecrated leg. On September 15 he met the president General J. M. Salas, who asked him to take command of a new Army of Liberation. Thus "the Liberator" was still another title added to Santa Anna's string. It was exactly what he always wanted: to be free of the cares of government and enter on another glorious campaign. His intentions to avenge Mexico had already been made clear a month earlier in Vera Cruz where he told a wildly cheering crowd:

> Mexicans! There was once a day, and my heart dilates with the remembrance ... you saluted me with the title of Soldier of the People. Allow me to take it again, never more to be given up, and to devote myself until death to the defence of the liberation and independence of the Republic!

In other words *all* Mexico—and Texas as well—would be restored beneath the emblem of the eagle and the snake; and President James Polk reading those words knew that he had been tricked and that this costly war he did not want would now continue.

72

Battle of Monterrey

~ HARD UPON THE ARRIVAL OF TAYLOR'S UNWELCOME VOLUNTEERS there appeared at the Camargo camp a wave of volunteer generals even less gladly received: Major General William Butler and Brigadiers John Quitman, Gideon Pillow, Thomas Hamer and James Shields. It was quite a cluster of stars and obviously intended to remind Old Rough 'n' Ready that he was still answerable to his commander in chief in the White House.

To say that James Knox Polk found Taylor's booming popularity not quite to his liking would not do justice to the instincts of this most political animal ever to prowl the gilded kennel on Pennsylvania Avenue. To the still-naive Taylor, a "general" such as Gideon Pillow—a militia creature of political and social "service" with no active or combat duty whatsoever to his credit—was more a nuisance than a threat. He had no way of knowing that Pillow, once a law partner of Polk's, was where he was as a reward for his help in securing the Democratic nomination at Baltimore in 1844. He was also Polk's spy assigned to watch Taylor, not only to report any signs of military misfeasance that could be magnified in the Stateside press, but especially to sniff out any signs of presidential fever seizing this dangerous national hero of unknown political preferences. Although Taylor received Pillow with customary courtesy, Pillow conceived a bitter hatred for his chief when he learned that Taylor had laughed outright when he heard that "the general" had ordered an entrenchment dug with the parapet on the wrong side of the ditch.

Not much was known about William Butler except that this militia general from Kentucky had served under Andrew Jackson during the War of 1812: a distinction that seems to have been claimed by every southern politican with military ambitions. But Taylor was glad indeed to shake the hand of General Quitman of Mississippi, whom he judged to be "a gentleman of intelligence" after leading a body of troops to Texas in 1836. Shields was also comparatively unknown, except for his recruiting feat of raising fourteen regiments of Illinois volunteers rather than the requested four. Arriving at Camargo in a fancy buggy, he did not exactly endear himself to Ol' Rough 'n' Ready. Neither did General Hamer of Indiana, who had enlisted as a private and by dint of vigorous politicking had had himself elected a lieutenant. "In the name of God," one of Taylor's soldiers wrote to his senator, "don't let Hamer be a brigadier general. He is talented, but doesn't dare undertake to drill a squad." Of the five, Shields—twice wounded—and Quitman proved themselves capable and courageous. But in May of 1846, Zachary Taylor expected little or nothing from any of them, relying instead on those young and eager West Pointers who provided him with such a handsome corps of junior officers, and his own pair of regular war dogs: Brigadiers David Twiggs and W. J. Worth. Twiggs has been best described by Justin Smith in his monumental two-volume *The War with Mexico,* writing:

> His robust and capacious body, powerful shoulders, bull-neck, heavy, cherry-red face, and nearly six feet of erect stature represented physical energy at its maximum. With bristling white hair and, when the regulations did not interfere, a thick white beard, he seemed like a kind of snow-clad volcano, a human Aetna, pouring forth a red-hot flood of orders and objurgations from his crater of a mouth; and he was vastly enjoyed by the rough soldiers even when, as they said, he "cursed them right out of their boots." In a more strictly human aspect he made an excellent disciplinarian, and he could get more work out of the men than anybody else in the army; but as a warrior, while he always looked thirsty for a fight, he was thought over-anxious to fight another day—to be, in short, a hero of the future instead of the past; and as a general, Scott had already said that he was not qualified "to command an army—either in the presence, or in the absence of an enemy." His brains were, in fact, merely what happened to be left over from the making of his spinal

cord, and the soldiers' names for him—the "Horse" and the "Bengal Tiger"—classed him fairly as regarded intellect.

Worth was perhaps the exact opposite of Twiggs, being rather more intellectual than physical, and also resembling Ol' Fuss 'n' Feathers Scott just as Twiggs was a larger copy of Ol' Rough 'n' Ready Taylor. Though of average height, he was a man of trim and muscular build and a graceful horseman almost the equal of U. S. Grant, who remains to this day the finest equestrian in the history of the U.S. Army. Worth carried himself like a born soldier and was thoroughly at ease with his staff, with whom he conversed in the style of an elegant gentleman. Yet he seldom smiled and his handsome dark features were stern even in repose. It was generally believed that General Worth burned with martial ardor, but both Grant and Meade—unusually perceptive observers for men so young—thought otherwise. Grant found him "nervous, impatient and restless on the march, or when important or responsible duty confronted him," while Meade wrote that he "has the great misfortune of being most rash and impetuous, and of constantly doing things which cooler reflection causes him to repent. This infirmity, in my opinion, renders him unfit to command, but on the field of battle, under another, his gallantry and bravery are well known and most conspicious."

It was perhaps inevitable that two commanders of such disparate character should quarrel, and again not surprising that the dispute should be over rank. At Corpus Christi Worth claimed that as a brevet brigadier he was the logical successor to Taylor should Old Zack for some reason cease to command, while Twiggs, then a regular colonel, contended that the honor of seniority belonged to him. The argument so divided Taylor's officer corps that it threatened to erupt into armed conflict, and Taylor quickly referred the question to Washington. Major General Winfield Scott promptly decided in favor of brevet rank. This so incensed a group of about one hundred officers that they appealed the decision to Congress. Taylor might have ended this dissension if he had openly taken a stand in either direction rather than to have appealed to Washington. Instead he ordered a general review and in spite of Scott's ruling placed Twiggs in command. But then, realizing that he had inadvertently given both sides a *casus belli*, he countermanded his own orders.

This provoked from Worth the caustic comment: "Whether an idea, strategic or of any other description, has had the rudeness to invade the mind or imagination of our chief is a matter of doubt. We are literally a huge body without a head." But then Worth was further outraged when President Polk entered the controversy, overruling Scott and deciding that regular rank took precedence over brevet. Worth, a man of great vanity, sulked for five days before resigning from the army and leaving camp, thus missing both Palo Alto and Resaca de la Palma.

But he returned just before the Monterrey campaign and was politely welcomed back by Taylor. Although Old Zack seems to have disliked Worth and secretly resented his having quit his army on the eve of the two battles with Arista, he respected him as an experienced regular officer much to be preferred to any one of that quintet of volunteer generals who had come to Camargo. Thus General Worth commanded Taylor's 2nd Division—while his rival General Twiggs led the 1st—when Taylor's army in mid-September of 1846 started marching southwest on Monterrey.

General Pedro de Ampudia, who had commanded briefly at Matamoros, was in charge at Monterrey, where he was none too popular with the populace, which detested him for his execution of a revolutionary named Sentmanat, after which he had had the man's head cut off and fried in oil so as to preserve it when, in the quaint custom of Mexican authorities, it would be stuck up on a pike in a public plaza. A big man and handsome in a cruel and sensuous way, with his military bearing, guardsman's mustache and dude's goatee, but for all his ferocious visage outside, inside he was rather more timid, especially in the vicinity of the heart; yet because of his unswerving devotion to two high principles—promotion and survival—he was now the chief general of the Mexican north. In Monterrey, as near a fortress city as any center in Mexico, he felt reasonably secure.

Monterrey was a formidable cluster of easily fortified stonewalled houses standing on high ground forward of the swift-flowing little Santa Catarina River, which effectively guarded its rear. To defend it Ampudia had seven thousand men and some forty guns, what would seem more than enough to repel Taylor's six thousand Americans attacking without supporting heavy artillery.

Zachary Taylor, however, now that he confronted his objective, was as confident as though he were still fighting Seminoles. Invincibly ignorant as he might be, he was still indomitably courageous; and thus, relying as always on the bayonet, and unwisely dividing his forces as always, he prepared simultaneous assaults on the city's eastern and western flanks.

On September 20, Worth took two thousand regulars and Texas cavalry on a long swing north to come in on the two fortified hills to the west. Running into difficult going, the column could make only five miles in the first four hours, and at nightfall the men encamped in the hills northwest of the city. Taylor's force was now split and separated, vulnerable to defeat in detail; but Ampudia, who had seen this precious opportunity, made no move to sally from the city.

Next morning, September 21, 1846, the Battle of Monterrey began in earnest. Worth in the west repulsed a determined charge of Mexican lancers and began attacking Federation Hill on the southern side of the Saltillo road. By nightfall the position was taken with a loss of fewer than twenty men, and the Mexican guns were turned against Independence Hill across the road. In the east, however, the Americans were not so fortunate.

Here the city was guarded by the bastioned Black Fort one thousand yards to its northern front and on the fort's east by a series of redoubts chief of which was Fort Tenería, or the Tannery. Here red-necked Dave Twiggs's regulars were to charge almost without artillery preparation. But Twiggs was not with them. He was sick, and command passed to Lieutenant Colonel John Garland.

Garland was to create a diversion for Worth engaged to the west. Whatever the purpose, the regulars pressed forward bravely—bayonets against bastions—and they were scourged from the Black Fort on the right, the Tannery on their left and loopholes and housetops in front of them. Americans flew into the air or stumbled and fell to pour out their blood on the hot earth. Scurrying low, the broken Americans sought shelter where they could find it, until, unit by unit, they could withdraw. One small unit that had gotten into a building behind the Tannery remained to pour musketry into that redoubt.

A second charge surged forward and was also broken in blood. Mexican marksmen picked off the Yankee officers with dreadful accuracy. Lieutenant Hoskins, he whose keg of whiskey had once won transportation priority over a case of books, came gasping up to Lieutenant Grant to borrow his horse. Minutes later he was shot dead from the back of the beast. Now, as the second line withdrew, General Twiggs came onto the field in "very unmilitary garb" to explain why he had arrived late.

"I expected a battle today," he said, "but didn't think it would come off so soon, and took a dose of medicine last night as I always do before a battle so as to loosen my bowels. A bullet striking the belly when the bowels are loose might pass through the intestines without cutting them."

No one then appreciated the humor of the situation, for a third attempt, at a fortified bridge farther to the right, had also been hurled back. Now Taylor turned to his volunteers. Brigadier General John Quitman sent the Tennessee and Mississippi regiments through a canefield that shielded them from enemy fire until the final dash at the Tannery. The moment they became visible, the Mexican guns roared. One solid shot killed seven volunteers and wounded others. One of the wounded clutched his rent abdomen while he crawled onto a rock, crouching there to sing a death psalm as he held in his intestines. But now the regulars behind the Tannery were picking off the Mexican gunners while the volunteers charged.

"Now is the time!" Jefferson Davis roared at his men. "Great God! If I had thirty men with knives I could take the fort!"

It was taken with a final rush, Tennesseans and Mississippians tumbling in together. They would quarrel for a decade over who had been the first inside. Now the field artillery came flying into the suburban streets, one battery becoming caught and rendered useless, another driving off Mexican lancers who rode over the field spearing American wounded and killing medical attendants. And then it was night, and Taylor, who had won a little fort at the cost of nearly four hundred casualties, ordered everyone back to camp except the troops holding the Tannery.

Before daylight, the attack was resumed. Worth's men, who had gone for two days without food and who had crouched all the rainy night at the base of Independence Hill, began crawling slowly and silently up its slopes. With dawn they charged and drove the Mexicans off its summit.

To the east there was no action, except that General Ampudia, having lost his western outposts, decided to abandon all his fortifications except the Black Fort and to concentrate his defense in the blocks of stone houses surrounding the plaza. On September 23 the Americans renewed the assault on the east.

They did not move through shot-swept streets, but instead had their artillery shoot down them while doughboys armed with picks and crowbars burrowed through the walls of the houses. Worth, meanwhile, hearing the firing and having no orders, pressed in from the west and began shelling the plaza. Caught between two fires, General Ampudia next day offered to surrender.

After a day of haggling over terms, Taylor accepted. His conditions—allowing the Mexican army to withdraw intact with its arms, even agreeing to an armistice of eight weeks—were more than generous, and the armistice itself was angrily rejected by President Polk. But as much as Taylor was criticized, he could hardly have done better. His little army was down to five thousand effectives, he was running short of supplies and ammunition, he was deep in enemy country, and if renewed assaults against a still superior enemy should fail, he would run the dreadful risk of retreating through a jubilant and vengeful countryside. If anyone was to be censured, it was Ampudia for having given up so readily.

And so, on September 25 the Mexican flag over Monterrey came down and Old Glory went up. The Mexican soldiers, neat in trim uniforms and freshly pipe-clayed belts, came marching out; and the Americans, "as dirty as they could be without becoming real estate," went marching in to the tune of "Yankee Doodle."

73

Polk and His
Generals Squabble

~ALTHOUGH TAYLOR'S VICTORY AT MONTERREY EXALTED HIM POLITI-
cally, it did not set the nation exulting as had his earlier triumphs.

Monterrey made it plain that Mexico was not going to be defeated
easily. Bereft of Texas, shorn of New Mexico and California, and now
menaced by American arms south of the Rio Grande, Mexico took
courage from the wrathful oratory of General Santa Anna, spurning
all offers to negotiate and swearing to fight on.

Thus the United States gradually became disenchanted with the
war. Even Taylor privately proposed a defensive stance, holding just
enough Mexican territory to force payment of claims. The idea was
popular enough to attract Polk, who feared what an extended war
might cost in men and money; if, indeed, he could persuade the
nation to support it. But then it also became clear that to surrender
the initiative to Mexico would incur a great loss in trade, prestige and
national honor. Seizing a neighbor's provinces and holding them for
ransom might strike the world as piracy. And so Polk and his advisers—who had begun the war with no real plan—at last decided on the
obvious step of striking at the enemy's heart in Mexico City.

From the outset it was clear that the route from the Rio Grande, an
advance across eight hundred rugged miles, was out of the question.
The best approach was from Vera Cruz on the Gulf. Cortés himself

had followed this route in his campaign against the Aztecs. It had been recommended to Polk by no less a person than General Santa Anna in the days when the new Mexican commander in chief was talking treason. Taylor was for it, and so were Winfield Scott and the powerful Senator Thomas Hart Benton. But it took a Whig victory in the congressional elections of 1846 to make Polk realize, at the repeated urgings of Senator Benton, that "a rapid crushing movement" was necessary to win the war and retrieve Democratic political fortunes.

Next came the question of a commander. Again in the partisan spirit of his times, Polk looked around for a trustworthy Democrat. But there was no such general acceptable to the army. There were only Taylor and Scott, and because Taylor was in the habit of criticizing Polk's administration, and because Scott, clearly Taylor's superior in generalship, was also now considered politically harmless, it was Scott who received the command.

Certainly there were considerations of a nobler cast motivating Polk's decision, chief among them the fact that Scott still outranked Taylor, together with Taylor's belief that the season of the yellow fever—*el vomito*—was too near to make an attempt on Vera Cruz. Nevertheless, Scott had inadvertently qualified by committing political suicide during his dispute with Polk the preceding spring.

Polk had then ordered Scott to take command in the Rio Grande. Scott intended to obey, but about that time the alarmed Polk was also preparing to name a half-dozen Democratic generals. Scott thought he "smelt the rat" and bluntly told Secretary of War Marcy that he saw "the double trick, to supersede me, and, at the end of the war . . . disband every general who would not place Democracy above God's country." Next Scott explained his failure to move quickly to the Rio Grande by informing the secretary: "I do not desire to place myself in the most perilous of all positions:—*a fire upon my rear, from Washington, and the fire, in front, from the Mexicans.*" That ended Scott's brief career as field commander, for the infuriated Polk directed him to remain in Washington. Scott's political career was concluded by his next epistolary indiscretion. He explained to Marcy that he had not been in his office to receive him one day because he had stepped outside "to take a hasty plate of soup." The remark tickled the country and Scott, in a pun upon the name of the great French soldier, Marshal Turenne, became known as "Marshal *Tureen.*" As the Boston *Courier* announced, Scott had "committed suicide with a goose-quill." Still, Scott endured these professional and political setbacks with an admirable dignity. He remained devoted to his task of organizing and directing the expanding army. He might have been too fond of plans and calculations, as his nickname Ol' Fuss 'n' Feathers suggests; he may actually have been so prim and prissy that, as one general's wife disdainfully observed, you could cover his mouth with a button; but he was nevertheless the most professional and scientific soldier the United States had yet produced—and without him there might not have been much of an army.

So Scott hurled himself into the Vera Cruz expedition. On November 14 the navy presented him a splendid gift: the port of Tampico, which would make an excellent staging area for America's first joint amphibious operation. On November 24 Scott departed for the Rio Grande and a hoped-for conference with Taylor at Camargo.

He had not been long gone before President Polk had reservations about appointing him. He still did not like him, and he liked less the prospect of seeing a second Whig trailing clouds of martial glory. Polk was not himself seeking re-election, yet he naturally wanted a Democrat to succeed him. And so it occurred to him to ask Congress to create the post of lieutenant general for Senator Benton, who would then supersede Scott. Congress, however, refused. The harsh, domineering Benton had made too many enemies among his own party, and no Whig would desert Scott.

This "vile intrigue," as Scott called it, so infuriated Ol' Fuss 'n' Feathers that he was later to write: "A grosser abuse of human confidence is nowhere recorded." So the Polk-Scott rift widened, even as a Scott-Taylor quarrel began developing.

Scott had written to Taylor of his intention to come to Camargo. But his letters either went astray—one was intercepted by Santa Anna—or arrived after Scott did. In the meanwhile, General Taylor had slanted off on a southwestern excursion against Victoria, the capital of Tamaulipas. Why, is not clear. Inland Victoria was of no use to Taylor. To march on it was only to weaken his position on the Monterrey-Saltillo-Parras line. Yet the march did have the effect of taking him away from Camargo, and Scott on his arrival there was unable to inform Taylor personally of the disagreeable truth that he needed his troops. Instead, he had to tell him by letter that he was taking most of Taylor's regulars and half his volunteers for the Vera Cruz–Mexico City operation, and that Taylor would have to act "for a time" on the "strict defensive."

Taylor blew up. He was not only a general being stripped of his troops and stopped in his tracks; he was also a candidate halted in mid-career. Full of wrath, he accused Scott of "worming himself" into the chief command by promising to kill him off as a presidential candidate. He said he was being sacrificed to the ambition of others, meaning the partisan Polk and the sly Scott, and although Taylor was himself on record as believing that Vera Cruz required twenty-five thousand men, ten thousand of them regulars, this was but a puny piece of logic that would not even scratch the gorgeous political theme of "The Martyrdom of Old Zack." So if Taylor did lose half an army, he did advance another giant step toward the White House— even as Santa Anna began advancing north against him with a brand-new army.

74

War Opposed/
Santa Anna Fields New Army

∼ IN AMERICA OPPOSITION TO THE WAR WITH MEXICO HAD BEEN FORCED underground by the popularity of Taylor's victories, but it erupted with renewed vigor after the Whig Congressional triumph, and its leaders included Northern Democrats as well. As in 1812, New England was the center of the movement, where it had powerful support from influential religious sects such as the Quakers, Congregationalists and Unitarians. Unitarian William Henry Channing went so far as to say that if he served in this "damnable war" he would be on the side of Mexico. Once again the cry of a "slavocracy plot" was raised, and the poet James Russell Lowell warned his Yankee neighbors:

> They jest want this Californy
>   So's to lug new slave-states in
> To abuse ye, an' to scorn ye,
>   An' to plunder ye like sin.

Less restrained were the remarks of Senator Tom Corwin of Ohio, who declared: "If I were a Mexican, I would tell you, 'Have you not room in your own country to bury your dead men? If you come into mine, we will meet you with bloody hands, and welcome you to hospitable graves.'"

Outraged American soldiers might hang "Black Tom" Corwin in effigy, but the net effect of his speeches—and those of Daniel Webster—was to create in Mexico the expectation of a joint *pronunciamento* from Whigs and Northern Democrats forcing the American government to withdraw its troops. Meanwhile, Santa Anna was busily trying to raise his army, and in this he was again aided by the activity of his enemy.

This time it was the volunteers, more ferocious at Monterrey than they had been at Matamoros. Their severest critic, Lieutenant Meade, wrote home of them:

> They are sufficiently well-drilled for practical purposes, and are, I believe, brave, and will fight as gallantly as any men. But they are a set of Goths and Vandals, without discipline, laying waste the country wherever we go, making us a terror to innocent people.... They cannot take care of themselves; the hospitals are crowded with them, they die like sheep; they waste their provisions, requiring twice as much to supply them as regulars do. They plunder the poor inhabitants of everything they can lay their hands on, and shoot them when they remonstrate, and if one of their number happens to get into a drunken brawl and is killed, they run over the country, killing all the poor innocent people they find in their way, to avenge, as they say, the murder of their brother.

The cause, Meade said, "was the utter incapacity of their officers to control them or command respect." And the cause of this was the old evil root of elected officers: men simply will not curb men who were once their civilian equals, their clients or their customers, and who will soon be so again. So the volunteers remained rapacious, making it easier for Santa Anna to recruit troops among the northern Mexicans they had ravaged.

Not all of Taylor's volunteers were so rapacious. Those commanded by General Quitman and Colonel Jefferson Davis, both of Mississippi, were almost as well disciplined as the regulars. Davis's Mississippi Rifles emerged as probably the finest body of non-regular troops in the Mexican War. This was because of their commander's great skill in training soldiers and because he held his men to his own strict code of honor. Thus if they stole food from a Mexican farmer he rebuked them and paid for the pilfered provisions himself. Not one of them dared to despoil a Mexican church knowing full well that the punishment would be severe. What they did not know was that as a boy Davis had been sent to a school in Kentucky conducted by Dominican priests. Once he became aware that he was the only Protestant there he asked to be baptized a Catholic, but the fathers wisely declined, so that when he returned home to Mississippi he was still a Protestant, but without a trace of the average Southerner's foaming hatred for the ancient faith.

They also were unaware that Davis had once been the son-in-law of General Taylor. As a young officer out of West Point, Davis had fallen in love with the general's eighteen-year-old daughter Sarah. Taylor opposed the match because he did not want his daughter to follow the hard life of a soldier's wife, but he made no attempt to stop their wedding in 1835. Three months later Sarah was dead of malaria and Davis so weakened by the same disease that it was years before he recovered. But now he was back in uniform, easily one of the most striking presences in Taylor's army: a shade under six feet and ramrod straight, slender and graceful, handsome in a refined and slightly haughty way with his large, deep-set gray-blue eyes, his thick wavy blond hair and perfectly proportioned features. Secretly, Ol' Rough 'n' Ready admired Davis, and he planned to use him and his fabled Rifles when the Liberator came riding north from San Luis Potosí.

Santa Anna had been elected President of Mexico. Technically, however, he was not free to exercise both political and military command, and so he passed executive power to Vice President Gomez Farias while he took the field with a brand new army.

Santa Anna had no fears about the Gringos entering Mexico through the side door at Vera Cruz, with the prize of the national capital only 250 miles away, because he seems to have believed that the yellow fever season would begin there before the Americans arrived. Rather, he fixed his eyes on the front door in the north, though much farther away. Here he hoped to gain that single, smashing victory that would send Taylor reeling backward, after which he would bar the road south while worrying "the war-weary" Americans to such an extent that they would be clamoring for peace before the winter of 1846–47 came to an end. In this he seems to have been encouraged by the antiwar sentiment in the United States.

As he marched north gathering recruits along the way he found to his delight that the depredations of the Yankee volunteers had made it easier to reenlist men from the areas they had ravaged. Even so, the Liberator still had to struggle against the old hatred of the northern provinces, which could not forget his own oppression. They refused him men and money, and even tried to combine against him. In San Luis Potosí members of a secret society called the Red Comet swore: "Nobody is bound to obey one who has no right to command."

Even the federal government seemed powerless to help Santa Anna. The treasury was empty, and *El Caudillo* was forced to the extreme expedient of seizing Church property. Predictably, such tactics produced little funds and by their violence alienated the Church and set the old anticlerical fires burning. Yet, by forced loans, seizures, remittances from state and local governments and his personal credit, the Napoleon of the West eventually had enough money to support an army of twenty thousand men. In all military history few captains have possessed Santa Anna's rare capacity for making a new army stand where none had stood before, even though, like the soldiers of Ivan the Fool, many of its men were made of straw. On January 27, 1847, the Liberator began marching north from San Luis Potosí.

75

Battle of Buena Vista

〜 OF SANTA ANNA AND HIS MEXICANS, GRUFF OLD ZACK SAID: "LET them come. Damned if they don't go back a good deal faster than they came." But it was Taylor who went back, once his scouts reported Santa Anna to his front. Fearing that the Liberator might outflank him and strike Saltillo in his rear, Taylor withdrew ten miles to an excellent defensive position at a place called La Angosture, or the Narrows, near Buena Vista ranch, about eight miles south of Saltillo. Here the Saltillo road became a narrow defile passing through a ravine-slashed plateau on the east, or Taylor's left, and a maze of gullies fronting a mountain on the west, or right. Because the right was considered impassable, it was the left that was fortified.

The road itself was barred at the Narrows, after which infantry and artillery stretched away east on the plateau in a rough arrowhead pointing south. The left or eastern side of this arrowhead was more vulnerable because there were not enough units to form a continuous line there. Still, it was a strong position; the ravines would nearly paralyze the Mexican cavalry and artillery and hamper their infantry. Thus, thought Taylor, Santa Anna's numerical superiority of about fifteen thousand to five thousand would be largely discounted. Santa Anna, however, did not agree. He warned Taylor that he was surrounded by twenty thousand men and would meet catastrophe unless he surrendered. His letter was carried under a flag of truce by a German surgeon, and after it was interpreted, Old Zack snorted, "Tell Santa Anna to go to hell!" Turning to his chief of staff, he said, "Major Bliss, put that in Spanish and send it back by this damned Dutchman." It was done, with considerably more courtesy, and in the late afternoon of Washington's Birthday, 1847, Santa Anna attacked.

His artillery began roving over the American lines while his right, under General Ampudia, tried to gain the slopes of a mountain above the lightly held American left. Both sides skirmished until after dark, when the Americans withdrew to the valley.

That night Taylor returned to Saltillo with an infantry regiment and a squadron of dragoons. He feared that the Mexicans might have flanked him and be moving on the city. Finding himself in error, he started back toward Buena Vista next day—February 23—just as the Mexicans gained the summit of the mountain and opened on the American left with long-range artillery. Brigadier General John Wool at once began shifting his troops to the threatened left. Volunteer riflemen and a battery of artillery under Lieutenant John Paul Jones O'Brien rushed toward the left-center where two Mexican divisions were coming up a slope. O'Brien's trio of guns dashed forward to within musket range of the Mexicans, unlimbered, and began battering the enemy. In turn, a Mexican battery on his flank struck at O'Brien. To his rear, the American riflemen had quit the field—most of them retreating all the way back to Buena Vista ranch. O'Brien and his gunners stayed on, stemming the Mexican tide until he had no more cannoneers. Then, leaving one gun behind among its dead gunners and horses, he pulled the other two out.

But now there was a break in the American left-center, and the Mexicans quickly began driving in the entire Yankee left. Only the right continued to face south, both center and left being bent back to face east. Masses of Mexican cavalry and infantry were moving along the base of the mountain to strike at Buena Vista in the American rear. At this moment, Taylor trotted up on Old Whitey. He went directly to the center of the line to direct the battle, and also, by his calm presence, to steady his men. Meanwhile, the riflemen he brought back with him checked the Mexicans in the center, while a composite command of horse, foot and guns was rushed to the rear to block the Mexican cavalry moving on Buena Vista.

With a gathering gallop, the Mexican lancers came charging forward. The Americans countercharged and split the enemy column in two. From American sharpshooters on Buena Vista's rooftops and behind her walls came a withering small-arms fire that emptied Mexican saddles and sent one wing of the broken column flying back the way it had come, and the other fleeing west to make a complete circuit around the American position.

Now the battle reached a critical point with Colonel Davis commanding about 360 red-shirted "rifles" at its center. After a formation of Indiana volunteers gave way on the left flank, Davis and his sharpshooters stopped the oncharging Mexicans before they could get in the American rear. Just then General Taylor rode up with his staff, watching while Davis prepared to receive General Torrejón's splendid brigade of Mexican lancers bearing down on them. Matchless horsemen that they were, they seemed to fly over the ground, the sun glinting off the tips of their uplifted long blades and their polished breastplates. If they could break through Davis's position, they could turn the tide of battle—an ominous possibility clearly perceived by Old Zack as he watched the enemy horse approach the thin line of Mississippi riflemen barring their path.

"Steady boys!" Taylor cried. "Steady for the honor of Old Mississippi."

Taylor watched approvingly while his former son-in-law arranged his Red Shirts in an upside-down V with the open end toward the foe. If they rode into it and Davis's forward wings swung shut behind them, they could be massacred in a miniature Cannae. They did sweep forward with shouts and yells, beautifully massed with pennons waving and their mounts tossing their heads. Suddenly, inexplicably, they halted. Someone, probably Torrejón himself, saw the trap. At once they tried to turn their rearing horses, just as the American rifles began to crack.

As though swept by a giant scythe, Mexican cavalrymen tumbled from their saddles. Stricken horses screamed horribly. Some of them squirmed and kicked atop riders they had crushed. Now the brigade of lancers was a milling, screeching, struggling mass—men jumping to the ground to flee on foot, mounts rearing and pawing the air. At once Davis's riflemen threw down their weapons to draw their Bowie knives. Yelling ferociously they charged forward on foot to seize the horses by the bit, hacking them to their haunches and driving their long curved blades into their riders' hearts.

"*Diablos!*" the Mexicans screamed. "*Camisas coloradas!* Devils! Red Shirts!"

Pulling desperately on the reins, they calmed their mounts to wheel and flee en masse.

Behind them General Taylor swung his cap in exultation. "Well done, Jeff!" he shouted in paternal pride. "Hurrah for Mississippi!"

Davis had indeed executed a splendid maneuver, although he paid for his gallantry with a painful foot wound that put him on crutches, and he was still hobbling on them in 1847 when he took his seat in Congress as a U.S. senator from Mississippi.

Now a second, more serious threat developed. A column of lancers prepared to charge the American infantry forward of Buena Vista. For a time Captain Braxton Bragg's guns broke up the enemy formation, but eventually it came on. At once two regiments of volunteers formed a V with the open end to the enemy. Into those yawning jaws came the lancers, at first at a trot, and then slowing to a walk, and the storm of fire that came from each side of the V of Buena Vista annihilated the head of the enemy column and broke the tail in a dozen pieces.

With its cavalry repulsed, the Mexican infantry withdrew. The tide of battle had flowed to the Americans, but then, for reasons never made known, a flag of truce passed between both armies and firing ceased. In that interval, Santa Anna prepared his last stroke. It came against what had been the American center and was now the left, and it fell just as three volunteer regiments were deploying. Once again, it was the guns of Lieutenant O'Brien, together with one gun under Lieutenant George Thomas (not yet "The Rock of Chickamauga"), which flew into the breach. With blown horses and weary men, the American artillerists drove forward to a position from which they could rake the enemy rear. After volunteer units came running forward to plug the gap, the Mexican tide halted and flowed back again.

The Battle of Buena Vista was over. A handful of artillerists backed up by volunteers fighting bravely when bravely led had repulsed a superior force executing a well-conceived and well-nigh successful turning movement. Taylor's losses were high—746 killed, wounded and missing—but Santa Anna's were five times higher. And on the morning of February 24 he turned his troops and began his horrible retreat to San Luis, arriving there with half of the force he had led north and with the next best thing to victory: the announcement of one.

As might have been expected, those materialist critics who always overlook the moral factor of war thought Taylor never should have fought Santa Anna. But Buena Vista denied the Liberator that single smashing victory he desired so desperately, while reviving the drooping spirits of the American nation. That new determination to go on with the war and win it was solemnized by the poet Theodore O'Hara, celebrating Buena Vista in the lines:

> On Fame's eternal camping-ground
>   Their silent tents are spread,
> And Glory guards, with solemn round,
>   The bivouac of the dead.

After Buena Vista the Mexican War shifted to the side door at Vera Cruz, and Zachary Taylor, who had fought his last battle, raised his sights still higher on the presidency. To the newspapers, which rebuked his partisans for their unseemly haste in discussing Old Zack's candidacy before the Whig National Convention, one Kentucky volunteer replied: "National convention be damned! I tell ye, General Taylor is going to be elected by spontaneous combustion!"

76

Vera Cruz
Besieged/ "Polko" Rebellion

~ ON FEBRUARY 21, 1847—THE DAY ON WHICH TAYLOR'S SCOUTS
sighted Santa Anna's banners below Buena Vista—General Scott
reached his staging area at Lobos Island about fifty miles south of
Tampico.

Here Scott found nothing like the twenty thousand troops he had
been promised, but only a few thin formations of volunteers already
ravaged by smallpox. Although he had organized his campaign against
Vera Cruz and Mexico City down to such thoughtful details as special
landing boats built to fit inside one another in "nests" of three, the
inevitable delays attendant upon this first amphibious operation in
American history were unraveling all his finely spun plans. Meanwhile,
Scott was frantic to be off to Vera Cruz before the season of *el vomito*
should arrive to turn the city into a pesthouse.

Gradually his troops appeared. Worth and Twiggs came to Lobos in
transports loaded with their regulars. There was another volunteer
division under Major General Robert Patterson, a wealthy Democrat
to whom Polk at one time wanted to give the chief command. There
were also the volunteer brigades of Quitman, Pillow and Shields.

Scott had culled the cream of the West Point corps for his command. His most valued officers were the engineers, men such as the
stocky, aristocratic Lieutenant P. G. T. Beauregard or testy George

Meade, but most of all the splendid Captains Joe Johnston and Robert E. Lee, two old friends who were both forty and who bunked together aboard Scott's flagship, the steamer *Massachusetts*. Crusty Jubal Early was at Lobos, too, along with Sam Grant and the tall young artillerist, Lieutenant Tom Jackson. The future would bestow the nickname of "Stonewall" on Jackson; now he was known for a painful reserve broken only by such terse remarks as: "I should like to be in one battle." Tom Ewell was Jackson's exact opposite. He liked to laugh, and he was convulsed at a camp along the Rio Grande one day when Ol' Fuss 'n' Feathers rode up to praise the "scouts" he had seen "peering at him from behind every bush." Ewell knew that the men were not on duty but rather doing their duty, for, as he wrote home: "The water here . . . opens the bowels like a melting tar."

At last some ten thousand men and about eighty ships were assembled, and on March 2 the fleet of paddle-wheelers and sailing ships—plus one queer steamer driven silently through the sea by an underwater propeller—upped anchors and made way for Vera Cruz about two hundred miles south. On March 5 the vanguard ships began arriving at Antón Lizardo, twelve miles below the target city. Two days later Commodore Conner took Scott and his general and engineers aboard the little steamer *Secretary* to reconnoiter Vera Cruz and its huge stone fortress of San Juan de Ulúa on a reef across the bay. This was the 128-gun fort that British naval officers swore could "sink all the ships in the world," yet little *Secretary* slipped in close until Ulúa began to puff and roar and raise splashes all around her, whereupon she turned and sped for safety. Back on his flagship, Scott announced that he would land his army on beaches a few miles southeast of Vera Cruz and out of Ulúa's range.

March 9, 1847, was a glittering blue day. Far away west the snowy peak of Mount Orizaba glistened like a noble beacon for the soldiers and sailors of the American fleet moving north for the landing beach. Off Vera Cruz men with glasses swarmed through the rigging of the foreign war vessels while ladies twirling parasols crowded the rails. At one o'clock in the afternoon Conner's bombardment ships with double-shotted cannon were in place offshore. In closer were seven gunboats armed with grape. Now 4,500 regulars led by Worth began clambering over the sides of their steamboats into 65 of Scott's surfboats. Ashore, a few hundred Mexican lancers cantered nervously along the beach. In the city, housetops and walls were black with humanity. All American eyes turned toward Orizaba. The moment the setting sun touched the mountain's peak the assault would commence. It happened: red ball met white mountain, from *Massachusetts* came the flash of a signal gun, from Vera Cruz and Ulúa came the roar of cannon making futile dimples on the silken sheen of the Gulf, from the American ships came the thunder of guns driving off the Mexican cavalry, and as cheer after cheer and the crashing of bands bursting into "The Star-Spangled Banner" chased the sound of the cannon across the water, the American soldiers ducked their heads beneath their gleaming bayonets while the sailors bent to their oars.

Men and officers still aboard ship watched anxiously as oars bit and flashed and the line of boats caught the swell of the Gulf. "Why don't they hit us?" a salty old sailor muttered. "If we don't have a big butcher's bill, there's no use in coming here."

But the enemy beach was silent. Suddenly, the boat carrying Worth shot out in the lead. It grounded with a lurch and the impetuous general leaped out, followed by his officers. Now the Americans were jumping into the surf, holding muskets and cartridge boxes high overhead. They waded in, sprinted up the sand of the crest of the first dune, raised their standards and burst into cheers. From the fleet offshore came answering huzzas, and as the bay reverberated to the triumphant cries and music of the Americans, Conner's blue-jackets rapidly brought another 5,500 troops ashore.

By midnight Vera Cruz was invested without the loss of a single man, and ten thousand Americans were eating pork and biscuit in the sand. It was a splendid feat, so dazzling that General Scott could scarcely believe that he had been able to bring it off unopposed.

The first American D day had been a stupendous success simply because Santa Anna had chosen to fight Taylor elsewhere and because Mexico had been shaken by the "*Polko* Rebellion."

This complicated conflict was in essence a struggle between the *Puros,* those doctrinaire democrats who, coming to power under Acting President Farias, "passed sentence of death" on Mexican society, and the equally fanatic *Polkos,* conservative merchants, professional men, craftsmen, clerks and, chief of all, the clergy. The *Polkos* got their name from the polka music played by the bands of the four independent battalions they had formed, as they said, to defend private property against the designs of the *Puros.* Actually, the *Polkos* were clericals and the *Puros* anticlericals, and the *Puros-Polkos* duel was in many ways an adumbration of the bloody factional strife of the Spanish civil war as well as the dualism that still divides Latin America.

The apple of discord was Church property. The Mexican government, inept as well as corrupt, and so eaten by loan sharks that in

1845 it was entitled to only 13 percent of the money entering its treasury, was at last bankrupt. But the Church was still wealthy, and even
other parties such as the *Moderados* regarded her property as the solution to the problem. The thinking of many Mexican leaders, not only
the ferociously anticlerical Farias, who would just as soon cripple the
Church as defeat the invaders, was best expressed by the congressman
who said: "If the Yankee triumphs, what ecclesiastical property or what
religion will be left us?"

But the Church could not agree, and so, after Congress passed laws
levying on her estates, she secured the allegiance of the *Polko* battalions. This was in February of 1847, by which time all of Mexico was
aware of the impending American invasion of Vera Cruz. Farias, not
daring to disarm the *Polkos,* decided to get rid of them by ordering
them to march to the defense of the imperiled city. The *Polkos* refused.
When Farias and the *Puros* attempted to disarm them, the *Polkos* took
to the barricades. Bloodcurdling cries arose from either side, there was
much firing back and forth, but, as had happened so often in Mexican
uprisings, most of the casualties were among innocent civilians.

President Santa Anna, meanwhile, refrained from taking sides
openly. Secretly, however, he worked for the downfall of Farias and
toward a *rapprochement* with the Church. Although the hierarchy distrusted him, he was obviously a lesser evil than Farias; and the *Moderados,* believing in his "victory" at Buena Vista, also rallied to his support.
And so when President Santa Anna came to Mexico City, a *"Te Deum"*
was sung to celebrate his defeat of the Americans, and on March 23,
1847, he formally superseded Farias in office.

Thus the penultimate result of the tragicomic *Polko* Rebellion. The
last step completed the farce: to get rid of Farias, the office of vice
president was abolished, and a *Moderado* "substitute president" was
appointed while Santa Anna again put aside the politician's coat-and-
collar to vest himself in "glory and the robes of war." But before he
could march to the rescue of Vera Cruz, American cannon were
already smashing at the city's walls.

Winfield Scott had all but placed the siege of Vera Cruz in the hands
of his engineers. Day after day they went out—Lee, Johnston, Beauregard, George McClellan and the others—to study the city's defenses
and terrain and to site gun emplacements. Sometimes Sam Grant of
the infantry went along to watch them work. Once Grant and Beauregard were inside an adobe hut when a Mexican shell slammed into it
and exploded. They were only stunned, for Mexican shells were notoriously weak.

Gradually, American soldiers, toiling in sweat and ankle-deep sand, built an investing line in the sand hills behind Vera Cruz, while others cut the city's water supply or dragged artillery into position. Many of Scott's officers fretted at the delay. The idea of a siege bored them and they were impetuous for a charge.

"Ugh," General Twiggs snorted, "my boys'll have to take it yet with their bayonets."

But Scott still wanted to take Vera Cruz "by headwork, the slow, scientific process." He did not want to lose more than one hundred men, and said: "For every one over that number I shall regard myself as his murderer."

On March 22, with his cannon emplaced, Scott summoned Vera Cruz to surrender. The Mexicans refused and the American siege artillery opened with a rising roar. Yankee gunboats began bombarding the city from the water, running in so close that Ulúa began growling again. Commodore Matthew Perry—the younger brother of Perry of Lake Erie—had relieved Conner the day before, and he at once recalled his overbold gamecocks. Soon heavier naval cannon were brought ashore, and Perry's sailors, trained in the naval way not to flinch at the flash of cannon, eventually learned that on land it was no disgrace to take cover: one day four sailors standing erect in the open had the tops of their heads blown off.

Night and day the guns roared until the artillery load rose to 180 shells an hour and there were fires burning throughout the city. On March 26 a white flag fluttered at Vera Cruz. Scott sent Generals Worth and Pillow to meet the Mexican commissioners. Worth came back grumbling: "General, they're only trying to gain time—they don't mean to surrender. They evidently expect forces from the interior to come to their aid and compel us to raise the siege, or else to keep up dilly-dallying until the yellow fever does it for them. You'll have to assault the town, and I'm ready to do it with my division."

Scott thanked Worth, took from him the Mexican note and called for interpreters with the remark: "Now, let's hear the English of what these Mexican generals have to say." To his annoyance, but not entirely his surprise, Scott heard language indicating that the Mexicans merely wanted to save face. He at once dictated acceptable terms, and on March 29, 1847, both the city of Vera Cruz and the fort at San Juan de Ulúa surrendered.

Scott the Scientific had been better than his word. He had lost only sixty-seven killed and wounded against what were at first reported as enemy losses of four hundred soldiers and five hundred to six hundred civilians. He was criticized, of course, particularly in the foreign press, for his "inhumanity" in bombarding the city into submission. His traducers, ignoring the plain fact that Vera Cruz was a fortified city that had refused to surrender, presumably wanted Scott to take it by syllogism. They certainly could not have wanted him to storm it, for to have done so would have been to guarantee a frightful slaughter. Actually, the British naval commander on the scene estimated that the Mexican Army lost eighty men killed and that civilian deaths numbered about one hundred.

Few shooting sieges have been less bloody, and yet Scott was soon to learn that the America of his day really loved a big butcher's bill. Upon the announcement of the capture of Vera Cruz in New Orleans, a man in the crowd called out: "How many men has Scott lost?" The reply was: "Less than a hundred," and the man cried: "That won't do. Taylor always loses thousands. He is the man for my money."

77

Scott Gets a "Shadow"/Wins a Battle

WHILE WINFIELD SCOTT WITH HIS CUSTOMARY ORGANIZING SKILL WAS turning Vera Cruz into a base for operations against Mexico City, President Polk in Washington decided that there should be a "peace commissioner"—i.e., a shadow—attached to Scott's army. The man chosen was Nicholas Trist.

Trist was the chief clerk of the State Department, in effect its second-in-command but not so designated officially. He was, of course, a loyal Democrat, a man of pleasant and impressive appearance. But he was not considered too dangerous in that any success in achieving a treaty might make him a candidate for the White House, but rather—if he were indeed successful—the glory would redound to the benefit of the Polk administration, especially Secretary of State James Buchanan, his patron.

In a sense Nicholas Trist was a diplomat in the mold of Tobias Lear, if he were not indeed an exact replica of him. Like Lear he had been the confidant of great and famous men, having been associated with Jefferson as a law student and become his grandson by marriage. He had also been Jackson's private secretary. Having dwelt upon Mount Olympus and drunk the nectar of the gods, it seems to have made him rather light-headed so that if he did know where he wanted to go—

Pennsylvania Avenue to be specific—he was uncertain of how to get there. He seems also to have been woefully deficient in two qualities that are the sine qua nons of high ambition: common sense and a sense of humor.

His training for this mission, however, was excellent: he had studied at West Point, and as a longtime counsel in Havana he not only had become a native speaker of Spanish but learned to understand the thinking of Spanish Americans. Even so, his position was more tenuous than exact: though officially styled "Commissioner Plenipotentiary," he was really nothing more than Polk's agent and paid out of State Department contingency funds.

Another somewhat more formidable drawback was that Trist disliked Winfield Scott with a passion. Although he had never met Scott, he knew that Polk and his cabinet abhorred the general; and Buchanan, perhaps fearful that the artful Scott might draw him into the Whig orbit, took great pains to warn him of the general's wiles while also, his baby blue eyes so innocent and guileless, casually hinting that a diplomatic triumph in Mexico might well lead to the Democratic nomination for president of the United States—an honor that the Secretary also coveted and would receive in 1856. Finally, President Polk urged Trist to trust no one but Gideon Pillow. So minded, Nicholas Trist traveled incognito to New Orleans and thence to Vera Cruz, where to his dismay he learned that General Scott and his army had departed for the interior.

Winfield Scott had been in a rage to get his command out of the coastal flats and into the cooler highlands before the dreaded *vomito* arrived in mid-April. His immediate objective was Jalapa, seventy-five miles away and four thousand feet above sea level, but his immediate difficulty was in obtaining animal transport. Washington had failed to forward five hundred draft horses needed to pull the siege guns, and so, as a poor substitute, Mexican mustangs were rounded up. On April 8 Twigg's division stepped out on the march to Mexico City, 260 miles west.

Old Davy Twiggs, a man with an oxen back and matching brain, "led" his foot soldiers on horseback. Paced by a horse, floundering in sand, broiling in a brazen sun and ravaged by diarrhea, the men simply melted away. By the end of the first day's march a third of the division was missing, and the route was strewn with abandoned equipment. On the second day the Americans came to the national highway, the way of Cortés, which the Spaniards had graded, paved and guttered, and used

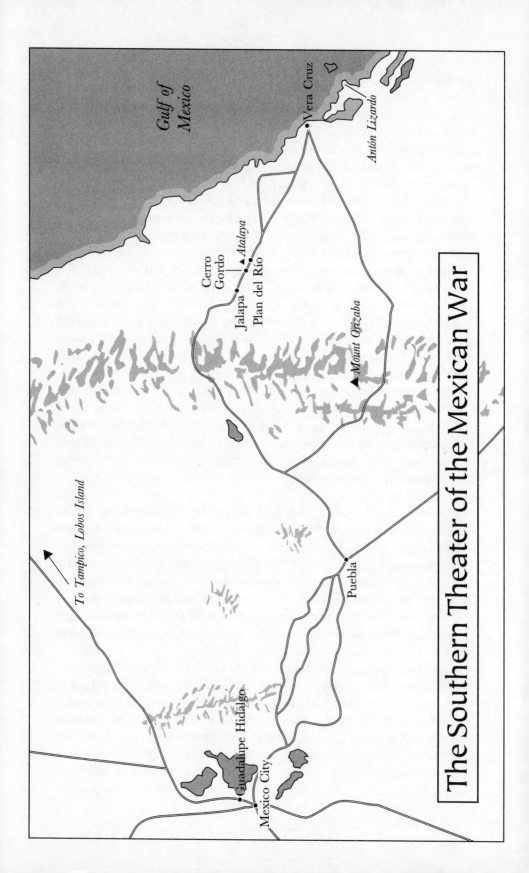

The Southern Theater of the Mexican War

Gulf of Mexico

Vera Cruz

Antón Lizardo

Atalaya

Cerro Gordo

Jalapa
Plan del Rio

Mount Orizaba

To Tampico, Lobos Island

Puebla

Guadalupe Hidalgo

Mexico City

for three centuries. Now, however, it was in disrepair; but it was nevertheless a better road than most of the ones the Yankee soldiers has
seen. To either side of it, all the way from Vera Cruz to Jalapa, were
the estates of Santa Anna. Here the going was not only easier but also
gorgeous, and the step of the soldiers quickened and their eyes brightened to behold the birds and flowers and trees of the exotic paradise
through which they tramped. On April 11 they crossed a stone bridge
into the village of Plan del Río, where the road winds and begins to
climb the highlands. Here the Americans sighted Mexican lancers.
Next day, Captain Joe Johnston and his engineers went scouting. Johnston came back with bullet holes in his right thigh and arm and the
report that Santa Anna was at the pass of Cerro Gordo.

Limping on his wooden leg, the Liberator had left the capital on April
2, and by April 5 had reached Jalapa. Here he took command of about
six thousand men, most of them veterans of his northern campaign,
and led them about twenty miles east to the point where Cerro Gordo,
the "Big Hill," guards the brow of the cordillera. Here he expected to
bar the American advance and keep the invaders so far down the
slopes that they would be within reach of the *vomito*.
    Santa Anna's position was a good one. To the right or south of the
road was a heavily fortified ridge. To the left or north was Cerro
Gordo itself, also fortified, and a half mile to the northeast was
another fortified hill, Atalaya. Thus the Americans trying to climb the
road would be caught between two plunging fires. They could not get
behind the fortified ridge on the south for its rear was guarded by a
canyon and Plan del Río. And Santa Anna thought the north flank was
protected by terrain so impenetrable that a rabbit could not get
through it.

Though a bit larger than cottontails and also somewhat more rational,
the West Point engineers on Scott's staff had no doubt that they could
solve the Liberator's defenses, and the general assigned Lieutenant
Beauregard and Captain Lee to reconnoiter the Cerro Gordo area.
    Robert Edward Lee was probably Scott's favorite West Pointer, as he
was also certainly a descendant of one of the most distinguished families of the era: the Lees of Virginia. Two of his forebears—Richard
Henry and Francis Lightfoot Lee—had been signers of the Declaration of Independence, and his father, "Light Horse Harry" Lee, had
been Washington's favorite officer. He was the same man who had
been so brutally tortured and disfigured by the riotors of Baltimore,
and when Robert was only eleven years old his family received word

that this famous cavalry leader had died on March 25, 1818, while sailing home from Barbados where he had failed to recover from his broken health.

Because Robert's three brothers were away from home, he became the head of the family, charged with caring for his invalid mother and his younger sister Anne who was hardly better. Yet, he accepted the duty cheerfully, until the day he left for West Point in the summer of 1825. Cadet Lee was popular at the academy, being graduated second in his class and holding the rank of adjutant, the highest for a cadet, and without a single demerit. This last might suggest a prissy character, but Lee was no namby-pamby. Warm-hearted and good-humored, though not exactly witty, he was able to win friends easily. His dignity was natural and his gravity probably the consequence of the misfortunes—financial as well as physical—that had overwhelmed his father. He was almost incredibly handsome, called the Marble Model by his classmates. At maturity he stood five feet eleven inches tall, weighing 170 pounds with a powerful torso and lean, athletic hips, big hands and surprisingly small feet. Upon a horse which he sat with easy grace, his long torso made him appear taller. Lee's wide-set eyes were dark brown, sometimes seeming almost black in dim light, his hair thick, black and wavy, his mouth perfectly formed. His entire countenance was manly and appealing, beaming as though illuminated from within by the glow of friendship. As a brevet lieutenant of engineers he quickly grew a pair of narrow black sideburns.

It was as an engineer that Robert Edward Lee gained the reputation of being one of the finest young officers in the U.S. Army. Between his graduation and the outbreak of war with Mexico he was assigned to stations where he developed his high skill at building fortifications. His first service in Mexico was with Taylor's army in the north, but then he was transferred to Winfield Scott's invasion force where he quickly caught the eye of Ol' Fuss 'n' Feathers. So did another younger officer with the fanciful name of Pierre Gustave Toutant Beauregard.

P.G.T. Beauregard, as he came to be known, was only sixteen years old when he arrived on the Plains of West Point in March of 1834. By then he had reached his full height of five feet seven inches, weighing a wiry 150 pounds and moving both on horseback and on foot with the grace of an athlete. Both his hair and eyes were dark and his complexion olive, so that when he commanded at Fort Sumter as the first general in the history of the Confederate Army his troops could say of him fondly, "How we love that little black Frenchman!"

As a youth Pierre had been deeply interested in military history, and it was said that at the age of seven as he walked up the aisle of St. Louis Cathedral in his native New Orleans to make his First Communion, he heard a rattle of drums behind him and turned to rush out of the church. To encourage his military studies, his father, one of the few Creole planters in Louisiana who spoke English, sent him to "the French School" in New York City conducted by the brothers Peugnet, who had served under Napoleon. Their war stories encouraged Pierre to steep himself in a study of the Napoleonic Wars.

Romantic stories seemed to follow Beauregard throughout his life, chief among them the tale of an unhappy love affair with Winfield Scott's beautiful daughter Virginia. Scott and his wife insisted they were too young to marry, and Mrs. Scott took Virginia to Europe, out of Pierre's reach. Yet the young lovers exchanged letters, although Virginia's mother intercepted Pierre's and failed to post her daughter's. Virginia became converted to Catholicism and then became a nun. In 1845 she is supposed to have learned of her mother's perfidy on her deathbed, summoning Pierre to her bedside. But by then he was already married.

True or false, the love affair had no effect on Beauregard's studies, for like Robert E. Lee he was graduated second in his class, and became—again like Lee—a distinguished army engineer. Known in Scott's army as the Little Creole, it was he along with Zebulon Tower who began to scout Santa Anna's "impenetrable" position at Cerro Gordo. Soon they began to find that if a cottontail could not get through it, they could—but then Beauregard fell ill of a fever, probably malaria. On April 15 Captain Lee picked up where Lieutenant Beauregard had left off.

Lee probed far to his right, slowly working his way up the ravines. He came to a spring and a well-trampled path leading from the south. He heard voices speaking Spanish and saw a party of Mexican soldiers approaching the spring. Silently, he dropped to the ground behind a log. The voices grew louder. There were more of them. Lee lay still in the moist heat while insects whirred in his ears and stung his flesh. Suddenly a Mexican sat on the log. Then another. Their backs were not three feet from the American. Then they arose and walked away. But more soldiers came and went and Captain Lee lay still until dark. Then he lifted his stiffened limbs and crept away. Down the treacherous ravine he went, moving stealthily with that intuitive feel for ground which is among the greatest of soldierly qualities. At last he reached headquarters and reported: it seemed possible that the Mexican left could be turned.

Encouraged, Scott ordered Lee to reconnoiter the area again on the 16th. He did, using a party of pioneers to cut a path still farther to the right. Next day he began to guide Twigg's division around the enemy left.

Sweating soldiers in light blue toiled up and down chasms so steep that animals could not climb them. Artillery was let down the steeps by rope and hauled up the same way. Suddenly, at noon, the Americans were discovered by Mexicans on Atalaya. A sharp fight for the hilltop began. Both sides fed in forces, until Colonel William Harney, a man as fiery in color as a red fox, led a charge over and around Atalaya. In fact, the charge was too impetuous. It carried forward to the slopes of Cerro Gordo, where the Americans were pinned down and picked off until light artillery from Atalaya enabled them to break off and withdraw.

Now Scott reinforced Twiggs with Shields's volunteer brigade. Under Lee's direction, they dragged three 24-pounders onto Atalaya's crest. That night Scott issued his battle orders: Twiggs was "to move forward before daylight, and take up position across the national road in the enemy's rear, so as to cut off a retreat towards Jalapa." Pillow's brigade was to attack the Mexican right on the fortified ridge. Worth's division was to follow Twiggs and Shields.

On April 18 the attack began. Twiggs sent the brigades of Shields and Colonel Bennett Riley on a swing right to get at the Mexican camp in the rear of Cerro Gordo and Atalaya. Shields moved directly on target, but Riley veered to his left and struck the western flank of Cerro Gordo. As both brigades moved, Colonel Harney's regulars went yelling down Atalaya, swept across the intervening hollow, and charged up Cerro Gordo's slopes. Within one hundred yards of the crest, they threw themselves down to catch their breath, jumped erect and followed the shouting Harney over the enemy's breastworks.

As the Mexicans fled, Captain John Magruder turned their abandoned guns on them. At this moment, Shields's troops burst upon the Mexican camp. A blast of grapeshot carried clear through Shields's body to deal him a wound that was miraculously not mortal; but his men rallied and routed the startled enemy. At the same time, Pillow's brigade, delayed in its advance to a jumping-off point, fell upon the Mexican right. Here the Americans suffered their severest losses, and Pillow was himself wounded in the arm. But once the Mexicans here realized that they were cut off to the rear, they surrendered.

By noon the Battle of Cerro Gordo was all over. Scott lost 63 killed and 337 wounded, but half of Santa Anna's army was captured and many others must have fallen. The Liberator did not wait to tally his losses. He fled toward Jalapa leaving his baggage wagon behind. Inside it the Americans found his military chest containing coin to pay his soldiers, cooked chicken, and—most precious prize of all—Santa Anna's spare wooden leg. Soon, in the tradition of the more grisly "Tecumseh razor strops," "Santa Anna legs" became fashionable in the States.

And within a few days Winfield Scott's triumphant little army was safely inside Jalapa. Behind the Americans lay the *vomito* and before them the exposed capital of a stunned nation.

78

Scott Burns His Bridges

~ SCOTT WAS EAGER TO PURSUE THE RETREATING SANTA ANNA, BUT before he could leave Jalapa he had to reorganize and eliminate shortages that had begun to afflict his army.

The first was in troops. On April 27 he was informed that the "new" regulars recruited under the Ten-Regiment Bill were being diverted to Taylor on the Rio Grande. Next his twelve-month volunteers began clamoring to go home. Most of them had only a month or six weeks left to serve, and they objected that if they waited until their discharge date they would have to leave the country through Vera Cruz just when the yellow fever was raging strongest. General Scott accepted the force of this argument, and on May 4 about three thousand men, the remnant of seven volunteer regiments, left Jalapa for the Gulf.

Scott's next shortage was in ready money with which to pay his troops and to purchase supplies. He also lacked cavalry and did not have enough teamsters and wagon masters, specialists who in those days were hired civilians rather than soldiers trained for the task. But even such serious problems as these were as nothing compared to the one raised with the arrival in Jalapa of a communication from Polk's peace commissioner, Nicholas Trist.

The Honorable Mr. Trist seems to have become convinced of the magnitude of his mission and the importance of his person. Upon his arrival in Vera Cruz, therefore, Trist did not go forward to Scott's headquarters as instructed. Instead, he wrote him a letter that may stand as a model of how a civilian may harry an already harassed soldier into apoplexy.

Trist told Scott that he, Trist, "was clothed with such diplomatic powers as will authorize him to enter into arrangements with the government of Mexico *for the suspension of hostilities.*" With this he sent a *sealed* letter for Scott to forward to the Mexican minister.

Scott flew into a rage. A rash letter-writer himself, he dashed off a reply stating that the "Secretary of War proposes to degrade me, by requiring that I, the commander of this army, shall defer to you, the chief clerk of the Department of State, the question of continuing or discontinuing hostilities." The sealed letter, which was nothing more than a refusal of earlier Mexican demands, together with a notice that a peace commissioner was now with the American Army, was disdainfully returned.

It was all a dreadful misunderstanding, chiefly due to Trist's preconceived notion that he disliked Scott and his inflated sense of his own importance. If he had met the general personally and shown him the confidential papers in his care, as he was instructed to do, he would not have provoked a rancorous quarrel likely to have most destructive consequences for the government they both sincerely served. But after Trist's first letter, all was cross-purposes. Scott, already aggrieved by the diversion of the "new" regulars to Taylor, became, like Taylor, convinced that all Whig generals were to be crucified. He wrote to Secretary Marcy and asked to be recalled, and at one point he wrote to Trist: "The Jacobin convention of France never sent to one of its armies in the field a more amiable and accomplished instrument. If you were armed with an ambulatory guillotine you would be the personification of Danton, Marat and St. Just, all in one."

Fortunately, the good offices of the British minister in Mexico helped to heal the rift. Scott and Trist met, found that they liked each other, and then, after Trist fell ill and Scott sent him a peace offering in the form of guava marmalade, they became close friends.

By then, mid-June, Scott had lost the friendship of his old comrade-in-arms William Worth. After the army had advanced to Puebla, about 150 miles west of Vera Cruz, Worth issued an ill-founded warning to his men that the Mexicans were mixing poison with the food they sold them. Scott ordered Worth to recall his circular, and Worth demanded a court of inquiry to judge his action. The court found him in error and subject to reprimand, and although Scott sought to soften the censure, Worth could not forgive him. Nor could he abide the fact that John Quitman and Gideon Pillow had been breveted to major generals senior to him. But he remained with the army.

Such difficulties made it ever more plain to Scott that he dared not tarry much longer at Puebla. He had already written to Secretary Marcy: "Like Cortés, finding myself isolated and abandoned, and again like him, always afraid that the next ship or messenger might recall or further cripple me, I resolved no longer to depend on Vera Cruz, or home, but to render my little army a self-sustaining machine." Like Cortés, he was burning his boats. He had received enough volunteer reinforcements, among them a brigade under Brigadier General Franklin Pierce, one of the few easterners to lead combat troops in "Mr. Polk's War." He had now about 10,500 effectives to march against an enemy city of 200,000 persons defended by a force he believed to be three times his own.

On August 7, 1847, the drums beat, bugles blew and the long lines of men in faded blue went swinging away to the Halls of Montezuma. In Europe the Duke of Wellington said: "Scott is lost. He cannot capture the city, and he cannot fall back upon his base."

79

Battle of Padierna-Contreras

〰 THE MEXICAN GOVERNMENT HAD PASSED THROUGH ANOTHER CONVUL-sion, only to lay quiescent once more beneath Santa Anna. The Liber-ator had outmaneuvered his numerous enemies by offering his resig-nation as a "sacrifice," after which, gratified by the public protest, he made the second sacrifice of withdrawing it. "What a life of sacrifice is the General's," a Mexican newspaper sneered. "A sacrifice to take the power, to resign, to resume; ultimate sacrifice; ultimate final; ultimate more final; ultimate most final; ultimate the very finalest."

Amid such dissension, Santa Anna prepared his defense of the capi-tal. He did not have thirty thousand men, as Scott thought, but rather about twenty-five thousand. Nevertheless, he disposed them artfully in a system of defenses—both natural and artificial—that made the hearts of the Americans sink as they marched down the road into the magnificent Valley of Mexico in which lay the capital city of their desires.

Scott's engineers could give him nothing but discouraging reports on the screen of lakes and marshes guarding Mexico City. Passage between the lakes was possible only on causeways raised above the marshes, and most of these were heavily guarded. Santa Anna had been careful to fortify the area around Lake Texcoco and the hill El Peñon in the north, for he expected Scott to come in here from the

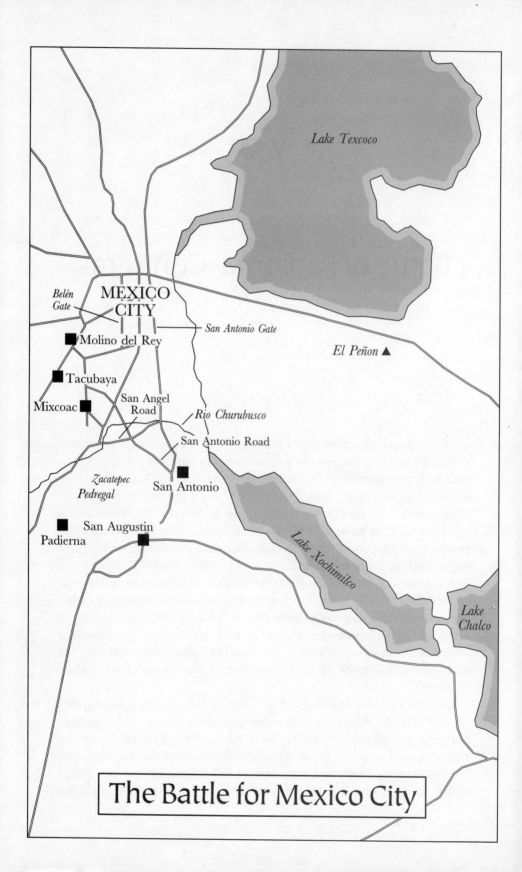

Lake Texcoco

Belén
Gate

MEXICO
CITY

San Antonio Gate

Molino del Rey

El Peñon ▲

Tacubaya

Mixcoac

San Angel
Road

Rio Churubusco

San Antonio Road

Zacatepec
Pedregal

San Antonio

Lake Xochimilco

San Augustin

Padierna

Lake
Chalco

The Battle for Mexico City

east. But Scott saw clearly that such an attempt would mean frightful losses. He ordered reconnaissances south of Lakes Chalco and Xochimilco. Here a rough but passable road was discovered, and on August 15 the army began movement to the village of San Agustin, modern Tlalpán, nine miles south of the city.

Here also the Americans seemed stymied. A few miles ahead of them was the well-fortified hacienda of San Antonio, and two miles farther north a fortified bridge over the canalized Rio Churubusco. Supporting the bridge was the thick-walled convent of San Mateo, inside which were the deserters of the San Patricio Battalion—excellent gunners who would lovingly blast away at their former tormentors of the parade ground. The route north, then, seemed barred. Could it be turned? Not on the right or east where Xochimilco lay; not, it seemed, on the left through the Pedregal, a great gray field of lava looking like a storm-tossed sea of stone. What about the other side of the Pedregal? There was a road there—the San Angel road—but there also seemed no way across the Pedregal.

Scott kept probing, however. On August 18 a party of engineers under Captain Lee entered the Pedregal, while others pushed north toward San Antonio escorted by dragoons under Captain Seth Thornton, the man whose ambush on the Rio Grande a year ago had touched off the war. From the hacienda came cannon fire, and the first shot cut Thornton in two. As the Mexican cannonade continued, the Americans withdrew.

Captain Lee, meanwhile, had found a tiny track in the Pedregal. Following it, he came to a piled-up mass of volcanic rock called Zacatepec. He climbed it and saw the San Angel road to the west. There were enemy troops on the slope of the hill at the village of Padierna to his left. Suddenly Lee heard firing. His escort had met a Mexican picket and exchanged shots. Realizing that these men had come from the San Angel road, Lee concluded that he could get there too, and that was the gist of his report to General Scott.

That night Scott decided to try to improve the Pedregal track so that guns and wagons might move over it. Early in the morning of August 19 working parties were sent out, and by one o'clock in the afternoon a road had been brought to within range of Padierna. But then enemy soldiers were met once more and cannon shot fell among the Americans. Padierna, it was seen, was now held in force by the Mexicans.

They were there because of the insubordination of General Gabriel Valencia, commander of the Army of the North. After Santa Anna had seen that Scott was not going to attack in the north, he had sent Valencia south to block the western road at San Angel. Valencia, however, had his own ideas and his own pretensions to glory. On August 18 he moved south from San Angel to the slope at Padierna, refusing, that night, to obey Santa Anna's orders to return to San Angel. By the afternoon of August 19 he was emplaced on the hill in full view of American officers standing atop Zacatepec.

To these officers it seemed that Valencia's left could be turned. General Pillow gave the word to Riley to take his brigade to the right, cross the San Angel road, and cut off Valencia's retreat to Mexico City. Then he ordered Brigadier General George Cadwalader to follow Riley, after which Brigadier General Persifor Smith, moving on his own initiative, took his brigade along the same route. By late afternoon all three units—about 3,500 men—were safely across the San Angel road. By then General Scott had come out to Zacatepec to approve what had been done, and also to see about 3,000 Mexican reinforcements start coming south from Coyoacán to take up station at San Angel.

The Americans west of the San Angel road were now caught between Valencia to their left or south and the reinforcements on the north. But neither Scott nor Persifor Smith, who had taken command west of the road, appeared to be concerned. Scott merely sent Captain Lee to Smith and calmly awaited developments.

They began after dark when Smith told Lee that he was going to move around Padierna during the night and attack it from the rear before daybreak. He told Lee that he would like a diversionary attack to be launched in front of Padierna, and Lee volunteered to carry that request to Scott. In rain and lightning, Lee crossed the road and began working east across the Pedregal. As he did, Santa Anna sent orders to Valencia to spike his guns and return to San Angel in darkness before an American attack in the morning should cut him off. Valencia, certain that he won a "victory" that afternoon, scornfully disobeyed the order.

On the rain-swept Pedregal, meanwhile, Captain Lee and a few men picked their way among lava rocks and chasms, leaping across fissures when they saw them outlined in fitful flashes of lightning, guiding on the gloomy bulk of Zacatepec when it, too, was thrown into relief. Lee's greatest fear was of blundering into a trigger-happy American sentry. Once, hearing the tramp of feet ahead of him, he paused and saw in a glare of lightning that they were the men of General Shields moving to reinforce Smith. Detailing a man to guide them, Lee plunged on. At last he came to Zacatepec. But Scott was not there. Weary and bruised, soaked to the skin, Lee pressed on to San Agustin, where he found his general.

Scott approved Smith's plan and ordered Franklin Pierce's troops to make diversion in front of Padierna. Pierce himself was injured, and command passed to Colonel Trueman Ransom. Lee found Ransom's men bivouacked on the Padierna and guided them into position.

West of the road, the arrival of Shields raised the American strength to four thousand men. At three o'clock in the morning of August 20, 1847, the rain-plastered Yankee soldiers began moving out. Once again those invaluable engineers showed them the way. Slipping and stumbling on the slippery track, they stole into Valencia's rear.

In front of Valencia, Ransom's men opened up. Valencia's soldiers returned the fire. Suddenly, they heard wild yelling to their rear. A tide of blue was flowing down the hill toward them, led by the huge Riley. Firing as they came, the Americans rushed headlong into the Mexican position. For a while the Mexican gunners worked wildly to reverse their guns. But then they broke and ran, joining the infantry already being trampled by fleeing Mexican horse. In seventeen minutes the battle was over. Day had hardly dawned before the San Angel road was black with Mexican soldiers streaming north. Among them somewhere was General Valencia, who had disappeared at the commencement of the battle. Left behind were seven hundred dead, more than eight hundred prisoners and a great store of military supplies.

The Americans had lost fewer than sixty killed and wounded, and now General Scott was free to push up the San Angel road to come down upon San Antonio in the rear.

80

St. Patrick's Battalion

⌇ IN APRIL OF 1846 AFTER ZACHARY TAYLOR'S ARMY HAD ARRIVED ON the north bank of the Rio Grande across from the Mexican city of Matamoros, the flow of desertions among the foreigners who comprised 47 percent of his fighting force threatened to weaken his strength considerably. Many of these foreigners were Catholics—especially the Irish who constituted about a quarter of Taylor's army—and Mexican recruiters made deliberate appeals to their religious loyalties. They also offered land bounties as further attractions, while those pretty Mexican girls who bathed naked in the river were also a powerful though unwitting inducement. To plug this leak Taylor began executing soldiers caught trying to desert, a most illegal policy since the United States was not yet at war. But the desertions continued, and this was because of the contempt and cruelty with which the veteran American officers—crusty old Indian fighters from the frontiers—tormented their foreign regulars.

None of the West Pointers, such as Lee and Beauregard, Grant and Meade, were sadists, if only because they had been trained to believe that if they wished to gain the respect and affection of their troops, they had to treat them as human beings and be sincerely concerned for their welfare. But the frontier fighters seemed to care more for the comfort of their horses than for their foreign-born enlisted men. Probably the most sadistic of them all was Colonel William Harney, commander of a regiment of dragoons: a foul-mouthed little bow-legged, red-haired, red-faced ferret of a man hated by every soldier in his command as well as any Doughboy unfortunate enough to be confined to the guardhouse when Harney was acting as provost marshal. Trooper Samuel Chamberlain has described Harney's style. Chamberlain was himself in the guardhouse when Harney appeared for an inspection brandishing a whip, and curtly asked two other prisoners why they were there.

"For nothing, sir," they replied.

"*Nothing!* God damn you, *nothing!* Lieutenant Buford, tie the damned sons of bitches up by the thumbs for two hours. The next time you come here, come for *something!*"

Hanging a man by his thumbs was Harney's favorite punishment, which he inflicted for such horrendous offenses as "disrespect" or "silent contempt." A soldier would have his thumbs tied to a rope thrown over a tree limb. Hauled erect he would be compelled to stand on tiptoe to keep his thumbs from being torn from his hands—a torment that usually did not end until he fainted. "Riding the horse" was to mount a prisoner on a pole supported by two uprights about ten feet high. Then his ankles were bound and as he struggled to maintain his balance his comrades were ordered to hoot and mock him and sometimes also to spit on him. "Bucking and gagging" was the most painful of these "company punishments." A bayonet or stick was forced into a man's mouth and held in place by a string tied behind his ears. Next he was seated on the ground and made to bring his knees up to his body so that a stick could be placed under them. His arms were then placed under the stick and tied to it. The cramps and thirst induced by this fixed position were excruciatingly painful and sometimes continued for hours.

By such means monsters like Harney sought to bend their men to their will, and when they deliberately singled out the foreigners for these disciplinary delights the "leak" that so dismayed Taylor turned into a veritable flood. It became worse with the arrival of those Southern volunteers whom Ol' Rough 'n' Ready also despised. By their atrocities against innocent Mexican civilians they so outraged these foreigners—again the Irish in particular—that the number of San Patricios, as the Mexicans called them, is supposed to have risen past seven hundred. Their commander was Thomas Riley, a former sergeant in the Fourth Infantry who was commissioned a colonel in the Mexican Army. They were far and away the one Mexican formation feared most by the American Army, having scourged Taylor's troops at Buena Vista. In 1847, fighting in defense of Mexico City against Scott's army, they took a fearsome revenge upon their tormentors at the bloody Battle of Churubusco.

81

Churubusco and the Molino del Rey

~ GENERAL SANTA ANNA DID NOT SIT STILL FOR HIS ENVELOPMENT AT San Antonio. Instead, learning of Valencia's defeat, he abandoned the position and ordered its troops to withdraw to inner defenses behind the Churubusco River. Other soldiers moved into those *garita*, or gates, which guarded the heads of the causeways and which were actually fortified stone buildings used as police and customs stations. It was at the Churubusco bridgehead-and-convent complex, however, that the main defense was concentrated, and here the pursuing Americans smacked "butt-end first" into the stubborn enemy.

Worth's division took the San Antonio road: Garland's brigade moved through a cornfield to the right of the road, and Colonel Newman Clarke's men advanced up the road itself. On the left of the road was Cadwalader's brigade, trying to punch between bridgehead and convent. Cadwalader could not, and his men finally crossed the road into the cornfield. Farther left, Smith's brigade struck at San Mateo, while still farther left Riley hit the convent in flank.

Across the Churubusco, Franklin Pierce, barely able to keep to his saddle, faced his brigade east and tried to cut the Mexican line of retreat. Pierce was eventually reinforced by Shields, and by riflemen and dragoons guided into battle by Captain Lee.

Santa Anna was now engaged across his entire front, and he fought back skillfully, rapidly countering Scott's cross-river attempts to turn him. For three hours the battle raged. From San Mateo, where the San Patricios were "fighting with a halter around their necks," came a dreadful drumfire. The hoarse cries of stricken men were counterpointed by the mad screaming of horses and mules. Smoke drifted everywhere, and in the cornfield the sound of bullets popping stalks was counterpointed by the uglier one of lead smacking flesh. Across the river Franklin Pierce was down again with a twisted knee, but he urged his men on until consciousness left him.

By three o'clock in the afternoon Scott had shot his bolt. All his available men were engaged—six thousand against eighteen thousand—they were falling by the hundreds, and they seemed stopped. One officer near Scott said to himself, "We must succeed or the army is lost."

But the Mexicans were low on ammunition, and the Americans had worked their way into position for the final heave. Almost at once, they arose on three fronts and charged—and they were irresistible. Only at San Mateo did the fight continue, and here the San Patricios fought with clubbed muskets until at last there were only eighty of them alive to be taken prisoner. With his bridgehead gone, the convent fallen and his line of retreat threatened, Santa Anna ordered another withdrawal.

Mexican soldiers went streaming north for the safety of the San Antonio Gate, and the American infantry let them go. Suddenly bugles blew a charge and a squadron of American dragoons under hawk-nosed Captain Philip Kearny, nephew of the conqueror of New Mexico, went clattering up the road in full pursuit. They were a stirring sight, matched iron-grays moving nose to tail with their riders ramrod-straight and grasping gleaming sabers that rested, blade up, against their right shoulders. On toward the gate they charged, into a storm of enemy fire, with Kearny unaware that behind him Colonel Harney had blown recall and his rear horsemen were dropping off by fours.

Kearny had only Richard Ewell and a handful of troopers with him when he reached the gate, dismounted and tried to force it on foot. But the Americans were fighting at the cannon's mouth. Blast after blast cut them to the ground. They withdrew, with Kearny clinging to his mount with the one arm that was to remain to him and Ewell escaping on his third horse.

Perhaps the chance to enter the San Antonio Gate and drive straight into the city of Mexico had been missed. At any rate, the Battle of Churubusco was over. Chiefly because of the dreadful fire of the

San Patricios, it had been far more costly than Padierna: about 1,000 casualties in all. Santa Anna's losses for the day were about 3,200 soldiers captured, among them eight generals, and 4,000 killed and wounded, plus a paralyzing loss of arms and ammunition.

Winfield Scott, convinced that he had "overwhelmed the enemy," did not occupy the capital, as he might easily have done. Instead, he agreed to a cessation of hostilities during which Nicholas Trist and his Mexican counterparts might negotiate a peace. But the armistice lasted only two weeks. Trist's territorial demands provoked the Mexicans into advancing unacceptable terms of their own, and on September 7, learning that Santa Anna had used the truce as a breather in which to refresh his forces, Scott brought the armistice to an end.

The Molino del Rey, or "King's Mill," was part of the bastion of Chapultepec that guarded the western approaches to Mexico City. Chapultepec Castle itself stood on the brow of a hill about two hundred feet high. To its west was a park and then the massive Molino del Rey built in a north-south line. About five hundred yards west of the Molino lay another strong building, the Casa de Mata. Between the two was an artillery battery supported by infantry. Perhaps eight thousand Mexicans held the entire position.

Scott decided that he must have this most formidable strong point after observing Mexican troop movements in that direction and hearing that Santa Anna was using the Molino as a foundry in which to cast cannon out of church bells. So he ordered General Worth to take it and destroy its contents.

Worth had a force of about 3,250 men, nearly half the 7,000 soldiers to which Scott's army had been reduced. He also had nine guns, but Worth, perhaps even more than Twiggs, scorned artillery when bayonets could be used. Cold steel, not exploding shells, was Worth's solution to stone walls. Thus the Americans jumped off in the morning of September 8, 1847, with the barest bombardment. As Molino's walls glowed white in the dawning day, two 24-pounders barked ten times apiece—and then the blue lines swept forward.

The entire Mexican front blazed with musketry and cannon. The blue lines were riddled and ripped apart. In the center, eleven of fourteen officers were struck down and the ranks suffered in proportion. On the left at the Casa de Mata two commanding officers fell, followed by a third. Broken, the left rallied—just as swarms of Mexican cavalry appeared across a ravine on the left. If the Mexican horse could get across the ravine under cover of Casa de Mata's guns, they could charge the American left and perhaps roll up the entire line.

American bugles blew and 250 dragoons swept toward the enemy lancers. Galling fire from Casa de Mata and a battery to the right emptied forty American saddles, but still the dragoons rode on, bluffing and outmaneuvering the more numerous Mexicans.

On the right, at the southern end of the Molino, battle was confused, with units advancing independently and fighting other units in the swirl of smoke. Finally a gate was battered in, and shouting Americans went pouring into the murk of the Molino. They chased the enemy up on the roofs of the buildings.

Up on the left, even as the reinforced center was returning to the attack, the enemy was also cracking. Mexican guns unwisely left outside the Casa Mata were captured and turned against the enemy. Still fighting stubbornly, the Mexicans twice mounted counterattacks. Beaten back, they began retreating east from the Casa de Mata to Chapultepec.

The position was now completely in American hands, and Worth, scenting total victory and glory, asked permission to press on to Chapultepec itself. Scott refused, repeating his order to destroy the enemy "cannon" and withdraw. But there were no newly cast cannon, not even any old church bells. And the Mexican church bells which caroled away joyously in the mistaken belief that an all-out assault on Chapultepec had been repulsed seemed to mock Scott's decision to launch the attack at all.

Even though the enemy had lost 680 prisoners and between 1,000 and 2,000 casualties, Worth's losses were close to 800 men, or a quarter of his attacking force and nearly an eighth of Scott's army. As one of Scott's officers wrote in his diary: "We were like Pyrrhus after the fight with Fabricius—and a few more such victories and this army would be destroyed."

82

To the Halls of Montezuma!

∼ GENERAL WINFIELD SCOTT HAD TO ATTACK. HIS POSITION, THOUGH not exactly desperate, was at least disquieting. Here he was with his army down to seven thousand men and at the end of a supply line 250 miles long the base of which at Vera Cruz could not be used until the *vomito* vanished in November. Before Santa Anna could become conscious of the vulnerability of this line, Scott had to strike him and seize the enemy capital of Mexico City. Thus, on September 9 when he assembled his generals and those beloved young West Pointers of his "cabinet," the question was not so much when to attack but where.

Scott began the meeting by informing those present that after the severe losses in the valley battles it was now imperative to strike a heavy and decisive blow at the capital city itself. He was determined that the meeting should not end without deciding at what point that stroke should fall. In his own analysis, Scott preferred to attack by the western gates, but because he sought independent judgments he kept that preference to himself.

Gideon Pillow arose and in a long wandering speech concluded that an attack on the southern gates should be launched. Scott's engineers led by Captain Lee supported that opinion. So did Generals Quitman, Shields, Cadwalader and Pierce. For some reason Scott's eye then fell on Lieutenant Beauregard sitting quietly in a corner, and he said: "You, young man, in that corner, what have you to say on the subject?"

What the general in chief did not realize was that the Little Creole was not so much speechless but rather sulking. Having recovered from his fever he had been dismayed to discover that Lee and Tower had each received three brevets for continuing the reconnaissance that he had begun, while he was given none. That soured him on Ol' Fuss 'n' Feathers, whom he now referred to sarcastically as "our glorious old chief," and whom—in his ignorance of the feud between Polk and Scott—he constantly criticized for having cut loose from his base at Puebla to go hurrahing off to the Halls of Montezuma.

But now, having been ordered in effect to give a command performance, he sprang eagerly to his feet to deliver an anaylsis that almost exactly duplicated Scott's own estimate of the situation. He began by saying that his own reconnoitering of the enemy's position indicated that he was steadily improving his southern defenses. For the very reason that Santa Anna expected an attack there and was preparing to receive it, the assault should be made elsewhere. At best a feint should be made in the south with the main blow to fall on Chapultepec. Success there would unmask two easily traversed causeways into the city.

After Beauregard sat down, a dead silence ensued, broken when General Franklin Pierce—who would one day become the 14th President of the United States—arose and declared "after what he had just heard, he was now in favor of the attack by Chapultepec." Another silence gripped the conference, ended this time by Scott who arose in all his commanding presence and said:

"Gentlemen, we will attack by the western gates!"

On the morning of September 12 American soldiers seized the vacant Molino del Rey and Casa De Mata on the western end of the Chapultepec complex. With daylight, American artillery roared, battering Chapultepec's buildings and walls in the fiercest bombardment of the war. Inside, General Nicolas Bravo called for reinforcements. But Santa Anna had no wish to feed more troops into what might become a slaughter pen. He kept some four thousand troops available on the western causeways, but they did not enter Chapultepec. Santa Anna's eyes were fixed south, where a convincing diversion by Twiggs had deceived him as to the American intent. So Bravo had to hold with fewer than one thousand men, of whom one hundred were cadets quartered at the Military College in Chapultepec.

Against them came Pillow's division issuing out of the Molino and Quitman's division moving north from Tacubaya against Chapultepec's eastern end. On the west the Americans met a withering fire as they dashed whooping through a grove of giant cypresses. Here Pillow was wounded, and his men were brought to a cowering halt in a ditch beneath the castle, and here it was found that the storming party had forgotten to bring scaling ladders. In desperation Pillow called for Worth to bring up his division before all was lost. But then the scaling ladders arrived, and the Americans jumped into the ditch, swung the ladders against the stone wall and went swarming up them.

Lieutenant James Longstreet, rushing up with a flag in his hand, fell to the ground wounded, and the colors were caught up and carried forward by Lieutenant George Pickett.

On the left of Pillow's advance, Mexican musketry had cut down the men following Lieutenant Tom "Stonewall" Jackson as he tried to manhandle a single gun forward. Alone among dead gunners and kicking horses, the tall young officer called to his vanished troops: "There's no danger! See, I'm not hit!" But his gunners heard the peening of the enemy bullets, and they returned only after more guns and a column of regulars appeared.

On the east, Quitman was attacking and taking heavy casualties. Colonel Ransom died, so did Major Levi Twiggs of the Marines—no relation to the general. The fight was hand to hand, with crossed swords and clubbed muskets, and the Mexicans stood firm for a time. But then all gave way.

All but the cadets of the Mexican Military College, many of whom fought on to the death and entered Mexican history as *"Los Ninos,"* the Little Ones. Six of them, aged thirteen to nineteen, gave up their lives rather than surrender. One of these, eighteen-year-old Agustín Melgar, battled the Americans step by step, dueling with them up the stairways until he reached the roof of the college where American bayonets ended his gallant young life. Over his prostrate body stepped Lieutenant George Pickett—famous or infamous in American history as the leader of the ill-fated "Pickett's Charge" at Gettysburg—to haul down the green, red, and white Mexican tricolor and run up the Red, White and Blue. Around him the men on the rooftop cheered, and so did the Doughboys hastening down the unguarded causeways into Mexico City—for the battle was now a race for possession of the capital itself.

The contest was between the divisions of Quitman and Worth, and Quitman was moving along the closer route, for his men marched on the causeway running directly east to the Belén Gate. Worth had to follow one causeway north before turning hard east to drive on the

San Cosmé Gate. General Scott had sent both generals reinforcements, personally joining Worth, accompanied by Captain Lee. But
Captain Lee, on his feet or in the saddle for nearly three days without
respite, suddenly fell from his horse exhausted and unconscious.

Both of the causeways the Americans followed carried an arched
aqueduct down their middles while roadways ran to either side. Both
were barricaded and covered with troops and artillery. Nevertheless,
the Americans slugged ahead. At 1:20 P.M. Quitman's troops crashed
through the Belén Gate into the city's outskirts. The Mexicans fought
back from the massive Citadel and Belén Prison. They were led by
Santa Anna, who had hurried north from his fruitless vigil in front of
Twiggs. At Belén the Americans hung on desperately against mounting casualties.

Worth also took losses as he slugged north and then swung east.
Once again the Americans began burrowing through houses with
picks and crowbars. They drove up to the San Cosmé Gate. Alarmed,
Santa Anna rushed to San Cosmé, but his presence made no difference. The Americans burst the barrier and kept on fighting after
nightfall.

Aware, now, that Mexico City's defenses had been breached, Santa
Anna returned to the Citadel at Belén. Here, in a council of war, he
decided to evacuate the city. He still had five thousand infantry and
four hundred cavalry, but he chose to move north to Guadalupe
Hidalgo. Before he did, some two thousand convicts were "liberated"
to prey upon the invading Gringos.

On the morning of September 14, 1847, General John Quitman
prepared for a stiff fight at the Citadel. Marching at the head of his
troops with his left foot bare—he had fallen into one of Mexico City's
numerous canals the night before and lost his shoe—he was sending
his units forward when a flag of truce appeared with notice of Santa
Anna's flight. Quitman quickly took possession of the Citadel, and
then, hearing that the freed prisoners were plundering the city, the
half-shod Quitman put himself at the head of his men and marched
into the Grand Plaza. He formed them on the great square in the
shadow of the cathedral and gave to the Marines the mission of cleaning the National Palace of thieves and vagabonds.

Atop the palace itself, the legendary Halls of Montezuma, Marine
Lieutenant A. S. Nicholson cut down the Mexican flag and ran up the
Stars and Stripes, unwittingly giving to his famous corps the first line
of its stirring battle hymn. And it was the sight of that speck of color
that brought the brief, bloody and glorious history of St. Patrick's Battalion to its grisly end.

83

A Noose for the Patricios

~ EXCEPT ON PAPER, GENERAL-IN-CHIEF WINFIELD SCOTT WAS NOT A vengeful man. He would have preferred mercy for all of the captured San Patricios. But the failure of the negotiations during the truce had made it impossible to decree clemency for men who had been the enemies of an army now expecting to suffer heavy casualties. Even so, Scott did succeed in obtaining non-capital punishment for Patricios who had deserted before the outbreak of hostilities, although the court-martial that doomed fifty of the captives to the gallows did not seem quite so compassionate in "forgiving" the others. Their sentence was to dig the graves of their executed comrades and "to receive two hundred lashes on the bare back, the letter *D* to be branded on the cheek with a red hot iron, to wear an iron yoke weighing eight pounds with three prongs, each one foot in length, around the neck, to be confined to hard labor, in charge of the guard during the time the army should remain in Mexico, and then to have their heads shaved and be drummed out of camp."

Colonel William Harney, of course, was placed in charge of the hangings. He had acquired a skill in this gruesome art by torturing and hanging Seminoles during service in Florida. It was natural, wrote Trooper Chamberlain, that a man "who had ravished Indian girls at night, and then strung them up to the limb of a live oak in the morning" would be eminently qualified for such work, and he must be admired for the matchless depravity by which he carried out his duties.

First, as the final insult to the Mexicans, he chose the plaza of the beautiful church of San Angel for erection of the gallows. Here the first eighteen or twenty of the condemned men were hanged. They were mounted on wagons hitched to mules, a noose around their necks. When a drum was tapped, the mules moved forward and the wagons pulled from beneath the Patricios' feet. But their fall was not sharp enough to break their necks, so that they kicked and squirmed in front of the church until they finally choked to death.

Next the "spared" deserters were lashed, and then hot irons pressed into their cheeks. Colonel Riley's brand was applied upside-down, and so, because Colonel Harney's guidebook did not quite cover the procedure to be followed in such a perplexing situation, he solved the predicament in true-blue "regulation" style by ordering the iron to be re-heated and applied right-side-up and thus "burn the other cheek." Still, Colonel Riley was not particularly dismayed to be so disfigured, for he had gained the love of a wealthy and beautiful senora, and he knew that upon his going free she would anoint his scars with golden kisses.

It did not occur to Colonel Harney that to whip, brand and hang these captive soldiers of Mexico would outrage enemy sensitivities and stiffen their will to fight on, thus prolonging the war and multiplying the casualties among his own troops; nor did it matter to him that however just the sentence, however normal the punishment was for the armies of the day—though these "deserters" were indeed rather more the fugitives from a cruel and heartless military system that accepted every sacrifice up to and including death and gave back torment in return—to have carried out these sentences in front of a church and by a method of execution considered by Mexicans as a profanation of the memory of the crucified Christ was nothing less than a vengeful and thoughtlessly cruel variation from the considerate and humane face that Winfield Scott had tried to show the Mexicans since his landing at Vera Cruz.

So far from regretting his barbarity, William Harney had gleefully reserved a special treat for the remaining thirty doomed Patricios. Another gallows had been erected at the charming little village of Mixcoac, sitting atop a hill in full view of the culminating battle for the National Palace—the legendary halls of Montezuma. When this should fall, and Old Glory be thrown to the winds, it would be visible at Mixcoac, and the mules would lurch forward again. How Harney must have congratulated himself. It could have been to him that the steward of the wedding feast at Cana had said: "But you have saved the best for the last!"

As General Pillow's division moved forward to the assault thirty lariats with dangling nooses were fastened to the Mixcoac gallows. Then the Patricios were mounted there seated on boards with their arms and legs tied. After the nooses were slipped over the heads of twenty-nine of them, the surgeon in charge told Harney that the thirtieth was already dying, having lost both legs at Contreras.

"Bring the damned son of a bitch out!" Harney snarled. "My order is to hang thirty, and by God I'll do it!"

So the dying man whose name was Murphy was brought out to the gallows in time to hear the order of execution read aloud. The Patricios burst out laughing at the order's absurdly formal language, and one of them taunted Harney: "If we won't be hung until yer dirty ould rag flies from the Castle, we will live to eat the goose that will fatten on the grass that grows on yer own grave, Colonel."

It has been said that when the American flag did fly from the castle, the doomed men cheered lustily. But this is preposterous. They had made their choice and they would never salute a banner under which they had suffered such injustice and indignity. They did cheer, however, but only for "Old Bravo," the Mexican general conducting the defense of Chapultepec.

As the battle raged on, the Patricios turned to baiting Harney again. "Colonel!" one of them called to him. "Oh, Colonel, dear—will yez grant a favor to a dying man, one of the old Second, a Florida man, Colonel?" When Harney asked what he wanted, he continued to the rising laughter of his comrades: "Thanks. Thanks Colonel. I knew yez had a kind heart. Please take my dudeen (clay pipe) out of me pocket and light it by yer eligant hair, Colonel, dear." As his comrades roared again with laughter, the infuriated Harney struck the man in the mouth with his saber hilt. Spitting out blood and teeth and chuckling, the man cried: "Bad luck to yez! Yez'v spoilt me smokin' intirely. I shan't be able to hold a pipe in my mouth as long as I live."

Seeing Harney gape in enraged incredulity, the doomed Irishmen guffawed again—just as the flag became visible above the palace. At once Harney gave the order for the wagons to move, but not before another deserter—seeing the legless Murphy begin to jerk in the Dance of Death—saluted Harney with the final taunt: "Oh, ye old brick top, it is kind ye are to make Murphy dance on nothing, now that he has lost his legs!"

So ended the sad saga of St. Patrick's Battalion; and yet, between brave men who could joke and jest with a rope around their necks and the foul William Harney sending them to their deaths snarling curses, history should have no difficulty judging the true winner of what began as a somewhat unequal contest.

84

Mexico Capitulates

∿ AT EIGHT O'CLOCK ON THE MOMENTOUS MORNING OF SEPTEMBER 14, 1847, there came into the Grand Plaza of Mexico City the blare of bugles and the rising clatter of horses' hooves. General in Chief Winfield Scott, superbly mounted and splendidly uniformed, those plumes that had given him his unwelcome nickname waving from his gleaming helmet, swept into the great square accompanied by an escort of dragoons with bared sabers. His officers followed, his bands played, his soldiers presented arms and whooped, and his Mexican audience—many of them visible on rooftops—cheered and waved handkerchiefs.

It was the high point of a great career, and Scott had earned those plaudits that he cherished so highly. He had led one of the most momentous fighting marches in military history. Hernán Cortés may have conquered Mexico City for Spain, but the Mexican nation is no longer Spanish; whereas Winfield Scott in conquering that same capital was the chief instrument in adding 1,193,061 square miles of territory—an area five times the size of France—to the national domain of the United States.

Here was one of the two great land grabs in human history that have remained permanent. The other was Czar Ivan the Terrible's conquest of Siberia in 1581. Although this was to add an incredible

5,330,896 square miles to the Russian Empire, this vast area by its frigid climate and its almost impenetrable perma-frost one thousand feet deep was almost entirely of little value to Russia except as a place of exile for the enemies of czars and commissars. Conversely, the area ceded to the United States by Mexico—including with Texas the modern states of Arizona, Nevada, California and Utah, together with parts of New Mexico, Colorado and Wyoming—was almost instantly productive in agriculture, industry, minerals and warm-water ports; and thus until a new technology unlocks the great treasures of Siberia still too prohibitively expensive to exploit, the American acquisition was in its value a greater achievement.

This area was ceded by Mexico after Nicholas Trist negotiated the Treaty of Guadalupe Hidalgo on February 2, 1848. Trist had been recalled by Polk, but after Santa Anna abdicated, Trist saw his opportunity and deliberately disobeyed orders. In return for the ceded land, the United States agreed to assume the unpaid claims and pay Mexico $15 million.

All this was achieved by a repudiated diplomat and a discredited general, for Polk the superb expansionist soon became "Little Jimmy Polk" the petty politician: he relieved Scott with a Democratic general and dismissed Trist from the State Department.

It had been an extremely vicious and nasty war, especially for one lasting only sixteen months (peace negotiations consumed nearly five months). The suffering experienced by the troops of both sides in climates that were alternating hells of heat and cold and terrain varying between desert and tropical jungle has never been fully appreciated and probably never will be. Because Mexico at that time kept no records of casualties among troops regarded as cannon fodder, its total losses are not known; although they almost certainly exceeded American casualties of 13,780 dead and thousands more wounded beyond recovery. Disease and accident killed far more Americans than enemy action: only one death in eight was inflicted by Mexicans.

Nevertheless, except for Alaska, the area of the continental United States was now rounded out. Now the "firebell in the night" could clang anew over whether the new lands should be slave or free. Almost all of the great protagonists in the dreadful debate lying ahead—especially the generals trained in the Mexican War—were on the scene. They were already taking sides and even changing tunes. One freshman Whig Congressman, in criticizing Mr. Polk's War as unconstitutional, discussed the right to revolt in terms that could never have fallen from his lips a decade later. "Any people anywhere," he said, "being inclined and having the power have the right to rise up and shake off the existing government, and form a new one that suits them better. . . . any portion of such people that can may revolutionize and make their own of so much of the territory as they inhabit."

The speaker was Abraham Lincoln.

Selected Bibliography

Adams, Henry. *The War of 1812*. Washington: Infantry Journal Press, 1944.

Adams, James Truslow. *The Living Jefferson*. New York: Scribner's, 1936.

Bowen, Catherine Drinker. *Miracle at Philadelphia*. Boston: Little, Brown, 1966.

Brant, Irving. *The Fourth President: Life of James Madison*. New York: Bobbs Merrill, 1970.

Brett-James, Antony. *1812*. New York: St. Martin's, 1966.

Chidsey, Donald Barr. *The War with Mexico*. New York: Crown, 1968.

Chamberlain, Samuel. *My Confession*. New York: Harper, 1956.

Cleaves, Freeman. *Meade of Gettysburg*. Norman: Univ. of Oklahoma Press, 1960.

Coles, Henry L. *The War of 1812*. Chicago: Univ. of Chicago Press, 1965.

Dutton, Charles J. *Oliver Hazard Perry*. New York: Longmans, Green, 1935.

Dyer, Brainerd. *Zachary Taylor*. Baton Rouge: Louisiana State Univ. Press, 1946.

Eaton, Clement. *Jefferson Davis*. New York: Free Press, 1977.

Eckenrode, H. J., and Bryan Conrad. *George B. McClellan: The Man*

Who Saved the Union. Chapel Hill: Univ. of North Carolina Press, 1941.

Eisenhower, John S. D. *So Far from God: The War with Mexico, 1846–1848.* New York: Anchor, 1989.

Elliott, Charles Winslow. *Winfield Scott.* New York: Macmillan, 1937.

Engleman, Fred L. *The Peace of Christmas Eve: How the Young United States Was Rescued from Destruction by the Treaty of Ghent.* New York: Harcourt, Brace & World, 1960.

Footner, Hulbert. *Sailor of Fortune: The Life and Adventures of Commodore Barney.* New York: Harper & Bros., 1940.

Forester, C. S. *The Age of Fighting Sail.* Garden City: Doubleday, 1956.

———. *The Barbary Pirates.* New York: Random House, 1953.

Freeman, Douglas Southall. *Lee's Lieutenants.* 4 vols., New York: Scribner's, 1942–44.

Gonan, Gilbert, and James W. Livingood. *A Different Valor: The Story of Joseph E. Johnston.* New York: Bobbs Merrill, 1946.

Harwell, Richard. *Lee: An Abridgement of Freeman's Four-Volume Study.* New York: Scribner's, 1961.

Hassler, Warren W., Jr., *General George B. McClellan: Shield of the Union.* Baton Rouge: Louisiana State Univ. Press, 1957.

Hebert, Walter H. *Fighting Joe Hooker.* New York: Bobbs-Merrill, 1944.

Henry, Robert Selph. *The Story of the Mexican War.* New York: Ungar, 1950.

Hickey, Donald R. *The War of 1812.* Urbana: Univ. of Illinois Press, 1989.

Horsman, Reginald. *The War of 1812.* New York: Knopf, 1972.

Jacobs, James Ripley. *Tarnished Warrior: Major General James Wilkinson.* New York: Macmillan, 1938.

James, Marquis. *The Life of Andrew Jackson.* New York: Bobbs-Merrill, 1954.

Johnston, R. M. *Leading American Soldiers.* New York: Holt, 1907.

Ketcham, Ralph. *James Madison.* New York: Macmillan, 1971.

Kraus, Michael. *The United States to 1865.* Ann Arbor: Univ. of Michigan Press, 1959.

Leckie, Robert. *The Wars of America, 1609–1991.* New York: HarperCollins, 1992.

———. *Great Battles of American History.* New York: Random House, 1968.

Lecky, W. E. H. *England in the XVIIIth Century.* Vol. I. New York: D. Appleton & Co., 1888.

Lewis, Lloyd. *Captain Sam Grant.* Boston: Little, Brown, 1950.

Long, Jeff. *Duel of Eagles: The Mexican and U.S. Fight for the Alamo.* New York: Morrow, 1990.

Lord, Walter. *A Time to Stand: The Epic of the Alamo.* New York: Harper, 1961.

Lossing, Benson J. *Pictorial Field Book of the War of 1812.* New York: Harper, 1968.

Mahan, A. T. *Sea Power in Its Relation to the War of 1812.* New York: Greenwood, 1968.

McFeely, William S. *Grant,* New York: Norton, 1981.

McWhiney, Grady. *Braxton Bragg and Confederate Defeat.* New York: Columbia Univ. Press, 1969.

Morison, Samuel Eliot. *The Oxford History of the American People.* New York: Oxford, 1965.

Muller, Charles G., *The Proudest Day: Macdonough on Lake Champlain.* New York: John Day, 1960.

————. *The Darkest Day, 1814: The Washington-Baltimore Campaign.* New York: Lippincott, 1963.

Nicholls, Edward J. *Zach Taylor's Little Army.* New York: Doubleday, 1963.

Pack, A. James. *The Man Who Burned the White House.* Emsworth: Naval Institute Press, 1987.

Petrie, Sir Charles. *The Four Georges, 1714–1830,* Boston: Houghton Mifflin, 1936.

Piston, William Garrett. *Lee's Tarnished Lieutenant: James Longstreet.* Athens: Univ. of Georgia Press, 1987.

Remini, Robert V. *Andrew Jackson.* New York: Harper & Row, 1977.

Robertson, James I. *General A. P. Hill.* New York: Random House, 1987.

Roland, Charles P. *Albert Sidney Johnston: Soldier of Three Republics.* New York: Thomas Yoseloff, 1961.

Ruiz, Ramon Eduardo. *Triumphs and Tragedy: A History of the Mexican People.* New York: Morrow, 1992.

Seitz, Don C. *The "Also Rans."* Freeport: Books for Libraries Press, 1968.

Sellers, Charles Grier, Jr. *James K. Polk: Jacksonian.* Princeton: Princeton Univ., Press, 1957.

Smith, Justin H. *The War with Mexico.* 2 vols. Gloucester: Peter Smith, 1963.

Tallant, Robert. *The Pirate Lafitte and the Battle of New Orleans.* New York: Random House, 1951.

Tucker, Glenn. *Dawn Like Thunder: The Barbary Wars.* New York: 1963

————. *Tecumseh: Vision of Glory.* New York: Bobbs-Merrill, 1955.

Van Deusen, Glyndon G. *Life of Henry Clay.* Boston: Little, Brown, 1937.

Werstein, Irving. *Kearny the Magnificent.* New York: John Day, 1962.

Whipple, A.B.C. *To the Shores of Tripoli.* New York: Morrow, 1991.

Williams, T. Harry. *With Beauregard in Mexico.* Baton Rouge: Louisiana State Univ. Press, 1956.

———. *P.G.T. Beauregard: Napoleon in Gray.* Baton Rouge: Louisiana State Univ. Press, 1955.

Index